The People, Maybe

DUXBURY PRESS SERIES IN POLITICS

General Editor
Bernard C. Hennessy
California State University, Hayward

A Logic of Public Policy   L. L. WADE AND ROBERT CURRY

American Political Interest Groups   BETTY H. ZISK

Analyzing American Politics   WALTER A. ROSENBAUM, JOHN W. SPANIER
                                                            AND WILLIAM C. BURRIS

An Introduction to the Study of   CHARLES O. JONES
Public Policy

Campaign Finance in America   DAVID W. ADAMANY

Political Images and Realities   DONALD REICH AND PAUL DAWSON

Political Life and Social Change,   CHARLES ANDRAIN
2nd edition available April 1974

Political Life and Social Change,   CHARLES ANDRAIN
Readings

Public Opinion, 2nd edition   BERNARD C. HENNESSY

Saving Appearances   HENRY S. KARIEL

Social and Political Inquiry   J. D. MAY AND KARL J. BEMESDERFER

Social Psychology of Political Life   SAMUEL A. KIRKPATRICK
                                                            AND LAWRENCE K. PETTIT

Techniques of Political Analysis   LYMAN TOWER SARGENT
                                                            AND THOMAS A. ZANT

The Black Politician   MERVYN M. DYMALLY

The Congressional System   LEROY N. RIESELBACH

The Irony of Democracy,   THOMAS R. DYE AND L. HARMON ZEIGLER
2nd edition

The People, Maybe, 2nd edition   KARL A. LAMB

A Guide to The People, Maybe   LEN SHIPMAN

SECOND EDITION

The People, Maybe

E 70

Karl A. Lamb

University of California, Santa Cruz

Duxbury Press
North Scituate, Massachusetts
A Division of Wadsworth Publishing Company, Inc.
Belmont, California

Duxbury Press
North Scituate, Massachusetts
A Division of Wadsworth Publishing Company, Inc.

L.C. Cat. Card No.: 73-84241
ISBN: 0-87872-061-8
Printed in the United States of America.

1 2 3 4 5 6 7 8 9 10 78 77 76 75 74

Quotations appear in this book from *The People, Yes* by Carl Sandburg,
copyright, 1936, by Harcourt Brace Jovanovich, Inc.; renewed, 1964, by
Carl Sandburg. Reprinted by permission of the publishers.

Quotations from Alexis de Tocqueville's *Democracy in America* have been
translated from the French by Karl A. Lamb.

Designed by Malcolm Grear Designers.
Illustrations by Edward Koren.
All photographs courtesy of Magnum Photos, Inc.
Production editing by Sid Seamans.
Type set by Craftsman Type Inc.
Printed and bound by Kingsport Press.

For Amy, Marty, and Steve

"The people will live on."

The people, yes, the people,
Until the people are taken care of one way
or another,
Until the people are solved somehow for the
day and hour,
Until then one hears "Yes but the people
what about the people?"
Sometimes as though the people is a child to
be pleased or fed
Or again a hoodlum you have to be tough with
And seldom as though the people is a caldron
and a reservoir
Of the human reserves that shape history . . .

The people is the grand canyon of humanity
and many many miles across.

The people is pandora's box, humpty dumpty,
a clock of doom and an avalanche when
it turns loose.

Carl Sandburg

To the Reader

The Wisdom of Carl Sandburg

In 1936, when three years of President Roosevelt's New Deal had done much to lift the nation's spirits, although economic conditions remained stagnant, Carl Sandburg published a book-length poem entitled *The People, Yes*. Sandburg portrayed the tragedies and contradictions of the era, but he expressed a fundamental faith in the American people—in their ability to overcome adversity, in their capacity to speak as a whole people (in spite, or because of, their human differences), and in their ability to control their own destiny. Sandburg acknowledged the power of special interests, and he recognized the violence that hides below the surface of society. But his basic faith was unshaken. He believed the institutions of American government can be held accountable to the people.

The power and conviction of Sandburg's work came from the fact that he was also a biographer of Abraham Lincoln. In Lincoln's life, he studied the interaction between a democratic leader and the democratic population. The shadow of Lincoln—both the triumph and the tragedy—lay upon *The People, Yes*. Sandburg knew the dimensions of human misfortune, and he realized the degradation that can be imposed by men upon their fellows through war and economic exploitation. But his memories of Lincoln gave Sandburg and his poem a reason for cautious optimism.

President Nixon's Interpretation

Early in 1973, President Richard M. Nixon cited Sandburg's three words—*The People, Yes*—as summarizing the meaning of America. The context of his speech is described below, pp. 437-439. On that occasion, the president gave a curious twist to Sandburg's meaning. According to President Nixon, government should be prepared to say "yes" to the aspirations of the people, and the people should be prepared to say "yes" to the requirements of their government, including the decision to wage war, even an undeclared war.

Sandburg's poem was written in rather a different spirit. It was a spirit close to that of the Declaration of Independence, which asserts that, when government fails to protect the people's liberties, it is their right "to alter or to abolish it." President Nixon was speaking as head of a stable government empowered by the Constitution, a final and unchanging authority. Later in the year, when the Watergate conspiracy investigation pointed toward himself, President Nixon cited the Constitution, rather than any need or privilege of the people, as the source of his own right to remain silent.

The Uncertainties of Our Time

Carl Sandburg's title did summarize his understanding of the American nation in 1936. But the questions raised in his poem cannot be answered so optimistically today. It is no longer possible to speak with Sandburg's assurance about the American people—all of the people—as a singular force in history, with a significance that transcends the internal divisions within them. It is less certain now than it was to Sandburg that the destructive forces unleashed by the Civil War have been contained. It is not clear that American government can respond appropriately to the accelerating problems of the twentieth century. Nor is it clear that the people can indeed enforce responsibility upon the far-flung enterprises of government. In the 1970s, it is difficult to share completely Sandburg's faith in either the good intentions of the people or the adequacy and responsiveness of American democratic institutions. The people, maybe.

Anyone who surveys the contemporary political scene may feel overwhelmed by the ironies and paradoxes that it presents. They include the contrast between the intentions of those who designed our institutions, and the present reality; the high hopes for technological advance turned sour by the ruin of natural resources; the realization that bigness in government does not insure efficiency; and the discovery that American power can be bent to evil purposes, both at home and abroad. Yet to understand the history of those contradictions is prologue to an understanding of modern America.

A Personal Book

This is one man's effort to comprehend and portray America's political and governmental system at a particular point in time: the middle 1970s, not long before the two-hundredth anniversary of the United States. Because the interpretations are highly personal, the reader is not expected to agree with all he finds. But he ought not to remain indifferent.

The book's intellectual hero is Thomas Jefferson. Its political heroes and villains are more diffuse. It is concerned with understanding the political conflicts of our time within the context of American political history, the interpretations of contemporary political science, and the operation of our current political institutions.

A central conviction of the book is that the abstract discussion of American political institutions does not capture the interest of the reader. Nearly every day, political events raise compelling questions about those institutions and their present performance. Therefore, each chapter is divided into two parts with distinct functions: the kaleidoscopic parade of contemporary events displayed in "images," and an examination of the issues raised by those events in "reflections."

"Images" and Their Inspiration

The technique of the images section was inspired by the novels of John Dos Passos. Images are real events, ranging from a few sentences out of the evening newspaper to the summary of an organization's ten-year history. Largely, they are written in the present tense. They involve public figures as well as private citizens. There is no effort to "let the facts speak for themselves." The images are selected, and juxtaposed, to portray the contradictions and ironies, the successes and failures, of American democracy. At the same time, they provide an introduction to contemporary political history.

There are a few fictional vignettes, based on real events, but with fictional protagonists, written with an eye to dramatic impact. Dos Passos, like Hegel, gains additional merit when stood on his head.

"Voices from Middle America"

Some of the images sections contain segments of interviews conducted by the author with registered voters in Orange County, California. The names of the respondents have been fictionalized to protect their privacy.

This research involved tape-recorded interviews with twelve families who reside in a single upper-middle-class neighborhood. Interview times extended to as much as forty hours per family. In *The People, Maybe*, their voices function like a Greek chorus, commenting upon the drama, and voicing the reaction of the common man to heroic aspirations. The research from which they are extracted is reported in *As Orange Goes: Twelve California Families and the Future of American Politics* (New York: W. W. Norton, forthcoming.)

"Reflections" and Methodology

The questions that are raised implicitly in an images section are discussed explicitly in the reflections section of the same chapter. Written more often in the past tense, the reflections segment may plunge into colonial history or the concepts of long-dead political theorists. Historical and theoretical perspectives help define contemporary dilemmas, but they seldom prescribe remedies. The reflections section usually progresses forward in time until it again presents the same issue or event highlighted in the images section. The chapter ends much as it began. Few final answers are offered; the reader must bear the burden of judgment.

The method of the book, therefore, may not seem very methodical. Episodic, discontinuous, tumultuous, and non-linear are applicable adjectives. The book attempts to imitate certain qualities of political life itself. If it is animated by any methodological conviction, it would be that the phenomena of politics are best re-created from the viewpoint of the political actors themselves. No pretense is made of separating fact from value. The findings of quantitative research are used when applicable, but quantification is not accepted as the sole equivalent of reality. The book's purpose is to introduce American politics, not the methods (or debates about methods) of the social sciences. The reader will seldom find the narrative interrupted by tables or graphs. He will find plenty of graphics—photographs and cartoons which are part of the narrative and underscore its purposes.

There are, however, recurrent themes. The conflict in American values between equality and achievement is one example. First defined in Chapter 1, it reappears in Chapters 2, 5, 8, and 11. In the final chapter, this value conflict is discussed as a clue to the significance of the Watergate scandals.

The author can also reach out and tap the reader on the shoulder, when the point at issue is controversial, or a judgment is offered that ought not to be buried in the textual narrative. Like this.

Introducing American Politics

The first edition of *The People, Maybe* was widely read by college classes in American politics. This second edition has been updated and reorganized to better meet the needs of such classes. Revisions were based on the experience of the many students and instructors who used the first edition.

The sequence of chapters, as well as the organization of individual chapters, follows the conviction that the clash of political issues, the disagreement over what should be done, stimulates a concern for the institutions of government and how they operate. The first chapter delineates the conflict over values in the arena of public education, including higher education, and asks students to consider what kind of enterprise they are part of. The second chapter, using the 1972 presidential election as an example, examines the performance of the political parties in linking public opinion and governmental policy through the electoral process.

Only after this immersion in the local and national political process is the reader introduced to the three branches of national government. Again, the approach is to portray issues interacting with institutions, citizens, and politicians. Rather than a separate chapter on the origins and development of the Constitution, there are three accounts of the constitutional source and subsequent development of the powers of governmental branches—executive, legislative, and judicial.

The progression of the six remaining chapters may seem more random. The discussion of Vietnam and American foreign policy precedes a description of the urban crisis and evolving patterns of federalism. But this was an arbitrary decision. The chapter on education, and the one concerning policemen, judges, and prisons deal with topics that are not usually covered so extensively in introductions to American government. Both educational and penal institutions (there are similarities) highlight problems that the political system has yet to resolve.

Some readers may feel that the most important issue in the study of American politics is the structure of power in society. The debate between pluralists and elitists is deferred until the seventh chapter, where it is considered essential to the discussion of pressure groups and public opinion. The final chapter attempts to summarize the preceding ten chapters by confronting the two central questions raised by the book: Can the people rule? If they can, are they likely to do it wisely?

Because of the intimate relationship between the images and reflections of a given chapter, the chapters should be read as whole units—although not necessarily at a single sitting. The sequence of chapters is hardly sacred. If the instructor agrees with Gabriel Eisenberg (see below, pp. 15-17) that the most important issue in understanding American politics is pluralism, he may ask students to begin with Chapter 7. The description of the National Rifle Association in Images 7 plunges the reader into the realities of politics as dramatically as any part of the book. On the other hand, if the book is read as an introduction to the people of the United States, before considering their politics, Chapter 8 could be the starting place, for it provides an historical chronology that will be useful in following the reflections segments of other chapters.

If a class chooses to emphasize the Constitution and the impact of its interpretation, the book could be read literally backwards. Together with the Declaration of Independence, an annotated version of the U.S. Constitution is printed in the appendix. The notations are to pages in the text where the Constitution is central to the discussion, and they are remarkably numerous. Using the appendix as a guide to relevant segments of the text, a course could be organized around an article-by-article examination of the Constitution.

Study Guide

The book presumes familiarity with certain terms, names, and incidents in contemporary politics. If he lacks that familiarity, the reader may become so engrossed in the detail of incidents described in the images sections that he will overlook data about political institutions and theories in the reflections sections. Or he may simply be confused by the procession of events and non-linear chronology. The publisher has supplied a map of the book's rocky terrain. A study guide for students, which supplements *The People, Maybe*, has been written by Len Shipman of Mt. San Antonio College. The guide emphasizes the institutions and concepts of American government. Mr. Shipman provides an outline-summary of each chapter, suggested objectives to be accomplished in reading it, definitions of important terms with an emphasis on historical and institutional detail, suggested topics and projects for discussion and further research, and student worksheets. The guide is available from Duxbury Press.

A Word of Thanks

In attempting to create a book that is both highly personal and non-conformist, an author incurs his greatest debt to those who support his vision. He becomes grateful for help received, for the restraint of associates invited to impose their attitudes upon the book who chose not to do so, and for those who contribute their own creative talents to the realization of his design. I should like to thank all of the following persons, both for their support and for their forbearance.

Robert Gormley is not only the publisher; he is, in the best sense, the Godfather of the book. It was first conceived in response to his suggestion. His enthusiasm for the book, which now extends to nearly five years, has been as unflagging as his patience with its author. Bob Gormley assembled the remarkable group who have given, in this second edition, a visual setting for the prose which matches its mood and purpose.

Malcolm Grear, and his associates, of Providence, Rhode Island, designed the book and assembled the photographs that make the pages of each chapter so vivid. I am delighted and grateful that Ed Koren agreed to match his formidable artistic talents to this manuscript. Although stimulated by the text, his cartoons stand by themselves as a commentary upon American politics. Sid Seamans, of Cambridge, Massachusetts, was the copy editor. He was sensitive to the substance of the material while paying careful attention to details. David Earle and Barbara Gracia capably coordinated production of the book at Duxbury Press.

Bernard Hennessy's supportive enthusiasm eased the transition from first to second editions; as advisory editor, he has been both restrained and helpful; our friendship continues.

With the second edition, as with the first, Pat Shuler has been involved in the book in a manner far beyond what could be expected in return for the modest sum she received as a research assistant. Her alertness to possible student reactions has been very valuable.

Charlotte Cassidy typed the manuscript with the same care and attention to detail that she gives all manuscripts. The price of a typist who is fast, efficient, and knows how to spell, is far beyond rubies.

I have accumulated a series of debts to colleagues for help in their areas of expert knowledge. I am particularly grateful to J. Herman Blake of the University of California, Santa Cruz, for reviewing my treatment of the black experience. Similarly, Ralph Guzman helped to formulate my—unhappily more brief—description of the Chicano experience. John Dizikes, who knows more about the nineteenth century in America than anybody, helped to tame some of my generalizations about the Civil War. I should also like to thank Peter Euben for suggestions, encouragement, and the loan of books; Stephen Cupps, for suggestions and the use of his data concerning the National Rifle Association; George von der Muhll, for recalling his childhood in Mason, Michigan; David Thomas, for perceptive comments on American government and its comparison with European governments; and John Hummel for reflections on the relevance of Rousseau.

The greatest measure of gratitude belongs to the dedicated teachers of American politics who cared about the impact of textbooks upon students, helped define what kind of book would be needed, and then monitored student reactions to the first edition. The original conception of the book was submitted to a group of California political scientists: Robert J. Latham, Max Lieberman, Garth Norton, S. Thomas Porter, Frank Poulos, Samuel Schwartz, John A. Walker, James F. Wickens, and Richard Zimmer. I am grateful for the suggestions and encouragement they offered on that occasion. Political scientists who have commented upon the first edition and its use, either voluntarily or upon request, include George Carey, Jeffrey M. Elliot, Paul Goodwin, C. W. Harrington, Bruce Larkin, Sue Leeson, Arthur B. Levy, Stanley W. Moore, Albert Palm, Harold V. Rhodes, Stephen Rubleman, Len Shipman, Sanford R. Silverburg, and Robert Wessel. I thank them for the positive thrust of their various suggestions and apologize for not being able to incorporate all of them.

The people listed here contributed much to whatever virtues the book may contain. But I have also expressed my thanks for their restraint, so I must extend to them a fervent absolution of responsibility for its faults.

Karl A. Lamb

Contents

National parties hardly exist, except when a presidential candidate is being nominated, but the performance of national parties forms identifications in voters' minds. This great psychological force is being weakened by the growth of independent voting, as parties lose their hold upon the electorate.

Parties have played their most creative roles after critical elections. Then they have become the vehicles of the people's will. No popular will was formulated in 1972.

The heroic nature of the presidential office is enshrined in the monuments that adorn Washington. The powers of the office are less than heroic, both in the Constitution and in practice. Congress doesn't give President Nixon what he wants; General Lavelle substitutes his own judgment; Daniel Ellsberg releases *The Pentagon Papers*.

Lyndon B. Johnson builds his own monument, while Richard M. Nixon tries to establish his relationship with the people through television. President Nixon's second term, under the shadow of Watergate, cannot celebrate the heroic potential of the presidency.

The presidency was hardly described in the Constitution, but it aroused fierce opposition based on a fear of kings. The office—hardly separable from its occupant—has been built by its strong incumbents, beginning with George Washington. Some presidents have been crippled by their own conception of the office, but the Constitution imposes permanent handicaps.

Modern presidents sit at the apex of a bureaucracy they cannot control. Yet they are surrounded by courtiers and other trappings of royalty, in danger of becoming isolated from the people.

The presidency is a tragically flawed office. The potential home of heroic leadership, it can also house disaster.

Washington, D.C. is a beehive of political activity, but do its residents stay in touch with the people? Senator Gravel grows disturbed by the *Pentagon Papers* and further publicizes them at midnight. Former Senator Brewster is charged with receiving an unlawful gratuity.

The Tax Reform Act of 1969 shows Congress at work. The old men, who have survived many elections, wield power. Congressmen are polite to each other out of necessity. Power cancels power, and the tax reform act does not really modify the economic structure.

The Constitution established Congress as an independent branch, and it still is. The critics would have Congress accept domination from some outside influence, to make it either less or more than the Constitution intended. But fashions change in political science; Congress is currently higher in esteem than the executive.

Congressmen intermingle four styles of representation: delegate, broker, trustee, and errand boy. Congress developed two important functions not mentioned in the Constitution: to oversee the operations of the executive branch, and to personalize the bureaucracy for their constituents. Congress is a deceptively healthy institution.

Campaigners for President Nixon point to his Supreme Court nominations as acts of lasting significance. Previously, the Court headed
by Chief Justice Earl Warren had greatly expanded the rights of
accused criminals, freedoms of speech and of the press, and the right
of newsmen to protect their sources. These rights are substantially
narrowed by the interpretations of the Nixon-appointed justices.

Supporting assertions of power by the executive branch is not the
same thing as restoring law and order.

The Court's power of judicial review is not explicit in the Constitution. It was established by John Marshall, the first great judicial
activist. The Court's power has waxed and waned throughout its history. A period of eclipse during the Civil War was followed by a time
of near-domination, as the Court joined hands with the corporations.
Constitutional crisis was resolved when the Court adopted self-
restraint regarding economic regulation after the Court-packing battle of 1937. The Warren Court blazed new trails in civil liberties,
racial equality, and legislative representation.

Neither judicial restraint nor judicial activism is praiseworthy in
the abstract. The question is: Does the Court advance the cause of
democracy?

The policeman is the street agent of the system of criminal justice.
Ronald August finds trouble at the Algiers Motel in Detroit. Black
power confronts blue power.

The path to a judgeship in Chicago leads through Mayor Daley's
party organization. Prisoners at Attica, in upstate New York, revolt.
In California, voters restore the death penalty. Crime increases.

If the Constitution is a social contract, citizens have given up certain
freedoms to obtain law, order, and justice. But these terms are of
uncertain meaning, and the institutions designed to guarantee them
are in trouble.

The policeman is underpaid, inadequately trained, and faced with
conflicting expectations. More money for police forces had little impact when prosecutors, courts, and prisons were unable to perform
their related functions. None could deal with the social causes of
crime, and the humane tradition in the Western concept of justice
was largely ignored by the people.

Serene in its Washington headquarters, the National Rifle Association
stands guard over the "right" of the people to keep and bear arms.
In spite of the assassinations of John F. Kennedy, Robert Kennedy, and
Martin Luther King, and the attempted assassination of George Wallace, the NRA firmly resists any move toward gun control, works to
defeat congressmen who vote for it, and undermines any legislation
that may be adopted. For thirty years, the people have favored gun
control. Shall the few rule, or the many?

The People against the Centers of Power   271
The authors of the Constitution were not concerned with the linkages
through which public opinion may control government policy. Modern methods measure public opinion; we now understand that opinion sets limits upon policy but does not determine it. While the influence of opinion upon elections is direct and immediate, the policy
process is dominated by the spokesmen for special interests.

Both pluralist and elitist theories acknowledge the power of private
interests and provide a fresh understanding of how American government does, or should, work.

The People against Themselves   297
One Nation, Divisible   299
Whether the American Dream is defined as equality, equal opportunity, or the duty of the individual to achieve, our social and political
institutions exclude entire groups from participation in that dream.
Malcolm Crockett, six years old and black, discovers this. The Moose
Lodge practices discrimination in private and the Ku Klux Klan flaunts
it in public. Blacks and Chicanos achieve a new political consciousness. Male chauvinism seems the last accepted prejudice.

But the charge of bigotry is too easily made. The "white ethnic,"
the Middle American, feels most threatened by the social and cultural
change of the last decade.

Creating a Nation: The Unfinished Story   315
Thomas Jefferson wrote that "all men are created equal." His assertion
did not apply to slaves, Indians, or women. The resident majority
soon denied its meaning to successive groups of immigrants. The
Civil War abolished chattel slavery, and more subtle forms of inequality were devised. Southern elites substituted racial hate for
economic interest as the basis of politics.

The Progressive concern for equality was killed by World War I.
The New Deal achieved new conceptions of economic equality. After
World War II, the struggle of black Americans toward equality met
some success and moved to the North.

Neil Armstrong landed on the moon.

Making Democracy Safe for the World   347
Some Lessons of Vietnam   349
Nobody can claim a monopoly of moral insight, but the United States
earned a prize for stupidity. The original commitment was made for
reasons of European policy, in total ignorance of the Vietnamese
people. "Stopping communism" became the justification.

The human costs of Vietnam are beyond counting. To call it a
tragedy is wrong: that implies noble motives in the first place. Vietnam teaches how American government can malfunction.

Power, Pride, and the People: Can Democracy Live by the Sword? 365
Since its birth, America has been ambivalent about its relationships
with the world. Shall we be a democratic example, or shall we intervene in the affairs of others? Isolation became the prevailing posture,
but interventions were regularly launched in the full conviction of
moral superiority.

After World War II, America had the power to act upon its convictions, and communism provided the target. The success of such
efforts as the Marshall Plan was followed by the absurdity of Vietnam.

The spiral of technology has increased the demand for new

weapons. Arming for war, President Nixon has sought peace based on an updated understanding of the world.

The misery of living in the central city can be symbolized by a block of decaying tenements in the Bronx. It can also be studied in the Pruitt-Igoe Project in St. Louis, an example of planned misery. Mayor Lindsay is leaving New York, and Carl Stokes has left Cleveland. Chicago prospers under Mayor Daley—or does it?

The places we live are being ruined by the appetite of the automobile. Suburbanites show small sympathy for the needs of core cities, and states are often slow in responding to federal policy initiatives. President Nixon handles the urban crisis by declaring the battle won and says revenue sharing will keep the peace.

President Nixon's planned "new federalism" would send new power to grassroots governments; but are the grassroots healthy? The states have developed new administrative competence as a result of the "marble-cake" federalism that developed out of the New Deal. President Nixon would change that recipe. Cities and counties tend to be controlled by local elites. Centralized taxation with decentralized administration will not necessarily advance the cause of democracy.

The relationship between the suburbs and the central cities is crucial to the survival of metropolitan areas. General revenue sharing offers more rhetoric than reform.

In 1969, President Nixon proposes redistributing the national income by providing poor families with cash in place of the ineffective service strategy of Lyndon Johnson's War on Poverty. Nixon's plan is labeled "revolutionary," but it is passed twice by the House of Representatives, only to die twice in the Senate Finance Committee.

The Students for a Democratic Society is founded in an atmosphere of hope, expressed in the *Port Huron Statement* of 1962. SDS gives inspiration and ideology to student activism during the 1960s, but it does not achieve miracles. SDS splits into factions, the Weathermen go underground, and the explosive end comes in 1970.

Americans were "born equal"; no revolution was needed to establish the doctrines of equality and opportunity. As a result, those who urge revolution are regarded as somehow un-American. The government established by the Constitution makes only incremental change in the status quo, except when critical elections adjust the political system to social and cultural advance.

The Watergate scandals challenge that ethic of exploitation based on elevating the value of achievement above the belief in equality. A prediction of fascism for the future is hard to establish, for the people can be inspired by noble motives. In partnership with trusted leaders, the people can exert a positive power for change.

CHAPTER 1

A Clash of Values:
The Case of Education

IMAGES 1

Who Am I?
Where Am I Going?

REFLECTIONS 1

Education and the
American Dream

Who Am I?
Where Am I Going?

Public education has touched more lives, employed more people, consumed more dollars, erected more buildings, and stimulated more controversy than any other activity of American state and local governments. It has been the fire under the melting pot, the gateway to status in a technological society, and the guarantor of equal opportunity. Educators claimed that education was the basis of democracy, and taxpayers supported it, often when they had no children of their own to benefit.

For nearly two decades, political controversy has raged over a matter presumably settled by the United States Supreme Court: the public schools shall not segregate their pupils according to race. That is, the schools should demonstrate an important aspect of democracy, instead of merely teaching about it.

Meanwhile, in grade school students learned about the nice fireman and the nice policeman, in high school about nice Thomas Jefferson, and in college the ideas of John Locke. Then they lined up to be interviewed by the nice personnel men from IBM, General Electric, and Dow Chemical.

But suddenly it didn't work any more. The students made fun of the slogans, and claimed that a lot they were required to study didn't really matter. They stopped lining up for job interviews. Before long, even the taxpayers began to have doubts.

Our Glowing History...

In 1961, the Texas House of Representatives passed a resolution urging that "the American history courses in the public schools emphasize . . . our glowing and throbbing history of hearts and souls inspired by wonderful American principles and traditions. . . ."[1]

Section 288 of the Texas Penal Code, passed in 1933, makes it illegal for teachers, principals, and superintendents to teach or conduct school business in any language except English, except when teaching a foreign language to English-speaking students. The glowing history of America can therefore be made available to Spanish-speaking students after they have mastered English. But the schools were prohibited from teaching English as a foreign language.

The law of 1933 may have been based on the assumption that Spanish-speaking citizens can never be more than second-class citizens.

July 4, 1776: *We hold these truths to be self-evident, that all men are created equal ...*

1. Quoted in Harmon Ziegler, *The Political Life of American Teachers* (Englewood Cliffs, N.J.: Prentice-Hall, 1967), p. 122.

"Created equal," all right, but what does that mean? What does it mean to students who are trying to understand the world and what it does to them? What did the student demonstrators of the 1960s really want? During a lull in campus activism, then Chancellor Roger Heyns of the University of California at Berkeley appeared on educational television to discuss the current generation of students.

At one point in the discussion, he said,

> These kids are not hung up on Karl Marx, they are hung up on Thomas Jefferson.

The Declaration of Independence says one thing, but what the National Guard and the state highway patrol *do* may convey a different message: stay in line, little friends, and don't make waves.

May 4, 1970: Kent State University in Ohio—four students are killed and eight wounded by rifle fire from the National Guard.

May 14, 1970: Jackson State in Mississippi—two students are killed and ten wounded in a thirty-second barrage of buckshot fire directed at a women's dormitory by state highway patrolmen.

November 16, 1972: Southern University in Louisiana—two students are killed by a shotgun blast fired by state troopers. Authorities later claim the shotgun shell was "mistaken" for a tear gas shell.

June 1973: The campuses are quiet, and students are more interested in making a place for themselves in the world than in changing the world into a better place.

Goodbye, Thomas Jefferson.

Guidelines for California: Klotz versus Moomaw
As the hippie culture grew, and even primary grade students challenged the wisdom of their elders, many groups demanded that the public schools of California accept moral indoctrination as a primary duty.

Thomas Jefferson, writing in 1820: ". . . We are not afraid to follow truth wherever it may lead, nor to tolerate any error so long as reason is free to combat it."

But students are not necessarily encouraged to exercise reason in the public schools; many parents claimed that their neighbors' children were escaping the moral instruction once provided by families and churches. (The real problem was that the social conformity, minimal academic skills, and mild celebration of the American Way, which the schools had long purveyed, were no longer selling so well—students doubted their relevance.) The state board of education had never suggested teaching moral standards, perhaps from a commendable reluctance at having to define them, and the authority of the state board is not binding upon local boards in any case. But, in the past, state board "guidelines" have usually been honored at the local level.

In 1969, a proposed set of guidelines for the teaching of morality was prepared by Edwin Klotz, a staff assistant to Max Rafferty, then state superintendent of public instruction. The eighty-one-page document was "accepted" by the board in May. It was described as a fundamentalist Protestant attack on the United Nations, the United States Supreme Court, mental health programs, and sex education, among other matters. It urged local schools to pattern their moral training after the moral leadership program of the U.S. Marine Corps. A flood of protest mail inundated the offices of state officials, and the board backed away from the proposed guidelines at its May meeting.

Governor Ronald Reagan's own pastor, Reverend Donn Moomaw of the Bel Air Presbyterian Church, was placed in charge of a committee assigned to prepare a more satisfactory proposal. The committee he assembled was largely composed of white Protestant southern Californians. He later added a Catholic priest and a Mexican-American. Drafts of the new report were circulated among interested groups in the state for comment.

In January 1970, the new proposal was presented to the board. It was generally nonreligious in content, stressing "truth, morality, justice, and patriotism." Supporters of the Moomaw report described the earlier Klotz report as omitting the entire doctrine of the brotherhood of man.

The Moomaw report was adopted by the board with but one dissenting vote. The board adopted amendments to the report, including one that listed the Klotz proposal in its bibliography as a reference, which permitted Mr. Klotz to claim victory for his point of view. However, most of Mr. Klotz's supporters walked out of the meeting, carrying Bibles, pictures of Jesus Christ, and homemade picket signs draped in red, white, and blue.

State Superintendent Max Rafferty, the flamboyant, conservative educator, author of *Suffer, Little Children* and *The Passing of the Patriot*, failed in 1968 to be elected to the United States Senate. In 1970, Rafferty was opposed for reelection by Wilson Riles, his own deputy. Riles was an acknowledged specialist in the education of minority children. The electorate apparently felt that all of Max Rafferty's rhetoric had not improved the performance of California's schools.

Wilson Riles was the first black man to win election to a state-wide office in California.

Max Rafferty became dean of the School of Education at Troy State University, Alabama.

In California, the state curriculum commission agreed that, hereafter, science texts used in the state will present both divine creation and evolution as opposing theories about the origin of man. Darwin's theory of evolution had been the sole explanation offered, but religious fundamentalists had been battling the use of such texts for ten years.

Henceforth, California students who choose to believe in the encounter of Adam and Eve in the Garden of Eden will find some support in their public school texts.

Wilson Riles said that this was only a symbolic victory for the right wing; the forces of enlightenment in education would save their influence for a more significant purpose.

A Political Institution

The secret is out, and it was never very well kept. The public schools, being public, have never concentrated much attention on the welfare of their students, as that welfare might be defined by the students themselves. Rather, they have served as transmitters of the dominant values of the surrounding culture, the convictions of the taxpayers who pay the bills, as interpreted by the middle-class professionals who run the schools. The professionals have defined what constitutes "achievement," and have predicted that the culturally disadvantaged will fall short, and they do.

This insight has been pushed to its ultimate conclusion, and applied to universities, by Maulana Ron Karenga:

> Everything moves in terms of political power, because without that power nothing is accomplished. The educational institution [is] one of the institutions that the power structure maintains, in order to reinforce its own position. One learns to be a "better American," I assume, by going to an American university; where else could one learn to be a better American than in a university? What you have to understand is that you should not fool yourself by thinking that education is an academic thing; it is basically a political thing, and it provides identity, purpose, and direction within an American context.
>
> If you are a white institution, for example, and blacks come in here, then the blacks come out "white," too, unless they have some different identity, purpose, and direction to shield them from all of this.[2]

The Coleman Report

In 1954, the Supreme Court of the United States, reversing the 1896 "separate but equal" rule for public accommodations, found that racial segregation in the public schools is "inherently unequal" and thus contrary to the Constitution. A year later, the Court directed that the integration of the schools should proceed "with all deliberate speed." *Brown* v. *The Board of Education of Topeka, Kansas* thus entered the textbooks as a landmark case in the march toward realization of the American ideals enshrined in the Declaration of Independence.

But the Court decision was met with more deliberation than speed. Token integration was established in some southern districts; segregation increased in the North. Ten years after the *Brown* decision, the Civil Rights Act of 1964 included the following section:

> *Sec. 402.* The Commissioner shall conduct a survey and make a report to the President and the Congress, within two years of the enactment of this title, concerning the lack of availability of equal educational opportunities for individuals by reason of race, color, religion, or national origin in public educational facilities at all levels in the United States, its territories and possessions, and the District of Columbia.

The survey of some 4,000 schools, 465,000 students, and 20,000 teachers was headed by James Coleman of Johns Hopkins University. It was a massive research effort, made possible only by modern data-processing. The findings were published in 1966. Its first conclusion was that

> The great majority of American children attend schools that are largely segregated — that is, where almost all of their fellow students are of the same racial background as they are. . . . Meas-

2. Quoted in Rhoda L. Goldstein, ed., *Black Life and Culture in the United States* (New York: Crowell, 1971), pp. 346–347.

ured by [the Supreme Court standard], American public education remains largely unequal in most regions of the country, including all those where Negroes form any significant proportion of the population. . . .

Thus, after twelve years, segregation remained the general rule. But the Coleman report encompassed many other matters. One of its cautiously stated conclusions was that the learning rate of minority students (as measured by standard achievement tests) does increase somewhat in integrated schools, without causing a decrease in the learning rate of majority pupils.

After Fourteen Years...

Racial segregation imposed upon a school district by its board results in a dual school system, one for whites and another for blacks. It was this kind of *de jure* segregation, established by the legal authority, and most common in the southern states, which the Court found in violation of the Constitution. But the Court's command to cease the practice was evaded in many areas through a variety of inventive delaying tactics. If schools had integrated their kindergartens in 1955, and another grade in each year following, the first students from those classes would have graduated from high school in 1967. After fourteen years, the Court decided that there had been ample deliberation, and that the time had come for action. In 1968, a unanimous Court declared:

> The burden on a school board today is to come forward with a plan that promises realistically to work . . . *now* . . . until it is clear that state-imposed segregation has been completely removed.[3]

Progress was slow at first, for cases moved slowly through the courts. When the Department of Health, Education, and Welfare began withholding federal support funds from segregated districts, the abolition of dual school systems gained momentum. By 1972, some 2,000 school districts were busing under court orders.

In the North, the style of segregation was known as *de facto*. It resulted, not from the command of a school board, but from racial patterns in housing. When blacks came into a neighborhood, whites fled. And school boards obligingly built new schools for them in the suburbs.

Whatever its source, the psychological damage to the segregated child, cited in the *Brown* case of 1954, remained the issue.

When the battle against racial separation in the public schools moved to the North, parents discovered remarkable virtues in the neighborhood school.

3. *Green* v. *County School Board*, 391 U.S. 430, at 439.

The Unanswered Question

Despite all its virtuosity as social-science research, the Coleman report merely documented, without explaining, the fact that is at the heart of all the controversy about ghetto schools, community control, busing, the Head Start program, and the definition of "quality" in education. It is that the learning rate of black children in the public schools — as measured by such tests as the grade level of reading ability — declines, the longer the black child attends school. To suggest that there is a natural racial inferiority would be a blatantly racist answer, and Coleman doesn't consider it. As a sociologist, he readily adopts an alternative hypothesis: black, and other minority children, are "culturally disadvantaged." Something in their home environment, or in their neighborhoods, does not support the process of learning, so the rate of learning declines.

The Coleman report contains data that both contradict the assumption of cultural deprivation and suggest an answer to the unanswered question. The report reveals that the parents of black children take a greater interest in their children's school work than do the parents of white children, when the families' incomes are comparable. And the desire of black children for educational attainment — including the hope of attending college — is higher than that of white children from families of comparable income. Coleman finds that black people view education as a means of "social mobility" more than whites. So, statistically, the black child does not necessarily suffer from a lack of support for scholarship at home. Furthermore, the learning rate of black and white children is very close in the early grades, when parental support for the child facing the adjustment to the new school experience is crucial. The gap in learning rates manifests itself, and grows wider, in the upper grades; the gap increases the longer the children remain in school!

There is an important clue here. Can it be that the school itself is somehow responsible? The relationship between the student and the teacher and the counselor and the other students and even the psychologist administering achievement tests?

It is common for teachers and psychologists to . . . conclude, from their interactions with the slum child, that the child is nonverbal.

Let me present an example. . . . The test is this: the child is shown four pictures — a policeman, a doctor, a farmer, and a sailor. He is asked why the four pictures go together, what they have in common. This is what is known as a test of concept formation . . . very much related to verbal performance. The middle-class first grader . . . comes up with a good, acceptable concept or category by saying that they are all men or they are all people. This gives great joy to the person who is giving the test, and he smiles approvingly at the little boy.

Now, when the lower-class child sees the four pictures, he might say that they go together because the doctor helps the other men and gives medicine to them, or he might say something really silly — they go together because they *like* each other. That answer really makes the test-giver frown. It . . . shows a failure to abstract, to form categories; it's just experiential.

Does this mean that the child doesn't *know* they're all men? Or all people? Of course he knows it; it's perfectly obvious. But he is not oriented to relating words to other *words*. He gets down to far more fundamental issues. He asks what these four men might do to each other. Do they like each other? Or hate each other? Will they help or harm each other? These are, after all, important questions in life. If they are largely irrelevant to the school situation, how relevant is the school situation to life?[4]

The notion of the "culturally disadvantaged" permeates the schools. It affects teachers, administrators, psychologists. They need not be conscious racists to have an ingrained lower *expectation* for the achievement level of minority students. And this expectation will influence their placement of minority students in different classes, the kind of performance that is judged adequate enough to receive a word of praise, the assignment of work to be done, and a hundred other daily teaching decisions. As the years pass by, the expectation of low achievement is revealed as a self-fulfilling prophecy: the minority student's level of achievement actually is lower. But it takes years.

So there is a reason why minority children do better in integrated classrooms. The teachers have higher expectations.

Of course, one can picture a high school in a liberal community that is strictly integrated. Students of a variety of races and economic backgrounds are free to meet in the schoolyard, if they want to, and everybody cheers the fullback, regardless of his race. But the students are rigidly tracked in separate classrooms, according to "ability," and the blacks are mostly in the lower track, and the lower track does not achieve very well at all. If it did, it would invalidate the procedures for testing "ability."

Why did the Coleman report fail to pinpoint the role of the schools in their failure to teach minority children effectively? Because Coleman felt that class differences—summarized as "cultural disadvantagement"—were so important in determining the rate of learning that he controlled for this variable, rather than attempting to explain it. According to psychologist William Ryan, the Coleman report is "a triumph of sophisticated research design over common sense."[5]

When President Nixon considered appropriate policies in the field of education, he depended heavily on the Coleman report, and he invited Professor Coleman to serve him as a consultant. In his speech of March 24, 1970, President Nixon discussed the inescapable fact of the poor performance of schools in the urban ghettos. He said, in part,

It is not really because they serve black children that most of these schools are inferior, but because, rather, they serve poor children who often lack the home environment that encourages learning.

The president promised to spend more federal money to support the programs of the ghetto schools. He did not mention teacher expectations.

The Big Yellow School Bus

If any symbol could replace, in the twentieth century, the one-room schoolhouse that served rural America in the nineteenth century, it would be the big yellow school bus. Buses bring the economies of

4. William Ryan, *Blaming the Victim* (New York: Pantheon, 1971), pp. 40–42. Emphasis in the original.
5. Ibid., p. 43. The thesis that teacher expectations influence pupil performance may be further examined in Robert Rosenthal and Lenore Jacobson, *Pygmalion in the Classroom* (New York: Holt, Rinehart & Winston, 1968).

scale to the consolidated rural and suburban districts. They are used by city districts to collect pupils from their homes and to carry students on field trips.

The U.S. Office of Education reported that, during the school year 1969-70, 43.4 percent of the nation's public school students were regularly transported by bus. No exact figure is available on how many of those students rode their buses to attend a school to which they were assigned to achieve racial balance. The Office of Civil Rights in the Department of Health, Education, and Welfare agreed with the U.S. Commission on Civil Rights that no more than 2 or 3 percent of the students were being bused to achieve integration. In fact, Congress was told by the secretary of Health, Education, and Welfare that more busing was done before 1970 to preserve segregated schools than was done in 1970 to support school integration. The number of pupils bused in Georgia, for example, rose slightly, but the number of miles traveled by school buses declined markedly. With integration, children need no longer be carried past one segregated school in order to reach their own segregated school.

However,

School buses were bombed and burned in Pontiac, Michigan.

School buses were overturned in Lamar, South Carolina.

Detroit, Denver, and Richmond, Virginia were among the cities ordered to desegregate.

Anti-busing was made the key issue by Governor George Wallace of Alabama, when campaigning for the presidency in 1972. He won the primaries in Florida and Michigan, where courts had ordered integration to be accomplished by busing.

Local judges continued to suggest that bus transportation was one of the methods that could be used to achieve school integration.

The Supreme Court Speaks Again

When he campaigned for the presidency in 1968, Richard Nixon spoke often of his determination to appoint only "strict constructionists" to the Supreme Court. This promise was related to his concern for the restoration of law and order. Candidate Nixon also, during the fall of 1968, spoke of his opposition to "forced busing" that would require the transportation of school children to achieve racial balance.

After two of his nominees to the Court were rejected by the U.S. Senate, President Nixon succeeded, by mid-1971, in appointing two justices who were confirmed and took their seats.

What does "strict construction" mean? Surely the authors of the original Constitution had never heard of school buses. Yet, in 1971, the justices of the Supreme Court—including the two Nixon appointees—spoke unanimously, declaring,

> We find no basis for holding that the local school authorities may not be required to employ bus transportation as one tool of school desegregation. Desegregation plans cannot be limited to the walk-in school.[6]

Voices from Middle America

Meet the Barberas. Fletcher, aged thirty-three, graduate of an eastern men's college, is an electronics engineer who recruits bright high school students in southern California for his alma mater. His wife, Maureen, is the daughter of a retired army colonel, a former professional model, and now the mother of three children. She is more alarmed than amused when her oldest son, aged seven, announces that when he grows up he plans to be a hippie.

Charles Gatewood

6. *Swann* v. *Charlotte — Mecklenburg Board of Education*, 304 U.S. 1, at 30.

A new school opened in their neighborhood two years ago, and they support it.

FLETCHER: *The key issue, to me, is the neighborhood-school concept. I would feel very strongly against having my kids bused to a school, say, five or ten miles away. And the reason is the close involvement of the community with the school, the fact that there are a lot of parents down there, particularly mothers, actually working in the school, helping the school. This is a real benefit to the school, to the children, and to the mothers and fathers. It would be a great loss not to have that. The way things are structured here, if our children have a problem, either a scholastic problem, or a disciplinary problem, we hear about it, we know the teachers, we can go down and talk to them. They're close at hand, and we've been able to solve all the major problems that have come up. I just don't think there would be that kind of cooperation if the school was ten miles away.*

MAUREEN: *One of the reasons we moved here was, we knew the schools were good. . . .*

FLETCHER: *And, no matter how you cut it, if you're going to integrate schools from an area with a lower tax base and schools from an area with a higher tax base, you're probably talking about degrading, to a certain extent, the schools in the higher tax-base area, and I don't want that.*

> The Supreme Court of California, in *Serrano* v. *Priest*, ruled that California's method of financing school districts, which relies heavily on local property taxes, violates the state constitutional guarantee that every citizen shall have the equal protection of the laws. California school districts vary from $103 of taxable property per pupil to $952,156 in a heavily industrialized area with few residences. The California court noted that this makes the quality of a child's education depend upon the wealth of his parents and neighbors; rich districts can supply expensive education for their children along with lower tax rates.

When Fletcher Barbera was asked about the California decision that school financing based on local property taxes was unfair, he admitted that the variation in wealth between school districts creates a problem.

FLETCHER: *I agree that every child should have a reasonable opportunity. And a lot of it has to do with education, there's no question about it. . . . It's very hard to measure what is the real output of an educational system.*

MAUREEN: *And I know that there are some school districts that spend a lot less than ours does, you know, money per pupil, and yet they get far better results.*

FLETCHER: *What are we really trying to do? I don't think we really even know what we are trying to do. Everybody agrees that there should be a reasonable amount of equality. I think most people would agree to that. I even agree to that. But the question is, what is it? . . . There's a direct connection between the amount of opportunity in the school and the average income of the families from which the children come. . . . So that says that there can't be any equality of opportunity unless you have a classless society. And that's, if you carry it to the extreme, that's socialism.*

The Supreme Court of the United States—with four Nixon-appointed justices—has not proven hospitable to policies that smack of socialism. In April 1973, the Court ruled that education is not one of the rights guaranteed by the U.S. Constitution. Therefore, said the Court in a 5-4 decision, the inequities that result from the property-tax system of educational finance cannot be challenged on the basis of federal constitutional guarantees; let the states act, for education is basically a state responsibility.[7]

Goodbye, Thomas Jefferson?

Inequality

In 1972, journals of education and the newsmagazines gave banner headlines to the publication of a study by Christopher Jencks, of Harvard, and his associates.[8] Jencks attacked the assumption that racial integration and the equalization of expenditures among the richer and poorer schools can lead toward racial and economic equality (or at least equal opportunity) in American life. Amassing mountains of data, he claimed to establish that schooling doesn't really make that much difference; the kinds of people leaving the high school door upon graduation are much the same as those who entered the kindergarten door so many years before. Adding new money to the school budget doesn't make much difference; "tracking" inside the classes doesn't matter much; smaller class size has little impact; hardly anything done for or with children in the schools modifies the inequalities they experience as adults. Much more important as formative influences are their experiences at home and in the street, and perhaps what they see on television.

Jencks suggested that Americans ought to abandon their usage of the schools as vehicles for social experimentation and reform. Instead, they should evaluate schools on the basis of whether students and teachers find them satisfying places in which to serve their time. As for society, Jencks proposed a remedy for inequality. Socialism.

The President Speaks

On March 16, 1972, President Nixon spoke on television. He did not minimize the amount of effort devoted to busing for the purpose of achieving racial balance. On the contrary, he stated that the lower federal courts had gone far beyond what the Supreme Court judged to be necessary. He said, in part,

> There's no escaping the fact that some people do oppose busing because of racial prejudice. But to go on from this to conclude that anti-busing is simply a code word for prejudice is a vicious libel on millions of concerned parents who oppose busing—not because they are against desegregation, but because they are for better education for their children.
>
> They want their children educated in their own neighborhoods. They have invested their life savings in a home in a neighborhood they chose because it had good schools. They do not want their children bused across the city to an inferior school just to meet some social planner's concept of what is considered to be the correct racial balance, or what is called progressive social policy.

7. *Rodriguez* v. *San Antonio Independent School District 409 U.S. 488* (1973).
8. Christopher Jencks et al., *Inequality: A Reassessment of the Effect of Family and Schooling in America* (New York: Basic Books, 1972).

President Nixon proposed two bills: The Equal Educational Opportunities Act, which would allow busing only as a last-resort remedy
for segregation and would provide federal funds for compensatory
education in impoverished schools; and the Student Transportation
Moratorium Act, which would bar the implementation of all new
court-ordered busing until July 1, 1973.

Professor James Coleman, principal author of the Coleman report,
was asked what he thought of Nixon's education policy, as first announced in 1970.

> Dr. Coleman told a reporter that he thought Mr. Nixon had
> exaggerated the problem of busing pupils to achieve desegre-
> gation and had softened the civil rights enforcement of the
> Johnson administration. But he said he supported unequivocally
> the president's efforts to spend money to ease the desegregation
> process and to overcome racial isolation.
>
> "It is weaker than past presidential statements with regard
> to legal enforcement, but it is much stronger than any other
> statement with regard to resource commitment," Dr. Coleman
> said.[9]

Waiting for the Court

President Nixon stated that the Constitution prohibits de jure racial
segregation, the kind decreed by school boards, but de facto segregation, resulting from residential patterns, is permitted. So, leaving
the black students in their ghetto schools, and the whites in their
suburban schools, federal money—$1.5 billion—would help upgrade
the ghetto schools. Meanwhile, the opponents of segregation argued
that so-called de facto segregation also resulted from governmental
action, such as Federal Housing Administration support for the mortgages of suburban homes, which drew middle-class whites away from
the cities. Thus it was not really distinguishable from de jure segregation. Across the land, lower federal courts began to agree.

The question of the constitutionality of de facto segregation was
presented by a case arising in Denver. The Supreme Court agreed to
consider that case. It arranged to hear arguments on it during the fall
term of 1972. By then, four of the nine justice were Nixon appointees.

Meanwhile,

> Congress passed a law delaying the implementation of
> court-ordered busing and debated further methods for limiting
> "forced busing";

> In their convention at Miami, the Democrats wrote in their
> 1972 platform that "transportation of students is another tool to
> accomplish desegregation. It must continue to be available,
> according to Supreme Court decisions";

> In their convention at Miami, the Republicans opposed busing
> and pledged to support a constitutional amendment, if necessary,
> to prevent it;

> School children climbed on board their buses; mostly they
> traveled in peace.

9. *New York Times*, March 26, 1970.

Class Discussion

Gabriel Eisenberg hurried to the desk so there would be no hesitation in his entry into the classroom. Some of the two-dozen seats were still filling with students. He was struck by the quietness; the students apparently didn't know each other, having been assigned to this particular room and time by a computer. Instead of greetings or conversation, they seemed withdrawn into themselves. Several were reading newspapers; Eisenberg wondered how many were reading sports sections, and if he should start by commenting on the previous day's game.

Eisenberg had lectured twice to the full class, but this was his first meeting with a discussion section. He looked around the room, wondering if he could really communicate with undergraduates, after the grinding years in graduate school. He decided against a discussion of athletics; better tend to business. He cleared his throat, not very loudly, and saw several students lay aside their papers.

"Maybe the easiest way to start," he said, "is for me to ask if there are any questions about the lectures I've given so far. The concept of pluralism isn't really difficult, but most of you won't have heard of it before. So, please, if there is anything you don't quite follow, now is the time to speak up."

Silence deepened in the room. Some students glanced down at their desks. Gabriel looked from one to the other, hoping somebody would return his gaze. In a middle row, a black youth stirred in his seat. Gabriel caught his eye and smiled encouragingly.

"It isn't really a question of understanding it," he said. "That doesn't bother me. It's a question of, well, I just can't relate to it."

"Can't relate? How do you mean?" the instructor asked.

"I heard you talk about all these multiple centers of power, and I followed all the arrows on those diagrams you drew on the board, and I just couldn't relate to it, and I don't think anybody from the inner city could. Because, whoever's got the power, it doesn't really matter, it's gonna be used to keep us down. It's all what we call The Man."

Gabriel Eisenberg saw that every student eye was trained on the young black; he imagined he felt an electric charge of sympathy and agreement in the room; he felt it himself.

"I think," he said cautiously, "that what you express is a problem of point of view. The difference between what one member of a political society sees, and feels, every day, and the viewpoint of an observer who attempts to gain an understanding of the system as a whole by constructing a model of it. Remember, the model is an abstraction which we must then test for its conformity to reality. And the impact of any abstract formulation is strictly intellectual. It can never have the impact of daily experience."

The boy nodded. "Sure," he said. "But the only way I have of testing your model—so far anyway—is whether it matches my own experience. And it doesn't match. All that talk about inputs and feedbacks, and all those arrows, it just doesn't fit anything. I don't see any place for me on that diagram. It doesn't account for unemployment in the ghetto. Or for police brutality."

Gabriel Eisenberg wished he had chosen a different topic to begin his lectures. He felt his face flushing with effort to say exactly the right thing.

"In terms of the model, what you are talking about is recognizing the outputs of the system—or, I should say, their absence. Because whenever some dominant interest in the system—the military structure, or the corporate structure—wins in the contest for the allocation of scarce resources, it means that the inner cities, the unemployed, the poverty stricken, get nothing. And the purpose of the model, the attempt to picture our pluralist system, is to explain how and why scarce resources are allocated in the way they are. Because it isn't inevitable, and neither is it an accident. It results from the contest of competing demands."

"But, Professor, if this is some kind of game, can you call it a fair game if there's one team that never has a chance to win?"

"Of course you can't. We'll be talking about the values of the culture surrounding the political system, and how they influence the performance of actors in the political system. The pervasiveness of institutionalized racism, for example. All of this leads up to my own criticism of the pluralist model, which is based on the fact that equality of access to the system simply does not exist. Narrowly based, well-financed pressure groups, concentrating on single issues—think of the oil lobby—have a power vastly out of proportion to their numbers, for example. And the disadvantaged groups of American society are doubly disadvantaged, because they don't have the political skills needed to organize effectively. Somebody who might become such an organizer needs to understand the entire political system, if he is going to organize and get results. That's the main reason for studying several models, or descriptions, of the American political system, in order to decide which one, or which combination of various ones, comes closest to describing the reality."

The black youth was slumped down in his chair now, his head nodding slightly. Eisenberg couldn't tell whether he was bored or indicating agreement. The instructor plunged on.

"As I've tried to indicate, another place where I part company with the pluralists is the conclusion of the analysis. For most of them wind up excusing the faults of the system and defending the status quo. But I think that the only reason for understanding the system is to be able to change it."

Eisenberg paused, looking around the room. All the newspapers were put away, a few students were taking notes, and three held up their hands. Eisenberg nodded at a thin figure in the back row dressed in patched Levis and a faded army jacket. The student's blond beard moved as he spoke.

"I don't relate to your diagrams either," the bearded student said, "but for a different reason. The whole thing is based on what you call 'the allocation of scarce resources.' That gives it away. The system you're talking about is the whole middle-class, capitalist, exploitative economic system that is using up what we have on this earth without replacing anything. It's the system that is polluting the air and water and napalming innocent peasants in Asia. Your model is based on the assumption that everybody wants to get into that system, but I say, 'no thanks.' And if enough people drop out of it, the whole thing will collapse from its own weight."

A girl wearing a frilly blouse answered without being recognized by the instructor. Her voice was heavy with contempt. "You talk about dropping out of the system," she said, "but I bet you're still driving around in some powerful convertible your parents gave you for high school graduation."

The blond bearded student responded gently. "Sorry," he said, "you're thinking of the wrong freak. I sold my car years ago. I get around on a ten-speed."

There was a rumble of amusement in the classroom. Stifling his own smile, Gabriel Eisenberg said, "I really think we ought to deal with concepts, not personalities."

The bearded student seemed to enjoy the attention of the class. He addressed himself to the black student in the front row. "People should think twice," he said, "before they work to get into this rotten, corrupting system. Because it's based on increasing consumption, satisfying artificial consumer demands created by Madison Avenue advertising. Consumption that will end up by destroying everything we have. Demands that change people into plastic, making them forget they're part of the animal kingdom, cutting them off from nature."

The husky black student frowned. "Man," he said, "I've never owned a car in my life. I think you ought to let me try one for myself, before you tell me it's a false value."

A girl in a front seat spoke up, only vaguely raising her hand. "That's right," she said. "When there are riots and looting in the ghettos, people are always asking, 'What's wrong with those people? What do they really want?' But they want the same things everybody wants—a decent home, a job, a chance to raise their families in peace. And maybe a chance to get away and go camping."

The comments came quickly now, and Gabriel Eisenberg had little need to say anything. He began to relax. The comments had less and less to do with pluralism, but he decided that was all right. When the hour neared its end, he was astonished that it had gone by so quickly. But he dismissed the class promptly, knowing some had to go across the campus before the next period.

On the way out of the room, he walked next to a young man he had noticed doodling furiously in his notebook, but never making a comment. "Pretty good discussion, don't you think?" the instructor asked.

"Mr. Eisenberg, what some of the kids said was kind of interesting, maybe, but I don't see what it has to do with that hour exam next month."

A Letter from Jerry

Vancouver, British Columbia

February 10, 1972

Dear Dad,

Thank you for the clippings about Senator Taft's proposal for amnesty in return for alternative service for "draft dodgers and deserters." It was nice of you to say that you'll understand if I don't think it's very relevant now, while the fighting is still going on in Vietnam, but that I ought to be thinking about the future.

Believe me, I think about the future a lot. And about the past, too. And about what it really means to love your country, as something different from your family and friends. Some of these things are hard to work out, but I'm getting a chance to do it for myself, which is the only way that makes a difference.

I think you know that it really broke me up last year when I couldn't even come down across the border to go to Grandma's funeral—or at least I thought I couldn't. At that point, it felt like the whole FBI, and most of the highway patrolmen, were looking just for me. I've since learned that there are at least 60,000 of us up here, and I've talked to some guys who've made several trips back to see their families, without any hassle. Maybe it's only a rumor that the FBI watches funeral notices in order to grab guys who go back for them.

I miss you and Mom and Joey and Melinda and a couple of old girl friends. But the more I think about it, the more I realize that I'm in no hurry to go back. Because I realize that I would be going back into a place that has always been kind of ready for me, although I didn't have much to do with making it. Those months I spent in the Marines weren't so different from the years of high school and junior college, only more concentrated. The schools and the Marines were telling me who I am, and where I fit in, and what I can expect out of life.

Up here, for the first time, I have to figure all that out for myself. It isn't easy, and it takes time. But I have a good enough job, and I have enough to eat, and I have some good friends, and some of them are bugged by the same things that bug me. I certainly don't have any reason to feel sorry for myself.

I don't know how long it will take, but I do know that, working on it from here, I am going to find out for myself just who I am, and where I am going. I don't want to have people try to teach me that any more.

I hope you and the family are well. I may try to visit you in another year. Meanwhile, why don't you think about bringing the family up here for vacation this summer?

With love to you all,

Jerry

Equal opportunity remained the goal, and public education was still recommended as the means of attaining it. But it was harder and harder to pretend that the schools in the central cities were equal to those in the rich suburbs. What bothered taxpayers the most was that some students seemed ungrateful for their education, and others criticized America instead of fighting for it.

Education and
the American Dream

When the words about equality were written into the Declaration of Independence, education was a private affair. Parents who could afford it hired tutors, or paid tuition to private schools. Thomas Jefferson felt that free public education was essential to democracy, but public schools were not established extensively in most states until the nineteenth century neared its close. Since that time, the public schools have developed a special role in American society. Exactly how that role should be defined and implemented was never completely clear. Now, more than ever, it is in question.

Nearly everyone complains about education. Are the schools really to blame, or are they victims of a deeper contradiction in the structure of American values? Do we expect too much from education, and not enough of America?

Becoming a Citizen

Most governments are concerned with affording protection for the rights of their citizens. The Declaration of Independence asserts that governments are instituted among men in order to secure such rights ("Life, Liberty, and the pursuit of Happiness") and that the powers of government are derived from the consent of the governed.

This assertion raises a number of questions, including the manner in which citizens indicate their consent to be governed, and under what circumstances they may withdraw that consent. Another basic issue is the very definition of "citizen." How does one become a citizen? The matter was not dealt with in the Constitution until the Fourteenth Amendment was adopted in 1868. It states that "all persons born or naturalized in the United States . . . are citizens of the United States and of the State wherein they reside. . . ."

Citizenship by birth is a principle of ancient Roman law known as *jus soli*, or "right of soil." Persons born in the United States are immediately citizens; there is no probationary period. Congress has also implemented the Roman principle of *jus sanguinis*, or right of blood. This means that the children of American parents, or of only one American parent, born in foreign countries, may also claim American citizenship.

For an immigrant to become a naturalized citizen is more complicated. Five years of continuous residence in the United States is required (three years in the case of the spouse of a citizen, or aliens serving in the United States armed forces). A course of instruction in the principles of the Constitution and the obligations as well as the rights of citizens is required. Finally, the new citizen swears an oath of allegiance before a federal judge. The only legal difference between the rights of native-born and naturalized citizens is that naturalized citizens may not be elected president or vice president of the United States.

> In *Hawaii*, James Michener wrote of the elderly Japanese and Chinese immigrants who had lived all their adult lives in the islands. After World War II, when Asians were permitted to become naturalized, many did so upon the urging of their children. Michener pictures the elderly applicants for citizenship wandering through their daily routines and mumbling "executive, legislative, judicial; executive, legislative, judicial. . . ."

A Voice from Middle America

Piotr Pavel was born in Russia in 1907. His grandfather was a rabbi, his father an attorney, and his mother a physician. When the Communist revolution triumphed, Piotr's family was viewed as part of the bourgeois enemy. Piotr was not permitted to study engineering. He left Russia, pleading ill health. He completed his training as an electrical engineer in France and worked in the pioneering days of French radio. Shortly after Hitler came to power in Germany, Piotr emigrated to the United States. He became a citizen in 1940.

PIOTR PAVEL: *I wasn't privileged to be born in this country, so I take my Constitution seriously. I think a naturalized citizen takes things much more seriously, because the native thinks of it as something that can be taken for granted. The naturalized citizen may have lived under regimes that are far from democratic, and that makes him appreciate America more. For one thing, he tends to respect the flag as a symbol of the good things America stands for.*

Political Socialization

Do native-born American citizens take their citizenship for granted? They are not required to take courses or pass examinations or even swear an oath; citizenship comes with birth. In several American states, the legislatures have reacted by passing laws that require the study of the American and state constitutions in the public schools, including colleges. Most modern nations provide in their schools the formal study of national traditions and values, and authoritarian governments usually regard the indoctrination of children as a primary task. Compared to the Hitler Youth Organization of Nazi Germany, or the Russian student's progression through various apprenticeship organizations like the Young Pioneers (joined at age ten) to the Komsomol, from which the future leaders of the Communist party are recruited, the civics classes of American high schools are best described as dull.

But do citizens learn about citizenship only in classes? Quite the contrary. Children develop a sense of belonging to a particular nation, and a sense of its government and figures of authority, at a very early age. Such attitudes are present in their environment—in the home, school, church, youth organizations, even neighborhood gangs, and in the media of communication like television, and they are absorbed without the child being particularly aware of their absorption, just as he learns the language spoken by the other members of his family. This is known as the process of political socialization, which is defined as "induction into the political culture."

The process continues into adult life and is never really completed. There is nothing to sharpen one's vague impression of the authority of the police, for example, like being arrested for reckless driving. And one's evaluation of legislative bodies may change if the city councilman or congressman responds favorably to a special request.

But the rather heavy-handed attempts of state legislatures to require the formal study of American traditions in the states' public schools may indicate a lack of confidence in the outcome of the natural process of political socialization. The natural process may include a lot of negative feelings:

Policemen known only as "pigs" or "the fuzz";

Building inspectors who serve the interests of the landlords, rather than the tenants;

Urban renewal projects that destroy poor people's homes, without finding new places for them to live;

Tax collectors' bookkeeping requirements that drive small businessmen out of business;

Caseworkers in the welfare office that disqualify one's family;

Orders for induction into the armed forces issued in the name of the president of the United States.

With such potential for negative experiences with government, it is only natural that legislators would wish to assure that young people also learn about the positive attributes of government. So,

The school day begins with pledging allegiance to the flag;

"God Bless America" and "The Star Spangled Banner" are sung in school assemblies;

Pupils learn about the inspired work of the founding fathers and the great principle of the separation of powers, without learning that some countries have perfectly satisfactory governments without a separation of powers or even a written constitution;

School children are taught that, in America, every citizen is equal, regardless of race, creed, color, or sex;

They are also taught that the accused is innocent until proven guilty.

In short, students are taught a great deal about the *ideals* of American democracy, often with the implication that those ideals have been completely realized. Sudden confrontation with reality may come as a shock. In the last few years, a number of college students have reacted violently to that shock.

Knowledge that the Ohio National Guard was routinely issued live ammunition for riot duty was not widespread on the campus of Kent State University. When the shots first rang out, students asked one another, "They're shooting blanks, aren't they?" And some members of the faculty assured them that live ammunition would never be used in a crowd.

> The professors may have been confused, but there were some students who knew. From the very beginning, they knew. Cindy Sudberry must be one of the most beautiful girls at Kent State. . . . She is a black—in her case, a golden tan. Of the shooting she says, "It was pathetic for a black like me to watch the nice white boys and girls growing up so fast. 'Are the guns loaded?' they asked. 'Are they using real bullets?' What in hell did they think the Guard have in their guns? You didn't hear any black asking damn-fool questions like that. But the poor white kids never knew what hit them. So many came up to me later and said, 'We never knew it was like that.' And I had to bite my tongue to keep from saying, 'I knew when I was born. The guns are always loaded.' "[1]

1. James A. Michener, *Kent State: What Happened and Why* (New York: Random House, 1971), p. 376.

We Hold These Truths...

To look at the Declaration of Independence reposing in its case of shatterproof glass, you would think that it is a document unique in all the world: a gathering together of priceless and original ideas in a document that, while imitated, has never been equaled.

It was the product of a particular time in human history, of a particular place (Philadelphia) and to a large extent, of a particular human mind (Thomas Jefferson's). But it was also a typical product of the eighteenth century and its faith in human reason, based on analyses of human society that began with the ancient Greeks. It was an expression of the liberal challenge to the medieval belief that forms of government were established by divine will; that in serving those governments, men somehow served God. The liberal belief was that *man* should always be considered more important than any social or political institution. Governments (including kings, princes, and prime ministers) resulted from arrangements made between men to fulfill their recognized needs. If those needs were not met, the institutions should be replaced. A chief spokesman of this belief was the English writer John Locke. Locke held that men, simply by being born, acquire the right to preserve their own lives, their own liberty, and such property as they are able to acquire. Governments are formed to protect these three rights.

The primary purpose of the Declaration of Independence was to tell the world that the thirteen colonies were withdrawing their allegiance to King George III and Great Britain. This could have been done in a sentence or two. But the signers of the document wanted to explain their reasons. They listed both general and specific grievances against the British government. The Declaration was phrased as an appeal to all mankind for understanding and support of the new nation.

> We hold these Truths to be self-evident, that all Men are created equal, that they are endowed by their Creator with certain Unalienable Rights, that among these are Life, Liberty and the pursuit of Happiness—That to secure these rights, Governments are instituted among Men, deriving their just Powers from the Consent of the Governed that whenever any Form of Government becomes destructive of these ends, it is the Right of the People to alter or to abolish it ...

Thus wrote Thomas Jefferson, Virginia gentleman, slave-owner disturbed by the institution of slavery, amateur inventor, author, spokesman for an age. He was thirty-three years old. He was a member of the Establishment of his time.

The Declaration of Independence was a revolutionary document—not because it promised to tear down the social order, abolish private property, or redistribute wealth. It did none of these. What it did was to state the American ideal: equality, liberty, and the right of the majority to establish and control its own government. And to abolish that government, if necessary.

"All men are created equal." A noble sentiment, but what does it mean? What has it traditionally meant, in America? According to one comfortable myth, the Declaration of Independence defined in 1776 the American Ideal, and the Constitution, adopted in 1789, provided the enduring governmental framework to realize that ideal.

That myth has been discredited.

For one thing, the Constitution not only condoned slavery but valued each slave at three-fifths of a man, for purposes of representation. So much for equality.

For another, the principle of checks and balances, the fundamental structure of the Constitution, was adopted by the founding fathers as a means of preventing the common people from having complete or continuing control over the decisions of government. Their pessimistic view of human nature extended both to the few and to the many. They wished to avoid a tyranny exercised by the majority, as well as the despotism of a few.

So what does "all men are created equal" really mean? To Thomas Jefferson, it certainly did not mean that all men are equally endowed with native talent and ability. He felt that aristocracy was inevitable; his concern was that it be based on merit, not the accident of wealthy parentage.

The More General Diffusion of Knowledge

In 1779, Jefferson introduced a bill in the Virginia Legislature which provided for the "more general diffusion of knowledge." It proposed a complete system of public education. The state would be divided into areas of five or six square miles each and a schoolhouse built in each area. There, at the expense of the taxpayers, every boy and girl (except for the children of slaves) would receive a minimum of three years' education. Second, there would be established a system of residential grammar schools, where the children of adequately wealthy parents would pay tuition for their schooling, but the best male pupils from the elementary schools would be educated at public expense. Third, the most able graduates of these grammar schools would attend the College of William and Mary, again at public expense. Fourth, the College of William and Mary, which was then serving largely as a secondary academy, would be converted into a university.

The first section of the bill, defining its purposes, stated Jefferson's conviction that universal education is the appropriate means for making the people the guardians of their own liberties. Since governments have shown nearly universal tendencies to become tyrannies, the study of history should enable the people "to know ambition under all its shapes, and . . . exert their natural powers to defeat its purposes."

We marvel today that such an outcome could be promised on the basis of only three years' schooling; but the idea of any education at all being supported by public funds was considered dangerously radical at the time. The bill did not pass in 1779, nor for forty years thereafter. Jefferson turned again to plans for public education after he had retired from the presidency.

A major purpose of the bill of 1779 was to encourage the development of an aristocracy of merit at public expense, by providing free education for the truly talented whose parents could not afford to provide it themselves.

> Those persons, who nature hath endowed with genius and virtue, should be rendered by liberal education worthy to receive, and able to guard the sacred deposit of the rights and liberties of their fellow citizens, and that they should be called to that charge without regard to wealth, birth or other accidental condition or circumstance; but the indigence of the greater number disabling them from so educating, at their own expense, those of their children whom nature hath fitly formed and disposed to become useful instruments for the public, it is better that such should be sought for and educated at the common expense of all. . . .[2]

In later describing this plan in his *Notes on the State of Virginia*, Jefferson described this selective feature of his plan of education as a method through which "the best geniuses will be raked from the rubbish annually."[3] This statement of 1781 should not be held against the man who later led the assault upon the Federalists and their posture of privilege. Jefferson's conception of Virginia in 1779 had been of a society fairly rigidly separated into social classes; only the educated, upper class would be the governing class. Equality of opportunity — movement from the lowest to the highest class — could only be realized through selective free education.

An Aristocracy of Wealth?

The founding fathers were men of established means. They were concerned above all with creating a government able to defend itself against foreign enemies and secure the liberties of its citizens. But a secondary motive was protecting the economic advantages of their own class against what they took to be the natural jealousy of the poorer classes. Rather than seeking, with Jefferson, the selection of an aristocracy based on merit alone, they were at least in part concerned with the protection of an aristocracy based on birth and wealth.

The governmental structure they designed has become a more democratic system, at least in a formal sense, than they intended. The people now have a larger share of power. U.S. senators are elected directly by the people; the presidency has become a popular office, responsive to the people and in contact with their lives in a manner completely unknown in the days of George Washington; the right to vote has been extended to progressively larger groups of the population.

However, the system of checks and balances still works as intended. Particularly in the realm of domestic policy, it is much easier to protect the status quo than to establish new policies. It requires organized outrage on the part of a very substantial part of the people to overcome the special advantages guarded by established interests who block or delay change.

How does the ideal of equality fare today?

The contrast between the very rich and the very poor is more striking than it was in the eighteenth century. Jefferson's beloved independent yeoman farmer has vanished, along with the frontier and the horse-drawn plough. The sharecropper remains.

But, you may argue, the concept of equality was never intended to guarantee equal comfort or wealth; all it guarantees is an equal chance.

2. Bill 79 of 1779, reprinted in James B. Conant, *Thomas Jefferson and the Development of American Public Education* (Berkeley and Los Angeles: University of California Press, 1962), p. 88.
3. Ibid., p. 7.

Very well. Perhaps equality is realized in one important sense if everyone shares the cost of government fairly, according to his ability to pay. Look into the maze of special privileges and good legislative intentions exploited for unfair gain that is the tax structure of the United States. Count the hundreds of citizens with gross annual incomes of more than $200,000 who legally avoid paying a single penny of taxes to the national government.

Or, is equality better defined as equal treatment by the agents of the law? Compare the treatment given, in most prisons, to draft evaders, with that accorded mere thieves. Five of the nine Supreme Court justices counted the number of blacks and poor people who were executed, compared to those indicted for similar crimes, and concluded that the death penalty, as administered by the states in the 1970s, is "cruel and unusual punishment," and unconstitutional.[4]

Can equality be defined as the humane application of rules established by legislative bodies? Look into the offices of welfare agencies and other bureaucracies.

Is equality the equal chance to express one's personality? Consider the controversies in high schools over dress codes and hair length.

Achievement: A Conflicting Value

Long before Thomas Jefferson asserted man's equality in the Declaration of Independence, the lives of American colonists were guided by rather a different conviction about the role of man on earth. It began as a very deep religious conviction. The first settlers of New England were religious radicals, who believed in a more immediate relationship between God and men than was preached by the established churches of Europe. Protestant clergymen who accompanied the first settlers saw the hand of God at work in conquering the North American continent. It seemed as if He had delayed its very discovery and settlement until that special group which enjoyed His favor but was persecuted by the older churches might come here, bend the resources of nature to their own usage, and multiply.

The early Puritans believed strictly in predestination. Men were marked for salvation or damnation at birth. But this belief was soon obscured by the tendency of the believers to act in a manner that might seem to demonstrate their select (saved) status. Sociologist Max Weber has written that

> it is not the ethical *doctrine* of a religion, but that form of ethical conduct upon which *premiums* are placed that matters. . . . For Puritanism, that conduct was a certain methodical, rational way of life which — given certain conditions — paved the way for the "spirit" of modern capitalism. The premiums were placed upon "proving" oneself before God in the sense of attaining salvation . . . and "proving" oneself before men in the sense of socially holding one's own within the Puritan sects.[5]

The idea of demonstrating the truth of one's predestined salvation stimulated an ideal type of behavior that became the norm of conduct, even when its religious origins were largely forgotten. The ideal man of New England was independent, hard-working, and did not

4. *Furman* v. *Georgia*, 408 U.S. 238, decided June 29, 1972.
5. H. H. Gerth and C. Wright Mills, tr. and ed., *From Max Weber* (New York: Oxford University Press, 1958), p. 321.

squander his wealth on frivolous entertainment. Rather, he hoarded an inheritance for his family. He asked for special favors from no man, and certainly expected none from government. Governments existed to maintain order and ensure the enforceability of private contracts. The individual was free to get on with his job, which was the conversion of the endless natural resources of the new continent to human usage.

Count Alexis de Tocqueville perceived this truth when he visited America in 1831. He wrote to a friend at home in France:

> The whole world here seems a malleable substance that man turns and fashions to his pleasure; an immense field whose smallest part only has yet been traversed, is here open to industry. Not a man but may reasonably hope to gain the comforts of life; not one who does not know that with love of work his future is certain.[6]

"Love of work." A determination to work hard oneself, and to prescribe hard work for others, became a central ethical precept for Americans, even before our independence was won from Great Britain. The idea would be elevated into mythology by Horatio Alger, Jr., and it would be exploited by the "robber baron" capitalists of the nineteenth century, and it would be used to hide their own racism from themselves by some Americans in the 1970s. But the idea that each individual must achieve his own wealth and comfort in economic competition with his fellows remained a basic American conviction.

During the presidential campaign of 1972, Richard Nixon attacked George McGovern's plans for reforming the welfare program by a redistribution of wealth. McGovern's plan, said President Nixon, would destroy the "work ethic." And the work ethic, he stated, is a source of America's greatness.

The feeling shared by America's early settlers that they were serving a divine mission had other consequences. The Puritans were seeking religious freedom, all right—their own freedom. It was not religious toleration as we understand it today. Being members of a congrega-

6. Alexis de Tocqueville to E. de Chabrol, tr. in George Wilson Pierson, *Tocqueville in America* (Garden City, N.Y.: Anchor, 1959), p. 87.

tion specially favored by God, they were not particularly friendly toward other people who failed to see the divine light. The American Indians were often regarded as heathens who should be taught the truths of Christianity, by force if necessary. A few of the early Puritans regarded the Indians as allies of the devil, concluding that there was no alternative to force. Modern ecologists may say that the Indians of the eighteenth century lived in close harmony with nature. The Puritans thought the Indians were lazy. And laziness was sinful. What better proof of their connection with the forces of darkness?

Later, when black Africans were imported as slaves, those who became converts to Christianity were granted their freedom. This soon proved unprofitable to their owners, however, and the practice was abandoned.

Jefferson's assertion that "all men are created equal" did not really fit the colonial practice. The conviction of the moral benefit of hard work, and the belief that the worker should be able to retain and enjoy the fruits of his labor (and of his father's and grandfather's labor) remains deeply ingrained in the American system of values. The belief that, in some sense, all men are created equal, is also ingrained in the American system of values. The fact that these two beliefs are contradictory receives little attention.

Why are they contradictory? When a man of talent works hard, exploiting his chances and the resources of nature, he founds family fortunes and business enterprises of a scope that affronts the ideal of equality. This encourages the development of an aristocracy of wealth and inherited privilege. When such families and businesses dominate a particular field of the economy, the chance of success by an individual who possesses only talent is greatly reduced.

How may the contradiction between the belief in equality and the moral worth of individual achievement be resolved? One way is to define equality as "equal opportunity," the chance for an equal start in the race of life. Given the nature of a complex technological society, how may equality of opportunity be assured? By providing all with equal access to education, so that the skills needed to succeed in life's competition may be learned.

This "solution" avoids other, more painful, alternatives. For the wealthy family need not share its income, or its tax writeoffs, with the poorer family. And the poorer family tolerates its poverty, secure in its hope that its children will have an education enabling them to rise to riches. Having acquired middle-class comfort, those same children can then condemn proposals for the redistribution of national income as socialist schemes for destroying the national moral fiber.

> The public schools' task is no less than obscuring the differences between wealth and poverty, implanting the work ethic in its pupils, and teaching everybody to share the values of the middle class. Public education is the motive force behind the American Dream of Success.

The Principles of Horace Mann

The architects of public education did not necessarily set out to make it the servant of the established order. When Horace Mann was asked to give up his career as a state legislator to become secretary of the Massachusetts Board of Education, reducing his income by at least half, he confided his reason for accepting to his diary: "I have faith in the improvability of the race—in their accelerating improvability."[7] The date was June 30, 1837.

7. Jessie Treichler, *Educating for Democracy: Horace Mann* (Chicago: Encyclopedia Brittannica Press, 1962), p. 86.

During his twelve years as secretary to the Massachusetts Board of Education, Mann's annual reports to the legislature expounded his developing ideas about education. Widely read, they influenced the developing pattern of education far beyond the borders of his state.

Significantly, Mann's efforts were begun in Massachusetts; the first steps toward urbanization and an industrial economy were taken in New England, and it was natural that New Englanders should first perceive the limitations of the haphazard system that abandoned most of the responsibility for education to church organizations and permitted many children to receive no education at all. Even in the 1830s, illiterates moving from the country to the city could not be readily placed in positions in the growing economy; and their very presence made men of property nervous. They began to support free education, fearing that the urban poor, cut off from opportunity by illiteracy, would attack the social order.

In his travels around Massachusetts, Mann practically shamed the townships into taking seriously their legal responsibility for providing primary education. In 1839, he founded the first normal school, intended for the preparation of teachers. Gradual acceptance by the states of the responsibility to support such institutions meant that teachers would no longer be casually prepared as spokesmen for some religious sect. However, since most of higher education remained under the control of religious bodies, Mann later decided that an institution such as Antioch College was essential for proving that the nonsectarian principle could be extended throughout the educational system. Mann became the first president of Antioch.

Horace Mann did not succeed, where Jefferson had failed, in establishing a complete system of free education. Nevertheless, his name is forever associated with basic features of American public education:

> Separation of church and state through the elimination of sectarian bias in publicly supported instruction. (Reverend Moomaw was thus a follower of Horace Mann; Edwin Klotz was not.)

> Popularization of Jefferson's conviction that an adequate educational system is essential to the development of democracy.

> Support for the education of teachers by the state.

> Support for local schools by the local taxpayers, accepting education as a general responsibility: schools are supplied for both rich and poor, without cost to parents.

Education for All

Horace Mann did not live to see the nationwide adoption of free public education. Just as they had done in Jefferson's time, childless taxpayers resisted the notion of financing the education of other people's children. The more common practice was the "rate-bill" system through which publicly managed schools, only partially supported by taxes, charged tuition. The school trustees of each town were empowered to assess a tuition charge against all but poverty-stricken parents, in proportion to the number of days their children had attended school during the year. Parents had little incentive to discourage truancy.

The rate-bill system was finally abolished in New York in 1867 and in all other states by 1871. One decisive factor was the vote of immigrants, who wanted education but could not pay for it. Another was the vote of wealthy men, who feared the disruptive consequences if the children of the poor were denied the education that promised opportunity.

Schools became the instruments of social mobility, the fires under the melting pot. This was true for the students, and, increasingly, it became true for the teachers. For teaching was one of the occupations open to the children of lower-class parents that lifted them out of blue-collar status and seemed to promise a more genteel way of life.

Just as the public schools had a ready-made clientele, so did the schools of education. If the high schools were to prepare students for college, it was only reasonable that the high school teachers be college products themselves; so Horace Mann's normal schools were upgraded in status, whether or not their programs were improved.

> The colleges must, in effect, run an intellectual economy-class service to meet the needs and suit the style of teacher-candidates. It isn't that these are necessarily less able, although by ordinary standards (such as norms on standard intelligence and achievement tests) they do tend to be less able than liberal arts or science and engineering students in the same institution. But their ideology and mental texture are different and less distinguished, and the educational curriculum has evolved to match their experience and peculiar intellectual style. It is frequently hortatory and pontifical rather than analytical; pompous and philanthropic but basically contemptuous of intellectual distinction and insensitive to its demands. The intellectual atmosphere of ed courses is, in fact, much the same as that of the high school itself.[8]

With the new status of teacher training, the teachers of teachers reached out for influence and professional recognition. Soon the states began adopting requirements for the certification of teachers that were largely administered by professional educators; and they usually stipulated that a number of hours be spent in professional education classes.

All in the name of establishing decent standards of instruction.

From good intentions, vast bureaucracies grow.

Closing the Alternatives

Teachers seeking acceptance into the middle class tended to identify with the values and attitudes of that class. For many years, those values were the most pervasively stated of any in the American culture. To their students, and the students' parents, the public schools were not so much in the business of preparing citizens for democratic responsibilities as they were keepers of the gateway to the middle class: a training ground for small businessmen, managers, salesmen; preparation for study leading to the professions, including teaching.

This usage of the schools, although not exactly that intended by Thomas Jefferson and Horace Mann, worked fairly well as long as two preconditions were present. The first was that students could indeed gain admission to the middle class—once their accents and manners were smoothed out—provided they demonstrated a modicum of individual ability. The second precondition was that there be

8. Edgar Z. Friedenberg, *Coming of Age in America: Growth and Acquiescence* (New York: Vintage, 1965), p. 263.

alternative courses open to the young person. If he did not choose to submit to whatever pain was involved in changing his manners and attitudes to conform to middle-class standards, he could still find a meaningful place in life as a largely uneducated, largely unskilled worker.

This alternative was closed off by the midpoint of the twentieth century. School attendance was compulsory until at least age sixteen in most states; and employers found it convenient to employ only those with a high school diploma even for unskilled jobs. The diploma served as a screening device, automatically reducing the number of applicants worthy of consideration.

The status of poverty had never been respected in American society, but, before the advent of television, the poor person was not surrounded with quarter-hourly reminders of the gulf of comfort separating him from a higher economic class. Cynics eager to attribute a personal motive to an entire system found that, with the development of a consumer-oriented economy, the function of the schools had become the training of consumers: instilling the materialistic values that assured competitive consumption—keeping up with the Joneses. Businessmen supported campaigns aimed at keeping the potential dropout in school.

Great Expectations

Everybody involved with the public schools had expectations of what the schools should accomplish. But those expectations were in conflict.

Poorer parents expected the schools to give their children opportunities they themselves had not known. Immigrant families expected to learn the language and attitudes of the dominant culture. Employers expected workers who were trained to cope with the complexities of industrial society. But the greatest task of the schools was to obscure the contradiction between the values of equality and achievement. For, if all students have an equal opportunity to succeed supplied by education, their actual success depends on their own ambition and labor. They need blame nobody but themselves for failure, and the inequalities of American society can be explained away.

But it became painfully clear that the schools were not equal to each other. As the cities decayed, parents who could afford it either sent their children to private schools or moved to suburbs with good public schools. Removal of the upper-middle- and middle-class students accelerated the decline of the schools they left behind, as experienced teachers sought higher pay in the suburbs.

Then the federal courts began to consider cases challenging the de facto segregation of the races in the schools resulting from the segregation of housing. The contradiction in values had become obvious and painful. People believed in equality of opportunity, but not if it meant that their own children were required to travel by bus to a school no better than the local one, and possibly worse.

Disbanding the dual school systems of the South had been comparatively simple. No school board or state legislature should assign to a separate race the badge of inferiority explicit in the establishment of separate schools. Breaking up the patterns of de facto segregation raised more-difficult questions. If the school-age population of a city contains 35.7 percent black children, must every school in the city contain 35.7 percent black pupils? Must the city district be combined with the districts of the surrounding suburbs (containing 1.3 percent black children) to the end that no school in either city or suburb shall contain more than 11.2 percent black pupils? How many hours of bus travel should be allowed, in order to achieve this ideal? Or, assume that a grade school in a Chicano neighborhood carries on a program of instruction in both English and Spanish. Is equal opportunity achieved by dispersing Spanish-speaking students to other schools, none of which can provide instruction in two languages?

In addition to all the other expectations, the schools were being asked to assure the success of American multiracial society. But how much reform in the society outside can be accomplished by changes in the schools? Students are more influenced—their attitudes more definitely formed—by experiences at home, in their neighborhoods, and by exposure to the mass media, than by study in the classroom.

Yet, what is the impact of the school?

A Training Ground for...Democracy?

In spite of Jefferson's belief in the benefits of subject matter, particularly history, the impact of a school or any other institution comes from the total experience it provides. Who can argue that a high school that expends more energy in checking hall passes than in producing Shakespeare provides the best training for entry into an open society that respects individual liberties? If the hierarchy of school authority treats the student as an object rather than a person, will the student learn to expect, or to offer, human understanding to others, when he himself becomes an adult? Can the school prepare the student for citizenship if it treats him as an inmate?

> What is learned most thoroughly ... is certain core assumptions that govern the conditions of life of most adolescents in this country and train them to operate as adult, if not as mature, Americans. The first of these is the assumption that the state has the right to compel adolescents to spend six or seven hours a day, five days a week ... in a specific place, under the charge of a particular group of persons in whose selection they have no voice, performing tasks about which they have no choice, without remuneration and subject to specialized regulations and sanctions that are applicable to no one else in the community nor to them except in this place. ... Compulsory school attendance functions as a bill of attainder against a particular age group, so the first thing the young learn in school is that there are certain sanctions and restrictions that apply only to them, that they do not participate fully in the freedoms guaranteed by the state, and that, *therefore, these freedoms do not really partake of the character of inalienable rights.*[9]

What profit does a student gain from reading John Stuart Mill's *On Liberty*, and learning of the free marketplace of ideas, if he does this reading in a school that rewards only the most conventional attitudes and regulates the manner of his dress, the length of his hair, and prohibits the exercise of his vocal chords in the cafeteria?

Can the American high school be pictured as an institution that imperils the future of democracy? Of course there are brilliant, dedicated, and inspired teachers. They are rare, and each should be treasured. Of course there are administrators who care for students as persons, not statistics. There are even schools that encourage students to pursue intellectual matters that excite them, even when they violate the boundaries of the curriculum.

9. Ibid., p. 42. Emphasis in the original.

Yet what graduate of an American high school can report that he found the experience truly *liberating,* in the sense intended in the phrase "liberal education"? It is a time and place surrounded by pressures: the pressures of middle-class parents anxious about college admission; juvenile court officials keeping their charges off the ghetto streets; teachers wanting the class to make a good record on the achievement tests. The most compelling pressure comes from the student culture itself. That culture may regard any show of special distinction in academic matters, or any sign of enjoying intellectual pursuits for their own sake, rather than for what rewards a good grade-point average can bring, as being at least undemocratic and probably perverse.

Like social workers, missionaries, and colonial administrators, teachers may enter their professions for the most noble of motives. Those motives define their attitudes, rather than the response of the students. Their clients, the students, truly a captive audience, have the least ability to influence the teachers' actions. Both actions and attitudes are shaped by the teacher's training as a professional and modified by pressures transmitted from the surrounding community and by the school administration. The teacher finds that his professional ideology provides a response to the pressures upon him — and it is a response that frequently ignores the real needs of students:

"Good citizenship" may be equated with not chewing gum or not talking during study period. Thus a noble concept, born in Athens, is reduced to piffle.

Ignorant of cultural patterns other than his own, the teacher may explicitly or implicitly refuse to recognize that black, Chicano, Puerto Rican, or Chinese students possess cultural traditions.

The teacher may substitute administrative classification for interpersonal relations; a "behavior problem" can be sent to the counselor, rather than being confronted as a human being.

Deviations from conventional attitudes or techniques may be quashed, even when they are the sign of a rare spirit of independence or spark of creativity.

The teacher may become an expert at constructing self-fulfilling prophecies: How can a "disadvantaged" child be expected to attain other than a low level of achievement?

Edgar Z. Friedenberg has described the outlook of middle-class teachers assigned to Indian schools operated by the Bureau of Indian Affairs:

> Here the teachers insist enthusiastically that the children have
> no culture at all: no music, no language — they can't even speak
> English; no ethical code — they *help* each other on tests!; and no
> experience of life — they have never seen an escalator or a super-
> market. For the Oglala Sioux themselves, and for their way of
> life, most of the teachers express contempt and fear; and they
> avoid any contact with the Indian community out of school.[10]

This could just as well be used as a description of the interaction (or
lack of it) between many urban teachers and the ghetto communities
they are expected to serve.

The Right to Be Different
At one time, the public schools had been the chief instrument for
achieving the concept of America as a great melting pot, where citizens of varied racial, religious, and national backgrounds were converted into patriotic Americans (and consumers).

But at the same time that school integration was proceeding in the
name of equal opportunity, the conception of the melting pot was
attacked. Imitation of the white, Anglo-Saxon, Protestant virtues was
no longer seen as the means of creating a viable society. The cost of
giving up one's cultural heritage was seen as too great a price for
acceptance in the American economic system. Some black spokesmen preached separatism, rather than integration. The children and
grandchildren of immigrant parents sought to recapture the folkways
that their elders had abandoned. No longer was there a single dominant cultural style. Americans looked toward a society of increasing
diversity, rather than the melting-pot ideal of homogenization. Perhaps the most disturbing development of the 1960s — at least to their
parents — was the abandonment of the middle-class work ethic by
affluent young people, who chose alternative life styles, a return to
more simple ways of living, natural foods, and the traditions of individual craftsmanship, in place of the mass production of the Plastic
Age.

Not only was the dominant cultural tradition of the middle class
under attack from without, as minority groups insisted upon the validity of their ethnic identity. It was also under attack from within,
as its own children consciously developed a counter-culture that challenged the established values. This conflict between life styles and
generations was aggravated, until 1973, by the war in Asia, which
some of the older generation supported while the younger generation
was required to fight.

Education — particularly the colleges — got caught in the middle.

What Is a University?

Thomas Jefferson proposed university education at public expense
for the most talented, in the expectation that they would there be
prepared for careers in the public service. They would be rendered
"worthy to receive, and able to guard the sacred deposit of the rights
and liberties of their fellow citizens." Jefferson saw no conflict between this conception of education and his insistence upon universal
suffrage. For it was a *representative* democracy that he sought to

---

10. Ibid., p. 261. Emphasis in the original.

establish; the daily work of government would be done by those best prepared by ability and training to handle it; their stewardship of the public trust would be held to account by the entire citizenry.

In Jefferson's time, and long thereafter, American universities were largely controlled by Protestant denominations, and their courses of study were of a rigid classical mold. In founding the University of Virginia, Jefferson foresaw the elective system, suggesting that students should be free to concentrate their attention upon those subjects they felt would be most useful to the vocations they would pursue after graduation. When it opened in 1825, the University of Virginia was one of nine state institutions of higher education; but a former president of Harvard assures us that it was the only one that attempted to be a university in the European sense, and its example influenced the newer states as they considered providing for higher education. "One could almost say," he adds, "that the shape of higher education in the West before the Morrill Act was largely fashioned in Virginia."[11]

The European university of the time was an elite institution, largely aloof from affairs of the marketplace. Before this pattern was well established in America, the Morrill Act of 1862 provided grants of the public lands (held by the national government) for the support of educational institutions. The resulting land-grant colleges, which assumed the task of educating young people for the mastery of the agricultural and mechanical arts, were very much part of the marketplace: they perceived their duty as being to apply the power of science to the needs of free enterprise. They also approached higher education as suitable to a broader range of the population than did the Harvards and Princetons.

The American university had not clearly defined its own function when it was overtaken by the knowledge explosion and a nearly universal desire for higher education. Each scholarly specialty became more narrow. The number of scholars (charged with making at least one "original contribution to knowledge" in order to acquire the doctorate admitting them to the scholarly fraternity) was increased dramatically so that the burgeoning student enrollment would have teachers; and the most prestigious universities promoted teachers only if they published further contributions to their specialties.

If professors had ever been disinterested seekers of the truth (and the very name university, which suggests that there *is* a single, unified, and discoverable Truth, was soon challenged), they were easily tempted to operate in that particular corner of the search for knowledge that was favored by those in government and in the foundations making research grants.

What, in this arrangement, was to become of the students? Particularly the undergraduate students — whom Jefferson wanted prepared for public service?

As long as the bright students were treated as junior apprentices, being initiated into the mystical world of foundation applications, "publish or perish," and the search for truth, while the average students stayed in their fraternities until the recruiter from the corporation of their choice appeared on campus, all was well. But, in the 1960s, students discovered that all was not right in the world, that universities made many decisions affecting their lives without consulting them, and that the places in society for which the university seemed to prepare them were not completely attractive. They charged that many of those places were based on acquiescence in institutionalized injustice.

11. Conant, *Thomas Jefferson and Public Education*, p. 29.

Students led the lunch counter sit-ins that challenged southern racial discrimination, but did not immediately end it. Students were involved in the drive to organize the Mississippi Freedom Democratic Party; but the demands of that group were largely rejected by party leaders at the 1964 Democratic National Convention. Expeditions from the campuses into surrounding society did not tumble the historical walls of injustice, so the students brought their convictions and techniques back home to the campus.

Across the nation, student spokesmen claimed that their own universities were microcosms of the larger society; reforming the universities was a step toward the salvation of society. Compared to southern towns, the disruption of universities proved relatively easy, and many student demands were realized: the termination of defense contracts here, the abolition of ROTC there, consultation on faculty promotions elsewhere. And, nearly everywhere, undergraduates received more attention than they had gotten for years. Students demonstrated that universities are essentially voluntary institutions which can be paralyzed when large numbers of students reject the voluntary arrangements.

As students attempted to protest national policies by attacking the serenity of their campuses, public authorities tended to invade those campuses to restore order, recognizing that the college deans commanded no battalions. Public opinion usually did not favor the students.

Constantine Manos

Their Own Executioners

When the Democratic National Convention of 1968 became immortal, not for the acts of the delegates, but for the battle between antiwar demonstrators and the forces of Mayor Daley in the streets outside, wise men worried about the future of the nation. One who did so was Harry N. Ashmore, former southern newspaper editor:

> Coming back from the convention hall in the early morning hours after the National Guard had replaced the blue-helmeted police outside the Hilton I found that the confrontation was now confined to one side of the generation gap. The soldiers, standing shoulder to shoulder with their rifles across their chests, were of an age with those who writhed along their front scattering taunts and jeers and obscene invitations. These were boys from Skokie and Peoria and East St. Louis, largely bypassed by the affluence that underwrites the middle-class protest movement that has taken on the sound of revolution but so far has not achieved much more reality than the television dramas upon which all these young were suckled. . . .
>
> There would always be a line somewhere manned by very young men in combat fatigues under orders to hold at any cost —and if they were pressed long enough and hard enough the time would come when the elevated gun barrels would come down and live rounds would slide home. This would be the ultimate tragedy, and the ultimate irony, for if reality ever overtakes the rhetoric the old and corrupt will be somewhere else when the young provide their own executioners.[12]

Harry Ashmore's prophecy came true months later, at Kent State University, when a line of young, but tried, National Guardsmen fired live rounds toward a taunting crowd. The nearest student was twenty yards away. The four students who died were in a parking lot one hundred yards behind.

12. From "Limits of Dissent (A Center Symposium)," *The Center Magazine* (Santa Barbara: Center for the Study of Democratic Institutions, November 1968).

The shootings at Kent State were followed quickly by the killing of students at Jackson State, Mississippi, by highway patrolmen. The two disasters seemed a kind of culmination of what the politicians called "campus disorders" and professors called "student unrest." Campus demonstrations did not end the invasion of Cambodia. Bombing continued in Vietnam for two more years, although American ground troops were largely withdrawn. The draft lottery removed individual uncertainty as to whether or not one would be called to serve in the armed forces. The campus mood changed; the vote was extended to eighteen-year-olds. When George McGovern confronted Richard Nixon in November 1972, young people didn't seem particularly excited about it.

But things could never be quite the same. The assumption that universities existed to serve the established powers through research with profitable applications, while students are prepared like other cogs to take their place in the industrial machine, had been mortally wounded.

Perhaps no new idea of what a college should be was developed, but it was clear that the purpose of higher education could easily be perverted by the concerns of the surrounding society.

And what is the purpose of higher education? In 1820, Thomas Jefferson wrote about the University of Virginia:

> This institution will be based on the illimitable freedom of the human mind. For here we are not afraid to follow truth wherever it may lead, nor to tolerate any error so long as reason is free to combat it.[13]

What Is Education For?

Jefferson's statement can stand as a noble definition, not only of the purpose of a university, but of the goal of education in a free society. However, the bulk of members in every human society—whether or not we grant it the label "free"—do not pursue the implications of "the illimitable freedom of the human mind." The pursuit of such freedom can be painful, and it can lead to prescriptions for change in the established order. In America, public expectations for public education have been quite different.

Education has been perceived traditionally by parents and by most students as the instrument of social mobility, the road to "success."

Employers have used the achievement of a school diploma or a college degree as a convenient screening device to sort out job applicants.

Asserting their influence over local school boards, citizen groups have insisted that it is the duty of school to deny the existence of alternatives to the prevailing local standards—particularly in matters of sex and race.

Responding to community pressures, the schools (normally with the help of students themselves) have expressed little interest in

---

13. From a letter to William Roscoe, reprinted in Conant, *Thomas Jefferson and Public Education*, p. 29.

nurturing the "freedom of the human mind"; rather they have concerned themselves with preparing students for a preexisting niche in life.

American colleges, concentrating not upon the vision of the "educated man" as a product (for who in a democracy could agree on what that would be?) but upon training apprentices for graduate and professional schools or the corporations, developed the "credit hour" as the lowest common denominator of education and the grade-point average as the standard measure of achievement.

Thus both secondary schools and the colleges became expert at providing certificates and degrees for those who did not challenge bureaucratic authority, accepted prevailing attitudes, and spent the required number of hours in the classroom.

The public expected the educational system to be, and in most cases it became, a servant of social stability, rather than an inspiration for social change.

The controversy over the busing of school children demonstrated something about the nature of American education. So did campus rioting. One lesson is that, when public educational institutions stand at the forefront of social change, taxpayers who resist social change may be willing to destroy the institutions, rather than yield to the forces of history. Many of its neighbors supported a proposal for converting Kent State University into an insane asylum.

If education is called upon to resolve contradictions in the value structure of society, when society itself refuses to recognize them, the first victims may be the rights of the students themselves — their rights to pursue truth, and their own identity, in the company of friends.

CHAPTER 2

Parties and Elections:
So the People May Choose

IMAGES 2

Prelude to a
Lonesome Landslide

REFLECTIONS 2

Parties, Voters,
and Critical Elections

IMAGES 2

Prelude to a
Lonesome Landslide

Every four years, the election of a president, the only official who speaks for the entire people, gives the United States an opportunity to define its goals anew. Candidates can offer competing visions of the nation and its purposes. The interaction between the people and their leaders can provide new energy and a renewed sense of purpose.

It didn't work in 1972. Largely unknown early in the year, George McGovern swept toward the Democratic nomination, but won it in circumstances that divided his party. The flow of enthusiasm generated by "the Prairie Populist" on the primary trail was dissipated. McGovern seemed to vacillate over the question of retaining Thomas Eagleton as his running mate. Then his efforts were devoted to clarifying past statements and apologizing for the policy preferences of his most visible supporters. George McGovern was finally unable to challenge the incumbent, for McGovern himself was the issue, not his vision of the nation's future.

For his part, Richard Nixon surrounded himself with the dignity and symbolism of the presidential office, allowing the feeling to grow that questioning the president's wisdom is akin to attacking the Constitution.

President Nixon was reelected by an historic landslide. But his party did not win a majority in either house of Congress. This left the suspicion that the people did not choose between opposing visions of the national future, but only — as had happened before — between contesting personalities. Voters split their tickets as an expression of distrust in both parties and candidates. And many eligible citizens did not bother to vote at all.

What difference did it make?

The Democratic Recovery

No account of the 1972 election can begin with that year. The seeds of public attitudes, as well as candidate actions, were planted long before. One explanation of the Democratic defeat is that the party was still suffering from its dramatic rejection by the voters in 1968, which followed only by four years the historic landslide victory of Lyndon Johnson, and by five years the martyrdom of John F. Kennedy.

The Democrats had been the "normal majority" party since the election of Franklin D. Roosevelt in 1932. The eight-year interlude of President Eisenhower (who carried a Republican majority into the

House of Representatives in 1952 that endured for only two years)
merely emphasized the Democrats' majority status. The full smile of
political fortune was turned upon the Democrats in 1964. Yet by 1968,
the nation was torn by discord: riots, demonstrations, and a growing
sense that events could no longer be influenced; the world, and the
government of the United States, were simply out of control.

Tradition held that the reelection of an incumbent president could
not be challenged within his own party. Cool Senator Eugene Mc-
Carthy agreed to become the candidate of a group of young Democrats
determined to battle against that tradition. McCarthy's handsome
showing in the New Hampshire primary led Robert Kennedy to announce his candidacy. With his Vietnam policy a shambles and his
popularity plunging, Lyndon Johnson then withdrew his candidacy
for a second term.

The battle for the nomination wound through the primary states,
with the climax coming in California, where, during the celebration
of his primary victory, Robert Kennedy was murdered.

Next, Chicago exploded in bloodshed. Antiwar demonstrators in
the streets were unable to determine the party's decisions, but their
clash with the forces of Mayor Daley preempted press and television
coverage of the convention itself. Vice President Hubert Humphrey,
who had not offered himself as a candidate in the primaries, received
the nomination. Lyndon Johnson dared not appear at the convention,
but his men controlled it. Looking at the wreckage of the convention,
Senator George McGovern commented, "This party has got to reform
itself, or die."

Hubert Humphrey began his campaign with the prospect of running third, behind Governor George Wallace of Alabama. But Humphrey was finally able to distinguish his own position on Vietnam
from that of President Johnson, so young protestors began to listen instead of heckling. The leaders of organized labor mustered all their
political muscle to win their members back to the Democratic banner
from George Wallace. Richard Nixon (who won the Republican nomination without much fuss) opened the campaign with a 15 percent
lead in the polls, but he finished less than 1 percent ahead of Humphrey in November. The Wallace vote was held to only 13 percent,
and the Democratic party maintained a majority in both House
and Senate.

Attempting to reverse this situation, President Nixon campaigned
hard for Republican congressional candidates in 1970. Addressing
himself to the discontents of what he called "the silent majority,"
the president used themes that were somewhat similar to those
used by George Wallace two years before. But the president's great
effort was largely a failure, and Democrats were encouraged to believe that there was no substantial Middle American backlash directed against the welfare policies of the Democratic party.

Meanwhile, substantial reforms in the method of selecting delegates for the 1972 Democratic National Convention had been proposed by a committee, first headed by George McGovern, and they
were accepted by most of the states. Warfare continued in Vietnam;
no longer was it "Lyndon Johnson's War"; it was Richard Nixon's.
As an early opponent of the war, George McGovern seemed likely
to inherit the youthful enthusiasm that had sustained the preconven-
tion campaigns of Eugene McCarthy and Robert Kennedy in 1968.

By the spring of 1972, Democrats felt that their party fortunes
were much restored from the disasters of 1968, and they would have
a fighting chance of unseating the incumbent president, Richard
Nixon. The Democratic delegates gathered in Miami for serious purposes; they did not care to engage in an exercise in futility.

Protecting the Image

In Book Seven of *The Republic* is Plato's fable of the cave. Plato imagines persons chained in a cave who can see only the shadows cast on the wall before them by persons passing in front of the fire-light behind them. With no contradictory experience, the people chained in the cave would base their entire concept of truth upon the images of shadows.

There is an important parallel between Plato's notion of the cave and the experience of watching the drama of the world unfold in black and white, or pastel, shadows flickering across the picture tube of a television set. Those shadowy images provide most of the information about politics for the American people.

A candidate for national leadership can be seen in person by only a sample of the American people. He can be touched by even fewer; he can converse with hardly any. The people can know and judge their prospective leaders only on the basis of the shadows—pictures on the screen, and word shadows written by the journalists who are our professional politician-watchers. There is no way for the people to measure any gap that develops between image and reality.

Richard Nixon and the Image-Makers

Richard Nixon's political career began after World War II, when television sets were becoming a feature of American living rooms. In 1952, he delivered the famous "Checkers speech" (Checkers was the name of the family dog), which squelched a move in the Republican party to force Nixon off the national ticket as General Eisenhower's running mate. He was generally regarded as a master of the new medium, but he remained aware of its artificiality, of its electronic imposition between himself and the people. He refused to wear makeup, although his heavy beard tended to make him seem something of a thug on the TV screen, for he was suspicious of television's manufactured reality. In 1960, when nominated for the presidency, he promised to campaign in every one of the fifty states, to be seen in person by as many Americans as possible. Attempting to meet this commitment, even after an accident confined him to bed for two weeks, he became tired and underweight, and that was how he appeared in his first television debate against John F. Kennedy. The historic first debate had an audience of eighty million, while the following debates never drew more than sixty million viewers. Nixon felt that he had the best of that argument, in matters of substance, but he simply did not match John Kennedy's vigorous and youthful image.

In 1968, Richard Nixon placed himself in the hands of the experts —television producers, speechwriters, and makeup men. His presentations to the public through television were carefully staged, and he did not tire himself with endless face-to-face campaigning, as he had done in 1960. He stayed rather aloof from the contest. The turmoil that racked the nation was clearly associated with the Democratic party, and he was willing to benefit from discord among his opponents. (He must have been shocked at the closeness of the final outcome.)

In 1970, President Nixon felt that he had to increase the representation of Republicans in Congress, if he were to have a chance of enacting his most important programs. His advisers talked of a "southern strategy" which would win votes that had gone to Democrats in the South and appeal to the "silent majority" in the Midwest and southern California. Winning these areas, he could easily ignore the Northeast, where "an effete corps of intellectual snobs"—as Vice President Agnew labeled them—edit magazines and write television news commentaries.

So he returned to outdoor campaigning. He renewed the joyous partisanship that had been his assignment as vice president. He persuaded Republicans who had safe seats in the House of Representatives to become candidates for the Senate. Young hecklers were admitted to his rallies in limited numbers, so that he could point to an example of the degradation of American values. In San Jose, California, he became involved in a confrontation with long-haired youths, which received widespread publicity but did not succeed in reelecting Senator George Murphy.

In all, the president engaged in some rather undignified activities. And they didn't work. As planning began for the 1972 campaign, his advisers worried about the contrast between President Nixon being received in great dignity by the rulers of Russia and China and the image of Candidate Nixon shaking his fist at an airport rally in Dubuque, Iowa. No, the spontaneity of campaigning directly among the people could only be dangerous. Better to keep the image-makers in control. One of the earliest decisions was to protect the dignity of the office; he would be the president of the United States seeking a renewal of his mandate, not Richard Nixon indulging in partisan controversy with some candidate who only aspired to that great office. His campaign committee was named the Committee to Reelect the President. It was supported by the Finance Committee to Reelect the President.

Campaign workers would later call registered voters, saying, "The president of the United States has asked me to call you...." For the first time, a presidential campaign developed a computerized, direct-mail and telephone campaign. By the end of the campaign, the Committee for the Reelection of the President would have so much money that nearly every registered voter could receive a personally addressed letter in the form of a telegram from Richard Nixon urging the voter to "participate" in the election. Some of the surplus money would be paid to G. Gordon Liddy to finance "dirty tricks."

Republicans did not plan the campaign of 1972 as a contest between equals. They knew that incumbent presidents who sought reelection in the twentieth century have not been rejected by the voters, with the exception of Herbert Hoover, whose first term was tied to economic disaster.

The devaluation of the dollar and the skyrocketing price of meat happened only after President Nixon's reelection was secure. By then, the press and Judge Sirica made details public about the Watergate break-in of Liddy and his accomplices.

Choosing the Candidates

Whatever problems confronted Richard Nixon, they were not the same as plagued Herbert Hoover in 1932. For Richard Nixon had made historic journeys in the cause of world peace, and he had withdrawn troops from Vietnam, and he had affirmed his opposition to tax increases, and he hinted that his solutions for domestic problems would be adequate, if only the Democratic Congress would stop frustrating their passage. (Conservative Republicans also opposed a great number of them, such as the Family Assistance Plan proposal.)

Richard Nixon's America was a studied contrast to that of Lyndon Johnson's. Under President Nixon's guidance, the nation seemed believable again; in the winter of 1968, before Johnson's withdrawal, it had seemed to be coming apart at the seams. Richard Nixon let it be known that he would discourage the disruptive elements in American society by ignoring them. Meanwhile, he hastened to modify the policies that led to discontent and disruption. By the spring of 1972, he seemed to be in a nearly impregnable position. Nevertheless, a challenger arose within the ranks of the president's own party.

How quickly traditions can change. In 1968, leading Democrats refused to run against Lyndon Johnson for months, until Eugene McCarthy agreed to do it; McCarthy wanted to oppose the war, and he had no further political ambitions.

Congressman Paul McCloskey of California, who won national attention by defeating Shirley Temple Black in a Republican primary, announced his candidacy for the Republican nomination, in order to give antiwar Republican voters an alternative to President Nixon. Himself a combat veteran, McCloskey felt that the continued bombing in Vietnam was a moral outrage. McCloskey's challenge died in the snows of New Hampshire, where he was soundly defeated. His defeat seems, in retrospect, a symbol of the fact that President Nixon had neutralized the Vietnam war as an issue, by progressively withdrawing ground troops.

But the war remained a leading issue to the Democratic candidates. Senator George McGovern of South Dakota had been asked to oppose Lyndon Johnson in the 1968 primaries but had refused, although McGovern had been one of the first senators to speak out against the war. Following the assassination of Robert Kennedy, McGovern did mount a last-minute candidacy. He then decided that, if the presidency is worth seeking, it is worth seeking properly, with plans and an organization established long in advance.

As the 1972 primary season began, Senator Edmund Muskie of Maine (Humphrey's 1968 running mate) was labeled the front-runner. Muskie had gained national attention in 1968 as the most level-headed and sensible of the four candidates; this impression was reinforced in 1970, when Muskie answered President Nixon's broadcast of the San Jose confrontation with youth. And Muskie won the primary in New Hampshire, his neighbor state. But George McGovern's young organization was there, and the South Dakotan (largely unknown to the nation) finished a surprisingly strong second.

Edmund Muskie did not win any more primaries. People remembered a show of emotionalism in the New Hampshire snow that presumably signaled the end of his candidacy. But it was more fundamental than that. As the acknowledged front-runner, Muskie seemed to have little to win and everything to lose if he should take aggressive campaign positions, for he was certain to make enemies. So he did very little. And he made no new enemies. But his friends began to drift away, eager to find a leader who would take them into the center of the action.

> Muskie, in keeping his campaign cool, was following expert advice. But there were forces at work in the Democratic party which the experts did not understand.

Where Did the People Stand?

In the period between the 1968 and 1972 elections, there were a number of analyses of the changing relationship between the American people and their two great, historic, political parties. The one credited with supplying Richard Nixon's picture of the electorate was written by Kevin Phillips, who served in 1968 as an adviser to John Mitchell, then Nixon's campaign manager. He called it *The Emerging Republican Majority*.[1] He argued that there is a cycle in American political history that is due to be repeated; the Democrats will become a permanent minority party, while the Republicans capture a majority. They will do this by ignoring the eastern cities with all their problems, and by responding instead to the wishes of the suburbs and the fastest-growing areas of the country in the Midwest and Southwest. Wallace's 13 percent vote in 1968 was cast by persons all-but-ready to change from the Democratic to the Republican party. They merely used Wallace as a stepping-stone on the way.

It was easier to criticize Mr. Phillips's book in the spring of 1972 than in November. If Richard Nixon was ignoring the East and New England, they didn't seem to mind: he got everybody's vote except for Massachusetts and the District of Columbia.

In answer to Phillips, Richard Scammon and Ben Wattenberg published *The Real Majority*.[2] They argued that the Democratic party would court defeat if it attempted to form a coalition of minorities. The American voter, they said, is "unyoung, unpoor, and unblack." He is also middle-aged, middle-income, and middle-minded. Candidates who appeal to the fringe elements of the political spectrum will be beaten, for the voter is passionately middle-of-the-road. He is also distressed by drugs, street crime, the generation gap, and welfare "chiselers." Such problems combine to make up the "social issue," which will be crucial to all future elections.

Humphrey's Claim and Wallace's Achievement

When, at the end of April, Hubert H. Humphrey managed to win the Pennsylvania primary, he announced that the "great, moderate middle" of the Democratic party had spoken, appointing him its leader. Thus he attempted to picture himself as the only kind of candidate Scammon and Wattenberg claimed could win. Humphrey felt comfortable with the claim. Active in national politics since 1948, he was one of the best-known figures in the party. Once discounted as a doctrinaire liberal, he had learned the practical arts of politics under the tutelage of Lyndon Johnson when Johnson was Majority Leader of the Senate. Humphrey had made his peace with the traditional leaders of the party, particularly including organized labor. He had sought the presidency for years and narrowly missed it in

---

1. Kevin B. Phillips, *The Emerging Republican Majority* (Garden City, N.Y.: Doubleday 1970).
2. Richard Scammon and Ben J. Wattenberg, *The Real Majority* (New York: Coward-McCann & Geoghegan, 1971).

1968. He probably felt himself better-qualified for the office than George McGovern. Although many of the young activists could never forgive him for supporting the Vietnam War so faithfully when he was vice president, he was in the best position to unify any breach between the established party leadership and the new volunteer workers, if the party itself could only unite behind his candidacy.

It was not to be. Humphrey could win primaries in Ohio and Indiana, and he would "take off the gloves" in battling McGovern in the California primary. McGovern's young supporters regarded Humphrey as a tired figure out of the past. Having won seven primaries and captured many delegates in the nonprimary states, McGovern had the certain support of 45 percent of the delegates when the convention opened.

Even while Hubert Humphrey was staking his claim upon the moderate middle, the performance of George Wallace suggested that a large segment of the people were little interested in middle-of-the-road candidates. Wallace won the Florida primary handsomely on March 14, just one week after the season's opening in New Hampshire. He would go on to capture Tennessee, North Carolina, Michigan, and Maryland, for a total of five wins, as compared to Humphrey's three. Gunned down in a Maryland shopping center on the eve of that election, his quest for the nomination was abruptly halted. He appeared at the Democratic National Convention in a wheelchair.

Wallace's career had been strongly identified with racism. But his campaign message in 1972 was an attack upon the Establishment, a shout of disdain for the educated folk who presume to run the country, a call for a return of the country to control by the plain, hardworking people who pay its taxes, fight its wars, keep its factories running and its farms producing. Wallace's favorite example of presumptuous bureaucrats imposing their will upon the people was school busing to achieve racial integration.

In George Wallace's vision of the people, there was no room for political leaders like Humphrey who dealt with the recognized power brokers. Nor was there a place for a McGovern, who showed a special affinity for young people, blacks, and movements like Women's Liberation. It was time for the plain people to recapture the direction of affairs. Early on, Wallace decided not to repeat his third-party venture of 1968, but to concentrate on building a power base within the Democratic party. He would claim that he forced both the Democratic candidates and Richard Nixon to pay more attention to the plain people.

Party Reform and McGovern's March to the Nomination

What was George McGovern's vision of the people? He perceived that the 1968 Democratic National Convention, dominated by delegates who were designated long before the key political events of that year, did not represent the people, nor even the rank-and-file workers of the Democratic party. Young people had played a special role in those events, but eighteen delegations to the convention had no members under thirty years of age. Women, who make up at least half the electorate, were represented by only 13 percent of the delegates. And a number of delegations effectively excluded blacks and the poor by requiring a substantial party donation from all those attending the convention.

Such methods for choosing delegates, McGovern felt, could not be tolerated at a time when major policies were contested. A convention dominated by servants of the incumbent administration is in no position to repudiate its policies. The intent of Eugene Mc-Carthy's candidacy had been to repudiate Johnson's Vietnam policy, but his supporters, in many nonprimary states, were excluded from participation in delegate selection.

The McGovern Commission adopted guidelines for the state parties to follow in choosing delegates to the 1972 convention. Such decisions were not to be reached before a calendar year in advance of the convention. All forums for making the decision—precinct and district caucuses, county and state conventions, and primary elections—were to be open to the widest possible participation by party members. Nobody should be prevented from seeking the position of delegate because of the cost, or because of a mandatory party contribution. There should be no discrimination on the basis of race or sex; the easiest way to prove discrimination had not occurred would be if the minority representation on the delegation were roughly proportional to the minority population of the state. (Most states treated this as a suggestion to fill their delegations with a quota of minority delegates. But many liberals consider quotas to be illiberal.) Finally, McGovern endorsed a decision that had been made by the 1968 convention. The unit rule, which required entire delegations to vote with their own majority, should be abolished. Following this logic, the winner of a primary election should not receive all the delegates, but only a share proportional to the votes he received.

In the years between 1968 and 1972, political activists increasingly abandoned the streets to work within the system, including the Democratic party. Black Americans showed new political sophistication, eighteen-year-olds got the vote, and women's organizations burgeoned. Each of these groups was promised a fair share of influence by the McGovern Commission reforms, and each tended to identify its own interests with Senator McGovern.

McGovern won his first primary victory in Wisconsin on April 4, following it with Massachusetts in late April and Nebraska in May. The capstone on his march through the primary states came from winning the last four contests—Oregon, Rhode Island, New Mexico, and California. The total votes cast in the seventeen primary states did not suggest that McGovern was overwhelmingly popular: Hubert Humphrey, 4 million; George McGovern, 3.9 million; George Wallace, 3.6 million; Edmund Muskie, 1.8 million.

Hubert Humphrey made his last stand in the California primary. He attacked McGovern's position on welfare, and he emphasized McGovern's association with radical youth. He told aerospace workers that McGovern's intention to cut defense spending threatened their jobs. Before the Humphrey campaign was intensified, polls showed McGovern winning by 15 percent; his final margin was reduced to less than 5 percent.

At this point, an ironic twist occurred. The McGovern Commission had recommended changing primary elections in which the winner receives all the delegates. This recommendation was not adopted in California; it would have required the amendment of state law. Humphrey and the other candidates challenged the outcome, asking a federal court to allocate them a share of delegates proportional to the votes each received. On appeal, a higher court said that this matter could only be settled by the party's national convention.

George McGovern was outraged at this attempt to change the rules after the game had been played. He regarded it as an attempt by Humphrey's forces to win on a technicality what they could not win from the voters. The bitterness of this conflict destroyed any chance for achieving real party harmony. On the crucial question of seating the California McGovern delegation, however, the convention voted in the affirmative. This was the signal that George Mc-Govern would be nominated.

The Convention Does Its Work

The McGovern Commission guidelines for the selection of delegates had a marked impact. This was no gathering of party hacks; more than 80 percent of the delegates had never before attended a national convention. Only sixty Democratic members of Congress made it to the convention as delegates. Mayor Richard J. Daley of Chicago, whose influence had set the tone of the 1968 convention, particularly in the streets outside, was defeated when the right of his 1972 delegation to take its seats was challenged. This symbolized the lessened influence, or outright defeat, suffered by traditional party leaders in state after state. The spirit of the new delegates was personified by Yvonne Braithwaite Burke, the assistant chairman, a black woman. She wielded the gavel with authority and humor. In November, she was elected to Congress from California.

The delegates took the business of the convention seriously, worked hard, and shouted down motions to adjourn, well into the small hours of each morning. They were not there as actors in a drama staged for prime-time television. Reflecting the McGovern reforms, 15 percent of the delegates were black, 40 percent were women, and 25 percent were under thirty years old. This was a threefold increase in each of these categories over their representation in the 1968 convention. Groups within the convention met continually to be sure that their concerns were presented forcefully to the candidates and to the platform committee. There were caucuses for women, blacks, Chicanos, young people, Indians, and the elderly.

One observer labeled the proceedings a "convention of grievance groups." They were there to support George McGovern and to further their own policy preferences, not necessarily in that order. When McGovern encouraged the defeat of platform planks calling for abortion-on-demand and truly radical reform of the tax and welfare systems, he was charged with reverting to an older, nastier kind of politics. In fact, he was attempting to broaden his base of support.

A Classroom Explanation: I

Gabriel Eisenberg hurried to meet his first class meeting after the close of the Democratic National Convention. His sense of excitement, which had risen as he watched the convention unfold, remained high.

"The best explanation for what's likely to happen this fall," he said, "comes from the work on American electoral history by Walter Dean Burnham.[3]

"Burnham tells us that the American political system is basically resistant to change. It sets up many persons and institutions that share the power and authority of government and gives each of them what amounts to a veto power. The only factor that leads them to share responsibility is the party system, so that members of the same party in the executive and legislature, for example, will work together. Since both parties have a stake in the status quo, they don't normally take up fundamental issues. This means that the parties

3. Walter Dean Burnham, *Critical Elections and the Mainstream of American Politics* (New York: Norton, 1970).

sound a lot like each other, and the people don't pay very much attention to the issues in elections; they vote according to party identification, staying with the parties they are used to. One party therefore remains the normal majority party, and the other gets used to being in the minority.

"But, every thirty to forty years, we have a critical election. A critical election comes about because of rapid changes in the economic and social systems that the political system can't keep up with. These changes create a group or groups who find the political system unresponsive to their needs. They form a coalition favoring change, which takes over one of the parties, or else, as was the case with Lincoln's Republicans, forms a new party. A coalition opposing change develops in opposition to them. People become interested in political issues, and voting participation increases. The result of the critical election is to change the coalitional base of both parties and to install a new normal majority. That party then leads in modernizing the political system to take account of the needs of the groups that had such a major part in carrying it into office.

"The exciting thing about 1972 is that it may just be one of these critical elections. The last one took place with the formation of the New Deal coalition, in 1932 and 1936. So it's time for a critical election. There have been terrific pressures for political change building up, stimulated further by the Vietnam War, which haven't been handled yet by the system—look at the decay of the cities, poverty, the rise of feminine consciousness, the civil rights revolution, and a long list of others. The groups concerned with those issues were well represented at the convention, and they nominated George McGovern.

"I think McGovern signaled that he knows he's leading a new and important force by choosing Senator Eagleton as his running mate. Usually, the nominee tries to balance the ticket by selecting a running mate from a different section of the country and from the opposite end of whatever range of policy attitudes exists in the party. This is done to unify the party and also to dull the voter's perception of the issues. But Eagleton doesn't come from a different section— Missouri isn't that far away from South Dakota, at least psychologically—and his voting record on the big issues in the Senate is about the same as McGovern's. This suggests that McGovern intends to sharpen the issues and make them more important than usual.

"But you should remember that the coalition favoring change doesn't always win. It did in 1932, when Roosevelt forged a new coalition made up of urban voters, organized labor, minority groups, and intellectuals—while keeping the solid South—that has lasted ever since, although for years now there have been signs that it is breaking up. In 1896, though, the coalition favoring change was soundly defeated. The Democrats' nomination of William Jennings Bryan meant that Populism was absorbed by the Democratic party. But Bryan never had much appeal to the workingman in the eastern cities. When he was defeated by William McKinley, it established the Republican party as the normal majority, the party of eastern industrialism, of sophistication, and of respectability, while the Democrats became the party of peripheral protest. When reform sentiment next arose, its vehicle was the middle-class Progressive movement within the Republican party. The Republicans remained the majority party until the Depression created newly disadvantaged groups.

"So, the question about the election this November is this: will it be a rerun of the election of 1932? Or will it be a rerun of the election of 1896?"

The Troubles of George McGovern

They said he never could believe that Ted Kennedy would turn him down. When it happened, George McGovern did not have a well-developed second choice for the vice presidential slot. He turned his attention rather quickly to his handsome and accomplished Senate friend, Tom Eagleton of Missouri. (Eagleton? Eagle Scout? Who could fail to see in that distinguished profile the very image of the good American, the practitioner of civic virtue, the director of the local Red Cross drive?)

Unhappily, Thomas Eagleton's rapid climb to the top of the political heap had exacted its costs. He had suffered mental disorders and had been hospitalized for electric shock treatments. George McGovern did not know this, although it was no secret in Missouri, and his staff could easily have discovered it. When McGovern learned it, his first thought apparently was for Eagleton's reputation and feelings. He declared "1,000 percent" support for Eagleton, allowing the Missouri senator the option of withdrawing gracefully.

But Tom Eagleton wanted to stay on the ticket. He remembered what had happened twenty years before, when a young California senator named Richard Nixon was brushed by scandal after being nominated for vice president. Nixon was threatened with removal from the ticket, but he fought back against his detractors in public, and he won. Tom Eagleton quickly mounted a campaign to win public support, and he met with much sympathy.

But the pressures on McGovern to dump Eagleton were redoubled, and he yielded, stating that Eagleton's continuation on the ticket would obscure the real issues of the campaign. This came when the press had been filled with speculation about Eagleton for a solid week. McGovern had some difficulty finding a replacement. But Sargent Shriver (practically a Kennedy) finally accepted, and the "real" campaign could begin.

Bob McNeely

Some would say the campaign really ended then. (Others would say that Nixon became unbeatable when he mined Haiphong Harbor without starting World War III.) The voter likes to think of presidents as having super-human qualities of moral certainty and decision-making ability. In the primaries, George McGovern established the image of a plain-spoken man who was guided, above all, by moral conviction. His apparent vacillation in the Eagleton matter did not fit the image.

President Nixon, poised far above the sordid verbiage of the campaign, sent out his assistants to renew the charges that Hubert Humphrey leveled against George McGovern during the California primary. John Connally, former governor of Texas and the only Democrat in the Nixon cabinet, led the exodus of Democrats from the party fold into the Republican presidential column. George Meany, president of the AFL-CIO, the nation's largest conglomeration of labor unions, insisted that labor remain neutral, although it had supported nearly every Democratic nominee for four decades.

Senator McGovern was attacked for the dress, habits, and attitudes of some of his supporters. He was accused—unfairly—of favoring unregulated abortions, marijuana plants in every garden, and the destruction of the armed forces of the United States. He had casually suggested a welfare reform scheme based on granting every man, woman, and child in the United States an income of $1,000 per year, then taxing it back from those who would not need it. He had to assemble an advisory group of economists to help explain exactly what he was talking about, although his plan had major features in common with the Family Assistance Plan proposed by President Nixon in 1969.

Secure in his patriotic position as a veteran World War II bomber pilot decorated for bravery, and convinced of the moral horror of the Vietnam War, Senator McGovern proposed granting amnesty for those young men who fled to foreign countries to avoid the draft, as well as those who deserted after experiencing those horrors firsthand. This proposal offended many Democratic voters.

On to November

George McGovern campaigned on, explaining his positions, frustrated because President Nixon never offered him a clear target, angered because he was subjected to a kind of critical attention from the press that the president never seemed to receive. He was convinced of the rightness of his cause, but he had trouble convincing the people.

His workers shared his conviction, however, and they let their sense of moral superiority show, when confronting the old and creaky party structure. The Democratic party—the party of Thomas Jefferson, Franklin D. Roosevelt, and John F. Kennedy—was not really based on mass participation. The Republican party could always muster a fine turnout for ladies' club luncheons and ring in the real estate salesmen and junior executives for a precinct caucus. But the Democratic voters who were the traditional backbone of party support at the polls rested content with the operations and decisions of the professional leaders. The McGovern Commission's reforms opened the processes of the party to well-organized political minorities. Since their participation had previously been discouraged, they were disdainful of the established hierarchy.

George Meany said that the "New Politics" arrogantly excluded members of the old coalition, the party members and labor, in favor of an elite of suburban and student types.

The idea that the McGovern campaign was being run by a group of elitists out of touch with the common man turned up in the private polls conducted for President Nixon. That this conception was the basis of George Wallace's campaign appeal did not deter President Nixon from considering it with great care.

The programs proposed by Senator McGovern had a familiar sound. The good things he wanted to accomplish appeared to depend on new agencies in, and new spending by, the federal bureaucracy. His proposals seemed very much like the ideas of what conservative Republicans call "the liberal establishment," the ideas that were rushed into law by Lyndon Johnson in the early days of his administration, and failed to win the war against poverty, or restore the cities, or get the kids to cut their hair.

Richard Nixon enjoyed the position of standing for those who opposed the establishment. It was an unusual position for the incumbent president of the United States. In terms of votes, it was very profitable.

Ten days before the election, George McGovern's standing in the opinion polls climbed back up to the level it had reached at the time of the Democratic convention, before the "Eagleton incident."

Election day came. Without many public appearances, hardly even submitting to the tiresome adulation of his supporters, and the taunting of the hecklers, that had exhausted him in 1960, Richard Nixon was reelected.

He was elected with a smashing majority of the popular vote, winning some 61.3 percent to McGovern's 37.3 percent, with less than 1.5 percent going to minor candidates. (What would have happened if George Wallace had been on the ballot?) President Nixon carried every jurisdiction except the state of Massachusetts (the Kennedy charm still operates) and the District of Columbia (Washington is a city with a substantial black voting majority).

But even that landslide failed to carry a Republican majority into Congress. The Democrats gained 2 Senate seats, for a 57–43 majority; lost 12 seats in the House, but retained a majority, 244–191. Democrats even gained a governor. Ticket-splitting was widespread, for the Democrats who deserted George McGovern did not therewith desert their party. The turnout was the lowest it had been since 1948, as only 55 percent of the eligible voters—76 million of the 140 million Americans over 18 years old—got to the polls. Perhaps the youthful voters were not used to exercising the franchise. But George McGovern's cause was hopeless without solid youth support, and he got only 52 percent support from those casting their first ballots. Whatever their age, voters did not feel excited by, nor much involved in, the national process of decision-making.

A Classroom Explanation: II

Gabriel Eisenberg sat casually on the desk in the front of the class-room. Looking out at the students, he suddenly labeled his own feel-ing: sad, but a little older, and maybe a little wiser.

"You will remember," he said, "that I told you at the beginning of the course this fall, that the election would be either a rerun of 1896, when William McKinley buried Populism and the Democratic party, or a rerun of 1932, when Franklin D. Roosevelt made the first steps toward establishing the New Deal coalition, which was firmly launched in 1936.

"It is now clear that neither of these historical models is applica-ble. In fact, we have not yet had the critical election that is needed so desperately to modernize the political system and bring it into adjustment with the economic system.

"Instead, we have just witnessed a rerun of the election of 1920, when Warren Gamalial Harding defeated James M. Cox and Franklin D. Roosevelt, who was nominated for vice president that year. The 1920 election came at a time of moral exhaustion, after a period when the people had supported political leaders in a cause of high moral purpose. In his first term, Woodrow Wilson achieved a striking record of domestic reform; in his second term, he led the nation into a war which was intended, as he put it, to make the world safe for democracy.

"But the nation was tired of the high pitch of Wilsonian idealism. Some felt those ideals had been betrayed in writing the Treaty of Versailles; others were simply eager to retreat into their private con-cerns, and turn their attention away from great public issues. Cox and Roosevelt supported Wilson's dream of a League of Nations, but not very enthusiastically. Cynically, and maybe with a sigh of relief, the country turned to Senator Harding, a small-town newspaper editor from Ohio. Harding won by a landslide, but it was no critical election; the coalitional base of the parties was undisturbed.

"The parallels between 1920 and 1972 are striking.[4] The United States has led a frantic political life for a long time now. The last really peaceful time was the administration of Dwight Eisenhower. When John Kennedy was elected, he claimed that urgent problems had accumulated under Eisenhower, that the nation had grown stag-nant. 'Let's get America moving,' he said. He also called for a spirit of selfless, idealistic dedication, symbolized by organizations like the Peace Corps.

"After Kennedy's tragic death, Lyndon Johnson became president, and he enacted into law many of the domestic reforms that Kennedy only talked about. As a southern president, he took great pride in guiding the first really meaningful civil rights law since the Civil War to passage. But law alone was not enough, and the civil rights move-ment sought support on the basis of justice and morality.

"Meanwhile, Kennedy had increased the commitment in Vietnam, and Johnson sent in American ground forces to win. The young men who had to fight there increasingly recognized it as a dirty war fought for no good purpose. The abstractions like 'containing communism' and 'assuring self-determination for the people of Vietnam' came to have a hollow sound. Communism can't be as menacing as we've been told, when Richard Nixon can go to fancy parties in Peking and Moscow.

4. The comparison between 1920 and 1972 was also suggested by Walter Dean Burnham. See his memorandum, "The 1972 Election: Pre-Mortem," (Mimeo, Cambridge, Mass., October 12, 1972).

"Along comes George McGovern. He calls for immediate withdrawal from Vietnam, which to many people sounds like a surrender. He also calls for welfare reform, and day-care centers, and help for the cities, in the name of equality and achieving the ideals of the Declaration of Independence. But, to a lot of people, it sounds like giving a lot of things to ambitionless people who haven't earned it. People are tired of achieving justice. All they want is some domestic tranquillity, translated as law and order, and a chance to get on with making a living and paying off the loan on the camper.

"And this is what the reelection of Richard Nixon promises. No more abstractions, no more sense of high moral purpose. He fits the cynical mood exactly. The people know that politicians, regardless of their brand of rhetoric, are crooked. So, when the burglary and bugging of the Democratic headquarters—the so-called Watergate scandals—are revealed, the voters only find it boring, and go to the polls and vote for Richard Nixon.

"Welcome to normalcy, and the second Nixon administration."

President Nixon's Vision

Had the election decided any fundamental issues? When it came to the value conflict between achieving equality or furthering individual achievement, Richard Nixon, the poor boy from Whittier, California, had taken a firm stand long before. In accepting his party's nomination in 1968 — the closing event of the convention, after the in-fighting is over, when the candidate can express what is closest to his heart — he said:

Tonight I see the face of a child. He lives in a great city. He's black or he's white, he's Mexican, Italian, Polish. None of that matters. What matters is he's an American child. . . . He sleeps the sleep of a child, and he dreams the dreams of a child. And yet when he awakens, he awakens to a living nightmare of poverty, neglect, and despair. He fails in school, he ends up on welfare. For him the American system is one that feeds his stomach and starves his soul. It breaks his heart. And in the end it may take his life on some distant battlefield. . . .

I see another child tonight. He hears a train go by. At night he dreams of faraway places where he'd like to go. It seems like an impossible dream. But he is helped on his journey through life. A father who had to go to work before he finished the sixth grade sacrificed everything he had so that his sons could go to college. A gentle Quaker mother with a compassionate concern for peace, quietly wept when he went to war but she understood why he had to go. A great teacher, a remarkable football coach, an inspirational minister encouraged him in victory and also in defeat. And in his chosen profession of politics, first there were scores, then hundreds, then thousands, and then finally millions who worked for his success.

And tonight he stands before you, nominated for President of the United States of America.[5]

5. See the analysis of the Nixon speech in Theodore H. White, *The Making of the President 1968* (New York: Atheneum, 1969), pp. 253-6. The quoted segment of the speech is on p. 256.

Rags to riches. Log cabin to White House. Corner drugstore to Hollywood stardom, or a Wall Street law firm. Although Richard Nixon
could understand the agony of the cities in his head, his heart was
committed to a different version of the American Dream. It was the
old dream of success, based on individual ambition and achievement.

What did this mean in 1972? In the closing days of the campaign,
President Nixon granted an interview to the *Washington Star*, on the
condition that it not be published until after the election. He said,
in part:

> The average American is just like the child in the family. You
> give him some responsibility and he is going to amount to
> something. He is going on to do something. If, on the other
> hand, you make him completely dependent and pamper him
> and cater to him too much, you are going to make him soft,
> spoiled and eventually a very weak individual. . . .
>
> This is a case where the American people were confronted
> with a choice of one candidate who promised to spend billions
> more of their money, basically . . . to help them, and the other
> candidate said, no, we are not going to promise to do that. We
> are going to promise to give you the chance to help yourself. . . .
>
> It is our responsibility to find a way to reform our govern-
> ment institutions so that this new spirit of independence, self-
> reliance, pride that I sense in the American people can be
> nurtured. I think it is out there.[6]

The president did not discuss the new sense of self-reliance "out
there" very completely during the 1972 campaign. If the people were,
by their votes, making such a choice, the terms of that choice were
not spelled out.

*A lonesome landslide, then. A president, overwhelmingly reelected,
who sits in the White House, brooding over the spirit of the people,
and decides he has a mandate to reduce the scope and cost of government. Returned to Congress is a Democratic majority, which feels
that it must have a mandate, too—if not from all the people, at least
from those disadvantaged groups who swelled the electoral majority
in individual districts. Their agenda did not include dismantling
government programs intended to aid the poor, the uneducated, and
racial minorities.*

*The election did not settle great issues. But it established the terms
of political conflict for the next four years.*

6. The Nixon interview was distributed by the Washington Post Service and published in
the *San Francisco Chronicle*, November, 1972.

REFLECTIONS 2

Parties, Voters,
and Critical Elections

Elections are the basic rituals of democratic government. The spectacle of an entire nation coming together to designate a single man as its president has inspired poets, journalists, and foreign observers. In 1972, much of the excitement was missing. Richard Nixon won by a great landslide, but the election did not appear to unify the people or the government. The choices made by the voters did not look clearcut; the majority had no confidence in its ability to determine the course of the nation.

The people seemed tired, even cynical. They did not show disappointment, so much as apathy. What is the relationship, in history and in the 1970s, between the American people and their political parties? Are the parties the instruments of the people, enabling them to control the government? Or do the parties so limit the alternatives available to the people as to make their choices meaningless?

To Express the People's Will

When the seventeenth- and eighteenth-century authors labored to establish the moral authority of government by the people, they paid little attention to the machinery that would connect public opinion with the policies of government. They assumed that, when the authority of the people to govern was established, communication between government and people would take care of itself; democratic government, by its very nature, would preserve the essential "chain of connection" with the people.

The activities of private — even secret — organizations in attempting to influence public, political decisions were common in the colonies long before the active rebellion against British rule. In 1763, John Adams confided to his diary his discovery that a caucus met regularly in Tom Dawes's garret and agreed to support candidates who were later confirmed in the Boston town meeting. Later, Massachusetts and other colonies developed political clubs, such as the Sons of Liberty, which agitated for independence both publicly and in private.

By the time the Constitution was drafted, its framers were no longer compelled to organize an opposition to the British governors; independence was an established fact. In the legal sense, the operations of the Sons of Liberty had been aimed at fomenting treason against British rule. The possibility that an organized opposition could oppose the policies of an incumbent government, yet remain staunchly loyal to the form of that government, was not clear in the British Parliament towards the end of the eighteenth century, nor was it obvious to the authors of the Constitution. They did not anticipate the development of political parties as we now understand them.

This failure of anticipation is abundantly clear in the provisions of the Constitution for electing a president. The first proposal to come before the Constitutional Convention, sponsored by James Wilson of Pennsylvania, was for the direct popular election of the president. This was overwhelmingly rejected; the Convention was meeting in part to counter what they considered the excesses of popular rule developed in the state governments. Although initially favored, a proposal for the election of the chief executive by Congress was defeated when the delegates were convinced that this would make the president a servant of the legislature. (One of their complaints about the state governments of the era, where, in most cases, the governor was elected by the legislature, was that the executive power had been weakened.) A compromise solution was worked out by an eleven-member committee. It provided for election of the president by an intervening body of presidential electors, chosen in a manner to be designated by each state. To protect small states, two electors would be selected in every state, equalling their number of senators; to protect large states, additional electors would be selected, equal to the number of House members. Electors would meet in each state and send their ballots to the Senate for counting, where the candidate with the largest number of votes would be declared president, the second largest number vice president; and, if no person received a majority, the election would be decided by the House of Representatives.

The Electoral College was thus established, and functioned well in choosing George Washington. By 1796, identifiable Federalist and Republican parties had developed, and the electoral vote was divided between John Adams and Thomas Jefferson. Jefferson became vice president. In 1800, Jefferson and Aaron Burr received equal numbers of electoral votes, and the lame-duck Federalist House nearly declared Burr president, for the Republican electors had not designated which candidate was preferred for which office. This weakness of the system was repaired by the Twelfth Amendment, passed in 1804: henceforth, both president and vice president would be members of the same party; and the party would designate which man should hold which office. The party would pose the alternatives for decision by the electorate.

Neither Article II, Section 2, of the Constitution, nor the Twelfth Amendment, specified *how* the electors should be designated by the states. In the beginning, they were selected by the legislatures, but this practice was followed by only ten of sixteen states in 1800, and it had disappeared by 1832. Instead, the presidential electors were themselves elected by the voters. Their customary pledge to support the candidate of their own party was rarely enforced by state law, although they seldom betrayed it.

The system through which we choose our president was thus well established within half a century of the adoption of the Constitution. The system depended then, as it does now, on the existence of national political parties. But such parties are not mentioned in the Constitution, and they were not envisaged by the founders.

> Yet the Constitution would have been unworkable without political parties. They provide the essential link between the people and their government.

Democracy in a Large Nation

The ancient Athenians felt that the number of citizens a democracy could contain was equivalent to the number of persons who could gather in the public square and listen to the debates of the orators. The size of a democracy was limited by the range of the human voice. Even so, Athens found it necessary to designate representatives (although this was at one time done by means of a lottery); and the Athenian *archons*, or elected generals, were the leaders of recognized parties. Government was recognized as an important responsibility; its tasks were performed by representatives responsible to the people. Although its boundaries did not exceed the limits of the city, Athens functioned to a large extent as a representative democracy for those who were fortunate enough to be citizens.

The founding fathers were aware that the experience of Athens might not be applicable to a large nation; but the Athenian experience was the only previous democratic example that could guide them, beyond the developing institutions of Great Britain. James Madison argued, in the Federalist Papers, that the multitude of interests (or factions) in a large nation would prevent any single faction from becoming a threat to liberty.

As it turned out, nationwide factions—the political parties—had to be developed so that the voice of the people could find expression.

Hamilton v. Jefferson: The Beginning of the Party System

Just as the caucus was secretly formed in Tom Dawes's attic to control the legislative decisions of the Boston town meeting, the first stirrings of national partisanship occurred not among the people, but within Congress. The able but arrogant Alexander Hamilton felt that the new government would be established on permanent foundations only if it protected the interests and nourished the prosperity of the wealthy classes. In his position as national hero, George Washington was a figure of vast prestige eclipsing sectional and economic differences. His position was above factionalism and ideology. Hamilton suspected that American institutions would develop British practices. If George Washington were cast as the equivalent to the king, symbol of the majesty of the state and therefore publicly aloof from the political contest, the role of prime minister, commander and champion of the political forces, would be taken by himself, Alexander Hamilton. His position as secretary of the Treasury would become the most important in the cabinet. But the British prime ministers of the era were not popular leaders; their position had evolved from the role of king's adviser, normally a master of court politics. Hamilton sought personal gain through private intrigue, rather than public persuasion.

Thus, while Hamilton's advice repeatedly persuaded President Washington, and his programs (including the establishment of a national bank and the assumption of state debts by the new national government) were adopted by the first Congress, the political party he built and captained was not broadly based. Hamilton was an elitist at heart, and the Federalist party had little taste for the work of recruiting and organizing followers among the common people.

In his position as Washington's secretary of state, Thomas Jefferson grew increasingly restive. While Hamilton wanted government to arrange benefits for selected classes in society, in order to assure the Constitution's permanency, Jefferson began with great faith in the good sense of the people and a belief that the power of public opinion would almost automatically direct the course of government. His faith was soon challenged; public opinion was not so powerful. Jefferson was particularly distressed at the influence of "stock-jobbers," speculators who purchased state bonds at depreciated value and profited handsomely when the national government redeemed them at face value. Yet Jefferson shared the feelings later expressed in Washington's Farewell Address, which warned against "the baneful effects of the spirit of party" that would "distract the public councils and enfeeble the public administration." It was "a spirit not to be encouraged."

The notion of groups of men meeting secretly to plan their tactical moves against the administration still seemed both treasonous and antidemocratic. Jefferson retired to Monticello in 1793. James Madison organized the opposition to Federalist policies in Congress; and Madison directed the first efforts toward establishing a party organization among the electorate. Jefferson did not yet accept the propriety of partisan opposition.

Madison's group in Congress was by then labeling itself "Republican," although the title "anti-Federalist" was more descriptive. For many members of the Republican group, and the areas in which it boasted popular strength, had fought the adoption of the Constitution and now opposed the nationalist policies of Hamilton.

In 1796, the Republican congressmen drafted Jefferson—without consulting him—to be their nominee for president. Receiving the second largest number of electoral votes, he was installed as vice president with Federalist John Adams. The new Constitution, innocent of the concept of party, did not suggest that the winning party should control the administration. As vice president, Jefferson maintained his stance as reluctant opposition leader, and Adams was dismayed at the failure of his old friend to cooperate. But Adams was even more dismayed at the bitterly partisan actions of the Hamiltonians. Like Washington, Adams felt that party interest should never be equated with the national interest.

The French Revolution Divides Americans

Events increased the tendency toward partisan division among both the politicians and the people. The French Revolution, advertised by Tom Paine and emblazoned with familiar slogans, seemed akin to the struggle of the colonies against Britain; yet the Federalists were horrified by the terroristic actions of the French revolutionaries and sided with the British monarchy. Federalist policies favored the seacoast merchants, at the expense of the frontiersmen of the interior; Colonel Alexander Hamilton himself led the troops called out to put down the Whiskey Rebellion. The treaty negotiated by John Jay with Great Britain, which seemed an affront to France, crystallized the growing division in the country. The Federalists enjoyed a burst of popularity in 1798, when the "XYZ Affair" turned public opinion against France; but the passage of the Alien and Sedition Acts made new enemies. Congressmen chose sides; neutrality became untenable.

In 1800, Jefferson's misgivings had vanished. He was ready to lead an opposition party, and he envisaged that party as a vehicle of the popular will. Jefferson's election was the first "critical election." Thomas Jefferson's party gave a voice to groups who felt that the Federalist leadership did not respond to their needs.

President Jefferson discovered the secret of democratic politics: the party must keep the devotion of its original supporters while adding enough new groups to form a workable majority. Unlike the Federalists, Jefferson's Republicans actively organized their following among the common people. In 1800, the vote of New York City was seen as crucial; the Republican leaders worked through the Tammany Society, a newly founded fraternal organization; and New York's electoral votes provided Jefferson his narrow victory.

Jefferson's greatest accomplishment was his use of the party to govern. He managed the election of congressional party leaders; he selected his cabinet on the basis of their party positions; he wielded patronage to reward the faithful and denied it to punish potential enemies. He denied all rewards to Aaron Burr, who had attempted to steal the presidency in the Electoral College. Although the rallying slogans of his party included hostility to strong executive action and a conviction that the national government should be kept weaker than the states, Jefferson casually announced that he would not let principle prevent actions demanded by the times. He proceeded with the purchase of the Louisiana Territory from Napoleon in spite of objections that his actions were contrary to the Constitution. Jefferson conceded the dubious legality of the act but claimed that it would be vindicated at the next election. He was reelected by a wide margin in 1804.

Toward the end of Jefferson's second term, his party began to come apart. Its majority in Congress was top-heavy; the Federalists did not provide a coherent opposition; without a challenging opposition to demonstrate that its common party purposes are more important than its interparty differences, any majority may waste its energies on minor disagreements.

James Madison followed Jefferson into the presidency. Madison had been an intellectual leader in the Constitutional Convention and, as co-author with Hamilton and John Jay of the Federalist Papers, was a leading propagandist in the contest for its ratification. Madison's name is forever linked with the articulation of the theory of checks and balances, the decision to establish a "separation of powers" between executive, legislative, and judicial branches which would deter the development of tyrants as effectively as it would prevent the government from being captured by an impassioned majority. The president could veto congressional legislation, for example, but the Senate could refuse consent to the president's appointments and to his treaties. Each branch was enabled, at crucial points, to intervene in the other's sphere of authority.

James Madison was the champion of this theory; his skill in the Constitutional Convention and as a congressman is undisputed; yet he was a disappointment as president. Herbert Agar concluded that "Madison could write a Constitution of divided powers, but he could not administer one."[1]

For, in making "ambition balance ambition," the Constitution established a governmental structure designed for stalemate. Its potential for paralysis could be overcome—and was overcome, first by Hamilton's Federalists, then by Jefferson's Republicans—only by the imposition of a common party purpose upon the divided governmental structure. In order to prevent the stalemate of conflict between Congress and the executive branch, the president had to perform skillfully as the leader of his party. James Madison did not develop this skill. Yielding to pressures and seeking private compromise, rather than using his available authority, Madison lost control of the party and thus of the government. Jefferson had been able to deal with congressmen from a position of strength based on his popular support in the congressmen's own states; Madison could not claim that essential ingredient of national political leadership.

The administration of Madison's successor, James Monroe, is commonly mislabeled an "era of good feelings," because there was no opposition party. Actually, it was a time of factional bitterness, as the overextended Republican party fought internal battles that brought its disintegration. Party caucuses in Congress had been making presidential nominations. In 1824, separate factional caucuses

1. Quoted in James MacGregor Burns, *The Deadlock of Democracy* (Englewood Cliffs, N.J.: Prentice-Hall, 1963), p. 44.

nominated four different candidates. The disparate elements of the nation could not be encompassed within the boundaries of a single party, particularly when no charismatic national leader emerged to unify its separate parts. Andrew Jackson was such a leader, but he was denied the presidency in 1824 after winning a plurality of the popular vote when the Republican factions in the House of Representatives selected John Quincy Adams. Jackson then constructed a new party from the ruins of the old; but the old party had been so discredited that a new name was adopted. Jefferson's Republicans became Jackson's Democrats. And the congressional caucuses had been so discredited that presidential nominations were thereafter made by party conventions.

The American party system was, in essence, reestablished as a result of this critical election of 1824. Jackson led the Democratic party, and the opposition came together in the Whig party. No longer were John Adams's private, and Washington's public, misgivings about the spirit of party held by politicians. The functions of political parties, and their nature as the vehicles of democratic choice, were understood and accepted.

When the one-party system was firmly established in the South as a bulwark of white supremacy, various devices were developed to exclude blacks from voting in the Democratic primaries. One by one, these devices were struck down by the U.S. Supreme Court. In 1944, South Carolina erased all legislation concerning party primaries from its books. Blacks were then excluded from the primary on the basis that this was a contest open to the members of a private club (the Democratic party organization) and that any private club could exclude individuals from membership on account of race—even when county clerks administered its elections.

In striking down this subterfuge, the Supreme Court was called upon to define the nature of a political party:

> The party may, indeed, have been a mere private aggregation of individuals in the early days of the Republic, but with the passage of the years, political parties have become in effect state institutions, governmental agencies through which sovereign power is exercised by the people.[2]

Democrats, Whigs, and Slavery

Andrew Jackson's Democratic party had adherents in both the North and the South. Martin Van Buren, the sly political manipulator from New York, welded the most popular elements of Jefferson's old Republican party into nationwide support for the popular military hero. But Van Buren had few of Jackson's leadership qualities, and, after succeeding the hero, Van Buren was denied a second presidential term by the Whig candidate, himself an aging military hero, William Henry Harrison. The Whigs, beginning as a congressional party, boasted the illustrious names of Henry Clay and Daniel Webster; but, in 1840, the ability of the Whigs to organize among the voters on a national basis (and to choose a candidate because of his personal popularity rather than his legislative ability) demonstrated that the party system had achieved maturity.

As the nation began to witness the unforeseen consequences of the compromise with the slave interests that had made framing the Constitution possible—the use of the cotton gin brought an expansion of

2. *Rice v. Elmore*, 333 U.S. 875 (1948).

the slave system, rather than the expected contraction—each of the national parties began to split into sectional factions, with the nation held together, and that only temporarily, by compromises worked out in Congress.

The Democratic party divided. Its northern Free Soil wing remained as true as could be expected to the spirit of Jackson; the southern wing committed itself to the doctrines of John C. Calhoun, holding that states could "nullify" national laws they found unconstitutional. The Whigs were divided between the "Conscience Whigs" of the North and the "Cotton Whigs" of the South. The Whigs never succeeded in installing a vigorous party leader in the White House— because they never nominated one. After 1856, the Whigs had vanished as a meaningful political force; Clay and Webster both died in 1852.

When the established parties abandoned the duty to speak for a national constituency and retreated into sectionalism, civil war was the result.

The Founding of the Republican Party

Expecting to win the presidency with the help of southern Democrats, Senator Stephen A. Douglas introduced in 1854 the Nebraska Bill, which repealed the previously established boundaries on the expansion of slavery into the territories. American politics exploded, much to the surprise of Douglas, who hoped to build political power by constructing a transcontinental railway. Like some modern politicians, he underestimated the emotional power that could gather around an unresolved issue. In the North, remnants of the Whigs, Free Soil Democrats, and the nativist Know-Nothing party came together in a new, *sectional* political organization, which took the already familiar name of the Republican party. They were a coalition united by their opposition to the expansion of slavery. In 1856, the Republicans nominated John Fremont, a war hero (thus following Whig habit). The Democrats selected James Buchanan, a northern man with southern sympathies, and he carried the Electoral College with but 45 percent of the popular vote in a three-way contest. (The third candidate was former-President Millard Fillmore, nominated by the dying Know-Nothings.) Buchanan could not provide the decisive leadership which alone might have saved the situation. He was little more than

the servant of the southern congressmen; his instincts were for indoor maneuver, not public leadership. His inaugural address was an example: he pleaded for the people to accept and obey the pending Supreme Court decision in the case of Dred Scott,[3] *whatever it should be*. Even as he spoke, Buchanan knew the content of the decision and had helped persuade the Court to make it; he knew that it would invalidate the Missouri Compromise.

As crisis followed crisis—the Dred Scott decision, bloodshed in Kansas, John Brown's raid—the split in the Democratic party widened, and each faction nominated a candidate in 1860. The Republicans consolidated their strength in the North with a radical platform that promised free land (the Homestead Act) to be settled by free men (no slavery in the new territories). In 1860, the Republicans nominated an obscure, moderate Illinois lawyer they were confident they could dominate. When civil strife broke out, however, Abraham Lincoln governed through orders and proclamations, without consulting Congress, and he maneuvered to keep Congress out of session as much as possible.

Lincoln was well aware of the fatal limitations—fatal for the nation—of a party that is exclusively sectional. He chose to take his stand upon the principle with the broadest popular appeal, preservation of the Union.

He wrote, "If I could save the Union without freeing any slave, I would do it; and if I could do it by freeing all the slaves, I would do it." His first cabinet included members of the old parties, the Free Soil Democrats and the Whigs. It was a Union cabinet. He gave hundreds of appointments, including officers' commissions, to Democrats, and he reached for the support of the border states and the War Democrats by proposing moderate policies for Reconstruction. In 1864, he chose Andrew Johnson, a War Democrat, for his running mate. Thus, even as the Civil War raged, Lincoln was intent upon building the peace: it could be accomplished, he was sure, only by a *national* political organization. Even the Republican name was abandoned. Lincoln and Johnson were the Union ticket.[4]

The Radical Republicans in Congress had a different vision. Motivated by animosity toward the southern aristocracy, the former slaveowners, they intended to treat the South as a conquered province. When Lincoln was assassinated by John Wilkes Booth, their path was made easier. For Andrew Johnson lacked Lincoln's chief asset: a base of support in the electorate, independent of the congressional constituencies. Johnson held no love for the southern aristocracy, but, as a Tennesseean, he did respect the South as a region, and he soon determined to pursue Lincoln's moderate policies.

The Radical Republicans impeached Johnson. Although they failed by a single vote to convict him, Johnson's authority as president was effectively destroyed, and further Reconstruction in the South was directed by Congress. The Constitution provides that the national government shall guarantee to each state a "republican form of government," but does not specify who shall decide if a state qualifies. Congress asserted that right and established the "carpetbag" governments, which caused each state to be ruled by a colonial adminstrator, backed by military force.

The Republicans expected to dominate national politics indefinitely through a coalition made up of northern Republicans and the

---

3. Dred Scott, a black slave, claimed he had become a free man by being taken into free territory. The Court ruled that the black race was intended for servitude, and the national government could not change the matter. See below, pp. 192-193.
4. The meaning of the Civil War in the context of conceptions of equality is discussed at length in Chapter 8, pp. 323-327.

newly enfranchised southern blacks. The instruments chosen for achieving this grand design were far from delicate. Although Reconstruction brought some benefits to the South, notably including the founding of public schools where few had ever existed, the excesses of the new rulers drove the southern moderates into the arms of the extremists. It may be that not even Abraham Lincoln could have reconciled the South to the bitterness of defeat, or prevented it from trying to win back through political manipulation what it had lost on the field of battle. The slaves were emancipated, but they were not long to enjoy the rights of citizenship.

When the Republicans agreed to end Reconstruction in return for installing Rutherford B. Hayes in the White House, they in effect abandoned a concern for the welfare of the freedman. The foundation was laid for a one-party system in the South devoted to white supremacy.

1896: A Critical Election

The one-party systems developing in the southern states had their counterparts in northern areas where the Republicans held a virtual monopoly of political power. But the Democrats maintained electoral strength in the North, particularly in New York, and the southerners were wise enough not to nominate one of their own for the nation's highest office. The Democratic party remained such a vital national force that it was able to capture a majority of the popular vote for president in four of the eight elections from the end of the Civil War until the end of the century. The victors were Samuel Tilden in 1876 and Grover Cleveland in 1884, 1888, and 1892. Hayes was installed in place of Tilden in the Compromise of 1877, which ended Reconstruction. The national balance between political forces was so even that the majority choice was not ratified through the operation of the Electoral College in 1888, when Benjamin Harrison was installed in place of Cleveland.

This balance was destroyed with the election of 1896. In that year, the Democrats nominated William Jennings Bryan, candidate of the Populist party, although Democrats in most southern states had already acted to bury Populism by renewing racial hatred as the dominant force in politics, in place of the economic interest urged by the Populists when they asked black and white sharecroppers to combine against their landlords.

Bryan's appeal was just as sectional as Lincoln's had been; but Bryan did not understand the need for a national appeal. "Free coinage of silver" won the support of the Rocky Mountain mining states, and the South was safe in the Democratic column in any case; but William McKinley's promise of "four more years of the full dinner pail" was more appealing to the workers of the North and East. Bryan's candidacies (he was nominated three times) represented the unsuccessful reach for political power of a coalition favoring change.

The election of 1896 was a critical election, establishing a new majority. But both parties retreated into sectional strongholds, and the most unfortunate consequence was the impact upon state parties. Northern states ranging from Maine through Michigan to California developed Republican one-party systems. Without two competitive parties, the voice of the people could not be effective, and the reformers established primary elections—so that the citizen members of the parties could make nominations, rather than a convention of the party leaders—in states both North and South.

On the national scene, the Republican party remained dominant for four decades by serving as the political handmaiden of the corporations, bringing fantastic development (as well as striking inequalities) to the economy. It was the party of the cities, the urban workingman as well as his employer, and the universities. With the end of Populism, reform sentiment was reborn in the middle-class Progressive movement, which began in the Republican party and produced Republican Theodore Roosevelt and Democrat Woodrow Wilson as its national leaders.

The hold of the Republican party upon the imagination of the national electorate, temporarily weakened by Wilson's election, remained in effect until the economic crash of 1929 shook the very foundations of capitalism.

The New Deal Coalition: Rise and Decline

Franklin D. Roosevelt did not need to make specific commitments during the 1932 campaign. President Herbert Hoover was so completely associated with the suffering of the Depression that FDR needed only to reap the harvest of discontent.

By 1936, however the New Deal had an established record, and millions identified their own well-being with it. The voting turnout increased by some five million over 1932. The shape of the new majority coalition was revealed. FDR kept the Solid South. He worked with the Democratic city bosses and rolled up huge majorities in the cities, where Republican domination had already been broken by the candidacy of Al Smith in 1928. Roosevelt was supported strongly by Catholics, Jews, blacks, and what are now called "white ethnics" —the children and grandchildren of immigrants from Southern and Eastern Europe. The affiliation of the Irish to the Democratic party was well established.

The vigor and excitement of the New Deal made the Democrats the party of the intellectuals and academics, of the cities, of organized labor, and, generally, of youth. The Republican party retained a strong following in urban centers among businessmen large and small, but the constituencies that regularly elected Republicans tended to be rural. Reversing the situation established by the election of 1896, the Republicans after 1936 were the party of "peripheral protest."

The Republicans could not count on the farm vote, however. Farmers supported the reelection of Harry Truman in 1948, assuring his narrow victory, in spite of defections in the Democratic ranks by the Dixiecrats and by the Progressive party led by Henry A. Wallace, FDR's former secretary of agriculture.

The interlude of two Eisenhower administrations only emphasized the majority nature of the Democratic coalition, as the election of Woodrow Wilson had shown the tenacious power of the Republican majority established in 1896.

Then, in 1960, came John F. Kennedy: the young president elected by a narrow margin, whose promise would never be fulfilled.

In 1963, with Kennedy assassinated in Dallas, Lyndon Johnson became president. He defeated Barry Goldwater easily in 1964, but then he tried to win a war in Vietnam.

The forces pressing for change grew in numbers and found a voice. Denied effective representation in the Democratic National Convention of 1968, they were well represented in the convention of 1972. The New Deal coalition seemed on the verge of explosion. The tension between its traditional members (as blacks confront white ethnics in the cities, for example) was more powerful than their allegiance to the party.

Richard Nixon led the forces opposing fundamental change in the political system. But his personal victory in 1972 did not guarantee the party realignment that comes with a critical election.

Bob Adelman

Excluded Groups

If our nation merits the title "democracy" only to the degree that its political parties respond to the needs of the people, *excluding no significant group*, a major failure must be recorded in the South, where blacks have been systematically excluded from political participation. Black people have been permitted, even encouraged, to vote in the North; the question of how *responsive* the parties have been to the needs of black voters requires an answer of more complexity.

Republican orators for years have called for the development of a two-party system in the South. Historically, parties have marched with the advance of democratic participation. They have led the battle to enfranchise new groups, expecting to win the gratitude and votes of these new members. But this process requires competition between two rival parties, each seeking support of the new group. To permanently freeze out the blacks, one-party systems were essential in the southern states. Franklin D. Roosevelt never seriously challenged southern racism; he needed southern votes in Congress to support his foreign policies.

In 1948, Harry Truman's overtures toward blacks stimulated the growth of the Dixiecrat party; Strom Thurmond of South Carolina was its nominee; he carried four states in the Deep South.

In 1952, many southerners defected to vote for Ike; they were called "Presidential Republicans," for they continued to vote in Democratic primaries for local and congressional candidates. The Republicans increased their attempts to assemble live political organizations in the southern states. They succeeded so well that the South provided the base of votes that nominated Barry Goldwater in the Republican National Convention of 1964.

But what of the classic theory of parties competing against each other to increase democratic participation? In the Deep South, Republican parties seemed more segregationist than the Democrats, and Republican Governor Kirk of Florida tried to prevent court-ordered school desegregation in 1970. The South provided the bedrock support for Richard Nixon in the 1968 convention; Strom Thurmond kept any convention waverers in line; in November, Nixon carried Thurmond's South Carolina; throughout the nation, some 95 percent of America's blacks voted for Hubert Humphrey.

Almost at once, the Nixon administration announced a modification of the policy that withheld federal funds from segregated school districts. Judges Haynsworth of South Carolina and Carswell of Florida were nominated by Nixon to the Supreme Court, only to be rejected by the Senate; President Nixon charged that the Senate would reject any conservative southerner, but he later successfully appointed a Virginia attorney, Lewis Powell.

In 1972, for the first time since 1944, the South voted solidly for a presidential candidate. This time, it voted solidly for a Republican —Richard Nixon.

Did this represent the Americanization of the South, or the Southernization of America?

When the political parties of the 1850s no longer attempted to speak for national sentiment and became sectional factions, the result was civil war. The message of the 1972 election seemed to be that the Republican party of Richard Nixon would not attempt to speak for all races and economic classes. If blacks, Chicanos, and the poor felt excluded from the governing majority, the future outcome of efforts to achieve the promise of equality by peaceful means seemed grim.

The Accomplishments of Political Parties

The past record of American political parties is remarkable. They were not provided for in the Constitution, which divided the authority of government to prevent unseemly influence by the people. The parties have made the system periodically responsive to the wishes of the people. The potential for stalemate established in the Constitution is normally realized, and only minor adjustments are made in the status quo, until the pressures for change build up, and a critical election takes place that revises the coalitional base of the parties and establishes a new majority. This has been done peacefully, except for the era preceding the Civil War, when the parties were unable to perform their historic role and splintered into fragments.

Equally remarkable is the fact that, while parties of minority protest have come and gone, American political history has been dominated by two major parties since the disappearance of the Federalists. Thomas Jefferson's party is the ancestor of the modern Democratic party; the Republican party, formed from the wreckage of the Whigs, traces its ancestry to John C. Fremont and Abraham Lincoln. The Democratic party is the oldest functioning democratic political organization in the world.

Why a Two-Party System?

For many years, Americans have congratulated themselves on the sensibility of their two-party system, ignoring the fact that, in many states, one party has dominated politics almost exclusively, while in others, parties have been so weakened as to be made ineffective.

The basis for this self-congratulation has been a twofold assumption: (1) a belief that multiparty systems (as in France's Third and Fourth Republics) lead to governmental paralysis and political chaos; (2) a conviction that one-party systems are the essence of dictatorship. These assumptions deserve brief comment.

A large number of parties, rather than one or two, tends to develop when the almost exclusive function of the party is seen as *representation*. Logic requires a larger number of parties, simply because the diverse groups of a modern society are so unlike each other that no party could claim to represent (for example) both cotton sharecroppers and executives of the electronics industry. As political positions grow more elaborate, political parties are likely to proliferate.

To facilitate the duplication in the legislature of the division of opinion within the country, multiparty systems often provide proportional representation within multimember districts. A party that wins the support of 10 percent of the electorate may win 10 percent of the seats in the legislature. When a legislature, like the American Congress, is made up of single-member districts, the individual winning the largest number of votes is the only victor; lesser candidates and parties win nothing.

When representatives of many parties win legislative seats, and no party wins a majority, the legislature can organize to carry on its business (electing officers, appointing committees, considering legislation) only when parties combine to form a coalition. No single party bears responsibility for the decisions made by the coalition; the electorate, rather than turning to a recognized opposition as substitute for the government that displeased it, may turn against the system itself. This has been the pattern of the French nation since the Revolution of 1789. Periods in which the national legislature dominates national affairs and many parties express the interests of specialized constituencies, while government is marked by instability and a failure to resolve major problems, have alternated with periods when a single charismatic leader, with support broader than any party could provide, dominates the government. The first of these executives was Napoleon I; the latest was General Charles de Gaulle.

The tradition of American national politics has been quite different from that of France. Rather than pursuing intellectual precision and careful representation of a narrowing constituency, American parties, in the pragmatic tradition, have sought victory by whatever means available. The frequent charge that American parties are without principle has some foundation; but the actions giving rise to the charge can also be interpreted as "responsiveness to the people."

Whenever serious third parties have strongly challenged the dominant parties, their programs or their supporters have been stolen by one or both of the major parties. This was true of the Populists (who were absorbed by the Democrats in 1896), the Progressives (who began under Theodore Roosevelt and ended under Robert La Follette as an insurgent wing of the Republican party),[5] and the Socialists. When an emotional issue divides the nation, and the major parties' similar approaches to that issue alienate a large group of voters, a spokesman for that alienation may seek the presidency, yet his "party" never

5. Henry A. Wallace was the Progressive candidate for president in 1948. In spite of using the same name, the protest movement he headed had little historical connection with the earlier Progressive party.

contests congressional seats. Major party congressmen in the alienated region can adopt the third party's slogans without fear of serious retribution at the hands of their own party. Thus George Wallace's lonesome campaign of 1968.

One-Party Politics

Political parties have been the vehicles through which twentieth-century dictators have grasped and consolidated power. Because that consolidation has involved the stifling of opposition parties, it is an easy assumption that one-party politics is likely to be authoritarian politics, suppressing at least a minority, and frequently a majority, to serve the interests of a narrow clique.

This assumption underlies the dismay of Americans that so few of the new nations of Africa and Asia have developed two-party systems. Yet, in most of these nations, a single nationalist party gathered into its folds all those groups that desired an end to colonial rule, even if they could agree on little else. Attracting nearly all men of education and technical knowledge, these single parties became the natural means for building a nation.

Americans conveniently forget that the movement for American independence was an intolerant movement. Citizens of the thirteen colonies who chose to remain loyal to George III were, by and large, driven out. Many emigrated to Canada. Similarly, the new national government provided by the Constitution was launched by the Federalist party, and several years passed before Thomas Jefferson and his friends became convinced that forming an opposition party would not constitute an act of treason.

Americans also forget our own long experience with one-party state politics. Whether in Republican Michigan (of the 1920s) or Democratic Texas (of the 1950s), these systems have fallen far short of providing ideal arrangements for the political participation of all citizens. Yet they could hardly be classified as totalitarian governments. Even when blacks and Chicanos were frozen out of the political system and prevented from serving in all but the most menial positions in the economic system, the option to move to another state, or to a city that promised better conditions, was always available, at least in theory.

As single parties developed into monopolies, reformers insisted that party nominations be made through primary elections, rather than by a convention of party leaders. This further strengthened one-partyism, for second parties lost their chief asset: the monopoly of opposition to the incumbent officials. Party primaries are not a good substitute for party competition. When two strong parties compete for electoral support, there is at least a chance that politics will be conducted on the basis of clear responsibility for the conduct of public affairs. When the only meaningful choice is made in the primary of the dominant party, a politics of personal factionalism results, candidate personality obscures relevant issues, and an unpopular administration replaces a scapegoat official, rather than yielding to the opposition.

American local one-party politics has produced a roster of legendary political leaders. Mayor Richard J. Daley of Chicago and Governor George C. Wallace of Alabama are but the latest in the tradition. The American voters have yet to elect a blatant demagogue to the White House, however. The Depression of the 1930s was a ripe time for the rejection of the traditional parties, and Huey Long of Louisiana was a likely candidate; but the actions of the New Deal, aimed at restoring economic health, and New Deal attention paid to Long's natural constituents (the poor, particularly the rural poor) ended the threat even before an assassin's bullet ended Long's life. Huey Long is credited with stimulating President Rooveselt's "left turn" of 1934-1935.

The national significance of such leaders has been due to their impact upon the major parties. Mayor Daley dominated, at least in spirit, the 1968 Democratic National Convention. Governor Wallace articulated a widespread feeling among the electorate in 1968, but he won only 13 percent of the vote. In 1972, his efforts were concentrated upon influencing the course of the Democratic party, although his major success may have come in persuading Richard Nixon to appeal to the same voter instincts that Wallace stimulated.

The Nature and Operation of National Parties

The argument thus far can be summarized in the words of E. E. Schattschneider:

> The political parties created democracy and modern democracy is unthinkable save in terms of parties. . . . The parties are not therefore merely appendages of modern government; they are in the center of it and play a determinative and creative role in it.[6]

If the parties are indeed this important, certain questions must be asked about them:

What kind of organizations are the national parties?
How do they go about performing their vital functions?

Do the voters appreciate the important functions performed by the parties?

Are the parties likely to perform those functions in the future as well as they have in the past?

These are important questions if the survival of Lincoln's "government of the people, by the people, and for the people" is important.

The Meaning of a Presidential Nomination

The important and paradoxical fact is that, as organizations, national political parties hardly exist in the United States in the intervals between presidential elections. The president is clearly designated as the leader of his party, but he can reward or punish individual senators and congressmen in only limited ways. Their political futures rest with the voters of their districts. A senator may fight the party's program, yet ride the president's coattails to reelection.

Finally, the party that loses the White House has no recognized leader—it is only a confused jumble of opposition voices, including senators, congressmen, the defeated presidential candidate, former presidents of that party, and the governors of large states.

The major American parties (i.e., Republicans and Democrats) may be defined as coalitions of state and local political organizations

6. E. E. Schattschneider, *Party Government* (New York: Rinehart, 1942), p. 1.

coming together every four years to prepare a program and to nominate a candidate for the presidency. They are held together only by
a desire to win, and this may mean selecting the candidate with the
greatest promise for helping the local ticket.

The presidency is the leading prize of American politics. To elect
a president, the nation is an enormous single-member constituency.
Unlike the British system, the American executive is a single person;
he cannot be divided between two or more parties. The prizes of national politics are not shared between the parties, except in situations
like Lincoln faced, when broadening the base of the president's own
party was required.

Since around 1836, the parties have nominated their presidential
candidates through national conventions. Traditionally, these have
been gatherings of the leaders of state and local organizations. Since
the Progressive era, an element of popular participation has been
introduced by the presidential primary elections held in several
states. The results of such primaries are not always binding upon the
delegates of the states in which they are held, and they are certainly
not binding upon the conventions, which are free to ignore the
candidate who emerged as the popular choice in the primaries, in
favor of one who did not so test his popularity.

> In 1968, the Democrats nominated Hubert Humphrey, who ran in no
> primaries. In 1952, they nominated Adlai Stevenson, a dark horse
> who had not sought the nomination. Who can be found to argue that
> the 1952 candidate should have been Senator Estes Kefauver of Ten-
> nessee, patient investigator and wearer of the coonskin cap, the victor
> on the 1952 primary trail?

National Conventions as Party Rallies

Enmeshed in unending, ritualistic speeches, and punctuated by bursts
of both maudlin sentiment and mindless emotion, American national
party conventions have been criticized (usually by Englishmen) as
the most characteristic and juvenile features of an immature political
system. If politics is a spectator sport, the conventions are its circuses.

Modern conventions are planned to fit the convenience of television viewers, although the 1972 Democratic convention delegates
were too serious-minded to be mere actors in a drama. The noise and
confusion have not been eliminated, for they are part of an important
purpose. Conventions bring together the separate party organizations
of the richly varied states and localities of America; these organizations disagree as to which program and candidate will help elect
the local candidates; conflict is inevitable. Some delegations will have
to go home disappointed, members of the losing faction; or a compromise will be reached which really satisfies nobody. The purpose of
the convention is to dissolve that disappointment by generating an
emotional head of steam that will power the organization with enthusiasm. Ideally, it will only reach its peak on election day.

National conventions, therefore, carry on the deadly serious business of forging a renewed national party in a circus atmosphere rich
in the slogans of the old party, nostalgia for past party heroes, and
fear that the same emotions which must weld the unity of the party,
given free rein, will tear it to shreds. The management of a national
convention combines the flair of the circus ringmaster, the deviousness of Machiavelli, and the craft of the television producer.

The convention is held before the television cameras. The networks battle against each other for the most lively and dramatic

coverage and thus the largest share of the audience; only the appearance of drama will ensure any audience at all. (When the American network stations of Detroit are filled with the sound and fury of national conventions, the audience share of the Canadian Broadcasting Company, also received in Detroit, rises dramatically.) So the television cameras busily probe the conventions, seeking conflict, even stimulating it, for drama is made from conflict. But a party torn apart at the summer convention is unlikely to win the November election. The party wants a convention that attracts attention—but favorable attention. The agreements and compromises that hold the party together are usually made in private, then ratified amidst a blast of music and a shower of balloons on the convention floor. If the convention, or a faction within it, cannot accept a private compromise, then the issue will be fought out on the floor of the convention.

Because the parties are not bound together by devotion to an ideology, party leaders appeal to party loyalty, a vague emotion akin to, but harder to identify than, the glow of good feeling that a member may feel when meeting with his fellow Elks or Rotarians. That appeal may not be successfully directed to young delegates who find the Elks and Rotarians irrelevant.

Each delegation brings to the convention certain needs and convictions. They want to return from the convention with the best possible candidates and platform statements to invigorate the local party. They want to show they carried some weight in the deliberations. If the convention awards none of its prizes to the faction with which a state delegation identifies itself, the appeal to party loyalty may not be enough to win the active help of that local organization.

The classic devices for restoring party harmony after the devisive process of selecting a single nominee include:

1. *Selecting a running mate who is the champion of the defeated party faction.* In 1960, John F. Kennedy chose Lyndon Johnson, thus insuring considerable support from southern Democrats and his own election. In selecting Thomas Eagleton as his running mate in 1972, George McGovern acted as if it were a critical election, when traditional elements of the party coalition are abandoned to attract new ones.

2. *Yielding to the desires of the opposing faction in drafting the party platform.* In 1952, the Eisenhower forces permitted the supporters of Senator Robert A. Taft a full share of symbolic victories in contests over platform language. When George McGovern opposed radical platform planks, to allow the party's

traditional wing some symbolic victories, his supporters did not understand; and this action contradicted his selection of Eagleton. Many McGovern delegates, as amateurs, saw contradiction and compromise as betrayal, rather than political necessity.

Although the platform may be ignored by the candidate and seldom wins the attention of the electorate, it is serious business to the delegates, because it does deal with the manipulation of political symbols into the semblance of a party program. The platform may certainly be read by the opposition after the election, when it seeks ammunition to renew the partisan debate. The Democratic platform of 1964 did not promise the steady escalation of the Vietnam War, which began in 1965. When the war became unpopular, the Democrats could not claim a mandate for its expansion.

How to Read a Party Platform

Party platforms are not intended as sacred contracts with the public. Political circumstances are likely to change dramatically between election and the inauguration of a new administration; since the platform is adopted before the nomination of the candidate, he feels himself free to ignore it at will.

Platforms are part of the total convention, the crucial operation through which the national parties *pose the alternatives of political choice*. Platforms are worth reading, not because they predict the policies of a new administration, but as a portrait of the party at a particular point in time. For the platform contains that combination of appeals that can be supported by the party and, in the judgment of party leaders, has the best chance of winning support for the party. Ideally, the platform is designed to yield the *maximum party cohesion* consistent with *optimum public appeal*.

The history of American politics, therefore, is on display in the party platforms. They record the issues that excite the public at convention time and the judgment of the party concerning what interests may be lured into the party fold. Reading between the lines, one can sense the compromises required to hold the party together for yet another presidential election.

Platforms usually make forthright and ringing declarations on matters that have long since been resolved, particularly when they are matters that once found the party out of step with the people. The Republican party declares its devotion to the right of unions to organize and to bargain collectively; it also pledges its support for social security and other programs of assistance to the senior citizenry. Both parties indicate their steadfastness in the face of challenges to the American Way of Life. The party occupying the White House points with pride to its accomplishments; the opposition deplores the failures of the incumbents.

A second type of platform plank is that designed to win the support of an identifiable special interest, such as agriculture. This task is complicated because the same promises may not attract both corn and wheat; and what pleases corn and wheat the dairy farmer may find appalling. The resulting compromise may be comprehensible only to the farm leaders who are its main audience; the general public shows little interest.

In 1972, a number of groups supporting George McGovern were mor interested in publicizing their own causes—through such means a platform committee statements—than in furthering the nominee campaign. "Gays for McGovern" attracted few votes from Midd America.

The Platform Committee, generally made up of two delegates from each state, holds a week of public hearings prior to the opening of the convention. This may be preceded by regional hearings. The official purpose is to allow every interest group in every section a chance to be heard (and to make its own bit of news) while demonstrating that the party is attentive to the grassroots. But the working draft of the platform is produced by the convention leaders. When an incumbent president is being renominated, the platform may be drafted by his cabinet. The final decisions are based on the finest political calculations by the leadership.

On controversial issues, the questions that actually divide the national electorate, the party position is likely to be vague, if not completely inscrutable. One would think that, with the advent of dependable public-opinion polling, the parties would simply cast their lot with the sentiment of the majority. But the politician's nightmare is the *intense minority*, and pollsters have no reliable way of measuring opinion intensity. Assume, for example, that 30 percent of a national sample felt that the soil-bank program should be continued, while 70 percent opposed its continuance as a waste of national resources. For the party to oppose continuance of the soil-bank would be disastrous if the 70 percent did not feel strongly about the question; while the 30 percent (many of them farmers prospering from the program) make their decision on the basis of *this issue alone*. Similarly, 95 percent of the public might oppose the oil depletion allowance, once it was explained to them, yet not make its choice on that issue alone. If only one party opposed the allowance, it would cause concentration of the oil industry's habitual financial support upon the opposition party. (In 1969, the depletion allowance was reduced by a bi-partisan congressional majority. But it was not eliminated.)

These are examples of narrow economic interest. What of the great issues of national policy, the questions of war and peace, the problems of the quality of our national life?

Parties, Presidential Campaigns, and the People

Because each party wishes to retain its hard core of supporters (which the Democrats failed to do in 1972), while attracting enough new voters to form a majority, both parties compete for roughly the same group of voters. They are the middle group who have not made the emotional investment required to identify themselves strongly with one party or the other. Parties devote considerable energy to appealing to special interest groups (farmers, organized labor, even professors); but their main public appeal, during most of America's political history, has been to this group in the center. Yet these appeals have often glossed over the most explosive issues.

The appeals addressed to the center group have, on occasion, sounded quite alike, and the differences between the party proposals have been hard to define. What was the difference between the Republican Protective Tariff and the Democratic Tariff for Revenue, in the 1890s? Where did Herbert Hoover actually stand on the question of Prohibition, which he called a "noble experiment," in 1932? In that year, the problems of saving the American economic structure—which had collapsed—from total destruction, were little discussed. Yet both candidates were agreed that federal spending should be curtailed, and

Franklin D. Roosevelt castigated President Hoover for his reckless and spendthrift attitude toward the national budget.

What were Hubert Humphrey and Richard Nixon actually prepared to *do* about the Vietnam War, according to their 1968 campaign statements?

In the word of V. O. Key, American politicians have long approached campaigning as an exercise in "humbugging" the electorate. From the kegs of whiskey set up outside voting places by Andrew Jackson enthusiasts, through the brass bands marching for "Tippecanoe and Tyler Too," and including Richard Nixon's slickly produced television commercials, political campaigners have avoided the highest level of intellectual discourse.

The Image-Makers

In an age of mass communication, when campaigns are directed by professionals and guided by survey research, anxiety is frequently expressed for the future of democracy. Implicit in this anxiety is the assumption that the voters are an inert mass whose opinions can be readily manipulated. Awe at the presumed power of the public-relations men is coupled with worry about the people.

In writing his history of the 1968 campaign, Theodore White recorded the growing influence of the polls and the increased use of public-relations techniques. After describing the nature of opinion polling, he declared that

> the strategy of the candidates was an attempt to comprehend and sway the voters as if they were digits, whose quality could best be profiled in percentages. . . .
>
> . . . The fall of 1968 could, conceivably, be the last in which an election in America is best understood by trying to understand what the leaders sought to do and tell the people.[7]

Richard Nixon distrusted the television producers and public relations experts in 1960, and he lost the election. They served him so well in 1968 that several were placed at the top of his White House staff. Involvement of these men in the Watergate affair during the 1972 campaign led to their dismissal, publicly disgraced, in 1973.

7. Theodore H. White, *The Making of the President 1968* (New York, Atheneum, 1969), p. 319. Mr. White was not deterred from writing another volume about the 1972 election.

Volunteer workers, political managers, and even candidates themselves have only a partial view of a national political campaign. Presidential campaigns are hastily assembled, uncertain in their direction,
expensive, and complex in their operation. Any campaign worker is
likely to think that his own role is the most important one, for he is
too busy to comprehend what others are doing. The man who manages the television shows assumes that his management determines
the outcome; the speechwriter detects a public response to a well-
turned phrase; the man who orders bumper stickers may assume that
the outcome depends on him.

Campaign workers might be astonished to learn that a considerable
body of political science literature holds that campaigns have little,
if any, influence upon the outcome of elections. For, in several elections, public-opinion data revealed that most voters made their voting
decisions *at the time of the national conventions.* This early decision
time had a psychological payoff. With the decision made, the voter is
free to ignore the advertisements and oratory and to pay only casual
attention to the performance of his own candidate. He is in a position
to turn off the frenzied activities of the campaign. Any guilt at failing
to be a "concerned citizen" is balanced by cynicism regarding the
campaign behavior of politicians.

It is clear that the power of the image-makers is limited by political
circumstances. No conceivable campaign could have overcome the
handicaps with which Barry Goldwater began the 1964 campaign.
The public relations men call a campaign successful that increases
the product's share of the market by a few percent. But a presidential
candidate needs 51 percent (of the Electoral College).

It is equally clear that campaigns have an impact. Nobody can review the periodic opinion data of 1968 — the surge and decline of
support for George Wallace, the recovery of Hubert Humphrey from
a position of abject helplessness at convention time — without becoming convinced that the images projected during the campaign can
affect the outcome. In 1972, the polls measured George McGovern's
decline in public esteem after the Democratic convention.

In the final analysis, it is not the words and the polished images
that have the greatest impact upon voter's decisions. It is *events.*
Events make issues important to the voters. And usually these are
events that no PR man can contrive. During the 1964 campaign,
China exploded a hydrogen bomb. This news distracted the public
from a recently publicized scandal concerning a member of President
Johnson's staff. More important, it reinforced voter concern that
Barry Goldwater might impetuously lead the nation into a major
war. Democrats had carefully cultivated an image of the Republican
candidate as "trigger-happy." The action of China, by reminding the
voter of international dangers, made this image a more important
element in his decision.

The events that most influenced the 1972 election occurred before
the campaign began. They were the visits of President Nixon to
China and Russia, and the fact that he was received with respect,
in spite of ordering Haiphong harbor to be mined.

What the Parties Mean to the People

The task of the image-maker supporting a party and a presidential
candidate is not the same as that of an ad man merchandising a bar
of soap. The party is an established organization; the voter has formed
previous opinions about it; to change parties requires much greater

effort and cost to the voter's self-image than to casually pick a different cosmetic off the drugstore shelf.

A special relationship exists between each of the traditional parties
and large segments of the American people. This relationship provides an element of stability in American politics, partially shielding
it from shock waves of popular emotion. Yet, in providing this desirable stability, the major parties also protect customs and institutional
structures that make American politics less open to participation by
the people. And a sense of participation gives democratic government
its legitimacy.

> In 1972, the Democratic National Convention was opened to par-
> ticipation by formerly excluded groups. But their very participation
> may have frightened habitual Democrats away from supporting
> George McGovern.

The Cost of a Federal Union

American parties hardly exist at the national level, except when a
presidential election is being held. The focus of party organization
is on the local, and occasionally on the state, level. The national
parties are voluntary coalitions; national headquarters have no authority over local organizations. Yet the attitudes of most voters
toward the parties are formed by the events of national politics. This
is why the national convention is so important to the local parties
that participate in it. In an organizational sense, the national party
is almost nothing; in a psychological sense, the national party is
nearly everything.

When the United States Constitution was written, the thirteen
states had individual histories of self-government under the Articles
of Confederation, and each boasted a sense of individual identity
stretching back over many generations of loosely controlled colonial
rule by the British. A new nation would only be possible if the individual states retained their identities and a large measure of independent power. Only a federal system of national government was
possible. One student of American politics has written that federalism
is like a heavy mortgage; meeting the payments is agonizing, but the
house would not be possible without it.

The chief cost of American federalism is found in our political parties. Rather than describing ours as a two-party system, it would be more accurate to say that we have 102 parties—two permanent party organizations in each state, and two temporary organizations at the national level. Why is this costly?

> The rules governing the organization of local parties and the methods through which the people can participate in its management are established by state law—laws passed by party members in the state legislature. Any national standards which may be imposed upon the practices of local parties originate in the Constitution, particularly the Fourteenth Amendment.
>
> Ideally, the localism of the party system should provide a chance for groups to participate and be represented on a local level when their numbers are insufficient to make a national impact. But local parties are often managed by the local social and economic elite, more interested in maintaining their own position than in ensuring popular participation—or even winning elections.
>
> Congressmen respond to the cues of local parties, not national parties. They get no rewards for responding to the national interest, if that seems inconsistent with the local interest. If they become so involved in national politics that local needs are neglected, a young challenger will rise to oppose them in the party primary.
>
> State parties (governed by state laws) determine the methods of selecting delegates to the national conventions. In the past these ensured a convention made up of local party barons, rather than representing the party membership. In 1972, the McGovern Commission reforms opened up participation in the convention, but rank-and-file party members were not organized to take advantage of it.
>
> The fact of party localism means that our parties are less responsive to *national* needs than they should be; the entrenched hierarchies of most of these local parties make them less responsive to *local* needs than they could be.

Party Identification as a Psychological Force

An important theory about American politics holds that it can be understood by studying the activities of interest groups.[8] Individuals with a common interest form groups; political parties appeal for the support of these groups, adding them together to create a majority.

Unhappily for the theory, most narrow economic interests (oil producers, for example) cover their bets by contributing to both parties, while interest groups with a mass membership are not easily controlled by their leaders. In 1940, John L. Lewis, president of the multiunion Congress of Industrial Organizations, supported the Republican nominee, Wendell Willkie. So few workers followed Lewis's advice that he resigned his position. By 1972, the Democratic allegiance of union members had been so shaken that AFL-CIO President George Meany's neutrality was probably an accurate reflection of the ambivalence of rank-and-file members. One could not imagine Ralph Abernathy or Roy Wilkins asking black Americans to vote for Richard Nixon. If they somehow became convinced that this was the best political stance for blacks in 1972, they still could not have

8. See the discussion of pluralism in Chapter 7, pp. 280-295.

urged it, for the attachment to the Democratic party of those black Americans who vote has roots stretching back to Franklin D. Roosevelt, too strong to be shaken by the events of a single election. (President Nixon did have the support of Sammy Davis, Jr. — but it did not bring him a bonanza of black votes.)

The party serves as the most important *reference group* in the political sphere. Identification with a party becomes part of a person's image of himself, and it need not be related to specific issues or campaigns. Studies have shown that American students formulate a clear party identification as early as the fourth grade. Party identification provides a filter for perceptions of the political contest, just as an early decision regarding the presidential candidates permits a voter to tune out the campaign. Not surprisingly, it is voters with the stronger party identification who tend to make their decisions at the time of the conventions. When their identification is very strong, they work in the campaign, rather than tuning it out.

> Arthur Garfield Lamb was born on election day in 1880, in a staunchly Republican town in Wayne County, Michigan. His loyal parents named him after the Republican ticket — James A. Garfield and Chester A. Arthur. He became a carpenter-contractor and participated in the home-building boom brought to Detroit by the expansion of the automobile industry. Later, he became active in township politics. When we conversed, he had been retired for a quarter of a century.
>
> "Great Uncle Arthur, have you ever voted for a Democrat?"
>
> "No, sir. If there's a Republican on the ballot I can't support, I just leave it blank."

The political party was a much greater psychological force for the individual American voter in the late nineteenth and early twentieth centuries. Political campaigning was devoted to turning out the party faithful, and its characteristic form was the torchlight parade. There were few independent voters, for nearly everyone was known as either a Republican or a Democrat, and very few were indifferent. Turnout rates were comparatively high.

This result may be explained by the closeness of party competition in the years between the Civil War and the critical election of 1896, coupled with the strength of the parties as organizations. Nearly all elections (even for township office in Michigan) were partisan. The candidates were nominated by parties, lesser officials were appointed by party leaders, and, in the absence of widespread civil service systems, all employees of local government were hired by the party. It was the heyday of the urban political machine. Political parties served as the principal agencies for integrating the succeeding waves of European immigrants into American society, asking only their votes in return. The practices of the Republican bosses in Philadelphia were little different from those of the Democratic leaders in New York City.

The first election to be based on a new kind of campaigning was that of 1916, when Woodrow Wilson needed to win adherents away from the normal Republican majority.[9] (He won his first term because of the split between the regular Republicans supporting Taft and the Progressives supporting Theodore Roosevelt.) Advertising techniques, rather than the mere mobilization of the faithful, were

9. The designation of 1916 as the turning point in campaign styles was first made by Richard Jensen, "American Election Campaigns: A Theoretical and Historical Typology," (paper delivered at the 1968 convention of the Midwest Political Science Association), quoted in Walter Dean Burnham, *Critical Elections and the Mainstream of American Politics* (New York: Norton, 1970), pp. 72, 73, 95, 96, 112.

Bob Adelman

needed. The "selling of the president"—so much decried as a description of the 1968 campaign—was first used to reelect that noble idealist.[10]

American politics has since been converted from a participatory into a spectator sport. The strength of the parties has been progressively weakened. Local nonpartisan elections are now widespread; civil service examinations have replaced patronage as the source of government employment; and the poor are cared for by bureaucratically administered welfare programs, rather than the generosity of the precinct captain.

With population growth, urban crowding, and the spread of electronic media, the parties continued to lose their importance for the people. Increasingly, voters depended upon the media, rather than personal contact by party workers, to supply the information relevant to the decision between candidates.

The number of persons who claimed they were "independent," rather than Republican or Democrat, increased after 1916, to rise dramatically in the 1960s. It had long been fashionable to say, "I vote for the man, not the party."

Two Pictures of the Independent Voter

During the 1950s, academic students of voting behavior established a picture of the independent voter which revealed the independent hero of the civics texts—calm, rational, and nonpartisan—as a myth. This research established the psychological importance of the party to the individual voter and found that party identification was the best predictor of the voting decision. That is, knowing whether a voter considered himself to be a Republican or a Democrat gave a better chance of knowing how he would vote than knowing any other characteristic. This research also found that the stronger a person's party identification, the more likely he was to be interested in politics, to be informed about the issues, and to feel that his vote was important.

10. See Joe McGinnis, *The Selling of the President 1968* (New York: Trident, 1969).

The independent, with no strong party identification, was less well educated, less interested, and found more often in the lower reaches of the socioeconomic scale. The research was conducted during the relatively quiet years of the Eisenhower administration, when political issues did not unduly agitate the electorate, and a critical election was not anticipated. Picturing the independent as one who decides on the basis of whim, if he participates at all, this conception promoted the strongly partisan voter to being the mainstay of the system.[11]

By 1970, however, the situation, and the electorate, had changed. Voters identified themselves as:

Republicans   25%
Democrats   43%
Independents   31%[12]

Was this ignorant and apathetic type, the independent voter, determining the outcome of elections? Political scientists wondered if a democratic system based on rational judgment by the electorate were possible, but campaign managers called in a platoon of advertising experts to suggest how the waverers could be won over.

In his final book, the late V. O. Key argued that this picture was misleading. Voters come closer to making a rational choice than political scientists imagine, he argued. And the electorate is not made up of fools.[13]

> In his 1970 attempt to elect Republicans to Congress by activating dismay at young people and their radical habits, President Nixon exhibited a low opinion of the electorate. He failed. But he continued to draw his top staff assistants from the ranks of advertising agencies.

Key's analysis was soon supported by other scholars, using a range of different techniques. They developed a new picture of the independent voter—the kind who emerges when a critical election is in the offing. In contrast to the "old" independent, he is better educated, has a higher income, is relatively active in politics, and is concerned with the issues. Also, he tends to live in suburbia, where the patterns of city machine politics never had a chance to develop.[14] Specifically, the Republican party can no longer count on domination in the affluent suburbs, and the attachment of working people to the Democratic party has been progressively weakened, without a corresponding turn to the Republicans. Furthermore, even persons who do not think of themselves as independents show an increasing tendency to split their tickets.

In sum, the parties are no longer so important to individual voters. If voters appreciate the fact that parties play "a determinative and creative role" in modern government, they have not responded by offering to the parties the same kind of loyalty their grandparents did. Viewing politics as a spectator sport, they have abdicated the responsibility for supporting campaigns to special-interest organizations. Revelations emerging from the Watergate investigations demonstrated that such interests expect, and receive, undue influence in the councils of government.

11. The survey-research-established picture of the independent voter is aptly summarized by Walter de Vries and Lance Tarrance, Jr., *The Ticket-Splitter* (Grand Rapids, Mich.: William B. Eerdmans, 1972), pp. 39-48.
12. Data source: Survey Research Center, University of Michigan, November, 1970. The categories of "strong" and "weak" identifiers have been combined. Similar proportions were identified by the national commercial polls.
13. V. O. Key, Jr., with the assistance of Milton C. Cummings, Jr., *The Responsible Electorate* (Cambridge, Mass.: Belknap Press of Harvard University, 1966).
14. See Burnham, *Critical Elections*, pp. 91-134, and de Vries and Tarrance, *Ticket-Splitter*, pp. 57-73.

When the scandals reached his highest staff members, President Nixon hastily suggested reforming the laws governing campaign finance. After the horse is stolen, attention turns to the barn door.

Parties and Critical Elections

Sociological analyses of the voting public have confirmed a theory that politicians have always acted upon: that there are identifiable groups which tend to support one party at the expense of the other. At least before 1968, labor tended to be Democratic, but union members even more Democratic. The degree of Republican party identification increased with education, until most college graduates were Republicans. But graduate study, particularly in the social sciences, seems to convert everyone to Democrats. Catholics are more likely than Protestants to vote Democratic, while hardly any Jews are Republicans—but remember Senator Jacob Javits (Republican, New York). Residents of large cities tend to vote Democratic, while those in suburbs and small towns (outside the South) are more Republican. Ninety-nine percent of black voters supported Lyndon Johnson in 1964 and 95 percent selected Hubert Humphrey in 1968. In 1972, President Nixon scored impressive inroads in all the traditional Democratic voting groups except for black people.

None of these attachments is all-inclusive. There are Republican workers and Democratic businessmen; voters will turn against their traditional party to support a popular candidate (Eisenhower in 1952 and 1956) or because that party has scored a conspicuous policy failure (1968).

For decades at a time, the parties will sound quite like each other. Each attempts to build a majority by appealing to the same group of voters, whose attitudes are found in the center and who have few partisan attachments. With neither the parties nor the electorate raising fundamental issues, one of the two parties functions as the normal majority, and the opposition party gains what advantage it can from conflicts occurring within the majority party.

But American political institutions were not designed as instruments sensitive to changing convictions on the part of the people. The system of checks and balances provides ample opportunity for those interests which benefit from it to protect the status quo.[15] The result is that America's political system lags behind developments

15. This argument is developed in the remainder of this book, particularly in Chapters 3, 4, 7, 10, and 11.

in her dynamic economic and social systems. Often too late, and painfully, adjustments are made in the political system by critical elections, which establish new coalitional bases for the two major parties and establish one of them as the new majority. At this point, parties play their most creative role by giving voice to the new convictions of the people and implementing their changed desires. In the periods between critical elections, the parties' role is more negative. They are available as organizations to be held responsible for the failures of government.

> The majestic—but seldom used—power of a democratic electorate is the power to pass judgment upon the performance of an incumbent administration and, if dissatisfied, to turn it out of office.
>
> Beyond that power, the message communicated by the voters in an election is far from clear.

The Future of American Politics

The election of 1972 revealed a paradox. It marked a continuation of the process through which the Republican and Democratic parties are losing the loyalty of their traditional supporting groups. The tendency of voters to split their tickets resulted in a Republican president and a Democratic Congress. It also resulted in a number of states with a governor of one party and a legislative majority of another, and many with one U.S. senator from each of the parties.

Ticket-splitting today probably indicates an increasing attention to politics and political issues on the part of the electorate; it also suggests a growing cynicism, directed against both parties and politicians.

The result is that, with the agencies of government divided between the two parties, no clear thrust for change can be developed. No party has emerged as the clear spokesman of the people. In spite of Mr. Nixon's talk of a new majority, the people did not find their voice in 1972.

The critical election of our era is yet to come. The next presidential election will take place in 1976, the 200th anniversary of the Declaration of Independence. Will it be a time of rededication to American ideals and the adaptation of their meaning to the needs of a post-industrial society? Will it be a time when the agonies of the cities and the claim of the poor for a decent share in the bounty of America will be recognized, and the United States will again take a place of honor among the family of nations on the basis of respect for accomplishment, rather than the awe inspired by military power?

All of that could happen—if it were willed by the people, urged by a candidate, and supported by a renewed political party.

Such a will was not present, nor was it expressed, in 1972.

CHAPTER 3

The National Executive:
Power or Paralysis?

IMAGES 3

An Office of Awesome Power

REFLECTIONS 3

The American Presidency:
Paradox and Personality

An Office of Awesome Power

The president commands the awesome power of the United States, including nuclear weapons. The resources of the federal government are available to serve his purposes—transportation, communication, or administration. He is the central figure of American politics, and he often seems the most important actor on the world's political stage, as American fleets prowl in Middle Eastern waters, and the president or his advisers fly to international conferences.

On closer examination—particularly of the Constitution—the presidential powers look less impressive. And the accomplishments of contemporary presidents seem somehow insignificant compared to the legendary heroes who held the office in the past.

Two Monuments

They are found at opposite ends of the Mall in Washington. Follow the image of one in the reflecting pools, and it will lead you to the other. You have to visit both to know what the presidential office has meant to America.

The Washington Monument is a single shaft, its design inspired by the obelisks built in ancient Egypt and dedicated to the sun god. It stands there, rising 555 feet into the sky of the city that takes its name from the man it commemorates, George Washington, Father of His Country. Austere, forbidding, essentially male, it commemorates in stark simplicity the act of foundation, the birth of the nation. Everybody knows that the nation began with the Declaration of Independence, which was written by Thomas Jefferson—and you can see his memorial not far away, at the Tidal Basin. But the Declaration of Independence consists of words—words that would no longer echo down the pages of history without the acts of George Washington, who commanded the military forces that made the Declaration into the reality of independence for the thirteen former colonies. When that independence was threatened by internal dissent, he became the first president of the federal union established by the Constitution of the United States.

The Washington Monument. Purity of action, unsullied by words. The Foundation. Fatherhood. Wellspring of the national awareness.

The Lincoln Memorial is entirely different. It is a temple; the inspiration is Greek, not Egyptian. Inside is the massive statue of the saddened, brooding Lincoln. The atmosphere is reverent. On the walls are engraved the immortal words, the Gettysburg Address and the Second Inaugural. Compared to Washington's shaft, the values commemorated in Lincoln's temple are feminine, and its massive enclosure enfolds the visitor in pensive solemnity. What Washington founded, Lincoln strove to preserve: the Union. And he was martyred at the summit of his accomplishment. His phrases of simple eloquence are the words of reconciliation. They give voice to a great, aching need to bind up the wounds of a nation and make it whole again — not only whole, but dedicated to noble purposes.

The foundation of national purpose and the preservation of the Union — the presidential office has been bound up with fundamental issues. It still is.

The Home(s) of Presidents

Elsewhere in Washington, at 1600 Pennsylvania Avenue, is the home of the men who attempt to fill the office once graced by Washington and Lincoln. The White House is surrounded by eighteen acres of grounds, with mounds graded by Thomas Jefferson to add visual interest, a majestic elm tree planted by John Quincy Adams 150 years ago, and lawns tended by a dozen gardeners. As rebuilt in 1952 at a cost of over $5.7 million, the White House has four floors above ground, a two-story basement, and 132 rooms. The ground floor is used for diplomatic and ceremonial occasions and for public tours. There are living quarters and guest suites in the upper three floors. The basement is used as office space by the many members of the presidential staff, as are the East and West Wings, both added in the twentieth century.

Serene in appearance, the White House is connected by the most modern communications equipment to the far-flung bureaus and outposts of the national government. From it, President Nixon telephoned the moon.

However, presidents need not remain in their official residence. President Richard Nixon maintains homes in California and Florida. The "Western White House" in San Clemente, located on a seventy-five-foot bluff overlooking the Pacific, has a modest ten rooms, in a five-acre setting bordered by palm trees. One minute away by golf cart, on Coast Guard property, are presidential offices built at a cost of $250,000 and costing $100,000 yearly to staff and maintain, for use when presidential whim takes the center of government to San Clemente. This may, however, be a wise investment; in 1971, a presidential aide reported, "At times it seems that the President can get more done in California in a day than in a week in Washington."[1]

The staff facilities at President Nixon's home in Key Biscayne, Florida, are less elaborate, but $10 million in government funds have been spent on the two houses. If he seeks a retreat closer to Washington, he can move to Camp David in the Maryland mountains.

To move from one home to another, or for other purposes of travel, the president can call upon a fleet of air force helicopters; an armored Lincoln Continental limousine, valued at half a million dollars; and the presidential jet plane, a Boeing 707-320B, which cost $9.1 million. For pleasure outings, there is the presidential yacht *Sequoia*, plus a new twenty-eight-foot hydrofoil, outfitted with silver drinking cups and wildcat-skin carpets, the gift of Russian leader Leonid Brezhnev.

> Can a president ever take a trip that is devoted, purely and simply, to pleasure? Wherever he goes, he is accompanied by an officer carrying a briefcase. The briefcase is known to its carriers as "the football."

1. Quoted in *Newsweek*, September 6, 1971, p. 29.

Stanley Tretick

It provides communication with the network of national defense command posts. It is not a simple "panic button," nor even a telephone. Rather, it contains sheets of precoded orders worked out to fit a number of options for the use of nuclear forces. The missiles it can launch, the planes it can send into the air, command a destructive power that could destroy a hundred million lives in a few minutes and probably make the earth uninhabitable.

All recent presidents have said that the nuclear forces of the United States will never be activated in anger. "Deterrent" nuclear forces exist to insure the possibility of retaliation. Their existence, it is claimed, insures that their use will never be necessary.

In the fourteenth century, the English longbow was hailed as the ultimate military weapon.

Ike's Dilemma
Presidents share authority with the legislative and judicial branches. Presidents—and often Congress—delegate authority to lesser officials of the executive branch. As a result, the president must persuade others of what they should do, on their own authority, to fulfill their separate conceptions of responsibility.

> In the early summer of 1952, before the heat of the campaign, President Truman used to contemplate the problems of the General-become-President should Eisenhower win the forth-coming election. "He'll sit here," Truman would remark (tapping his desk for emphasis), and he'll say, 'Do this! Do that!' *And nothing will happen.* Poor Ike—it won't be a bit like the Army. He'll find it very frustrating."
>
> Eisenhower evidently found it so.... "The President still feels," an Eisenhower aide remarked to me in 1958, "that when he's decided something, that *ought* to be the end of it . . . and when it bounces back undone or done wrong, he tends to react with shocked surprise."[2]

2. Richard E. Neustadt, *Presidential Power* (New York: Wiley, 1960), p. 9.

A Congressional Scorecard

The president can command awesome power. This does not necessarily mean that his vision of the public welfare is enacted into law. Richard Nixon, in 1969, was the first president since Zachary Taylor in 1849 to enter his office facing opposition party majorities in both houses of Congress.

In 1969, President Nixon won 74 percent of the congressional roll-call votes that presented clear tests of support for his views. The comparable figure for 1970 was 77 percent, and for 1971 it was 75 percent. However, not all of his proposals even received the full consideration symbolized by a roll-call vote. In 1970, the 92nd Congress enacted into law just ninety-seven (46 percent) of President Nixon's specific requests.[3] In general, the less significant proposals were adopted, while major items like welfare reform and governmental reorganization languished.

Throughout his first term, President Nixon met more resistance in the Senate than in the House of Representatives. The 1972 elections increased the Democratic majority of the Senate by two members.

The Executive Branch

The president can command awesome power. This does not mean that the nearly 3 million civilian and over 2 million military employees of the federal executive branch are immediately responsive to his wishes.

The Department of Health, Education, and Welfare employs some 127,000 civil servants and administers 270 federal programs. In the first few years of the Nixon administration, disagreements between the HEW employees and Nixon's conservative White House advisers made frequent headlines. Some of the top HEW administrators resigned noisily, like Civil Rights Director Leon E. Panetta, who charged that the White House prevented him from properly enforcing civil rights. When liberal Robert Finch served as HEW secretary, the department's employees publicly cheered him in his apparent disagreements with the White House. One administration official charged that HEW employees felt they constituted a separate policy-making arm of the government. When Elliot Richardson, who would later become President Nixon's super-administrator, was named HEW secretary in 1970, gradual changes began.

General John D. Lavelle commanded all United States Air Force units in Vietnam for eight months, beginning in August 1971. During that time, the selection of U.S. Air Force targets was strictly limited by Rules of Engagement approved by President Nixon. Other targets could be attacked only as a matter of "protective reaction"—that is, because of an actual or impending attack upon the aircraft involved. Lavelle was aware of the buildup of North Vietnamese forces for the offensive of April 1972. During a four-month period, he ordered at least 128 attacks upon unauthorized targets in North Vietnam, which were reported as "protective reactions." His entire chain of command was involved in this deception, which came to light only when an enlisted man wrote about it to Senator Harold Hughes of Iowa.

Lavelle's raids probably contributed to the collapse of Henry Kissinger's secret peace negotiations in Paris in November of 1971. For the North Vietnamese knew Kissinger was saying one thing, while the U.S. Air Force did something else; and Kissinger believed

3. Figures are from *Congressional Quarterly*, August 12, 1972, pp. 2002, 2003.

that all those enemy attacks, which made so-called "protective reaction" necessary, had actually taken place. A few weeks later, President Nixon ordered the same kind of bombing that Lavelle had performed without orders, believing that the previous restrictions had not elicited an appropriate response from North Vietnam.

Removed from his command, General Lavelle was permitted to retire, upon reduction of his rank from four to three stars, with a pension of $2,250 a month. Called to testify at a congressional committee hearing, General Lavelle admitted that he had "interpreted too liberally" the presidential limits in the selection of targets and that he had ordered pilots to falsify their reports. The general stated that he would take the same actions again in the same circumstances.

The Constitution specifies that the president is commander-in-chief of the armed forces of the United States. The founding fathers' intention was to insure civilian control of the military power.

A Visit to the Lincoln Memorial

In the first week of May, 1970, some 100,000 college students were converging upon Washington to protest the invasion of Cambodia and the shooting of students at Kent State University, Ohio, by National Guard troops. Colleges across the nation were closed by their administrations; in California, they were closed by the order of Governor Ronald Reagan. On May 8, President Nixon held a televised press conference. Retreating from his attitude of the previous October, when he sent word that he was watching football on television while thousands of student protestors gathered around the White House, the president expressed understanding and sympathy for the student goals—end the war, end the killing, end the draft.

Excited and unable to sleep, President Nixon summoned his valet and the Secret Service and drove to the Lincoln Memorial at five o'clock the following morning. There he found a group of eight students, who had gone to the Lincoln shrine to renew their own faith in national values. The student group quickly grew to number fifty. The president engaged the students in a rambling conversation, mentioning his own conviction, as a student, that England's Prime Minister Neville Chamberlain was a man of peace, only to realize later that Winston Churchill was right in urging war; recommending that demonstrations be kept peaceful; hoping that black students would abandon separatism as a policy; and listing places in the world that should be visited while one is young. When he talked to individual students, however, and learned what colleges they attended, the president could only think to ask about the fortunes of their football teams; when he learned that students were from California, he asked if they enjoyed surfing. Outraged, the students said his questions were at least irrelevant, at most insulting.

> The genius of Abraham Lincoln was that he understood and expressed the anguish of the people. He knew their thoughts and fears. He had no public opinion polls to consult, but he did not need them.

Landslides

Careful count has been kept of the popular vote received by presidential candidates since 1824, when John Quincy Adams was elected. From then until 1920, no president was elected with more than 57.4 percent of the vote, which Theodore Roosevelt garnered at the time of his reelection in 1904. In 1920, Warren G. Harding was elected by an impressive landslide, 60.4 percent of the popular vote. Three other presidents have been chosen by similar margins: Franklin D. Roosevelt, reelected with 60.8 percent in 1936; Lyndon B. Johnson, reelected with 61.1 percent in 1964; and Richard M. Nixon, reelected with nearly 62 percent of the vote in 1972.

The magnitude of his popular majority does not assure a president the favorable judgment of history. The question is, how does he interpret the mandate? Then, what does he do with it?

Temple to a Long-Forgotten Deity

The Washington Monument was completed in 1884; the Lincoln Memorial in 1922; both were constructed long after the greatness of these two presidents had been acknowledged by succeeding gener-

ations. The Presidential Libraries Act of 1955, institutionalizing a practice begun by Franklin D. Roosevelt, authorized the federal government to accept and operate any presidential library presented to it as a gift. It provided former presidents with a chance to supervise the building of their own monuments.

On May 22, 1971, the Lyndon B. Johnson Library was dedicated on the campus of the University of Texas in Austin. The party was attended by the Nixons, the Agnews, former White House staff members, Texas politicians, and a bevy of senators, including Barry Goldwater, Johnson's opponent in the historic 1964 campaign. The building they came to dedicate was an "eight story monolithic mass" designed to house the 31 million documents and 500,000 photographs that record Johnson's life-long political career. The library cost $17 million. The money was largely contributed by the state of Texas, but a hefty $1 million came from the Johnsons themselves. An unfriendly critic described the new building:

> There is no doubt that the detail of the collection, the stretch of history it represents, are impressive and unique. Used as a standard, it is difficult to imagine what Presidential libraries may grow to be in another decade. This one is obviously a tribute to a man. Archeologists, stumbling upon it in some far-distant century, might well mistake it for the remnants of a temple built to a long-forgotten deity.[4]

George Reedy, a former press secretary to President Johnson, reflected upon his experience and wrote a book about the presidential office.[5] He stated that the presidential institution makes it entirely too easy for the president to isolate himself from political reality. Able to limit his public appearances to staged television productions, he needs to see — and be seen by — only the staff members whose jobs depend on serving, and even flattering, him. A president could suffer from serious neurosis, according to Reedy, and the people would have no way of knowing it, unless the president slobbered at the mouth in public.

Mr. Reedy was not invited to the dedication ceremonies in Austin.

During the campaign of 1972, Richard Nixon largely tended to his presidential responsibilities; political speech-making was done by his helpers. He ignored the charges of corruption and political espionage leveled by his opposition. When he was reelected by an historic margin, President Nixon said that he sensed, in the nation, a new spirit of self-reliance, a rejection of the "permissiveness" that had marked the preceding years. His first domestic priority, he said, would be to reorganize and streamline the national government, making it "leaner but stronger."

A president immersed in the technicalities of public administration would provide a contrast with past presidents (including some aspects of the first-term Nixon) who offered dramatic proposals for securing the public welfare.

Had the people outgrown their need to have a hero in the White House?

4. Nicholas C. Chriss, "Lyndon Gets His Library," *The Nation*, June 7, 1971, p. 712.
5. George E. Reedy, *The Twilight of the Presidency* (New York: NAL-World, 1970).

The American Presidency: Paradox and Personality

The president of the United States is a familiar figure to his country-men and to much of the world. He is sometimes loved, frequently respected, often hated or feared. His office is hardly described in the U.S. Constitution, and its present dimensions would shock the authors of that document. The presidency has been built by the forces of history and the men who have held it.

Woodrow Wilson stated that the Constitution permits the president "to be as big a man as he can." Richard Neustadt adds that "nowadays he cannot be as small as he might like." Heading an executive establishment of millions, he is at the center of political events in the nation and in the world. In the eyes of the people, he has the responsibility for shaping those events to further the national interest, although they may be outside his control. This expectation on the part of the people can be, for the president, a source of great strength. It can also lead to tragedy.

Shared Authority

The founding fathers of the American nation drew their theoretical convictions from the galaxy of political thinkers that flourished in England and Europe in the seventeenth and eighteenth centuries. John Locke supplied several of the concepts stated in the Declaration of Independence. The founders drew only a single idea from the writings of a French Baron, Charles de Montesquieu. But that single idea became an organizing principle of the United States Constitution and of the structure of government in the fifty states. It is the principle of the separation of powers.

Baron de Montesquieu was convinced that the best form of government is a monarchy, for a monarch symbolizes the permanency of the social order. But he sought the best organization of government to preserve individual liberty. In common with his age, he perceived the power of government as the most certain threat to liberty, but he felt that liberty could flourish only within an orderly system: he was concerned with freedom *under* law, feeling that any claim for freedom *from* law was a delusion that could lead only to the destruction of society.

Montesquieu's *The Spirit of the Law* was published in 1748 and translated into English in 1750. He found the model for a properly constructed government in the then-current theory (although the practice was something else) of the English government. Montes-

quieu declared the essence of tyrannical government to be the practice of combining in the hands of a single man, or a single body of
men, the power both of determining and administering the law.
That single person or group, seeking its own interest alone, could
both establish tyrannical laws and execute them in a tyrannical manner. This could only be prevented by establishing separate institutions to share the authority of government. In England, he wrote,
the Houses of Lords and Commons represented different interests
in society, yet neither could make laws without the concurrence of
the other; and the monarch, attuned to yet different interests, executed the laws, with the result of guaranteeing individual freedom.

The supremacy of Parliament over the monarchy had been established in 1688, and the authority of the House of Lords was becoming
less important, to be extinguished in all but name by 1911. Complete
authority is lodged with the House of Commons, and its exercise is
made accountable to the people through periodic elections. But this
outcome was not clear in 1748, either in France, in the American
colonies, or in England itself.

The term "separation of powers" is misleading, for the power of
government operating upon an individual citizen is a single power.
When the citizen receives a draft notice or an income tax return, the
interruption of his life is the same, regardless of the degree to which
that interruption results from the writing of a law by Congress, its
interpretation by the courts, or its administration by the executive
branch. In applying the doctrine of the separation of powers, the
founders established separate institutions which *share* the authority
of government.

The fact of sharing authority was made explicit in the concept of
"checks and balances," which is usually listed as a twin concept
along with the separation of powers. Famous number 51 of the Federalist Papers declares:

> In order to lay a due foundation for that separate and distinct
> exercise of the different powers of government, which to a cer-
> tain extent is admitted on all hands to be essential to the pres-
> ervation of liberty, it is evident that each department should
> have a will of its own. . . . The great security against a gradual
> concentration of the several powers in the same department,
> consists in giving to those who administer each department the
> necessary constitutional means and personal motives to resist
> encroachments of the others. . . . Ambition must be made to
> counteract ambition.[1]

A Single Executive

The men who met in Philadelphia were determined to preserve the
infant nation. They were convinced that the Articles of Confederation were too weak to provide the framework for an enduring nation. And the main flaw of the Articles was the lack of executive
authority. But the people of their states had known the impact of
arbitrary and capricious executive power exercised by kings and royal
governors, and the war for independence had been fought against
such authority. The founding fathers were faced with a delicate problem. They wished to establish a strong and independent executive
power; yet they dared not revive memories of the English king, or
the new Constitution might be rejected by the states.

1. *The Federalist*, 51, various editions (first published, 1788). The authorship of number 51
has been ascribed to both Alexander Hamilton and James Madison, but modern scholarship favors Madison.

Four of the states then had plural executives, in which councils shared the executive power. Nine of the states had a single executive, given the title either of president or governor, but he was subservient to the legislature. Executives served a term of a single year, except for two years in South Carolina and three in New York and Delaware.

When, in convention session, James Wilson of Pennsylvania moved that the executive consist of a single person, a hush fell over the delegates. It was a proposal of marked audacity, calling forth memories of royal pretensions. In the end, the framers adopted a description of the presidency that was quite sparse, based on the powers of the state governors, and made up both of very specific provisions and very general ones. The exact wording of the oath to be recited by the president upon taking his office was prescribed, for example; but the only hint that a vast executive bureaucracy might develop is contained in the sentence "he may require the Opinion, in writing, of the principal Officers in each of the executive Departments." The framers were very clear about two matters: the military should be under civilian control, and the new nation should speak with but a single voice to other nations. They explicitly provided that the president should be the "Commander in Chief of the Army and Navy of the United States, and of the Militia of the several States, when called into the actual service of the United States." The president was empowered to receive "Ambassadors and other public Ministers" and to appoint the diplomats of the United States, with the advice and consent of the Senate. This makes him chief diplomat of the nation.

Other roles performed by the president are barely hinted at in the Constitution. From his constitutional right to address Congress on the state of the Union has grown his role as chief legislator, establishing the congressional agenda through legislative proposals. Because "the executive power" is vested in the president (and it is his duty to "take care that the Laws be faithfully executed"), he is the chief executive, confronted with perhaps the most challenging managerial task in the world. Nowhere in the Constitution is mentioned a role that was adopted by George Washington and has been thrust upon every president since. This is his responsibility to lead his political party. Legislation enacted in 1946 made explicit a duty that the electorate had long since assigned to the president. He is to be the manager of the economy, attempting simultaneously to achieve full employment, good profits for industry, and hold down the cost of living.

Many analyses of the presidency divide the office into these separate duties or roles. But such a separation obscures the fact that the president is indeed a single person, performing his executive responsibilities simultaneously. This is a source of both strength and weakness. His position as chief of party may strengthen his ability to perform as chief executive or chief legislator. But his performance in one role may also make other roles more difficult. When Lyndon Johnson's attention became concentrated upon his decisions as commander-in-chief, and the war in Vietnam lost popular support, his ability to perform his other tasks was increasingly weakened.

The president's power of decision—his ability to launch nuclear war, for example—seems the ultimate power. But his days are actually spent in coping with the separation of powers system. The Constitution encourages each branch to encroach upon the authority of the others. The president was guaranteed a negative influence upon the work of Congress, if he chose to exercise the veto power. The State of the Union message hardly suggested the great positive impact that his legislative leadership could provide. Thomas Jefferson continually made rhetorical bows to the independence of Congress. Because of his subtle and powerful exercise of party leadership, however, he became its leader.

Congress was given the power to "advise and consent" to the president's appointments, and to any treaties negotiated by him, as well as the ability, by an extraordinary majority of two-thirds in both houses, to override his veto. Laws could be established only through the joint concurrence of the Senate, the House of Representatives, and the president.

Congressmen and the president—and, later, the lesser officials of the executive branch—tended to identify as the will of their constituency a course of action that would also advance their personal ambitions. This was not a hypocritical claim, for performance of the public will is bound to bring credit to the public's agent. But the Constitution arranged for each official to serve a different constituency, so that each perceived a different version of the people's wishes. Thus was ambition made to counteract ambition.

The founding fathers exercised the full power of their ingenuity in designing the Electoral College as a device for electing the president. They assumed that each section of the nation would put forward its own candidate, and that the final choice would frequently be made by the House of Representatives. They did not foresee the development of political parties of national scope, which soon made the Electoral College a mere formality. (It remains a potentially dangerous institution, if the electors as a group should choose to disregard the instructions of their party.) The result was to make the president the only representative of the whole nation, the man who claims to speak for all. This claim permitted him to expand his authority—in the name of democracy—into areas where the Constitution is vague or silent.

> There was a powerful reason for describing the powers of the president in general and unlimited terms. The delegates knew that the first president would probably be their own presiding officer, George Washington. Confident of his ability to establish the office with appropriate dignity and authority, they did not wish to embarrass him with a lengthy discussion of the possibilities of a plural executive.
>
> From the very beginning, the scope and prestige of the office were intimately connected with the personality of its occupant.

A Fear of Kings

The opponents of the new Constitution attacked the proposed executive vigorously. In the Federalist Papers, Alexander Hamilton replied to their charges with a sarcastic pen:

> The authorities of a magistrate, in few instances greater, and in
> some instances less, than those of a Governor of New-York,
> have been magnified into more than royal prerogatives. He has
> been decorated with attributes superior in dignity and splendor
> to those of a King of Great-Britain. He has been shown to us
> with the diadem sparkling on his brow, and the imperial purple
> flowing in his train. He has been seated on a throne surrounded
> with minions and mistresses; giving audience to the envoys of
> foreign potentates, in all the supercilious pomp of majesty. . . .[2]

Hamilton then took some pains to demonstrate that the formal
powers accorded the president by the proposed Constitution were
less than those accorded the governor of New York.

Some of the powers of state governors are still, in a formal sense,
greater than those of the president. Most notable is the "item veto"
power, which the president lacks, but which the governors of thirty-
nine states enjoy. This is the power to strike out individual items of
an appropriations bill, without invalidating the entire appropriations
package. It gives an executive greater control over the budget, for
often the passage of some appropriations bill is essential for the continuation of government.

In 1972, President Nixon asked Congress for what was in effect an
item veto power, in order to hold federal spending to Nixon's planned
level. The bill was passed by the House but met fierce opposition in
the Senate, where several Republicans joined the Democratic majority in defeating the proposal by a wide margin. Regardless of
party, senators did not wish to establish precedents that would limit
the power of Congress.

Hamilton was on firm ground in comparing the powers of the president with those of the governor of New York. For the presidential
office had been modeled on New York, which had the strongest
executive of any of the thirteen states. Gouverneur Morris was the
chief draftsman of the relevant constitutional provisions for both
New York and the United States.

Continuing his argument, Hamilton wrote that comparisons of
the presidential office with the king of England were preposterous.
For the king occupied an hereditary position, from which he could
be removed only by violence. And King George III successfully asserted that his own judgment should prevail over that of Parliament.
The president would be elected, returning to the people for a renewal
of his mandate after four years. And he would be confronted by a
Congress possessing equal and independent authority.

2. *The Federalist*, number 67 (first published March 11, 1788).

Was Hamilton putting his readers on? As a delegate to the Convention, Hamilton had proposed a monarchy; when he later became George Washington's secretary of the Treasury, he acted as though he felt Washington's position was equivalent to an elected monarch, with himself cast as a kind of prime minister. Hamilton eventually got into so much trouble with the Jeffersonians in Congress that he was forced to resign.

Even then, it was becoming clear that a president is his own prime minister. As president, he is the symbolic head of the state, like a king. But he does not have the permanent tenure of a king. He is also the leader of the government and must be intimately involved with the politics of the people, like a prime minister. Unlike a prime minister, he cannot be sure of a favorable majority in the national legislature.

> Harold Laski wrote, of the twentieth-century president, "he is both more and less than a king; he is both more and less than a prime minister."[3]

When the new government of the United States took office, a number of seemingly trivial details remained to be settled. One was the form of address, or title, to be applied to the president of the United States. John Adams, then serving as vice president, felt strongly that the authority of the office would be enhanced if its occupant were customarily addressed with a title demonstrating ceremonious respect. Adams favored "His Most Benign Highness." The U.S. Senate agreed in principle with Adams, who was their presiding officer. A Senate committee recommended the title, "His Highness, the President of the United States of America, and Protector of the Rights of the Same."

The House of Representatives disagreed vigorously. There were to be no trappings of royalty in this new democracy. The president, they decreed, would be addressed simply as "Mr. President." And so he has been, from 1790 to the present day. The American ambivalence toward authority thus was demonstrated in the beginning. The president occupies his office on a lease that the people may choose not to renew. During his tenure, he shall be reminded that his temporary status is really no higher than any of his countrymen.

Some of the most outrageous criticism directed by a free press at an incumbent president was directed at George Washington.

Washington and Adams: Strength and Weakness
The confidence of the Constitution's authors in the dignity and judgment of George Washington proved well founded. Washington was aware that his acts would give the presidential office its form. He adhered to the Constitution; where the Constitution was silent, he asserted executive authority. He originated the practice of claiming "executive privilege," a precedent still followed by presidents and their assistants. The House of Representatives had requested the right of examining documents relating to the mission of John Jay to negotiate a treaty with Great Britain. Washington replied that, under the Constitution, the House had no role to play in the approval of treaties, and the conduct of foreign relations requires confidentiality. "A just regard to the Constitution and to the duty of my Office," he wrote, "forbids a compliance with your request."

Congressmen have been able only to grind their teeth in frustra-

3. *The American Presidency* (New York: Harper, 1940), p. 11.

tion during more than a century and a half since then, when presidents and their helpers have followed Washington's example.

Testifying before a congressional committee interested in the Watergate scandals, then-Attorney General Kleindienst asserted that "executive privilege" could be extended to all 3 million members of the executive branch. If Congress didn't like that, he said, they would have to impeach President Nixon.
    Some weeks later, Mr. Kleindienst resigned from his position.

> Washington's relationships with Congress were formal and correct, if not cordial; he left the dirty work of getting his policies passed to Alexander Hamilton. Washington formed the cabinet, nowhere mentioned in the Constitution, of the heads of his executive departments. His work as chief administrator was energetic and diligent. Above all, he maintained his popularity with the people. He kept in touch with public opinion by maintaining an extensive correspondence, and he toured the thirteen states to emphasize national unity. He was a masterful leader of the Federalist party, although he hardly admitted, even to himself, that his supporters had formed a political party. He sensed that the people did not completely share the disdain of the House of Representatives for pomp and ceremony.

> His natural taste for regal display was freely indulged. He ventured forth in a handsome coach drawn by six cream-colored horses or on a white steed mounted with leopard-skin housing and saddlecloth with gold binding. The Presidential household operated on a large scale, with fourteen white servants, seven slaves, and frequent elaborate dinners done with a high formality conveyed by the presence of powdered lackeys in the entrance hall.[4]

George Washington thus brought a sense of style to his office. Other presidents have displayed a style that lifted them above the common man, but served, paradoxically, to cement the respect and affection of the people. Contemporary examples include Franklin D. Roosevelt and John F. Kennedy.

George Washington was a success as president, establishing the broad outlines of the office, and demonstrating its potential, particularly when occupied by a man who enjoys political support that is independent of Congress. Washington—and other presidents who have won the admiration of history—used such popular support to overwhelm the potential for frustration and stalemate written into the Constitution as the principle of the separation of powers.

John Adams, the second president, was not so fortunate. As author of the Massachusetts Constitution, Adams had been one of the most important American theorists of the separation of powers doctrine. The liberty of the people, he felt, would be best protected if the personnel and powers of the executive, legislative, and judicial branches were carefully separated. Washington had performed ably as party leader, a presidential role that is nowhere mentioned in the Constitution. John Adams may have possessed the most outstanding intellect of any president in American history. But he was unwilling to concede the necessity of leading a party, or "faction," and the Federalists in Congress acknowledged Alexander Hamilton (who did not then even hold a public office) as their leader. Because he failed to understand the need for party leadership, Adams was unsuccessful

4. Louis W. Koenig, *The Chief Executive* (New York: Harcourt, Brace and World, 1964), p. 32.

in the related roles of leading Congress and managing the administration. His frustrations reached a climax when he was defeated for
reelection.

The Constitution had applied the principle of checks and balances
so well that only an adroit political tactician enjoying great popular
support — usually expressed as effective party leadership — could realize
the potential authority of the presidential office.

George Washington demonstrated the strength of the presidential
office; John Adams demonstrated its inherent weakness.

Learning on the Job

The presidency is an office that, despite its traditions, is intimately
bound up with the incumbent's conception of the office, and the
challenges to the president's skill and authority posed by the issues
of the time. The president has no "boss," in the sense of a person who
can prescribe, and later criticize, the way he works. He can implement the merest whim for a change of scenery by calling for the
presidential helicopter and aircraft to whisk him away to a more
amenable climate. This seems to give him freedom to organize his
days and his tasks to suit himself. But he is, in the deepest sense, the
servant of the people — not only the temporary coalition of individuals
and groups that elected him, but also of "generations yet unborn."
Seeking the favorable judgment of history, and sworn to protect and
defend the Constitution, he has the most demanding judges of his
performance that can be imagined.

How does one learn to be a president? There is no dependable
preparation for the job. Presidents come to understand the nature of
their office, and their own capacity to fill it, through experience. However, they may bring preconceived notions that affect their performance. Some have held a restricted view of the scope of their authority.
William Howard Taft, for example, declared that "the President can
exercise no power which cannot be fairly and reasonably traced to
some specific grant of power" in the Constitution, or in a law passed
by Congress. President Taft was not very happy in the White House.
Neither was Herbert Hoover, who held a similarly restrictive view of
presidential power.

Other presidents have felt that nearly any action was open to them
that was not specifically prohibited by the Constitution. Theodore
Roosevelt was such a president. Abraham Lincoln and Franklin D.
Roosevelt went further, claiming that, in grave emergencies, the
president can exercise almost unlimited powers to preserve the nation.
Upon his inauguration, Roosevelt claimed that the Depression was as
grave an emergency as a war; he hinted he would model his assertions
of authority after the wartime practices of Lincoln and Woodrow
Wilson. All evidence suggests that Franklin Roosevelt very much
enjoyed being president.

Presidents often change their conceptions of the nature of the office. John Kennedy was interviewed after two years in office. He said,
in part,

> I think the Congress looks more powerful sitting here than it
> did when I was there in Congress. . . . When you are in Congress
> you are one of a hundred in the Senate or one of 435 in the
> House, so that the power is so divided. But from here I look at
> a Congress, and I look at the collective power of the Congress
> . . . and it is a substantial power.[5]

5. "After Two Years — A Conversation with the President," Television and Radio Interview,
December 17, 1962, in Public Papers of the Presidents of the United States, John F. Kennedy, 1962 (Washington, D.C.: U.S. Government Printing Office, 1963), p. 892.

Scoring the Presidents

An occasional pastime of American historians is polling their colleagues about the "greatness" of past presidents. The presidents winning the highest scores include Washington, Jefferson, Jackson, Lincoln, Theodore Roosevelt, and Franklin D. Roosevelt.[6] They were presidents who held office during times of crisis, who fought successful battles with Congress (or, like Lincoln for a time, managed to ignore Congress completely), and who had a very generous interpretation of the powers of their office. We may be tempted to conclude that American historians prefer the executive over the legislative branch. A more complete interpretation is that historians agreed with the positions taken by those particular presidents, instead of the dominant attitude of the Congresses which opposed them.

Similarly, presidents are scored during their terms of office by journalists who keep track of their key proposals before Congress, reporting with dismal sorrow the ones that fail to win support. When Congress votes to override a presidential veto, the stuff of headlines is produced.

Conflict makes news. The Constitution assures conflict. It is an easy matter to cast the president as hero, and Congress as villain, of the contest.

But the president is not always pictured as the hero. In 1951, President Truman's action in sending troops to Korea without the approval of Congress was attacked by a number of congressman, including the late Senator Robert A. Taft, Sr. The president, said Taft, had "usurped authority." Scholars favoring strong presidential authority rallied to Truman's side. One of them was Arthur Schlesinger, Jr. In 1972, when substantial sentiment in Congress opposed the continuance of hostilities in Vietnam, the same historians were not so willing to argue that the Constitution grants more certain authority to the president than to Congress in the field of foreign affairs. Schlesinger recalled the 1951 controversy and felt compelled to confess:

> The present writer, with a flourish of historical documentation and, alas, hyperbole, called Taft's statements "demonstrably irresponsible."[7]

Senator Taft's 1951 criticism resulted in the passage of a Senate resolution stating that no further troops should be sent to Western Europe without congressional approval. Among those voting for the resolution was Senator Richard M. Nixon of California.

When the president is attacked on constitutional grounds for exceeding his authority, one can only be certain that the attacker disapproves of the president's policy.

The Bureaucracy: Helpers or Rivals?

As the responsibilities of government expanded to meet the demands of an industrial, and then a post-industrial, society, the executive branch grew in personnel, power, and cost. Officially under the direct

6. One of the first of these polls of historians was conducted by Arthur M. Schlesinger, Sr., in 1945. For an account of it, see W. E. Binkley, *The Man in the White House* (Baltimore: Johns Hopkins Press, 1958), p. 81 ff. Arthur Schlesinger, Jr. repeated the exercise in 1962.

7. Arthur Schlesinger, Jr., "Congress and the Making of American Foreign Policy," *Foreign Affairs* 51 (October 1972): 96.

control of the president, these burgeoning offices quickly became more than any man could keep under his personal supervision, or even coordinate through meetings of the cabinet. It is the nature of bureaucrats to become experts in a narrow field; a president may think twice before insisting that his own knowledge matches that of the expert.

The federal bureaucracy became yet another center of fragmented power. It is made up of persons and organizations separate from the president who share his executive authority. The problem of any president is to somehow make his position at the head of the executive branch meaningful. He sits at the apex of a bureaucracy of some 3 million civilian employees. (In 1790, the entire federal government employed just 780 people.) In the 1970s, the largest enterprise of the federal government was the Department of Defense, and the president as commander-in-chief ruled over some 2 million additional persons in the armed forces of the United States.

Not only the armed forces, but also the civilian employees, were scattered around the nation and around the world. There were, for example, nearly as many federal employees working in California as in the District of Columbia.

How is a president to be sure that the vast network of bureaus, departments, and agencies that is the executive branch are responsive to his will, and thus, ultimately—at least in theory—to the people? The original answer was to staff the executive branch with political supporters of the president. George Washington sought men of good character for government positions; coincidentally or not, they were also Federalists. When Thomas Jefferson became president, he removed hundreds of Federalists from office and replaced them with his own partisans. This use of patronage served two useful functions. It assured that the president's subordinates would be committed to implementing his policies. It built up his party, for the possibility of obtaining a job in government added personal motivation to any disinterested concern for party goals. When President Andrew Jackson dismissed hundreds of the previous administration's appointees, one of his supporters enthusiastically exclaimed, "to the victor belong the spoils." Party patronage was thereafter called the "spoils system," and it began to earn a deserved bad reputation, when public position was used for private gain. But congressmen were also party men, and the use of patronage to staff the federal government was not modified until President James A. Garfield was assassinated by a disappointed office-seeker in 1881. The Civil Service Act was passed in 1883. It established a commission charged with selecting federal employees on the basis of merit, rather than partisan affiliation.

Civil service is a mixed blessing. Presidents need no longer be surrounded by a swarm of office-seekers as they launch their administrations. (Abraham Lincoln's direction of the Civil War had been hampered by demands for the dispensation of patronage.) However, one attraction of civil-service status is that the employee cannot be dismissed, except for just cause. Disagreement with the policy approach of the president does not constitute just cause, unless it can be proved that it has led one to sabotage the department's operations. With civil service, presidents cannot engage in the wholesale replacement of government personnel, but a president taking office can appoint some 2,000 officials whose positions are not part of the civil service system.

Former Congressman John Schmitz of California (the American Independent party nominee for president in 1972) liked to remind his constituents that the election of Richard Nixon did not place the federal government in the hands of the Republican party. The same "New Deal bureaucrats" were running things, he said, who had done so for forty years.

A number of civil servants working in the Department of Health, Education, and Welfare were dedicated to the policy of racial integration in the public schools. They did not change their minds simply because President Nixon questioned the wisdom of school integration accomplished through busing.

The bureaucracy is vast; Congress may reduce the appropriation of a particular office or bureau, but to actually abolish one is rare. Once a particular function is accepted as a task of government, and an office is established to perform it, the proclivity of bureaucracies to protect and expand their functions begins to operate. As the number of American farmers has decreased, the number of employees of the Department of Agriculture has increased.

Presidents come and go, as the White House gets a new tenant periodically. Career civil servants plan on lifetime employment. Presidents, seeking reelection and the vindication of history, want to solve problems, shake up organizations, and make a record of accomplishment. Civil servants are likely to take a longer point of view. Problems are not so much solved as they are ameliorated; organizations don't like to succeed so well that they are put out of business.

Management organizations that have reached a certain critical size can exist quite happily with nothing to manage. When the Krupp munitions works were destroyed by bombing in World War II, the headquarters building was untouched. The management functioned happily for the rest of the war, writing memoranda to each other.

The affairs of a government bureau are carried out according to fixed rules, which are the quintessence of fairness. Ideally, nobody gets preferential treatment simply because he once aided the president's campaign, or because he belongs to a group—Indians, say, or blacks —who have historically confronted the cold treatment of bureaucratic "fairness." Elected officials may want to make things happen, and civil servants may share their goals. But the internal needs of the bureaucracy require that nothing shall happen until the proper forms have been filled out, with the appropriate number of copies.

Governmental agencies normally develop sources of support in Congress, and in the nation, that are independent of the president. The Army Corps of Engineers serves as consultants and contractors to Congress, on very nearly a direct basis. Congressmen prove their dedication to their constituents' needs by providing construction projects. Failing new construction, routine maintenance—harbors always need dredging—can be announced from Washington with a flourish. Government bureaus maintain their own congressional lobbyists to assure a favorable consideration of their budget requests, not necessarily in coordination with the recommendations of the Office of Management and Budget in the Office of the President.

The president is not the master in his own house. He may appoint a cabinet member who is favored by a powerful, organized group, in order to woo the political support of that group. If he becomes dissatisfied with the official's performance, he risks losing that support if he discharges the official. An effective cabinet officer is likely to develop a separate constituency, even if he has none at the time of his entry into the cabinet. As the cabinet member's independent political support grows, the president must conduct relations with him with greater care.

There are eleven cabinet-level departments—State, War (now the Department of Defense), and Treasury created in 1789—and others established in response to the historical expansion of the functions of the federal government. Even within a giant department, there may be bureaus that operate independently of the cabinet officer who is the department's nominal head. The classic example was the Federal Bureau of Investigation under the directorship of J. Edgar Hoover. According to organizational charts, the FBI was and is part of the Justice Department, headed by the attorney general of the United States. But J. Edgar Hoover was an independent power. First appointed by President Calvin Coolidge, establishing the FBI's reputation in the gang-busting days of Prohibition, Hoover was reappointed by the six following presidents. He died, in office, in 1972.

In addition to the cabinet departments, there are numerous independent executive agencies—"independent" because they are not part of any cabinet department. Some, such as the Veteran's Administration, have more employees than most cabinet departments. Among these executive agencies are such well-known and powerful units as the Central Intelligence Agency and the Selective Service System, and such obscure ones as the American Battle Monuments Commission. Also in this category are government corporations such as the Tennessee Valley Authority.

Newly recognized issues may not fall automatically within the jurisdiction of an existing department. When a problem has been identified (violence in the cities, heroin addiction, or the increased sale of pornography), the president demonstrates his concern by appointing a group of distinguished citizens to a commission or task force. Hearings are held, reports are issued, and recommendations made. The president is free to—and frequently does—ignore the report and its recommendations. Since the New Deal, presidents have often responded by asking Congress for a new agency and a new appropriation.

There is a third major type of executive agency. These are the independent regulatory commissions. In this case, the word "independent" is more than justified. Members of these commissions are appointed by the president, with the advice and consent of the Senate, but their members are not responsible to him, and he cannot remove them from office. Their task is to regulate complex industries, to protect the public against unfair practices, and to license the commercial usage of public assets, through such actions as granting routes to airlines and licenses to television stations. Oldest of the regulatory commissions is the Interstate Commerce Commission, established in 1887; youngest is the Civil Aeronautics Board, established in 1938. Their constitutional authority comes from Article I, Section 8, of the Constitution, which empowers Congress to "regulate Commerce with foreign Nations, and among the several States, and with the Indian Tribes." Congress has delegated this authority in specific areas to the regulatory commissions, attempting to establish them as agencies independent of Congress, of the president, and of the regulated industry.

The decisions of these commissions often involve millions of dollars. The license to operate a television station (particularly the only one in a moderately sized market area, like the station formerly operated by Lyndon Johnson's family in Austin, Texas) has been described as the equivalent of a license to print money. Periodic investigations reveal that the regulatory commissions do not remain independent of the industries they regulate. Presidents have too frequently appointed commissioners with close ties to the regulated industry whose habit of mind is more in tune with industry needs than with the public interest. Presidents are in no position to determine the decisions of the regulatory agencies, but a major scandal involving one of the agencies may implicate the president and his administration, at least in the public mind.

Perched at the apex of the executive pyramid, the president may only seem to be in control. His real position may be like that of a cat on a hot tin roof.

Tools of Coordination

How can any president impose a common sense of purpose upon the far-flung executive branch? It grows by increments, as Congress responds to public demands. Today's new agency may be in direct conflict with the purpose of yesterday's bureau. Following World War II, the federal government insured the mortgages of suburban homes through the Federal Housing Administration. This encouraged middle-class families to move away from the central city. Then, as city problems multiplied, the federal government attempted to arrest the decay of the central city through a helter-skelter array of programs perhaps climaxed by Lyndon Johnson's conception of a Model Cities program. President Nixon created the cabinet-level Urban Affairs Council in an effort to coordinate such policies.

Jurisdictional disputes between various agencies have been famous since the feud between Harry Hopkins and Harold Ickes in Franklin D. Roosevelt's administration. And the contest between army, navy, and air force for available funds was only made less public by their combination into a single Department of Defense.

The cabinet has not functioned as a strong agency of coordination for the last half century, if it ever did so. Even George Washington's first cabinet eventually failed to serve this purpose, due to the fundamental disagreement between Secretary of the Treasury Alexander Hamilton and Secretary of State Thomas Jefferson. A modern cabinet fails for more complex reasons. Each department head is a specialist, and he may have little to contribute to general matters. His attention is captured by the complex demands of his own department. Furthermore, the cabinet officer is normally committed to serving the convictions of his own staff—if he is an effective leader—and particular groups in the population. Since the president must serve a broader constituency, he may discount the cabinet member's advice.

Robert Finch, Richard Nixon's political friend of longest standing, became the secretary of Health, Education, and Welfare. As a progressive Republican, he hoped to serve the disadvantaged sectors of American society and thereby expand the membership of the Republican party. Some of President Nixon's advisers had quite a different political strategy in mind. Finch was unable to choose between loyalty to his own convictions and those of his subordinates at HEW, on one hand, and concern for Richard Nixon's political fortunes, as interpreted by the White House advisers, on the other. When Finch withdrew the nomination of Dr. John Knowles as assistant secretary for health because of political pressures led by the Political Action Committee of the American Medical Association, his authority with his assistants at HEW was severely damaged. The ambiguity was resolved only by promoting Finch to the position of White House Counselor, and appointing a new secretary of HEW.

The president is a single executive; the power of decision rests with him alone. Abraham Lincoln is said to have announced a cabinet vote, "Seven noes, one aye. The ayes have it." But how can the president be sure that he has the appropriate information for making the decisions that reach his desk? More important, how can he be sure that the important decisions—the decisions that affect his own political fortunes—*do* reach his desk, while those that can safely be handled elsewhere, in accord with his wishes, do not? And how can he impose a grand design upon the pattern of his decision-making?

Presidents have adopted a number of devices for coordination, both formal and informal. Some of these have become established by law, so that the presidency is not only an office with an incumbent, it is also an institution. To coordinate the far-flung bureaucracy of the executive branch, the president has developed his own bureaucracy, the Executive Office of the President. Originating in 1939, it now includes nearly 3,000 employees in the Office of Management and Budget, the National Security Council, Domestic Council, Council of Economic Advisers, and some ten other agencies.

Before 1939, presidents borrowed their staff assistants from the existing executive departments. A distinguished commission studied the management problems of President Franklin D. Roosevelt and concluded, "the President needs help." President Roosevelt agreed. Congress gave FDR permission to hire six administrative assistants who would have "a passion for anonymity." Thus began the evolution of the presidency from office to institution. Although each president organizes the staff to suit himself, none has been able to stem its inevitable growth; for the responsibilities of the president are overwhelming, and he can best delegate authority to people who have his confidence, understand his thinking, and have no separate constituencies to serve—men and women who can be reprimanded, replaced, or permitted to fade into the background, without the public conflict that would come from such treatment of an official appointed by the president with the consent of the Senate. The president's management of his staff is hardly even noticed, except by the political gossip columnists, who regard it (with some justice) as the equivalent of the palace guard, or the group of courtiers, surrounding a king.

The eighteenth century portrait of presidential power ("surrounded with minions . . . giving audience to envoys") painted by opponents of the Constitution came to pass in the twentieth century, as a result of growth of the powers and duties of the executive branch.

Richard Nixon came to the presidency with a rich fund of experience. He had, as vice president, worked for eight years on the fringes of the Eisenhower administration. Some Eisenhower assistants treated Vice President Nixon as a superfluous appendage to the administration. Nixon remembered this, and he was determined that the Nixon White House would have no equivalent to Eisenhower's assistant, Sherman Adams. Further, he was convinced that the size of the White House staff should be reduced, and more executive authority wielded by cabinet officers. The first responsibility of a president, he told Theodore White, was in the field of foreign affairs. A competent cabinet should be largely able to deal with domestic matters.[8] Both of these ideas were shattered by the realities of Washington. President Nixon's cabinet officials were caught up in the problems of their own departments, and the struggle for influence within Nixon's circle of advisers and assistants got off to an early start, culminating in the division of the White House staff into warring factions when the Watergate scandals were more fully revealed.

> Little was heard of Nixon's desire that policy be made by Cabinet members collectively and individually to permit a much smaller White House staff. Once planted in the fertile bureaucratic soil of Washington, the White House staff began growing at a frantic pace while the proposed rejuvenation of the Cabinet was never pursued with much seriousness.[9]

President Nixon's preoccupation with foreign affairs continued for the first two years of his first term. The elections of 1970—when he failed to increase substantially the number of Republicans in Congress—drew his attention back to domestic matters. In his 1971 State of the Union address, he proposed a massive legislative program of proposals old and new. He called for enactment of his earlier welfare reform and revenue sharing proposals, adding new proposals for national health insurance and environmental protection. He also asked for a major reform of governmental structure, combining cabinet departments to serve the "New Federalism" that would revitalize government at all levels by restoring local initiative. President Nixon indulged in rhetorical flourish by naming his program a "New American Revolution." Congress yawned, but many normally critical commentators reacted favorably. Soon thereafter, he decided to invade Cambodia; after that, the campuses exploded. The New American Revolution was largely forgotten.

During the 1972 campaign, President Nixon gave an interview to the Washington *Evening Star*, which was published only after his historic election victory was added up. Nixon said that the emphasis of his second term would be upon reforms designed to make government "leaner and stronger," renewing America's faith in governmental institutions, assuring responsiveness on the local level to local needs. He said, in part,

> It is our responsibility to find a way to reform our government institutions so that this new spirit of independence, self-reliance, pride that I sense in the American people can be nurtured. I think it is out there.[10]

The first step in trimming governmental fat, he said, would be to reduce the size of the White House staff.

In the basement of the White House, Henry Kissinger commanded his own staff as President Nixon's chief adviser on foreign affairs and director of the staff of the National Security Council. By 1972, Kissinger's personal assistants outnumbered the White House staff (fifty-five people) that assisted Franklin D. Roosevelt at the climax of World War II. Kissinger was named Secretary of State in 1973.

8. Theodore H. White, *The Making of the President 1968* (New York: Atheneum, 1969), p. 147.
9. Rowland Evans, Jr., and Robert D. Novak, *Nixon in the White House* (New York: Random House, 1971), p. 45.
10. Quoted in the *San Francisco Chronicle*, November 10, 1972.

The Lonesomeness of Power

When he assumed office in 1969, President Nixon was determined to keep foreign policy firmly in his own hands. The appointment of William Rogers, practically a novice in foreign affairs, as secretary of state, served this determination. It was doubly served by bringing Henry Kissinger into the White House. Kissinger recruited leading foreign-policy experts for his own staff. The foreign-policy innovations of the first Nixon administration came from the basement of the White House; Kissinger moved to the State Department in 1973.

No domestic-policy staff sprang into being during Nixon's first term to match the efficiency of Kissinger's foreign-policy operation. President Nixon continually shifted the positions of his domestic advisers, tinkering with the organization of the staff, circulating staff memoranda that proposed a theoretical basis for a program of domestic legislation.

A modern president easily becomes isolated. He is surrounded by men who serve him alone. Their power is their ability to speak for the president; that ability vanishes if they lose the president's confidence. Consciously or not, his advisers may formulate only the opinions he wants to hear. Sharing with him the special environment of the White House, they are not likely to contradict the president's understanding of events outside.

President Nixon, striving to manage his time, reads few newspapers himself. Staff members prepare a summary for him. Not eager to disturb the serenity of his breakfast, they may omit news items and opinions of potential importance, until crises have developed that clearly demand presidential attention. Meanwhile, the helpers who open his mail hasten to report the magnitude of support for the president's policies, ignoring the intensity of opposition. Intent upon serving their master, the president's staff itself may close off direct contact with the world outside.

> The reality of American folly in Vietnam was hidden for years from Lyndon Johnson; how much President Nixon knew or did not know of the Watergate plans and coverup has inspired controversy of immense significance.

The last best hope for the intrusion of the outside world, whether the president wills it or not, lies in the periodic conferences he holds with members of the press. Franklin D. Roosevelt developed the press conference into high art, using it to charm and inform the reporters who interpreted his actions to the country, while asking them about developments in their home areas. Now, press conferences are live television productions. Appearing before the cameras, President Nixon recognizes the reporters whose questions he will accept; he interprets their questions to suit himself; he reveals as much information as he cares to reveal; and there are no followup questions. The reporters are there to communicate the state of the president's mind to the country; they have no method (under Nixon's press-conference arrangements) for telling the president about the country's state of mind.

Can the president exercise his potentially great powers of public persuasion, if he grows out of contact with the worries and concerns of the people? Pursuing his noble dream of world organization, Woodrow Wilson did not realize the extent of the people's moral exhaustion at the close of a war, nor did he see the need for compromise with his political opponents. The result was tragedy.

Some writers about presidents (and some presidents) have emphasized the loneliness of the office. President Nixon makes his big de-

cisions in absolute solitude. Presidents are concerned with the forces of history; they know that the ultimate responsibility for decision cannot be shared.

Some of the most celebrated presidential "decisions" turn out to be hardly decisions at all. Harry Truman's decision to use the atomic bomb against Japan is an example. The bomb was developed to be used. Its use seemed the only way of avoiding an invasion that would cost the lives of many American military men. Truman's advisers were unanimous in recommending its use. The possibility of *not* using the bomb was hardly considered.

Presidents are in grave danger of becoming isolated from meaningful human contact. Surrounded by those whose mission is to serve his every whim, the president lacks critics who can challenge his goals, his assumptions, his very view of the world.

The authority of the president's helpers depends on the confidence he places in them. Members of the White House staff are not elected, and their appointments are not confirmed by the Senate. Yet, when they speak for the president, they wield awesome power.

Richard Nixon invited some old and trusted friends to serve him in the White House. Their loyalty was to Richard Nixon's welfare, as they conceived it, and only secondarily to the party or the nation. Some of these aides were charged with treating members of Congress —even Republican members—with studied arrogance.

When H. R. Haldeman and John D. Erlichman were required by the president to resign as a result of Watergate scandal revelations, many members of the Republican party were not without joy.

It was the modern equivalent of eighteenth-century court intrigue, when the king was forced to withdraw his favor from a particular group of courtiers.

The political issue of Watergate was deeper than that of any court intrigue. If the president's men so eagerly broke the law to prevent the truth of Watergate from being publicly known, what other laws would they wink at to further their own interests at the expense of the people?

An American Invention

A single, powerful, energetic, but democratically elected executive. The presidency. It is an American invention, much imitated by other nations. Yet the office is particularly dependent upon the personality and habits of its incumbent.

Since adoption of the Bill of Rights in 1791, the U.S. Constitution has been amended some sixteen times. On six of these occasions, the presidential office has been mentioned, but on none of them has the power of the president been further defined. Three amendments (numbers XII, XX, and XXV) have been concerned with designating the occupant of the office. Public uncertainty as to which candidate or which public official should exercise the vast presidential powers could be a national disaster—and nearly was when the electors of 1800 did not specify whether Thomas Jefferson and Aaron Burr should serve as president and vice president, or vice versa.

Two amendments have provided guarantees of the right to vote for president and vice president, the only nationally elected officials. Amendment XXIII granted this right to the residents of the District of Columbia, and Amendment XXIV guarantees that the right to cast such a vote shall not be denied on account of failure to pay a poll tax. This indicates the symbolic power of the office. The ability to vote for president may establish the legitimacy of the national government in the mind of the individual citizen.

Amendment XXII limits the service of a president to two terms. Largely a slap at the memory of Franklin D. Roosevelt, it was supported by party leaders hungry for such patronage as will come with a change of administrations. This limitation weakens the office, for both associates and enemies know that a president nearing the end of his second term can have no third term in which to retaliate for political injuries or insults. But the amendment does nothing to define further the powers of the office.

> The dimensions of the presidential office have been created by the forces of history. They are drawn anew by each of the incumbents.

The Tribune of the People

It remains there, a frozen moment of time, because your memory imprints the sights seen, the stunned words spoken, when you learned of death in Dallas. Sooner or later, you got to a television set, and then you were glued to it for that longest weekend, observing yet somehow taking part in the drama that unfolded, its various acts constantly replayed and commented upon. No one could deny the sense of national loss; the power and charm and persuasiveness and determination to march in step with history of John F. Kennedy became clear only as genuine tragedy transmuted the reality of the man into legend. We all knew that something infinitely important—all the more important because we were late in recognizing its importance—had been stolen by the assassin's bullet. The sense of desolation was complete.

The national experience of 1963 was not unique. A massive outpouring of national grief was called forth by the assassination of Abraham Lincoln and the death in office of Franklin D. Roosevelt. These were men of heroic stature, their greatness grudgingly recognized even while they were alive. Yet the national reaction was hardly less at the deaths of William McKinley and Warren G. Harding. When a president dies, the political discord of the moment is revealed as insignificant, and the sense of loss is the loss of direction, of the continuity of history, of the protection afforded its people by the very existence of the nation.

The president is the only significant official elected by the entire nation. The vice president remains insignificant, in spite of regular promises by presidents (including Johnson and Nixon, who had themselves been vice presidents) that it will be different for their newly elected junior colleagues. For the vice president has meaning only as a potentiality; his sole important purpose in the Constitution is to become president, if needed, and his sole purpose in his party's national convention and campaign is to help the president win the election.

In ancient Rome, the plebeians, the lowest order of citizenry, who had little going for them other than citizenship, elected a *tribune* to protect their rights and interests in the councils of the mighty. The word has come to mean "defender of the people."

For most Americans, in time of crisis, the president is their defender.

Winning the respect and even the affection of the public (as John Kennedy did) is not the same as creating a demand for a program that the public understands and insists upon. Lyndon Johnson constantly read opinion polls, carrying them in a coat pocket, fondling them like a peasant telling his beads. But all the mass media expertise available to the government and to the Democratic party could not substitute for the irreplaceable act of leadership. President Johnson could not adequately explain the need for an Asian war; he dared not call upon the nation to make real economic sacrifices in its behalf. Finally, a realization of the human sacrifice involved (which many in Congress knew, and told of) came upon the people, and President Johnson withdrew, to avoid being repudiated.

Democratic political leadership results from interaction between the people and the leader in particular circumstances; it is not a formula to be learned by rote. Achievements of electronic technology such as television have greatly affected the ways in which it can be exercised, but technology cannot create leadership. It springs from a two-way relationship between the leader and the people. That relationship sometimes draws upon the best instincts of the people; and the experience of that relationship has frequently called forth previously hidden resources of magnanimity and good judgment from American presidents.

If a political leader does not develop an instinct for this relationship and explore its uses, his leadership will never achieve its full potential, regardless of how skillfully he manipulates the formal powers of his office.

Before he died, John Kennedy had overcome the psychological handicap of his narrow plurality and had tasted the joy of a leader's interaction with the people. But he had not yet tested the power of his leadership by pitting his image of the people's will against that held by the United States Congress.

The American presidency has furnished many images for the national Pantheon of heroes. Giant faces are carved into the side of Mt. Rushmore. Three presidents—Washington, Jefferson, and Lincoln—have inspired monuments in the national capital that are at the top of any tourist's list. Two of these—the Lincoln and Jefferson Memorials—seem to be temples of the national spirit, permanent reminders of the origins and tempering of the American soul.

But are presidents accorded the status of hero only after death? Must memories of mortal men be revised into legend, before presidents become heroes? Is our glorification of past presidents only a yearning for an earlier time, which must have been less crowded, less complicated, and more comfortable? Or does the notion of the president as hero, or tribune, of the people, explain a continuing relationship between the people and their elected leader?

> Reporters noticed that the lines of tourists waiting to tour the White House were undiminished at the peak of revelations concerning the Watergate scandal. One couple waiting in line was interviewed. The wife said that one touches history, merely by walking though the White House. Her husband said that all politicians are crooks.

A Tragic Flaw

Ancient Greek dramatists developed the vision of tragedy as a religious insight and a mirror of the human condition. The tragic vision sees man as the victim of an implacable fate. The tragic hero achieves nobility by struggling against that fate. The Greek tragic hero is a man of good character and admirable intentions. He pursues those intentions with a devotion that is more than human, and calls down the vengeance of the gods, who resent mere men pretending to divine abilities.

Herodotus, the first historian, portrayed the fate of nations as bound up with the tragic misfortunes of their leaders. Herodotus saw the Greek defeat of Persia as but an extension of the fall of Xerxes, the Persian king, following from his tragic flaw of overweening pride. Modern historians offer a more complicated explanation of the forces that determine the fate of nations. It can be argued that presidents are products of their times, and that the individual personality does not make that much difference. One can ask, "How would the national course be different now if it had been directed in the past by presidents Alf Landon (1936), Wendell Willkie (1940), Thomas E. Dewey (1944 and 1948), or Adlai Stevenson (1952 and 1956)?" A good case can be made for the answer, "Not very different at all." For these were nominees chosen by an opposition party, which wanted to win; and the opposition's understanding of the temper of the times and the needs expressed in public opinion was not very different from that of the party which won the White House.

But such an answer begs the question. The feelings of the nation are bound up in the fortunes of the president. The stock market rose and fell with reports of President Eisenhower's health in the 1950s, and with the testimony given at the Watergate hearings in 1973. The psychological relationship between president and people is demonstrated when presidents die in office. This relationship has been made more firm by television. Whether the president is loved or hated, he is familiar; his voice and gestures, brought into the family living room, are more familiar than those of the state's two senators, or even the mayor of the town. The president personifies the government, and the political party, which he leads. A judgment directed against him may fall with equal weight against them.

The president is praised, and reelected, when events go well, even when they are events he does not control. The morale of the nation can be lifted by the jaunty words of a president like Franklin D. Roosevelt, or the friendly grin of an Eisenhower. The public can be enraptured by the eloquence of a John F. Kennedy, and admire (at least in retrospect) Harry Truman's devil-take-the-hindmost bluntness. A president buoyed by public support can accomplish much. Even the entrenched committee chairmen of Congress must pay him heed. Just as presidents can ride high on a surge of public sympathy, however, they can plunge to the depths of despair when the public turns against them. The president is the most convenient scapegoat for public disappointment. Everything seemed possible to Lyndon Johnson when he scored a record win over Barry Goldwater in 1964; by 1968, Johnson withdrew from public office, a frustrated and embittered man. Herbert Hoover, a humane engineer and energetic public administrator, won election easily in 1928. By 1932, his name was so thoroughly associated with the economic suffering of the Depression that any nominee of the Democratic party was bound to defeat him.

The history of the presidential office is replete with personal tragedies; and the tragedy of the president has often been a tragedy for the nation. Woodrow Wilson's stern adherence to principle made him a successful leader of domestic reform in his first term; he led the nation into war under a banner of high moral purpose; but his very sternness became obstinacy. Refusing to compromise with Republicans in the Senate over the Treaty of Versailles, he permitted the League of Nations to be born without American membership. Driving himself in a speaking campaign to prevent this outcome, he collapsed physically and finished his term as an invalid in the White House.

The office tends to damage its occupants. Wilson's successor, Warren G. Harding, can only be reckoned a mental and moral midget by comparison—yet Harding died in office, perhaps in part because of confronting his own inadequacies. Franklin D. Roosevelt, who thrived in the presidency, was finally worn out and destroyed by its burdens. Lyndon Johnson was destroyed politically, and lived only four years after his "abdication."

The presidential office ruthlessly magnifies the personality of the man who holds it. Woodrow Wilson's austere moralism, Franklin D. Roosevelt's patrician charm, Lyndon Johnson's contemptuous, and

Richard Nixon's resentful, reactions to criticism—all have been traits that influenced the course of the nation. Presidents need not answer directly the challenges of a legislative opposition, as English prime ministers must do. Presidents are assured of occupying their office, barring impeachment or death, at least until the next election. If presidents have flaws in their character (Warren Harding's inability to say "No" to his friends, for example), the office will magnify them. If they are tragic flaws, the nation may well be bound up in the president's tragic fall.

The possibility must be confronted that the presidency is a tragically flawed *office*. Created as one of three coequal branches of the federal government, it has assumed in recent times a position and importance that outweigh both Congress and the judiciary. In political terms, it is the president personally, and secondarily his administration, which receives credit in the polling booth when national affairs progress well, and blame when they do not.

> The majestic power of a democratic electorate is its ability to express displeasure with an incumbent administration and sweep it out of office.

In spite of its institutionalization into the confusing array of agencies, commissions, departments, and committees we know as the executive branch, the presidency still functions within the confines of the Constitution; in legal form, it remains one of three coequal branches.

> The electorate holds the president responsible for the fortunes of the nation, but he does not possess authority to match that responsibility.

Not only is a president confronted by the independent power of Congress and of the courts; he cannot effectively control the myriad activities of the executive branch. The tragedy of the presidency is thus a constitutional tragedy. The office is prevented from developing the power and influence that would be necessary for a full discharge of its responsibilities.

Should the traditional concept of the separation of powers, the basic principle of the Constitution, therefore be abandoned? Should we recognize the fallacy of the mechanical metaphor that so fascinated the founding fathers, and adopt some other principle upon which to organize the national government?

Such questions are easily dismissed for being "academic." The Constitution of the United States is unlikely to receive such a fundamental revision. All amendments to the Constitution so far adopted have originated with a two-thirds majority in both houses of Congress. One of the most serious limitations upon presidential effectiveness in domestic affairs comes from the parochialism and propensities for obstruction of congressional committee chairmen. But congressmen like it that way.

Have other democratic systems yielded better results? The French system, oscillating for the last two centuries between the unquestioned rule of an admired leader and stalemate in the representative assembly, has proven at least unstable, if not actually dangerous. The British parliamentary system—admired by many American political scientists—has produced moments of despair, as well as moments of glory. America has known ineffective presidents like Harding; England has produced its Chamberlains and Asquiths. It would almost seem that democracies, regardless of their institutions, tend to choose and accept leadership that is no better than they deserve.

The authors of the Constitution desired above all to limit the authority of government; the imperative of the twentieth century may be to empower the government to act. Much is spoken about the dangers of "repression" in modern times. There is a kind of repression generated by the rigid habits of bureaucracies, whose agents are uncomfortable in the presence of cultural values and symbols (beards? long hair? black skins?) different from their own. They seem to seek a degree of conformity with their own cultural standards as the price of accommodation. But a far greater danger is the danger of paralysis.

Paralysis—

of a Congress ruled by men immune to the forces of political and cultural change;

of agencies that repeat the actions of established habit, although their original purpose, whether achieved or not, has long since been forgotten;

of a citizenry wearied of crisis and change, eager to withdraw its attention from public matters in the pursuit of private pleasures;

of a vast and complicated federal organization that runs on inertia, in the absence of a new sense of energy and direction;

of a president (Wilson? Lyndon Johnson?) so firmly committed to a policy that he ignores all signs of the people's opposition to it.

Presidents can overcome the paralysis. They can reach over the heads of Congress and appeal to the people. Aroused public opinion can bring action. Presidents can energize the bureaucracies, infusing whole agencies with a new sense of mission.

Presidents can do this when they lead a convinced public, a public no longer mired in its cynical disdain for politics; a public tied to the president by hope, trust, and expectation. Above all, a public united in its dedication to a cause, acknowledging the president as leader of that cause.

Such unity comes when the nation is caught up in evangelistic zeal (1917-18), suffers from economic misery (the Depression), or is devoted to conquering evil (World War II). The pressures of circumstance have led the people to perceive their president as hero; supported by their trust and confidence, the president has been able to perform acts of heroic leadership. If, however, events go awry, the people turn against the president, or the ideas he has championed, making him the scapegoat for what may have been, in large measure, failures of the people themselves.

The presidency is an office of paradox. Americans have always been ambiguous about political authority. The Constitution is designed to prevent full authority from resting with a single person or institution. The president is only one man; but he works miracles when the people invest him with more than human dimensions, regarding him as their heroic leader. No mortal man can possess the heroic qualities that are ascribed to hero-presidents. When they are revealed as merely human, the public may turn against them. Government will continue, but with no sense of direction, no feeling of unity.

Disaster for the man can mean disaster for the nation.

Days in the Life of a Congressman

The days of a U.S. congressman can seem unending. He is surrounded by a thousand pressures, demands, messages, and temptations. He must study hundreds of reports, to know what he is voting on. He is in Washington to do the will of the people of his district, if they have a single will, and if he can find it out. It is much easier to determine the desires of a special interest group, and the price they may pay, in ways both direct and subtle.

The congressman is in Washington to serve the needs of the people. Whether he does so effectively doesn't matter too much. For the voters to think that he serves them effectively is what counts. Therein lies reelection. With enough reelections comes power. The course of the nation is affected by the decisions and actions of the old men of Congress, the ones who have survived.

The days of a congressman can stretch into unending years, as he waits to accumulate the seniority that will bring him real power. By then, he may have forgotten what noble cause it was that he had planned to serve.

Boulevard of History

Pennsylvania Avenue, Washington, the District of Columbia. The path of war protesters and presidential funeral processions, main artery of politics and history. At its lower end, set among a jumble of federal buildings, theaters, hotels, and department stores, is the White House, gleaming behind its screen of noble trees. At the upper end, dominating a substantial hill, stands the Capitol, its classic outlines the inspiration of much American civic architecture. The perfect dome bears a statue called Liberty. Sharing the hill are the Library of Congress, the Supreme Court, and an urban slum now being renewed.

The mile-long length of Pennsylvania Avenue symbolizes the separation between the executive and legislative powers, a basic principle of the American Constitution. The avenue is busy, crowded with autos, buses, and taxicabs. Congress, which governs the District of Columbia, sets taxi fares on the basis of zones. The Capitol and the downtown business district are included in a single zone, so that congressmen and their helpers can traverse the length of Pennsylvania Avenue for the lowest fare. Such a trip need not represent a bridging of the separation of powers; more likely, it means a visit to a lobbyist's office, or a meeting with constituents, or being entertained by agents of the power centers of American society.

What Does Washington Lack?

Washington is a capital city only in a political sense—and it was hardly even that before 1933. It is not the capital city of American commerce, nor of American culture, nor of American education. As for the theater, Washington is a road-show town.

The preoccupation of Washington is politics. Although their families live in suburban Maryland or Virginia, each day Washington is crowded with hundreds of thousands of public officials, diplomats, civil servants, party workers, lobbyists, and newspapermen, all intent upon the latest shift in the winds of political fortune. Gossip, scandal, and political speculation are ingested with the martinis at embassy cocktail parties and with the cheeseburgers in the Library of Congress cafeteria.

Is it possible that the unique community of Washington, those hundreds of thousands who keep their mental antennae quivering, ever alert to the subtle changes of political power, generate the excitement they so enjoy within their own ranks? Is it possible that (lacking close contact with commerce and culture) they have few real ties with the American people?

> Not long after the inauguration of Richard Nixon, Hubert Humphrey reported, with uncharacteristic chagrin, that, as vice president, he had neither understood nor appreciated the extent and the bitterness of the opposition to the Vietnam War. Only when he left office and went among the people did he realize the extent of their disillusionment.

Larry L. King, son of a night watchman, was born in a west Texas town and grew up in Midland. He accepted the values of west Texas without much examination. He hardly knew a black person until he was serving in the army, where he experienced the efforts of his unit to conform to President Truman's order integrating the armed services. After the army, he attended Texas Tech, in Lubbock, and became a journalist. His college included not a single black student; but, by then, King no longer accepted such arrangements as ordained from on high. In 1954, he went to Washington as assistant to a Texas congressman, and he learned that Washington's internal political affairs were managed by southerners on the District of Columbia committees who felt that "integration" was the foulest word in the English language. Washington was becoming the first American city with a black majority among its residents, and the congressional committees seemed determined to encourage the worst potentialities of that fact, as if to teach the northern liberals a lesson.

When riots occurred in Watts and other cities, Larry King heard talk at cocktail parties in segregated Washington living rooms of the reasons why "it can't happen here." And it didn't, until an April evening in 1968.

> An old friend with whom I had served Capitol Hill time telephoned my Washington home: "Have you heard what happened to Martin Luther King?"
>
> I knew as surely as an eyewitness. "Oh goddamn! Somebody shot the poor son of a bitch!"
>
> "The lid will blow now," I said. "Especially if he dies. They'll burn it all down." Within a short time King's death was confirmed. I called my friend back, noting his excellent White

House connections while I was currently in bad odor there: he should contact a mutual friend on LBJ's staff and beg that all possible conciliatory gestures be made—a shutdown of business operations, all manner of pledges to employ unlimited federal power in bringing the assassin to justice, the President's promise to attend the funeral service or a promise to transport the body to wherever Mrs. King might choose.

My friend called back within the hour: "They're reserving Sunday as the official day of mourning. Business will be closed, and everything." Was that all? "Yes."

"Well, fuck that! It's not enough. Most businesses are closed on Sunday, anyway. Dammit, they've got to do something meaningful. Otherwise, it will be construed as an insult."

"They seem to think they know what they're doing over there," my friend said. "The President's going on TV here in a little bit and tell everybody to simmer down." Though we did not know it then, the first plate-glass windows were being kicked in around 14th and U Streets.

Through most of a sleepless night I listened to the radio, picking up reports of violence and random burnings. Near dawn I fell into a drugged sleep, awaking in midmorning when my brother telephoned from Texas to see if we were safe. "Sure," I said, groggy and puzzled. "Why?"

"You'd better wake up," he said. "Your town is on fire. I'm watching it on television."[1]

That night, wrote Larry King, he did not sleep until he had made a billy club from a broomstick and placed a butcher knife next to his bed.

Rats

Seven months before the death of Martin Luther King, the House of Representatives debated a bill, recommended by President Lyndon Johnson and approved by the House Committee on Banking and Currency, to provide $20 million of matching funds for the control of rats in urban slums. The title of the bill was the Rat Extermination Act of 1967.

Being largely unacquainted with the ravages brought to the slums by these rodents, congressmen almost laughed the bill to death. There were references to "throwing money down the rathole" and to "the civil rats act." Representative John Bell Williams of Mississippi said,

I have an alternative suggestion which could save the taxpayers money.

Let us offer a bounty of twenty-five cents a rat. It would put youngsters to work, and get rid of poverty and rats at the same time.[2]

The House rejected the Rat Extermination Act by a wide margin the day after it approved, by a similar margin, the Anti-Riot Act which brought "The Chicago Seven" to trial for conspiring to disrupt the Democratic National Convention of 1968.

One year after the death of Martin Luther King, the Senate Select Committee on Nutrition and Human Needs took field trips to Florida, Illinois (East St. Louis), and the District of Columbia. At one point,

1. Larry L. King, "Confessions of a White Racist," *Harper's*, January 1970, p. 62.
2. *Congressional Record* (daily edition), July 19, 1967, p. H 19441.

Senator Charles Percy of Illinois described the committee's visit to slum dwellings in the District of Columbia:

> I was interested yesterday in going around, Mr. Chairman, to find the very high cost of rents. One apartment with eight children in it, was $195 a month, and it was a pigsty. It was terrible. Nothing had been done in that apartment to repair it, in the three years that the family had apparently lived there. . . .
>
> We tried to call the owner of that apartment, and I demanded to know why they had not filled up the ratholes, got the toilets to work, and had hot water on. I have a report this morning, I am happy to say, that this morning for the first time two plasterers and a general repairman showed up at 7:30 this morning. They are plugging the holes, they are setting rat traps in the alley behind the buildings, and with the spotlight of attention on them, something is going to be done.[3]

The senators were told, among other things, that the District of Columbia had the highest infant mortality rate in the nation, except for Mississippi, and that, while 100,000 people in the District needed and were eligible for the food-stamp program, only 26,000 were using food stamps, because of their high cost.

Congress was not insensitive to social problems—only slow to notice.

What Really Matters?

Senator Mike Gravel of Alaska grew increasingly restive at the contrast between the horrors of warfare in Vietnam and the business-as-usual conduct of the United States Senate. The breaking point came when the *Pentagon Papers* were exposed to public view. Other senators were torn between distress at the content of the papers, on the one hand, and dismay over the irregular and perhaps illegal method of their disclosure, by Daniel Ellsberg, on the other. Gravel wanted to force a more speedy publication.

He first attempted to read previously unpublished portions of the papers into the *Congressional Record*. This was objected to on the legitimate—but rarely utilized—ground that there was not a quorum present in the Senate chamber. Senator Gravel then called a midnight meeting of his own subcommittee of the Senate Public Works Committee. The television cameras were there, and Senator Gravel read from the *Pentagon Papers* for over three hours, often with tears rolling down his face.

As part of his concluding remarks, Senator Gravel said:

> The greatest representative democracy the world has known, the nation of Jefferson and Lincoln, has let its nose be rubbed in the swamp by petty warlords, jealous Vietnamese generals, blackmarketeers, and grand-scale dope pushers.[4]

Senator Gravel felt strongly about what he had to tell. Other senators seemed more concerned with the propriety of the way he chose to tell it. Gravel's insistence upon feeling that a higher, external morality should take precedence over the Senate's procedural rules did not endear him to many of his senior colleagues.

3. *Hearings before the Select Committee on Nutrition and Human Needs of the United States Senate*, 90th Congress, 2nd Session, and 91st Congress, 1st Session, 1969, p. 2206.
4. Mark T. Green, James M. Fallows, and David R. Zwick, *Who Runs Congress?* (New York: Bantam, 1972), p. 174.

Bob McNeely

Tax Reform (Act I)

Prologue: Yes, Boys, That's Where My Money Goes

Unless it repeals previous policy, each new government decision is added to the mass of existing decisions enshrined in the U.S. Code. Most government actions are piecemeal decisions, taken at a particular time to satisfy some demand or redress some grievance presented through the political system. Before long, the body of the law is marked with contradictory provisions, conflicting purposes, and special benefits that have become obsolete.

Nowhere is this result more obvious than in the tax laws of the United States. It is obvious because the dollar has an established value. Unlike power or prestige, dollars can be measured in terms of simple quantity. Special privileges written into the tax laws provide a portrait of the power wielded by special interests in times past. And there were contradictions: a person with an income of $600 a year had to file a tax return; a family could be living below the poverty line, receiving federally subsidized welfare payments for part of the year, yet still be required to pay income tax on its modest salary income. Uncle Sam giveth, and Uncle Sam taketh away.

Of course, some of the more striking inequities resulting from tax loopholes are not really planned that way by Congress. For example, in 1968, Mrs. Horace Dodge, ninety-eight-year-old heiress to the automobile fortune, received an income of roughly $2 million on which she paid *no income tax at all*. Her income came from the interest paid by a $50-million investment in municipal bonds, and income from municipal bonds is tax exempt.

Municipal bonds are a main source of revenue for cities, but their rate of interest is low. To make the bonds attractive to investors, the federal government made their interest income exempt from the income tax. It was an indirect way of helping the cities, and Congress was not really upset at helping Mrs. Dodge.

Scene I: The Kennedy Tax Cut

Congress accepted the goal of reforming the tax structure, in order to plug loopholes and distribute the impact of taxation more fairly, in 1959. But no bill was reported that year. Minor reforms were accomplished in 1962. In 1963, the Kennedy administration began to develop a tax-reform proposal.

But it soon became obvious that "every legislator's favorite reform closed some other legislator's favorite loophole."[5] Vice President Johnson advised that any modification of the oil-depletion allowance would imperil the entire tax bill, as the friends of oil would combine to defeat the entire bill.

President Kennedy began to consider the claim of some of his economic advisers that federal tax rates, set in wartime to control inflation, drained off private funds needed for economic growth. A general tax cut (unrelated to tax reform) might well serve to increase employment and general prosperity, although the economy even then was on an upswing. The idea followed the logic of economic theory developed by John Maynard Keynes; but, before then, presidents had proposed and Congresses had adopted tax cuts only in times of obvious recession.

The tax cut was finally enacted after the assassination of John F. Kennedy. It brought a period of national boom and nearly full employment, which has been rare in peacetime. Mr. Keynes was vindicated.

> Mr. Keynes also prescribed tax *increases* in times of inflation. Unhappily, peacetime legislatures, anticipating public reactions, find it much more difficult to raise taxes than to lower them.

Scene 2: Paying for Lyndon Johnson's War

Rapid escalation of the Vietnam War began in 1965. In every modern war, including the limited Korean "police action," the American people have accepted economic sacrifice in the form of higher taxes and even wage controls, price controls, and rationing. President Johnson did not ask even for higher taxes in 1965. Perhaps he knew that Congress would not provide them; Congress and the people kept a peacetime outlook. It was intended to be a quick war, even a cheap war, and it was taking place on the other side of the world.

Scene 3: Surtax

The war remained far away and hard to understand, but it proved neither quick nor cheap. It was soon costing $30 billion a year. To finance it, the Treasury borrowed money, which was inflationary, and the funding of domestic programs was cut, particularly health, education, and the War on Poverty. The poor were, in essence, financing the Vietnam War, and sending their sons to die in it. In 1967, President Johnson asked Congress for a 10 percent surtax on personal and corporate income taxes. Congress grumbled that this across-the-board "tax on a tax" did nothing to share the burden of taxpaying more equitably. When Lyndon Johnson withdrew from the contest for the Democratic nomination in 1968, it was no longer possible to question the purity of his motives, and the surtax was passed as a temporary measure until June 10, 1969.

The measure was too little, and far too late, to control inflation resulting from the financial pressures of the war effort. President

5. Theodore C. Sorensen, *Kennedy* (New York: Bantam, 1966), p. 484.

Johnson had asked the Treasury to look into the need for tax reform as early as 1965, and that department had launched a four-year study.

Scene 4: Outrage

On January 17, 1969, three days before the inauguration of Richard Nixon, President Johnson's secretary of the Treasury, Joseph W. Barr, reported upon his department's four-year study. He predicted a taxpayer's revolt.

> The middle classes are likely to revolt against income taxes, not because of the level or amount of taxes they must pay out but because certain provisions of the tax laws unfairly lighten the burdens of others who can afford to pay. People are concerned and, indeed, angered about the high-income recipients, who pay little or no Federal income taxes. For example, the extreme cases are 154 tax returns in 1967 with adjusted gross income above $200,000, including 21 with incomes above $1 million, who paid the U.S. Government not one cent of taxes.[6]

Mr. Barr's testimony touched a responsive nerve in that group called "Middle America," which had seen the wealthy take up the cause of the poor and the black, and the sons of the wealthy challenge authority at Berkeley and Harvard, while they themselves paid increasing taxes and saw the power of higher wages drained away by inflation.

Outraged letters flooded congressmen's offices. The language used, they said, matched in violence that used by the protesters against the war. The Treasury Department got more mail demanding tax reform in the first ten days of February 1969 than it had gotten during all of 1968.

On February 18, the House Ways and Means Committee began hearings on tax reform.

Scene 5: President Nixon Recommends

On April 21, the Nixon administration sent to Congress its recommendations regarding taxes. They followed the same lines as the program proposed by Lyndon Johnson's departing Treasury officials, and Speaker McCormack predicted that they would prove acceptable to the Democratic majority in Congress. President Nixon requested, among other things:

> A low-income allowance, beginning in 1970, which would insure that families below the poverty level would not be required to pay federal income tax.

> A "limit on tax preferences," so that wealthy persons receiving their incomes from nontaxable sources would nonetheless be required to pay income tax—in essence, a minimum tax.

> Abolition of the 7 percent tax credit allowed businessmen against investment costs (adopted in 1962 to promote economic growth, this incentive to invest in new plant and equipment was clearly inflationary in 1969).

> Several technical adjustments in claiming of deductions by both individuals and corporations, aimed at more equitable treatment.

6. *Congressional Quarterly*, January 24, 1969, p. 147.

A continuation of the 10 percent surtax until January 1, 1970,
when it would be reduced to 5 percent, and then expire on June 30.

At this point, the level of expected revenues remained the same,
for the elimination of tax favors for the wealthy was to be balanced
by tax relief for the poor.

Scene 6: A Promise from Wilbur Mills

Wilbur Mills, chairman of the House Ways and Means Committee,
stated in 1969 that the proposed "limitation on tax preference," without specific reforms, would distract attention from the inequities
provided by various tax loopholes. He said there was a momentum
for tax law reform in the House that should not be lost.

In considering the surtax extension, the Democratic Study Group
(an association of young, liberal Democrats) stated their reluctance
to extend the surtax without being assured that tax reform would be
forthcoming. They wrote to Chairman Mills to ask about the prospects for tax reform legislation. Mills replied that he expected to bring
a bill to the floor of the House by October. Satisfied, his colleagues
passed the surtax extension and elimination of the investment tax
credit, as proposed by the Nixon administration, by a vote of 210 to
205.

The Senate was less confident. They approved only an extension
of the 10 percent surtax until December 31, 1969.

(Curtain)

Charles Gatewood

How to Get Along

High in the new Senate Office Building, before a window with a magnificent view of the Capitol, the senator leaned back in his chair and spoke to a college student seminar about the habits of senators.

"The rule for addressing Senate colleagues during formal debate," he said, "was set down for all time by Alben Barkley. (You remember Alben Barkley, he was Senate Majority Leader before he became Harry Truman's vice president.) As near as I can recall, Alben Barkley said, 'if you're convinced that your opponent is a son-of-a-bitch, you refer to him as "my distinguished colleague." But if you're sure that he's a *dirty, stupid* son-of-a-bitch, you call him "my *noble, learned,* and distinguished colleague."'"

A dark-haired student at the back of the group did not join in the gentle laughter.

"That's the kind of hypocrisy," he said, "that is going out of style. The whole tradition of verbal ass-kissing has got to go. How can you justify tolerating some reactionary, when you should be fighting him?"

"Son," the senator replied, "the only reason is this. The issues change. And the lineups change. You make as few enemies as possible today, because you may need all the friends you can get tomorrow."

But Watch Out for the Rules

Washington, November 18, 1972 (Associated Press) — Former Senator Daniel B. Brewster of Maryland was convicted yesterday of receiving an unlawful gratuity while a member of the Senate.

Lobbyist Cyrus T. Anderson was found guilty of bribery and the mail-order firm of Spiegel, Inc., pleaded guilty to two charges of payment of an unlawful gratuity. . . . Brewster faces a maximum sentence of six years' imprisonment and a $30,000 fine. Anderson faces a maximum sentence of 45 years imprisonment and $60,000. . . .

The government charged that Anderson gave Brewster $14,500 to influence the senator's vote on third-class mail rates legislation in 1966–67. . . . Anderson received the funds from his employer, Spiegel, Inc., a Chicago-based mail-order firm which stood to lose hundreds of thousands of dollars if the legislation to raise third-class postage rates was approved by Congress.

Brewster was found guilty of all three counts of a lesser bribery charge of "receiving an unlawful gratuity" which means that the Senator accepted the funds "with no corrupt intent." . . .

The defendants admitted giving and receiving $12,500, but said the funds were campaign contributions. Brewster also emphasized that he supported low postal rates long before the money exchanged hands.

Prosecutor James E. Sharp urged the jury to convict both men to bring a quick halt to influence peddling in Congress. After the verdict, he was asked if he thought the verdict would cause "bells to ring on Capitol Hill."

"I hope so," he replied.

The Old Men Have the Power

On July 27, 1972 Senator Allen J. Ellender of Louisiana, aged 81, died at the Bethesda Naval Hospital of a heart attack. Ellender had interrupted his campaign for reelection to a seventh six-year term, to come to Washington for the vote on an agricultural appropriations bill. The most senior member of the Senate, Ellender was chairman of the Appropriations Committee and former chairman of the Agriculture Committee.

Allen Ellender was a floor leader of the Louisiana Legislature when Huey Long was first elected governor, and he was Speaker of its lower house when Huey Long continued to dominate Louisiana politics while serving as a U.S. senator.

Espousing the populism that was basic to Huey Long's political program, Ellender was first elected to the Senate in 1936, when Franklin D. Roosevelt was winning his second term as president. In those days, Ellender was a liberal supporter of FDR, and he authored the original bill supplying school lunches from agricultural surpluses. In recent decades, however, Ellender was marked as a fiscal and social conservative and a dependable opponent of civil rights legislation.

> Ellender was succeeded as president *pro tem* of the Senate—presiding officer when the vice president is absent—by Senator James O. Eastland of Mississippi. Born in 1904, Eastland was first elected to the Senate in 1940.

Tax Reform (Act II)

Prologue: Wilbur Mills, Country Lawyer

He was born in Arkansas on May 4, 1909, the son of a country banker. He received his B.A. from Hendrix College in 1930 and entered Harvard Law School, completing his work in 1933. He returned from Harvard, married, and established a law practice in Searcy, Arkansas. Two daughters were born. He served as Probate Judge of White County, Arkansas, from 1936 until 1938, when he was first elected to Congress. He was then twenty-nine years old.

Adopted as a protegé by Speaker Sam Rayburn of Texas, Wilbur D. Mills was assigned to the Ways and Means Committee in his second term, an unusual assignment for a newcomer. He began quietly to build a reputation, helping to shape the legislation associated with the late New Deal of Franklin D. Roosevelt, and Harry Truman's Fair Deal. In 1957 and 1958, the confrontation over school segregation took place in Little Rock, Arkansas, between Governor Orval Faubus and President Eisenhower. Mills' seat seemed threatened for a time, when his district was merged with that of arch-segregationist Dale Alford. But Alford decided to run for governor. Although usually tagged as a conservative, Mills supported President Kennedy's position 87 percent of the time in 1961, and President Johnson's position 60 percent of the time in 1967.

In 1958, Wilbur Mills became chairman of the Ways and Means Committee. He quickly developed a reputation for possessing the best technical mind in the House, if not all of Washington. With Republican Richard Nixon in the White House, Mills' committee became the major congressional source of ideas in the realm of social legislation. In 1972, Mills would be backed as a possible Democratic presidential nominee.

Scene 1: The Right of Petition

The Ways and Means Committee held public hearings on proposed tax reforms fairly constantly from February 18 until April 14, 1969. Practically every interest group that asked for a hearing got a chance to testify; individual members of Congress and various retired and incumbent public officials were also heard.

The AFL-CIO called for tax relief for families in the low- and middle-income brackets. The United Auto Workers stated that the "chief inequity" of the system was the taxation of poverty-level incomes.

Spokesmen for the U.S. Chamber of Commerce and the National Association of Manufacturers opposed nearly all the suggested reforms, particularly the "arbitrary" minimum tax applied to everyone in order to keep a few wealthy individuals from paying nothing. They praised the system of special incentives for various types of business — depletion allowances, the capital gains tax, accelerated depreciation allowances on real estate — as necessary to the continued healthy functioning of the economy.

Oil industry representatives suggested *increasing* the oil depletion allowance; after all, neither the Johnson nor Nixon recommendations had asked that it be lowered.

Democratic Congressman Wright Patman of Texas renewed his crusade against social experimentation supported by tax-exempt foundations.

The Tax Committee of the U.S. Chamber of Commerce suggested simplifying the tax law. The complexity of the Internal Revenue Code, they suggested, was the main loophole.

Scene 2: Executive Sessions

The door closes at this point on the tax reform bill, for the features of the House bill were developed in executive "mark-up" sessions by the twenty-five members (fifteen Democrats, ten Republicans) of the Ways and Means Committee. However, it is possible to write with some confidence about what occurred, for two important studies of the operations of the committee and the leadership of Wilbur Mills have been published, based on interviews with all the committee members.[7] Furthermore, the door cracked open when word of voting on the oil depletion allowance leaked out.[8]

Ways and Means is one of the most influential committees in the House. Every congressional district in the nation contains individuals and enterprises affected by its decisions. In addition, its Democratic members serve, by long tradition, as the Democratic Committee on Committees, determining the committee assignments of Democratic members of the House. Even to be a junior member of Ways and Means is a position of considerable stature; every congressman wants friends on Ways and Means.

Members of the committee are practically united in their admiration, and even affection, for Wilbur Mills. Mills' national reputation, particularly in banking circles, is so great that a word of praise from Mills may help a congressman get crucial campaign fund donations. Members of the committee are attracted to it by its prestige and power; they have no ideological battles to wage, and they endorse compromise as a political way of life.

Mills regards his committee as a microcosm of the House, reflecting its moods and divisions. Mills is not interested in reporting a bill to the full House membership unless it can pass. His reputation for legislative astuteness depends on his ability to do this; he has only had one measure defeated on the floor in fifteen years. He strives to make the necessary compromises within the privacy of the committee meeting room, rather than permitting an unpredictable public con-

7. John F. Manley, "The House Committee on Ways and Means: Conflict Management in a Congressional Committee," *American Political Science Review* 59 (December 1965): 927; and "Wilbur D. Mills: A Study in Congressional Influence," ibid. 63 (June 1969): 442. See also Manley's *The Politics of Finance* (Boston: Little, Brown, 1970).

8. "How Ways and Means Committee Voted on Depletion," *Congressional Quarterly*, August 8, 1969, pp. 1466-1467.

flict on the floor of the House. Such conflict is certain if a sizable group of Ways and Means members files a minority report when a bill leaves the committee.

The committee ratio of fifteen Democratic members to ten Republicans would seem to make it a likely instrument of Democratic party policy. In fact, at least two of the Democrats are normally of the conservative southern variety and tend to align themselves with the Republicans. Mills thus casts the swing vote, and he always votes last.

> If an issue divides the Committee along liberal-conservative lines Mills and 12 Democrats can beat the Republicans and two conservative Democrats 13–12; or, in some cases, Mills and two conservative Democrats plus the Republicans can defeat the 12 Democrats 13–12. . . . It is a rare coalition that sees him on the losing side.[9]

Of course, Mills is not really interested in making decisions by a one-vote margin. Extremely reticent about his own policy preferences, he listens while all members of the committee express their views on an issue, paying particular attention to the views of the senior minority member and other Republicans. When all have been encouraged to speak out, Mills "responds to them in such a way that his conclusions, drawn from their discussion, become their conclusion."[10] Wilbur Mills states the consensus.

In 1969, that consensus favored limiting the special favors in the tax laws, although many had been public policy for forty years. Many committee members felt that the very symbol of tax privilege, the oil depletion allowance, should be lowered. Democratic Congressman Charles A. Vanik of Ohio led the attack within the committee, claiming that the House would pass a comprehensive tax reform bill *only if* the depletion allowance were decreased. In an attempt to compromise at a higher figure than others desired, George Bush of Texas, founder of several oil companies, proposed reduction of the allowance to 23 percent. The motion was defeated, 9–16. Chairman Mills was then on the losing side of a 12–13 vote against reducing the allowance to 22 percent. The final motion, reducing the allowance to 20 percent, was agreed to by a vote of 18–7. The most important defection from the forces of oil was Hale Boggs of Louisiana, traditionally a supporter of the 27.5 percent figure, who switched to vote in favor of the reduction. Boggs was then House Democratic Whip—the second highest party office—and second in Ways and Means seniority to Mills himself. News of his defection caused such a storm that Boggs called a press conference four days later, which lasted for two and a half hours. He said that the depletion cut was necessary to remove the oil indus-

9. Manley, "Wilbur D. Mills: A Study in Congressional Influence," p. 461.
10. Ibid., p. 447.

try as a "congressional whipping boy." An earlier statement issued by Boggs called upon "progressive members" of the industry to accept "these reasonable reforms and thus remove the issue as one of national controversy."

The committee did not achieve unanimity. There was no minority report, but seven members of Ways and Means signed separate statements; four of them had voted in the committee against the final agreement on reduction of the oil depletion allowance. Of the seven, only George Bush of Texas and Rogers C. B. Morton of Maryland, then chairman of the Republican National Committee, called for "further study" of the depletion allowance and other matters. Morton knew that President Nixon had promised to uphold the depletion allowance during his campaign.

Scene 3: A Closed Rule

The tax reform bill was known as HR 13270. After eight hours of discussion, it was granted a "closed" rule by the House Rules Committee. But a price was exacted. Wilbur Mills was forced to accept, on behalf of the Ways and Means Committee, a proposal for tax relief made by Rules Committee member Richard Bolling.

The closed rule, used when considering complex legislation with many interrelated provisions, prohibits the introduction of amendments during floor debate, except with the approval of the committee reporting the bill. Bowing to the expertise of the committee, the House becomes a stamp of approval for its work. Only Mills' Ways and Means Committee is regularly granted a closed rule for its bills. HR 13270 was a 368-page document. Among its notable provisions were:

Tax relief for those with low incomes:
Elimination of the requirement that families below the poverty level pay income tax. A family of four, for example, would have no tax liability unless its annual income were about $3,500. It would take 6 million poor people off the tax rolls.

An increase in the "standard deduction," simplifying the tax returns, and somewhat reducing the taxes, of 34 million people.

Abolition of the tax discrimination against single persons.

Anti-inflation provisions:
Abolition of the 7 percent tax credit for business investment.

Continuation of the 10 percent tax surcharge until December 31, 1969, and its reduction to 5 percent for six months thereafter.

Maintaining a steady level of tax revenues.

General tax reform provisions:
A "limit on tax preferences" so that wealthy persons could not escape all taxation by total investment in tax-sheltered enterprises.

A 7.5 percent tax on the investment income of private foundations.

Modification of the provision for deducting the appreciated value of property donated to private foundations.

Modification of specific tax benefits:
Reduction of the oil depletion allowance from 27.5 percent to 20 percent, with similar reductions in the depletion allowances granted to other extractive industries.

Gradual elimination, over a ten-year period, of the tax-exempt status of municipal bonds, with a program of federal interest subsidies to support municipal bond sales.

Strict limitation on the use of "hobby farming" losses as deductions to prevent the payment of taxes on nonfarm income.

The method of deducting accelerated depreciation on real estate was reserved for new homes, to stimulate new residential construction; it could no longer be used as a bonus by slum landlords.

Reduction in the tax incentives for corporate mergers.

Lowering the tax deductions allowed banks in connection with bad-debt reserves.

The closing of many even more technical tax loopholes known largely to accountants and tax attorneys.

HR 13270 was debated for six hours on the floor of the House on August 6, 1969, under the closed rule. The three hours of time allocated to the majority was managed by Wilbur Mills; the three hours allocated to the minority was managed by Congressman Byrnes of Wisconsin, then ranking Republican member of the committee.

In concluding his introduction of the bill, Chairman Mills stated:

> This bill is essential to reform our tax structure and to make our tax system fairer. It is urgently needed to maintain the morale of our taxpayers and to demonstrate to all that million-dollar incomes with no tax liabilities are a thing of the past. It is needed to grant tax relief to taxpayers in general and particularly to those at poverty levels. Finally the bill is needed to repeal the investment credit which has outlived its usefulness and to extend the surcharge on a temporary basis until mid-1970 so that we can complete the job of fiscal restraint needed to clamp down on inflation and to get the economy under control.[11]

Scene 4: The Will of the House

Even as Wilbur Mills spoke, he was preparing to introduce two amendments approved by the Ways and Means Committee after the bill was reported. The first of these, providing the same depletion allowance standards for oil extracted from oil shale as for oil pumped from underground pools, was relatively noncontroversial. (Since no commercially feasible process had been developed for extracting oil from shale, it seemed fair for those seeking to develop the process to have the same incentive as those drilling oil wells.) The second, however, was a modification in the tax rates, which, in providing modest tax reductions for everybody, reduced governmental revenues and threatened the anti-inflationary purposes of the bill.

This was the amendment that Wilbur Mills accepted in order to win a closed rule from the Rules Committee. A liberal critic has written of it:

> For a crucial period lasting less than a week in early August both Wilbur Mills and the Nixon Administration lost control of the

11. Reprinted in *U.S. Code, Congressional and Administrative News*, 12, 1969 (St. Paul, Minn.: West, 1970), p. A-834.

> situation. . . . Some "good guys" like organized labor and Repre-
> sentative Richard Bolling of Missouri discovered that the relief
> package would not help much the lower-middle-class citizens
> who owned their homes, as distinct from renting. In 24 hours,
> Mills' whole plan collapsed and his committee approved an
> additional $2.5 billion of tax rate reductions. . . . Perhaps the
> bill could not have passed the House without this. . . . For a
> brief instant the stern and sensible men lost control, and at that
> moment normal public and political sentiment about taxes
> made its beachhead.[12]

On August 7, the House of Representatives passed HR 13270, including the two committee amendments, by a vote of 394 to 30. Those
casting "nay" votes included 10 Republicans and 20 Democrats.
Nearly all came from oil-producing states. Negative votes were cast
by 12 of the 23 representatives from Texas, 4 of the 6 representatives
from Oklahoma, and 7 of the 8 representatives from Louisiana. The
lone exception was Hale Boggs.

(**Curtain**)

Alan Who?

A reporter for the *San Francisco Chronicle* accompanied Senator Alan
Cranston, California's senior senator, during a Cranston visit to the
Bay Area that sandwiched thirteen major events into a single day.

The most disconcerting discovery made by the reporter was that
nobody (other than his staff and other party leaders) recognized the
senator—not on the plane, not at the airport, not in taxicabs, not in
office building elevators. When he appeared at a television studio for
his appearance on an interview program, the receptionist asked Senator Cranston to spell his name twice before she called the inner office
to be sure that he should be admitted.

The Senator didn't seem to mind.

Congressmen are often more widely known in Washington, and feel
more at home there, than in the districts they officially represent.
Congressmen who retire from office, or are turned out of it by the
voters, tend to stay on in Washington.

They become lobbyists, and may expect a substantial increase in
income.

Tax Reform (Act III)

Prologue: An Old English Custom

The U.S. Constitution provides, in Article I, Section 7, that "All bills
for raising revenue shall originate in the House of Representatives;
but the Senate may propose or concur with amendments as on other
bills." The provision followed a practice well established in the
English Parliament. The House of Commons, being the lower branch
and closest to the common people, had charge of raising governmental
revenues. In fact, the king could only win the revenues he asked from
Parliament after receiving petitions for the redress of the people's
grievances and acting upon them.

---

12. Edwin L. Dale, Jr., "Revenues and Reform in the Tax Bill," *New Republic*, January 3,
1970, p. 13.

In mid-twentieth-century America, the House of Representatives was not always regarded as the branch of Congress in closest contact with the common people. Nevertheless, following the Constitution, the Senate waited for the House to propose a tax bill and then reacted to its details. The purpose and basic outline of the bill would be established by the House.

Thus it was in 1969. While Wilbur Mills and his committee were hammering out the tax reform bill, the Senate conducted its dramatic debate and vote on the president's proposal for further deployment of the anti-ballistic missile. Developments in the Ways and Means Committee were watched largely by the lobbyists for interests which were about to lose their special tax privileges. Thirty-three of the fifty-nine lobbyists newly registering with the clerk of the House of Representatives in September of 1969 indicated that their intention was to influence tax legislation.

Scene 1: Hearings before the Senate Finance Committee

HR 13270 went to the Senate Committee on Finance, chaired by Senator Russell B. Long, son of the legendary Huey Long. Senator Long is himself an oilman. His committee handles the taxation of the oil industry. Senator Long does not acknowledge a conflict of interest, for oil is a dominant industry in Louisiana. To represent oil, he says, is to represent Louisiana.

The Committee held twenty-three days of hearings, at which 300 witnesses appeared. Since HR 13270 had been published, interested parties were able to study its implications, and they flocked to the Senate to describe the horror that would be brought to their enterprises by the House bill.

One horror was described by representatives of America's cities. With the Nixon administration and the Federal Reserve Board attempting to control inflation through high interest rates, the municipalities found it nearly impossible to sell their low-interest bonds. It would be totally impossible, they argued, if that interest were to become even indirectly taxable. The Nixon administration had proposed revenue sharing with local governments. Even if Congress passed the plan, there would be no substantial funds until 1972 or 1973. And a hope of revenues in 1973 built no sewers in 1970.

Other witnesses made pleas on behalf of the oil industry, the real estate industry, private foundations, universities (which feared reduced gifts if the value increase of appreciated securities were made taxable), farm organizations (which, in general, resented the competition of wealthy "hobby farmers" who engaged in activities like cattle breeding to incur a deductible tax loss), and bankers.

Scene 2: Executive Session

It had been charged that members of the Finance Committee, including Chairman Long, were hostile to tax reform and would bottle up the bill, killing it for the session. Senator Long committed the group to reporting a bill by October 31, and the committee's recommendations were agreed upon in sixteen days of private meetings.

During the 1968 campaign, President Nixon had promised to protect the oil depletion allowance. In an effort to save at least the symbol, the Treasury Department proposed other taxes that would raise substantial revenues from the oil industry, in place of lowering the depletion allowance. But Congress was in no mood to save Nixon's campaign promises—particularly promises made to the oil industry.

As in the House, Senate committee voting on the depletion allowance was politically too explosive to remain confidential.[13] Oil lobbyists hoped for a 10–7 vote in favor of restoration of the full 27.5 percent allowance. Because of past Senate actions, oil lobbyists expected the support of Senator Vance Hartke of Indiana and Senator Eugene McCarthy of Minnesota. But Senator McCarthy did not attend the meeting, and Senator Hartke proposed reducing the allowance to 15 percent. The motion by Chairman Long to restore the 27.5 figure failed to carry on an 8–8 tie vote. The senators eventually agreed by a vote of 12–3 to set the depletion allowance at 23 percent, an increase of 3 percent over the House figure. Nevertheless, at the 23 percent figure, the oil industry would increase its annual contribution to the cost of American government by $215 million.

The sentiment for a fairer tax structure was as well recognized in the Senate as in the House. The Senate Finance Committee opened slightly some of the loopholes that had been closed by the House bill, but it closed some that the House measure had left untouched. Notably:

Municipal bonds retained their tax-exempt status; income from this source would not even be subject to a minimum tax (good news for Mrs. Dodge).

The "limit on tax preferences" of the House bill was replaced with a minimum tax of 5 percent on formerly nontaxable income.

More stringent regulations on private foundations were adopted, including a "death sentence," which meant that foundations will lose their tax-exempt status in forty years.

The financing of voter registration drives by private foundations was prohibited. This had immediate implications for the civil rights movement.

Provisions for deduction of the appreciated value of gifts of tangible personal property (such as works of art) to private foundations (such as museums) were reinstated.

Corporations were prohibited from deducting, as a business expense, penalties paid as a result of losing antitrust suits.
That is, breaking the antitrust law would no longer be subsidized by the tax law!

Confronted with the last-minute amendment reducing tax rates, which had become part of the House bill, the Senate made little effort to rebuild defenses against inflation. It lengthened the period over which the reductions would take effect, so that their full revenue loss would not take effect until 1973. But the Senate Finance Committee, at the same time, provided an increase in the personal exemption (which had been set at $600 for many years) to $700 in 1970 and $800 in 1971. This dramatic change would make the reality of tax relief more obvious to voters. But it would add inflationary pressures to the economy.

Scene 3: On the Senate Floor
The Senate does not debate measures under a closed rule. Amendments may be offered from the floor.

At one point, Senator Fannin of Arizona (a member of the Finance Committee) was defending an amendment restoring the tax shelter

---

13. *Congressional Quarterly*, October 31, 1969, p. 2132.

for pension plans established by physicians doing business as corporations, which had been eliminated by the Finance Committee over his objection. It was opposed by Senator Ribicoff of Connecticut. The amendment was also favored by the U.S. Treasury Department, which wanted more time to study the entire question of tax-sheltered pension plans. Senator Fannin suggested that it was improper for Senator Ribicoff to resist the recommendation of executive branch authorities. Senator Ribicoff replied:

> I think there is collective wisdom in the Senate of the United States, and I think that the collective wisdom of the Senate in many instances is superior to that of a bureaucracy or a department. I do not hesitate to have the Senate initiate the legislative process. What has been wrong with the legislative process over the last thirty years is that the Senate has failed to take the initiative and has waited, hat in hand, for a decision to be made at the other end of Pennsylvania Avenue.[14]

This appeal was heard by only a handful of senators, for routine Senate debate is sparsely attended. The amendment was accepted, and the doctors kept their tax shelter.

The general outlines of the bill—a combination of tax reform and tax relief—survived the process of Senate debate, and the Senate version was then passed.

Although Senator Long assured his colleagues that many of the complicated provisions of the House bill had been simplified, the bill grew from 368 to 585 pages.

Scene 4: Conference

When—as frequently happens—House and Senate pass different versions of the same legislation, the differences must be resolved in a conference committee. Each house appoints members (usually from the relevant committees) who are charged with shaping the final bill as nearly as possible on the model of that originally passed by their own house. Conference committees meet in secret sessions, in contrast to the public meetings of House and Senate.

The conference report on the Tax Reform Act time and again states that "the conference substitute follows the Senate amendment." But these are largely minor and technical matters in which the Senate's additional work may well have improved the original House provision. On matters of major disagreement, the will of the House prevailed as frequently as that of the Senate, or the differences were compromised.

14. *Congressional Record* (daily edition), December 9, 1969, p. S 16246.

Some of the notable provisions included:

Setting the oil depletion allowance at 22 percent.

Increasing the "personal exemption" in easy stages to a total of $750 in 1973, thus postponing the inflationary impact of the Senate action.

The "minimum tax" provision of the Senate was adopted; since it applied both to corporations and individuals, it would bring more money to the Treasury, although permitting a few individuals to escape with lower taxes than the House provision.

Municipal bonds continued to be tax-exempt.

Several provisions adopted by the Senate but not by the House were omitted in the final version. One of them would have provided a tax credit for parents paying college tuition.

On December 22, 1969, in separate actions, the House and the Senate voted to approve the conference report. The Tax Reform Act of 1969 was sent to President Nixon.

Scene 5: Finale

At 9:30 A.M. on December 30, 1969, one day before the surtax was scheduled to expire and thereby precipitate a financial crisis, President Nixon signed the Tax Reform Act of 1969 into law. It included an extension of the surtax.

(**Curtain**)

Epilogue: What Did It All Mean?

Congress acknowledged the need for tax reform in 1959; ten years later, the tax structure was indeed modified. Senator Long described the bill as the most significant tax measure since enactment of the original income tax in 1913. It limited long-established special privileges, eased the burden of taxation on low-income families, and eliminated a few notorious inequities.

In 1962, then-Vice President Lyndon Johnson suggested to the Kennedy administration that any attempt to lower the oil depletion allowance might scuttle any package of tax reforms. This implied substantial control of the U.S. Congress, on this issue, by the oil industry. In 1969, Congressman Charles Vanik claimed that no tax reform could be passed unless it *included* a reduction of the depletion allowance. Eventually, the depletion allowance was reduced from its historic 27.5 percent to a still generous 22 percent figure; not a single oil firm seemed threatened with bankruptcy as a result. Oil could muster only thirty House votes against the Tax Reform Act of 1969.

The reforms enacted by Congress exceeded in scope the proposals made by both the departing Johnson administration and the new Nixon administration. For, in the meantime, there had been a public outcry against unfair tax privileges, partly stimulated by departing Johnson Treasury officials, and Congress got the message better than the new administration. The final outcome depended on the skill and leadership of Wilbur Mills. Mills recognized the public demand and, more important, foretold the impact of that demand upon his House colleagues. He exploited the surge of public and congressional sentiment to formulate and enact significant legislation.

If it had been the first step toward true equalization of the tax burden, the Tax Reform Act of 1969 could indeed be described as a milestone. Unfortunately, it remains a quick end-run by Congress—and Wilbur Mills—to head off a middle-class taxpayers' revolt. Some notorious outrages of the tax laws were repaired, but basic changes were not made.

The tax structure of the United States still assigns the greatest financial burden to workers and the middle classes by heavily taxing wages and salaries. Income produced by *wealth*, on the other hand, is taxed lightly; and, in a number of special circumstances (such as Mrs. Dodge's famous municipal bonds), it is not taxed at all. Any number of enterprises have followed oil's example and petitioned Congress for a favorable tax loophole. Few have been disappointed.

When Wilbur Mills and his Ways and Means Committee worked out the Finance Act of 1971, they were again involved in the arrangement of special tax benefits, rather than a general reform of the tax burden.

The friendly ties between large business enterprises and the U.S. Congress have inspired a cynical description of the American economic system: *Free enterprise for the poor. Socialism for the rich.*

In the Public Interest

Appalled by the apparent ease with which the course of American policy was pointed in the direction favored by corporations, defense contractors, and other special interests with powerful lobbies, John Gardner decided to take action. He announced the formation of Common Cause, a public interest lobby. A former secretary of Health, Education, and Welfare, with impeccable ties to the Ivy League and fashionable society, John Gardner qualifies as a member of the American Establishment.

Gardner quickly enrolled over 200,000 citizens willing to pay dues of $15 per year. One of the first announced goals of Common Cause was to achieve reforms that would make Congress stronger and more responsive to the desires of the people. Gardner planned to attack the seniority system.

Once in a Decade
Every ten years or so, there is a major shift in the power structure of the House of Representatives, when the Speakership changes hands. It is well established that the House Majority Leader becomes the new Speaker. But who becomes the new Majority Leader, and thus the Speaker-elect?

The presumption is in favor of the Majority Whip, who is next in line, but the official decision is made by the majority party caucus through an election. When elderly Speaker John McCormack of Massachusetts, brushed by scandal, retired in 1971, Carl Albert of Oklahoma, the Majority Leader, was acclaimed as his successor. The Majority Whip was Hale Boggs of Louisiana. First elected in 1946, Boggs accumulated a moderately progressive voting record, and he was usually "sound" on issues of interest to organized labor. Having served nine years as Whip, Boggs was closely identified with the "insiders" of the House power structure. When Boggs announced his candidacy to succeed Albert as Majority Leader, somewhat to his surprise, four other congressmen also announced their candidacies.

In internal political maneuverings in the House, the most easily overlooked members are the freshman congressmen. Until a congressman is launched upon his second term, lobbyists and even colleagues may not invest much time or attention in him—for a freshman congressman may be only a political accident, and he may not be returned thereafter.

Of the 255 Democrats elected to the House in 1970, 33 were freshmen. And a very lively group of freshmen they were. They were the men and women of the "new politics" inspired by Eugene McCarthy's candidacy in 1968 and traumatized by the disasters of the Democratic National Convention in Chicago.

> New York's Bella Abzug attacked the Pentagon, war, the seniority system, and other revered targets ... California's Ron Dellums, up from the black ghetto, wore Afro hair and bell-bottoms ... Les Aspin of Wisconsin, former McNamara Whiz Kid, wanted to correct insanities he had discovered in the Pentagon ... James Abourezk—half-Lebanese, half-Sioux—was a peacenik who had grown up on a South Dakota Indian reservation, identified with have-nots and favored abolishing seniority. Father Robert Drinan of Massachusetts—first to wear a Jesuit collar in the House—kidded himself as the "Mad Monk."[15]

To the extent that the contest for Majority Leader represented a struggle between old and new, conservative and liberal, establishment and newcomer, it was a contest between Hale Boggs of Louisiana and Morris Udall of Arizona. "Mo" Udall came to Congress in 1961, taking the House seat vacated when his brother became President Kennedy's secretary of the Interior. Eager for action, Udall challenged Speaker McCormack's authority in 1968, after serving a scant seven years in the House. (McCormack entered Congress when Udall was six years old.) Udall was conceded to be the natural leader of rebellious newcomers in the House. By everyone except Hale Boggs.

Mark Godfrey

15. Larry L. King, "The Road to Power in Congress," *Harper's*, June 1971, p. 55.

Bella Abzug felt that the election of Hale Boggs was assured when organized labor backed the candidacy of James O'Hara of Michigan, splitting the liberal vote between O'Hara and Udall. Yet, there were three candidates marked with varying degrees of conservatism: Boggs from Louisiana, Wayne Hays from Ohio, and Bernard Sisk from southern California. No candidate could claim an ideological monopoly.

The decision was made by secret ballot in the Democratic caucus. Hale Boggs was elected overwhelmingly on the second ballot, when Hays and O'Hara withdrew. The source of Boggs' support cannot be exactly pinpointed. But he clearly received substantial support from the freshman members.

Who had helped the newcomers find homes, apartments, and schools for their children? Hale Boggs. Who had extended the welcoming hand of the House establishment to the newcomers? Hale Boggs. Who had introduced the newcomers to Wilbur Mills, chairman of the Ways and Means Committee that also handles the committee assignments of Democratic members? Hale Boggs, second ranking Democratic member of the Ways and Means Committee. Who had been there to explain how important a committee assignment is to a freshman, and to offer help with that crucial decision? Hale Boggs. And Hale Boggs had symbolically demonstrated the breadth of his legislative interests by voting to reduce the oil depletion allowance, when all the other Louisiana congressmen voted to retain it.

Congress is an institution that determines the boundaries and comforts of its members' daily lives. Power in the House of Representatives may be based upon the effective leadership of political causes. It is more likely to be accumulated slowly as the sum of individual gratitude for a series of small, humane kindnesses.

Hale Boggs entered upon his new duties. Boggs and Speaker Albert together appointed jovial, dovish Thomas P. O'Neill of Massachusetts as Majority Whip, although a number of members suggested that the position of Whip be made elective, since it seemed the sure starting place on the road to the Speakership.

In October 1972, Hale Boggs was missing and presumed dead on an airplane flight lost in Alaska. The House finally declared his position vacant. On January 2, 1973, the House Democratic Caucus voted for Thomas O'Neill to succeed Hale Boggs as Majority Leader. There was no opposition. Then, at O'Neill's request, the caucus voted, 123 to 114, to keep the position of Majority Whip an appointive, rather than an elective, office.

It is an easy matter to examine Congress and find it wanting. Its powerful men are old, and many seem out of touch, even with their own districts. Congress has acquiesced in the growth of bureaucratic power in the executive branch, and it has refused to exercise its constitutional authority to limit the funds that support the president in pursuing reckless foreign policies.

Is Congress, the national legislature, a withering branch? Is it so involved with its internal procedures and protocol that the vital taproot of contact with the people has been allowed to atrophy? Or have the functions of Congress so changed in the last half century that its critics expect it to do things it is not prepared for, ignoring its real accomplishments?

Time, Change, and the Response of Congress

There are 100 men and women in the United States Senate, and 435 in the House of Representatives. The Senate was originally conceived of as a small gathering of ambassadors representing the sovereign states, while the House was seen as directly representative of the people and intimately involved in their political affairs.

Now the average House district has half a million inhabitants: too many constituents with whom to maintain intimate contact. The congressman counts himself lucky if a sizable minority of his constituents even recognize his name. Senators do not win reelection because of the dignity with which they represent the sovereign independence of their states. They are more likely to win reelection because they have proven their ability to bring home federal projects and federal money.

If the circumstances in which congressmen operate have changed so dramatically, can Congress perform the functions specified for it by the Constitution?

A Sense of Dissatisfaction

Criticism of Congress is not hard to find. The daily press keeps a box score of legislation proposed by the president and disposed of by Congress, which reporters see as the natural villain of the checks and balances system. Members of Congress—particularly junior members—complain that it lacks a sense of urgency. Comparing the lackadaisical performance of Congress with the energy displayed by the executive, Senator Joseph Clark labeled it "the sapless branch" of national government. Other critics, identifying their own convictions with the public will, and finding that a congressional majority does not share those convictions, attack Congress for being undemocratic.

This sense of dissatisfaction remains vague and unfocused, however, until the critic specifies exactly which functions Congress ought, but fails, to perform. An ideal standard is then established against which the actual behavior of Congress may be compared. If dealing with an ideal standard seems too theoretical an exercise, then Congress may be compared with the national legislatures of other industrialized, democratic nations, or the Congress of today may be compared with Congress in earlier periods and with the intentions of the Constitution.

The quickest comparison of Congress with the national assemblies of other Western democracies reveals that Congress has an influence, an independence, and a sheer *presence*, which is nearly unique. For the experience of other nations, such as England and France, is that, in complex modern societies, the executive power tends to absorb the legislative power. In both England and France, the executive (cabinet) is chosen from the legislature and is, in theory, responsible to it. In practice, this has come to mean that all decisions of consequence are made by the executive and communicated to the legislature for discussion and approval. The legislature, then, exists primarily to make legitimate the actions and decisions of the executive. If they cannot accept the decisions of a particular cabinet, the legislature does not take command. Instead, a new cabinet is chosen that will enjoy the confidence of the legislative majority.

By contrast, the U.S. Congress formulates an independent judgment. It can modify, or even reject, the executive's decisions. The Constitution was founded upon the concept of a separation of powers, which meant a legal separation of the personnel who share the powers of government. That separation is as real now as it ever was, and just as frustrating. An English critic sums up the situation:

> Negatively, at any rate, the Congress of the United States possesses in fact the power given to it in form by the Constitution. Congress can and does hold up the program of even the most forceful and popular president, Congress can and does thwart with impunity the wishes of the American electors.[1]

Such criticism sees Congress failing to yield to some outside influence that seeks to control it. This outside influence may be the executive branch; it may be the political party that won the last national election; it may be "the will of the people"; or it may be the obviously superior wisdom of the experts in ecology, or whatever is the fashionable issue of the time.

Congress is blamed for remaining a separate branch and thus living up to its constitutional mandate.

Congress in the Constitution

Article I of the Constitution concerns Congress and the legislative power. It is the longest and most detailed section of the Constitution. The image of Congress held by the authors of the Constitution is fairly clear in its lines. The House of Representatives, elected in the same manner as the most numerous branch of each state legislature, was conceived of as being intimately involved with the politics of the people and quickly responsive to changes in the public mood.

1. Denis Brogan, writing the Introduction to Senator Joseph S. Clark, *Congress: The Sapless Branch* (New York: Harper, 1965), p. viii.

This implied a considerable turnover in the membership of the House; it suggested that the structure of authority within the House might change in accord with the tempo of popular opinion. That this was the case was demonstrated by the election of Henry Clay as Speaker of the House in 1811. Although Clay was a freshman congressman—he became presiding officer of the House upon being inducted as a member—he was the nationally recognized leader of the War Hawk faction of the Republican party, a political conviction that swept the nation.

Furthermore, membership in the House was very highly regarded. The direct relationship between the people and the House made it more alluring to some politicians than the Senate. After John Quincy Adams served as president, he was elected to the House as a Representative from Massachusetts. He established a new and distinguished career as a legislative opponent of slavery.

The Constitution provided that two senators be appointed by the legislatures of each state. The early Senate functioned somewhat as a gathering of elder statesmen, prepared gently to curb the democratic enthusiasms of the lower house. To the extent that there was an American aristocracy, its voice was articulated in the Senate. After the Civil War, however, corruption overwhelmed most state legislatures, and senators tended to purchase their seats outright. An aristocracy with no sounder claim for deference than the naked power of wealth could not be permanently tolerated, and the Seventeenth Amendment, ratified in 1913, brought the direct election of senators by the voters. This restored the prestige and influence of the upper house. But the Constitution's intention, that upper and lower houses should serve different constituencies and respond to different combinations of interests, was preserved. Agreements reached concerning specific issues in one house continued to be quite different from the agreements reached on the same issues in the other house.

Article I of the Constitution envisions Congress as the active branch of government, the initiator of new policies, the framer of decisions. Section 8 of Article I enumerates the powers of the new federal government and labels them the powers of Congress. There are seventeen specific grants of congressional authority, ranging from the power to "lay and collect taxes" to the power to grant patents that secure to inventors the exclusive rights to their inventions. The final magnificent catch-all provision stipulates that Congress shall have the power to "make all Laws which shall be necessary and proper for carrying into Execution the foregoing Powers. . . ." Chief Justice John Marshall was not long in seeing the splendid opportunities opened by that phrase.[2]

The balance of Article I neatly rounds out the description of the new government by describing those things Congress is prohibited from doing (no ex post facto laws, for example) in Section 9 and those things no state is permitted to do (such as making treaties) in Section 10.

Because of current controversy over the appropriate roles of Congress and the president in making and executing foreign policy, it should be noted that the Constitution does not clearly differentiate between the two kinds of policy, except to be very clear that it is the national government, rather than the separate state governments, that is empowered to conduct the foreign relations of the United States, including the regulation of foreign trade. The inability of the thirteen states, as organized by the Articles of Confederation, to

2. The expansion of national power under the guidance of Chief Justice Marshall is described below, pp. 189-192.

formulate a single foreign policy had, of course, been a major reason for writing a new Constitution. The enumeration of congressional powers in Section 8 of Article I intermingles domestic and foreign affairs, often in the same sentence, with perhaps a preponderance on the side of foreign relations. These powers are, of course, described in eighteenth-century language. Congress, for example, will "grant Letters of Marque." Clearly the broad outlines of foreign policy are to be made by Congress, as Congress is empowered to "declare War" and to "regulate commerce with foreign nations." But Article II makes it just as clear that the conduct of foreign relations shall be the function of the president; the nation will speak with but a single voice to other nations. The president will be commander-in-chief of the armed forces, and he alone is empowered to receive the ambassadors of foreign powers.

> If the president of the United States has come to exercise extraordinary, and even arbitrary, power in the conduct of foreign affairs, who is to blame? Have presidents usurped powers that belong to Congress, or has Congress abdicated those powers by refusing to exercise them? The Constitution itself does not provide a clear answer. A very conservative Supreme Court wrote in 1936 a hymn in praise of "the very delicate, plenary, and exclusive power of the President as the sole organ of the Federal government in the field of international relations."[3] The President, not Congress, is the sovereign.

Modern Practices of Congress

Many attributes of the modern Congress contrast starkly with the intentions of the Constitution and earlier congressional practices.

The first of these is an apparent reversal of the relationship between the two houses. The House of Representatives was conceived of as the popular house, the register of mass passions. The first House had 65 members, each representing about 60,000 persons. The House member was a figure of stature, known and admired within his rural community. The present House has 435 members, each with roughly half a million constituents. A few congressmen are substantial figures in their home towns. Those representing districts arbitrarily carved from the center of metropolitan areas are strangers to most of those they represent. They cannot gain attention from the local mass media that serve areas containing many millions. Because the House has so many members, its business is conducted by strict rules that prevent individual members from playing such a distinct role in its deliberations that they will attract attention from the national media. Facing an election every two years, the House member is continually running for reelection. He may hesitate to embrace those controversial causes that pose as great a danger of losing votes as of gaining them. Furthermore, real power in the House is wielded by the elderly men from safe districts who are chairmen of the standing committees. They need not be overly concerned with achieving reelection. In any case, their power is exercised quietly and in a gentlemanly manner; they need not embrace controversial (and ungentlemanly) causes in order to enhance it.

The House of Representatives seems to be the most conservative, drab, and settled of the two houses. Groups with a vested interest in maintaining the status quo may look first to the House for allies. It is less responsive to the whims of public opinion because the activities of its members attract less attention from the media.

The Senate contains two members from each state, as it has from

3. *United States* v. *Curtiss-Wright Export Corp.*, 299 U.S. 304 (1936).

the beginning; but they are no longer appointed by the state legislatures. The Senate was designed as the home of the elder statesmen, who would restrain populist impulses in the House of Representatives and protect the rights of property. As the number of members of the House increased, the prestige of the Senate, as a more exclusive body, grew during the nineteenth century. Prior to the Civil War, the compromises arranged in the Senate by great orators such as Clay and Webster held the nation together. Although the tradition of great oratory has died almost as completely in the Senate as in the House, and the Senate also accomplishes its real work in committees, Senate procedures are much less formal, and a senator can gain national attention through his participation on the Senate floor, even if only by leading a filibuster that blocks normal business. Senators each represent an entire state, with a much greater variety of interests and opinions than are contained by a House district. Because he has easier access to the media, a senator has some opportunity, if he works at it, to become a television celebrity. He may well embrace controversial causes: the publicity will get his name and face known to the voters, but, since he confronts an election only once in six years, they may forget the nature of the cause he espoused. Senator George McGovern was reelected in 1968 from the conservative, Republican state of South Dakota.

The Senate now seems the house in closest touch with the people. At least senators receive much more attention from the communications media than do representatives.

The Senate offers an additional focus of interest. Four of the last five presidents have been former senators. All of the last six major party candidates for the presidency have been senators. Senators are very aware of this fact.

The second striking paradox of the modern Congress is its loss of initiative. In the 1880s, Woodrow Wilson found that the national government was, in essence, ruled by the standing committees of Congress. No longer do individual congressmen, nor the House or Senate as institutions, recognize great national problems and struggle to forge resolutions out of their own knowledge, insight, and experience. In a post-industrial society, government is too complex, and great issues arise too frequently. The executive branch has superior sources of information. Now the agenda of Congress is determined, in its broad outlines, by the requests of the president for specific legislation. Legislative proposals are considered by standing committees of the House and Senate, which impress their own judgment upon the details of each bill. The committee proposals are discussed and amended, then accepted or rejected, on the floor.

Thus, although Congressmen like to refer to themselves as members of the world's greatest deliberative body, neither the House nor the Senate does much deliberating, and floor sessions are neither important nor well attended, except for the final votes on crucial issues. The real work is done in the committees of each house.

Power of the Purse

Congress was granted an historic power by the Constitution which it retains and jealously guards. That is the power of the purse, which the English Parliament developed to control the king before it won legislative powers.[4] Only Congress can appropriate the funds used to operate the national government. The power of establishing the

4. See the discussion of the development of the right of petition, above, pp. 134-136, 140, and below, pp. 279-280.

budget is the power to determine the activities and priorities of government. However, Congress has not wielded this power very systematically. It has no method for weighing the budget as a whole. Instead, appropriations are made piecemeal, and tax laws are written by a separate committee. Authorizations for the spending of money —for the armed forces, or for education, or road-building—are recommended by the subject matter committees, and passed as legislation. But the actual money to be spent is specified in separate appropriations bills. The specialist subcommittees of the House and Senate Appropriations Committees each make their separate contributions to an appropriations bill. The custom of reciprocity means that each subcommittee respects the expertise of the others. Authority is fragmented, for the subcommittees operate practically autonomously, with little control by the full Appropriations Committees. When decisions have been made by the House (where money bills originate), the Senate Appropriations Committee listens to appeals.

Congress developed the General Accounting Office as a legislative staff agency able to perform some surveillance over the total budget. But it is no match in size, competence, or knowledge to the Office of Management and Budget in the president's office. The president has a staff of professional economists with whose expertise Congress has little hope of competing. In short, while Congress guards its power of the purse with care, it does not always use it wisely nor comprehensively.

In August 1972, Congress passed a bill appropriating more than $30 billion for the programs of the Department of Health, Education, and Welfare. It was nearly $1.8 billion more than the Nixon administration had requested. Congressional leaders were proud of their action and announced that the spare funds would be subtracted from the Defense Department budget. Senate Majority Leader Mike Mansfield stated that the bill demonstrated Congress's sense of the nation's priorities.

President Nixon vetoed the bill, labeling it inflationary. His opponent in the presidential election campaign, Senator George McGovern, charged that President Nixon exhibited a "confused sense of values" when he denied the possibility of spending an additional $1.8 billion on human needs in 1973, but requested an increase in defense spending of $4 billion.

In the House of Representatives, 42 Democrats joined 129 Republicans in voting to sustain the veto, and the two-thirds required to override a veto could not be mustered. The veto was upheld.

Standing Committees and the Status Quo

Another characteristic of the modern Congress that might surprise the founding fathers is the role of the standing committee. The press of business has grown so great that, in the House, the Rules Committee devotes its time to deciding which matters reported by legislative committees will be discussed on the floor, and the circumstances in which they may be debated. Every bill is given a "rule," which specifies the length of debate and the method of introducing amendments. The Rules Committee thus has the ability to kill proposed legislation it dislikes.

Congressmen could not handle the diverse and complicated modern issues if they did not specialize. The result is that the principal work of Congress is done in the standing committees of the Senate and House. The necessary compromises are worked out in committee, often in executive session, so the bending of political principle need not take place in public view. The committees function as miniature legislatures, for, if their report is unanimous, it will probably be adopted on the floor with little amendment.

Committee chairmen can wield great authority over the conduct of committee business. They set meeting times, establish agendas, appoint staff assistants, and schedule hearings. They also appoint the chairmen of any subcommittees deemed necessary. A committee chairman is in a position to shape the content of any legislation his committee considers.

Committee chairmanships are won on the basis of seniority—the span of uninterrupted membership on the committee. Although this system is much criticized, for its places the elderly occupants of safe congressional seats in the positions of power, congressmen have never agreed on an acceptable alternative. Although modified in 1971, the seniority system remains the key to congressional organization. Congressmen feel that any other method could lead to conflict between personalities in which issues of political substance would be only implicit. The gentlemanly nature of legislative business would be threatened; legislative purposes would be forgotten as personal animosity flourished.

The power to make authoritative decisions is decentralized to the committees and fragmented among their senior members. This protects the integrity of Congress as an institution and impedes the efforts of external forces (such as the executive branch) to control Congress. However, such external forces often operate in the name of the people; the president, after all, claims the entire nation as his constituency. The decentralization of congressional knowledge and decision-making has the effect of making the entire Congress biased toward those established interests that are in the closest contact with the standing congressional committees.

Congress is best equipped to defend and perfect the status quo. Somebody else must break bold new paths of public policy.

The Advantages of Incumbents

The seniority system pervades both the Senate and the House of Representatives as a method of determining the distribution of authority. This fact suggests that one of the Constitution's expectations is no longer realized: although members of the House submit their records to electoral judgment every two years, the turnover in membership is not very impressive. Incumbents tend to get reelected.

If the House were very closely tied to changes of mood in the electorate, this would suggest that members of the House are able readily to adapt their principles and policies to conform to electoral whim. In fact, individual voters are seldom well informed about the voting record and other actions of their own congressmen. They tend to judge the incumbent, and Congress itself, according to how well national affairs are progressing. A favorable electoral judgment on presidential performance seems to rub off on congressional incumbents—even, paradoxically, incumbents whose party opposes the president.

> The most obvious explanation of the lonesome landslide of 1972 was also the most persuasive. The people gave Richard Nixon an overwhelming vote but did not allow him a Republican majority in Congress. Apparently they wanted Congress to continue checking and balancing.

Incumbents enjoy marked advantages in the race for reelection. They are able to keep their names before their constituents through many legitimate and semilegitimate uses of the congressional "franking" privilege—or free postage. Most congressmen send newsletters and circulate questionnaires on the issues among their constituents. They can take credit for any federal money coming into the district, whether or not they were involved in the decision. They do their best to handle "casework"—the special requests of constituents for help in dealing with the bureaucracy—in such volume, and with such satisfactory results, that a reservoir of sheer gratitude is built up in the district, which is independent of issues, parties, and the way the congressman votes on particular bills.

Incumbents also enjoy an advantage in financing their campaigns. Figures collected by the Nader Congress Project show that incumbents regularly outspend their challengers, and by about the same proportion; incumbents are simply a better investment for campaign contributors.

> The first advantage incumbents have is that they already have been assigned to committees. A corporation or labor union knows whether a given Congressman is likely to serve on a committee with jurisdiction over subjects important to them. For example, if a Representative has been assigned to the House Agriculture Committee, it is a good bet that he will continue to serve there if reelected—which means that a farm conglomerate will be more likely to give money to him than to his opponent, who might well be assigned to the Public Works Committee. Conversely, trucking executives will sooner support a Public Works Committeeman than his opponent, who may end up on Agriculture. . . . As the treasurer of the Truck Operators Nonpartisan Committee [put it], "We do what we can for those on the committees who might help us. It's as simple as that."[5]

Of course, the longer a member remains in Congress, and the more seniority (with its potential for power) he accumulates, the easier it is for him to attract campaign support. The tendency of incumbents to retain their offices has important consequences, both for Congress as an institution and for congressmen as individual members of it.

5. Mark J. Green, James M. Fallows, and David R. Zwick, *Ralph Nader Congress Project: Who Runs Congress?* (New York: Bantam, 1972), pp. 230-231.

The Sense of Urgency

An important institutional consequence is that Congress has a much greater air of permanence than does the group of political appointees and elected officials who make up the presidential administration. A president must make his mark in four years, or, at most, in eight. Senators cannot expect to have much impact upon Senate business during their first six-year term, and a representative must expect to labor in powerless anonymity for many years. Seldom does Congress as an institution generate a sense of urgency to match that issuing from the executive branch, although individual senators may address themselves to particular issues with a very great sense of urgency. Years ago, freshman senators who insisted on contributing to Senate debate were practically ostracized. Senators now realize that the electorates of large states are highly volatile, and a freshman senator needs to attract some public attention if he is to have a chance for reelection.

Another reason for the lesser sense of urgency in Congress is that congressmen know they will be dealing with each other for years to come. If individual members insist on the moral rightness and urgency of their position on today's issue, they may alienate colleagues whose support they will need on tomorrow's issue.

Because the issues it deals with are potentially so explosive, moral righteousness, when indulged in by congressmen, is primarily for public display. The working habits of both House and Senate emphasize reverence for the rules, willingness to compromise, and elaborate politeness to colleagues. The institution developed these habits for the same reason that tigers have claws — self-preservation.

The Structure of Power within Congress

A second institutional consequence of the tendency of incumbents to be reelected is that lines of authority and influence within the House and Senate tend to be established on a permanent basis and to be little affected by the outcome of any particular election. In essence, the structure of power is fragmented and elitist; the power to make decisions that will probably be legitimated through floor voting rests with a small group of senior members.

Leadership is of two kinds: the "elected" leaders of the party; and the chairmen, automatically designated through seniority, of the standing committees. In the House, the party leaders are the Speaker, the Majority and Minority Leaders, the Majority and Minority Whips,[6] and their assistants. Although these officials are elected by the party caucus, length of service in the body is not irrelevant, for it permits a member to build the chain of debts and gratitude that may result in his election to a position on the leadership ladder.

Party officials are important in establishing agendas, agreeing upon procedural points, and organizing the body for its work. The Speaker of the House, as its presiding officer, exercises strategic authority. He can refuse to recognize members who desire the floor; he can refer bills to committees that may be favorably inclined, or not, to consider them; he appoints the House members of the all-important conference committees that reconcile the differences between House and Senate versions of the same bill. As leader of his party in the House, the Speaker is responsible for the conception, presentation, and pas-

6. The term "Whip" comes to parliamentary usage from the English hunt, where the "whipper-in" is responsible for bringing together the hounds and organizing their chase of the fox. Thus, a Party Whip is responsible for making sure that members of his party are in attendance when crucial issues are to be decided.

sage of a party program. If the president is of the Speaker's party, the Speaker becomes the main spokesman in the House for the administration's program. If the president is of the opposition party, he must make some arrangement with the Speaker for seeking common objectives, or the administration's legislative proposals may be quietly forgotten.

However, the Speaker cannot blatantly use his authority as presiding officer to further partisan purposes, for he is responsible to all members of the House for the orderly conduct of its business. In the fragmented power structure of the House, he can be no more than the first among equal members of the ruling elite. He cannot decide on, and achieve, a course of action that is opposed by the Rules Committee and the Ways and Means Committee, for example.

> Power was not always so fragmented. Late nineteenth-century Speakers were referred to as "czars." In the early years of this century, Speaker Joseph Cannon ruled the House with absolute rigidity. He appointed the standing committees and named their chairmen; he served as chairman of the Rules Committee, which ran the House. Progressives organized a revolt in 1910 that resulted in the limitation of the Speaker's powers; they have never been restored.
>
> Speaker Cannon was vindicated posthumously. One of the three House office buildings was named for him.

Walter Dean Burnham has analyzed data gathered by Nelson Polsby that delineate the "institutionalization of the House of Representatives." One important measure of the phenomenon is the percentage of committee chairmanships assigned strictly on the basis of seniority. Burnham demonstrates that the peak era for consolidating the use of the seniority device was around the critical election of 1896. The essentially negative purposes of the victorious coalition of 1896 were well served by the fragmentation of authority among committee chairmen who were not amenable to the influence of party. Burnham argues that the 1910 revolt against Speaker Cannon and the consequent limitation of the Speaker's powers was a result of the earlier acceptance of the norm of seniority appointments, rather than cause for a new acceptance of the role of seniority. Cannon had formed his own image of the Speakership in an even earlier time; when he tried to mold his behavior in that image, it was no longer acceptable to the general membership of the House.[7] No longer at ease with the notion of a party majority, articulated by the Speaker, as equivalent to the will of the people, they wanted to keep authority fragmented, held by an elite, and less responsive to external influences.

Power within Congress remained fragmented and elitist throughout the period of social and political upheaval that began with the Great Depression. Under the banner of the New Deal, Congress broadened the distribution of wealth and health in America. But the structure of the congressional institutions that developed these new policies remained as elitist as ever. They still are.

> The Constitution established a system of government that does not bend and sway to changes in popular whim. The political parties are the main weapons available to the people for forcing responsiveness upon governmental institutions. It is not at all clear that the parties continue effectively to perform this function.[8]

7. Walter Dean Burnham, *Critical Elections and the Mainsprings of American Politics* (New York: Norton, 197), pp. 100-103. The central thesis of Burnham's book is examined below, pp. 469-471.
8. The arguments supporting this conclusion can be found in Reflections 2, pp. 70, 86.

Congressional Careers

If Congress is the branch in closest touch with the wishes of the people, the result is not a marked turnover in congressional membership. The fact that incumbents are likely to win reelection has important consequences for individuals—the members themselves, and the entire apparatus of staff members that aid them. Lifelong careers can be planned in Washington. A member of Congress will retain his seat as long as possible, acquiring seniority, contacts, and friendships; serving the interests of his district, and possibly the public welfare. When he is ready to slacken his pace, or his constituents in their wisdom replace him, he can readily step into a new career in the so-called "third house" of Congress. He can become a lobbyist.

The possibility of forging lifetime careers operates to turn the member's attention inward, away from organizations, causes, and even moral convictions that might guide his activities. Instead, his actions will be increasingly cued by the internalized values, the social habits, and the definitions of prestige, that guide his fellow congressmen.

Freshmen congressmen, who often come to Washington committed to bringing a breath of fresh air into a stuffy institution, learn the reasons why Congress works as it works. They begin to relax, work hard to master the intricate details of matters considered by their committees (specialized knowledge based on plenty of committee "homework" earns the respect of their colleagues), and take a longer-range view of Congress and its future.

The most dependable critics of the seniority system are members who have the least seniority themselves.

Portrait of a Congressman

What kind of person is it who makes the trip from the local district to Washington? They are, of course, all manner of men and women, but Congress does not represent the people in the way that a mirror reflects an image. Congressmen are not a microcosm of American society, for there are vast subgroups that do not place a fair share of their members in Congress. Thirteen women were elected to the 92nd Congress, but approximately 53 percent of the electorate is female. If there was a definable, "woman's interest," they were in a poor position to insist upon its adoption. Racial minorities are notably underrepresented; there were eleven black representatives and one black senator (Edward Brooke, Republican of Massachusetts) in the 92nd Congress. The poor and uneducated must depend upon the educated and wealthy to protect their interests, for congressmen have

mostly gone to college and have achieved success in business or banking. More congressmen have been trained in the law than in any other profession.

There were 310 practicing lawyers in the 91st Congress. The role of lawyers in American politics has been recognized since Tocqueville's time; America's fondness for stating political issues in legal terms is unmatched by any other country. If legal training handicaps lawyers by narrowing their view of the world (a charge often made but impossible to prove), Congress is bound to suffer from such handicaps.

The most important fact about American congressmen is that they are products of the life and culture of their districts. Even a casual examination of official congressional biographies reveals the pattern: growing up in a stable famly, and living most of their early years in a single town or suburb; attending the local college; off to law school at the state university; a period of service in the armed forces, which provides the only experience of extensive travel; return to law practice in the home town; membership in the leading church, fraternal organizations, and service clubs; entering local party politics, winning lesser offices, and then the race for Congress. More important than his prior education in determining the outlook of the congressman is his prior experience: all congressmen are *elected*; they are required to be students of the political structure and distribution of power within thir home constituencies.

The congressman becomes a person of stature in his local community before he wins the nomination. The business, social, and professional elite of the district are the congressman's friends and the contributors to his campaign. He knows their opinions without asking. He is also influenced by the opinions of other voters in his district, although he seldom has a clear notion of their attitudes on particular issues. The matters Congress decides are highly technical and specialized, and the general public pays them little heed. Only the vital interests affected—as in the tax-reform bill—will press their point of view upon the congressman. Yet the congressman is sensitive to the indicators of general public opinion. He can become so convinced of the existence of a public demand for change—as in the tax-reform bill—that he will, at least temporarily, repudiate the pressures of special interests for a continuation of their privileges.

The congressman comes to Washington as a person well grounded in the dominant values of his local area; he is a provincial. He knows his continuance in office depends upon his not affronting those values too dramatically. Yet, once in Washington, he becomes the recipient of new experiences, and he tries to make a place for himself in an institution that has its own set of values and hierarchy of authority. The resulting tension may require the congressman to forge a new concept of himself as a representative of his constituents.

Styles of Representation

If a congressman conceives of himself as bound to the implicit and explicit wishes, or even instructions, of his constituents, he sees himself as a *delegate*. If, on the other hand, he feels that he has been elected because of the voters' confidence in his particular knowledge and judgment, which may be superior to their own, he sees himself as a *trustee*. Edmund Burke, famous eighteenth-century member of the English Parliament, felt that the duty of a Member of Parliament was to act as a trustee for the interests—which he was better able to define than they were—of not only his own district, but of the entire nation, including generations yet unborn. However, the theorists of the American Revolution, such as Thomas Paine, felt that a representative must be bound by the instructions of his district.

The modern congressman may go to Washington with the attitudes of his district so firmly in mind that he perceives them virtually as instructions. But his Washington experience may broaden his outlook. His committee assignment may make him aware of problems and groups that hardly exist at home, or at least are unknown to his accustomed social circles. Committee investigations may inform him of the problems of groups, such as migratory workers or the American Indians, that have enjoyed little effective representation in Congress, the way it did the Kennedy brothers. Congressmen come to think of themselves simultaneously as trustees and as delegates, adopting a different style of representation for different issues.[9]

A third style may be labeled that of the *broker*. In this conception, all claims upon legislative attention deserve response, and the congressman has no business imposing his own preferences upon them. Rather, it is his task to accommodate as many as he can, without causing anguish to other groups, or damage to the best interests of the nation.

Obviously, all three of these representational styles can contribute to the effective performance of Congress. To the extent that the congressman adheres to the internal norms of the institution and abandons his parochial concerns, however, he is likely to think of himself increasingly as a *broker* and a *trustee*.

In every election, a small number of senior members of Congress are retired by the voters, usually as a result of defeat in the party primary. These are the elder statesmen who have pursued and won the rewards of seniority, devoted themselves to the service of the national interest as they conceive it, and have gotten out of touch with the district.

9. See Roger H. Davidson, *The Role of the Congressman* (New York: Pegasus, 1969), Chapter 4.

None of these rather noble conceptions of the relationship between a representative and his own, or future, generations, encompasses the role that many congressmen adopt: *errand boy*. Americans regard their congressman as, above all, "their man" in Washington. It is his duty to smooth relations between the bureaucracy and the people of his district so that they will receive their fair share, or more, of whatever federal gravy is available. Is the local aerospace firm bidding on a contract for a new fighter-bomber? Let the congressman explain to the Defense Department why the local firm should have the contract, although its bid is not the lowest. (The district is beset by unemployment.) Is the local college asking for a loan to construct new dormitories? Let the congressman explain to the Office of Education that the college's new guidelines assure that it will no longer practice racial discrimination in its hiring practices. Does a local businessman (and major campaign contributor) require a loan from the Small Business Administration? Let the congressman convince the bureaucrats that the applicant's earlier bankruptcy was beyond his control. Has a constituent been denied admission to the local Veteran's Hospital because of a technicality? The congressman will clear up the matter.

Meanwhile, let the congressman entertain the busloads of students sent on civics class field trips, and show them the glories of democracy in action. Perhaps they will visit a session of either the Senate or the House and find more than a handful of members in attendance.

All congressmen are errand boys, to a certain extent. There is nothing quite like personalized attention to a constituent's needs to build up credit at home. Some of the requests that come to congressmen require special action by a bureaucrat, who would gladly do it even without the intervention of a congressman. But the congressmen like to play the role of humanizing the bureaucracy. The army, the navy, and the Veteran's Administration maintain liaison offices in Congress to make contact easier.

The Accomplishments of Congress

Some representatives may view themselves as trustees, others as delegates, a great many as brokers, and a few will admit that most of their energy is devoted to the running of errands. The important point is that all of these kinds of representation are practiced at the same time, by members of the same legislative body. The effectiveness of the institution—its total accomplishment—is made up of the sum of the relationships worked out between individual congress-men and their constituents. Legislation, in the final analysis, is the product of the entire institution; and so is representation.[10]

Any assessment of the functions performed by Congress must consider the performance of the total institution, rather than concentrating upon the shortcomings of a particular committee or the scandalous behavior of an individual member. The first and most obvious point is that Congress is not neutral. To portray Congress as merely an "arena" in which groups conduct their contest for power does not acknowledge what Congress does. Congress provides representation for the diverse peoples, interests, and causes of a far-flung nation of more than 200 million people. Congressional procedures decide which of those interests will be protected in the advantages they possess, and which shall receive new advantages. This decision is weighted in the direction of the biases that are built into Congress. Until the last few years, and the revelations of such legislators as Senator William Proxmire, the Armed Services Committees of both House and Senate were closely allied with the Pentagon and the industrial corporations that supply defense needs. The recommendations of the committees were accepted with little challenge. Everything else being equal (which it never is), the Senate will allocate to the less populous states benefits that are greater than their share of the population warrants. After all, Wyoming has two senators, and so do New York and California.

Nevertheless, Congress does facilitate a sense of representation and legitimacy—the feeling that one's voice can be heard in government. The ease with which incumbents are reelected suggests electoral satisfaction with the total performance of Congress; opposing candidates are unable to stimulate the voter outrage that would negate the incumbent's electoral advantage. The very fragmentation of congressional authority—making miniature legislatures of the standing committees—probably facilitates Congress's representative function, even while it renders the total policy output of Congress less coherent and less ideologically satisfying.

The bias of Congress is hardly toward hasty action. The legislative process is a time-consuming one, new policy must pass many points at which it can be vetoed, and each point is guarded by a different individual or group sympathetic to the existing distribution of governmental favors. Congress is unlikely to surprise the nation; but it is likely to reflect the public mood. When Congress is criticized for lagging behind public opinion, the criticism may be essentially invalid. For Congress is sensitive not so much to fluctuations of opinion on volatile issues as it is a register of changes in the basic national structure of values.

The Supreme Court spoke as the conscience of the nation when it called for the racial integration of the public schools. But not much integration took place until a decade later, when Congress, pressed by the civil rights movement, supported the Court decision with legislative policies.[11]

Congress has come to perform two important functions, made necessary by the modern growth of government, that are not envisioned in the Constitution. The first is the "watchdog" function, which is legally called the "oversight of administration." It is also called

10. See Hanna Fenichel Pitkin, *The Concept of Representation* (Berkeley and Los Angeles: University of California Press, 1967), p. 224 ff.
11. The history of school integration is dealt with in more detail above, pp. 6-14, 31-32, and below, pp. 337-341.

"surveillance." It is based on a recognition of the fact that, just as the president has an interest in the legislative program, Congress is concerned with assuring the responsible performance of the varied and complex agencies of the executive branch. Not only must Congress be alert to see that the duties of the executive branch are being carried out with efficiency and economy. Congress also has the right to determine whether the law is being administered in accordance with the intention of Congress in passing the law.

The principal weapon for overseeing the administration is the committee investigation. The present structure of congressional standing committees was established by the Legislative Reorganization Act of 1946, which authorized all standing committees to conduct investigations. Recognizing the need for oversight, the committee structure parallels the structure of the executive branch. Each standing committee is concerned with the duties and performance of particular departments and bureaus. It is conceded that Congress is better equipped than the British Parliament, with its differing traditions of ministerial responsibility and an aloof civil service, to require responsible performance by the executive bureaucracy.[12]

The system has obvious imperfections. Both House and Senate Armed Services Committees seemed to proceed for some years on the assumption that the Pentagon could do no wrong, and military installations and contracts should be shared among congressional districts in the same manner as dams and highways. The Agriculture Committees have been charged with overseeing the administration of the food-stamp program, for that program is administered by the Department of Agriculture. Both the department and the committees have been responsive to large-scale agricultural corporate interest groups who are not willing to admit that malnutrition is widespread in America. This particular gap was partially filled, under the stimulus of television exposés, by the Senate Select Committee on Nutrition and Human Needs.

Committee investigations are often criticized for having no legislative intent, and congressional investigations were generally in bad repute following the excesses of Senator Joseph McCarthy of Wisconsin in the 1950s. In fact, congressional investigations serve to educate the public as much as to educate the members of Congress. Investigations are a necessary and honorable means for fulfilling the function of overseeing the administration. That politically favorable publicity may accrue to the congressman conducting the investigation may be a bonus of the system.

> Senator Harry Truman of Missouri first came to national attention during World War II as the fair-minded chairman of the Senate committee charged with investigating the profits and performance of defense contractors.

Related to the function of overseeing the bureaucratic performance is the congressional function of personalizing the bureaucracy. Congressmen become their constituents' guides through the mystical maze of government agencies. Congressional intervention often is effective in cutting administrative red tape. To describe this activity as the "errand boy" function hardly does it justice; for its function is to bend a large and cumbersome governmental structure to the needs of the individual citizen. Such a function is essential to the continuing legitimacy of government.

---

12. See authorities cited in John S. Saloma, III, *Congress and the New Politics* (Boston: Little, Brown, 1969), p. 131, n. 2.

Perhaps congressmen are not the best agents for personalizing the bureaucracy. It is a function that should be performed impartially for all citizens, regardless of race, status, or party activism. The congressman's performance may be affected by political considerations. Many critics have recommended some imitation of the Swedish office of *ombudsman*, on a national or congressional district basis. It seems unlikely that congressmen will give up this role, however. While some complain that service to constituents distracts their attention from more statesmanlike duties, all recognize it as an important road to reelection.

Congress Changes, Too

The most common contemporary description of American government emphasizes the exotic growth in functions and power of the executive and leaves the impression that Congress watches helplessly as its constitutional prerogatives are eroded. This criticism is particularly levied in the field of foreign affairs, by those who are appalled at presidential actions and the reluctance of Congress to limit them.

The picture is not accurate. Congress has developed a structure of standing committees that serves the dual purpose of affording representation to the diverse interests of a pluralistic society and exercising surveillance over the far reaches of the executive branch. Congressmen have become the guides of individual citizens through the complexities of the bureaucracy. These functions—oversight of the administration and personalization of the bureaucracy—are nowhere anticipated in the Constitution, but have been ably developed by Congress in response to modern needs.

Congress remains overly dependent upon the information and expertise of the executive branch. However, hesitant steps are being taken towards redressing this balance, as the staffs of congressional committees are increased and Congress investigates the potential of computers for information storage and policy analysis.

But the willingness to modify procedures is the key. Such a willingness is the clearest sign of congressional will to survive. In 1970, the Congressional Reorganization Act revised committee and floor procedures for the first time since 1946. Compared to the 1946 changes, those implemented at the beginning of the 92nd Congress were neither basic nor wide-ranging. However, one dramatic procedural change authorized by the 1970 act could only be introduced in 1973, at the beginning of the 93rd Congress. The House of Representatives began to operate its newly installed electronic equipment for recording votes.

This innovation had been adopted over the previous half a century by thirty-six state legislatures. The House had both procedural and technological reasons for resisting the change. The lengthy call of 435 names gave members ample time to converge on the House chamber, in response to ringing bells in the corridors, from their offices, committee rooms, and the gymnasium in the Rayburn House Office Building. But each roll call consumed more than half an hour, and the House devoted more than a fifth of the time it spent in session to the roll-call formalities. House members do not have assigned seats in the House chamber, and computer technology was required to establish a dependable electronic system. The installation cost more than a million dollars.

Electronic voting may lead to new efficiencies in the legislative process, not alone through time saved, but by keeping the attention of members more closely attuned to the progress of matters on the floor. However, it may also reduce the ability of party leaders to influence the outcome of close votes, further weakening the influence of the party organization on the policy output of the House.

Meanwhile, in the Senate, liberals slackened their customary attacks upon Rule 22, which requires an extraordinary majority to limit debate and thus makes filibustering possible. Although filibusters have been used in recent decades largely to frustrate the passage of civil rights legislation, Senate liberals used the filibuster successfully during President Nixon's first term to defeat funding for the supersonic transport, Supreme Court nominations, and an anti-busing bill.

The strongest criticisms of Congress for violating democratic ideals are focused upon the seniority system. Partly in response to pressures organized by Common Cause, the citizens' lobby headed by John Gardner, the first crack appeared in the seniority system. In 1971, at the opening of the 92nd Congress, the House Republican caucus agreed to elect the top-ranking Republican member of each committee, instead of depending on the automatic designation of seniority. The Democratic caucus agreed to vote for a committee chairman whenever the person designated by the seniority procedure was objected to by ten members of the caucus. The effect of these changes could not be immediately measured, but they were a clear indication of a mood favoring procedural reform in the House of Representatives.

In 1972, Congress implicity recognized the inhibiting influence of senility. Pension benefits were liberalized, so that a retired congressman might receive a pension equaling 2.5 percent of his annual salary for each year of service. Fifty-seven House members either retired or were defeated in party primaries that year. By contrast, only thirteen House incumbents were defeated in the election of November 1972, and this was a larger number than usual. The defeat of nine of them largely resulted from the decennial reapportionment of congressional districts.

The dominant explanations of American government can change quickly. Thirty years ago, Congress was criticized because it did not yield to the efforts of the executive branch to control it. In the 1970s, Congress is condemned because it seems unable to control the president.

The Constitution established Congress as a separate branch. It remains, unique among industrial democracies, as a vigorous, active, and independent element of national government.

The legislative branch, contrary to appearances, may not be withered at all. Its elderly spokesmen do seem anachronistic in a time of rapid social change. But Congress as an institution has shown a remarkable ability to sense, indeed, to anticipate, changes in the public consensus, and to afford representation (although not always equal representation) to the many elements of a complex and dynamic society.

The executive branch still controls the most resources.

CHAPTER 5

The Constitution, Judges, and National Policy

IMAGES 5

Farewell to the Warren Court

REFLECTIONS 5

The Supreme Court and the Uses of the Constitution

Farewell to the Warren Court

Behind the marble Grecian columns of what the architect conceived as a temple of justice sit the nine black-robed members of the United States Supreme Court. They are the guardians of the Constitution's meaning. Their work is carried out with the dignity and solemnity appropriate to this responsibility. But the Court often becomes the focal point of political controversy.

Former Justice Oliver Wendell Holmes, Jr., explained. "We are very quiet there," he said. "But it is the quiet of a storm center."

A New Court

How does a president of the United States make an impact on history? Which of his actions will live on, long after his administration has ended, still determining the course of the nation? In 1972, the Finance Committee to Reelect the President expressed no doubt about one of President Nixon's accomplishments. In an appeal for funds to support the reelection of Richard Nixon, the committee advised potential contributors that "he has appointed four members to the Supreme Court . . . who can be expected to give a strict interpretation of the Constitution and protect the interests of the average law-abiding American."

Had the previous Court shown hostility towards the interests of law-abiding Americans? Getting down to specifics, the campaign finance committee wrote that "the courts are once more concerned about the rights of law-abiding citizens as well as accused law-breakers."

The charge that the highest court of the land had, before the 1968 election of Richard Nixon, disregarded the requirements of the law in order to express tender sympathy for criminals would seem absurd on its face, were it not for the apparent agreement of the voters, expressed by Mr. Nixon's 1972 landslide.

To see if the charge against the Supreme Court of former Chief Justice Earl Warren has substance, it is necessary to examine some of its decisions. To see whether the Finance Committee's claim of a new trend in the Court's decisions has validity, one must compare recent decisions, and assess the role of President Nixon's appointees in making them.

The Warren Court and the Rights of the Accused

Clarence Gideon's Lawyer

In deciding the case of an individual, the Supreme Court may initiate major changes in the operation of both state and national government institutions. Often the Supreme Court takes such action on behalf of one of the more marginal members of American society — one who would usually receive little notice from a rich and powerful government supported by the majority. Such a case began in 1962, when the Supreme Court received a petition written in pencil from Clarence Earl Gideon, an inmate of the state prison in Raiford, Florida. Mr. Gideon urged that the Supreme Court review his conviction and five-year prison sentence for petty larceny because he had been convicted by the state of Florida without "due process of law." Gideon had asked the judge to appoint a defense lawyer, for Gideon was a pauper. The judge told Gideon that Florida law required counsel to be appointed for those unable to pay for it only when the possible penalty was death. Gideon told the judge on that occasion, "the United States Supreme Court says I am entitled to be represented by counsel."

Gideon was wrong. In defining the Fourteenth Amendment of the Constitution, the Supreme Court for many years held that the "substantive" guarantees of the Bill of Rights — such as freedom of speech, press, and religion — apply to both federal and state governmental actions because of the Fourteenth Amendment. However, certain "procedural" rights are not necessarily protected from abridgment by the states.

Because most of the legal business of the country is conducted in state courts, it was felt that the different experience of the individual states would best be followed in establishing court procedures. A citizen charged with a certain crime might be assured of a jury trial in one state, but not in another; the court might appoint a lawyer for an impoverished defendant in some states, but not in others. In 1931, the Supreme Court ruled that the defendant in a capital crime — one punishable by death — must have a defense lawyer appointed for him, whether he requests it or not.[1] But other circumstances that might require the appointment of counsel were not defined, and a series of cases requiring a more clear definition of "due process" came to the Court. Finally, in 1942, the Court ruled in *Betts* v. *Brady* that impoverished defendants were required by the due process clause of the Fourteenth Amendment to have appointed counsel in state criminal trials only if a trial without a lawyer could constitute "a denial of fundamental fairness."

In the intervening twenty years, the Court defined a number of "special circumstances" in which the defendant must have an attorney's help to insure fairness. They included the defendant's illiteracy, ignorance, youth, or mental illness. But Clarence Gideon did not claim any of these special circumstances. The Supreme Court voted to grant "certiorari" (i.e., to bring the case up from the Florida court for consideration by the United States Supreme Court).

The Court specifically asked counsel arguing the Gideon case to discuss the following argument: "Should this court's holding in *Betts* v. *Brady*, 316 U.S. 455, be reconsidered?"

Although Clarence Gideon had no lawyer in his original trial, the Supreme Court appointed as his attorney Mr. Abe Fortas. A graduate

1. *Powell* v. *Alabama*, 287 U.S. 45 (1931).

of Yale Law School in 1933, Fortas had gone immediately to Washington, where he served in various offices in President Roosevelt's New Deal. In 1942 he became under-secretary of the Interior under Secretary Harold L. Ickes. In 1946, Fortas left government service for private practice and built his firm into one of the richest and most powerful in Washington, on the basis of access to leading government officials. Described as "an angry man—angry at injustice," Fortas nevertheless had made a substantial fortune representing the interests of individual and corporate clients. But Fortas served Clarence Gideon without pay. It is an honor to be appointed by the Supreme Court to represent an indigent petitioner.

Having appeared many times before the Supreme Court, and knowing through the study of its decisions the attitudes of each justice, Abe Fortas tried to prepare an argument that would counter the possible objections of all nine judges. He hoped, if the *Betts* v. *Brady* rule were overturned, that the decision would be unanimous. Meanwhile, Bruce Robert Jacob, an assistant attorney general for the state of Florida, prepared to argue the case against Gideon. Upon advice of his colleagues, he invited every other state to support Florida's case on behalf of states' rights in determining the procedures of criminal justice. Jacob did not know that thirty-seven states already provided counsel for impoverished defendants. After receiving Jacob's notice, twenty-three states signed an *amicus curiae* brief urging that *Betts* v. *Brady* be overruled. Only two states joined in the support of Florida's claim that it be upheld.

The briefs were printed and considered by the court; and the case was argued orally before the Court on June 15, 1962. Relaxed and confident, Abe Fortas explained his reasons for seeking the reversal of *Betts*. Jacob spoke on behalf of Florida, and other attorneys argued as friends of the Court. On March 18, 1963, Justice Hugo L. Black delivered the opinion of the Court in the case of *Gideon* v. *Wainwright*.[2] Justice Black had written a biting dissent in the case of *Betts* v. *Brady* twenty years before. It was with some satisfaction that he read an opinion that held, in essence, that the *Betts* decision had been a mistake and that the Court now overruled it. All nine justices supported the result, although four offered slightly different reasons. After twenty years, the Court changed its mind.

What were the results? Within six months, public defender laws were passed by eleven states to provide paid defense lawyers for impoverished defendants. Lawyers knew that injustice results when men accused of crime are forced to represent themselves before juries. They seemed to be waiting for a nudge from the Supreme Court to repair this flaw in the system of justice.

And what of Clarence Gideon? Receiving notice of the U.S. Supreme Court's decision, the Florida Supreme Court set a new trial for Gideon. It was held in Panama City, in the same courtroom, with the same prosecutor and the same judge, as the original trial. But Fred Turner, a local lawyer, was able to establish reasonable doubt in the minds of the jury whether Clarence Gideon did in fact break into the Bay Harbor Pool Room and steal a six-pack of beer and small change from the cigarette machine. Turner suggested that the state's only witness, who accused Gideon, had himself done the breaking in.

Clarence Earl Gideon, a white man then in his mid-fifties, who had served four previous prison terms for felonies—unable to settle down to steady work, he supported himself by gambling and rare thefts—was returned to his children and gainful employment as an automobile electrician.

2. 372 U.S. 335 (1963).

In accepting the 1968 Republican Convention's presidential nomination, Richard Nixon charged that "courts . . . have gone too far in
weakening the peace forces as against the criminal forces in this
country."

In referring to "criminal forces," did candidate Nixon mean impoverished defendants like Clarence Gideon?

Take the Handcuffs off the Police . . .

The tempo of cases determining the applicability of the Bill of Rights
to the states, through the Fourteenth Amendment's guarantee of
"due process of law," was accelerated by the Warren Court. The
Gideon decision aroused little objection. Fourteen months later,
when a no longer unanimous Court overturned the conviction of a
man who requested and was denied a lawyer during questioning by
the police, there were deeper repercussions. It held in the case of
Escobedo v. *Illinois* that a confession or other incriminating statements made by the accused before being advised of his rights cannot
be used as evidence in his trial. To deny the request for a lawyer,
even during the police investigation, was unconstitutional.

Prosecutors around the country protested that the decision would
hamper the police. No longer would it be possible to base a case on a
voluntary confession given to the investigating policemen, before
legal proceedings begin. But the Court anticipated this argument. The
opinion declared:

> No system of criminal justice can, or should, survive if it
> comes to depend for its continued effectiveness on the citizens'
> abdication through unawareness of their constitutional rights.
> No system worth preserving should have to *fear* that if an ac-
> cused is permitted to consult with a lawyer, he will become
> aware of, and exercise, these rights. If the exercise of constitu-
> tional rights will thwart the effectiveness of a system of law
> enforcement, then there is something very wrong with that
> system.[3]

This was followed by the case of *Miranda* v. *Arizona*,[4] in which the
Court barred the use of a confession obtained from a suspect in custody who had not been told that he could seek the advice of a state-
appointed attorney before responding to the questions of the police.
The failure to *offer* a lawyer was thus unconstitutional. Then, in
1967, the Court ruled that suspects have a right to counsel even in a
police lineup.[5] In these cases, as in others, the Court developed an
"exclusionary rule." This means that evidence obtained by the police
in an unconstitutional manner (as when the defendant has no chance
to consult a lawyer) must be excluded from consideration at the trial.

Unable to cope with rising crime rates, police chiefs blamed Supreme
Court decisions. The late police chief of Los Angeles, William J.
Parker, placed on his wall a chart that depicted the rise of crime.
Each jagged peak was topped with the title of a Supreme Court
decision.

The John Birch Society continued its campaign to impeach Earl
Warren. Bumper stickers blossomed, reading "Support Your Local
Police."

3. 378 U.S. 478 (1964).
4. 384 U.S. 436 (1966).
5. *United States* v. *Wade*, 388 U.S. 218 (1967); and *Gilbert* v. *California*, 388 U.S. 263 (1967).

Policemen claimed that their ability to preserve law and order was hampered by the Court's imposed rules for the treatment of suspects. The patrolman's morale plummeted when the defendant he believed guilty was acquitted because evidence gathered in an unconstitutional manner was excluded from the trial.

In 1968, the Court rendered a decision that yielded to the policeman's point of view. The Fourth Amendment of the Constitution prohibits the making of unreasonable searches and seizures (i.e., a judicially approved search warrant is required). It is applicable to the states because of the "due process" clause of the Fourteenth Amendment. Yet how should the eighteenth-century language of the Fourth Amendment be interpreted in the present era, when the "persons, houses, papers, and effects" of a citizen may also include an automobile, and modern technology has produced lethal weapons that can be concealed in a pocket or a handbag? In the case of *Terry* v. *Ohio*,[6] the Warren Court ruled that a policeman making a reasonable investigatory stop may conduct a limited protective search for concealed weapons when he has reason to believe that the suspect is armed and dangerous.

Under the right circumstances, a policeman may "stop and frisk."

The *Terry* ruling was decided by the Warren Court by a vote of eight to one. Justice William O. Douglas wrote a vigorous dissent.

Why was the Court so concerned about the right to counsel of an accused criminal? Rich men can bring their own lawyers to court, or the police station, with a telephone call, but a poor man cannot. The Constitution knows no distinction between rich and poor; all are citizens. It is entirely possible that favoritism toward the rich will be the result of police practices, if they conduct questioning before the accused is able to consult an attorney, although everyone has agreed since the *Gideon* case he must have a lawyer at the time of an actual trial.

Vacancies on the Court

The Departure of Warren and Fortas

In the first blush of his 1964 victory over Barry Goldwater, Lyndon Johnson nominated his good friend Abe Fortas as an associate justice of the Supreme Court. Although Republicans complained that Fortas had too frequently served as Johnson's political agent, the nomination was confirmed by the Senate.

As the 1968 election approached, President Johnson revealed that he had received a resignation from Chief Justice Earl Warren, conditional upon the Senate approving a new chief justice. Johnson nominated Abe Fortas to be chief justice and, for the vacancy thus created, he nominated another old friend, Judge Homer Thornberry of Texas.

By this time, political circumstances had changed. Republicans argued that Lyndon Johnson, as a lame-duck president, should not name a new chief justice—although the practice was instituted by the second president of the United States, John Adams. A group of senators declared their opposition to Fortas's appointment and revealed that Fortas had the previous summer received $15,000 for giving nine lectures at the American University Law School. The

6. 392 U.S. 1 (1968).

$15,000 had been raised by Fortas's former law partner, Paul Porter, from corporate clients of the firm—clients who were likely to have a case argued before the Supreme Court. A Senate filibuster to prevent the Fortas nomination began on September 25, 1968. When a vote to end the filibuster failed to attract the necessary two-thirds majority, Justice Fortas asked President Johnson to withdraw the nomination. Chief Justice Warren remained in office.

In early May 1969, *Life* magazine published the results of an investigation of the connections between Associate Justice Abe Fortas and Louis E. Wolfson, a financier convicted of stock fraud. The story was greeted in Washington as a major scandal. Fortas' enemies in Congress called for immediate impeachment proceedings.

> The Constitution provides that the House of Representatives "shall have the sole power of impeachment." In the case of Supreme Court justices, the House must charge them with a failure to maintain "good behavior." The charges are then tried by the Senate. One justice, Samuel Chase, has been impeached. He was a blatantly partisan judge who clearly misused his office in support of the Federalist party, which was then being turned out of office by the people and Thomas Jefferson. But even Justice Chase was not convicted by the United States Senate.

Abe Fortas had lived in the heady atmosphere of Washington since graduating from law school. Washington officials have the power to prosecute or not prosecute antitrust suits, to award defense contracts, to assign television franchises, and to regulate the securities market. After leaving government service himself, Abe Fortas earned about a quarter of a million dollars annually. He abandoned this income for the $39,500 salary of an associate justice. On the Court, Fortas dedicated his vigorous intellect to serving the liberal wing of the Court and, through them, the impotent and outcast, the Clarence Gideons of American society.

The Supreme Court is established as a disinterested tribunal, and the justices are appointed for life. The wisdom of the court had been attacked frequently, but its integrity had not. Although Justice Fortas wrote to Chief Justice Warren that "there has been no wrong-doing on my part," he saw that the suggestion of wrong-doing cast shadows upon the Court's reputation.

On May 16, 1969, Justice Fortas resigned in a two sentence letter to President Nixon. He was the first Supreme Court Justice in the history of the United States to resign in response to public criticism.

Warren Burger, President Nixon's Acquaintance

Richard Nixon let it be known that, in seeking a replacement for Chief Justice Earl Warren, he specifically passed over two well-qualified lawyers who were also personal friends. He did not want the Court open to the charges of "cronyism" which had been leveled at Lyndon Johnson's friends, Abe Fortas and Homer Thornberry.

On June 23, 1969, the courtroom of the Supreme Court building witnessed a unique ceremony. President Nixon addressed the Court, not as president, but as a lawyer-member of the bar. Mr. Nixon stated that the survival of free government is dependent upon continuity with change. "No institution," he added, "of the three great institutions of our government has been more responsible for that continuity with change than the Supreme Court of the United States." In reply, Chief Justice Warren stated:

> We serve no majority. We serve no minority. We serve only
> the public interest as we see it, guided only by the Constitution
> and our own consciences.[7]

Chief Justice Warren then administered the oath of office to his successor, Warren Earl Burger of Minnesota, a federal judge who had met
Mr. Nixon briefly on only two previous occasions. Newspapers reported that Mr. Burger's record had been conspicuously conservative
on issues except for civil rights where "he is considered a liberal or
moderate." In questions concerning the administration of criminal
justice, Judge Burger had criticized judges for being too particular in
setting down rules to protect every conceivable procedural right of an
accused. He wrote:

> Guilt or innocence becomes irrelevant in the criminal trial as
> we flounder in a morass of artificial rules poorly conceived and
> often impossible of application.[8]

The Seat of Justice Holmes

The departure of Abe Fortas left President Nixon with another Court
vacancy to fill. It was the seat once held by the great dissenter, Oliver
Wendell Holmes, then by Justices Frankfurter, Goldberg, and Fortas.
It was considered the "Jewish seat," if presidents cared to make the
Court reflect a religious balance. Judge Thornberry, Lyndon Johnson's
choice for the position, did not qualify on this particular ground, and
politicians and commentators hastened to point out that no president
should be required to follow the custom. The best man should be
appointed, regardless of religion.

In directing then-Attorney General Mitchell to seek candidates,
President Nixon sought regional, rather than religious, representation.
He was eager to demonstrate his solicitude for the southern states that
contributed to his electoral victory. Therefore, he defined his "best
man" as a southerner, a "strict constructionist" who would approach
the Constitution with less imagination than the Warren Court majority (particularly when dealing with criminal procedures), a man
with judicial experience, and, if possible, a Republican.

After due consideration, President Nixon nominated Judge Clement T. Haynsworth of South Carolina. Judge Haynsworth's qualifications were investigated by the Senate Judiciary Committee. The
representatives of labor unions and civil rights organizations, as well
as the American Bar Association, offered their opinions. The Constitution provides that the Senate shall "advise and consent" to the
president's nominations.

It became apparent that Judge Haynsworth, a quiet man, had been
little involved in the major social issues of our time. Furthermore, he
had once ruled on a case distantly involving a corporation in which
he owned some shares of stock. He was charged with "insensitivity"
to the ethical standards of judicial practice. His rejection was urged
as necessary to protect the prestige and integrity of the Court.

Those objecting to Judge Haynsworth on ethical grounds were not
the same senators who had objected to Judge Fortas on ethical
grounds. The liberality of Fortas's opinions made conservatives his
opponents; the anticipated conservatism of Judge Haynsworth's opinions made liberals his opponents. Although everybody proclaimed
concern for the prestige of the Court as their guiding motive, political

7. *New York Times*, June 24, 1969.
8. Ibid., May 25, 1969.

forces were contending for the outcome of future Supreme Court decisions and therefore the content of important national policies.

A coalition of conservative Republicans and southern Democrats could not control the Senate on this issue. Even Senator Hugh Scott of Pennsylvania, the Republican Senate Minority Leader, voted against Haynsworth. Seventeen Republican senators supplied the negative votes that made the defeat certain.

President Nixon next nominated G. Harrold Carswell of Florida, a federal circuit judge of even less prominence than Clement Haynsworth. This nomination also became the focus of intense pressures upon the Senate. As a young man, Carswell had endorsed white supremacy when campaigning for the Georgia legislature. As a judge, his decisions had been reversed by higher courts twice as frequently as those of the average federal judge, and his decisions were cited as authority by other judges only half as often. Carswell's opponents settled on the charge that he was "mediocre," a charge supported by protests from lawyers, judges, and law school deans. Senator Roman Hruska of Nebraska, forced to the wall during senatorial debate, unwisely asserted that mediocrity ought to be represented on the highest court (since there are so many mediocre citizens). Nixon wrote to a senator hinting darkly that another rejection would "usurp" his constitutional prerogative to name justices.

Judge Carswell was rejected by a vote of fifty-one to forty-five. President Nixon announced that the Senate "as presently constituted" would reject any nominee from the South. This was an attempt to aid Republican senatorial candidates in southern states, ignoring the fact that the margin of defeat for Carswell had come from the vote of thirteen Republican senators (including Senator Marlow W. Cook of Kentucky, who led the effort to confirm Judge Haynsworth), and that four southern Democrats had voted against Carswell.

President Nixon's third choice to fill the seat of Justice Holmes was Judge Harry T. Blackmun of Minnesota, a good friend of Chief Justice Burger and of Hubert H. Humphrey. Hardly a radical, Judge Blackmun was noted for humaneness, and he was no stranger to abstract thought. Republican senators heaved a sigh of relief, and the Senate quickly confirmed the nomination.

Impact of the Nixon Appointees

The Nixon Appointees

It was clear that Chief Justice Burger lacked some of the qualities that contributed to the greatness of his predecessor, Earl Warren. Jovial and diplomatic, Earl Warren had come to the Court without judicial experience. But his political experience was extensive and, perhaps, more relevant. Warren welded the diverse and brilliant legal intellects of his Court into the semblance of unified purpose. On the crucial, landmark decisions, they often spoke unanimously.

Burger's talents lay elsewhere. An able administrator, he turned his attention to the problems of the overburdened federal court system, and spoke out in favor of changes that would make the system of justice more orderly and certain in its operations. These were necessary and admirable actions. But Burger's inability to lead the Court itself in the manner of his predecessor meant that it could never be called "the Burger Court."

However, from the beginning of Harry T. Blackmun's service, it was clear that his legal attitudes were very much cast from the same mold as Burger's. They voted together so often that Court observers labeled them "the Minnesota twins."

Time worked its way with the stalwarts of the Warren Court. Hugo Black, the first justice appointed to the Court by Franklin D. Roosevelt, a man whose political and judicial career spanned the tumultuous social and technological changes of the twentieth century, resigned because of illness in September 1971. He died on September 24. John Marshall Harlan, grandson of the Court's first great chief justice, John Marshall, resigned at the same time and died on December 29. President Nixon had two more vacancies to fill.

The Nixon administration advanced a number of candidates for public discussion, including Herschel Friday, a bond lawyer who had represented the Little Rock, Arkansas, school board in its battle against desegregation. Friday and the three other serious candidates were opposed by the American Bar Association and other lawyers. President Nixon finally settled on Lewis Powell, a respected Virginia attorney, and William Rehnquist, an official in the Department of Justice. Rehnquist was young, vigorous, intelligent, and very conservative. But neither Powell nor Rehnquist could be charged with the deficiencies that led to the rejection of Haynsworth and Carswell. The Senate confirmed the nominations.

With the Court again at full strength, four of its nine Justices were the appointees of President Richard Nixon. What difference did it make?

Narrowing the Rights of the Accused

On June 7, 1972, the Supreme Court decided the case of Thomas Kirby, a citizen of Illinois. In February, 1968, Kirby and his friend, Ralph Bean, were stopped for questioning by a Chicago policeman. Among the papers they produced for identification were travelers' checks and papers bearing the name of "Willie Shard." Kirby and Bean were arrested. Records at the police station revealed that Willie Shard had reported being robbed the day before. Shard was brought to the police station and shown Kirby and Bean—no persons other than police officers being present in the room. Shard identified them as his robbers. The two were later convicted, although Bean testified that they found Shard's papers strewn in an alley.

The point at issue was that Kirby and Bean had no legal counsel at the time of their identification by Shard, and Shard would naturally feel inclined to agree with policemen who claimed to have arrested his robbers. He was certainly not asked to pick his assailants out of a group.

The Court decided that the holding of *United States* v. *Wade*,[9] which stipulates that the accused has a right to counsel even in the police lineup, did not apply. The Warren Court's rule, they wrote, applies only to accused persons who have been formally charged with a crime. The charge was made against Kirby and Bean only after their identification by Shard. Written by Justice Potter Stewart, the decision was joined or concurred in by the four Nixon appointees —Burger, Blackmun, Powell, and Rehnquist.

Four justices dissented. They wrote that the Court's opinion made a senseless distinction. If the accused criminal ever has a right to counsel, it must operate at the time when the accused is confronted by the accuser, regardless of whether he has formally been charged with a crime. And police lineups, intended to identify the suspect, are nearly always held before formal charges are made.

9. 388 U.S. 218 (1967). Also see above, p. 172.

The Court's opinion did not reverse the principle established by the Warren Court. Instead, it narrowed the definition of the right guaranteed in the *Wade* decision. Of course, in the eyes of the Nixon-appointed justices, the four dissenters were attempting to expand the *Wade* definition of the right to counsel.

The decision went the other way in the case of Otis Loper. Loper was convicted in 1947 of statutory rape and sentenced to fifty years in prison. The only witnesses at his trial were Loper, a physician, and the presumed victim, Loper's eight-year-old niece. Over the objections of Loper's attorney, the prosecutor questioned Loper about his previous convictions for robbery, which successfully discredited Loper's denial of guilt in the eyes of the jury.

The point of interest twenty-five years later was that Loper's previous robbery convictions (stretching from 1931 through 1940) were achieved when Loper did not have the advice of counsel. Thus, according to the 1963 case of *Gideon* v. *Wainwright*,[10] they were unconstitutional proceedings.

Consistent with other opinions holding that the principle of *Gideon* should be applied retroactively, the Court held that the unconstitutional robbery trials should indeed have been excluded from Loper's rape trial (although the judge could not have known it at the time) and returned the case to the lower court for further proceedings.[11] The opinion was written, again, by Justice Stewart, joined by Justices Brennan, Douglas, and Marshall. Justice White concurred in the result. The four Nixon-appointed justices dissented. Chief Justice Burger described the majority decision as an "extravagant result," for it applied the 1963 *Gideon* principle to a 1947 trial.

10. 372 U.S. 335 (1963). Also see above, pp. 170-172.
11. *Loper* v. *Beto*, 405 U.S. 473 (1972).

Stop and Frisk

Police Sergeant John Connolly was patrolling a "high crime area" in Bridgeport, Connecticut, at 2:15 A.M. Acting on the tip of an informant casually known to him, Sergeant Connolly approached a parked car. He had been told that Robert Williams, seated in the car, carried a gun in his waistband and that the car contained illegal drugs. Sergeant Connolly tapped on the window and asked Williams to open the door. Williams responded by rolling down the window. Connolly reached inside the car, grabbed the gun from Williams' waistband, and arrested him for illegal possession of a firearm. But it is legal to carry guns in Connecticut, whether concealed or not, provided the owner has a permit to do so. Connolly did not ask Williams if he had a permit. When other policemen arrived, a search of Williams's car was conducted. They found "substantial quantities of heroin on Williams's person and in the car, and they found a machete and a second revolver hidden in the automobile."[12] Williams was later convicted of possession of both the gun and the heroin. Williams's lawyer contended that the initial seizure of his gun, which led to the subsequent search and seizure of the heroin, was "unreasonable," and thus unconstitutional under the Fourth Amendment. The evidence, he claimed, should have been excluded at his trial.

The Court disagreed. The informant's tip constituted information reliable enough for Sergeant Connolly to act upon, and his actions were within the limits established by the Warren Court in the case of Terry v. Ohio.[13] The opinion was written by Justice Rehnquist, joined by the other three Nixon appointees and Justices Stewart and White.

Justices Brennan, Douglas, and Marshall filed dissents. Justice Douglas argued that actions of a vigorous gun lobby, which maintains the legality of gun-carrying in Connecticut, was the real culprit in the case.

Many people who come into contact with the police in "high crime areas" are poor. Many, also, are black. A major reason for supervising the procedures of policemen is to be sure that all citizens are accorded the same rights, regardless of their race or wealth.

Thurgood Marshall was the first, and only, black man ever appointed to the U.S. Supreme Court. He wrote a poignant dissent.

After carefully comparing the circumstances of the case before the Court and the Terry v. Ohio decision of four years earlier—a decision he had supported—Justice Marshall concluded:

Mr. Justice Douglas was the sole dissenter in Terry. He warned of the "powerful hydraulic pressures throughout our history that bear heavily on the Court to water down constitutional guarantees. . . ." While I took the position then that we were not watering down rights, but were hesitantly and cautiously striking a necessary balance between the rights of American citizens to be free from government intrusion into their privacy and their government's urgent need for a narrow exception to the warrant requirement of the Fourth Amendment, today's decision demonstrates just how prescient Mr. Justice Douglas was.

. . . The Fourth Amendment, which was included in the Bill

12. Adams v. Williams, 407 U.S. 143 (1972).
13. 392 U.S. 1. Also see above, p. 173.

of Rights to prevent the kind of arbitrary and oppressive police action involved herein, is dealt a serious blow. Today's decision invokes the spectre of a society in which innocent citizens may be stopped, searched and arrested at the whim of police officers who have only the slightest suspicion of improper conduct.[14]

The pattern was clear. In questions of police procedure, the four Nixon appointees sided with the policeman, in the absence of overwhelming contradictory evidence. In some cases, they might be joined by Justice White or Justice Stewart to constitute a majority, but not always. The result was not to reverse the Warren Court decisions that had granted new dignity to the impoverished criminal suspect. Instead, the trend of the Nixon appointees' decisions was to render the rights defined by the Warren Court more and more narrow in their application, until finally the point of meaninglessness might be reached.

The Death Penalty

A question that awaited the appointment of a full nine-member Court was the applicability of the Eighth Amendment's prohibition of "cruel and unusual punishments" to the death penalty as administered by the states. Six hundred prisoners on various death rows awaited the decision. The Court was unable to reach unanimity; in fact, there was no official opinion written for the Court, as five justices wrote separately to support the finding that, as currently administered in a manner that favors women over men, rich over poor, and whites over blacks, the death penalty is unconstitutional. The four Nixon appointees dissented, largely on the grounds that the Court was exceeding its authority.[15]

The Fourth Amendment was particularly designed to protect persons suspected of crimes — the guilty as well as the innocent — against arbitrary police practices. The Eighth Amendment recognized that even convicted criminals have rights. The First Amendment was designed to protect law-abiding citizens from other kinds of arbitrary governmental power.

Did the four Nixon appointees have a different attitude from the Warren Court concerning the First Amendment?

Free Speech, a Free Press, and the War in Vietnam

The First Amendment of the Constitution of the United States provides that "Congress shall make no law . . . abridging the freedom of speech, or of the press. . . ." For half a century the Supreme Court has ruled that the Fourteenth Amendment prohibits state governments as well from abridging these freedoms. But what constitutes an abridgment?

14. *Adams* v. *Williams.*
15. *Furman* v. *Georgia*, 408 U.S. 238 (1972).

The Tinker Children Go to Court

In December 1965, a group of adults and school children met in Des Moines, Iowa, to discuss ways of expressing their objections to the Vietnam War. They determined to wear black arm bands during the entire holiday season. Among the group were John F. Tinker, then aged fifteen, and his sister, Mary Beth, aged thirteen. When Des Moines school principals learned of the plan, they decided that any student wearing an arm band to school would be asked to remove it and if he refused he would be suspended until he returned without it. Mary Beth and John wore their arm bands on December 16 and 17, and they were suspended from school. They did not return until after New Year's Day. Their father asked the U.S. district court for an injunction to restrain school officials from further disciplining John, Mary Beth, and their friends. The district court dismissed the complaint, holding that the action of the authorities was reasonable to prevent disruption of school discipline, although no such disruptions had occurred. The case was appealed and found its way to the Supreme Court in 1968. On February 24, 1969, Justice Abe Fortas wrote the opinion of the Court.

He found that the wearing of black arm bands was "pure speech" of a symbolic sort and was protected by the Constitution, even if there was some risk that the expression of such an opinion might cause a disturbance—if, for example, the children wearing the arm bands were attacked by super-patriotic fellow students. Fortas concluded:

> In our system state-operated schools may not be enclaves of totalitarianism. School officials do not possess absolute authority over their students. Students in the school as well as out are "persons" under our Constitution. They are possessed of fundamental rights which the State must respect just as they themselves must respect their obligations to the State. In our system students may not be regarded as closed-circuit recipients of only that which the State chooses to communicate.[16]

David O'Brien Burns His Draft Card

There was, however, a difference between the symbolic speech of the Tinker children and other kinds of symbolic speech. In March 1966, David O'Brien stood on the steps of the South Boston Courthouse and burned his draft card in front of a large crowd, several agents of the FBI, and many television cameras.

Members of the crowd immediately attacked O'Brien and his companions. FBI agents took O'Brien to safety inside the courthouse and advised him of his right to counsel and silence. O'Brien stated that he had burned his draft card "so that other people would re-evaluate their positions with Selective Service, with the Armed Forces and re-evaluate their place in the culture of today," and that he knew he was violating a federal law.

The law violated by O'Brien was an amendment passed in 1965 to the Universal Military Training and Service Act of 1948. It declared that an offense would be committed by any person "who forges, alters, knowingly destroys, knowingly mutilates or in any manner changes any such [draft card]."

O'Brien argued that the 1965 amendment was unconstitutional because it was enacted to abridge free speech and because it served no legitimate legislative purpose. In delivering the opinion of the

16. *Tinker* v. *Des Moines Independent Community School District*, 393 U.S. 503 (1969).

Court, Chief Justice Earl Warren wrote that "the constitutional power
of Congress to raise and support armies and to make all laws necessary and proper to that end is broad and sweeping." The 1965 amendment, he found, was clearly within this power. The issuance of draft
cards, and the requirement that they be retained by young men who
were registered, helped assure the proper administration of the law.
The statute could not be held unconstitutional, even if O'Brien were
correct in saying that the purpose of Congress in passing it was to
limit free speech. For the results of the law, not the intent of Congress,
were what counted.

Wrote Chief Justice Warren:

> We cannot accept the view that an apparently limitless variety
> of conduct can be labeled "speech" whenever the person en-
> gaging in the conduct intends thereby to express an idea.[17]

That is, if O'Brien burns his draft card as an act of civil disobedience,
he should expect to be punished.

Charles Harbutt

17. *United States v. O'Brien*, 391 U.S. 367 (1968).

Julian Bond and the Georgia House of Representatives

In June 1965, Julian Bond was elected to the Georgia House of Representatives. Bond, a black, was a staff member of the Student Non-Violent Coordinating Committee. Several months later, SNCC issued a statement attacking American involvement in the Vietnam War and expressing sympathy with young men who resist the draft. In response to a radio interviewer's question, Julian Bond stated that he endorsed the statement, saying "I don't think that I as a second-class citizen of the United States have a responsibility to support that war."

When Julian Bond appeared, on January 10, 1966, to be sworn in as a member of the Georgia legislature, the clerk refused to administer the oath. Seventy-five members of the House had filed petitions seeking Bond's exclusion on the grounds that Bond could not in good faith take the prescribed oath supporting the Georgia Constitution and that of the United States. They claimed the SNCC statement gave aid and comfort to the enemy and violated the selective service laws.

A committee of the legislature, investigating these charges, asked Bond to testify. He reaffirmed his previous statement but pointed out that, while he admired those who refused to be drafted in the full knowledge of the legal punishment for that act, he had never advocated breaking the law; he had not counseled any person to burn his draft card, and his own card was secure in his pocket. The committee recommended that Bond be excluded, and the Georgia House refused him his seat by a vote of 184 to 12.

The Supreme Court held that the state of Georgia could not define freedom of speech more strictly for a legislator than for a private citizen. Exclusion of Bond because of his endorsement of the SNCC statement was an unconstitutional abridgment of free speech, prohibited by the First Amendment as applied to the states through the Fourteenth Amendment.

Freedom of speech is protected, no matter how distasteful others may find its content.[18]

The Case of the Obscene Jacket

In April 1968, Paul Robert Cohen was observed in the corridor of the Los Angeles County Courthouse wearing a jacket that bore the clear words, "Fuck the Draft." Cohen did not commit, nor threaten to commit, any act of violence. In fact, he didn't say a word. Cohen was arrested and later convicted for disturbing the peace by engaging in offensive conduct. Cohen said that the jacket expressed his revulsion against the Vietnam War and the draft.

The issue reached the Supreme Court in 1971, when two Nixon appointees were justices. The Court found that Cohen's jacket was more like the arm bands worn by the Tinker children than the card-burning of O'Brien. Justice Harlan wrote for the Court,

> We cannot indulge the facile assumption that one can forbid particular words without also running a substantial risk of suppressing ideas in the process . . . the State may not, consistently with the First and Fourteenth Amendments, make the simple public display . . . of this single four-letter expletive a criminal offense.[19]

18. *Bond* v. *Floyd*, 385 U.S. 116 (1966).
19. *Cohen* v. *California*, 403 U.S. 15, at 26.

Justice Blackmun dissented, joined by Justice Black and Chief Justice Burger, and by Justice White in part.

The Pentagon Papers

Also in 1971, the *New York Times* and the *Washington Post* began to publish sections of a classified documentary history of decision-making in the Vietnam War that had been supplied by a former government employee, Daniel Ellsberg. The Nixon administration sought and obtained injunctions preventing their further publication. Legally known as "prior restraint," this is censorship in its purest form. Otherwise, publication would proceed, and the question of whether any laws were broken by publication would be determined afterwards.

Courts in the District of Columbia and in New York both ruled that the government had not shown adequate justification for such restraint. The Supreme Court immediately agreed to hear the appeal of the government, and the Court's decision was issued just four days later.

The solicitor general of the United States argued that the guarantee of a free press in the First Amendment can be secondary to the duty of the executive branch to maintain the national security; and the executive branch should be largely free to define what the national security requires. The Court disagreed, the injunctions were vacated, and the publication of the *Pentagon Papers* proceeded.[20]

Chief Justice Burger, together with Justices Harlan and Blackmun, dissented. Basically, they wrote that the freedom of the press is not absolute, that the case was considered too hastily, and the government should have more time to prove that publication of the materials would indeed prejudice national security. It was the last case in which Justices Black and Harlan participated.

The trial of Daniel Ellsberg for making classified information public began before a jury in 1972. By 1973, revelations surrounding the Watergate scandal revealed that Richard Nixon's White House staff, in preparing a "personality profile" of Ellsberg on Nixon's orders, had the office of Ellsberg's personal psychiatrist burglarized. Two admitted Watergate thieves were implicated. The case against Ellsberg was dismissed because of government misconduct, emphasizing that constitutional restraints apply particularly to government officials; they cannot ordinarily be set aside by asserting the needs of "national security."

The Newsman's Source of Information

In the *Pentagon Papers* case, the first two Nixon appointees indicated their support for the proposition that the right of the government to protect its secrets (even long after the event) may be superior to the right of the press to publish information of public interest. After Nixon's appointees Powell and Rehnquist joined the Court, an opposite aspect of the question was presented to the Court: What right does the government have to demand information from a newspaperman? In particular, does the guarantee of a free press in the First Amendment mean that a newsman can refuse to divulge to a grand jury the identity of persons who reveal information to him, when he has promised to keep their identities a secret?

20. *New York Times Co.* v. *United States*, 403 U.S. 713 (1971).

Leonard Freed

The issue was presented by three separate cases. One was concerned with a reporter investigating drug abuse in Kentucky; the other two were concerned with reports of Black Panther activities in Massachusetts and California. In each case, grand juries investigating presumed infractions of the law issued subpoenas to reporters. The reporters were asked to share information they gained in the course of their work, but had promised not to reveal. The newsman in each case refused, asserting that the First Amendment implies a privileged relationship between reporter and informant similar to the confidential relationship between priest and penitent or physician and patient. The reporters chose to serve jail sentences for contempt of court rather than reveal their sources.

The Court's opinion was written by Justice White and joined by the four Nixon appointees, although Justice Powell wrote a concurring opinion to say that the decision should be applied narrowly. The Court wrote that, while a number of states have established such a privileged status for reporters by statute, neither Congress nor the legislatures of Kentucky, Massachusetts, and California have done so. And a long legal tradition holds that a grand jury should be able to call upon the information possessed by any citizen. The Supreme Court will not create a law that Congress and the state legislatures have refused to pass; the newsman will not be accorded privileged status under the First Amendment.

Justices Douglas, Stewart, Brennan, and Marshall dissented. Expressing his displeasure with the opinion, Justice Potter Stewart wrote:

> The Court in these cases holds that a newsman has no First Amendment right to protect his sources when called before a grand jury. The Court thus invites state and federal authorities to undermine the historic independence of the press by attempting to annex the journalistic profession as an investigative arm of government.[21]

In praising President Nixon's Court appointments, the Finance Committee to Reelect the President did not mention their tendency to support most assertions of authority by the government. The committee overlooked an important distinction. The interests of the average law-abiding American and the interests of the federal government are not always, or necessarily, synonymous. The Watergate investigations made this clear to millions of Americans.

It is quiet in the Supreme Court. The Court is one place where citizens can assert their rights against the power of the government. If they cannot do so with some hope of success, the streets could grow very noisy.

21. *Branzburg v. Hayes*, 408 U.S. 665 (1972).

The Supreme Court and the Uses of the Constitution

The Supreme Court of the United States—nine men in black robes, surrounded by symbols and slogans proclaiming "Equal Justice Under Law"—possess the power, in limited circumstances, to overrule the president, the Congress, and the people themselves.

The nine justices are the guardians and interpreters of the Constitution. Some years before he was appointed as chief justice, Charles Evans Hughes stated that "we are under a Constitution, but the Constitution is what the judges say it is." Did this mean that the clear words of the Constitution—such as the declaration that "Congress shall make no law . . . abridging the freedom of speech"—can be bent and twisted to rob them of meaning? Do the judges use the Constitution to enact their own policy preferences?

What is the source of the Court's power? Has it normally been used in the interests of all? Do these judges, who need not submit their actions to the public approval of an election, somehow preserve democracy?

The Origins of Judicial Power

Nowhere in its 5,000-word length does the United States Constitution explicitly state that the Supreme Court shall have the final say in constitutional questions. It does not provide that the Court can invalidate acts of Congress and of the president. Yet the Court has this power, which makes it more than the equal of the executive and legislative branches. The Court can be, in fact, supreme.

Examination of notes on the debates of the Constitutional Convention has shown that many delegates anticipated that the Court would come to wield such power. Some looked forward to this with pleasure, others with misgiving. But none wished explicitly to provide that power in the Constitution. It was presumed that the Court's power would be wielded to protect the very class of men who were drafting the Constitution—the conservative merchants and landed gentry. The delegates knew that the words written into the Constitution were general and would take on meaning when interpreted. They knew that such interpretations would be made by the Supreme Court. Perhaps it was a mark of their genius that they left unstated their belief that the final say concerning acts of the executive and the legislature would reside with the judges.

This likelihood was no secret from the men who first read the proposed Constitution. One of the major arguments against the Constitution in the debates concerning its ratification was the implicit threat that a national judiciary headed by the Supreme Court might overturn laws enacted by the representatives of the people.

In defending the document against these charges, the supporters of the Constitution claimed that the principal use of judicial review would be to protect all the people (not the upper class alone) against unfair laws by guarding popular rights and enforcing the constitutional checks upon public officials. Yet many held the private conviction that the Supreme Court, with the power of final interpretation, would be the basic guardian of the interests of the monied class.

In the Federalist Papers, Alexander Hamilton argued that the Constitution would be adopted by, and represent the will of, all the people. (The Preamble begins "We, the People . . .") Courts would have to void laws contrary to the Constitution, for the will of the people would certainly be superior to the opinion of their agents or representatives. Thus Hamilton made use of two "legal fictions" that have endured:

1. The Constitution in some real sense was written by the people.
2. The meaning of the Constitution would be plain to judges.

As the most brilliant strategist of the Federalist party, Hamilton believed that the strength and permanence of the new government could be assured only by involving it in the protection of the interests of the monied classes. When appointed secretary of the treasury in George Washington's cabinet, Hamilton labored to achieve this policy, over Jefferson's growing objections.

President Washington named only Federalists to the Supreme Court—thus establishing a practice honored by most presidents since his time. In 1789, the Federalist Congress adopted the Judiciary Act to fill in some missing details. It provided that the Supreme Court would review state decisions that invalidated any federal measure or upheld any state measure that had been challenged as being contrary to the national Constitution. This Congress, which included nineteen members of the Constitutional Convention, felt that state courts would have the power of judicial review and that the Supreme Court would have the last word. Section 25 of the Judiciary Act of 1789 remains the law of the land today. Nevertheless, it still does not make explicit the power of the Court to rule directly upon the acts of Congress and the president.

Because the system of subsidiary courts was not yet established, the first justices appointed by Washington sat as individual judges in courts meeting temporarily in various cities of the young country. As a result, the Supreme Court had little business as a Court in the first decade of its existence. Among the few matters that did reach it were suits brought against individual states by citizens who felt they were owed money by those states and knew they could not collect in the state courts. The Supreme Court upheld these claims, protecting the interests of money-lenders against the popular state governments and challenging the authority of the states. Acting quickly, Congress and the states adopted the Eleventh Amendment to the Constitution, which specifically banned such suits in all federal courts. Almost at the beginning, the ultimate weapon against an unfavorable decision of the Court was used: to reverse a Supreme Court decision, the Constitution can be amended.

This early defeat of the Court by the people did not make the Court an instrument of the popular will. Sitting as individual judges in the circuit courts, the justices next upheld as constitutional the limitations upon freedom of the press enacted by the Alien and Sedition Acts during President Adams' administration. The Federalists hoped to extend their lease on political power by suppressing political opposition, regardless of the Bill of Rights.

Justice Samuel Chase used his judicial position to deliver scorching speeches against the Jeffersonians. He was impeached by the House of Representatives in 1804 but never convicted by the Senate, partly because of uncertainty as to the meaning of "good behavior," which the Constitution requires of judges.

The Work of John Marshall

One of the Federalist reactions to Thomas Jefferson's political strength was the Judiciary Act of 1801. It established sixteen new judicial circuits and thus sixteen new federal judges to be appointed by President Adams from the ranks of the Federalist party before Jefferson and his Republican party should take office. The Federalists could be voted out by the people, but federal judges were appointed for life. This ploy was not successful, for the Republican Congress simply repealed the act of the "lame duck" Federalist Congress (lame duck because they served only until their already elected successors should take office). But the Republican Congress could not undo another act of lame-duck President John Adams. Shortly before leaving office, Adams appointed as chief justice of the Supreme Court the man who is usually recognized as the greatest chief justice of them all, John Marshall of Virginia. He would preside over the Supreme Court for the next thirty-four years.

Through a combination of his personal charm, superb sense of political tactics, and unswerving devotion to Federalist principles, John Marshall established the national government as superior to the state governments, the rights of property as more certainly protected by government than the rights of the poor, and the Constitution as a document that would support the growth and centralization of national authority. He prevented full achievement of the policies of the Republican party, which, with Jefferson, was devoted to the state governments and to the people. And he outlasted the twenty-four years of Republican administrations by yet another decade.

John Marshall knew that the power to define the general phrases of the Constitution would be as important for the future of the nation as the act of writing them. A ruling tradition of the English common law holds that judges are normally bound by the principle of *stare decisis*. This means that judges follow the precedents enunciated by previous judges, deciding similar cases in similar ways, so that citizens in their dealings with the law may be fairly certain of that continuity which President Nixon praised in his speech before retiring Chief Justice Warren. Because John Marshall was interpreting the federal Constitution, in most cases for the first time, he was not bound by previous decisions. But his decisions would stand as landmarks for future justices of the court.

The Landmark Cases

Marshall's Court laid an important legal basis for the American Industrial Revolution in the *Dartmouth College*[1] case, which held that the board of trustees, or corporation, which governed Dartmouth College was the equivalent of a person and thus was protected by the Constitution (Article I, Section 10, Paragraph 1) against New Hampshire when that state passed a law "impairing the Obligation of Contracts." (That small reference to contracts, which would forever

---

1. *Trustees of Dartmouth College* v. Woodward, 4 Wheaton 518 (1819).

favor money-lenders over borrowers, was placed in the Constitution largely at the urging of James Wilson, a delegate to the Constitutional Convention from Pennsylvania, who was one of George Washington's initial appointees to the Supreme Court.)

The *Dartmouth College* case came to the Supreme Court because the New Hampshire Legislature attempted to convert Dartmouth College into a kind of state university by passing a law that enlarged the number of trustees, and established a twenty-five member board of overseers. Twenty-one of them would be appointed by the governor of New Hampshire. In finding this act of the New Hampshire Legislature unconstitutional, John Marshall:

1. Defined the corporation governing Dartmouth College as a person.

2. Found that the charter establishing Dartmouth College, granted by the king of England in 1769, was binding upon the state of New Hampshire in 1816.

3. Declared that this charter was the same as a contract between the government and the "person" of the Dartmouth corporation.

4. Concluded that the New Hampshire legislature did indeed impair the obligation established in that contract.

This argument had no precedent; Marshall was clearing new judicial ground. The case was important in establishing the legal independence of institutions of higher education; it was even more important in establishing the power of corporations.

Marshall further expanded the power of the national government at the expense of the states in the case of *McCulloch* v. *Maryland*.[2] The Bank of the United States, established by Congress to bring some order to the chaos of state-run banks, tended to favor the interests of wealthy businessmen (mostly Federalists) and to be very demanding in their dealings with small borrowers (mostly Republicans). The state of Maryland placed a heavy tax upon the Maryland branch of the U.S. Bank in an attempt to drive it out of the state. The cashier, McCulloch, refused to pay. Maryland sued to collect.

John Marshall ruled that Congress indeed has the power to establish a United States Bank, although this power is nowhere listed in the Constitution. Rather, he claimed, it is inferred as a "necessary and proper" means required to achieve the great ends assigned to the national government, including the raising of taxes and the regulation of currency. Having found the U.S. Bank constitutional, he then found the Maryland tax upon its operations unconstitutional by declaring that "the power to tax is the power to destroy," and that no act of a state could place limits upon methods adopted by the national government to discharge its constitutional responsibilities.

The decision opened a line of legal development in which diverse governmental activities, unmentioned in the Constitution, are nevertheless declared Constitutional. If the goals are constitutional, so also are the means of achieving them. Instead of serving as a restraining influence upon the actions of government, the Constitution can be viewed as an instrument for legitimizing new methods for achieving long-established goals.

The supremacy of the national government was reenforced five years later in the case of *Gibbons* v. *Ogden*.[3] The New York legislature had given to Mr. Ogden a monopoly franchise to operate steamboats in

2. 4 Wheaton 316 (1819).
3. 9 Wheaton 1 (1824).

the state of New York. Gibbons ignored this, and Ogden sued to have Gibbons's boats taken out of the trade. The logic of the *Dartmouth College* case might have led Marshall to conclude that the monopoly granted by New York was a contract that could not be impaired. Instead, he turned to the clause of the Constitution that gives Congress the power to "regulate commerce . . . among the several states." Gibbons's steamboat service ran to New Jersey, and Marshall ruled that, when Congress is given a power, it cannot be exercised by a state. New York could not regulate interstate commerce in 1824. Today, no state may collect a sales tax on articles sold in the state but shipped to another state. This precedent become very useful to corporate attorneys when the states later tried to control the actions of powerful corporations that shamelessly exploited groups of citizens. The "steamboat decision" was very popular at the time, for the services provided in New York City by Ogden under his monopoly charter were inadequate. The growing commerce of New York needed more transportation facilities, or it would be strangled.

Thus, with broad strokes of the judicial brush, John Marshall and the Court he led established the supremacy of the national government over the state governments, and the legal privilege of free enterprise against governmental regulation. During his thirty-four years, the Marshall Court rendered 1,106 decisions; Marshall wrote the Court's opinion in 519, or nearly half of these; he dissented in only nine cases, less than 1 percent. This is a measure of the intellectual leadership Marshall provided for his Court—long after justices who were presumably his political opponents were appointed to it.

But the most famous of Marshall's cases was *Marbury v. Madison*,[4] which established that the Supreme Court may declare unconstitutional, and hence void, a law passed by the United States Congress. The decision also revealed John Marshall's political sense at work in combination with his legal deviousness.

Shortly before leaving office, President John Adams appointed forty-two new justices of the peace for the District of Columbia. But these so-called "midnight commissions" had been granted so late that there was not time to deliver them to the appointees. Newly inaugurated President Thomas Jefferson ordered James Madison, his secretary of state, to withhold the commissions. One of the justices of the peace to be commissioned, William Marbury, asked the Supreme Court to issue a court order or "writ of *mandamus*" to compel Madison to deliver the commissions. Marshall faced a quandary. If the Court ordered Madison to deliver the commissions, the administration could disregard the order, revealing the inability of the Court to enforce its decisions. If the Court said that Madison was within his rights in refusing to deliver the commissions, the judiciary would be admitting a subsidiary position to the executive. What he did was declare that Marbury and his fellow appointees were entitled to their commissions, but the Supreme Court did not have the power, on original jurisdiction, to issue the order which would compel Madison to deliver them. To do this, he declared unconstitutional Section 13 of the Judiciary Act of 1789. This section had empowered the Supreme Court to do exactly what Marbury asked. Marshall declared that the Court could not properly do so without violating its constitutional nature as a court of appeals. That is, instead of considering cases of this sort in the first instance, the Court could only handle them after they had been adjudged by lower courts. Thus Marshall gave Jefferson the immediate political result Jefferson desired—no appointments for Marbury and his friends. And the immediate practical result of

4. 1 Cranch 137 (1803).

the decision was to reduce slightly the authority of the Supreme Court. But, in the process, he established the principle that the Court may declare acts of Congress unconstitutional.

Any government established according to a written charter requires some authority to define the charter's meaning, and nobody was greatly surprised when Marshall asserted it. But he did so in circumstances that avoided any challenge to his assertion. As champion of the people, Jefferson could have protested that the voters have no check upon the judges, who are appointed for life, rather than being elected. With his immediate political objective secured, Jefferson did not issue such a challenge.

> Marshall established the Court as a *political* branch of the government, just as involved in making policy as the executive and the legislative branches. Perhaps it was inevitable — given the experiment with a written constitution, which required interpretation to become meaningful. When Alexis de Tocqueville visited the United States during the presidency of Andrew Jackson, he wrote that "hardly any political question arises in the United States that is not resolved sooner or later into a judicial question."
>
> Americans should be grateful that John Marshall resolved such political questions in favor of a stronger, more competent national government — a government that has survived war, rebellion, and economic collapse. But the task of interpreting the Constitution is not complete, nor has the meaning of democracy in American been permanently defined.

The Decline and Rebirth of Judicial Power

With the death of John Marshall in 1835, President Andrew Jackson appointed Chief Justice Roger Brooke Taney of Maryland. As secretary of the Treasury, Taney had handled Jackson's battle against the United States Bank, and his appointment to the Court was in part the payment for a political debt. Taney brought to the Court rather different attitudes from those that had motivated John Marshall. As a Democrat (which members of Jefferson's and Jackson's political party were now calling themselves), Taney represented the interests of southern and western farmers against the merchants and financiers of the East. Under his guidance, the states were permitted to regulate interstate commerce, provided that particular field had not been preempted by congressional action. Thus, while Marshall sought to expand national power at the expense of the states, Taney supported both state and federal power, provided it was exercised for the benefit of the agrarian interests Taney himself favored.

This general trend of decisions of the Taney Court is normally overlooked because of a single disastrous decision. In 1857, the case of *Dred Scott v. Sanford*[5] came before the Court. Born a slave, Dred Scott had been taken by his master from Missouri through the free state of Illinois into the Wisconsin territory, where slavery had been outlawed by the Missouri Compromise. Brought back to Missouri after twenty years, he went to court to establish his status. The Court was invited to resolve the problem which was threatening the continuance of the Union: Should slavery be permitted in the new western states? Chief Justice Taney was himself a slave-holder, and his agrarian concerns extended to the plantation owners of the South. He went far beyond the minimum necessary to decide the case of

5. 19 Howard 393 (1857).

Dred Scott. He branded as unconstitutional an act of Congress—the Missouri Compromise, which had in fact been repealed by the entrance of California into the Union. Citing the Fifth Amendment, Taney argued that to prohibit slavery in any of the new territories would deprive the slave-owner entering such territory of his property "without due process of law." But Taney even went beyond this. He held that, in the views of the founding fathers, persons of African descent "were not intended to be included" as citizens of the United States but were considered "a subordinate and inferior class."

This decision enraged the whole spectrum of anti-slavery forces, ranging from the Abolitionists who viewed the slave system as pure evil, to the laborers who wished to exclude the competitive slave labor system from the new territories. It led the New England states to threaten secession from the Union, and it sent scholars digging into the records to prove that the principle of judicial review was never intended by the founding fathers. The decision was never enforced. It became yet another milestone on the road to civil war.

Taney and his colleagues remained the Supreme Court of the Union during the Civil War, but their prestige and authority had vanished. On April 27, 1861, President Abraham Lincoln suspended the writ of *habeas corpus*, a procedural device for assuring an accused citizen of a speedy trial. Lincoln delegated to the military commanders the authority to hold persons suspected of disloyalty to the United States in prison without a court order. Taney, sitting as a circuit judge, issued a courageous opinion holding this practice contrary to the Constitution. Lincoln replied that his own action was completely in accord with the Constitution's provision that "the privilege of the writ of *habeas corpus* shall not be suspended unless when, in cases of rebellion or invasion, the public safety may require it." The South was rebelling; it was necessary, he claimed, to put down the rebellion by force of arms in order that *all* the laws of the Union could be enforced; to keep the single law regarding *habeas corpus* in effect threatened the achievement of that cause, so it must be suspended.

Abraham Lincoln was devoted, publicly and privately, to the defense of the Union and the Constitution. Yet he willingly suspended an important guarantee found in the Constitution because it was inconvenient. He argued that a physician may amputate a limb to save a patient; he will never sacrifice the patient to preserve the limb.

The Court as the Servant of Capitalism

In the closing years of the Civil War, the Supreme Court was little more than an appendage upon the American body politic. Within thirty years, its position was restored as a dominant branch of the national government. The Court accomplished this by leading the march to power and privilege of the emerging dominant force in American society—unregulated free enterprise and the corporation. By the 1890s, the Supreme Court had accepted the suggestion that the Fourteenth Amendment to the United States Constitution should be interpreted as preventing state legislatures from depriving corporations of "property without due process of law." Any effort of the people of a state, acting through their legislature, to tax or otherwise regulate private enterprises—even if they were monopolies—were found inconsistent with the Constitution and thus invalid.

During its history the Supreme Court has considered more than 1,000 cases concerned with the due process clause. The great bulk of these have had to do with the regulation of business on the theory established by Marshall in the *Dartmouth College* case that corporations are "persons." Only a handful, and those quite recently, have involved the original intent of the Fourteenth Amendment to remove from the black race those legal liabilities which constituted the "badges of slavery."

The most blatant example of the service rendered men of wealth by the Supreme Court came in 1895 with the case of *Pollock* v. *Farmers' Loan and Trust Company*.[6] This case invalidated as unconstitutional an 1894 law in which Congress imposed a tax upon individual incomes. Through a somewhat tortured definition of the taxing power of Congress (Article I, Section 8, Paragraph 1, and Section 9, Paragraph 4), the Court concluded that an income tax was a direct tax that could not be collected from individuals, without reference to the population of states. The impact of this decision was only reversed with the passage of the Sixteenth Amendment, in 1913, through the guidance and influence of President William Howard Taft.

> After the Civil War, the Court majority seemed determined to use the Constitution to restrain any movement by Congress or the state legislatures toward reform of the economic system. But crusading newspapermen continued to expose the injustices of rampant capitalism. And the Court decisions were not unanimous. In the opinions of dissenting justices, the decisions of the Supreme Court carried the seeds of their own reversal.

The Power of Dissent

The Supreme Court has been noted for including among its justices men of powerful intellect who dissent from the decisions of the majority and explain the reasons which would support the opposite ruling. The first of these was William Johnson, Republican of South Carolina, who served for thirty years in John Marshall's Court and regularly registered his objections to the Marshall rulings. The second was John Marshall Harlan, Republican of Kentucky, himself named after the first great chief justice. A former slave-owner who had little formal legal education, Harlan demonstrated his ability to cut through pompous legalisms in over 300 dissents that challenged the practice of the Court majority in making the rights of private property more nearly absolute than any other.

Harlan's dissent in *Pollock* v. *Farmers' Loan and Trust Company*, which declared the income tax unconstitutional and committed the federal government to dependence upon import duties to finance its affairs, pinpointed the economic motivation of the Court majority when he wrote that the decision

6. 158 U.S. 601 (1895).

strikes at the very foundations of national authority in that it denies to the general government a power which is, or may become, vital to the very existence and preservation of the Union in a national emergency, such as that of war with a great commercial nation, during which the collection of all duties upon imports will cease or be materially diminished.[7]

Justice Harlan's most famous dissent came in the case of *Plessy* v. *Ferguson* (1896), in which the constitutionality of the Louisiana law requiring separate railroad coaches for black people was challenged. In upholding the Louisiana statute, the Court majority casually stamped as a "fallacy" the argument that

the enforced separation of the two races stamps the colored race with a badge of inferiority. If this be so, it is not by reason of anything found in the act, but solely because the colored race chooses to put that construction upon it.

This casual assumption represented a misunderstanding of human psychology. It was also a perverse misunderstanding of the intent of the Fourteenth Amendment. Justice Harlan dissented in thundering words:

There is no caste here. Our Constitution is color-blind and neither knows nor tolerates classes among citizens.

Harlan's opinion was adopted by a unanimous Court in 1954. Opinion polls show that the public has increasingly accepted the principle of racial equality before the law. But the implementation of that principle has met white resistance in both North and South.

The Proper Bostonian

The most famous dissenting Justice was Oliver Wendell Holmes. A wounded veteran of the Civil War, a Boston Republican who remained devoted to the Republican party throughout his career, an aristocrat by nature and inclination, Holmes was passionately devoted to the democratic process and its guarantee of freedom of speech, of the press, and of thought. His record of biting dissents was directed against a Court that was determined to protect the rights of private property and free enterprise above all else. In economic matters, Holmes favored judicial restraint. He felt that the Court should not write its own economic theories into the Constitution but should find in the Constitution justification to permit democratically elected legislatures to undertake, particularly in the individual states, reasonable experiments with the organization of economic affairs and the regulation of corporations. In the area of individual liberties, however, Holmes was a judicial activist. He implored the Court to intervene in the protection of individual rights and to void laws which threatened the traditional democratic freedoms. He wrote, in echo of John Stuart Mill:

The ultimate good desired is better reached by free trade in ideas . . . the best test of truth is the power of the thought to get itself accepted in the competition of the market. . . .[8]

Justice Holmes's wit and wisdom won him undying fame, but it

7. Ibid.
8. Justice Holmes dissenting in *Abrams* v. *U.S.*, 250 U.S. 616 (1919).

seldom persuaded the majority of his colleagues. His dissents remained to guide later Court majorities.

Free Speech in the 1920s

Are the freedoms guaranteed by the First Amendment to the Constitution guaranteed absolutely? Does freedom of speech include the right to urge the abolition of free speech? Is it appropriate for the majority, speaking through its legislature, to limit the right of minorities to urge ideas that the majority finds despicable or even dangerous? These have been real questions since the Federalists themselves passed the Anti-Sedition Act of 1798. They were live questions during World War I, when a wave of anti-German prejudice swept the country, and in the period just following that war, when anti-Communist agitation was led by the attorney general of the United States. If a government official leads the harassment of an unpopular group, the group's only recourse may be the Constitution and the courts. For the elected servants of an aroused majority may feel little concern for the rights of individuals despised by that majority. Justice Holmes wrote a memorable opinion in the case of *Schenck v. United States* in 1919. The opinion upheld the constitutionality of the Espionage Act of 1917. Schenck and his associates were charged with conspiring to cause young men to resist conscription (i.e., the draft). They had circulated through the U.S. mails a pamphlet urging this course of action.

Because the finding of the case was contrary to Justice Holmes's general belief in free thought, it is speculated that he joined the Court majority in order to write its opinion and thus state as narrow grounds as possible for limiting the freedom of speech. What he devised was the test of "clear and present danger." He wrote:

> The most stringent protection of free speech would not protect a man in falsely shouting fire in a theater and causing a panic. ... The question in every case is whether the words used are used in such circumstances and are of such a nature as to create a clear and present danger that they will bring about the substantive evils that Congress has a right to prevent. It is a question of proximity and degree. When a nation is at war many things that might be said in time of peace are such a hindrance to its effort that their utterance will not be endured so long as men fight and that no court could regard them as protected by any Constitutional right.[9]

But Holmes's test did not prevail. His colleagues remained concerned that Socialist and Communist doctrines might pervert the American people and, before long, they devised a new test for laws that might limit freedom of speech in the case of *Gitlow v. New York*. Gitlow had been found guilty of "criminal anarchy" in that he had "advocated, advised and taught the duty, necessity and propriety of overthrowing ... government by force. ..." Gitlow claimed that no result had followed from his advocacy (i.e., no government was toppled), and therefore the law under which he was convicted was unconstitutional. The Court majority found, in 1925, that Gitlow

> advocated not merely the abstract doctrine of overthrowing organized government by force, by violence and unlawful means, but action to that end.[10]

9. 249 U.S. 47 (1919).
10. 208 U.S. 652 (1925).

Thus, free speech could be limited if it involved "advocacy to action." This meant that only the most abstract kind of criticisms of the American social and political system could freely be uttered. Mr. Holmes registered his dissent:

> Every idea is an incitement. It offers itself for belief and if believed it is acted on unless some other belief outweighs it or some failure of energy stifles the movement at its birth. . . . If in the long run the beliefs expressed in proletarian dictatorship are destined to be accepted by the dominant forces of the community, the only meaning of free speech is that they should be given their chance and have their way.[11]

The aristocratic Justice Holmes believed in human dignity and the right of dissent, but his application of the principles could vary according to the circumstances, as his different opinions in *Schenck* and *Gitlow* demonstrate. His suggestion that the government must ensure the existence of a free marketplace of ideas, even if the winning idea should result in the rejection of democracy in favor of communism, has not won wide acceptance by congressmen, state legislatures, or school boards. The conception of the Constitution as an instrument for protecting the rights of individuals and minorities against the operation of public opinion has not always won the total adherence of the Supreme Court itself.

F.D.R. versus the "Horse and Buggy Court"

The trend of Supreme Court opinions set in the closing years of the nineteenth century continued in the first thirty years of the twentieth century. In the prosperity of the twenties, the impact of these decisions was hardly remarkable. With the collapse of the economy beginning in 1929, it became clear that there is no "invisible hand" operating in otherwise unregulated free enterprise to insure that able-bodied men willing to work shall find employment or that widows, orphans, and the aged shall somehow be cared for. Over the years, the Court created a twilight zone in which neither the national nor the state governments could take effective action. If state legislatures attempted to regulate business, the Court claimed such regulation was prohibited by the due process clause of the Fourteenth Amendment. If the national government attempted regulation on a national basis, the Court found that such legislation exceeded the constitutional power to regulate interstate commerce, or that it violated the due process clause of the Fifth Amendment. The Supreme Court majority regarded the Constitution as requiring the restraint of government efforts to reform or regulate the economic structure. The majority held to this conception, even when the national economy collapsed after the 1929 stock market crash.

Franklin D. Roosevelt was elected president in 1932. Upon his inauguration in 1933, there followed 100 days of legislative activity never matched before nor since. A host of new laws and new federal agencies together constituted an attempt, on a national basis, to deal with the shortcomings of the economic system. Cases concerning the New Deal legislation did not come before the Supreme Court immediately. Beginning in 1935, however, the Court began systematically to invalidate the structure of the New Deal by finding its most important laws contrary to the Constitution.

11. Ibid., Justice Holmes dissenting.

But the Court did not find state efforts to deal with the problems of the time any more acceptable. In 1936, the Court voided a New York statute providing minimum wages for women who worked. The Court majority opposed social reform, whether attempted by the states or the national government. The "nine old men" of the Supreme Court had been appointed by Presidents Harding, Coolidge, Hoover, and Wilson. No vacancies occurred for Roosevelt to fill with judges sympathetic to the New Deal. The constitutional crisis was universally recognized. Even the 1936 Republican candidate, Alf Landon, insisted upon a plank in the Republican platform calling for an amendment to the Constitution to permit national legislation regulating the wages, hours, and working conditions of women and children.

President Roosevelt bided his time until, in 1936, he scored an historic election victory, winning every state except Maine and Vermont. With this evidence of public support, the president asked Congress to reform the Supreme Court—indeed the full federal judiciary—by appointing new judges to "help" those over 70. He specifically referred to the Supreme Court as a "horse and buggy court" in the airplane age, a group of old men who refused to keep up with the times.

Roosevelt made this charge when, in the case of *Schecter Poultry Corporation* v. *United States*,[12] the Court declared invalid, as an undue delegation of legislative authority to an executive agency, the National Industrial Recovery Act. The act had been rather sloppily drafted. It included minimum wage and maximum hour requirements as well as providing that a number of industries would establish "codes of fair competition." The Schecter brothers had shipped diseased chickens in interstate commerce in contravention of one of these codes.

Yet when Roosevelt's scheme for modifying the composition of the Supreme Court's majority was made public, it stimulated a great public outcry. For, by then, the Supreme Court had come to share the same symbolic function as the Constitution—a function similar to that performed in British government by the person of the monarch. An attack upon the Supreme Court seemed to be an attack upon the very foundations of America. Many who stated this argument hoped that the Court could continue to prevent the enactment of social reform legislation. For public consumption, they issued ringing declarations of the duty of the Supreme Court to protect individual liberties and claimed that FDR's plan threatened those liberties. When the Court headed by Earl Warren began twenty years later to protect individual rights with vigor and dedication, some of these same gentlemen declared that the Court was exceeding its authority.

President Roosevelt's bill was defeated after a long controversy. He was fond of saying that he "lost the battle but won the war." In 1937, the Supreme Court began finding that the legislation of the New Deal was possible within the limits of the Constitution.

The economic collapse was so complete as to affect nearly every American. Millions of ablebodied men found they could not find employment at any wage. Many families abandoned the eroded fields of the Southwest and became wandering migratory workers, seeking employment and food. Yet, in California, surplus oranges were burned or plowed under so that their presence on the market would not further depress the price. Franklin D. Roosevelt was elected in 1932 because of a conviction that any president would do better in

12. 295 U.S. 495 (1935).

meeting the crisis than Herbert Hoover. Roosevelt did not have to outline with great care what he anticipated doing.

President Roosevelt's reelection in 1936 constituted an enthusiastic public endorsement of his programs. When the Court majority decided, in 1937, in *National Labor Relations Board* v. *Jones and Laughlin Steel Corporation*[13] that the Fair Labor Standards Act was consistent with the Constitution, they signaled not only that labor unions could organize, they also indicated a rediscovered respect for the will of the majority as represented by legislative action. A critic wrote that "A switch in time saved nine," for this change of heart made President Roosevelt's "court-packing" plan unnecessary.

For half a century, the Court had effectively turned democracy on its head by protecting the rich corporate minority from majority attempts to regulate their activities. For thirty years, the Court had done this over the vigorous protests of Oliver Wendell Holmes. Holmes retired in 1932. In 1937, the Court majority adopted Holmes's policy of judicial restraint concerning economic regulation.

> Before he died in 1945, President Roosevelt had appointed nine Supreme Court justices—an entire Court. Included were Hugo L. Black and William O. Douglas, leaders of judicial liberalism.

Free Speech in the 1950s
Just as the end of World War I had signaled national hysteria directed against radicalism, the early stages of the Cold War stimulated an attack on American artists, intellectuals, actors, union leaders, and political activists who had been sympathetic to Russia during the 1930s. A generation suddenly convinced of the perils of International Communism placed the preceding generation on trial for being insensitive to such dangers, much as the college generation of the 1960s condemned its fathers for tolerating racism and imperialism. One result was the conviction of eleven leaders of the Communist party of conspiracy to advocate the overthrow of the government by violence. Was this a violation of the First Amendment guarantee of free speech? In deciding the *Dennis* case, the Supreme Court avoided the standards permitting limitations on speech established in the 1920s. Instead, the justices adhered to the ruling of the lower federal judge, Learned Hand, who claimed that the "gravity of the evil" advocated by revolutionaries could be such as to justify restrictions on free speech, even if the chances were slight that that evil should come to pass. Therefore, the Smith Act, under which the eleven men had been prosecuted, was ruled constitutional.

Justices Black and Douglas dissented. Justice Black said that Section 3 of the Smith Act was clearly unconstitutional. Justice Douglas agreed and wrote, in part:

> The Act, as construed, requires the element of intent—that those who teach the creed believe in it. The crime depends not on what is taught but on who the teacher is. That is to make freedom of speech turn not on *what is said*, but on the *intent* with which it is said. Once we start down that road we enter territory dangerous to the liberties of every citizen. . . .[14]

Six years later, the Court membership had changed markedly, and the constitutionality of the Smith Act was again at issue. Fourteen

13. 301 U.S. 1 (1937).
14. *Dennis* v. *United States*, 341 U.S. 494 (1951). Emphasis in the original.

"second-string" members of the Communist party had been convicted
of conspiracy to advocate the overthrow of the government. This
time the Court returned to the "advocacy of action" standard stated
in the *Gitlow* case of 1925.[15] The Smith Act was not invalidated, but
standards of evidence were established which led the government to
drop further Smith Act prosecutions, for they realized that it would
be next to impossible to obtain convictions.

> Throughout the period, Justice Hugo Black maintained his position
> that the guarantees of the First Amendment are absolute; when the
> Constitution says that "Congress shall make no law . . ." it means
> that Congress shall make *no law*.
>
> In the realm of civil liberties, then, Justice Black was a "strict con-
> structionist." Was this what President Nixon had in mind when he
> sought judges who would restore "law and order"?

A New Birth of Freedom

As Earl Warren, former governor of California, was beginning his
term as chief justice of the U.S. Supreme Court in 1953, his personality was analyzed by Professor Fred Rodell of the Yale Law School.

> Unblinded by the Tweedledum-Tweedledee twaddle of much
> that passes for learned legal argument, unblinkered into the
> narrow vision so often typical of those who have past judicial
> experience, he seems essentially a direct plain-spoken politician
> who knows that his is primarily a political job. Of such, when
> they combine humanity with honesty, are judicial statesmen
> made.[16]

Rodell next discussed the dissents entered by Justices Black and
Douglas to the majority decisions of the Truman-appointed Court,
which approved the limitations placed on free speech by a government made nervous by the Cold War. Professor Rodell concluded:

> O'Shaughnessy, the Irish poet, once sang: "For each age is a
> dream that is dying, or one that is coming to birth." Over eight
> score years and five, through age after different age, the men
> who are the Supreme Court of the United States have attended
> the birth and the death of different dreams. Today it would be
> a tragedy if the Black and Douglas dissents—which are rather
> affirmations of a faith—should prove a dirge for the bravest
> dream of all. For under the inspiration of those two great Jus-
> tices and the aegis of a potentially great Chief Justice, the Amer-
> ican dream of freedom may be reborn.[17]

After sixteen years, Chief Justice Earl Warren retired. How did the
American Dream fare at the hands of the Warren Court?

Toward Racial Equality
The landmark decision of the Supreme Court banning racial segre-
gation in the public schools came in 1954. It was the case of *Brown* v.
The Board of Education of Topeka, Kansas. It was the case that, in

15. *Yates* v. *United States*, 354 U.S. 298 (1957).
16. Fred Rodell, *Nine Men* (New York: Random House, 1954), p. 331.
17. Ibid.

essence, made valid law out of Justice John Marshall Harlan's 1896 dissent in *Plessy* v. *Ferguson*.

In reaching the decision, the justices considered social-science findings regarding the damage done to the personalities of children forced to attend segregated schools:

> To separate them from others of similar age and qualifications solely because of their race generates a feeling of inferiority as to their status in the community that may affect their hearts and minds in a way unlikely ever to be undone. . . .
>
> We conclude that in the field of public education the doctrine of "separate but equal" has no place. Separate educational facilities are inherently unequal.[18]

The Court then set a re-hearing of the case to determine what remedy might be provided for the complaining school children. In 1955, the Court fashioned its formula: that public schools should be desegregated "with all deliberate speed," and that lower courts should supervise the process.

School desegregation through the legal process was long and difficult. Lawyers are capable of substituting delay for deliberation. Ten years after the *Brown* case was decided, one of the school districts involved in that case, in Prince Edward County, Virginia, remained segregated. White children attended "private" schools, and their parents received a rebate of county taxes in order to pay the tuition. Black children had no school at all. In the 1964 case of *Griffin* v. *County School Board of Prince Edward County*,[19] Justice Black wrote a biting decision aimed at ending this practice. By 1964, however, Congress caught up with the Supreme Court. Title VI of the Civil Rights Act of 1964 provided that acceptable plans of desegregation would have to be supplied by all school districts before they could receive federal-aid monies. The pace of integration began to accelerate.

The Warren Court also treated other, noneducational, aspects of racial discrimination, including segregation in housing, restaurants, and public transportation; requirements for voting qualification; and miscegenation.

After its degradation in the service of private enterprise, the Fourteenth Amendment was again being used to support the purposes of its authors: to eliminate the "badges of slavery" that prevented all citizens from enjoying equal justice under law.

18. 347 U.S. 483 (1954).
19. 331 U.S. 218 (1964).

Equal Representation

The greatest impact upon the future of American democracy by the Warren Court may, in the future, be designated as a series of cases beginning in 1962 with *Baker* v. *Carr*.[20] At issue was the districting, or "apportionment" (i.e., drawing boundaries of districts from which representatives are elected), of the Tennessee state legislature. The Tennessee Constitution required that district boundaries be adjusted after each census to contain an equal number of residents. But the boundaries had not been changed for fifty years. The task of redistricting was assigned to the legislature, and the Tennessee Constitution provided no alternative if the legislators should refuse to do this duty.

Previous attempts to win the intervention of federal courts in such cases had been denied on the ground that districting is a "political question." This catch-phrase has been used generally to designate cases the Court finds too hot to handle. But it has overtones of the possible invasion of the separation of powers. That is, it may be improper for the judicial branch to tell the legislative branch what to do. In the *Baker* case, the Court held only that the matter could come into federal courts and that clearly something was wrong in Tennessee. Dissenting justices pointed out that the Court was not providing any guidelines to lower federal courts as to what relief might be offered. It was only suggesting that unfair schemes of representation might be prohibited by the Fourteenth Amendment.

The standard of fair representation was soon provided. In *Wesberry* v. *Sanders*,[21] decided in February 1964, and *Reynolds* v. *Sims*,[22] decided in June 1964, the Court held that state legislatures, to be constitutional, must be apportioned with districts of "substantially equal" population. One man, one vote would henceforth be the rule. And this rule should apply even if the people of a state, in a referendum vote, adopted some other plan of apportionment. (This was the holding in *Lucas* v. *Forty-fourth General Assembly of Colorado*.)[23]

The Supreme Court thus attacked one of the most difficult problems of modern American democracy—how in a rapidly changing nation, with a highly mobile population, representative institutions can be made responsive to the public will. Court supporters claimed that, in making state legislatures (and other representative bodies) more responsive to the people, the Court preserved the federal system and countered the tendency of cities to take their problems directly to Washington.

But it was soon clear that the cities needed all the help they could get, from whatever source available. And it was also clear that, while "one man, one vote" was necessary to call state legislatures to their duty, the application of the rule to all legislative bodies did not, by itself, insure fair representation, for computers could provide districts of equal population that were nonetheless politically gerrymandered.

> The Supreme Court justices were accused of "rewriting the Constitution" when they discovered the one man, one vote standard of fair representation to be included in the due process clause of the Fourteenth Amendment. Of course they were. But their predecessors in the 1890s had discovered in the Fourteenth Amendment a vehicle for the protection of corporations against regulation by state legislatures. Court critics who claimed it was usurping unintended powers were more concerned with what interests were affected by decisions than with the propriety of the Court. The Court has always been a political institution.

20. 369 U.S. 186 (1962).
21. 376 U.S. 1 (1964).
22. 377 U.S. 533 (1964).
23. 377 U.S. 713 (1964).

The Standards of Criminal Justice

As late as the 1920s, individual rights guaranteed in the Bill of Rights of the federal Constitution were held to be limitations upon the national government alone. Since then the due process clause of the Fourteenth Amendment has led the Supreme Court to apply many portions of the Bill of Rights to the states. Guarantees of the Bill of Rights may be divided between substantive rights (such as freedom of speech and of the press) and procedural rights (such as trial by jury). The procedural guarantees cover the rights of persons accused of crime. During the decade of the 1960s, the Warren Court used a standard stated in 1937 in the case of *Palko* v. *Connecticut*,[24] holding that those portions of the Bill of Rights are binding upon the states which are "of the very essence of a scheme of ordered liberty." Dealing with issues on a case-by-case basis, the Court has concluded that practically all those rights are essential. These have included the prohibition of unreasonable searches and seizures (including wiretapping); the prohibition of self-incrimination ("no person . . . shall be compelled in any criminal case to be witness against himself"); the right to a speedy trial; the right to a trial by jury; and the right to a lawyer.[25] And, when the trial is over, states may not impose cruel and unusual punishment.

This series of decisions has been called the "due process revolution." It called upon state governments to act with restraint in dealing with individuals on the lowest rung of society's ladder—the impoverished citizen accused of committing a crime.

Police chiefs and public prosecutors complained the Court was tying their hands. Hours of questioning to extract a confession were no longer permitted. The Court, they claimed, didn't understand police work. They forgot that Earl Warren had been a policeman in Berkeley, California, and had served as the district attorney of Alameda County. Perhaps he understood police practices very well indeed. As Tocqueville pointed out long ago, American officials are usually unrestrained in their officially prescribed duties, so long as their actions have the support of the majority. Attentiveness towards the rights of accused criminals does not, it seems, have widespread support within the American electorate. In 1968, candidate Richard Nixon charged that such decisions were strengthening the "criminal forces" at the expense of law and order.

What the "due process revolution" did was to apply to the states those limitations on the procedures of law enforcement officers that had always applied to the national government. Federal law-enforcement agencies—including the FBI—have long operated under these restraints. Is it reasonable to argue that these Supreme Court decisions leave state highway patrolmen and city policemen prostrate and helpless against the advancing forces of crime?

24. 302 U.S. 319 (1937).
25. For a discussion of the "right of counsel" cases, see above, pp. 170-174, 177-178.

Freedom of Speech and of Religion

Earl Warren became chief justice in 1953 when the most lively political issue in the United States, stimulated by the genius for publicity
of Senator Joseph McCarthy of Wisconsin, was the influence of domestic communism. The House Committee on Un-American Activities and a similar Senate subcommittee headed by McCarthy made
frequent headlines. State legislatures also joined the game of Communist hunting. Then in 1957, the Warren Court confirmed in the
Yates case the finding of *Dennis* that free speech may be limited.
With the retirement of Justices Whittaker and Frankfurter, the Court
embarked upon a more liberal construction of the rights of free
speech, free press, and free assembly.

In the late 1960s, political protest was directed against United
States involvement in the Vietnam War. The Court upheld "pure"
free speech against limitations of state authority, as in the *Tinker*
case. But it found that speech *plus action* (such as the burning of
draft cards) could indeed be limited.

In June 1969, the *New York Times* reported that the public school
classes of Clairton, Pennsylvania, and several others in the Mononga-
hela Valley, were holding religious ceremonies. These consisted of
reading of a passage from the Bible followed by the recitation of the
Lord's Prayer. This was a longstanding practice in Pennsylvania,
based upon a 1913 state law. The *Times* pointed out that the Supreme
Court in 1963 had invalidated the Pennsylvania law in the case of the
School District of Abington Township, Pennsylvania v. *Schempp*.[26]

The Warren Court was asked to interpret the meaning of the First
Amendment's declaration that "Congress shall make no law respecting an establishment of religion." Following the logic and precedent
of the *Flag Salute* cases,[27] the Court held in a series of cases culminating in the *Schempp* decision that school boards acting for the states
could not require religious exercises in the public schools.

The Court stated that the First Amendment was "incorporated" as
a limitation upon state governments by the due process clause of the
Fourteenth Amendment. And holding religious services in the public
schools represented a law "respecting an establishment of religion,"
in the words of the First Amendment.

Bible reading in Clairton was resumed because of pressure placed
on the school board by angry parents. The students themselves favored it. A survey by the student council among 201 seniors showed
that 116 favored prayer and Bible reading, 78 favored the former
practice of silent meditation, and only 7 favored no classroom religious observance.

An editorial in the Pittsburgh *Post-Gazette* asked, "How can children be taught to respect the law when their school authorities are
deliberately and boastfully defying it?"

Attorney William E. Duffield, president of the Fayette County
Anti-Tax Protest Committee, replied, "The Boston Tea Party was
illegal, too."

Resistance to the decision in Pennsylvania, where the case arose,
won public attention. But studies of other states revealed that quiet
resistance to the ruling was very common—not because school superintendents were eager to defy the Court, but because school boards
did not seek full knowledge of the decision, and they were determined
above all to avoid the controversies that can threaten the success of
school board elections. In many American states, a public school
teacher who feels that Bible reading is essential to the welfare of his

26. 374 U.S. 203 (1963).
27. *West Virginia State Board of Education* v. *Barnette*, 319 U.S. 624 (1943).

pupils is unlikely to be ordered to change his habits, unless challenged by parents and their lawyer.

The authors of a study of compliance with the *Schempp* decision drew some general conclusions about the likelihood that Supreme Court decisions will be followed.

> We may say with some confidence that (a) the greater the degree of change mandated, or (b) the more the objects are numbers of people rather than visible public officials, or (c) the more the ruling requires local invocation of courts for enforcement, the less likely the ruling is to be obeyed.[28]

That is, the definition of individual rights in the daily dealings of citizens with government remains largely in the hands of governmental officials and bureaucrats. They are most likely to respond to the attitudes of the public as they perceive them, as Tocqueville pointed out so long ago. The pressures of majority opinion are likely to control the expressions of minority opinion quite effectively.

The Limits of Judicial Authority

The wisdom of President Nixon's appointments to the Supreme Court were cited as an argument for his reelection in 1972; the fact that the Senate had rejected two of his appointees was ignored. By then, Mr. Nixon had named four members of the high tribunal; after the next retirement, he would name a fifth, and the Court majority would then consist of Nixon appointees. The impact of his first four appointments was becoming clear; this was a very different institution from that presided over by Chief Justice Earl Warren.

Was the Court beginning to reflect President Nixon's point of view? What would that mean? What are the dimensions of the Supreme Court's authority?

The Court does not serve as legal adviser to the president. He cannot ask in advance whether some action he contemplates is in accord with the Constitution. President George Washington requested such an advisory opinion and was refused, in 1793. Other presidents, and other Courts, have respected that precedent. The opponents of Abe Fortas's nomination as chief justice claimed that he offended the doctrine of the separation of powers by serving, strictly in private, as a counselor to President Lyndon Johnson.

The Supreme Court decides only "cases or controversies" (as specified in Article III of the Constitution) between parties who have "standing to sue." The meaning of the Constitution is determined only when the outcome of the case will affect the legally recognized interest of one of the parties; the Court will be able to "grant relief." This practice severely limits the ability of persons who claim no status other than "taxpayer" to sue the federal government on the basis that tax monies are being misused, for one of many million taxpayers contributes very little toward financing a particular government operation. It is similarly difficult for a devotee of the ecology movement to claim that some industry is damaging the environment and thus harming "the public interest." The "class action" suit has provided a partial solution to such problems, however.[29]

---

28. Kenneth M. Dolbeare and Phillip E. Hammond, "Local Elites, the Impact of Judicial Decisions, and the Process of Change," paper prepared for 65th annual meeting of the American Political Science Association, Washington, D.C., 1969, p. 13.
29. See below, pp. 292-294, for a discussion of "public-interest" lobbying.

Perhaps every American, in the spirit of the Constitution, should be able to take a claim concerning his rights to the Supreme Court. This is not feasible in a nation of 220 million people. Yet the Warren Court, in a case like Clarence Gideon's, reached down to help an impoverished citizen. In 1972, a distinguished commission appointed by Chief Justice Burger recommended the establishment of a new appeals court, which would reduce the number of cases (potentially more than 60,000 a year) for which the Court may consider granting a writ of *certiorari*. (No matter how many cases it considers each year, the Court remains a political institution.)

Although the Constitution specifies that the Supreme Court will have original jurisdiction in some cases (those affecting foreign ambassadors, for example, or when one of the fifty states is a party to the case), nearly all issues considered by the Court are appealed from a lower federal or state court. The Court itself determines which of the cases submitted to it involve a significant issue of constitutional interpretation. Such cases are granted a writ of *certiorari* (Latin for "make more certain") and are then argued before the Court. A case is refused when the justices feel that it is not properly within their jurisdiction, or because they feel that no new interpretation of the law is called for. The Court need not state the reasons for a refusal to grant *certiorari*. All of this means that the Court may have the last word in a controversy, but it will seldom have the first.

Yet in defining the meaning of the phrases of the Constitution, the Court can establish new trends in national policy. John Marshall's Court used the basic document as an instrument for establishing a strong federal government and for protecting the interests of property; Courts in the late nineteenth century made the Constitution the handmaiden of unfettered monopoly capitalism; the "nine old men" of the Court used the Constitution to invalidate the social legislation of Franklin D. Roosevelt's New Deal; and Earl Warren's Court used the Constitution to nudge public officials toward realizing the promise of the Declaration of Independence, that all men — regardless of race or financial status or the popularity of their convictions — are indeed guaranteed equal treatment under the law. In all of these cases, the judges were "activists." They were eager to call other elements of government to an accounting at the bar of the Constitution.

The opposing philosophy of "judicial restraint" holds that Supreme Court judges, appointed for life, do not have a grasp of the intricacies of policy questions comparable to that possessed by elected officials (or even, perhaps, by the cop on the beat). Since other officials are accountable to the public through elections, giving the people the ultimate weapon of the removal power, the justices should make a "strong presumption" that the actions of the other branches of government do, in fact, conform to the Constitution. A finding of unconstitutionality should only be made upon the strongest of evidence and the deepest of soul-searching. For, in an orderly system, policy innovations come from the legislature, not the judiciary.

Furman v. *Georgia*,[30] the death penalty case, showed these two approaches at work. Each justice wrote a separate opinion. All nine justices tended to agree that the death penalty does not deter crime; the main reason for its retention by an otherwise civilized nation is a public desire for visible revenge upon the criminal. Justices Marshall and Douglas felt that the time had come to put aside the essentially barbaric practice, and that the Court should lead the way.

30. 408 U.S. 238 (1972). See above, p. 180.

The justices appointed by President Nixon agreed, in essence, that the death penalty is barbaric, serves little purpose, and causes great anguish in judges who impose it. But they felt that only Congress can decide when the time has come to abolish it.

A Healthy Constitution?

Some of the most notable justices of the Supreme Court have been proponents of the philosophy of judicial restraint. Oliver Wendell Holmes tended to be an activist in the field of civil liberties but chose restraint in questions of economic regulation. Certainly, if the system established by the Constitution is working well, the Court need not perform an activist role. For the grievances of minorities will find a hearing in the legislature, and they will be dealt with justly to protect good order, which is in the public interest to maintain. If the Constitution is healthy, President Nixon's desire to appoint "strict constructionist" judges who will practice judicial restraint is a very sensible desire.

But is the Constitution healthy?

Consider two landmark areas in which the Warren Court flew its activist colors: legislative apportionment and racial desegregation. In neither field was the Court's action taken hastily. The legislatures of Tennessee and Alabama, required by their state constitutions to reapportion their legislatures every ten years, had taken no action within the twentieth century. The entire development of twentieth-century urbanization had taken place in those states, and in several others, with no adjustment in the system of legislative representation. Legislatures in which rural areas were overrepresented created federal congressional districts in which rural areas predominated, leaving the cities without adequate voice in either state or national legislative branches.

State courts could provide little relief. The Supreme Court considered the issue as early as 1946, dismissing a challenge to the congressional districting of the state of Illinois on the ground that it was a "political question," which could be settled only through the electoral process by the people of Illinois.[31] In 1946, the Court could perhaps assume that an enraged urban population would somehow force state legislatures to perform the duties assigned by the constitutions of their own states. By 1962, when *Baker* v. *Carr* came before the Court, the error of that assumption was clear. The "one man, one vote" doctrine promised city voters at least symbolic access to the political process from which they had been systematically excluded for decades.

The school integration decision was neither hasty nor ill-considered. In the *Plessy* case of 1896,[32] the Court had sanctioned legal segregation. The line of cases which would reverse *Plessy* began in 1938[33] and culminated with the *Brown* decision of 1954;[34] sixteen years were required for the Court to complete the reversal of the "separate but equal" doctrine that ruled for nearly sixty years. At no time in that period was there an indication that the cause of black Americans would be seriously and successfully championed by any

31. *Colegrove* v. *Green*, 328 U.S. 549 (1946).
32. *Plessy* v. *Ferguson*, 163 U.S. 537 (1896). Also see pp. 194-195, 201, and 332.
33. *Missouri ex rel. Gaines* v. *Canada*, 305 U.S. 337 (1938) was the first in a series of cases dealing with educational segregation. Others were *Sipuel* v. *Board of Regents of the University of Oklahoma*, 322 U.S. 631 (1948); *McLaurin* v. *Oklahoma State Regents*, 399 U.S. 637 (1950); and *Sweatt* v. *Painter*, 399 U.S. 629 (1950).
34. *Brown* v. *Board of Education of Topeka*, 347 U.S. 483 (1954)

other segment of government. Black people seeking equal treatment from the officials of their states could not turn to the very state legislatures that established the legal basis of segregation, nor could they find help from a Congress in which southern conservatives were so powerful. Their cause could be advanced in only minimal ways through Executive Orders of the president, such as President Truman's order that the armed forces be racially integrated. The Supreme Court was the only real hope.

The "right to counsel" cases constituted the intervention of the Supreme Court in behalf of impoverished citizens in their confrontation with local law-enforcement agencies. Again, the Supreme Court provided access. Its decisions, speaking with the force of a national conscience, reminded Americans that the Constitution applies to *all* citizens, regardless of their race, financial position, or place of residence.

> This ability to speak as the national conscience, when no other public officials will do so, delineating the rights of the least powerful members of American society, may not be found among the "strict constructionist" judges sought by President Nixon.
>
> If the system were healthy, it would not be needed.
>
> Who can say, with conviction, in the 1970s, that the nation no longer needs a conscience?

Obedience to Supreme Court Decisions

Of what use is a conscience, if it is not listened to? This question summarizes the dilemma of the Supreme Court. Joseph Stalin once asked of the Pope, "How many battalions does he command?" The Supreme Court has no forces at its disposal to assure that its decisions will be honored. If the Court gets too far in advance of public opinion, and the president, Congress, and local officials refuse to accept the decisions of the Court as relevant to the operations of their own consciences, the decision of the Court will not succeed in establishing new national policy.

Decisions of the Warren Court again demonstrate this principle at work. The legislative apportionment decisions called forth immediate action. By 1968, one or both houses of the legislatures of forty-nine states had been reapportioned in accordance with the distribution of population. The ruling of the Court ("one man, one vote") was clear and easily implemented by lower courts. The objects of the decisions were highly visible public officials (state legislators). Whether or not the Court's policy was being followed was easy to determine. Those legislatures failing to follow it could be readily identified and easily challenged in the courts.

Matters were not so straightforward in the integration and school prayer cases. The school desegregation ruling was clear (racial segregation sanctioned by the state is unconstitutional), but the remedy ("with all deliberate speed") was vague. The objects of the decision were hundreds of school boards with changing memberships and various degrees of sensitivity to the requirements of constitutional law. Furthermore, the desegregation decision attacked deep-seated feelings of racial superiority in a manner that the reapportionment decisions did not. The dual school systems of the South have now been substantially dismantled. But this result came only after the involvement of Congress and the executive branch in the question, and the agony of the civil rights movement. The question of de facto school segregation in the North is not resolved at this writing.

The school prayer decisions required the adoption of new policies by individual principals, teachers, and school boards, often located in areas that do not closely follow the trend of events in Washington. It required invocation of court assistance on the local level to be enforced. Parents who objected to the recitation of prayers by their children in the public schools could risk the ostracism of their neighbors if they insisted that local schools adhere to the Court's policy. However, if they were willing to take that risk, they would have the Supreme Court of the United States on their side.

The Warren Court is gone now. The path to be followed by the new Court is not yet certain. President Nixon's appointees are called "conservatives," but judicial conservatism includes a deep respect for the evolution of the law. The Warren precedents cannot be overturned wholesale, or immediately, although the Nixon Court's rulings on pornography show a different interpretation of the First Amendment.

Yet — in a vast, bureaucratic society, governed in accord with the wishes of society — will individual citizens and groups out of tune with majority opinion turn so readily to the federal courts for the defense of their rights? Will they find succor there?

Two great principles support the legitimacy of American government. The first is that the majority rules, through the mechanism of elections. The second is that certain fundamental principles, including the rights of individuals, are not subject to majority decision, but are guaranteed to all. The creative role of the Supreme Court lies in the area where these principles come into conflict.

Judicial activism is not praiseworthy in the abstract. The crucial question is not whether the Court justices uphold the actions of other branches of government. Rather, it is whether their decisions advance the cause of democracy, with all its nobility and contradictions.

Policemen, Judges, and Prisons

Most citizens are hardly acquainted with the Supreme Court decisions that give modern meaning to the phrases of the Constitution. But they have a great deal of contact with the streets of their own neighborhood, and they may have fears of the streets in other neighborhoods. "Law and order" has a concrete meaning. Yet, "justice" is somebody else's business, until the citizen himself confronts the power of the law.

Lawyers can spend weeks with their books, seeking precedents and refining arguments. Judges are well paid to apply the concepts involved in "justice." Professors can agonize in print over the social causes of individual maladjustment, but a convicted criminal can only expect punishment. Behind the bars, he will have months or years to pay his debt to society and plan how to please his parole board.

The "system of criminal justice" depends above all upon the policeman. He is its agent and symbol on the streets. He wields the power of government to limit the life and liberty of the citizen. The decision about who is arrested and who goes free, who lives and who dies, is made on the spot. It is made by the cop on the beat.

The Trial of Ronald August

Ronald August's trial was held in the county courthouse in Mason, Michigan, county seat of Ingham County. The courthouse in Mason is like a hundred others in midwestern towns. It forms the center of the town square. The shade trees are tall, and there are benches for the old men who gather at courthouses. The courthouse probably seemed elegant when it was completed, but it has grown dirty and dismal with age. The solidity that once symbolized the permanence of the law now only contributes to an air of outmoded ugliness. On the lawn, there is a monument to the dead soldiers of the Union Army, as if that were the one event in a hundred years to disturb the town's pattern of life.

Mason has about 5,000 people. It is not far from Lansing, Michigan's capital. But it is ninety miles from Detroit. So far that the flames of the 1967 Detroit riot did not light up the sky east of Mason. In the summer of 1969, a Mason jury was asked to consider the impact of that riot on the policemen called out to control it—and on the people who were caught in it.

Ronald August was a Detroit policeman. He was suspended in 1967, when he admitted involvement in the incident at the Algiers Motel, which later became the subject of a best-selling book by novelist John Hersey.[1] Ronald August's trial was delayed because of the book. So many people had read it, the defense attorney argued, that finding an unbiased jury would be difficult. After several delays, the trial was finally moved to Mason. Such a "change in venue" is often requested when an alleged crime receives so much publicity that a fair trial seems unlikely in the community where the crime took place.

By the usual random procedures, a jury of eleven women and one man was impaneled in Mason. All were white. Neither side accused the other of wanting an all-white jury; but Mason has few blacks. In his charge to the jury, Circuit Judge William Beer declared:

> This is not a racial trial. It was not brought to Mason to insure an all-white jury. Justice wears a blindfold. Our court must be colorblind. You must not reach a verdict that is based in any way on prejudice or on sympathy.[2]

Malcolm Little spent his early boyhood in a four-room house outside East Lansing, Michigan. He would win fame as Malcolm X; toward the end of his life, he would take the name of El-Hajj Malik El-Shabazz. But his memories of Michigan remained vivid:

> In East Lansing, no Negroes were allowed on the streets . . . after dark. . . . Every town had a few "home" Negroes who lived there. Sometimes it would be just one family, as in the nearby county seat, Mason, which had a single Negro family named Lyons. Mr. Lyons had been a famous football star at Mason High School, was highly thought of in Mason, and consequently he now worked around that town in menial jobs.[3]

Riot Duty

In the summer of 1967, Ronald August was twenty-eight years old. He was a five-year veteran of the Detroit police force. He played the clarinet in the police band, was a parishioner of St. Raymond's Roman Catholic Church, and the father of two small daughters. Fellow patrolmen described him as a "good family man" who regarded police work as a job to be done, rather than a special calling.

On Sunday, July 23, 1967, his day off, Ronald August was called back to duty by the police department. He was called at 7 A.M. After four hours of waiting in a precinct station, he was assigned to street duty, relieving a group of policemen who were obviously exhausted. He was amazed to see that the police simply stood guard in the streets without attempting to prevent the widespread looting of stores in the riot-torn area. He remained on duty until the early hours of Monday morning and returned to duty Monday noon. On Monday, he spent some time beneath his squad-car, for protection against apparent sniper fire. On Tuesday, after learning of the death of a popular fellow officer, he went to the Algiers Motel in response to reports of sniper fire.

---

1. John Hersey, *The Algiers Motel Incident* (New York: Knopf, 1968). This account of events in the Algiers Motel is based on material in Mr. Hersey's book.
2. *San Francisco Chronicle*, June 4, 1969.
3. *The Autobiography of Malcolm X* (New York: Grove Press, 1966), p. 7.

The Swinging Time Review

On Sunday afternoon, July 23, the Fox Theater on Woodward Avenue in Detroit was holding an annual week-long music show called the Swinging Time Revue. One of the groups consisted of five young black men who had played together since junior high school and had cut some records. They were called the Dramatics.

As the Dramatics finished their performance, the announcer came on stage to cancel the rest of the performances. He said that a riot had broken out, and recommended that the audience return to their homes. The Dramatics got on a Woodward Avenue bus. After several blocks, the bus was stopped by policemen who said there was shooting just ahead and the bus would not be allowed through. When the boys got off the bus, they saw the Algiers Motel across the street. The boys had just been paid fifty dollars each for their performance. With no way to get home, they saw the Algiers as a shelter, and also as an adventure. None had spent many nights away from home. They went across to the Algiers Motel and rented a room. They called their mothers to report they were safe and would be home later.

They met some friends at the Algiers and were introduced to two white girls, Juli and Karen, who lived there. The Dramatics stayed in the Algiers Motel Sunday night and all of Monday and Tuesday, watching television, shooting craps, using the swimming pool, and playing records. They called home again. Flames and the sounds of gunfire swept the city.

Around midnight on Tuesday, one of the boys took a small pistol, the kind used by track officials to start races, and fired two blank shots. His friends who were the "targets" did an elaborate pantomime of being shot down. It was a game of cops and robbers, or Wild West, played against the background of the real thing. (The pistol has never been found.)

The noise of the gun was heard by a National Guardsman assigned to protect the Great Lakes Mutual Life Insurance building, across the street from the Algiers Motel. He radioed a report of sniper fire to his headquarters. After this was transferred to the city police headquarters, it was received by Patrolman August and his two companions as a report that "the Army was under heavy fire."

When August and his companions arrived at the Algiers Motel Annex, they found various National Guardsmen and highway patrolmen already there. In the motel hallway were lined up eight black youths and the two white girls. August and his companions, Patrolmen Senak and Paille, joined in the search for the suspected sniper. The first search revealed nothing. Law officers returned to the ten people lined up in the hall. One by one, the suspects were systematically beaten. The policemen were particularly upset at the presence of the white girls and the hint of interracial sex. After the men had been bloodied, the girls had their clothes ripped away, until clad only in their panties. One unit of state patrolmen went away; they did not like what was going on in the Algiers Motel.

In the next effort to find a gun or sniper, young men were taken away one by one from the line-up in the hallway to nearby bedrooms. They were then told to lie down and be silent. A shot was fired. The law enforcement officials returned to the line-up and said that the person had been shot. The others must reveal the hiding place of the sniper and his weapon or share the same fate. It was a game of intimidation, a war of nerves.

But was it only a game? Three black youths were left dead in bedrooms of the Algiers Motel—Carl Cooper, age seventeen, Fred Temple, age eighteen, and Auburey Pollard, age nineteen. Patrolman Ronald August was tried for the murder of Auburey Pollard.

The Verdict

Ronald August's defense attorney claimed that the conditions in Detroit were nothing less than the conditions of war. The shooting of Auburey Pollard, he claimed, was "justifiable homicide committed under battle conditions."

If battle conditions existed by early Wednesday morning in Detroit, they had been created by the police, the highway patrol, and the National Guard. (Regular troops of the U.S. Army were also there. Unlike the National Guard, they obeyed orders not to fire.) On several occasions, when snipers were reported, National Guard tanks pulled up and directed machine gun fire upon the closest buildings. One young girl was killed when her uncle, standing in the window, lit a cigarette. The flash of his lighter was seen by the troops below as a discharging rifle.

Neither the governor of Michigan nor the president of the United States knew what to do about the violence in Detroit. Ronald August's attorney suggested that he could hardly be blamed if he became confused.

Patrolman August stated that he did indeed take Auburey Pollard into one of the motel bedrooms. But, he said, the shooting occurred when Pollard tried to snatch the shotgun away from him. In the scuffle, the gun discharged.

Judge Beer ruled that, as a matter of law, the jury must find Ronald August either guilty of murder in the first degree or innocent. If guilty, August would be sentenced to life imprisonment, which could only be reduced by a governor's pardon. (Capital punishment is outlawed in Michigan.) If innocent, he would go free. In most Michigan murder cases, the jury is empowered to reduce the charge to second degree murder or to manslaughter. In this case, the judge ruled that no reduced charge would be possible. For the prosecution's case was intended to prove that Ronald August deliberately and with careful forethought did murder Auburey Pollard.

The jury deliberated for two hours and fifty minutes. It concluded that Ronald August was innocent.

Rebecca Pollard, the mother of Auburey, wept bitterly, "I didn't look for them to find him guilty. All whites stick together."[4]

A Patrolman in Harlem

The storybook policeman of the early twentieth century earned the name "flatfoot." He patrolled on foot. He could spend years in a single neighborhood, and he became a fixture in it. The citizens for whom he preserved order came to regard him as a friend. And he performed important social services — calming family quarrels, interceding with the local political organization, finding jobs, helping drunks find their way home, calling for medical assistance.

All that changed. Social work agencies were developed. Policemen were put in cars and dispatched by radio. They could cover a

4. *Time*, June 20, 1969, p. 17.

larger area with greater efficiency, and concentrate on crime and its prevention.

But policemen descending from patrol cars could not always count on cooperation in a poor neighborhood; more than just efficiency was needed. The foot patrolman is coming into his own again. In New York, one of them is Jeremiah William Dunlop, age thirty-six, white. A six-year veteran of the force, he is on duty from four to midnight, in Harlem. Eighth Avenue, from 139th to 145th Streets.

Dunlop greets people in the street by name. He says he likes people. He points out it would be hard to survive in this area without the support of the community. He says, "When there's trouble, sometimes the friends will help you out." He adds, "Sometimes they won't."

The reporter who accompanied Dunlop on his beat wrote of Dunlop's area:

> The pedestrian arguments that continually rage on the streets would be arrestable offenses anywhere else. Petty thievery is almost overlooked for the welter of major thefts. The traffic offenses in a single block could keep a nightcourt busy for a week. . . .
>
> "You have to use judgment," said Dunlop. "If I arrested everybody who was breaking the law, I'd never get anything done. You have to use discretion."
>
> A man stops the cop and asks for a dollar. "I'm in a crap game," he says. "Give me a buck. What's it to you, anyway? Come on, give me a buck."
>
> Quietly, Dunlop refuses. "What the hell's the matter, cop?" the man continues. "What you got against black people? What's the matter, you don't like black people?"
>
> Legally, the man can be nailed. Dunlop, however, avoids arrest. He bites his lip until finally the man goes away. Dunlop explains that the offense was minor, that an arrest could have led to bigger trouble, perhaps violence. And as for his abused pride? "I'm a cop," he says simply, "I'm used to it."[5]

Dunlop continues on his beat. On Lennox Avenue, a man is stabbed in the head during an argument. The police say the victim will not sign a complaint if he recovers; he is too frightened of his attacker. A woman suffers a heart attack in a fifth floor room on 144th Street. The street is crowded, the stairway winding and cluttered, and the police spend thirty critical minutes moving her to the ambulance. On Eighth Avenue a woman comes out of a grocery store. A boy grabs her purse and runs out of sight.

On 142nd Street, there is a homicide.

Dunlop learns that some of the police call-boxes on his beat may be booby-trapped. They could explode when used. It is an old story. So far, it has never been more than rumor. A stout woman stops Dunlop outside a pawn shop and asks for help. She tells a confused story about a dollar being snatched from her by a young boy. Dunlop hails a bus and puts the woman aboard.

The next day is Dunlop's day off. He will inspect a home he is buying on Long Island. A colonial design, it has four bedrooms. The mortgage will amount to $20,000. It will be the first time that Dunlop, his wife, and his four children have lived outside an apartment building. To finance the house, Dunlop has taken a second job, driving a taxi twenty hours a week. Says Dunlop, "This city is just no place for people to live."

5. Tim Tiede, "A Night on the Harlem Beat with Policeman Dunlop," *Santa Cruz Sentinel,* July 25, 1968, p. 22.

Blue Power

When John Lindsay was elected mayor of New York, a major campaign promise was to modify the Review Board, which had existed since 1955. The purpose of the board was to handle complaints against police, but its decisions were controlled by the majority of its members, who were policemen. Lindsay expanded the membership of the board and installed a civilian majority.

The Police Benevolent Association (PBA), with the aid of at least half a million dollars and a professional public relations agency, campaigned against the Civilian Review Board in a referendum election. Ads suggested that the police force should be kept free of politics. Ads further suggested that Lindsay's Review Board would insure an increase in street crime. In November 1966, the voters of New York turned down the Civilian Review Board by a three-to-one margin. There is still a board, but all its members are policemen.

Since then, Mayor Lindsay and the Police Benevolent Association have clashed on several occasions. And a second association has been formed to represent the opinions of the rank-and-file patrolmen. It is called the Law Enforcement Group (LEG). Its attitudes are even more hawkish toward potential criminals than those of the PBA.

Since then,

Former Mayor Carl Stokes of Cleveland indicated that maintaining civilian control of the police is a major problem, not only in Cleveland, but in most cities.

In both Cleveland and Los Angeles, police have gone directly to the ballot for pay raises or retirement benefits when the city councils refused them.

In Los Angeles, three bond issues have passed to build more police facilities while school bond measures have been rejected.

Across the nation, police lobbyists have imitated the tactics of the California Peace Officers Association, one of the most effective lobbying organizations in Sacramento.

Years ago, sirens were removed from Philadelphia police cars. When asked about it, a police official who did not wish to be named replied that the patrolmen were really rather adolescent. The sirens were used too often when they weren't needed.
Of course, the policemen still have their guns.

What Is to Be Done

The recommendations are all familiar. The police need better pay and better training. Somehow, the job has to be made attractive to college graduates. Police forces should adopt the new technology: computer linkages providing instant information about the identity of stolen automobiles and the criminal records of arrested suspects; better communications; more money and energy for "police-community relations" programs. And integrate! The percentage of minority members on the force should match the percentage in the city.

But the police chiefs were in trouble. Many forces were hit with waves of early resignations. Recruitment lagged. At least 50,000 police jobs went unfilled across the nation. The recruiters went to the army posts where Vietnam veterans were being released from the service. Young men who entered the armed services before choosing an occupation might feel that their experience in uniform provided them with training leading to a new career.

To Each His Own Prejudice

All through the 1950s, the concentration of blacks increased in the central cities. Living conditions grew worse, and unemployment increased. The policemen came into the ghettos, looking for criminals, expecting cooperation and respect from everyone else. The hint of an attitude of anything less than deference seemed threatening, and they reacted.

Every morning, past midnight, brutally beaten black men were brought into the accident wards of major cities, presumably the losers of tavern brawls. But they were not injured with knives or guns. Hospital workers soon realized that these were the victims of "questioning" in the back seats of police cruisers. Nobody—not the nurses, not the accident ward doctors, not the politicians, least of all the police commissioners—questioned what was going on. The beaten men were charged with resisting arrest.

The pattern was not universal. Police brutality was the exception, not the rule. But each isolated incident was talked about in the ghettos. Policemen as a group were judged by the lowest common denominator, and the growing hatred of the blue uniform was expressed. Screamed obscenities stimulated further police violence. Policemen felt they could win respect only by showing superior strength. Black Power advocates would soon preach the need for self-defense.

But people outside the ghettos paid little attention. Dwight Eisenhower was president, seeking world peace. In 1960, John Kennedy brought new style and hope to the White House, but proposed no civil rights legislation. He needed southern Democratic votes for other measures in Congress. Legislation was proposed after Martin Luther King was jailed in Birmingham. Then the young president's life was taken, and his assassin in turn was murdered, while in the custody of the Dallas police force.

With John Kennedy buried in Arlington, and the eternal flame lit over his grave, Lyndon Johnson broke the logjam in Congress. Among the new laws was the Civil Rights Act of 1964. But the growing crisis of the northern cities could not be resolved by assuring voting rights for black people and the integration of public facilities in the South. Beginning with Watts in 1965, the ghettos exploded. Hundreds of other cities knew violence in the following years. Perhaps the importance of police behavior in precipitating the urban crisis was not clear in Oakland, or in Newark, or in Paterson, New Jersey. But the events surrounding the 1968 Democratic National Convention in Chicago made news around the world, and the problems faced by city police in handling angry crowds were painfully clear. Their lack of preparation for the task was also clear. The treatment of the Chicago demonstrators was labelled "a police riot."

There was a new birth of concern. The social commentators, and their audiences, including the liberal professors, discovered the police as a new "problem" for study. The police, on the other hand, prepared to defend themselves against criticism and sought conspirators to blame for inciting the riots. They were determined to fend off intrusions by outsiders.

Shocked by a pattern of events that seemed beyond control, each side felt a pressing need for action. And each side felt that its own understanding of reality was complete enough for action. Further study was not called for.

Listen to Professor William P. Brown. He is in a position to understand the prejudices of both groups. A retired Inspector of the New York City police, he teaches at the School of Criminal Justice at the Albany campus of the State University of New York.

Particularly in reference to the racial crisis, policemen and professors have assumed an unprecedented importance to our society, and, in a bitter debate as to whether we are headed toward
a police state or an unpoliced state, they have developed a mutually acrimonious relationship which bears significantly on our
prospects for reaching any solution to that crisis.

The scripts which the members of each group carry into their
discussions of the disorder problems show surprising similarities, if one basic rule of the game is recognized: policemen
speak only of blacks in connection with disorder and control;
professors addressing the same topic speak only of policemen.
Otherwise, in tone and content police views of black protestors
mirror many professorial views of the police who deal with
black protestors.

The policeman is worried about "Black Power." He wants
"law and order" restored. He is convinced—along, incidentally,
with a large percentage of the remainder of the blue-collar class
—that the main reason why crime is so frighteningly rampant is
that black activists have not been forced to comply with the
law. More stringent enforcement, a removal of the "kid gloves,"
is his remedy. The academic is worried about the growth in police power. He wants "due process," as reflected in the Supreme
Court restrictions on police power, fully respected. At least in
conversation, he sees a wide spectrum of causation for the problems of the day, but police violence constitutes a focal point
against which he can be definitely opposed. The Daniel Walker
Report on the Chicago riot or the John Hersey dramatization of
the Algiers Motel incident are cited as pictures of the general
pattern of police oppression, rather than as descriptions of iso-

lated incidents. The professor is convinced that only strong repressive action against the police can preserve freedom in our time.

The actions and opinions of each group are, of course, influenced by the stereotypes its members hold. Police view blacks and professors view police with greater awareness than ever before, but in terms of brutish, cardboard-thin caricatures and unrealistic expectations. The policeman's black activist is a dangerous figure. He has replaced the Negro of pre-1960, that passive, rather subhuman member of an isolated world characterized by crime and social and personal degradation. He exudes hate rather than apathy, and he hates the policeman most of all. Black protesters are assumed to be tied to radical groups. The word radical still has more than a slight coloration of Communist, and connotes overall, centrally directed planning of illegal and subversive activities. . . .

[In the view of the professor, the policeman] has the basic attributes of brutality and stupidity, rendered more dangerous by ignorance, insecurity and the lust for power and violent expression which led him into police work in the first place. . . . The professor is enamored of simple solutions from times recently but definitely past. Like the civil libertarians of yesterday, his major answer is to stop the police from committing illegal actions. Excesses from the protest side are ignored, the general view being that their control is not really a problem, that any effort other than to eliminate underlying conditions which resulted in the protest is somehow authoritarian and improper.[6]

Professor Brown called upon the professors to be true to their calling as scholars. He asked them to act only after investigation, to support proper police practice, and to work toward orderly reforms, avoiding the easy assumption that protesters are always right, police always wrong.

"Pig"

Black detective Ollie Glover of the Richmond, California, Police Department drove along a busy main street. At an intersection, he saw two small black girls standing at the curbing. They wanted to cross the street, but they were frightened by the cars zooming past.

Glover brought the police car to an abrupt halt. "Okay, little girls, come on and cross," he called.

When the girls reached the other side of the street, they turned and waved to him. "Thank you, pig," they called.

Pawns of the White Man

What is it like to be a black policeman? Police forces can be tight little societies. To be accepted, you don't dare disagree with the common values. Black policemen report that they must prove themselves in the eyes of their white colleagues by their treatment of black people. They must demonstrate no favoritism—and the best way to show no favoritism is to deal more harshly with blacks than with anyone else.

As the agony of the cities comes increasingly to be symbolized as a confrontation between police and blacks, what is the special role of the black policeman? Here is an explanation published as long ago as 1969:

6. William P. Brown, "Mirrors of Prejudice," *The Nation*, April 21, 1969, pp. 498-499.

> The white police administration has used black police against
> black people. This is the only reason black policemen are hired
> . . . black policemen have only one useful function and that is
> as pawns of the white man to be used against black people.[7]

The statement hardly seems astonishing. It could have been taken
from any collection of black militant rhetoric. The remarkable point
is that it was published by the Afro-American Patrolmen's League of
Chicago. It is one of the new associations of black policemen willing
to disagree openly with white colleagues over the treatment of black
people. Black policemen were slow in accepting militant tactics, and
many of the older black policemen are still uninterested in political
action. But the crisis of the cities can only be alleviated by changes
in attitude, and it was inevitable that black policemen would have
to declare whose side they are on.

In New York, the militant black policemen's association is called
the Guardians. The Guardians supported Lindsay's Civilian Review
Board, breaking away from the white Patrolmen's Benevolent Association. Explained a spokesman, "we had nothing to hide from black
people."

The black policeman should have a very special role in holding the
cities together. So far, he has not found it; nor are there signs that his
white colleagues will grant him this special role.

But what is the appropriate role of any policeman, white or black?
What exactly do we expect him to do? We supply him with a gun and
a badge, and we grant him the authority to use force, if necessary, to
maintain the law. Yet we also demand that he prevent violence and
treat all citizens with total respect for their rights.

In June 1968, Mayor Lindsay presented the New York Police Department's highest awards to twenty-six patrolmen and detectives for
being the city's most outstanding policemen in 1967. Three of the
awards were presented posthumously. All went to men who had been
in gun battles with armed criminals. None was won for other important aspects of police work, such as preventing a riot or conducting
an investigation that led to the non-violent arrest of a notable
criminal.

It had long been a tradition that the New York patrolman who
gets into a gun battle is the most likely candidate for promotion to
detective.

Testing by Ordeal

> *Chicago, Aug. 1, 1972 (Associated Press).* Two psychologists
> testified yesterday that their tests showed that 20 percent of
> Chicago policemen were "calculated risks" and were assigned
> to black, Spanish-speaking or poor white neighborhoods to
> "make or break them."
>
> Avrum Mendelsohn and Arnold Abrams testified at the
> last of four hearings called by Representative Ralph Metcalfe
> (Dem.–Ill.) to investigate complaints of police brutality. . . .
>
> Abrams, a psychologist with the Chicago City College sys-
> tem, testified that more than 20 percent of the city's policemen
> needed counseling for psychological difficulties, compared with
> 8 percent of the general population.

7. Quoted in the *San Francisco Chronicle*, September 9, 1969.

Not all police work—or even most of it—involves the use, or threat, of violence. Much more energy is devoted to keeping traffic flowing, getting old cars off the street, collecting drunks from the sidewalks, carrying sick people to the hospital, and interceding in marital squabbles.

In Washington, D.C., Internal Revenue Service lawyer George Grindle reported that his 1951 De Soto, which he maintained with loving care as a prize antique, was towed away by the police and crushed into scrap metal a few days after being ticketed for illegal parking at another location. "How could they have done it?" lamented Grindle. "It was parked on private property. It had up-to-date license plates and new tires."

Police Chief Robert Porter of the Washington suburb of Takoma Park said, "We were wrong. There's no doubt in my mind about it."[8]

The remarkable fact may be that policemen make as few mistakes as they do. After all, they are only human. When the police have done their work, the accused comes before a judge. Here, perhaps, he will see the majesty of the law at work, striving for disinterested justice.

More likely, if he enters the overcrowded court system of a large American city, he will confront the practice of "plea bargaining." Faced with crowded dockets, judges sanction the making of deals between the prosecution and defense attorneys. The charge is reduced to a lesser offense if the accused will plead guilty ("cop a plea"), thus avoiding the time and expense of a trial. Will he ever again believe that all are presumed innocent until proven guilty?

How to Become a Judge

The *Chicago Tribune* sent a task force of reporters to investigate the attitudes and careers of the 128 circuit court judges of Cook County, Illinois. Their first finding was that four out of five judges cheerfully admitted that they won a place on the bench by working their way up through the ranks of the party organization, beginning as precinct captains or ward organizers.

A classic account was offered by Judge Herbert R. Friedlund, aged sixty-three. Friedlund began his story in 1956, when he ran for county clerk as a Republican against Edward Barrett, a Democrat and close associate of Mayor Richard J. Daley.

> "You see, all the newspapers predicted that Eddie Barrett would beat me by 500,000 votes in the county clerk's race," Friedlund explained. "Well, he won by only 147,000 votes and I got a million votes.
>
> "Later on, Barrett said to Mayor Daley, 'Any guy that can get a million votes against me should be on my side.' And Daley said that he was right, anybody that could do that should be on his side. So, when 1960 came along, he asked me if I wanted to be a Democrat. I said I did."
>
> Then came the crucial conversation with Daley that would lead to a seat on the bench. Friedlund recalls it this way:
>
> Daley: "What do you want?"
>
> Friedlund: "I'd like a judgeship."

8. Reuters dispatch, *San Francisco Chronicle*, November 28, 1972.

Daley: "You do good work for us and you will be a judge. I think you should be one. I think you're qualified for it. Anybody who can poll a million votes against Eddie Barrett deserves to be on the bench if he wants to."

Friedlund: "That's my ambition."

Daley: "I'll back you."

"And the Mayor stuck by that," said Friedlund. "He was the only politician who ever kept his promise to me."[9]

The Chicago Bar Association proposes to replace the election of judges with an appointive system "based on merit." Candidates for appointment would be screened from the upper ranks of the legal profession by the Bar Association itself. John S. Boyle, Chicago's elected chief judge of the circuit court, replies that the electoral process is more likely to award judgeships to ethnic minorities and assure judicial representation to all segments of society. Judges nominated by the Bar Association, he says, would principally represent the wealthier classes and the corporations.

The charge leveled against judges who regard their office as the summit of a successful political career—a reward to be enjoyed—is not that they are unfair or corrupt. They tend to be quite honorable men. It is, rather, that they conduct court affairs according to habits established fifty years ago. They have no youthful energy, no understanding of modern record-keeping techniques, no new ideas at all. The courts groan under the load produced by an increased population and the growing urban crime rate related to drug abuse. Overburdened in this way, the courts are not able to handle with speed or efficiency the many civil cases that involve no criminal charge, such as settling liability claims arising from an automobile accident.

Justice remains an abstract notion. But one of its most commonly stated principles holds that "justice delayed is justice denied."

After the Trial Is Over

When the attorneys have argued and the jury votes, the accused can become a convict. Then he goes to prison. American prisons are increasingly overcrowded, understaffed, and unhealthy. In many states, they are known as "correctional facilities," in honor of the theory that they will take the outcasts and misfits of society, educate and rehabilitate them, and restore them to fruitful lives.

In fact, the overwhelming number of prisoners are those who have been in prison before. The rate of successful rehabilitation is low. At least two-thirds of those released from prison are convicted of new crimes and returned for further "correction." The prison system seems to confirm lawbreaking behavior, rather than changing it.

9. *Chicago Tribune*, May 17, 1971.

Think of all the city jails that are crowded with prisoners who have not been convicted of any crime but are detained awaiting trial. They cannot afford to post bail. Thus they must wait for the wheels of justice to grind, while they live in institutions that are most effective in serving a purpose for which they were not intended — training habitual criminals. If acquitted, they will probably have no job to return to, for someone else was hired during their stay in jail. "Justice delayed is justice denied" — but the rich man can afford the bail bond.

Attica

Twelve miles to the south of the New York State Throughway, in the green rolling hills of the fertile upstate agricultural district, lies the town of Attica. Its population is less than 3,000. With seven churches, a few banks, and a movie theater closed some years ago because of competition with television, it resembles a thousand other American towns.

But such a "skyline" as the buildings of Attica offer is dominated by the dismal turrets and thirty-foot-high walls surrounding the fifty-five acres of a major "correctional facility," one of the leading links in the New York prison chain. It is an "end-of-the-line" prison; many of the inmates are sent there because they have caused trouble in other prisons, and are serving life sentences. In 1971, it was also used to house first-offenders being introduced to the prison system. It was a harsh place, and the prison administration did not differentiate between first-offenders and hardened convicts.

The prison was the leading "industry," with the largest payroll, in Attica. The 383 guards were residents of Attica and the surrounding countryside. They were all white. In 1971, the Attica Prison held 2,250 convicts. Three-fourths of them were black or Puerto Rican. The guards recruited from the surrounding farm country did not understand the language and culture of the young ghetto residents they guarded. But verbal communication was not really necessary; guards signaled prisoners to line up for meals or work by banging their clubs against the walls.

There was little for the Attica inmates to do in the way of recreation or rehabilitation. Some of them worked in the prison metal shops, for wages of 25 cents per day. They were allowed to take one shower a week. Trips to "the box" — solitary confinement — were used to enforce prison rules. The box was conveniently located above the prison hospital, in case the convict was beaten too enthusiastically while being taken there.

The idea of "breaking the law" is based on the concept of the individual's responsibility for his own actions. The convict has clearly failed in the contest of life. When a society values individual achievement above nearly everything else, the best place for human failures is out of the public consciousness. Prisons are the garbage cans of society. In spite of the elaborate concern for the rights of an *accused* criminal, a *convicted* criminal is hardly considered to partake of the ideal of equality. State minimum wage laws are not applied to prison inmates, and convicted felons in thirty-seven states permanently lose the right to vote.

Discontent among the prisoners at Attica was widespread. Convict spokesmen complained of racist treatment by guards and the unyielding attitude of Superintendent Vincent Mancusi. Some of the leaders

called themselves "revolutionaries" and smuggled books by Bobby
Seale and Malcolm X into their cells. In July of 1971, Attica inmates
sent a petition (or manifesto) to Governor Rockefeller, listing their
grievances. It had no immediate effect.

Rioting began at 8:30 A.M. on September 9, 1971, and lasted for
four days. About half of Attica's 2,250 prisoners seized Cell Block D
and its yard. They held a number of guards as hostages. The first day,
eleven injured guards and civilians were released to receive medical
treatment. One guard died two days later, making the rioters liable
for murder charges. Trenches 200 yards long were dug in the yard
for defense against an attack, and the convicts set up their own organization to keep order. Thirty-seven hostages remained in their
hands.

New York Corrections Commissioner Russell G. Oswald came to
Attica the first afternoon. A newcomer to the New York system,
Oswald had won high praise for modernizing Wisconsin's prisons.
He had developed plans for Attica that included more meaningful
rehabilitation programs, evening vocational training classes, and a
better law library; but none of the plans had been implemented.
Oswald decided to talk to the prisoners in person. They rejected his
immediate demand for the release of the hostages, and they presented
their list of demands, which did not strike Oswald as unreasonable.
Some of the demands were: no more censorship of the letters they
wrote, permission to hold political meetings, the legal minimum
wage for work in the prison shops, regular procedures for the consideration of grievances, and religious freedom for Black Muslim
worship.

A group of "outside observers" trusted by the inmates was admitted to witness the negotiations. Oswald surprised the observers
by agreeing to twenty-eight of the thirty inmate demands. He would
not promise the immediate dismissal of Superintendent Mancusi —
which could hardly build the morale of the other superintendents in

the system — and he would not promise general amnesty against prosecution for any illegal acts committed during the riot. But he did promise that no administrative action would be taken against the rebels, and that they would not be physically punished.

The prisoners asked for Governor Rockefeller to come to Attica, but the governor felt there must be limits upon what responses rioting prisoners can demand. The governor was, however, in constant communication with Attica, and he approved Oswald's agreement to the twenty-eight demands. According to some observers, the rioters felt that Oswald's agreement to these items was too good to be true, and they simply could not trust his acquiescence. They feared reprisals by the guards. Meanwhile, state troopers and National Guardsmen gathered around the prison walls, preparing for an assault. Their commanders urged Oswald to order an attack. Instead, Oswald continued his efforts to negotiate. Although negotiations seemed to make progress at first, the attitude of the prisoners hardened when the prison guard, injured on the first day, died.

On Monday morning, Oswald reminded the convict leaders of the demands that had already been granted and insisted upon the release of all hostages. Their answer was to pose convicts next to several of the hostages with knives held to their throats, warning that all would be killed if the walls were stormed. Oswald felt that he had no further choice, and the attack was launched. Sharpshooters were mounted on the walls, helicopters dropped tear gas, and troopers swarmed into the yard. Visibility was poor, and there were many gunshots, although the orders had been to fire only in self-defense or to protect the life of a hostage.

Within an hour, the attack and the riot were over. Twenty-eight of the hostages were saved; only nine died. Twenty-six prisoners were dead or fatally wounded. The immediate official reaction was jubilant; the sudden attack had apparently saved three-quarters of the hostages from death at the hands of their captors.

Cornell Capa

A day later, the medical reports came in. All of the dead hostages, and all of the dead prisoners, were killed by gunshot wounds; there was not a single slashed throat. Only the attackers had guns. The prisoners' weapons were limited to knives, spears, and clubs.

Later, released hostages testified that they had been treated with surprising gentleness by the convicts. In fact, the actions of the convicts, throughout the four days, had never matched their rhetoric. Although some of their spokesmen used revolutionary language, the general thrust of their protest seemed an effort to say that, although they were convicted criminals, they should be treated as human beings.

"We are men," said one of the inmate statements. "We are not beasts, and do not intend to be beaten or driven. What has happened here is but the sound before the fury of those oppressed."[10]

But convicts are losers in the contest of life. When the walls were stormed by guards and troops, bent upon restoring order in the name of society, convicts were brutally beaten. It was reported that some convict leaders, holding their hands in the air in a gesture of surrender, were shot in the back.

Meanwhile, in California

In the aftermath of the Supreme Court decision finding the death penalty, as applied by the states, unconstitutional, an initiative measure was placed before the voters of California. It was based on the presumption that the death penalty would be found constitutional if it were truly mandatory, allowing no discretion on the part of courts in its application. Any person convicted of specific crimes would be executed.

The measure was most strongly supported by the organization of prison officials. They desired the reinstatement of a provision that a prisoner serving a life term who injures a prison employee will be executed if the employee dies within a year and a day. They argued that a "lifer" has nothing left to lose but his existence, and the threat of a death penalty was required to protect other prisoners, and guards, from his violent actions.

The easy answer was that prisons, and society itself, should be reformed, so that there would be no occasion for life-term prisoners to engage in violent acts. Even if that were possible, it would be a long process. Prisons must operate every day.

California voters approved the measure overwhelmingly.

Policemen, courts, judges; district attorneys, public defenders; trial courts and courts of appeal; city jails and state penitentiaries. Together they make up a system of criminal justice. Actually, the jurisdictions are confused and overlapping, and it is hard to dignify the result with the label "system." In the 1970s, the institutions are overcrowded and overworked. The police are able to capture and obtain convictions of less than 10 percent of the persons committing serious crimes. The courts are so overburdened as to make a mockery of justice. And the prisons perform best of all as training schools for criminals.

10. Quoted in *Time*, September 27, 1971, p. 22.

Can Order Be Preserved, if Justice Is Denied?

In the full flush of its technological pride, the United States sent a series of missions to the moon. At home, the administrations of major cities could not assure the safety of their streets, let alone provide efficient garbage collection.

New attention turned to the confusing mixture of institutions involved in establishing criminal justice—police forces, prosecutors, courts, correctional officers, and prisons. The maintenance of law and order was a major issue of national politics, although most of the agencies devoted to that purpose were controlled by cities, counties, and states. Police officers were distressed by the Supreme Court's tenderness for accused criminals, and so was President Nixon. Prisons were torn by riots, and a long, hot summer of discontent took shape every year in the inner cities.

When experts examined the instruments we must depend on to maintain an orderly society, they wondered if the sum total of their operation was not to encourage the growth of crime.

Meanwhile, Richard Kleindienst, then-attorney general of the United States, reported that the rate of increase in crime was slowed by the measures of the Nixon administration. Crime increased by 17 percent in 1968, but only by 6 percent in 1971. City streets remained unsafe at night—and often in the daytime—while crime rates increased in the suburbs.

Mr. Kleindienst resigned in 1973 due to his relationship to those implicated in the Watergate scandals.

Leviathan

In their efforts to rid ideas about politics of the traditions that encrusted them throughout the Middle Ages, seventeenth-century political thinkers developed the contract theory of the state. Disregarding any contrary historical evidence, this theory held that, at one time, men existed in a state of complete anarchy. Law, government, and other social institutions had not been invented. Men were completely free; but their very freedom endangered them. Each individual pursued his own passions and desires without protection from the passions and desires of others.

Thomas Hobbes, the greatest exponent of the contract theory, described in a famous passage written in 1651 the sorry condition of men in this "state of nature":

> In such condition, there is no place for Industry . . .; no Navi-
> gation . . .; no Building . . .; no account of Time; no Arts; no
> Letters; no Society; and which is worst of all, continually feare,
> and danger of violent death; And the life of man, solitary, poore,
> nasty, brutish, and short.[1]

In Hobbes' view, the only escape from this miserable condition
lies in each man giving up some of his freedom by entering into an
irrevocable contract with his fellow men. This contract establishes
the state. The state is absolute, the source of all law and authority.
It creates an order so profound that individual men are enabled to
seek their own destinies in an atmosphere of predictable relationships
with their fellow men. Men bound together through the social contract achieve unity; this unity creates a power that is awesome to
behold.

> The multitude so united in one person is called a Common-
> wealth, in Latin, *civitas*. This is the generation of that great
> *Leviathan*, or rather, to speak more reverently of that *mortal
> god* to which we owe, under the *immortal God*, our peace and
> defense. For by this authority, given him by every particular
> man in the Commonwealth, he has the use of so much power
> and strength conferred on him that by terror thereof he is
> enabled to form the wills of them all, to peace at home, and
> mutual aid against their enemies abroad. . . .[2]

Hobbes' use of terms such as "power" and "terror" has led some to
see in his thought a foreshadowing of the modern totalitarian state,
such as Stalin's Russia or Hitler's Germany. But his description contains an important truth about *all* governments. Government is only
possible if, at some point, it can use force to protect the social order
against individuals or groups that threaten it. It is impossible to imagine a government that does not hunt down bank robbers and attempt to recapture their loot and put them in jail. It is similarly
difficult to imagine a government that would encourage the dyna-
miting of railroad tracks or the hijacking of aircraft flying within its
borders.

Because we expect government to resist attacks upon the social
order, and since we permit only government to do so by force, the
state in modern times has been defined as that organization which
has a monopoly on the legitimate use of force. That is, only government may appropriately use force to achieve its policies.

Governments are universally endowed with symbols of authority
and nobility. Think of the pomp of a king's coronation, or the ceremony of a president's inauguration. Even (or particularly) in a democracy, the generals wear uniforms laden with medals and insignia.
The police wear uniforms and badges to symbolize their authority;
the judges wear robes. It is as if psychological warfare were being
waged in an effort to make a feeling of awe at the majesty of the state
substitute for the terror Hobbes felt would be required.

Of course, no government can rule through force alone. Neither
Hitler nor Stalin did so. Every government is accepted as "legitimate"
(lawful, or at least appropriate) by a large number of its citizens. Those
who break particular laws do not normally deny the need for government. The man who cheats on his income tax expects his savings
to be safe in the bank. The driver who speeds on the freeway hopes
the car will be safe from theft when it is parked downtown.

---

1. Thomas Hobbes, *Leviathan* (Oxford: Clarendon Press, 1958), p. 97.
2. Ibid., p. 132.

The Constitution as Social Contract

The authors of the United States Constitution accepted the contract theory. Although the American colonies could hardly be described as existing in a state of nature, it was felt that a new government was appropriately formed by the people entering into a contract. The authors of the Federalist Papers wrote that the Constitution was a supreme expression of the will of all the people. The Preamble itself made this claim.

> We the People of the United States, in Order to form a more perfect Union, establish Justice, insure domestic Tranquility, provide for the common defense, promote the general Welfare, and secure the Blessings of Liberty to ourselves and our Posterity, do ordain and establish this Constitution for the United States of America.

However, the founding fathers did not share Hobbes's gloomy conviction that man's propensity for evil is likely to rule his actions, in the absence of external restraints. Rather, they followed John Locke in believing that minimal restraints should be imposed by government, for men are capable of self-control as well as self-government.

The Constitution did not establish Hobbes's Leviathan of absolute authority. It provided for a national government that would enjoy certain specific, "delegated" powers. Both national and state governments were prohibited from taking certain actions. All other governmental powers were reserved to the states, or to the people themselves. (The Tenth Amendment somewhat redundantly specified that this was the intent of the document.)

Although the authors of the Constitution were anxious to create a strong national government and therefore an orderly social framework for the pursuit of their commercial interests, the people of the thirteen states, having recently cast off oppressive British authority, were concerned that the national government not be too strong.

The very fact that a *federal* government was being created gave considerable assurance of this outcome. For, under a federal government, the Hobbesian vision of unified and all-powerful government is very difficult to achieve. Every citizen in a federal system is subject to two governments — in the case of the United States, to the national government and to the state government. The Constitution established *dual citizenship*, making every citizen subject to two sets of laws — the national laws, and the state laws. One consequence is that most of the essential tasks of government listed in the Preamble are performed by state governments, and by cities chartered in the states, if they are performed at all. State governments must "establish Justice" and "insure domestic Tranquility"; the national government showed little interest in securing "the blessings of Liberty" for individual citizens until the Civil War established the right of the federal government to define the rights of citizenship. The national government did not attempt to "promote the general Welfare," in the sense of providing social services, until President Roosevelt's New Deal was established.

The regulation of human relationships (marriage, divorce, inheritance, education, selling of property, protection from fire and natural disaster, providing for widows and orphans) is accomplished according to laws established by state legislatures and administered by the agents of the state — cities, counties, and their various specialized bureaucracies. According to the old theory, it was the need for this very kind of regulation which led men to enter into a social contract and establish a government. Government can, if it must, use force to make citizens obey such regulations. In the cities, the agent of that force is the policeman.

> Can you imagine explaining that to a ten-year-old on a street corner in Harlem or Oakland or South Chicago? Explaining that we all entered upon a social contract symbolized by the Constitution written in 1789? That each of us, in order to participate in civilization, gives up some freedom for the good of all?
> *I know it's hot, but we've got to turn off that fire hydrant. The firemen are going to need the water.*

Insure Domestic Tranquility

Nineteen sixty-seven was a year of rioting in the cities. A president's commission made recommendations, but not much happened. The riots went on. Protests against the war in Vietnam ended Lyndon Johnson's presidency. In 1970, the war was still going on. College students occupied buildings and staged confrontations and issued demands. Colleges didn't change very much. Well in advance, the Nixon administration announced that the end of the Vietnam War would not provide untold billions for the massive attack on domestic problems that so many recommended. In fact, it declared, the Department of Defense would require an even bigger budget.

Violence in the cities, violence on the campuses. Nobody had to read the thoughts of Chairman Mao to know it could continue. In 1964, when Barry Goldwater talked about "crime in the streets," many commentators considered him in bad taste. In 1968 and 1972, every politician talked about "law and order." In the 1970s, the police were receiving more attention—both friendly and unfriendly—than they had gotten in years. Nearly everyone wanted them to do something. But what?

Law, Order, and Justice

What does the call for law and order mean? It may be related to the basic human desire described with cold logic by Thomas Hobbes. It is the desire for a dependable social order that will protect us from the unpredictable passions of our fellow men. On the other hand, it may be only a sign of resistance to change. It may be a call for protection against the quite predictable passions of the ghetto residents who cry out against their exclusion from the affluent society that surrounds them.

We pause for the identification of terms.

Law

One of the oldest sayings of American politicians and school teachers is that our government is "a government of laws, not of men."[3] Often the saying is joined with a suggestion that men (particularly politicians) are certainly undependable and probably corrupt, while laws, by nature, are enduring and noble. Used in this way, the phrase is blatantly antidemocratic in its implications. For laws are written by

---

3. The saying was first used officially in the "distributing clause" of the Massachusetts Constitution of 1780, drafted by John Adams, later the second president of the United States. The document declared: "In the government of the Commonwealth of Massachusetts the legislative, executive and judicial power shall be placed in separate departments, to the end that it might be a government of laws, and not of men." The principle of separation of powers is discussed in Chapters 3, 4 and 5.

men, interpreted by men, and enforced by men. A central concept of democracy is that laws are established in accord with the will of the majority, with due regard for minority rights. Citizens who accept the validity of the democratic process through which the law was formulated should accept the law itself. The true meaning of "a government of laws, not of men" must be that no citizen will be victimized by the arbitrary whim of a government official, for the actions of government officials are prescribed by policies (laws) made according to the procedures of democracy.

The late William H. Parker, much-admired chief of the Los Angeles Police Department, put it this way:

> As policemen we are guided by an artificial definition of right and wrong—the law. We do not pretend that it is all-wise, all-inclusive, or all-just. The student of ethics will find in it many flaws. . . . Law exists, not because we do agree on what is right and wrong, but because we do not agree. A universally accepted standard of ethics does not exist. To prevent anarchy, it is necessary to impose this artificial standard based on majority agreement.[4]

Majority agreement. Participation in electing the officials who make the laws is supposed to win the citizen's allegiance to the laws made. For, while he may disagree with the majority view in some cases, he is certain to join the majority on other issues. And he is at all times free to persuade his fellow citizens to share his viewpoint.

In the last few years, the right to vote has been extended to residents of the District of Columbia and to persons eighteen years of age. Some call this "co-optation," which they define as stimulating a meaningless sense of membership in the system.

Laws bring a measure of certainty and predictability to the relationships between men. Thus individuals are able to seek self-realization ("the pursuit of Happiness") within the framework of a relatively stable society. For this reason, laws change slowly. The principle of *stare decisis* means that the law should be predictable. Uncertainty breeds disorder, and the function of a lawyer may be defined as predicting how a court will decide. Legal scholars have gone so far as to say that it is more important that specific laws be *certain* than that they be just. The luxury of such an assertion can come only when most of a society is convinced that the basic thrust of governmental institutions is to achieve justice, at least for themselves, and probably for all citizens.

Order

The concept of order emphasizes predictability and certainty at the expense of adaptability. It includes the ideas of peace, quiet, discipline, subordination, obedience, and public tranquility.

Riots and mob violence are the antithesis of order. When entire neighborhoods are caught up in a spasm of destructiveness, reason is submerged by passion. Orderly human relationships are no longer possible. In such a situation, it seems strangely out of place for policemen to charge individuals with willful violation of the law.

Thomas Hobbes was concerned with how order may be established in society. Paradoxically, he felt that liberty could best be assured if

4. From speeches by William H. Parker (in 1950 and 1952) in O. W. Wilson, ed., *Parker on Police* (Springfield, Ill.: Charles C Thomas, 1957), reprinted in Laurence Veysey, ed., *Law and Resistance* (New York: Harper & Row, 1970). p. 313.

the individual felt terror at the power of government. If they are true to the heritage of John Locke, Americans will reject terroristic government. However, police tactical squads are being provided with plastic helmets, leather jackets, and exotic weapons. Few Americans protest the growing use of electronic surveillance devices, and fewer still seemed outraged when former Attorney General Mitchell asserted that the government may listen to (wiretap) whatever conversations it decides are relevant to the national interest.[5]

Justice

The concept of justice is fundamental to human relationships; it is considered the most important goal of a successful society. Among the ancient Jews, justice was considered not too different from the more violent conception of revenge. Its purpose was to punish the wrong-doer in proportion to his crime. Crime and punishment were matched as nearly as possible. ("An eye for an eye, a tooth for a tooth.") Watching over all was a harsh and vengeful God.

But justice is not only a negative concept, concerned with crime and punishment. It is also a positive notion encompassing the ideal human relationships that should exist within the framework of society. The *Republic* of Plato, a classic of Greek political thought, can be described as an effort to define the meaning of justice. In essence, Plato held that justice consists of enabling every man to perform well his recognized role in life. In this sense, justice partakes of both the value of achievement and the value of equality;[6] justice results from those social arrangements that permit every person to develop his abilities to the highest level he can attain.

Justice has a humane dimension. This was recognized by the Jewish prophets who periodically sang of a merciful God and suggested a kind of justice that is tempered by deep sympathy. Surely it is this connotation that is invoked by the Preamble to the Constitution, which asserts that one of the document's great aims is "to establish Justice."

In the developing tradition of Western law, justice was increasingly recognized as closely related to procedures and administration. (Amendments three through eight of the Bill of Rights are concerned with procedures.) In this definition, justice is equated with fairness. It is concerned with the impartial application of the law. We speak of policemen who "enforce" the law; but we speak of judges who "administer" justice. Perhaps the relationship is best summarized in the slogan carved above the entrance to the U.S. Supreme Court Building: EQUAL JUSTICE UNDER LAW.

But the daily operations of the system of justice are supervised by the states, rather than the federal government. Those operations are not always characterized by fairness. Consider these examples from three states:

Illinois:
The city of Chicago plays host to many conventions. When policemen find a well-dressed drunk wandering the streets of the Loop, it is normal practice to pick him up and return him to his hotel. When a drunk dressed in rags is found wandering in the slums, the practice has been to arrest him. If he protests, he is likely to be beaten.

---

5. Mitchell's assertion was denied by the Supreme Court, which found wiretapping legal only if authorized by a judicial warrant. The vote was 8-0. See *United States* v. *U.S. District Court for the Eastern District of Michigan*, (1972).
6. These concepts are introduced on pp. 23-28.

California:

> In Los Angeles, [a woman] was giving her children a bath when two plainclothesmen came bursting in and started to ransack her bedroom. The police had no warrant, but they had picked up [her] brother, who allegedly used narcotics, and they had decided to search her home. When she protested, they twisted her arms behind her back, snapped handcuffs on her wrists, and dragged her off under arrest. . . . Police in their illegal search had found a bottle containing pills. She had told them they were vitamin pills (which they were, as the police laboratory subsequently found out), but the arresting officers were obsessed with the idea that [the woman] must have narcotics secreted upon her person. She was ordered to undress. When she refused, two male cops held and half-strangled her while two policewomen stripped her, spread her buttocks, and examined her rectum.[7]

Missouri:

> When buildings were burning in the Kansas City ghetto and National Guardsmen and police were firing at real and imaginary snipers on the rooftops . . . the people who wanted protection from the rioters and looters didn't find it. White commercial interests outside the ghetto were well and successfully guarded. "We felt we were all being contained to destroy ourselves," Mrs. Samantha Cunningham angrily told a reporter. "Aren't the police supposed to protect me too?"[8]

If there is one version of the law for middle-class merchants, another for long-haired students, and a third for blacks, what has become of the ideal of equal justice?

Much Injustice Is Beyond the Control of Policemen

The interrelationship of law, order, and justice seems clear. It is hard to establish one if the other two are lacking. The Supreme Court has, over the last decade, interpreted the Bill of Rights in a manner aimed at improving the quality of justice in the procedures used for criminal investigation by the police. Enlightened policemen, and most judges, accept these rulings as proper and necessary.

Injustice created in the relationship between policemen and their suspects results from the attitudes and habits established on both sides, which control decisions of the moment. When the policeman is convinced that he will be met in the ghetto by hostility, and the black youth is certain that the police will enter the ghetto only with brutality, both expectations are likely to be fulfilled.

But there are kinds of injustice more permanent in nature and more damaging in their impact. Consider the following circumstances, over which no city policeman exerts direct control:

> With the automation of cotton and other crops, southern blacks are driven from the land to seek new lives in northern cities.

> Rather than administer welfare, some counties in the South have purchased one-way railroad tickets for welfare clients.

> Chicano and Puerto Rican youths attending city high schools often do not master the English language well enough to read simple texts in English.

7. Fred J. Cook, "Law and Limits," *Saturday Review*, February 4, 1967, p. 48.
8. Robert Pearman, "Black Crime, Black Victims," *The Nation*, April 21, 1969, p. 500.

Until very recently, urban renewal officials have been little interested in finding alternate housing for the slum families displaced by renewal.

Many craft unions, particularly in the building trades, have been reluctant to admit members of minority groups.

Many employers seeking completely unskilled labor consider only high school graduates; the diploma accomplishes the first screening of the applicants.

The practices of tax assessors combined with those of building inspectors encourage landlords to disregard the city codes and permit their buildings to remain unsafe and unsanitary.

The practices of welfare agencies penalize the families of men who find employment, for the welfare payment is reduced by the amount of wages earned. This can mean a 100 percent tax.

As frustration and despair explode, somebody lashes out at his family or his neighbor. Somebody else calls the police.

The Man

Confronted by the explosive dangers of the ghettos, both professional and amateur students of society have sought simple explanations. One is concerned with the diminished role of the father in black families. Another seeks the answer in the past experiences of the ghetto residents.

For generations, black American families lived in a state of virtual peonage in the South. As agricultural tenants, they were permitted to labor on the land; but a share of the crop had to be paid to the land-lord. It was a single crop, usually cotton, which was sold for cash. The sharecropper's money then was spent to secure food and clothing from the nearby village store. There was no other source of supply. Other merchants were too far away to reach by mule-drawn wagon; when automobiles were available to most, the sharecropper could not afford one. And it was only the local store which would extend credit against the next year's crop. Frequently, the local store was owned by his landlord. The sharecropper had no choice but to pay the prices set in the local store through the whim of its owner; but the value of the crop was established by distant market forces.

Although vicious, the system was simple. The oppressor was easy to identify. He was the white man living in the big house on the hill. He owned the land, and he owned the store. The landlord held "his" sharecroppers, both white and black, in economic bondage.

When sharecropping was no longer profitable for the landlord, the tenants were forced from the land and into the cities. They were thrust into a more complex society made up of bureaucratic institutions. The oppressor was not so easy to identify. In part, it was the city planners and their urban renewal projects; in part, it was the welfare agencies whose codes were based on middle-class assumptions; in part, it was the self-protective attitudes of labor-union members; in part, it was the practices of the public schools, where the teachers and administrators were ill-prepared to understand the psychic needs of children transplanted from southern soil to northern tenements.

One fact was clear. The dominant institutions of this society were white. And the ultimate enforcer of their various rules was the cop. He became the personification of oppression. He was The Man.

But no simple explanation can encompass the reality of the slum. The realities of slum life do not depend upon the race and past experiences of slum dwellers. Middle-class Italians trading sociological slogans at the country club have usually forgotten the indignities suffered by their grandparents at the hands of Irish cops. The slums have always been high crime areas, for human misery and despair naturally seek targets. And policemen are normally sent to areas where crime is anticipated.

The American Policeman

What functions can we realistically expect the police to perform? Can they, through daily contact with the human debris cast up by the ebb and flow of the American urban economic and social system, prevent crime? Can they enforce the law? Can they preserve order? Can they administer justice? Can they do all of these equally well, or do they have a better chance to achieve some goals than others?

An attempt to approach the answers to these questions can come only after considering the nature and practices of the American policeman.

Just as the ghetto cannot be understood through simple explanations, neither can the policeman. In spite of sociological record-keeping, each policeman is, after all, an individual, and the actions of policemen should be judged on an individual basis. But some statements can be made about policemen in general. In relation to the enormous responsibility he bears, the policeman is:

Underpaid.

Inadequately trained and poorly educated.

Uncertain as to the exact nature of his responsibility.

Increasingly convinced that he is discriminated against as the member of a minority.

The Recruitment of Police Officers
In sociological terms, policemen are recruited from the ranks of the lower and lower-middle classes. A police career is one of the few social roles with prestige and responsibility still open to men of little

education. Police departments operate under civil service; when a policeman has passed his probationary period, he can only be dismissed because of gross misconduct. The job affords both opportunity and security.

Police departments impose physical requirements upon recruits. In the belief that representatives of the law should be imposing, many seek recruits of great physical stature. When the New York City department abandoned the minimum height requirement of 5 feet, 9 inches, it was considered a major breakthrough. For this made many more Puerto Ricans eligible.

Mental requirements are seldom mentioned. Only a few departments administer tests in an effort to eliminate the psychological misfits—those for whom the carrying of a gun is important. Senior officers claim they can spot such types through an interview.

In the last fifteen years, only 5 percent of the entrants into the New York Police Department have had any college training. A survey of the occupations of their fathers showed that more than three-quarters were manual or service workers. Joining the police force was therefore a means of climbing upward on the social ladder. It was the gateway to middle-class status.

Policemen are recruited only for the beginning ranks. Promotion is from within. There is no provision for the "lateral entry" of persons from other fields into responsible positions.

With the exception of Depression times, when the general shortage of jobs led many college graduates to enter police work, the pattern of upward social mobility through joining the police force has prevailed in most American cities. The first nationality group to establish the pattern were the Irish of Boston and New York; other groups have followed. Columnist Ed McCabe reported that his high school friends in an eastern slum neighborhood who became neither priests nor hoodlums nor hod carriers joined the police force. When joining the force is seen as a pathway out of the slums, it is not surprising that policemen show little sympathy for those unable or unwilling to find a way out.

A modern exception to the historic pattern is the young black ghetto dweller. For several years, blacks have shown little interest in joining the police force. (Before that, they were not encouraged to apply.) Yet black militants demand black policemen for black neighborhoods. Black policemen report that they are regarded as Uncle Toms in the ghettos and as freaks in the white neighborhoods. Charged with inconsistency, the militant leaders reply that to join the police forces *as presently organized* requires a sell-out to the Establishment. The history of casual racist brutality exercised by white policemen in the ghettos is too long, and too well-documented, to be ignored. Ghetto dwellers regard the police as an occupying force.[9]

The Pay Scale of Police Officers

Although the pay of a policeman may be enough to give him a glimpse of middle-class pleasures, it is hardly enough to provide them, particularly for an entire family. The following figures, compiled for the City Management Association's *Municipal Yearbook* in 1972, give the salaries for patrolmen in selected cities during their first twelve months on the force in 1971: San Francisco, $11,700; Chicago, $10,788; Los Angeles, $9,855; Philadelphia, $9,578; New York, $9,499; Cleveland, $9,063; Detroit, $8,480; Kansas City, $8,352; Atlanta, $8,320; Boston, $8,300; Houston, $8,000; and San Antonio, $6,708.

Among the skilled workers who enjoy a higher income than policemen are painters, carpenters, plumbers, electricians, and mechanics. Of course, these trades generally require a longer period of apprenticeship than does any police force. But they have more certain hours. Policemen are encouraged to carry their guns and identification when off duty so they will be able to intervene on behalf of law and order if needed.

Adopting middle-class standards, but not paid enough to enjoy them, many policemen respond by taking second jobs. (Two-thirds of American policemen hold additional jobs, according to one estimate.) Policemen are regarded as steady and dependable part-time employees. However, slum residents unable to find any job at all resent the policeman holding two.

The Training of Police Officers

Several occupations can be legally carried on only by qualifying for and obtaining a license. A minimum amount of special training is required to become a candidate for these licenses. The minimum required *hours* of training for such positions are these: 11,000 for physicians, 5,000 for embalmers, 4,000 for barbers, and 1,200 for beauticians. The comparable figure for policemen is 200 hours. Few basic police academy courses last for more than five weeks. (In small towns, a new patrolman may strap on his gun and go out to maintain order after a half-hour lecture from his chief.) Of these occupations the two with the responsibility of determining life and death are physicians and policemen.

After completing the official course, the young policeman joins the ranks. Officially he is on probation. But few are discharged during this period. In the academy, he listens to lectures that present the official department viewpoint. On the streets, from his older col-

9. See James Baldwin, "A Report from Occupied Territory," *The Nation*, July 11, 1966, reprinted in Vesey, ed., *Law and Resistance*, pp. 318–328. See also Ramsey Clark, *Crime in America* (New York: Simon and Schuster, 1970), pp. 157–159 and 248–249.

leagues, he learns it the way it is. Police commissioners come and go, as mayors respond to public pressures by changing the top administration of the department. But the change at the top does little to mold attitudes and practices of the policeman in the patrol car.

The young policeman has joined a select fraternity, those who wear the gun and badge. Various studies of police forces have revealed two enduring attitudes which are practically universal.

Law enforcement officers close ranks around one of their members who is threatened by an outsider — either physically or by criticism. The "officer in trouble" call is the one which draws the quickest and most massive response from other police units. The "cop killer" is the most thoroughly hunted criminal.

The policeman who snaps under tension and beats a suspect — or even shoots him — can usually expect support, rather than criticism, from fellow officers. The Wickersham Commission, appointed to study law enforcement by President Hoover, reported in 1931 that "it is an unwritten law in police departments that police officers must not testify against their brother officers." That custom prevails today. None of the officers present at the Algiers Motel reported the murders committed there. The incident might have escaped public notice, except for an investigation launched by Detroit Congressman John Conyers after he talked to the victims permitted to escape with their lives.

Policemen identify with their roles. Acting as the agents of society, they are sensitive to attacks or criticism directed against the police, for they see these as attacks upon all authority. At this point the code of the street policeman is likely to diverge from the law. Persons who are breaking no law, but are acting in a manner that seems to challenge the authority of the police, may be arrested on some charge such as disturbing the peace. Then, when the citizen demands to know what he has done wrong, he is additionally charged with resisting arrest.

Policemen have implemented the attitudes they shared with the larger society, regardless of the letter of the law. Policemen have traditionally been very rough with suspected homosexuals, feeling that deviates are viewed with disgust by society and that an excess of zeal in handling them will only be applauded. The same attitude prevailed for years in handling black people and other minority groups that received little sympathy from the majority. As minority groups organize in politically effective clubs and committees, political pressure directed against the city administration sends a stream of new directives to be posted on the precinct station bulletin boards. The policeman is admonished to treat all citizens with equal respect.

From the beginning, the policeman finds his actions subject to criticism. Higher courts and such groups as the American Civil Liberties Union insist upon protecting the rights of individuals accused of crime. Yet, as the policeman grows in experience, he feels that he is an expert at recognizing criminals and would not make an arrest unless the person were guilty. And he may come to feel that anyone who challenges his authority, or who blatantly deviates from normal dress and behavior, is at least potentially guilty. An arrest seems in order, although the person involved has broken no law. After investigating complaints against New York policemen for more than a year, Paul Chevigny found that many fell into just that pattern: the policeman made an arrest without sound legal grounds, then he lied to provide a legal justification, by asserting a breach of the peace when there was none. If the arrested citizen complained verbally, the policeman might claim a physical attack, in order to justify a charge of resisting arrest.[10]

When complaints of police brutality reach the ears of public officials and are heeded, the policeman may argue that "politics" prevents the proper handling of his job. Let him arrest and harshly treat an influential citizen, with friends at city hall or the police commission, and he knows that politics prevents the impartial performance of his duties. The need to survive breeds cynicism. White youths are treated with respect; who knows who their fathers are? No such worries are attached to blacks.

James Q. Wilson, a leading student of the police, reminds us that policemen are not the products of graduate schools. They are working-class professionals. "This means," Wilson points out, "they bring to the job some of the focal concerns of working-class men—a preoccupation with maintaining self-respect, proving one's masculinity, 'not taking any crap,' and not being 'taken in' . . . the officer's behavior will depend crucially on how much deference he is shown, on how manageable the situation seems to be, and on what the participants in it seem to 'deserve.' "[11]

When the pride of a policeman confronts the pride of a Black Panther . . .

The Job of the Police Officer

When police forces were first organized in such cities as Boston and Philadelphia, the focus of their duties was upon maintaining order, not upon enforcing the law. They were expected to patrol the streets at night, to prevent riots, and to intervene in private quarrels before violence resulted from actions of the participants or from bystanders taking sides. The apprehension of criminals and the restoration of stolen property was the task of constables or detectives who were hired by the wronged parties to pursue the offender. The constable often received a share of the recovered goods.

In the early nineteenth century, detectives were bureaucratized by placing them on the police force and paying them a salary in place of the former fee system. By the end of the century, the detective was identified in the popular mind as the central figure, and the solution of crimes as the central drama, in police work. Sherlock Holmes was a leading figure of Victorian fiction. Capturing criminals began to eclipse maintaining order as the central police task.

Soon policemen were called upon to enforce the majority's notion of morality. Pimps, prostitutes, and gamblers had to make arrangements with the police in order to continue supplying their services, for which there was a lively demand. When the Prohibition amendment was passed, crime became big business, and policemen were seen as glamorous warriors against complex organizations.

But this was a change in image, not reality. The policeman still spends much of his time in maintaining order. Directing traffic is the leading—and most time-consuming—example. Policemen are called upon to provide services, to transport an ill person to the hospital, retrieve a frightened cat from a tree, or instruct school children in traffic safety. They are asked to intervene in private quarrels: teen-

10. Paul Chevigny, *Police Power: Police Abuses in New York City* (New York: Pantheon, 1969), p. 141.
11. Quoted in Seymour Martin Lipset, "Why Cops Hate Liberals—and Vice Versa," *Atlantic*, March 1969, p. 83.

agers at a dance, drunks in a tavern, or brawling husband and wife
in an apartment house. In such situations, the sight of a blue uniform
may cool the situation sufficiently to keep it from exploding. Yet
nobody is arrested; and, in a few days, the participants may forget that
the police were called.

Such intervention is a necessary and appropriate use of the majesty
of the state as represented by the policeman. But the television image
is of the gang-buster, and the surest way to promotion in the department may be through waging gun battles. When the public emphasis
is upon law enforcement, the policeman may easily come to regard
the minor and routine tasks of maintaining order as not "real" police
work.

But that function is basic to preserving civilization in the urban
setting. The police must strive both to maintain order and to enforce
the law. Unfortunately, the same habits and procedures are not appropriate for both tasks. James Q. Wilson has written that

> municipal police departments are two organizations in one
> serving two related but not identical functions. The strategy
> appropriate for strengthening their ability to serve one role
> tends to weaken their ability to serve the other. Crime deter-
> rence and law enforcement require, or are facilitated by, special-
> ization, strong hierarchical authority, improved mobility and
> communications, clarity in legal codes and arrest procedures,
> close surveillance of the community, and the avoidance of en-
> tangling alliances with politicians. The maintenance of order,
> on the other hand, is aided by departmental procedures that
> include decentralization, neighborhood involvement, foot pa-
> trol, wide discretion, the provision of services, an absence of
> arrest quotas, and some tolerance for minor forms of favorit-
> ism. . . .[12]

To be effective in maintaining order, the policeman must become
known and trusted, a participating member of the community. In this
role, his effectiveness depends on his prestige, not on his strength. The
old-fashioned foot patrolman had some of that prestige; he became a
member of the community.

But cities grew faster than police budgets, and crook-catching was
accepted as a high calling. Radio-directed patrol cars, headquartered
at fortified precinct stations, promised increased efficiency. If catching criminals was the way to promotion (some departments established arrest quotas), the patrolman had to look upon those he met
as potential criminals to be watched, not as fellow members of a community to be served. Policemen did not get out of their cars to pass
the time of day or to make friends. They got out to ask questions or
conduct searches or answer a specific call for assistance. They became
intruders in the slum community, enemies of its way of life, the long
arm of a distant city hall, the agents of the law. The Man.

> It is the haunting possibility of mass violence—on the campuses and
> in the city ghettos—plus mounting fear of crime in the streets, which
> have given policemen new and growing political power in America's
> cities. Yet the president's commission examining the major riots of
> 1967 reported that in half the cases, the final precipitating incident
> that triggered violence after simmering tensions were built up was
> action by the police—an arrest, or a questioning, or a confrontation.
> And heading the list of grievances of ghetto residents was "police
> practices."

12. James Q. Wilson, "What Makes a Better Policeman," *Atlantic*, March 1969, p. 135.

Policemen as a Conscious Minority

Surrounded by criticism, finding that his arrests may not lead to convictions because the evidence is excluded as illegally obtained, convinced that the first cry of "police brutality" will bring down the wrath of liberals and academics and possibly the city administration, policemen wonder if they can possibly conduct their jobs in a way that will satisfy their critics. Their bitterness grows when they realize that most of their critics have no interest in joining the shock troops that must respond to the next report of rooftop sniping while the ghettos burn.

At one time, the policeman was comfortable as the representative of the dominant values of society, for he knew what those values were. Insofar as they were related to financial rewards and better education, they represented the goals of himself and his family. In a time of social change, such values are no longer clear. President Nixon suggests that the courts have gone too far in restraining policemen; the Civil Liberties Union conducts systematic investigations of complaints against police practices. College students, who in former days were models of what the cop's children might become, scream obscenities and call him "pig." City hall calls for restraint in dealing with looters; white working-class families cheer harsh action. The policeman is surrounded by conflicting expectations as to how his job should be performed.

He turns to a certain source of unconfused sympathy: his fellow policemen. Their frustrations and uncertainties reinforce each other; the comfort provided is so soothing that contrary perceptions from outside the force are discounted. Soon an ideology develops: "we, the police, alone among all others, understand what is needed to enforce the law and protect the fabric of society. The politicians in city hall are pandering for votes, and the bleeding heart liberals in their suburban houses wouldn't spend ten minutes on skid row, for pay." The natural sense of solidarity shared by men who face common dangers is reinforced by political conviction, a perception of common interest, and the sense of shared enemies.

One natural result is concerted political action. First, to gain material benefits, such as better pay and pensions. Then, to modify the legal boundaries of police work by lobbying to persuade the state legislature to override court decisions. (New York's "stop and frisk" law, for example, permits searches on the basis of vague suspicion.) Finally, police enter politics to prevent the intrusion of outside authority upon their practices.

One of the most common recommendations for police reform is the establishment of the civilian review board, a body separate from the police force, to handle complaints against it and to act as a buffer between the police and ghetto residents. New York City policemen defeated Mayor Lindsay's expanded Review Board in a referendum vote. In other cities, such proposals have been defeated by police pressure exerted on city councils.

And, across the country, police are increasingly able to win political battles by appealing directly to the voters. For in a time of violence and change the public discovers anew its dependence upon the police.

> This is a twofold tragedy. It is a tragic mistake to assume that crime can be controlled simply by strengthening the police. For the police have no control over the root causes of crime. It is self-defeating to support the police in their opposition to reasonable proposals for external review. The changes needed in police attitudes, the development of a new conception of the police role, and the needed mediation between the police and the ghetto must come in large measure from outside the force.
>
> And even a relatively perfect police force will fail to control crime if the prosecutors, courts, and prisons fail to perform their related tasks.

The Role of the Prosecutor

When the facts have been developed by the police investigation, the prosecutor must decide the disposition of the case. His powers of discretion are very broad. If there is probable proof of a violation of the law, he should seek an indictment and bring the case before a court.

However, most prosecutors are elected officials. The temptation to gain some publicity, when public interest is aroused by a dramatic case, may be overwhelming. Prosecutors often describe to the press the evidence they have found, instead of reserving it for the court. This, of course, prejudices the possibility of a fair trial. The fruit of police investigations should not be given to the press, any more than reporter's investigations should be the basis of public prosecutions.

If he is not elected, the prosecutor is politically appointed; United States attorneys are usually the protégés of a United States senator, for such appointments are confirmed by the Senate, and the habit of senatorial courtesy prevails. Since prosecutors have many connections with the existing structure of power, political considerations may influence the decision as to what facts constitute a firm basis for seeking an indictment. When a prosecutor never indicts prominent citizens, the police will think twice before arresting them, even on the strongest evidence. Friendly prosecutors are even more important to organized crime than friendly judges.

If the prosecutor does not use the evidence developed by the police to prepare a case that will stand up in court, the accused will go free, and crime will be neither punished nor deterred. The relationship between the police and the prosecutor's office is crucial, and the prosecutor should be prepared to assume a leadership role. His guidance may determine whether the police use sound (and constitutional) procedures in their investigations. He may determine the fields in which police efforts are concentrated, by simply not prosecuting cases he believes are politically unsound, based on laws (such as a prohibition of "lewdness") that the people prefer to ignore. The interests of a community, and its respect for the law, may be greatly enhanced if policemen spend less time collecting drunks or observing topless dancers, and spend more energy investigating the incidence of "white collar" crime, such as price-fixing or the manipulation of time-payment contracts by middle-class merchants, or assign patrolmen to check the security arrangements of banks and all-night markets, in an effort to prevent armed robbery.

However, most prosecutors do not build up an office of experienced professionals. For the salaries of the prosecutor's assistants are set by a city council or a county board of supervisors who themselves want to demonstrate their stinginess with the taxpayer's money. So the prosecutor can enlist only young attorneys who want a few years of trial experience before going on to a more lucrative practice.

Sometimes the process of plea bargaining breaks down when the accused, believing himself innocent, insists on his right to a trial. The prosecutor does not have the case prepared, or has no assistant free to present it, so he can only ask the judge for a continuance of the trial. *Justice delayed is justice denied.*

Courts and Judges

The American judiciary varies greatly in its jurisdiction, competence, and authority. On the lowest rung are justices of the peace, who have limited authority and usually no requirement for legal training, but often — being paid a percentage of the fines they levy — show a passion for finding the defendant guilty. Then there is a structure of lesser courts — traffic courts, juvenile courts, district courts — and an intermediate level of courts of appeal. Each state has a supreme court for the final disposition of appeals and the authoritative interpretation of state law.

Judges reach the bench in a variety of ways. In some states, they are elected after a partisan nomination. In others they are appointed by the governor, and, after a time, the electorate is asked if they should be continued in office. That is, the judge runs, not against an opponent, but against his own record. Because the quality of judicial performance is hard to assess, incumbents are usually reelected. In some states, the Bar Association reviews a slate of nominees suggested by the governor. The practice of Missouri, copied by a dozen other states, is for the governor to appoint from a list submitted by a nominating committee composed of judges, lawyers, and the public.

Judges do not investigate crime; they do not rehabilitate prisoners. They are the intermediaries, the connecting links in the presumed chain of justice. Their duty is to protect the innocent, assure fair trials, apply the law, instruct the jury (when there is a jury; judges rule on cases when there is no jury), and fix penalties for those found guilty.

Fully half of those arrested for the commission of serious crimes are under eighteen years of age. Separate courts are provided for juveniles in which the procedures are private and informal, on the theory that the agony of a public trial would damage the child. Thus minors are not considered to possess all the procedural rights guaranteed to adults by the Constitution, including the right to counsel. The juvenile judge must, in many cases, decide whether an offender is returned to a home that rejects him or be sent to an institution that is likely to confirm his criminality.

The quality of justice depends uniquely upon the quality of the judge. His function is to determine the applicable rule of law, and then to apply it appropriately. Benjamin Disraeli, the nineteenth-century English prime minister, said that "justice is truth in action." That a judge has won political popularity does not guarantee that he will be an effective judge, for he is the servant of the law, not of public opinion. The notion of an elected judiciary did not occur to the founding fathers; all federal judges are appointed. Persons from other nations who have never known of an elected judiciary are often appalled to find it in the United States. The dignity of the law seems inconsistent with the popular judgment associated with an election. Yet the electoral process has produced some distinguished American jurists.

In fact, it is the politicians who decide who shall become judges, whether the decision is implemented by appointment or election. In some areas, opposing party leaders consult and share the judgeships, so that the nominees are not opposed by members of the other party. This protects the dignity of the bench while it preserves the authority of the party leaders. Yet judges receive no special training. The assumption has been that any lawyer can be a judge. In practice, the development of judicial skill and a judicial temperament has not always taken place, even with long experience. Increasingly, judges are forming associations through which they can share insights and experience, making the bench a less lonely assignment. But this is a recent development.

Judges are faced with crowded dockets, due to the increasing population and the impact of modern social forces upon individual behavior. Not all courts are administered in a manner that keeps the judge's time available for the crucial matters that he alone can decide. Judicial record-keeping is markedly anachronistic; county court-houses seem to provide the last refuge for ledgers and steel-tipped pens. Computers are rarely used to keep criminal records or to trace legal references. Yet their potential for easing the judge's task is very great. Similarly, the use of subsidiary personnel to handle the judge's administrative tasks, freeing him to concentrate on matters of decision, requires further development.

Not all delay is the fault of the court. The accused may wish to postpone his trial, knowing that prosecution witnesses will die or move away, that the prosecutor will lose interest in favor of fresher crimes, and that his chances of escaping conviction increase with each postponement. Insurance companies reluctant to pay claims may delay trials for the same reasons. And some trials are delayed because the prosecutor's office is not ready yet, or the defending attorney has a previously scheduled task in another court. *Justice delayed is justice denied.*

> When accused prisoners are released on bail to await trial — and criminal trials are delayed up to a year in many cities — they sometimes are arrested for fresh crimes. This has led to the practice of "preventive detention," which is a far cry from the Constitution's guarantee of a "speedy and public" trial.

What Are Prisons For?

Prisons as we know them today are an American invention. A young French magistrate, Count Alexis de Tocqueville, came to the United States in 1831 to study these new prisons, which replaced death pen-

Charles Harbutt

alties, mutilation, and public humiliation in the stocks as punishment for crime. They were called "penitentiaries," from the same Latin word as "penitence." The Quakers who first developed them hoped that criminals confined to solitary cells would consult their consciences, repent of their misdeeds, and prepare to face society as reformed men. But experience showed that strict solitude led instead to insanity. Programs of instruction and labor were added. Tocqueville got to see the inmates building the new prison at Sing Sing, in New York. He was astonished that 30 guards controlled 900 prisoners; he perceived that the harsh discipline had to be administered with justice, or the prisoners would rise and overwhelm their keepers.[13]

The penitentiaries built in the nineteenth century are gloomy fortresses. States seemed to compete with each other to see which could build the most imposing "pen." It was as if the criminal classes might be frightened into emigrating to a different area.

The century that followed Tocqueville's visit saw a long list of changes in American penology: the institution of parole boards, the establishment of separate juvenile courts, provision of separate facilities for females and children; abolition of the whip, the ball-and-chain, the striped clothes, bread-and-water (except as punishment), and the rock pile. Many states established single departments of corrections, and the guards, who had been patronage appointees, were granted the dignity of civil service status.

In fact, whole new professions and bureaucracies were developed, aimed at either the custody or the rehabilitation of the prisoner. The reforms were backed by ladies' clubs, charitable organizations, and political candidates, but they took place in the absence of general agreement among the members of society as to the function of prisons.

13. George Wilson Pierson, *Tocqueville in America* (Garden City, N. Y.; Doubleday, 1959), pp. 60–69.

At least four different definitions of that purpose could be identified as follows:

1. Prisons exist to punish lawbreakers. Thus the state takes over
the function of revenge, and the victim of crime need not create
further disorder by seeking his own revenge.

2. Prisons exist to punish criminals, not so much for the effect upon
them, but to create an example that will deter others from committing crimes.

3. Prisons are a regrettable necessity, for lawbreakers threaten the
order of society; but criminals are also the victims of social forces.
Prisons should be made as humane as possible; punishment should
no longer be their watchword.

4. Prisons should take the damaged human material sent to them
and treat the wounds inflicted upon it. Rehabilitation is the goal;
a range of educational, recreational, and psychiatric programs are
the means, coordinated with carefully supervised paroles.

The last two of these definitions have guided the twentieth-century
movements for prison reform; the first two, rather primitive, definitions were left to percolate among the general population, and among
the prison guards.

The evidence is growing that prisons do not actually achieve any
of these functions. None of the four common definitions of a prison's
purpose fits the facts.

1. The victims of armed robbery or forcible rape are hardly restored
to the status they enjoyed before the crime by knowing that the
criminal has been imprisoned. In fact, the rate of successful
prosecutions for such crimes is low; in three cases out of four,
nobody will be sent to jail. To the extent that the victim of crime
has entered into a social contract, the state has failed to uphold its
end of the bargain: order was not maintained. It would be more
sensible for the victim to receive direct monetary compensation
from the state, thus achieving a kind of symbolic revenge that need
not await the capture of the criminal.

2. The fact that persons convicted of particular crimes receive
long prison sentences does not deter others from committing those
same crimes. For one example, sentences for bank robbery average
seven years, yet bank robbery is the fastest increasing crime
handled in the federal courts.[14]

3. Prison terms have not decreased the individual's hostility
toward society. At least 80 percent of reported crimes are committed by persons who have already served prison terms. Furthermore, it is impossible to make the massive, walled penitentiaries
into humane institutions. Outbreaks like the riot at Attica would
seem to demonstrate this.

4. The total impact of all the "correctional" programs is hard to
measure. Much effort has been poured into prison educational
programs, and the literacy rate among prisoners has increased; but
the rate of successful rehabilitation has not. Prisoners have performed fruitful work in prisons; but who will employ an experienced license-plate maker upon his release? Group psychotherapy
has enabled prisoners to express their resentments verbally, but it

14. Clark, *Crime in America*, p. 203.

has not reduced the percentage of recidivism (return to prison after committing new crimes). The recidivism rate of prisoners detained in the most modern, comfortable, and healthy prisons seems to be the same, or greater, than that of the grim, old hell-holes. One study suggests that the promising "halfway houses" established to ease the ex-convict back into society may *decrease* slightly the rate of successful rehabilitation.[15]

A plausible explanation for this paradox has been offered by Robert Martinson, an associate professor of sociology at the City College of New York:

> Were the reformers on the wrong track all the time? Could it be that the prison regime *as such* (brutality, food, inmate subculture, etc.) has little or nothing to do with the causes of repeated criminality?
>
> Suppose ... that recidivism rates over the last 150 years were not affected by changes in the prison regime, that instead they simply reflect the *interruption of normal occupational progress*. Imagine what damage a five-year prison sentence would have on the chances for employment of a 20-year-old apprentice in 1800 as compared to a 20-year-old semi-skilled worker today. In 1800, the young apprentice could go on to a productive life. ... The released offender was needed in an expanding economy. He could take up a new life and did not leave the prison bereft of the minimum requirements — a strong back and a pair of willing hands. ... To "make it" in the 1970s requires a more exacting sequence of moves — high school or college, marriage, first job, bank account, next job, and so forth. Let us say that interference with this sequence produces "life cycle damage." The damage is most intense (perhaps irreparable) at just the ages when crime peaks — from 15 to 25. ... The prison produces its paradoxical result ... not directly through anything it does or does not do to the offender, but simply by removing him from society.[16]

Professor Martinson is not condoning prison brutality. On the contrary, he is suggesting that neither brutality nor its opposite ("softness," or "coddling") can be counted on to achieve rehabilitation. No matter how well they are designed and managed, modern prisons do not rehabilitate. They are filled with persons who have committed crimes against persons and property; among them, the poor, the uneducated, and the racial minorities predominate.

The way to decrease such crimes is to attack poverty, racism, and urban decay. Crime can never be entirely eliminated, but to reform the prisons is to treat symptoms, not causes.

However, any doctor unable to get at the root cause of a disease will treat its painful symptoms. A few professional corrections personnel are interested in reforming that part of society nearest to them — the

15. Another study shows that certain prisoners are prone to "institutionalization" — they become so accustomed to being told what to do every minute that they cannot cope when returned to society. Given the "comforts" of a modern prison, such people frequently commit crimes in order to be caught and returned to the familiar prison environment. See Yitzhak Bakal, ed., *Closing Correctional Institutions* (Lexington, Mass.: D. C. Heath, 1973). For a positive view of halfway houses for returning convicts, see Oliver J. Keller and Benedict S. Alper, *Halfway Houses: Community-Centered Correction and Treatment* (ibid., 1970).

16. Robert Martinson, "The 'Dangerous Myth,'" *New Republic*, April 1, 1972, p. 25. This account of the American prison depends heavily on Martinson's four-part series, collectively titled "The Paradox of Prison Reform," *New Republic*, April 1, 8, 15, and 29, 1972.

prisons. Recognizing the prisons' failures, they search for alternatives that better serve both the inmate and society.

Massachusetts reform schools were closed in 1972, and 95 percent of the children were placed in noninstitutional alternative settings, such as halfway houses. Some were returned to their families, with daily supervision. Recidivism dropped from its 86 percent level of 1969, to 72 percent in 1972. The delinquent young people (and thus society) were probably better served by this humane treatment.

If the treatment of juvenile delinquents can be reformed, why not the adult prisons? Because reformers are rare in the bureaucratic ranks. In the absence of public demand for change, bureaucracies cling to established habits.[17]

The Indeterminate Sentence

Those who are convinced that prisons remain at least potential agencies of effective rehabilitation support the concept of the indeterminate sentence, such as "one year to life." This places the convict's life in the hands of the correctional officials and his parole board. He will be returned to society, but only tentatively; the slightest mishap, and he can be yanked back behind the protective prison walls. A youth sent to prison for committing minor larceny can get into trouble while there, offend his parole officer later, and remain a client of the correctional system for the rest of his life.

Prisoners never know when a particular "debt to society" will be paid. They universally despise the indeterminate sentence, circulating the legend that the entire correctional system exists in order to supply employment for middle-class bureaucrats.

17. See Yitzhak Bakal, "The Closing Down of Institutions: New Strategies for Youth Services," Ph.D. dissertation, University of Massachusetts, Amherst, 1973. Recidivism figures are from Appendix D.

And What of the People?

Professor Martinson labeled the four-day riot at Attica an "expressive mutiny," a new method for prisoners to communicate their agony and despair to the public. He noted that the Attica riot signaled the bankruptcy of the theory that prisons can indeed "correct" their inmates.

If what happened at Attica was an effort at communication, is the message getting through? If it is, what steps could be taken in response to an aroused public opinion?

It seems obvious that—if money is part of the problem—the nation can easily afford greater financial support for the agencies of criminal justice. In 1970, the expenditure for all federal, state, and local policemen, prosecutors, courts, and correctional facilities was approximately $5 billion. At the same time, $9 billion was spent on tobacco and $12.5 billion went to purchase alcoholic beverages.[18]

But what would increased expenditures be used for? So far, the reaction has been to beef up the police force. In California, Governor Reagan increased the expenditures for police and reduced those for prisons. President Nixon established in the Department of Justice the Law Enforcement Assistance Administration. It has made grants to police departments. Some of the money has gone to support police training, but most of it has been spent on more patrol cars, improved two-way radio systems, and other technological marvels. Such equipment is probably useful. The point is that federal funds are used to make existing police forces more efficient, rather than to restore foot patrolmen or experiment with new ways of relating policemen more directly to their communities. And there has been no large-scale effort to improve the functioning of the courts or the penal system. The prisons will continue to release men who, having no ready role in society, will turn again to crime. The police will have plenty of use for their new equipment.

One useful function that public opinion could play shows no sign of developing. This would be a movement toward modifying the law so that policemen would no longer be required to enforce majority morality. Much police energy is now devoted to investigating the so-called "victimless" crimes—varieties of sexual conduct between consenting adults, bare-bosomed bars, pornographic movies, and private drunkenness. That energy could be better used in the detection and prevention of crime against persons and property.

But will the public demand the further closing of outmoded penitentiaries in favor of "community supervision" of convicted criminals? Only, one suspects, if the convicts are returned to somebody else's community—unless courageous political leaders succeed in educating public opinion.

Plato and the Jewish prophets conceived of a justice that includes mercy and the opportunity for self-fulfillment. That concept seemed hardly related, in the 1970s, to the practices of policemen in America's inner cities, the functioning of the overcrowded courts, or the product of the prisons' correctional efforts.

Nor did such a concept find much favor with the people themselves. A more common attitude was expressed on bumper stickers:

Support Your Local Police.

18. Clark, *Crime in America,* p. 123.

CHAPTER 7

Pressure Politics: Shall the Few Rule, or the Many?

IMAGES 7

The Friends of the Gun

REFLECTIONS 7

The People against the Centers of Power

The Friends of the Gun

On a Quiet Street

Washington, the District of Columbia, our nation's capital. A quiet downtown street, around the corner from the giant hotels and department stores that cluster near the White House. A tidy sidewalk, a few men in business suits walking in the humidity of a summer day. Unhurried. There are patches of well-kept lawn. Back from the lawn, a row of buildings, set wall-to-wall. Some are three floors high, some are more. The fronts of the buildings are decorated in cut stone, solid but somehow graceful, in the style developed by the American colonists when their ruler was King George III. It is a quaint street of office buildings, made to look like a row of colonial mansions.

Abruptly, among the Georgian fronts, there is a more modern building. Taller, with square windows and walls of black marble. Solid. An investment. The owner planning to stay in Washington for a long time—as long as there is a Washington to stay in. The building has a large, splendid doorway. On one side of the door, aluminum letters are fastened into the marble:

THE NATIONAL RIFLE ASSOCIATION OF AMERICA

On the other side of the door, more aluminum letters:

THE RIGHT OF THE PEOPLE
TO KEEP AND BEAR ARMS
SHALL NOT BE INFRINGED

Inside that quiet building, there is office space for 250 employees. There is a museum displaying more than 800 firearms. One of the items is a pistol that belonged to General Ulysses S. Grant, eighteenth president of the United States and (some years later) eighth president of the National Rifle Association. There are editorial offices for a monthly publication, *The American Rifleman*. There is an office to account for an annual budget of at least $6 million. Most of all, there is a nerve center linking this national headquarters with some 12,000 local shooting clubs, state rifle associations, wildlife, conservation, and police officer associations, gun manufacturers, and gun importers. There is a legislative and public affairs division, which informs any of the members of the organization (more than a million members, each paying annual dues of $6) of any legislative threat to "the right to keep and bear Arms" (or to buy or sell or transport them). Practically overnight, the NRA can send perhaps half a million letters of protest speeding to the offices of United States congressmen. If any city councilman or county supervisor or state legislator has the courage to offer legislation that would regulate the traffic in guns, the computerized membership list can supply the names of the gun enthusiasts in his district who should have a warning of the threat.

That the National Rifle Association should have such power with Congress, and with state and local legislatures, seems hard to believe, until one remembers that guns are important to Americans, historically, psychologically, and economically. Many figures of American history—Daniel Boone, Marshall Dillon, Sergeant York—are associated with guns and shooting. Endless hours of television time are spent showing reruns of the myth of the American frontier, where courage and the Colt revolver strode together into the noon-day sun. About 8,000 Colt revolvers were made each year during the height of the frontier period. At least 150,000 of them are made annually in the 1970s; a growing new sport is the fast-draw competition.

The sale of firearms, ammunition, and shooting accessories totals more than $300 million a year. The gun in America is big business; the industry has a $3 billion investment; it isn't just a few hardy sportsmen who support the National Rifle Association.

The mystique of the gun can be implanted in children's minds before they can even talk. There are teething rings in the shape of guns, and diaper pins with protective heads carved in the shape of pistols are available. American boys are given toy guns to enliven their play as casually as girls are given dolls.

After all, guns are guaranteed to us by the Constitution.

> The literature of the NRA does not quote the full text of the Second Amendment of the United States Constitution. They leave out the same important phrases that did not fit on the marble wall. The Second Amendment reads: "A well-regulated Militia, being necessary to the security of a free State, the right of the people to keep and bear Arms, shall not be infringed." Many claim this refers to a right of the people *collectively* to maintain an armed force—a right denied the colonists by King George. If so, the *individual* citizen has no constitutional right to keep a firearm in his home.

A Tale of Four Guns: Part 1

The 6.5-mm Mannlicher-Carcano Bolt-Action Carbine

In the middle 1950s, a step was taken by the armed forces of various European nations that affected a corner of the American economy. Agreements were reached concerning the standardization of personal weapons to be used by the soldiers staffing the armies of the North Atlantic Treaty Organization (NATO). In adopting a single sized cartridge—thus making ammunition interchangeable across national borders—NATO officials rendered obsolete the weapons carried by the foot soldiers of England, West Germany, Norway, Sweden, Belgium—and Italy. These rifles were suddenly useless as army weapons, but private citizens in the European countries were not allowed to purchase them. They were not useless to gun importers in the United States. At an average cost of $1 each, the rifles began to enter our country. Even with a 52 percent import duty, the cost to the importer was little more than $2 per rifle. They were eventually sold for from $12 to $40 each.

One of the items most heavily imported at the time was the bolt-action Mannlicher-Carcano, an Italian carbine first designed in 1891. Shortly before the NATO decision, this rifle had been declared unsafe for military use by the Italian government because its barrel showed a distressing tendency to explode in the face of the person using it.

In the years between 1955 and 1958, nearly a quarter of a million such rifles were received in the United States. By then, the sale of domestically manufactured rifles had declined by some 50 percent, and the profits of the industry had vanished. Several of the plants making sporting rifles for the American public were located in Massachusetts; the economy of the state felt the impact of foreign competition; and, on April 28, 1958, the junior senator from Massachusetts did his duty. John F. Kennedy introduced a bill to prohibit the importation into the United States of arms originally manufactured for military purposes. Kennedy's bill, co-sponsored by Representative Albert P. Morano of Connecticut, met unyielding opposition from the National Rifle Association. Because there was support in Congress for some kind of legislation, the NRA supported a substitute measure, which only prohibited the return to this country of military weapons sent abroad through the foreign assistance program. The substitute bill, passed on June 23, 1958, left the loophole that permitted the continued importation of Carcano rifles.[1]

On November 22, 1963, a bullet fired by a Mannlicher-Carcano rifle ripped into the brain of President John F. Kennedy as he was riding in the rear seat of an automobile in Dallas, Texas. The rifle had been purchased through the mail. Its purchaser had not needed to establish his mental stability or fitness to own a deadly weapon. The dealer had no way of knowing that Lee Harvey Oswald (he signed a different name, anyway) was a former Marine, now normally unemployed, who had been in and out of psychiatrists' offices, had visited Russia, was subject to occasional checkups by the FBI, and sought a place in history. There was no delay, no chance for local police to look into the record or character of the purchaser of the gun. Indeed, the local police were not notified that the gun was being mailed. To obtain his rifle, Lee Harvey Oswald had only to send a money order to the dealer.

A Voice from Middle America
John Wesley Weeks, electronics engineer and registered Republican, remembered after seven years his feeling of shock and outrage at the murder of President Kennedy. He says,

> We were mad, and I was mad, that this one clown, Oswald, could come along and strike out the vote of the people. We weren't really supporters of John F. Kennedy, but, nonetheless, he was the President and we supported him as President.

John Weeks owns a rifle, a shotgun, and a handgun. None of them has been fired for twenty-five years. He would be happy to register them with the police.

Congressman Dingell and Public Opinion
In late 1966, Robert MacNeil began working with NBC documentary producer Fred Freed on an hour-long program to be called *Whose Right to Bear Arms?*

MacNeil described their actions many months later:

> We were both convinced that the evidence pointed overwhelmingly to the need for federal legislation to restrict the sale of firearms. It was calculated that 17,000 people would die in the

1. Carl Bakal, *No Right to Bear Arms* (New York: Paperback Library, 1968), p. 147.

United States by gunfire in 1967. No other civilized people has such a high homicide rate. The issue seemed beyond argument. Every conceivable eminent and qualified authority in the nation — successive Presidents, the FBI, police chiefs, judges, and criminal psychologists wanted tighter laws. Countless bills had been introduced in the federal and state legislatures in recent years but almost none had passed. In Washington, they had not even come out of committee.

The reason was a powerful and well-financed lobby led by the National Rifle Association. . . .[2]

MacNeil and Freed felt that their topic was not really even controversial. Public opinion polls showed that 75 percent of the American public favored a law requiring the registration of rifles and shotguns and 80 percent or more favored the requirement of registration for pistols and revolvers. Rather than rehash familiar arguments, their purpose was to examine the motives and the techniques of those opposing gun-control legislation. The program concluded with an interview (cross-examination, really) of Franklin Orth, executive director of the National Rifle Association. According to MacNeil, the interview was "designed to bring out very clearly the inconsistencies —in fact, the hypocrisy—of the NRA position, which tended to support measures to limit misuse of firearms but in fact worked diligently against them."[3]

Even before the filming of the program was complete, however, producer Freed received a letter from Democratic Congressman John D. Dingell of Michigan. Dingell was a member of the House Committee on Interstate and Foreign Commerce, which is assigned the task of legislation concerning broadcasting and of studying the impact of legislation currently in force in the field of broadcasting. Dingell said that he took a considerable interest in commentaries involving firearms, and threatened that, if the program actively pressed for a particular legislative position and did not give full expression to the opponents of anti-gun legislation, he might find it necessary to bring the matter forcefully to the attention of the Federal Communications Commission and the chairman of the Commerce Committee. Shortly afterward, the advertiser who had intended to sponsor the program withdrew.

When the program was completed, it was shown to network executives, who decided that it should be shown, even without a sponsor. But the NBC legal department decided that it would have to be re-edited. Network executives would soon be called on to testify on other matters before congressmen, and they did not wish to do so in an atmosphere of hostility.

In the editing, material that tended to embarrass Mr. Orth of the National Rifle Association was removed. MacNeil's original conclusion had been that, in face of broad public support for gun control legislation, it was time for Congress to resist the pressures of the gun lobby and pass a bill. This conclusion was eliminated from the program.

In Dearborn, Michigan, the department of parks and recreation in the spring of 1968 developed a program of instruction in marksmanship. It was offered during weekdays, and there were classes specifically for women. And the TV cameras were there to record it. Targets in the shape of human silhouettes. The secretaries and suburban housewives

2. Robert MacNeil, "The News on TV and How It Is Unmade," *Harper's*, October 1968, pp. 79–80.
3. Ibid., p. 80.

and grandmothers and maiden aunts lining up and chatting happily as they waited for their turns. Taking the pistol, holding it in both hands, at arms length, a deep breath, a squeeze of the trigger . . . and on the first try most of them closed both eyes and missed and the instructors probably thought the safest place on the range would be down by the targets.

Why Dearborn? For five days at the end of July 1967, the night sky was alight with the flames of the Detroit riots. "When I looked at that sky," one of the lady marksmen said, "I decided that if any of *them* tried to come into my house, I'd be ready."

Why Dearborn? Perhaps because, many years ago, Mayor Orville Hubbard announced that Negroes would not be permitted in his city after sundown and he got reelected every time by a bigger margin.

A Tale of Four Guns: Parts 2 and 3

The Remington Target Rifle with Telescopic Sight

Following the assassination of President Kennedy, and for five years thereafter, legislation was introduced in Congress which attempted to control the easy purchase of deadly weapons. Such legislative proposals were not new; they had been made for years and were supported by every president from Franklin D. Roosevelt through Lyndon B. Johnson. This was a record of thirty years of active concern by the single man elected by all the people and expected by them to define and express the public interest.

In 1968, gun control legislation was introduced in the United States Senate by Senator Thomas J. Dodd of Connecticut and Senator Edward M. Kennedy of Massachusetts—both states which are centers for the manufacture of pistols, rifles, and shotguns. On April 4, 1968, the Senate Judiciary Committee, voting six to six, failed to support the gun-control bills on which they had held hearings. During the course of the debate, the angry Senator Dodd demanded, "How many more people have got to be assassinated in this country?"

An hour later, Dr. Martin Luther King, Jr. lay dying on the balcony of a motel in Memphis, Tennessee. His throat had been all but torn away by a sniper's bullet. The bullet was fired from a Remington rifle with a telescopic sight. It had been purchased a few days before in Birmingham, Alabama, over the counter of a sporting goods store. Cash money paid: no questions asked, none answered. No delay for a police investigation of the purchaser. No way to discover that James Earl Ray was an escaped convict, eager to fire the opening shot of a new racial war.

On April 5, Senator Dodd, with the aid of his supporters, Edward Kennedy of Massachusetts and Joseph Tydings of Maryland, did win Judiciary Committee approval of a gun-control bill—by a vote of nine to seven. To achieve this, however, he agreed to abandon the provision of the bill that completely prohibited the sale of rifles and shotguns by mail in interstate commerce—the way Oswald got the gun that killed President Kennedy.

Even while a narrow majority of the Judiciary Committee was being formed, the pictures of the dying Martin Luther King were shown on television screens—the pathetic, stricken faces of his assistant ministers, the haste of the ambulance attendants, the running policemen, the outstretched arms of those who, suddenly motionless against a gloomy sky, pointed across a vacant lot filled with trash towards the rooming house from which the shot had come.

This was no casual incidence of local brutality. This was the planned and carefully executed murder of the man who still believed that race warfare need not come, the man who believed that white America could still be led to remember the teachings of love professed by Jesus and the promise of equality written in the Declaration of Independence. His death was the signal or excuse for new rioting, looting, and burning.

As the funeral cortege of Martin Luther King wound through the streets of his home city, hundreds of black and white Americans joined together in the heartbroken refrain:

We shall overcome ...

The May 1968 issue of *The American Rifleman*, monthly magazine of the National Rifle Association, dismissed the murder of Martin Luther King somewhat casually. "No law," the magazine stated, "that human ingenuity can devise would have prevented the murder. . . ." The same issue illustrated an article called "Happiness Is a Warm Gun" with a picture of an eight-year-old boy holding some dead pheasants and a shotgun. *The American Rifleman* carries a regular column of legal comment which discusses court cases dealing with concepts such as that of justifiable homicide.

In 1970, 52 percent of all murders were committed with handguns. Since the twentieth century began, 750,000 Americans have been killed with privately owned guns—more than have been killed in wars. Of 126 policemen killed while on duty in 1971, 94 were killed by bullets from handguns.

The .22 Caliber Iver-Johnson Revolver

Sometime in the 1960s, a small target pistol moved off the assembly line of the Iver-Johnson manufacturing plant in Fitchburg, Massachusetts (home state of the Kennedy family). It was light, fairly accurate, and could be fired rapidly. It could be purchased for $15. It was sent to a sporting goods store in Los Angeles County, California.

In August, 1965, several days of unrest following an incident of police brutality culminated in riots in the Watts district of Los Angeles. The results: 34 persons dead, 4,000 arrested, $35 million of property destroyed.

Albert L. .Hertz lived several miles away in Alhambra, a more affluent suburb of Los Angeles. Mr. Hertz was seventy-two years old. He was probably hardly aware of the existence of the black ghetto of Watts except as an exit sign on the freeway. He learned of it through the television and newspaper reports of the riots. Concerned that the police power might no longer be adequate to protect his family, he went to the sporting goods store and purchased the Iver-Johnson target pistol. He registered his purchase with the authorities, in accordance with California law; that was to become important. Months later, Mr. Hertz died, and the pistol passed into the possession of his daughter, Mrs. Robert F. Westlake, who soon moved to a wooded suburb of San Francisco.

She came across the pistol in her attic and recognized it as a greater source of danger than of protection. Mrs. Westlake gave it to a neighbor, who gave it to her son, who traveled back to southern California and sold it to a casual acquaintance; the casual acquaintance was a dark young man born in the Arab country of Jordan. He was the brother of Sirhan Sirhan.

On June 5, 1968, Senator Robert Kennedy appeared among his jubilant supporters in the ballroom of a Los Angeles hotel. Early returns indicated that he had won the California presidential primary election. He spoke briefly of the triumph, spoke of his gratitude to his supporters, and held up his two fingers in the sign of peace. Senator Kennedy was then taken to the kitchen, so that he could go quickly to another room of celebrating supporters waiting to hear him. The senator paused to shake hands with members of the kitchen staff. Waiting for him beside the serving counters were Sirhan Sirhan and the .22 caliber Iver-Johnson.

This time, *The American Rifleman* did not treat the matter so casually:

> The rights of two hundred million law-abiding Americans to own and use firearms legitimately are gravely threatened because of three assassins, all of them possibly Communist tools.[4]

In September of 1968, the County Council of Montgomery County, Maryland, met to consider a proposed local ordinance to require the registration of guns. The most distinguished witness to testify at the Rockville hearings was Senator Joseph Tydings of Maryland, who urged this local action to match that proposed by himself and fellow senators on the federal level. The hall was crowded, and the most vocal members of the audience opposed gun control legislation. As Senator Tydings spoke, loud voices, unidentified, shouted out from the crowd:

Go back to your niggers!

Two years later, Tydings would harvest the full wrath of the friends of the gun. Declared the number one target of the gun lobby, which would finance the campaign against him, he would be defeated in the 1970 election by Republican J. Glenn Beall, Jr.

It was four and a half years since the assassination of John F. Kennedy in Dallas. During that time, nearly 97,000 other Americans died by the gun — 35,000 murders, 50,500 suicides, and 12,000 accidents. During that time, Martin Luther King, Malcolm X, Medgar Evers, and George Lincoln Rockwell were murdered with guns.

The death of Robert Kennedy was, for many, a last straw. Congressmen carried market carts full of letters favoring gun-control legislation into the hearing rooms. Petitions were circulated. New bills were introduced. Congressmen discovered that they had always been opposed to violence.

The friends of the gun pointed out to Congress that the regulation of gun use was a matter for the states. When the drive against the unrestricted sale and use of guns spilled over into the state legislatures, the friends of the gun insisted that any regulation of the weapons industry was the responsibility of Congress.

Meanwhile, Michigan had a law requiring the registration of guns when purchased. But it was an easy drive from Detroit into Ohio, where it was reported that guns could be purchased near Toledo at drive-in restaurants. *Two cheeseburgers and a Colt revolver, please.*

Perhaps the people were beginning to realize that the traditions of the frontier were no longer appropriate in an urban, industrial society. Perhaps they could no longer bear to think that their political leaders — men who embodied hopes and dreams for a better life — faced constant danger from guns held by madmen or professional killers. Perhaps the time had come at least to take action that might prevent

4. Ashley Halsey, Jr., "Can Three Assassins Kill a Civil Right?" *The American Rifleman,* July 1968, p. 16.

Burk Uzzle

guns from being acquired by the very young, known criminals, dope addicts, and the mentally deranged. Perhaps the time had come to require gun users to make themselves known to the public authorities, just as those who drive cars or keep pet dogs are required to obtain licenses.

In fact, support for gun-control legislation was nothing new. The Gallup Poll began asking for opinions as early as 1938. At that time, 80 percent approved of the idea of gun control. Similar surveys indicate that nearly half of American households contain one or more guns; but surveys over a period of years show that even gun owners favor submitting to a police examination before purchasing a gun. And they favor this by a margin of two to one.

Polls taken after the assassinations thus did not reflect a sudden change of opinion. What happened was that an existing opinion became *intense*—strong enough to lead people to write letters to their congressmen, organize petition campaigns, and attend public meetings. The opinion polls again showed nearly 80 percent in favor of legislation aimed at controlling guns, and many were now ready to insist that Congress act.

Articles in *The American Rifleman* took on a more defensive tone. Legislators were urged not to act in haste during a moment of public panic due to the revulsion at yet another Kennedy assassination. The magazine expressed surprise and shock that segments of the public seemed to be willing to yield up part of their "constitutional right" to bear arms. A major article attacked the public opinion polls: they predicted the wrong presidential winner in 1936 and 1948; the samples are numerically quite small; surely no citizen would modify a constitutional right, so that the polls had to be in error—or perhaps even incorrectly reported by those conducting them. As further evidence, *The American Rifleman* reported that, on TV talk shows in a score of cities, when gun-control legislation was the subject, a majority of those calling in *opposed* gun-control legislation. Here was proof of the polls' error![5]

Or was it a demonstration of the quickness of the trigger finger on the telephone dial—so that calls from the friends of the gun got there first?

5. Ashley Halsey, Jr., "Do Americans Really Want Gun Laws?" *The American Rifleman*, April 1968, p. 16.

The Gun Control Act of 1968

The effort to achieve some kind of federal gun control began in the Congress of the United States in March of 1964, just after the murder of President Kennedy. The contest still continues. And the proponents of gun control have little to show for their efforts. Yet those efforts had been supported at their peak by the greatest outpouring of public sentiment expressed on any issue for many years. Senator Tydings received 1,200 letters *per day* supporting gun control, spilling out of his Senate office suite and into the hallway. Tydings sponsored a bill calling for the registration of all firearms and the licensing of gun owners. This would be done by the states—just as automobiles are registered and their drivers licensed by the states—except that the federal government would be prepared to step in if the states did not establish the needed machinery within the required time.

Upon urging by the attorney general of the United States, President Johnson submitted a similar bill to the Congress. Advertising agencies volunteered their help; astronaut John Glenn headed an emergency gun-control committee. Department stores in large cities bought expensive advertisements in major newspapers to point out that they had discontinued the sale of firearms. A newspaper canceled *Dick Tracy* and *Little Orphan Annie* because of their constant depiction of violence. Television executives announced that the displays of violence on dramatic programs would be curbed. When the legislation went before the Senate Judiciary Committee, its chairman, Senator James Eastland of Mississippi, received 3,000 letters and 16,000 telegrams in only three days during June 1968.

Congress was faced by technical issues of some complexity: the definition of ammunition; the question of the gun collector whose antique weapons might be incapable of firing; the best method of providing financing for the program of registration and licensing. But the public campaign of both sides in the controversy was reduced to raw emotion. Supporters of the legislation were denounced as "Communists." Said the National Rifle Association, "No dictatorship has ever been imposed on a nation of free men who have not previously been required to register their privately owned firearms." (When this assertion was investigated by the Library of Congress, at the request of Senator Tydings, it reported that gun-control laws in force in Italy before the advent of Mussolini were relaxed by his dictatorial administration but have been returned to their original strength by the democratic government in power since Mussolini's death. The Library pointed out that gun registration laws have existed in Switzerland since 1874 and in England since 1831.) Opponents of gun control argued that lists of gun owners would fall into the hands of any invading foreign power and permit the invader to crush opposition by seizing all privately held firearms. Senator Tydings replied that the greatest treasure an invader could find would be the membership list of the National Rifle Association, conveniently stored on computer cards at the Washington headquarters.

The Anti-Gun Pressures Fade

The spontaneous outpouring of support for gun control was beginning to recede. The supporters of gun-control legislation also attempted to reduce the issues to raw emotion. Their advertisements urged voters to "write to your Senator, while you still have a Senator," hinting that firearms in the hands of the deranged would soon destroy the United States Senate. Another ad showed a man lying on the ground, shot down by a bullet. The caption stated that "there is only one thing a gun is built to do." These ads were prepared on a volunteer basis by a small Chicago agency, North Advertising. (The National Rifle Association published a story concerning the ads, including the names of seven clients of the agency. Gun fans began to write to the firms involved, threatening a product boycott.) Any person questioning the proposed legislation was depicted as a "gun nut." Elizabeth Taylor Burton of Hollywood financed an anti-gun advertisement in several large metropolitan dailies, signed by twenty-two senators and twenty-one congressmen. (The National Rifle Association published these names, so that its members would identify the legislators on the opposition side, in case their members missed the original ad in the *New York Times* or the *Washington Post*.)

The full force of the issue broke over a Capitol Hill bustling with the frenzy to adjourn and return to the districts to get on with the campaign for reelection. Could any action blunt the impact of the issue on those campaigns? And what kind of action would lose the fewest votes? Nearly every congressman had an opponent traveling the length and breadth of the home district castigating Congress and his incumbent opponent for a failure to enact legislation that would control crime and violence ... perhaps some voters who were not particularly disturbed by the deaths of Martin Luther King and Robert Kennedy would nonetheless see some form of gun control as necessary to the preservation of law and order.

Lyndon Johnson had endorsed a strong gun-control bill, but gun control was not very high on the president's list of priorities. Months before, those problems became overwhelming, and Lyndon Johnson announced a limited bombing halt in Vietnam and his decision not to seek reelection. Thus the president of the United States formally acknowledged a failure of moral leadership and renounced political power. On most issues, the position and activities of the president create a strong, inescapable force around which the political maneuverings of individual congressmen ebb and flow like the tides at the edge of a breakwater. In the summer of 1968, however, President Johnson was serving out a self-limited term.

Congress was left to react to the pressures operating upon it without the catalytic influence of presidential leadership. Gun control was only one of many issues that disturbed voters. However, when senators and congressmen returned home, they were told that a strong gun-control bill would be political suicide. For the friends of the gun were little interested in the general voting record of their representatives. Their judgment would be made on this single issue. In the words of former Senator Joseph Tydings,

> The gun lobby, like any other extremist, single-issue organization, was able to make its voice heard louder and longer than any other group. Supporters of reasonable gun control tend to be multi-issue people, willing to judge their representative on a variety of issues. But the gun extremists, it is widely believed, make their judgment on the gun issue alone. And single-issue people frighten office-holders more than any other threat.[6]

How could a congressman do something for law and order, yet not seem to threaten the enjoyment of sportsmen and gun owners? The answer was the Gun Control Act of 1968, which regulated the shipment of ammunition, rifles, shotguns, and "destructive devices," such as timebombs, in interstate commerce. Four months earlier, such shipments of pistols in interstate commerce had been similarly regulated as part of the Omnibus Crime Bill.

6. "Americans and the Gun," *Playboy*, March 1969, p. 80.

The Gun Control Act of 1968 did not regulate the use of guns; it did not prohibit the sale of guns in interstate commerce. It provided that persons buying rifles or shotguns in interstate commerce now must swear that they are at least eighteen years old. Shipments of guns across state lines can be made only from one licensed manufacturer, importer, collector, or dealer to another. The license fees for importers are set at $50, for dealers at $10. And guns cannot "knowingly" be sold to fugitives from justice or the inmates of jails or mental hospitals.

No registration. No licensing of gun users. No sure way to establish the mental competence or criminal record of gun purchasers. It was a grand victory for the friends of the gun.

But no unseemly celebration marred the air of dignity surrounding the black marble headquarters of the National Rifle Association. The voting records of all legislators concerned with gun-control legislation were researched; the computer supplied the addresses of NRA members in each district.

In January of 1969, *The American Rifleman* featured an editorial welcoming Richard M. Nixon to the White House as the sixth United States president to hold membership in the National Rifle Association. (The five previous presidents were U. S. Grant, Theodore Roosevelt, William H. Taft, Dwight D. Eisenhower, and John F. Kennedy. The NRA did not remind its members of the ironies involved in Kennedy's paid membership nor the fact that Nixon's NRA membership had been presented without charge to him earlier in his political career.)[7] The same issue featured an article titled "Effect of Gun Issue Seen in Vote Results," in which the "voting of thousands of outdoorsmen and conservationists" was credited with "a decisive part" in the victory of at least seven new United States senators. Singled out as the brightest achievements in this electoral sweep were the defeats of veteran senators Joseph H. Clark of Pennsylvania, Wayne Morse of Oregon, and Mike Monroney of Oklahoma, whose distinguished careers meant nothing to the NRA; for these senators advocated gun control.

All through this period, the National Rifle Association enjoyed a privileged status. In 1938, the Internal Revenue Service classified it as an organization "exclusively for the promotion of social welfare." Buttressed by this ruling, the NRA never registered as an organization attempting to influence legislative policy, as lobbies are required to do. The NRA pays no taxes on its income.

In early 1969, an official of the NRA did register individually as a lobbyist—when the FBI began to investigate his organization.

Following Through

A surge of public outrage nearly accomplished the passage of strong gun-control legislation. But public attention turned elsewhere, while the relenting opposition of the NRA remained. With an election at hand, congressmen did not want to seriously offend these one-issue voters. So the Gun Control Act of 1968 was a very weak substitute for the strong measures that had been urged by the supporters of gun control.

7. In September, 1969, President Nixon was presented with an eighty-nine-year-old shotgun that once belonged to his uncle, Charles Wright Milhous. Accepting the gift from the neighbors at the San Clemente Western White House, President Nixon remarked, "I've never shot a gun."

When legislation has been passed, it must be implemented. The NRA and its allies were prepared to follow through the entire process by which congressional intent is translated into administrative regulations.

The Alcohol, Tobacco and Firearms Division of the Internal Revenue Service was charged with implementing the Gun Control Act of 1968. The division proposed strong administrative regulations, which IRS Director Sheldon Cohen felt expressed the intent of Congress, and which he described as a compromise. When public hearings were held, so that "interested parties" could discuss the proposed regulations, fifty-two groups and individuals gave oral testimony or submitted written statements. One statement—a letter from Senator Dodd of Connecticut—endorsed the proposed rules as "reasonable and necessary." The other fifty-one statements, coordinated by the NRA, sought to weaken, modify, or even eliminate the proposed regulations, claiming they went far beyond the intent of Congress. Confronted by such apparent unanimity, government officials accepted many of the weakening amendments recommended by the gun lobbyists.

The Saturday Night Special

In 1972, Congress was concerned with an important loophole that had been overlooked by the Gun Control Act of 1968. The act prohibited the importation from abroad of handguns which the secretary of the Treasury found to be of "no potential use to sportsmen." This had an immediate impact: 1,239,930 handguns were imported into the United States in 1968; by 1970, their number had fallen to 279,536.

The act did not, however, ban the importation of the *parts* of handguns. Gun dealers found they could make their own gun frames and add cheap, imported barrels, triggers, firing pins, grips, hammers, cylinders, and springs. No very complicated tools were required; the manufacture of these cheap weapons became a "cottage industry"

(like pottery or rug weaving) in a number of states. Selling the results for $10 or less, gun dealers received at least a 100 percent profit. About 60,000 of these weapons were assembled in the United States in 1968; an estimated 1 million were produced in 1970. They are called "Saturday night specials." That name came from the Chicago gangster vocabulary of the 1930s. Minor hoodlums would go down to Cicero on Friday afternoon, pick up a cheap pistol, and use it in Saturday's armed robbery. It could then be thrown away.

America's passion for guns became an issue in foreign relations. Seven nations complained that forbidding the importation of cheap handguns, but permitting their domestic manufacture, was contrary to American obligations under the General Agreement on Trade and Tariffs, which stipulates that whatever a government allows to be manufactured domestically it should also allow to be imported.

Senator Birch Bayh of Indiana held hearings of his Juvenile Delinquency Subcommittee in early 1972 and worked out proposed legislation that would ban the manufacture and sale of such guns. Even the National Rifle Association agreed that cheap handgun parts should no longer be imported; guns ought to be reliable.

The sense of public outrage generated by the 1968 assassinations had died down, and Senator Bayh's bill did not then seem terribly pressing to the Senate.

A Tale of Four Guns: Part 4

The Charter Arms .38 Caliber Revolver

Arthur Bremer, aged twenty-one, an unemployed bus-boy, disappointed in a love affair with a sixteen-year-old girl, packed up a suitcase and his two guns and drove to Canada in a rented car. The month was April 1972. Bremer's purpose was to assassinate President Richard Nixon during Nixon's visit to Ottawa. Why? In order to get some attention—he imagined the bulletins interrupting television programs—and bring some drama (including his own death at the hands of the Secret Service) into his rather ordinary life.

Arthur Bremer had no difficulty obtaining the weapons he planned to use. They were a Browning 9-mm automatic pistol and a Charter Arms .38 caliber revolver. However, in preparing to cross the border into Canada, Bremer pushed the Browning pistol into a recess in his trunk, and it fell down in front of the right rear wheel. He could not retrieve it.

On April 13, Bremer saw President Nixon pass by in a motorcade, but he was unable to carry out his plans. He caught other glimpses of the president but was again prevented from firing. He finally decided that the president was too well-protected while traveling in Canada and decided to follow him to Washington. On April 24, depressed at his repeated failure to carry out his mission, Bremer wrote in his diary,

I'm as important as the start of W[orld] W[ar] I [.] I just need the little opening and a second of time. . . . I go crasy with delight when I hear Jhonny Cash's new record, *"You but me Here."*

"I shot you with my .38
And now I'm doing time"[8]

8. From excerpts published as "An Assassin's Diary," by Arthur Bremer, *Harper's*, January 1973, p. 62 (Bremer's spelling is reproduced).

Bremer went to see the film *A Clockwork Orange*. While watching, he conceived the idea of substituting George Wallace for Richard Nixon as victim, in spite of his worry that a Wallace death would not merit as much television coverage.

Bremer followed the Wallace campaign. He attended a number of rallies in Michigan, becoming a familiar figure to some of the Wallace workers. Then, at a rally in Laurel, Maryland, on May 15, 1972, his chance came. As George Wallace stepped from behind his bulletproof rostrum to shake hands with the crowd, Arthur Bremer's hand holding the .38 caliber revolver came out through the crowd, and the firing began. George Wallace fell to the ground, seriously wounded. Stray bullets struck three other people. Arthur Bremer was captured. CBS Television News recorded every second of the assassination attempt. Bremer got his moment in the sun.

George Wallace was permanently paralyzed by a bullet that lodged in his spine. After a five-day trial, Bremer was found guilty by a jury which felt his diary revealed him as sane, not insane. He was sentenced to sixty-three years in prison, on various counts of assault. When the judge asked if he had a statement to make before imposing sentence, Bremer said, "Looking back on my life, I would have liked it if society had protected me from myself."[9]

The Senate Acts

The attempted assassination of George Wallace, while in the midst of his campaign for the Democratic presidential nomination, rekindled public interest in the topic of gun control. A bill moved through the legislative process and was passed on August 9, 1972. It outlawed the manufacture and distribution of the Saturday night specials made in the United States from imported parts. The gun lobby followed the progress of the bill and succeeded in including a provision eliminating the requirement of the 1968 law that dealers keep records of the sale of .22 caliber rim-fire ammunition. This was viewed by the gun dealers as essentially a harassment and the most objectionable feature of the 1968 law.

Because it seemed certain that some legislation would pass, friends of the gun lobby introduced two weakening amendments. One permitted the continuing sale of the Saturday night specials, banning only their manufacture and the importation of their parts. Senator Bayh, sponsor of the bill, said that this amendment would "gut" it. The amendment was defeated by a roll call vote of 70-27. A slightly less overwhelming vote defeated the second gun-lobby amendment, which would have banned cheap handguns on the basis of unreliability, rather than because of unsuitability for "sporting purposes."

The purposes of the proposed bill were preserved against attacks by the National Rifle Association. However, a comparison of 1972 with 1968 voting showed the gun lobby had acquired the support of ten new senators. Ten senators elected since the 1968 debates voted for the NRA position, whereas their predecessors had voted against the lobby.[10] The most notable example was Senator J. Glenn Beall of Maryland, who defeated Senator Joseph Tydings in 1970 with the help of a gun-lobby campaign.

But the purposes of the Senate bill were very limited. Floor debate gave a glimpse of what a bill with real teeth in it could have looked like. Amendments were introduced that would have made the law into real gun-control legislation. For example:

9. *San Francisco Chronicle*, August 5, 1972.
10. For the complete list, see *Congressional Quarterly Weekly Report*, August 19, 1972, p. 2105.

Senator Philip Hart proposed an amendment that would have outlawed the possession of handguns by any persons except the military, the police, approved security guards, and federally licensed target-pistol clubs. The amendment was defeated on a roll-call vote, 84 to 7.

Senator Edward M. Kennedy of Massachusetts (his two brothers slain by assassins) proposed an amendment requiring the registration of every civilian-owned gun and the licensing by the federal government of every person owning a gun. The amendment was defeated on a roll-call vote, 78 to 11.

A Gallup Poll conducted in late May, 1972, showed 71 percent favoring a law that would require a person to obtain a police permit before he or she could buy a gun. Those owning guns felt the same as those who did not. Only 25 percent opposed the policy, and 4 percent had no opinion. Dr. Gallup commented that these were the same results his poll had obtained for more than thirty years.

Even the limited purposes of the Senate bill were too strong for the House of Representatives. The House took no legislative action on the issue, and it died for the 92nd Congress.

Four assassinations. Three completely successful, one very nearly so. The shooting of George Wallace removed the Alabama governor from the presidential campaign. His absence from the ballot probably insured the reelection of Richard Nixon, who had been Arthur Bremer's first intended victim.

The political decision of the people can be frustrated by senseless violence. Some of the people resent it. These crazed assassinations drew attention to the widespread and largely uncontrolled ownership of guns in the United States and their frequent use to "settle" family arguments, contests with the police, and conflicts between street gangs.

Public opinion favored the registration and licensing of guns. Gun owners agreed. The public had held this opinion for more than thirty years.

The National Rifle Association, claiming to speak for gun owners, disagreed. Guns, they said, do not kill people. Only people kill people. The friends of the gun stood by their motto:

When guns are outlawed, only outlaws will have guns.

The People against the Centers of Power

Assassinations, cop-killings, and murders in the family. Robert Kennedy killed, and George Wallace shot, by "Saturday night specials." These events intensified, at least for a time, a public opinion that had been established for three decades. That opinion favored the universal registration and licensing of guns.

But the National Rifle Association and its allies in the gun lobby disagreed, and they prevailed, either crippling or blocking meaningful legislation.

The gun issue was important enough by itself. More important was what it demonstrated about the nature of government in America. It suggested that overwhelming majority opinion can be frustrated by the operations of an interest group. If the gun lobby has such power, imagine the influence, on other issues, of the oil lobby, or the American Medical Association, or the AFL-CIO. More frightening still, think of decisions made without debate in the public arena. President Nixon did not consult opinion or even congressional leaders before invading Cambodia, or launching the saturation bombing of North Vietnam in December 1972. Cozy relationships between a president's administration and large corporations are revealed by muckraking reporters.

If public opinion is impotent, unable to control the outcome of policy decisions that are made in the full glare of national attention, what hope has public opinion of influencing decisions made by officials who do not consult public feeling?

The question is fundamental. Where is power in America?

The Will of the People

In spite of their desire to make "ambition counteract ambition," by establishing a system of checks and balances, and removing the selection of most officials from direct action by the people, the founding fathers claimed that the Constitution established a system of government, in which, ultimately, decisions rested with the people.

James Wilson described the new government to the Pennsylvania ratifying convention:

> When you examine all its parts, they will invariably be found to preserve that essential mark of free governments — a chain of connection with the people.

James Wilson spoke of this "chain of connection" with easy confidence. He enjoyed the benefits of ignorance, for the American government was an experiment. The colonists, far from the center of government in England, had enjoyed much influence upon their own government. Attempts of George III and his ministers to curb that influence led to the War for Independence. The eighteenth century was rich in speculation about the nature of government by the people and claims of the moral rightness of such a government over all others. But Locke, Montesquieu, Rousseau, and Harrington (to name authors who established the intellectual climate in which the Constitution was written) did not much examine the nature of that chain of connection. There had been little experience of democratic government. Athens, in ancient Greece, had developed a workable form of democratic government; but the authority of that government extended only to a city. Thus there was no conflict between national and local interest, for the "nation" and the city were the same. Democratic government in a large nation remained to be tried.

On the crucial question of the connection between opinion and policy the founding fathers followed the lead of the eighteenth-century political theorists, by ignoring it. It was assumed that, when the government was bound to follow the general will (or, in more modest terms, be guided by public opinion), this fact alone would stimulate the formation of public opinion and ensure its effective communication. The actual connection, or *linkage*, between public opinion and public policy was hardly discussed. The possibility that the people might be little interested in the new power bestowed on them was not considered. Rather, efforts were concentrated on limiting the scope of that power. The frequent shortcomings of a democratic electorate, apathy and ignorance — which in the twentieth century cause many to despair for the future of democracy — were little mentioned 200 years before.

What Do Elections Mean?

The election was planned as the most important link in the chain between the government and the people. The Constitution provided for periodic elections. The incumbent president or at least his party is judged on the basis of performance every four years. Congressmen must renew the support of their districts every two years. The Constitution provided six year terms for senators; the Seventeenth Amendment provided for their direct election by the people.

But what does an election mean, as a guide to the making of government policy? The National Rifle Association claimed that the 1968 election proved that supporters of strong gun-control legislation can expect the end of their political careers. Four new supporters of the NRA joined the U.S. Senate in 1968, six in 1970. Opponents of the Vietnam War after the defeat of Hubert Humphrey proclaimed the rejection by the people of "Lyndon Johnson's War." The war was still going on years later. The message of the 1972 election was, at best, ambiguous. President Nixon won a personal endorsement but so did his partisan opponents in Congress.

The chain of connection between the people and their government is clear in an election: the people decide, among alternatives posed by the political parties, who their rulers shall be. The people pass judgment upon their incumbent officials. But their electoral voice does not prescribe the decisions to be made or the direction taken when new crises shall arise, or old issues be joined anew.

When the election is over, the people no longer speak with a single voice. The office-holder attempts to predict and anticipate the reactions to events of his constituents. Trying to anticipate public opinion, he attempts both to lead and to follow it. But where is the fine line between "leadership" and "manipulation"?

The Measurement of Public Opinion

Surely, if the will of the people lives at the moment of an election, it does not die when the ballots are counted. Public opinion is recognized as a real force by dictators, as well as by democratic politicians. But how does anyone know the content, the degree of unanimity, and the importance of public opinion on a given question?

Since democracy began, politicans have done their best to keep in touch with the public. Every congressman scans the newspaper of his home district, including the letters to the editor. He reads his mail or has it read. The *pro* and *con* opinions are counted on each issue. He keeps track of what the people tell him when they visit his office, attend a campaign rally, or write him a letter. Many congressmen send lengthy questionnaires to every postal address in the district (postage being free to U.S. congressmen) to ask the opinion of their constituents on a variety of issues awaiting governmental decision.

But do such contacts really reveal the nature of public opinion? Letters to the editor are written by those who are so concerned that they will use the necessary time and energy. And they may do this much only at the urging of an organized group. The same is true for writing a letter to a congressman. For a constituent to pay a special visit to a congressman costs both time and money. Unless this is part of a vacation tour, the constituent is undoubtedly very interested indeed in a particular piece of legislation. In short, the congressman is in ready contact with special and local interests, but probably not with national public opinion—or even with general opinion within his district, because of the highly selective process that results in people seeking to communicate with congressmen.

Careful research reveals that no more than 10 percent of the electorate have *ever* written a letter to a newspaper editor or a congressman. And nearly all the mail received by congressmen comes from about 2 percent of the voters. In 1964, and probably in every other year, the political opinions of these letter-writers were strikingly different from the attitudes of the general public.[1]

Only in the last thirty-five years have techniques been developed for measuring public opinion in a way that does not depend for accuracy on asking an entire electorate to choose between alternatives, as is done in an election. These techniques are grouped under the name "survey research." They are based upon the science of probability, a

1. P. E. Converse, A. R. Clausen, and W. E. Miller, "Electoral Myth and Reality: The 1964 Election," *American Political Science Review* 2 (June 1965): 333.

branch of mathematics. Survey research was developed initially to serve industry: as the American economy changed from a focus on production to a focus on consumption, the future of vast industrial empires came to hinge upon anticipating (and influencing—thus Madison Avenue) the whim of the consumer. The choice made at the drugstore counter between Brand X mouthwash and Brand Y can mean profit or bankruptcy for the mouthwash maker. So he is willing to spend quite a lot for market research.

Survey research is based upon asking questions of a sample of persons selected carefully to represent the opinions of the entire population being sampled. The opinion pollsters soon got into the business of predicting the outcome of elections. Newspapers were willing to pay for stories about who would win, "if the election were held today." And commercial firms might hire the pollster with the best election prediction, feeling that this proved the accuracy of his techniques. Nearly all the pollsters were wrong in 1948. They predicted that Thomas E. Dewey would defeat Harry Truman for the presidency. But this humiliation led to improved techniques, and the pollsters have been remarkably accurate—at least in predicting American national elections—since then. This ability of the pollsters to predict elections and to discover what kind of people prefer which party fascinates campaign managers. It provides many hints for running an election campaign. But does it help explain that "chain of connection" which should exist between the people and their government?

Priorities of Public Opinion

Students of public opinion have developed techniques that can, for a fleeting instant, describe its content. But attitudes on specific issues can change rapidly. (The pollsters picked Thomas Dewey because they stopped interviewing ten days before the election. They thought the campaign was over. Harry Truman didn't think so.) It requires little study of the output of the American political system—presidential decisions, congressional voting—to realize that the connection between public opinion and the content of public policy is difficult to discover. There are several reasons.

To begin with, public opinion is not a single force. There are at least two sides to every question; opinion will be divided on every issue. It is hard to imagine most of the people of the United States accepting a given *idea* at a given time. The closest one can come would be to cite instances when the entire nation seemed to feel the same *emotion*. Outrage when Japan attacked Pearl Harbor in 1941. Or shock and grief when President Kennedy was murdered. On the normal kind of issue, public officials will receive messages from opinion holders with a wide variety of convictions.

Second, opinions are of varying degrees of importance to the persons holding them. When opinions are intense, they are more likely to lead to some kind of action: writing to a legislator, marching in a demonstration, or changing one's voting habits.

When a minority holds an opinion with great intensity, and the majority does not, the minority may receive more attention. As former Senator Tydings expressed it, those who opposed gun control were "single-issue" people; those who supported it were not as likely to judge their representative on this issue alone. But the public opinion polls have not found reliable methods for determining the intensity of opinion.

Another reason for the failure of public opinion effectively to guide public policy is that, in the modern world, the decisions to be made by government are very complex and become the concern of experts. Congressmen themselves make no attempt to become informed about every issue. Congressmen do most of their work in committees that specialize in particular policy areas. Other congressmen give much weight to the opinions of the leaders of these specialist committees, and committee members normally insist upon handling all matters within their assigned fields. The committees depend upon other sources for gathering information. These sources include the agencies and bureaus of the executive branch of government. And they particularly include organized interest groups that feel their welfare is affected by specific legislation.

It is clear that the "general will," in the sense of an opinion held almost unanimously by the public—thus having greater moral force than the sum of individual wills—is an invention of the eighteenth-century philosophers that seldom, if ever, exists in real life. Public opinion is not a single phenomenon. In fact, there are "attentive publics," the citizens who pay enough attention to particular public issues and care about them enough to form an opinion and to act upon it.

The impact of public opinion on a given issue, therefore, depends on its *intensity*, its *distribution*, and its *stability*.

Intensity means strength. How important is his opinion to the person believing that particular way? What will he do about it? Will it determine his vote? Will he form or join a group of people who believe the same way he does? The members of the National Rifle Association and its related organizations apparently believe very strongly that any effort to regulate the sale of guns eventually threatens the possession of their own guns.

Distribution refers to how the holders of a particular opinion are distributed in the nation and within the social structure. For example, if nearly all persons holding a certain opinion are Democrats and live east of the Mississippi, congressmen from safe Republican districts in the West are unlikely to pay them much attention. The friends of the gun, although particularly strong in the South and West, are distributed throughout the nation. They belong to both major parties, and some minor ones. They come from all walks of life. They share in common only their opposition to gun control. On this one issue, they prevail.

Stability refers to the permanence of opinion. Do the people holding a particular opinion continue to believe it, and act upon it, no matter what? Or is the opinion highly volatile, subject to change as world or national events change? (A number of people claimed that all wars are immoral, until the Six-Day War between Israel and her Arab neighbors.) Stable opinion is likely to have the greatest political impact. The friends of the gun seem permanently opposed to the control of guns. They did not change their minds with the murders of Medgar Evers, John F. Kennedy, Martin Luther King, or Robert Kennedy, or the attempted murder of George C. Wallace. Rather, they increased their emphasis on the use of guns for self-defense. And their lobbyists continued to thwart attempts at gun control. As the example of the National Rifle Association demonstrates, group activity is often more important than public opinion in determining the outcome of policy issues. Frequently, the position of the winning group may be quite contrary to the opinion of the majority of citizens who have paid attention to the issue.

Opinion and Policy

The connection between public opinion and public policy is more subtle and complicated than the eighteenth-century democratic theorists imagined it would be. Political leaders understand the properties of opinion very well, and they know that an accumulation of months or years on the calendar will bring their performance before the judgment of the electorate. The public may turn against them because of conditions the public officials cannot influence. But elected officials know they are courting certain defeat if they habitually act in a manner contrary to public opinion that is both intense and stable.

The next election exerts a greater influence over incumbent officials than the previous one. They become experts at predicting public reactions. This has been called "the law of anticipated reaction"; it means that, on issues which stir wide public controversy, the elected official formulates an idea of how his constituents will react before reaching his decision.

> In the 1950s, there was a movement in academic circles calling upon the Eisenhower administration to recognize diplomatically the People's Republic of China. The argument ran that it was absurd to isolate from contact with the West a polity that included so many millions of the world's population.
>
> The most common answer was that "public opinion wouldn't stand for it." The Cold War was at its height, and the national distaste for the methods and values of totalitarian communism presumably demanded that "Red" China be ignored and the fiction be maintained that the "real" Chinese government was that of Chiang Kaishek, on Taiwan.
>
> In the 1970s, Richard Nixon (who had been vice president in the Eisenhower administration and a leading Cold Warrior) visited the People's Republic of China and arranged for its admission into the United Nations. Television cameras followed his progress through a round of official banquets and his tour of the Great Wall.
>
> It turned out that public opinion would stand for quite a lot.

In fact, the public conviction that communism was the nemesis of democracy and must be resisted with overwhelming military power was an echo of convictions held by President Eisenhower and his austere secretary of state, John Foster Dulles. There is a two-way relationship between government officials and public opinion. Elected officials seek simultaneously to follow and to lead public opinion.

> In 1972, candidate Nixon stated repeatedly that the public would not stand for a welfare system that supports "chiselers" unwilling to find their own jobs. By then, the U.S. Congress had rejected a number of proposals for welfare reform, including those advanced by President Nixon.

The relationship between general public opinion and the decisions of public policy can best be described as a negative, rather than a positive, relationship. Public opinion, *as perceived by public officials*, establishes broad boundaries for the outcome of the process that determines policy decisions. Public officials' assumptions about what they feel general public opinion will tolerate limits the range of policy options they are willing to consider and support.

In 1968, Lyndon Johnson discovered that the public would not tolerate the commitment of even more ground troops to the apparently futile war in Vietnam. In 1972, Richard Nixon surmised that the public would not care too much if American airmen, safe above the clouds, rained unprecedented destruction upon the "primitive" society of North Vietnam below. And he was right—until Russian-made missiles brought down more and more B-52s, and their crewmen were taken prisoner.

The predictions of public officials about the state of public opinion determine which policy alternatives are thinkable, and which are unthinkable. Policy proposals that deeply offend the values of the national culture might be called *sacrilege*, although without narrow religious connotations. A proposal that the federal government seize all privately owned farmland, food processing plants, and retail markets in order to operate the entire food-production industry would be so foreign to American habits of private enterprise that it could only be entertained by a few esoteric academics. The chance of immediate public agreement with such a proposal would be zero.

At the opposite end of the spectrum are the *traditions* of a society that are so ingrained that they can hardly be challenged. An example might be the conviction that the Constitution is a noble and time-proven document. A proposal to scrap the Constitution in favor of, for example, a parliamentary form of government (which would also destroy federalism and the states) would, at least initially, meet with nearly solid opposition. Figure 7-1 shows how the continuum can be diagramed.[2]

Figure 7-1. Public-Opinion Continuum.

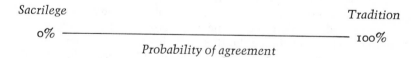

Important concepts may be located between the extreme ends of the continuum. Proposals for change in policy begin as *private ideas*. When they have won the backing of a substantial group, they become *proposals*. Proposals are the object of attention in the communications media, and they are discussed in legislatures and political party conventions. When the proposal is accepted, it becomes a new *policy*. The policy may be controversial, and it may not win public support. This was the case of Prohibition, which was made part of the U.S. Constitution in 1919, but removed in 1933. It was also the case with President Johnson's expansion of the ground war in Vietnam, a policy adopted without being publicly considered as a mere proposal. When policies are implemented and win broad public support, they are no longer part of the public debate. They gradually assume the properties

2. This analysis is based on that of Bernard C. Hennessy in his *Public Opinion* (2nd ed.; Belmont, Calif.: Wadsworth, 1970), pp. 396–400, by permission of the author.

of traditions. This was the case of the Social Security system adopted by the New Deal, attacked by Republicans in 1936, but accepted and even expanded by the Eisenhower administration in the 1950s.

Ideas, proposals, and policies may all be described as "issues" that are debated and amended, then accepted or rejected. They are the raw materials, or "inputs" of the political process. Traditions and sacrilege, obviously, cannot be thought of as issues. An idea which is too outrageous to win the support of others and become a proposal recedes to the status of sacrilege. A policy which fails to win broad endorsement never becomes a tradition. The complete continuum, therefore, is shown in Figure 7-2.[3]

Figure 7-2. Relationship between Opinion and Public Issues.

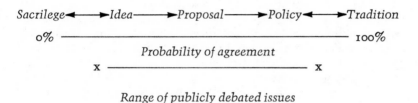

Range of publicly debated issues

Figure 7-2 suggests why there is a built-in advantage for the status quo: established policies do partake of the qualities of tradition, and those persons who suffer from them must convince others of the evil of that suffering, before enough strength is gathered to formulate a proposal for consideration by governmental institutions. The policy of racial segregation in public facilities in the southern states, although given constitutional sanction only in 1896,[4] was regarded as a sacrosanct tradition by the southern white power structure. Many years of effort were required before the abolition of segregation could be presented even as a proposal. This was first done successfully before the Supreme Court, the branch of the national government least directly responsive to public opinion.

Figure 7-2 also reveals the function of political leaders, which is to bring new ideas before the public as proposals and persuade a substantial segment of the public that they deserve to become policies. When we approve of the proposals, we call this process the "leadership" of public opinion. If these ideas were initially considered sacrilegious, we call it "courageous leadership." When we do not approve of proposals, we accuse their sponsors of "manipulating" public opinion. When political leaders object to our favorite proposals on the grounds that "public opinion would never accept them" (sacrilege!), we accuse those leaders of "pandering" to public opinion.

> John F. Kennedy wrote a prize-winning book called *Profiles in Courage.* Spanning American history, it was a series of biographical sketches of a handful of politicians who risked their careers by opposing the clearly understood wishes of their constituents.
>
> The number of politicians with that kind of courage is a small and select number. Is this an admirable property of the American political system?

3. Ibid.
4. *Plessy v. Ferguson,* 163 U.S. 537 (1896). See also the more detailed discussion of the civil rights movement, above, pp. 10-14, 200-201, and below, pp. 318-343.

Two Kinds of Politics

While an election may seem the finest hour of free institutions, when public opinion is both determined and implemented, the actual accomplishment of an election is more modest. It is a device for changing government officials peacefully. Victorious candidates may speak of a "mandate," but it is difficult to prove that the electorate was attempting to transmit any particular message along with its vote. For public opinion can be volatile, transitory, and seriously divided. It can also be ignorant.

Campaign activities are one kind of politics, and the process through which public policies are determined—a process that takes place between elections, with the knowledge of the previous and, more important, forthcoming elections hanging over it like a shadow—is a rather different kind of politics. The role of public opinion in electoral politics is remarkably straightforward, compared to the role of public opinion in the process of policy formation. This second kind of politics seems to be dominated by the activities of spokesmen of special and private interests, and self-appointed spokesmen for public opinion. Long before democratic theorists invented the notion of the public will, the right of individuals and groups to testify concerning the policies of direct interest to them was well established. That right is specified in the First Amendment of the United States Constitution:

> Congress shall make no law . . . abridging . . . the right of the people peaceably to assemble, and to petition the Government for a redress of grievances.

The Right of Petition

The National Rifle Association may be unique in that it claims a section of the United States Constitution (the Second Amendment concerning the right to bear arms) as being somehow its own personal property. No other interest group can lay claim to such authority for its single legislative purpose. (The Prohibition amendment reflected the strong will of a single group, but it was eventually repealed.) The strength of the NRA and all other interest groups (which are called "pressure groups" or "lobbies" when we don't agree with their positions) can be traced to the First Amendment and its guarantee of the right of petition.

Right of petition. The very words have a medieval sound. The humble citizen, presenting a claim upon the sympathy of his king. A "petition for the redress of grievances." Not an appeal to law, but an appeal to the good grace of the sovereign, who would grant the request from a deep sense of justice.

The British Parliament built its power as an institution upon this privilege of individual citizens. As Parliament grew in authority, it claimed the power of the purse: the king could not raise money for whatever projects he had in mind without the permission of Parliament. It became the custom that, before Parliament granted his monies, the king was first required to heed a number of petitions and respond to the complaints they contained.

The right of petition came to be considered a fundamental right. Its linkage in the First Amendment with the right of assembly was completely natural; for individuals, then and now, normally form into like-minded groups (interest groups) more effectively to seek a change in governmental policy.

The right of petition, guaranteed in the Constitution, is a primitive form of communication between the citizen and his government. It is a guarantee that the subject will be heeded when he addresses a specific request to his ruler. It was a right established before rulers were democratically elected.

But the medieval picture of a humble citizen petitioning his sovereign has quite vanished when we look at modern democratic government. Gathered around the seats of governmental power, we find clusters and constellations, so numerous as to be uncountable, of spokesmen for special interests. These political satellites are unlike the heavenly bodies, because their orbits are not fixed. Their attractions to each other, and their influence upon the makers of policy, are constantly changing. Their power has, at times, overshadowed even that of government.

Interest Groups in a Complex Society

Modern government could hardly function without interest groups. For modern government deals with a society infinitely more complex, and its interrelationships with that society are much more difficult to understand, than any scheme of things dreamt of by ancient kings. The need for some new decision is normally brought to the attention of the political system by an interest group; the debate on what that new action should be is carried out by, or with the aid of, interest groups; interest groups lead a chorus of complaint if the new policy threatens their welfare; and, when a new policy is adopted, persons benefiting from it usually form a group to defend that policy against change.

In addition, interest groups possess special knowledge. Legislators or bureaucrats who succeeded in ignoring all such groups would operate in a vacuum of ignorance. A proposal to regulate working conditions in a particular industry could hardly be formulated without listening to representatives of the workers and employers in that industry. When Congress considers setting tariff rates on imported goods, the representatives of domestic manufacturers flock to Washington. Even the departments and bureaus of government have lobbyists — to convince Congress that their programs merit the requested appropriations.

Interest Groups Are Everywhere

Americans have a certain fondness for joining. Some groups are strictly local in membership and may have little interest in politics. In 1948, the small town of Amherst, Massachusetts, had

> well more than one hundred Clubs, Lodges, Leagues, Guilds, Tribes, Granges, Circles, Unions, Chapters, Councils, Societies, Associations, Auxiliaries, Brotherhoods, and Fellowships. Their specialties or special interests, to name a few, include cards, cameras, stamps, gardens, churches, teachers, speakers, voters, horses, business, service, golf, nature, eating, fishing, gunning, parents, grandparents, ancestors, needlework, temperance, travel, and kindergarten.[5]

5. L. Doran, *University of Massachusetts Alumni Bulletin*. December 1948, p. 4, as cited by Earl Latham, "The Group Basis of Politics, Notes for a Theory," *American Political Science Review* 46 (1952): 376.

One result is that any enterprising land developer who lays out a new subdivision provides a community-center building, so that citizens' groups will have a place to meet.

In a similar way, the building boom in downtown Washington has for years depended on the construction of office buildings to house the many groups that seek to influence the federal government. Some groups are so permanent and well-financed that they erect their own buildings. The National Rifle Association building is one example. The AFL-CIO building, a handsome structure almost in the shadow of the White House, is another. A block away is the imposing structure of the United States Chamber of Commerce; it is both older and larger than the AFL-CIO structure. Executives from the business and union groups eat lunch in the same restaurant in the Lafayette Hotel, but not with each other. Both groups, however, dress like executives, and you can't tell them apart. Open class warfare doesn't go on at the Lafayette. Each group of lobbyists recognizes the other's right to work within the system.

Washington, D.C., has no manufacturing industry. Its industry is government; its workers are the employees of government and the staff members of the organizations who seek to influence government. The latter are called "lobbyists" because of the former practice of stopping legislators in the antechamber, or lobby, of the chamber where formal legislative business is conducted. The lobbyist sought the last chance to whisper into the legislator's ear before he went in to cast his vote. It was also the last chance to press some favor, including money, upon the legislator.

Practices are no longer quite so crude, but the name remains.

A political interest group is organized, at least in part, because of its concern for a particular area of public policy. The group may have either a large or a small membership; it may or may not be operated along democratic lines, so that the members have a voice in determining the organization's policy position. In the United States, many pressure groups claim to be organized along democratic lines and to have a large number of members, who, if they cannot carry an election through their personal voting, will at least be able to provide (or withhold) the money or precinct work essential to a political campaign. Some groups may be consulted for the usefulness of their information, but the threat of intervention in the electoral process is the best weapon for gaining the rapt attention of legislators during the consideration of new policy. Many lobbies that work closely with Congress use campaign contributions as their sanction and reward. Groups which lack such financial resources — such as the public-interest lobbies associated with Ralph Nader — depend for effectiveness on mobilizing public opinion.

Because pressure groups are such a permanent fixture of the American political landscape, and their activities are to be found wherever public decisions have to be made (go to your local city council and listen to the homeowners' association protest a change in the zoning law), some writers speak of a "pressure system" that surrounds the officials of government.

This might be democratic and even fair if every citizen had an equal chance to be represented by organized pressure groups. But do they?

The Bias of the Pressure System

The bias of the pressure system is toward the further success of groups that are already strong, well-organized, and led by men who understand how government works. Associations of manufacturers fit this description; so, nowadays, do labor unions. Such groups owe their strength to established government policies. Their lobbyists are well placed to delay, modify, or entirely prevent the change of those policies. The structure of American government—the many chances of a veto in Congress, the coziness of government departments with the clients they serve—reinforces their power.

Does every citizen have an equal chance to have his needs represented by an effective interest group? Think upon the hundred or more "Clubs, Lodges, and Leagues" in Amherst, Massachusetts. This is surely organization—much of it political—at the grassroots. Supposedly anybody can join, but do they? To be effective requires some understanding of parliamentary procedure. To attend the meeting, the young mother has to be able to pay a baby sitter. And she'll want clothes that are new enough and stylish enough that she won't seem out of place.

Groups may be found everywhere, geographically speaking, but they are not found at every point on the social scale. Group membership presupposes a certain amount of education, a certain level of income. It is a middle-class phenomenon. The poor, the socially outcast, and the uneducated are seldom found in the ranks of interest-group organizations. Furthermore, although interest groups often claim to represent the wishes of a broad-based membership, the membership is unlikely to be as well informed as the lobbyist leaders on the scene, who normally make their own decisions and portray them as those of the membership. In short, few, if any, interest groups are run democratically.

Some of the most effective pressure organizations have no mass membership and avoid operating within the public view. For example, a number of antitrust suits prepared in the Department of Justice have been settled by "consent decrees" after the quiet persuasion of lobbyists has brought the intervention of the White House staff. A settlement by consent means that the offending corporation says, "We don't admit doing anything wrong, but we'll stop." There is no trial, fine, or other punishment.

Political scientists have been fascinated by interest groups for at least the last half century. Groups have been studied from a variety of viewpoints, and a collection of case studies has been gathered. They show, in sharp detail, the power of pressure groups on specific issues in the policy-making process, as compared to the candidate images and party identifications which play such a compelling role in the politics of the electoral process. They also show that, within the broad limits set by public opinion, the contest between groups, or the relationship between private groups and public agencies, may determine the policy decision.

Bob Adelman

In general, a pressure group will be most effective if:

1. Its attention is limited to a small range of issues, perhaps to a single issue. *Gun control.*

2. Its membership is widely distributed, making a difference in the political balance in several districts of a given legislature. *The NRA claimed credit for the defeat of six incumbent senators in 1972.*

3. When the organization does not have a widely distributed membership, or any mass membership at all, it seeks to influence key government officials, but it will do so in private. *Dita Beard of ITT contacted Richard Kleindienst, then deputy attorney general of the United States.*

4. The mass membership should be united upon the goal of the organization but permit its leadership great flexibility in its selection of tactics. *The NRA leaders report the success of their efforts, after the fact, in* The American Rifleman. *They need not consult the members before implementing their tactics.*

5. Funds should be readily available for use at the crucial time. *The NRA has at least $6 million a year.*

6. The goal of the organization is not clearly contrary to the prevailing opinion of the time. *Although public opinion favors gun control, it is not an intense opinion. The NRA hitches a ride on the ecology issue by making alliances with conservationist groups.*

7. Opposition is either unorganized or poorly organized. *The supporters of gun control are also interested in other issues. The NRA is only interested in defeating gun control.*

In light of these standards of effectiveness, let us consider some currently famous pressure groups, and one from the pages of history.

Organized Labor: Too Many Issues

Many political interest groups do not have influencing public policy as their primary purpose. The National Rifle Association, for example, was originally formed to promote marksmanship among civilians. Similarly, a labor union exists so that its members can band together as a single force to seek agreement with the employer on wages, hours, and working conditions. Unions had to win the right of collective bargaining—the very right to exist—through the political process. Having won this right, union members are not necessarily committed to a further program of legislative action.

Just as the organization in the 1960s of poor people and black people was viewed with alarm by groups with a greater share in the benefits of the economic system, the organization of unions in the 1930s (and before that in the 1890s) was feared as the vanguard of a social revolution. Some American labor leaders had indeed read their Marx; but their members, by and large, had not. The tradition of union militancy was smothered by success. The fear that organized labor would become a political army dedicated to revolutionary change proved unfounded.

The political effectiveness of a mass organization depends upon the relationship between its leaders and its members. The leaders of American labor (with notable exceptions in the Teamsters and the building trades) have interested themselves in a broad range of liberally oriented legislation, from civil rights to legislative reapportionment. But they have not been able to mobilize the full political potential of organized labor in support of these goals. The membership was often indifferent, and George Wallace's 1968 campaign showed that it could be hostile to the union leadership's involvement in social-reform issues.

Labor has exerted undeniable political force since the 1940s only when the health of the union movement itself has been threatened. Labor has mobilized to battle proposed right-to-work laws in state after state. Such laws make union membership completely voluntary, permitting workers to enjoy the advantages of collective bargaining without paying dues to support the union. Right-to-work laws have been adopted only in states where labor unions have been small in number and politically ineffective. In states where the right-to-work law was proposed, union members turned out in full force to defeat the referendum measures and the candidates endorsing them.

Access and Opinion Change: the Case of Oil

There are many points at which the decisions of government can be influenced. One does not appeal to Congress to install a new stoplight at the corner of Fourth and Main. Both national and local governments are further subdivided into executive, legislative, and judicial branches. The gun lobbyists were present wherever the action was: first in Congress; then at the Internal Revenue Service hearing; and always at meetings on gun control in state legislatures and city councils.

Selecting the point of access is the basic decision of strategy. Individuals and groups who can claim their rights are being denied appeal to the courts. If the Constitution is involved, the final decision is determined by the United States Supreme Court. Groups in tune with the prevailing public sense of what is important usually look to the legislative branch to protect and expand whatever favors they receive from public policy. This depends on using a knowledge of the fine points of the legislative process. They may, in addition, play a game of balancing one element of the federal system against the other. When oilmen won the depletion allowance in 1924, they entrenched themselves to protect it—to protect it long after the industry became a stable giant, rather than a collection of wildcat firms, long after scientific procedures were perfected to take much of the uncertainty out of exploration for oil. It was this uncertainty that justified the depletion allowance in the first place. Seekers after oil were presumed to take the risk of sinking a dry hole only if assured that a successful strike would be protected with this tax advantage. In the 1920s, oil exploration was one of the burgeoning industrial (and financial) activities that supported the business boom and the feverish speculation of the stock market. The boom died with the stock market crash of 1929, but the oil depletion allowance remained.

Oil developed special friends. One was the late Senator Robert Kerr of Oklahoma, an oil-producing state. A current friend is Senator Russell Long of Louisiana, son of the great Huey. Huey Long founded a national Share Our Wealth movement with the slogan, "Every Man a King." Russell Long makes speeches against welfare chiselers.

Oilmen have not been partisan; they have freely contributed to the campaigns of whichever candidates have a chance of winning. Protection of the rights of American companies to seek oil in exotic corners of the world has been an important factor in determining American foreign policy under both Democratic and Republican administrations.

In 1968, an oil well being sunk in federally leased underwater lands off the shore of California tapped a high-pressure pool. Millions of gallons of crude oil flooded the beaches around Santa Barbara. Marine and bird life was destroyed. In 1969, Secretary of the Interior Walter J. Hickel announced a study of the oil depletion allowance that could modify or eliminate it. Secretary Hickel, formerly the governor of Alaska, was considered a friend of oil. But it was clear that protecting the special privileges of the oilmen was no longer in tune with the climate of opinion. The methods of Congress are so complicated— majorities must be held together at so many stages of the process— that it is much easier to defeat a bill than to pass it. It is easier for a group to protect an existing privilege than to win a new one. The modest reduction of the oil depletion allowance in 1969 signalled a change in the public climate of American politics.[6] Protection of the natural environment would be every politician's declared goal in the early 1970s.

The giants of the oil industry have not been wounded by the cut in the depletion allowance. In six months of 1971, the major oil companies' after-tax income was $3 billion; its profits were a fifth of all industrial profits in the U.S., and double the combined profits of the auto companies.

This result is achieved by controlling supply and adjusting prices to hold up profits, a pattern established by the first John D. Rockefeller. The major oil states of Texas and Louisiana regulate production in the interest of the major companies, while the federal government limits the importation of cheap foreign oil. Small, independent companies that launch price-cutting wars are dealt with severely.

At present, the oil companies are buying into the natural gas, coal, and uranium industries, in order to establish monopoly control of fuels and avoid present and future competition in the marketplace.

6. The history of the tax-reform bill of 1969, which included a reduction of the oil depletion allowance, is recounted above in Images 4.

ITT: The Real Scandal

The International Telephone and Telegraph Company is one of the "conglomerate" firms that have grown so phenomenally in recent years. Conglomerates are based on the same concept as the "holding companies" that were held partially to blame for the stock market crash of 1929 and were presumably ruled out of existence by the stock market reforms of the New Deal.

The public revelation that ITT offered $400,000, through its Sheraton Hotels subsidiary, to support holding the 1972 Republican National Convention in San Diego, California, brushed the Nixon administration with scandal only when it was matched with the fact that the administration soon thereafter negotiated a consent decree which resulted in dropping an antitrust charge against ITT, the eighth largest industrial corporation, permitting it to proceed with the acquisition of the Hartford Fire Insurance Company, fourth largest company in its field. President Nixon agreed to hold the convention in Miami, Florida.

Conglomerates provide exotic profits for financial manipulators, but the growth of giant companies involved in diverse businesses has proved the antithesis of efficient management. Their growth was encouraged by economic pressures resulting from the Vietnam War. The Johnson administration made no effort to regulate conglomerates, claiming that regulatory legislation would have to be perfected, and this required the initiative of Congress. The Nixon administration holds that existing legislation is adequate, thus stifling whatever congressional initiatives are developed.

Reporter I. F. Stone charged that ITT corrupted Democratic officials in Connecticut to win state approval for the merger with Hartford Insurance. This fact, he wrote, inhibited the Democrats from developing the issue raised by ITT relationships with the Republican White House. Stone then described the real economic and political scandal that he claims lies behind the story of ITT:

> The biggest issue in the ITT affair is that these huge corporations can make up in political influence what they lack in the capacity to survive the normal tests of the free market. ITT got its consent decree . . . by negotiating from a position of weakness, by pleading that unless they were allowed to get away with their acquisitions they might collapse, adversely affecting the stock market and Nixon's reelection chances. . . . Economic power paid off in political power at the expense both of good business management and of good government.[7]

The example of ITT posed the question in a stark manner: to what extent may the decisions of a democratic government be made in secret for the benefit of private or partisan interests, and that government still merit the label "democratic"?

The Watergate scandal made that issue inescapable.

The Anti-Saloon League: An American Success Story

Perhaps the most successful pressure group in American history was the Anti-Saloon League, provided that success is defined in terms only of achieving the group's goal.

The Anti-Saloon League operated in the second decade of the twentieth century. It was a time of enthusiasm for social reform. Muckrakers exposed big business, and Theodore Roosevelt defined

7. I. F. Stone, "Behind the ITT Scandal," *New York Review of Books,* April 6, 1972, p. 10.

the presidency as a "bully pulpit" for the practice of moral leadership. Gathered together in the Progressive movement were "good citizens" (often pompous and certainly optimistic representatives of the middle class in towns and small cities) determined to battle the evil influences of Wall Street, corporate trusts, and political parties.

The league regarded the use of alcoholic beverages as evil, and drunkenness as sinful. The saloon—which took fathers away from home and their paychecks away from wives and children—was labeled the greatest blot on a presumably Christian society. The goal of the league was to strike at the very source of this evil by prohibiting the manufacture, importation, sale, and use of alcoholic beverages. The American national government had never before attempted thus to limit personal behavior. It would take an amendment to the Constitution.

The Anti-Saloon League enjoyed the active support of most of the Protestant churches in the United States. But its organization was separate from the structure of the churches. This arrangement permitted the churches to remain uninvolved in the hurly-burly of practical politics. And it gave league leadership great flexibility in choosing strategy. Many churches held special Temperance Sundays. The collections taken on those days went to the Anti-Saloon League headquarters.

The league, in turn, encouraged church members to judge congressmen and state legislators solely according to their positions on Prohibition. They were remarkably successful. Legislators soon found that the league could deliver—or withhold—crucial numbers of votes. This was true not only for the United States Congress but also for the legislatures of most states. Opposition to the concept of banning alcohol by constitutional amendment was diffuse, and less well organized, although probably numerically superior. The Prohibitionists were one-issue people. Their campaign was relentless. Two-thirds of the House and Senate eventually proposed, and the legislatures of three-fourths of the states ratified, the constitutional amendment.

The Eighteenth Amendment was adopted on January 29, 1919, and endured until it was repealed by the Twenty-first Amendment on December 5, 1933. The era of optimistic reform that produced Prohibition was ended by World War I. The mood of the Roaring Twenties was set by press agents, the explosive growth of automobile ownership, feverish business development, flagpole sitters, a revolution in moral standards, and an apparent desire by Americans to catch up with the more sophisticated societies of Europe. Prohibition killed the saloon—but it was replaced, first by the speakeasy, and later by the cocktail lounge. Prohibition was the law, and the fashion was to break that law. Bootlegging became big business. From bootlegging, organized crime branched into other fields, and the remnants of the bootlegging empires prey upon American society today, managing gambling, prostitution, extortion, and much of the drug traffic.

A determined pressure group achieved Prohibition. When it went into effect, however, most people rejected its purpose. Failure to respect this particular law not only destroyed that law but led to lessened respect for the law in general. The Eighteenth Amendment did not turn out to be in the public interest, nor did it stop Americans from drinking.

What will become of marijuana?

A Problem of Theory and Practice

The phenomenon of pressure politics in the United States poses a difficult question for any student of the subject. That the role of government has been expanded far beyond the founding fathers' vision cannot be denied. In general, the public, to the extent they are represented by the two major parties, accepts this expansion. But private interests have been able to use the expanded authority of government to assure their own welfare. (Think of the federal loan guarantee that saved Lockheed from bankruptcy, or the tax and foreign-trade advantages of the oil industry.) Such advantages have seldom been totally congruent with public needs, yet public opinion has tolerated them.

American government is not operating in the manner anticipated by the theorists of democracy who influenced the authors of the Declaration of Independence and the Constitution. The problem for the student of government is this: should the theory be changed to fit the practice, and arguments sought to demonstrate that current practice nevertheless achieves some of the same goals as the original theory? Or, should one recognize the contrast between theory and practice, and support the change of the practice, by peaceful means or otherwise, to return it somehow to a closer match with the original theory?

The first of these alternatives has been followed by scholars called *pluralists*; the second by some of those who are called *elitists*. Both are attempting to acknowledge the power of private interests in American government and incorporate that knowledge into a fresh understanding of how American government does, or should, work.

Pluralism: The Primacy of the Group

Pluralism takes its very name from the multitude and diversity of groups. It holds that the structure of power in America is not a single structure, not a monolithic hierarchy consisting of a few rulers and a mass public. Rather, the constellation of power varies from time to time and from issue to issue. Organizations develop (trade associations, unions, other alliances of the like-minded), which protect their own specific interests in public policy. When one of these has grown overly strong (as corporations did in the nineteenth century), opposing groups (such as labor organizations in the twentieth century) develop to counter-balance their power.

But unions, threatening a strike, can win wage increases that the employer adds to his prices, rather than subtracting from his profits. This is not competition; it is accommodation; and the public pays the cost.

Constantine Manos

The common man is available as an ally who can be persuaded to support the goals of these interest groups; public opinion, in appropriate cases, can thus be mobilized. But each group becomes important only in that corner of public policy that concerns it, and even there it must contend with groups organized by its opponents. To the extent that pluralist theory is an extension of the economic concept of free enterprise, it includes the assumption that the competition between self-seeking groups in the political arena operates to assure the good of society through the operation of some kind of "invisible hand." Some pluralists recognize the bias of the pressure system against participation by the less wealthy and the less educated, but insist that the interests of such people can be well represented in the political contest by activist group leaders. Furthermore, there is no conspiracy to limit participation, and individuals are free to rise above their social handicaps and become activists themselves. Recognition of the possibility of participation, and the availability of periodic elections that determine which officials will serve as referees in the contest between groups, provides a feeling that public policy is indeed influenced by public feelings, and that the chain of connection between the people and their government is real, if sometimes invisible.

Nevertheless, the people do not have a very predominant role. A leading theorist of pluralism, Robert Dahl, explains:

> The fundamental axiom in the theory and practice of American pluralism is, I believe, this: Instead of a single center of sovereign power there must be multiple centers of power, none of which is or can be wholly sovereign. *Although the only legitimate sovereign is the people,* in the perspective of American pluralism *even the people ought never to be an absolute sovereign;* consequently no part of the people, such as a majority, ought to be absolutely sovereign.
>
> Why this axiom? The theory and practice of American pluralism tend to assume, as I see it, that the existence of multiple centers of power, none of which is wholly sovereign, will help (may indeed be necessary) to tame power, to secure the consent of all, and to settle conflicts peacefully. . . .[8]

8. Robert A. Dahl, *Pluralist Democracy in the United States: Conflict and Consent* (Chicago: Rand McNally, 1967), p. 24.

Dahl thus acknowledges that the connection between the people and their government is indirect, perhaps even vague. In a later work, he concedes that it may not be strictly accurate to label American government constructed on this model as a "democracy," in the classical sense. The more exact term for a system characterized by multiple centers of power is "polyarchy."[9]

Portraits of a Power Elite

Elite theorists look at some of the same phenomena as do the pluralists, but arrive at an interpretation that is quite the opposite. Instead of emphasizing the tendency of private interests to balance each other, they emphasize the cases in which powerful interests hold sway with no effective countervailing force at work. Rapacious corporations of the late nineteenth century were able to prevent the growth of real labor unions until the 1930s; an alliance between military planners in the Pentagon and the corporations that build their hardware dominated the Armed Services Committees of both House and Senate through the 1950s and 1960s, and the recommendations of these committees were accepted by Congress without serious question.

One strain of elite theory concentrates upon the social backgrounds of the politically powerful. These men attended the same universities, belong now to the same clubs, serve as directors of the same companies, take their vacations at the same resorts, and share the same view of the world.[10] Holding the key positions in the executive branch of government, the large corporations, and the huge private foundations, they are in a position to coordinate the activities of the institutions they lead and thus base national policy upon their shared view of the world. Furthermore, they can manipulate public opinion, for they influence (through foundation grants) the research topics of academic experts, and they control the mass media.

The contest between interest groups is a reality too strong to deny; many elite theorists follow the lead of C. Wright Mills by asserting that this contest, largely carried on in the halls of Congress, is concerned only with secondary issues, while the power elite decides the questions of economic policy, war and peace, the life, comfort, or death of men and nations. Congress deals in "the middle levels of power," diverting public attention from the really crucial issues.[11]

9. Dahl, *Polyarchy: Participation and Opposition* (New Haven: Yale University Press, 1971).
10. See G. William Domhoff, *Who Rules America?* (Englewood Cliffs, N.J.: Prentice-Hall, 1967); and his *The Higher Circles* (New York: Vintage, 1971).
11. C. Wright Mills, *The Power Elite* (New York: Oxford University Press, 1957), pp. 244, 245.

The most extreme form of elitist theory holds that the two great American political parties are financed and controlled by the same power elite; even labor leaders have been co-opted by the rulers of corporate capitalism; elections, therefore, are a fraud, conducted at the times specified in the Constitution to provide the electorate with the illusion of choice and thus construct a spurious legitimacy for the regime. Any connection between public opinion and public policy is equally fraudulent, for the content of public opinion is determined by the messages disseminated at the behest of the power elite through educational institutions and the mass media.[12] However, other elitists hasten to add that the power elite is not necessarily lacking in concern for the welfare of the masses; indeed, one of its main motives could be a concern for that welfare, as understood by the elite.

The more gentle critics of the pluralist position are content to charge that they incorporate major elitist principles into democratic theory. Excusing the inability of the common people to participate directly in political decision-making, they offer the multiple power centers of the interest-group system as a substitute means of achieving democratic goals in a large and complex social system.[13]

Echo of a More Settled Time

The development of pluralist theory as an explanation of the nature of American government, and perhaps as a justification for the relatively small role played directly in it by the people, largely occurred during the decade of the 1950s. When, during the same era, C. Wright Mills's *The Power Elite* was published, it was greeted with scorn.[14] This was a period of self-congratulation in many sectors of American life, and citizens seemed content to place their confidence in President Eisenhower, turning their attention from politics to private profit or pleasure. Upon leaving office, President Eisenhower warned of the growing power of a "military-industrial complex."

In the 1960s, social problems largely unaccounted for in pluralist theory, and largely deferred by the Eisenhower administration, exploded. Riots in the cities and riots on the campuses indicated that large segments of the people were distressed by their apparent inability to influence the governmental decisions that affect their lives. The best efforts of the Urban League and the National Association for the Advancement of Colored People had not made the ghettos of northern cities livable. Martin Luther King, who called for patience, passive resistance, and faith in the ultimate ability of the system to react favorably, was murdered. War in Vietnam sustained national prosperity while it consumed resources that could have been devoted to cleaning up the cities and the environment. Lyndon Johnson and the Democratic party appeared no more eager than Dwight Eisenhower and the Republican party to curb the power excesses of huge corporations; and, on re-reading, much of John Kennedy's glorious rhetoric struck readers as empty of insight.

Overriding all was the reality of the war. Conceived in the executive branch, fed by the technological ingenuity of the defense industry, and conducted in private by members of the liberal establishment who seemed blind to the moral dimensions of their actions, the simple fact of the Vietnam War seemed the strongest possible argument for adopting the elitist interpretation of American government.

12. Ibid., pp. 305, 310–311.
13. Peter Bachrach, *The Theory of Democratic Elitism* (Boston: Little, Brown, 1967).
14. G. William Domhoff and Hoyt B. Ballard, *C. Wright Mills and The Power Elite* (Boston: Beacon Press, 1968), provides excerpts of the criticisms directed at Mills by liberals, radicals, and "highbrows."

But—

the power of rampant capitalism was finally opposed, and
with success, by organized labor;

the Senate did eventually question the recommendations of
its Armed Service Committee, and only the vote of Vice President
Agnew saved the anti-ballistic missile;

public realization of the futility, if not the immorality, of the
Vietnam War drove Lyndon Johnson to quit the White House;

in the four years of his first administration, Richard Nixon did
move American forces from the ground to the air.

Serving the Public Interest

The reaction of many to the events of the 1960s was to take to the
streets. But the March on the Pentagon failed to levitate that formidable structure (as Abbie Hoffman had promised), and the 1968
demonstrators in Chicago radicalized each other, with the help of the
police, but could not block the nomination of Hubert Humphrey and
failed to get a peace plank written into the Democratic party platform.
By 1972, the Yippies in Miami's Flamingo Park were largely a tourist
attraction.

Perhaps it was because the street demonstrators spoke in violent
and revolutionary rhetoric, which general public opinion was not
ready to accept. Perhaps it was because the self-styled radicals never
hid their contempt for the common people whose help they needed
to create a mass movement. Whatever the reason, street politics as
a vehicle for change was dead and buried in the bowels of the earth
by November 1972.

But the imbalance of the pressure system remained: the producing interests normally could prevail over the protests of the unorganized consumer. People who had no illusions that the system could be changed overnight sought ways to reform it by playing its own game. The role of consumer advocate was invented and personified by Ralph Nader. The function of the citizen's lobby was reinvented and redefined by Common Cause. The way to overcome the bias of the pressure system was the application of new pressures.

Ralph Nader burst upon the public consciousness as the author of *Unsafe at Any Speed,* an attack upon the auto industry's casual attention to the safety of its products, with particular attention to the Chevrolet Corvair. General Motors sought to discredit Nader by hiring detectives to uncover dark secrets in his private life. Revelation of this fact in a congressional hearing did more to advance the cause of auto industry regulation than any other factor: for General Motors to react to a serious, documented charge with a show of naked power was at least a tactical error, and possibly the revelation of a deep-seated public-be-damned attitude.

His reputation secure, Nader organized a variety of crusades in the interest of the consumer. Students and young lawyers flocked to his banner. A series of "Nader Reports" were issued, to be greeted with mixed reviews. The master project, enlisting the efforts of some thousand helpers, was a study of Congress, and of each incumbent running for reelection in 1972. Ralph Nader became something of a giant-killer.

Meanwhile, John Gardner, a Stanford psychology professor, educator, World War II intelligence officer, registered Republican and foundation executive, who served President Lyndon Johnson as secretary of Health, Education, and Welfare, became restless at the apparent unresponsiveness of government to the concerns of ordinary people. In September, 1970, he formed Common Cause as a citizen's lobby. Within a year, it had enrolled 200,000 members willing to pay dues of $15 per year. By then it had launched active lobbying projects in Washington and in several states. John Gardner commented on the group's birthday,

> If there is anything I have learned in the past year, it is that this discontent—this sense of being "had"—runs right through the American people. The sense of being dispossessed and separated from the decisions governing your own lives is not limited to the black, the poor, and the young. It's the average American. It's even the upper-middle-class American. . . .
>
> But there is hardly an issue where a malfunction of government occurs that doesn't hit the poor harder. . . .[15]

There was about John Gardner and the movement he founded a sense of middle-class confusion mixed with outrage. A conservative critic charged, anonymously, that Gardner is a member of the ruling (liberal) power elite whose function, conscious or not, is to draw public attention away from fundamentals. Wrote the critic, "the diminution of establishment power can never take place so long as the establishment's 'house rebel' is leading the rebellion."[16] But Gardner chose to concentrate on issues where real accomplishment would be possible. Many of his efforts were focused on making government more open and responsive. The organization quickly com-

15. Quoted in Judith G. Smith, ed., *Political Brokers: People, Organizations, Money, and Power* (New York: Liveright, 1972), p. 267.
16. Unsigned article in *Human Events*, July 10, 1971, quoted in ibid., p. 263.

piled a record of noble causes joined, together with some modest
successes in influencing policy. For example:

Congressional reforms: The Common Cause publicity campaign
against the evils of the seniority system helped convince both
Republican and Democratic caucuses to adopt resolutions
providing that committee chairmen designated through seniority
can be removed by a vote. It provided hope that the most abusive
and autocratic chairmen can indeed be removed. Even if no
chairmen are voted out of office, it will no doubt encourage some
to be less abusive and autocratic.
   In the 1972 campaign, Common Cause monitored the finance
and spending of congressional candidates.

Ending the war: Common Cause supported successful efforts
in both houses, which were aimed at cutting off funds, or the
supply of troops, by certain dates. But the same legislation or
resolution was never passed by both houses during the
Vietnam War.

Ecology: Common Cause efforts may have tipped the balance
in a close vote on funding for the super-sonic transport.

Welfare reform: John Gardner worked with President Nixon's
Secretary of Health, Education, and Welfare Richardson to perfect
the bill passed by the House under the guidance of Wilbur Mills.
But the Nixon administration did not keep up pressure on the
Senate, and the Senate could not agree on an alternative to the
Nixon proposals. The legislation died.

Expansion of the electorate: Common Cause was a major
source of support for legislation, with a constitutional amendment
proposed to the states as a clincher, which awarded the vote to
eighteen-year-olds.

In spite of its strong beginning, the future effectiveness of Common
Cause was not assured. John Gardner, however, offered a clear perception of the organization's function:

> We are going more and more into the kind of issue that isn't
> going to be settled easily. When you're talking about the gut
> questions of who holds power and how deep are the defenses
> that prevent somebody else from getting power, you are talking
> about final questions over which people will fight to the death.
> Matters like seniority, lobbying controls, campaign spending,
> exposure of conflict of interest get right to the heart of how the
> power structure maintains itself. . . . We're working in a terri-
> tory that no politician can work. They can't afford to. It's too
> close to the bone. . . .
>   You have to understand that for a public-interest lobby the
> most important weapon is public information. It isn't like a
> special-interest lobby, which wants to keep most things quiet.[17]

Enlightened public opinion, therefore, has the potential for counter-
balancing arbitrary authority within the power structure. It was a
conviction as old as the Constitution, no doubt shared by the authors
of the First Amendment.

17. Quoted in Smith, *Political Brokers,* p. 266.

That some public decisions should be influenced by private interests is inevitable, and even praiseworthy; remember the right of petition. When the power of private interests is not checked by competing power centers and is able to prevail in spite of contrary public opinion, then the viability of governmental structures must be questioned.

In a contest between the people and the centers of power, the people are not certain to win. Because of the complexity of such legal artifacts as the tax structure, the people are not certain even to realize they have lost something.

Some version of the power-elite theory was adopted by the street demonstrators; they were never able to enlist widespread public support. Others, who did not expect overnight change, but who wanted to make the system more responsive, became consumer advocates and formed public-interest lobbies.

Slowly, painfully, changes were made.

CHAPTER 8

The People
against Themselves

IMAGES 8

One Nation, Divisible

REFLECTIONS 8

Creating a Nation:
The Unfinished Story

One Nation, Divisible

A restless nation. Expanding to fill the continent, conquering the wilderness, damming rivers to make fruit trees bloom in the desert, the people cluster in cities which then have their centers destroyed by great, arching freeway interchanges. Pathways are thus provided for the automobile, the very symbol of restlessness, individuality, and freedom. But they cannot be built fast enough; the lesson of the traffic jam comes home: assuring the freedom and mobility of individuals brings paralysis and collapse to the social structure.

Americans do not find the root of personal meaning in the places of childhood. You can't go home again; the old homestead has been uprooted for a McDonald's hamburger stand. Nor is the source of personality found in pride of function as craftsman, manager, or worker. There is no feudalism here; all are invited to strive upward, and this means that some will sink downward, and others will find their way blocked by spoken or unspoken judgments that they are not worthy of the competition.

What, then are the bonds that hold a nation together? Is it a common adherence to those great charters of our freedom, the Declaration of Independence and the Constitution? When all citizens take the Constitution seriously, caring what their elected representatives do, preaching and practicing the freedoms of speech, press, and religion, a commitment may be formed that can overcome the divisions which beset America.

But everybody does not take the Constitution seriously. American society, most of the time, and her political system, too often, operate to exclude whole groups, not only from economic opportunity, but from equal treatment by the law.

What value, then is the American dream of equality?

Liberty and Justice for All

Malcolm Crockett ran along the sidewalk, late for school. His breath came in gasps, because of running and because he was trying not to cry. It was hard not to cry. After two blocks, he remembered how to stop. He remembered what his mother taught him to say to himself, half a year before, when he came home after a fight at school.

I am Malcolm Marcus Crockett. I am six years old. I am black. Black is beautiful. I am Malcolm Marcus Crockett sixyearsold. I am black is beautiful.

The words passed through his mind in time with the rhythm of his footfalls on the crumbled sidewalk. His breathing came easier, and

soon it fell into the same pattern as the pounding of his good leather
shoes. Because breathing was easier, the other thing came crowding
back into his memory.. . .

He was ready to leave for school early. His mother told him to take
it easy, there was plenty of time. He did not ask her about the bicycle,
afraid she would say no. He knew he would not dare ride the bicycle
to school, but there would be just time to ride to the end of the street
and back, maybe even twice. He had only been able to ride the bike
for the last four days, because his legs had just grown to reach the
pedals, although it had been a Christmas present from his grand-
father.

His father left the garage door open when he went to the plant, so
it was easy for Malcolm to wheel the bike out of the garage, and he
got it started down the driveway after only two false tries and made
a turn into the street that hardly even wobbled. The street was empty.
Three blocks away, the pavement would end in cactus and desert sand
on the edge of the gully he wasn't allowed to throw trash into any
more. There would be wild flowers on the desert from the spring rains.
The morning sun felt good, and when he pumped faster and faster on
the pedals, the bike went so fast that the wind made his eyes water.

The street ended too soon. Regretfully, he slowed down, swung
wide, and managed a turn in the street without stopping. He rode more
slowly back toward home. As he passed a corner, he heard a car turn in
behind him. He moved over toward the gutter so there would be plenty
of room for it. The car passed him, pulled over to the curb ahead, and
he saw it was a police car, like he had seen on television. Men got out
of each of the car doors, waving their arms at him. Malcolm saw he
could not get past the fat man walking into the middle of the street,
so he stopped. He swung his leg over the bike seat quickly, before it
could fall to the ground.

O.K., boy, where did you get the bike?

The fat policeman had a red face.

The other one came over quickly and pulled the bike away. Malcolm's hands slipped off the handle grips and he reached out for the
bike but it was pulled several feet away, and the tall policeman bent
down to look at it. Malcolm tried to follow, but the fat policeman
grabbed him by the shoulder.

Boy, I asked you, where did you get that bike?

The hand on his shoulder hurt and the bike was out of his reach
and Malcolm felt a hot new wetness rush into his eyes.

*It's mine. I got it from my grandpa. From my grandpa for Christ-
mas.*

*I don't believe that. It's brand new. I bet you stole it from one of
those new houses on Segundo Terrace.*

The tall policeman straightened up. *There's no license on it,* he
said. *No license anywhere.*

The policeman's fingers tightened on Malcolm's arm. He tried to
pull free, to go to the bike, but the hand only became tighter.

*No license! Now you really are in trouble. Every bike in El Paso
County has to have a license. Maybe we'll take the bike and you too
down to the jail and then you can remember where you got it.*

The words tried to rush out, to explain, but they got caught in his
throat and hurt so that he started to cry. And because he was crying
and ashamed the hurt was worse.

But the thin policeman did wheel the bike back towards him and
seemed a little interested in what he was trying to say.

The fat policeman turned his head towards the sidewalk and let go
of Malcolm's arm. Looking around the bulk of the policeman's stomach, Malcolm saw his mother. She was hurrying into the street. Not

running, and her head was held high, but she was still hurrying. The great, soft ball of her hair coming beneath the branch of an elm tree seemed like a signal of safety.

Later Malcolm realized that she had seen him ride away on the bike and went into the street to look for him when he didn't come back. But then, when she came up to the police car, all Malcolm knew was that maybe at last it would be over. The tears came flooding out, and he was even more ashamed, because the painful grip was gone from his shoulder.

Mommy, don't let them take me to jail.

Malcolm could tell that she was angry, because he had seen that flash in her eyes before, but the loud words did not come. Instead, she was biting her lip to keep the loud words back. She explained that he had only been able to ride the bike for the last few days, they had never even thought about a license, and anyway Malcolm had never ridden the bike farther than the end of the street.

It wasn't a bike like this that we were watching for, the thin one finally said. *But I'll call headquarters and check the serial number, just to be sure.*

Malcolm, his mother said, *you run on to school before you're late. I'll take care of the bike.*

Malcolm ran on down the block and across the vacant lot towards the school. But he could not make the crying stop.

When he got to the schoolroom, the class was standing. He slipped down the row to his desk and turned to face the front of the room where the flag hung from a long pole. Miss Simpson frowned at him but didn't say anything. The voices rose around him:

I pledge allegiance. To the Flag. Of the United States of America. And to the Republic. For Which it Stands. One Nation. Under God. Indivisible. With Liberty and Justice for All.

Malcolm moved his lips in time with the words, but no sound came. The wetness still welled into his eyes, and the flag was a blur of red, white, and blue.

A Liquor License for the Moose Lodge

In the aftermath of the Civil War, Congress passed, and the states ratified, the Fourteenth Amendment to the United States Constitution. Southern states ratified it in order to be readmitted to the Union. The amendment was intended to assure that the newly freed blacks (freedmen) would not only be released from the bonds of slavery, but would enjoy the full status of citizenship. But how could the full status of citizenship be secured? In the civil rights cases of 1883,[1] the U.S. Supreme Court held that the Fourteenth Amendment applies only to the official acts of state governments and does not apply to the actions of private citizens, such as the owners of hotels, restaurants, and railroads, who could exclude persons from the use of their facilities on account of race. Therefore, Congress cannot control the discriminatory acts of private citizens, unless those acts are supported and intertwined with the policies of the state.

The effect of this decision was to nullify a large part of the intention of those who passed the Fourteenth Amendment. Justice John Marshall Harlan said as much in his vigorous dissent from the decision. Historians have argued that this trend of decisions permitted the South to win back in the Supreme Court much of what it had lost

---

1. 109 U.S. 3 (1883).

in military defeat in the Civil War. However, still following the principle of these cases, the courts were left with room to maneuver in defining what constitutes the "implication" of the power of the state government in the discriminatory practices of private individuals. This distinction permitted the Supreme Court eventually to invalidate the actions of states taken to enforce racial restrictions in property deeds,[2] and to rule that restaurants open to the public must serve all races.[3]

A question of state "implication" came before the Supreme Court in 1972. A member of Moose Lodge number 107, in Harrisburg, Pennsylvania, brought a black guest to the clubhouse. Mr. Irvis, the guest, was refused service at the bar on the grounds of his race, and for no other reason. Irvis argued that such discrimination is unconstitutional, and that the liquor license granted Lodge 107 should be revoked until the practice was discontinued.

In a six to three decision, the Court held that the mere granting of a liquor license did not involve the Commonwealth of Pennsylvania in the private practices of the Moose Lodge. The Lodge could keep its license. However, the Lodge could not invoke the aid of the Pennsylvania Liquor Control Board in enforcing its racially discriminatory practices.

Justices Douglas and Brennan wrote dissenting opinions, and were joined by Justice Thurgood Marshall, the only black member of the Court. The dissents pointed out that Pennsylvania manages the sale of alcoholic beverages as a state monopoly through state-run stores; the resale of liquor, by the drink, may take place only in licensed hotels, restaurants, and private clubs; and private clubs remain open at hours when hotels and restaurants may not legally serve drinks. Furthermore, the total number of liquor licenses granted in a particular area is proportional to the population, thus giving the possession of a liquor license something of a monopolistic flavor. Liquor licenses have been revoked by Pennsylvania in order to control a variety of conduct presumably offensive to the majority: homosexuality, topless dancing, and even noisy and disorderly establishments. This seems to indicate that the authority of Pennsylvania has been rather intimately implicated in the liquor business.

Wrote Justice Douglas,

> Government may not tell a man or woman who his or her associates must be. The individual can be as selective as he desires. So the fact that the Moose Lodge allows only Caucasians to join or come as guests is constitutionally irrelevant, as is the decision of the Black Muslims to admit to their services only members of their race. . . .
>
> [But] the State of Pennsylvania is putting the weight of its liquor license, concededly a valued and important adjunct to a private club, behind racial discrimination.[4]

Justice Brennan wrote that the Court majority overlooked the fact that organs of government are intended to promote "liberty, justice, fair and equal treatment, and the setting of worthy norms and goals for social conduct. Therefore something is uniquely amiss in a society where the government, the authoritative oracle of community values, involves itself in racial discrimination."[5]

2. *Shelley* v. *Kraemer*, 334 U.S. 1 (1948).
3. *Garner* v. *Louisiana*, 368 U.S. 157 (1961).
4. *Moose Lodge No. 107* v. *Irvis*, 32 L Ed 2nd 627 (1972).
5. Justice Brennan was here quoting his own opinion in a previous case, *Adickes* v. *Kress & Co.*, 398 U.S. 144, at 190 (1970).

The constitution of the Moose Lodge provide that "the membership of the lodge shall be composed of male persons of the Caucasian or White race above the age of twenty-one years, and not married to someone other than the Caucasian or White race, who are of good moral character, physically and mentally normal, who shall profess a belief in a Supreme Being." It has since been changed.

The Crosses Burn Again

Indianapolis, Indiana, December 10, 1972 (Victoria Graham of the Associated Press). The Ku Klux Klan that ruled Indiana with pageantry and terror in the 1920s says it's rebuilding its empire in the 1970s with ballots, bumper stickers, and ballpoint pens.

The hooded order that dominated Indiana from the roadhouse to the Statehouse today holds conventions at Holiday Inns . . . combining wiener roasts with white supremacy and selling KKK decals and trinkets to support the free enterprise system. . . .

Grand Dragon William Chaney, a part-time paper server in Indianapolis . . . said, "Our new Klan doesn't want to burn and destroy. We're going to bring change in the political arena."

But, if the ballot box doesn't work, King Kleagle Paul Book, a jukebox repairman in Kokomo, readily admits the Klan will use other means.

"We are training vigilantes and will use them for self-defense if blacks, socialists, and Communists take over and we lose individual freedom," says Book. . . .

The Klan is holding more and more ceremonial cross-burnings on farms and full-robed streetwalks to distribute literature in courthouse squares. . . .

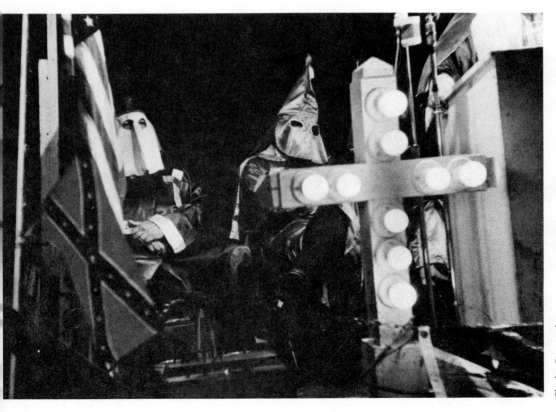

Charles Gatewood

Klansmen distribute reams of anti-integration, anti-Jewish, and anti-Communist literature, racist joke cards, doggerel and green plastic pens that say "United Klans of America."

When Alexis de Tocqueville, the great French student of American democracy, visited the United States in 1831, he spent several weeks in Philadelphia and Baltimore. He reported the following conversation with a citizen of Pennsylvania:

"Please explain to me why in a State founded by Quakers, and known for its toleration, free blacks are not allowed to exercise the rights of citizens. They pay taxes; is it not fair that they should vote?"

"You insult us," replied his informant, "if you believe our legislators could have committed so gross an act of injustice and intolerance."

"Then in your State, the blacks have the right to vote?"

"Certainly."

"Then why did I not see a single Negro at the polling booth this morning?"

"That is not the fault of the law. The Negroes have the right to vote, but they don't show up at the polls."

"That's very modest of them!" Tocqueville exclaimed.

"Oh, they don't *refuse* to go to the polls, but they are afraid of being harmed there. In this country, the law is sometimes unable to maintain its authority without the support of the majority. In this case, the majority entertains very strong prejudices against the blacks, and the magistrates are not able to guarantee them the rights conferred by the legislature."

"I see," said Tocqueville. "The majority claims the right not only of making the laws, but of breaking the laws it has made?"

Six years later, in 1837, the Pennsylvania legislature did enact a law denying the vote to free blacks.

Some Ideas Can Be Taught, Some Can't

From the wires of the Associated Press, June 6, 1969. Somerville, Massachusetts—Sheila McNabb, twelve, wrote in her seventh-grade composition on the Vietnam War: "My brother was killed and it just gets me sick when you read in the newspapers about them burning their draft cards and ducking the draft."

(Sheila's brother, John, was killed in action in 1967.)

Her teacher, Eleanor Sobel, wrote on the paper: "Was this war worth your brother's life? Maybe he should have burned his draft card."

Sheila's parents, Mr. and Mrs. Henry McNabb, protested to the superintendent of schools, and the school board Wednesday night suspended Mrs. Sobel, with pay, pending a hearing.

Earlier, Mayor James F. Brennan had demanded that Mrs. Sobel be fired immediately. "We do not want this sort of teacher in our system one day longer than necessary," Brennan told school superintendent Leo C. Donahue.

Mrs. Sobel said she was trying to bring out further thoughts by questioning, and felt her notation on the paper was a question, not a statement.

Mrs. Sobel said the class was assigned to write on one of two subjects—"I am against U.S. involvement in Vietnam" or "I support the war in Vietnam."

"I couldn't tell from her essay whether she was for or against the war," Mrs. Sobel said.

The Jury Is the Majority

In cool, moderate San Francisco, off-duty policeman Michael O'Brien came home from an outing feeling out of sorts. As he was putting his boat away in a rented garage in a black neighborhood, the boat trailer was scraped by a car owned by Carl Hawkins, a black. O'Brien leapt from his car and brandished his .38 revolver at Hawkins, offering to kill him in exchange for the scratch. According to witnesses, O'Brien shouted, "I want to kill a nigger so bad I can taste it." Policeman O'Brien habitually wore a tie-clip reading "Gas Huey" (Huey Newton) when on duty in black neighborhoods.

Twenty-five year old George Baskett, also black, picked up a two-foot long piece of wood and tried to knock the gun from O'Brien's hand. Baskett was shot through the chest and died in the street.

O'Brien was tried for murder in January 1969. The only black juror called was peremptorily dismissed by the defense attorney, Jake Erlich. The testimony of four black witnesses agreed substantially as to the events that had transpired. It was contradicted by a policeman who was a late arrival on the scene and by O'Brien, who claimed he fired in self-defense. When David Anderson, a white college student, supported the testimony of the black witnesses, Erlich spent three days attacking the credibility of Anderson on the basis of presumed left-wing associations in college.

In his summation, Erlich charged that O'Brien was brought to trial because of Mayor Joseph Alioto's desire for black votes. He suggested that the black witnesses and David Anderson were conspiring to destroy the reputation of the police and the fabric of order. The judge did not challenge Erlich's argument, no matter how blatantly racist its content became.

Michael O'Brien was acquitted.

Alexis de Tocqueville wrote in his great book, *Democracy in America:*

> When an individual or a party suffers injustice in the United States, to whom can he appeal? To public opinion? Public opinion constitutes the majority. To the legislature? It represents the majority and implicitly obeys it. To the executive power? It is appointed by the majority and serves as a passive tool in its hands. To the public force? The public force is nothing but the majority under arms. To the jury? The jury is the majority invested with the right of hearing judicial cases; and the judges themselves, in certain states, are elected by the majority.

A Name of One's Own

Before 1836, the southwestern part of the modern United States, stretching from Texas westward to the Pacific, was the territory of Mexico. President James K. Polk was determined to annex California to the Union, but Congress was not eager for war. Polk settled the matter by sending U.S. troops into territory claimed by Mexico. They were attacked as invaders by the Mexicans. "Our boys" were being fired on, so Polk got his war. (Sound familiar?)

Any decent school history of California reveals that, prior to the end of the Mexican War in 1848, many Mexican citizens lived in the Southwest. It may even say that the treaty of Guadalupe Hidalgo provided that they could become American citizens (with appropriate rights and obligations) if they chose to do so, and the United States government would honor the titles to their property, which consisted largely of vast tracts of land. At that point, the Mexicans drop out of the history books: they become invisible in the later narratives of

California, Arizona, and Texas. (A few families remain in the history of New Mexico and even send members to Congress. Texas and California have each elected a Mexican-American Congressman in modern times.)

But the story of the long battles within the boundaries of unfamiliar Anglo-Saxon legal traditions, the exploitation by the Yankees flooding in to seek their fortunes, the practices of the Land Commission, and the economic disasters that combined to decimate those landholdings and move them into the hands of the Anglos are not told. The former Mexican citizens, and their descendants, lived on, sinking gradually to lower status in the bustling new commercial economy that followed the coming of the railroads.

Ten years of revolution began in Mexico in 1910. During that decade, about 800,000 refugees crossed the border into the United States. Some traveled as far north as Detroit, where they became yet another immigrant strain, a new ingredient in the agonized cauldron of the industrial "melting pot." Those remaining in the Midwest and Southwest were segregated in groups of hovels on the wrong side of dusty rural towns. They occupied the lowest rung of the employment ladder, working as miners and as migratory farm laborers, wandering from field to field, never staying in one place long enough to become important in local politics, or even send the children to school where they could learn the English language, which was needed to take the first step up the ladder.

There were status differences between those who traced their presence to the Spanish settlers of the sixteenth century and the newcomers from Mexico. But, in 1930, the Bureau of the Census designated all as members of "the Mexican race." And, after that, as the Depression and dustbowl spread over the Southwest, and Anglos resented the necessity of welfare support for impoverished families, local officials sent whole families back to Mexico, not differentiating between the parents, the majority of whom were not American citizens, and the children, who were.

But World War II came, and jobs burgeoned in the aircraft and defense industries of California and Texas. Young men served in the armed forces, and many felt this service entitled them to a fair chance in the postwar economy. A new sense of identity and purpose called for a new name: Mexican-American. But some of the soldiers who died in combat were denied burial in their home-town cemeteries. That Mexican-American GIs had won 10 percent of the nation's highest medals for bravery was of small consequence back home. The war brought urbanization. On the west side of San Antonio, in east El Paso and east Los Angeles, whole communities developed which were separate but self-contained, with businesses, schools, churches: the *barrio* (ghetto).

By 1950, officials of the Census Bureau were more sensitive. Categorization was now under the heading "Spanish surnamed." And the researches of the Census Bureau permitted a measurement in the 1970s of how far the nation's second largest minority still falls short of realizing the promise of economic equality. In southwestern cities, the average Spanish-surnamed worker earns sixty cents for the dollar earned by his white counterpart. And the income of the family averages two-thirds that of the white family, in spite of the greater likelihood that the women and children of the family will also be employed.

But change was in the air. Beginning from nothing in Delano, California, Cesar Chavez built the Farm Workers Organizing Committee and showed that one of the "Spanish surnamed" could challenge the power of the elite leadership of southwestern agricultural business.

President Nixon, hoping to add a new dimension to the Republican party, appointed some thirty of the newly successful Mexican-Americans to his administration, including Mrs. Romana Acosta Bañuelos, a Los Angeles tortilla manufacturer, who became treasurer of the United States. (Let the Republicans divide themselves from the Democrats on the basis of wealth and success, not race and nationality.)

But a sense of unity, overriding economic divisions, was offered. The new group of militants disdained the confusion of labels inherent in "Spanish-speaking," "Mexican-American" and "Spanish surnamed." They accepted, and gloried in, the name *Chicano*. It was originally a term generated by poverty and racial discrimination; an in-group expression among the poorest of the poor that separated *Mexicanos* living in America from *Mexicanos* still living in Mexico. The sharp Aztec sound for the x in *Mexicano* became *Chicano*, a distinctive term, a symbol of pride, the rallying cry of a new political consciousness.

Voices from Middle America: I

Richard Rinehart, in his middle fifties, is an executive engineer with a public-utility company. Although Richard was born in Oregon, his father was a German-speaking Swiss who emigrated to the American Northwest as a young man and married the daughter of Norwegians. Richard is a comfortable man who spends much time in his rose garden and is pleased that his wife does precinct work for the Republican party.

RICHARD RINEHART: *We went to our daughter's graduation from college. We couldn't help noticing that there were some long-hair type kids there. Well, when the flag goes by, I get kind of a little emotional. So, The Star-Spangled Banner was played, and everybody stood up. And this one individual with the long hair, he just sat in his chair. And, you know, did the clenched fist thing. So I sounded out to nobody in particular, but to him in general, "This is a free country, either love it or leave it."*

I got the impression he would have liked to come up there and bust me in the nose.

The Last Acceptable Prejudice

Women ran the mimeograph machines and brewed the coffee that sustained the fighters for freedom of the 1960s. Some began to wonder why they should always be relegated to the back room, serving as maids and clerks of the movement, but never as the leaders. Looking around, they discovered that the status of women in America hardly fit the assertion in the Declaration of Independence that all are created equal.

For example:

In 1955, the median income of full-time male workers was $4,250;
of females, $2,700. The sex differential was $1,550. In 1970, the
median income of full-time male workers was $9,000; of females,
$5,300. The sex differential was $3,700. In 1955, the average
woman's salary was 64 percent of the average man's salary; in
1970, it was 59 percent of the man's average.[6]

The more education a woman had, the greater would be the
gap between her income and that of a male with equivalent
education and experience. In 1969, a college-educated woman
working full time had a median income of $7,400; her male
counterpart received $12,960. The average sex differential was thus
$5,560, but it masked some real outrages: two fiction editors of
comparable monthly magazines — the male earned $50,000 per
year, the female $15,000. In 1971 at the J. Walter Thompson
Advertising Agency, a male public relations coordinator earned
$25,500; a female, with comparable experience and years with
the firm, earned $16,500; solid-state physicists doing research in
private industry in New York state, both with Ph.D.s and
comparable experience: the male received $24,000, the female,
$18,500.[7]

National agencies hesitate to issue credit cards to women; in
fact, a married woman becomes practically a non-person in the
eyes of banks, who consult only the husband's credit rating.
Meanwhile, a single woman may be able to take out a mortgage
on her house only if her father co-signs the document. When a
couple applies for a loan, only a few banks will credit the income
of a working wife as part of the family's assets. In California and
other states with "community property" laws, assets earned by
either husband or wife are owned jointly, but management is
legally vested in the husband alone. Thus, even if women should
receive equal pay for equal work, they would be unable to spend
money on a basis equal with men.

Until a January 1973 decision of the United States Supreme
Court, women were not free to manage the most intimate
processes of their own bodies.[8] Abortions were prohibited or
controlled in nearly every state of the Union, largely because of
nineteenth-century laws passed when abortion was a dangerous
medical procedure; but their modernization was opposed on the
basis of philosophical conviction and religious faith. The Court
ruled, 7-2, that the state may prohibit abortions to protect the
unborn person only in the final ten weeks of pregnancy, and
may regulate abortion in the interests of the mother's health only
after the first three months.

As women won political recognition, some of them came to
preside over large gatherings. They were addressed as
"Chairperson." Men who fulfilled the same roles were called
"Chairmen"; men are men, but women now get to be persons.

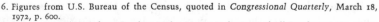

6. Figures from U.S. Bureau of the Census, quoted in *Congressional Quarterly*, March 18,
   1972, p. 600.
7. Income comparisons from Caroline Bird, "Money Is the Root of All Freedom?" *Ms. Magazine*, December 1972, p. 84.
8. *Jane Roe* v. *Henry Wade*, 35 L Ed 3nd 147 (1973). Three of the four justices appointed by
   President Nixon voted in favor of permitting abortions; the president had frequently
   stated his opposition to abortion.

The Nineteenth Amendment to the United States Constitution, which secures the right of voting regardless of sex, was ratified by the states in 1920. A few feminists — but only a few — felt it was only a beginning. Three years later, an equal rights amendment was introduced into Congress. It read:

Equality of rights under the law shall not be denied or abridged by the United States or by any state on account of sex.

Forty-nine years later, that amendment was passed by both houses of Congress and sent to the states for ratification. If ratified, it would become the Twenty-seventh Amendment to the Constitution.

It was a milestone, like the winning of the vote; but this time it was more likely to be recognized as winning a battle, rather than achieving a truce. One of the proponents of the amendment stated that sexism is "the last socially acceptable prejudice."

She could not have had much experience of the city streets, or of country towns in the South and Southwest. Because people tend to construct an identity on the basis of their hatreds, and shared hatreds define the boundaries of some social circles.

The Neighborhoods of Chicago

Uprooted from villages, countryside, or cities, driven from their ancestral homelands by economic distress or political oppression, the immigrants came to America believing in her promise. Nine-tenths settled in cities, in neighborhoods where they would be surrounded by others of their own national origin. In the beginning, it was a way to ease the transition to the ways of a new homeland. But it could also become a prison for the soul: no longer bound by the constraints of the old country, they were unable fully to taste the freedoms promised by the new one.

Mike Royko writes about the way it was in Chicago:

Chicago, until as late as the 1950s, was a place where people stayed put for a while, creating tightly knit neighborhoods, as small-townish as a village in the wheatfields.

The neighborhood-towns were part of larger ethnic states. To the north of the Loop was Germany. To the northwest Poland. To the west were Italy and Israel. To the southwest were Bohemia and Lithuania. And to the south was Ireland.

... You could always tell, even with your eyes closed, which state you were in by the odors of the food stores and the open kitchen windows, the sound of the foreign or familiar language, and by whether a stranger hit you in the head with a rock. . . .

The ethnic states got along just about as pleasantly as did the nations of Europe. With their tote bags, the immigrants brought along all their old prejudices, and immediately picked up some new ones. An Irishman who came here hating only the Englishmen and Irish Protestants soon hated Poles, Italians, and blacks. A Pole who was free arrived hating only Jews and Russians, but soon learned to hate the Irish, the Italians, and the blacks.

... Go that way, past the viaduct, and the wops will jump you, or chase you into Jew town. Go the other way, beyond the park, and the Polacks would stomp on you. Cross those streetcar tracks, and the Micks will shower you with Irish confetti from the brickyards. And who can tell what the niggers might do?

But in the neighborhood, you were safe. . . . So, . . . people
stayed in their own neighborhood, loving it, enjoying the closeness, the friendliness, the familiarity, and trying to save enough
money to move out.[9]

But suppose that a faceless planner in the school board office downtown decrees that your child should be transported by bus from the
warm friendliness of your own neighborhood to a school in enemy
territory? Then what?

George Wallace knew. Adopting "forced busing" as a key issue,
he entered the 1972 Democratic primary contests. His campaign headquarters prepared campaign brochures in Spanish, German, Italian,
Polish, Yiddish, and Chinese.

Asked about his goals, Governor Wallace replied, "My efforts are
concentrated on trying to straighten out the Democratic party, trying
to make it the party of the people again."[10]

Who, Then, Are the People?

There is a long tradition, in this country and elsewhere, of intellectual
sympathy for "the common people." Russian professional people and
some of the nineteenth-century nobility expressed profound admiration for the peasants who exhibited such a healthy oneness with the
soil. Marx looked toward the working man as the vehicle of the revolution; the bourgeoisie (and their property) must be washed away in
the blood of revolution. The pattern repeats itself: persons at the
upper end of the social scale (but who do not actually command the
forces of the state) look down with understanding (perhaps true empathy, maybe only condescension) at the people at the very bottom
who support with their labor the entire social and economic structure (as in the nineteenth century) or have no technical skills to sell
(as in the twentieth century). The intellectuals at the top blame the
middle groups for the sordid condition of the lower classes, forgetting
their own complicity.

When students at elite colleges speak disdainfully of racists, they
are talking about the redneck farmer, a secret adherent of the Ku
Klux Klan, in Georgia, or the white working-class policeman who
fired shotgun pellets into a crowd of black students at Southern University in Louisiana. Their sympathies are for the victim, for the
sharecropper behind his mule or the black child pulling leaded paint
from the walls of his ghetto room in the city. The bigot is not deemed
worthy of understanding.

Their empathy does not extend to the policeman, or to the assembly-line worker who knows no other trade and feels threatened
that his bosses have become "equal opportunity employers," or to the
mental hospital attendant who pumps gas on his days off, owes money
for his new living room furniture, and can't afford to take his family
to the movies.

The cost of "making it" — of moving from the ethnic neighborhood
to the suburb, of sending kids to college, of learning how to ski — that
cost, for the striving member of the working class, is the denial of
present gratifications in favor of long-range goals. Instead of going to
the movies, one scrapes together the mortgage payment that keeps
the family one more month in a "good" school district. This denial
of present pleasures — uptightness — is scorned by the children and
grandchildren of those who completed the upward journey years ago.

9. Mike Royko, *Boss: Richard J. Daley of Chicago* (New York: New American Library, 1971),
pp. 30-32.
10. Quoted in *U.S. News and World Report*, April 10, 1972, p. 34.

Children of affluence, they know that whatever happens, there will be another meal, another ride to hitch down the highway, another telephone to call Daddy in case of trouble.

So the students marched down the slope at Kent State and made "obscene gestures" at the National Guardsmen. They knew the rifles couldn't be loaded.

Voices from Middle America: II

Eldene Markus grew up in a Polish neighborhood in East St. Louis that was normally locked in conflict with the Irish area that bordered it. She went to work as a seamstress before graduating from high school. She married an electrician, and they migrated to California during World War II. He worked in an aircraft plant and she sewed parachutes. They have retired now, and live in a modest but new home not far from a beach in southern California. Eldene's nephew is a lieutenant in the Marine Corps; she looks forward to his visits from Camp Pendleton.

Eldene vividly recalls her reaction to the Kent State incident:

ELDENE: *I read in the paper where one of the girls that got shot, had a flower in her hand. And she took it and put it in the gun, the muzzle of the gun, and made some remark to the soldier. Now, that's antagonizing. She needed her face slapped. That's provoking! If they hadn't already been in lots of trouble, the National Guard wouldn't have been there in the first place.*

Eldene's husband, Jan Markus, joins the conversation, and he talks about various groups in America and the amount of power they wield in American politics.

JAN MARKUS: *Well, I think there are some groups of people that are a minority in this country that have too much to say about our government. And I don't have to tell you who they are!*

Marc Riboud

ELDENE: *It's the colored.*

JAN: *No, not only the colored. There's others, I don't have to tell you.*

ELDENE: *Well, who is it?*

JAN: *Do I have to say it? Well, I mean the Jews, for one thing. They have too much to say. Like, they're trying to get us tangled up in the Middle East, and they're using pressure to get us in there. And I just don't think that's right.*

But the Markuses feel that tax laws favor the rich, and they say that "a little more socialism" would be good for the country.

What George Wallace Understood

Those members of the upper-middle and upper classes, secure in the sanctity of their particular suburb, who denounce widespread bigotry in American life, may be practicing a bigotry of their own. Michael Lerner, a student of psychology and political science, writes that

> the upper class has reached a plateau of security from which its liberal-radical wing believes that it can mock the politics of the policeman and the butcher and slight their aspirations while still living genteelly in the space between them.[11]

Dismissal of the "white ethnics" because of their apparent racism is a common reaction. But it only reveals the tip of the emotional iceberg. In fact, writes Lerner, the student is rejecting the value system and psychological orientation of the lower- and lower-middle-class persons he labels "bigots." Psychologists encourage him, by suggesting that upper-class values do more to liberate the psyche. It is easy to make fun of Mayor Daley's grammar or tell a Polish joke. To do so is a confession that one fails to understand the concerns of those groups that feel most threatened by the social changes of the last decade.

George Wallace understood this.

Richard Nixon learned it.

Even the social scientists are catching on. If the 1960s were the time of exploring the dark side of life in the ghettos, of understanding the psychic costs of racial prejudice, and investigating the impact of segregation upon the minds of children, social scientists in the 1970s have discovered Middle America and realize that it must be taken seriously.

The middle groups—white ethnics, the working poor, the lower middle class, the union members, the wage earners who don't have much chance of ducking income taxes because they are taken from the paycheck every week—however they are defined, these groups constitute the majority.

You cannot begin to understand the American people until some empathy for the majority is developed.

Away in England, George McGovern reported that he had been taking a nap while Richard Nixon delivered his inaugural talk.

Later, in Oxford, Senator McGovern said that the majority of Americans are "dispirited."

11. Michael Lerner, "Respectable Bigotry," *The American Scholar* 37 (Autumn 1969); reprinted in L. K. Howe, ed., *The White Majority* (New York: Random House, 1970), p. 202.

Even before delivering his inaugural address, President Nixon nominated Peter J. Brennan of New York to be the new secretary of labor. Mr. Brennan was president of the New York Building and Construction Trades Council. He was the "hard hat" voter personified, a representative of the conservative wing of organized labor, a spokesman, perhaps, for Middle America.

Brennan was opposed by the NAACP and other civil rights spokesmen because the construction unions have resisted most strongly the entry of black and other minority members into their ranks. Some labor leaders expressed pleasure that one of their own number was appointed to the position, but others regarded it as the simple payment of a political debt.

The Senate consented to the nomination.

Voices from Middle America: III

Jerry Willis sits forward in his chair, his powerful shoulders suddenly thrust back with the importance of what he has to explain: his opposition to the admission of blacks to his union's apprentice program is not based on bigotry.

JERRY: *It's tough work, layin' brick. The hourly rate is all right when you're workin', but construction slows down first thing when there's a recession, and a spell of bad weather lays you off without any warning.*

He waves his hand around the modest living room. The color television set has its sound turned down so we can talk.

JERRY: *I won't have much to leave my son. Even when this house is paid for, the way taxes are going up, he might not be able to afford it. But I can leave him my trade. I can leave him my place in the union. Then I'll know that he can always earn enough to eat, if he's willing to work.*

Waiting to See the Parade

On January 20, 1972, a bearded young man climbed fifteen feet up a utility pole at the corner of Pennsylvania Avenue and Fourteenth Street in Washington, D. C. He had a fine view of the route of President Nixon's inaugural parade. The District Police Force backed a van up to the pole and sent policemen to its roof. But they could not reach the young man.

A group of antiwar protesters, seeing this drama, chanted encouragement to the young man. One girl screamed, "Watch the mace, cover your face, Brother!"[12]

Taller policemen were sent to the roof of the van, but still they could not reach the young man.

Then the president's limousine came by, and the antiwar protesters went to shout and throw bottles and fruit toward it, and the policemen went to round up the protesters and herd them into a nearby park.

Forgotten, the young man began to climb down the pole.

But one of the patrolmen spotted him before he could get away, and, at the command of the sergeant, six patrolmen grabbed the young man and hustled him off — not very gently — to a nearby patrol wagon.

Around the youth's neck, flapping in the wind, was a sign that read, "Peace on Earth, Good Will Toward Men."

12. United Press dispatch, *San Francisco Chronicle*, January 12, 1973.

Alexis de Tocqueville wrote:

> In general, the law leaves American officials far more independ-
> ent within the limits of prescribed authority than the French
> civil officers. Sometimes they are even allowed by the majority
> to exceed those bounds. They are protected by the opinion and
> backed by the power of the majority, so they dare do things that
> shock a European, accustomed as he is to arbitrary power. By
> this means habits are formed in the heart of a free country
> which may some day prove fatal to its liberties.

Sweet Land of Liberty

In her twenty-ninth year, Sarah Simpson was not quite able to accept
the path that stretched before her, the established role of spinster
school teacher. But she realized that she had to find her challenge and
reward in her teaching, or she might wind up with nothing at all.
(Except her membership in liberal organizations that no longer
seemed to attract unmarried men.) So she volunteered to teach first
grade in the most integrated school in the city, because that would be
the greatest challenge and the greatest reward.

She had thirty of them, first graders of every color: several Chicano
children who could hardly speak English, a handful of black children,
the twin daughters of a Japanese gardener, and a number of white
children. A few of these were from the new tract development at
Segundo Terrace. They came to school each morning dressed cleanly
and, if they were not eager for the day's activities, at least they had
eaten good breakfasts and could be counted on to last until noon without growing drowsy. But already at age six they were infected with the
beginnings of hate directed toward those with darker skins.

Sarah Simpson tried to deal with each child as an individual, bringing first one and then the other out of his shell of shyness to blossom
in the glow of pride of a drawing mounted on the board for all to see
or the responsibility of some job like cleaning the blackboard.

This morning, she was worried about Malcolm Crockett. He had
been an early success. For months now, she had watched his intelligence bloom as he hurried eagerly into such unexplored corners as
the first-grade curriculum provided. But today he seemed withdrawn
and distracted, and she wondered why.

It was time to practice for their part in the spring assembly. Sarah
had the children arrange their chairs in a semicircle around the bat-
tered piano.

"We'll play the song through once," she said, "to see how well you
remember it from our last practice."

She struck some introductory chords and began in her own clear
voice, loud enough to encourage, but not loud enough to dominate,

> My country, 'tis of thee,
> Sweet land of liberty,
> Of thee I sing . . .

The uncertain voices joined her own. Sarah looked at the many-
colored faces of her students, and suddenly she felt a surge of pride
and accomplishment. At least at that moment, they were striving together towards a kind of harmony.

But, at the back of the group, Malcolm Crockett sat silent in his
chair.

Creating a Nation:
The Unfinished Story

The words about freedom and equality were there in the Constitution and the Declaration of Independence for everyone to read. For millions, they defined the promise of America. But the words did not affect the practices of the American people very much. Was it possible that Americans could claim liberty for themselves at the same instant they were denying it to their fellow citizens? Or do the concepts of freedom and equality acquire new meanings as society changes? Can their meaning ever be permanent?

Who Are We?

In June 1968, as Senator Robert Kennedy lay dying in a Los Angeles hospital, the City University of New York held its commencement. The speaker was Arthur M. Schlesinger, Jr., Harvard historian and former adviser to President John F. Kennedy. His topic was "The Politics of Violence."

> The world today is asking a terrible question — a question which every citizen of this Republic should be putting to himself: what sort of people are we, we Americans?
>
> And the answer which much of the world is bound to return is that we are today the most frightening people on this planet.
>
> We are a frightening people because for three years we have been devastating a small country on the other side of the world in a war which bears no rational relationship to our national interest.
>
> We are a frightening people because we have already in this decade murdered the two of our citizens who stood preeminently before the world as the embodiments of American idealism — and because last night we tried to murder a third.
>
> We are a frightening people because the atrocities we commit hardly touch our official self-righteousness, our invincible conviction of our moral infallibility.
>
> The ghastly things we do to our own people, the ghastly things we do to other people — these must at last compel us to look searchingly at ourselves and our society before hatred and violence rush us on to more evil and finally tear our nation apart. . . .[1]

1. Arthur M. Schlesinger, Jr., "The Politics of Violence," *Harper's*, August 1968, p. 19.

Thomas Jefferson and the American Ideal

Thomas Jefferson wrote in the Declaration of Independence that inalienable rights include "life liberty, and the pursuit of happiness." By making this change in Locke's traditional formula of "life, liberty and property," Jefferson suggested a more open society, a more universal participation, than in any government of his day. For "property" traditionally meant property *in land*. The feudal society of Europe was based on a small and powerful landowning class. In Jefferson's own Virginia, only landowners ("freeholders") could vote.

Jefferson was well aware that the protection of equality, in a government by the majority, would rest with that majority. He wrote that, although "the will of the majority is in all cases to prevail, that will, to be rightful, must be reasonable." The "minority possess their equal rights, which equal laws must protect, and to violate which would be oppression."

In following John Locke, who held an optimistic view of the likelihood that free men may find fulfillment under limited government, Jefferson largely ignored the writing of Thomas Hobbes. Hobbes was a pessimist. He held that men are so enslaved by their passions, so certain to perpetrate evil upon their fellow men, that the only hope of safety lies in submission to an all-powerful government. Locke had a certain amount of faith in the ability of the people to be decent to each other.

The kind of government envisioned by Thomas Jefferson would prove workable only if, as he claimed, the people were "the safest repository of their own rights."

But the definition of the rights of citizens is left mostly to the Supreme Court, that part of American government which is least directly responsive to majority opinion.

Even as Jefferson penned his definition of the American ideal, realities of American society ignored his claim that "all men are created equal." The American Indian was being systematically bribed, betrayed, and slaughtered. In Jefferson's Virginia, two-fifths of the population were black slaves, persons treated as property to be bought and sold, rather than human beings with human rights. Jefferson was aware of this contradiction, and he proposed to the Continental Congress that the list of grievances against the British monarch include the fact that the slave trade was permitted to continue. Jefferson recorded in his notes, taken at the time, that the clause

Bruce Davidson

reprobating the enslaving [of] the inhabitants of Africa, was struck out in complaisance to South Carolina and Georgia, who had never attempted to restrain the importation of slaves, and who on the contrary still wished to continue it. Our Northern brethren also I believe felt a little tender under those censures; for tho' their people have very few slaves themselves, yet they had been pretty considerable carriers of them to others.[2]

The nation thus was born carrying within itself that contradiction which may yet destroy it: How can the equality asserted by the Declaration and demanded by the Bill of Rights have meaning when it is denied by the social structure?

Inequality Enshrined in the Constitution

The Declaration of Independence created a new nation, but it did not establish a new national government. It provided that the colonies would henceforth be "Free and Independent States." All that was specified about the new nation was that it should be known as the United States of America. The Articles of Confederation were finally drawn up by the Continental Congress and submitted to the states for ratification in July 1777. But they provided for little more than a league of friendship between independent states.

This arrangement was tolerable, as long as all energies were devoted to defeating England. The common enemy imposed unity. While engaged in throwing off the power of the strong central British government, the Americans were unlikely to establish one of their own.

With no central government of consequence, the state governments grew in authority. And, in the state governments, the executive power languished, for the war had been fought against the arbitrary British executive power. The state governments came to be dominated by their legislatures; and, in that time (when the representation of special interests by pressure groups was not so well developed) the legislature was particularly close to the people. This proved very distressing to those who were suspicious of the people—the moneylenders, the merchants, the large landowners—in short, the "rich and well-born." They feared that the governments of the several states would prove unable to protect life, liberty, and property.

By and large, the well-to-do supported the Constitution of 1787; some of them helped to write it. Determined to form a new government, the founders did not permit disagreements to thwart their purpose. Instead, they sought compromises that all could accept, even if the results did not fit neatly with ideals previously stated.

After two months of deliberations, the Convention was stalled by disagreement over the method of representing the states in the national government. With the exception of Benjamin Franklin, who was intrigued by the idea of a single-house legislature, the delegates were agreed that the legislature should consist of two houses based on different conceptions of representation. Lords and Commons, the two houses of the English Parliament, presented a powerful model. The solution, known as the Connecticut Compromise, provided that two members would be sent to the Senate from each state, regardless of its wealth, population, or power. Thus the "Free and Independent States" of the Declaration of Independence would be represented as states, in equal status. Furthermore, the selection of senators was to

2. Quoted in Max Beloff, *Thomas Jefferson and American Democracy* (London: English University Press, 1948), p. 66.

be done only indirectly by the people. Senators would be elected by the state legislatures. James Madison argued that the aristocratic body thus created would be less open to the "fickleness and passion" of the directly elected lower house. It would protect minorities from the majority will. But he insisted just as firmly that the people should be represented directly in the lower house.

Thus were established the Senate of the United States and the House of Representatives. The majority of the Convention apparently felt that property, and only property, should be the basis for voting. They tended to equate property-owning with wisdom, sound principle, and support for the continuity of society. However, as delegate George Mason pointed out, eight or nine states had already "extended the right of suffrage beyond the freeholders. What will the people there say, if they should be disenfranchised?" The need for approval of the final document carried the day. There was no reason to expect the voting citizens of any state to accept a national government that denied them the privilege of voting. The founders, in the end, specified that states would be represented in the lower house according to population, and that those voting would have the same qualifications as specified by the state for voting in elections to the most numerous house of the state legislature.

Another question concerning representation remained to be settled. Southern delegates argued that, whether people or property were the basis of representation, the number of slaves held in each state should be counted in determining its representation in Washington. Northern delegates, naturally enough, objected. The final compromise was written into the Constitution without mentioning the word "slave."

> Representatives . . . shall be apportioned among the several States which may be included within the Union, according to their respective numbers, which shall be determined by adding to the whole number of free persons, . . . excluding Indians not taxed, three fifths of all other persons.[3]

"Taxation without representation is tyranny" had been a slogan of the War for Independence. Indians paying taxes would be represented. Whether they would be encouraged to vote would be a matter for the states in which they lived. It was not contemplated that slaves would vote, nor that they should enjoy other legal rights. Their status as property was recognized in the Constitution, and their political value was set at three-fifths of a free citizen. The slave trade, which Jefferson abhorred, was provided for in Section 9 of Article I. Congress was prohibited from ending the slave trade before 1808. White superiority was enshrined in the Constitution.

The Origins of Slavery

The institution of chattel slavery had not been imported. It was an American invention, or at least a re-invention of an ancient practice, developed as economic practices were reinforced by legislation. In the seventeenth century, the word "slave" had rather a vague meaning in the English language. It was roughly equivalent to "servant." In the European feudal system, the status of serf (or "villein") was inherited and could not be changed. The serf was bound to the land on which he was born, and his master was the landowner. Nevertheless, the serf was recognized as a person, and he enjoyed certain legal rights.

3. Article I, Section 2, Paragraph 3.

Bruce Davidson

There were other kinds of servitude in which the term of service was specifically limited in a contract between servant and master.

Serfdom did not develop in the colonies, for the problem was to attract new settlers for conquering vast areas of unsettled land. Not a stable labor system, but a rapidly expanding one, was needed. At the beginning of the seventeenth century, white and black servants were of approximately equal status. But the colonial settlers needed to attract skilled laborers from Europe. It was necessary to assure them that any servitude would be of fixed duration; at its end, the former servant could himself become a landowner. This seemed appropriate in the case of workers who brought with them the cultural experience of England, Ireland, or Scotland, and shared with their masters the Christian religion. The black men who were increasingly imported into the colonies following the establishment of African trade did not share these attributes. For a time, black men converted to Christianity were freed. But that was expensive. In the southern colonies (particularly South Carolina and Georgia) it was discovered that crops suitable to a tropical climate could best be produced on large units with the constant attention of labor. The most profitable form of labor on the large plantations was slavery. The notion that black men *by nature* should be condemned to a lifetime of servitude developed quickly. The myth of white superiority supported it. By the year 1700, several colonies defined the black slave as property, to be bought and sold. Racial intermarriage was prohibited, and the domination of the master was assured by law.

When the eighteenth century brought intense speculation about the natural rights of man—which culminated, as far as America was concerned, in the Declaration of Independence—the southern plantation owner excluded the black man from his theorizing. The Puritan conviction of a heavenly mission had excluded first the Indians and then the blacks. Northerners did not insist that black men were created equal to white.

Complete chattel slavery was hardly seventy-five years old, but a generation was so accustomed to it that white superiority—the feeling that black men didn't count as human beings—seemed a part of the natural order.

Men tend to be defined by their hatreds; racial prejudice damages the bigot as well as the victim.

Regardless of their moral convictions, New Englanders knew that slavery was incompatible with the economic conditions of their region. In approving compromise with the slave interests, they expected that, following the end of the slave trade in 1808, slavery would prove economically advantageous in a decreasing area of the country and would eventually die out. However, Eli Whitney of Connecticut invented the cotton gin in 1793. This process for separating cotton fibers from seeds made the plantation system (and chattel slavery) profitable in a much greater area. It was not the last time that technological change would mold American social institutions and modify the American concept of equality.

Jefferson, Jackson, and the Meaning of Equality

Thomas Jefferson realized that the assertion of the equality of all men did not settle the political discussion but only began it. He did not believe that men were equal in ability nor that they would be equal in achievement. But he felt strongly that no man should have a superior position simply because of the wealth or power of his parents. He knew that, in the world of politics, a few men would become leaders, while the majority would remain followers. Jefferson anticipated that the leaders would be drawn from what he called a "natural aristocracy" or an "aristocracy of merit." He believed that, given an equal chance, this leadership would emerge. To encourage the process of selection, Jefferson favored a system of free, public education.[4]

But the expanding frontier and growing industries provided opportunities that did not depend upon education as Jefferson understood it. By the time of Andrew Jackson's presidency, the distinction between leaders and followers, which Jefferson found so natural, had largely disappeared in the conviction that no special training was needed by those who held positions of public trust.

Both Jefferson and Jackson felt that the greatest threat to freedom came from government itself. They did not conceive of government as a force that could intervene in society to preserve and protect individual liberties or individual welfare; they did not predict that positive governmental action—beyond support for a schooling system—might be needed to assure equality of opportunity.

During the presidency of Andrew Jackson, Alexis de Tocqueville made his famous visit to America. He was struck by the moral authority and political power of the majority. He was fearful of the excesses the majority might commit and for which he saw no restraint. He wrote of the president,

> General Jackson is the slave of the majority; he yields to its wishes, its feelings, and its demands. Indeed, he discovers the feelings of the majority in order to make himself its leader.

4. The relationship between democracy and education is examined in Chapter 1.

In closing the first volume of his long analysis of the American democracy, Tocqueville pointed out that he had been describing the society established by Americans of European descent, the white men of America. In order to make predictions about the future of America, Tocqueville found it necessary to examine the implications of the fact that America was inhabited not by one race, but by three: white, Negro, and Indian. After describing the process of driving the Indians ever farther westward, he predicted their eventual extinction. Concluding his study of the abolition of slavery in the North, Tocqueville predicted a conflict between whites and blacks:

> I do not regard the abolition of slavery, in the Southern states, as a means of warding off the struggle between the two races. The Negroes may long remain slaves without complaining; when once raised to the level of freemen, they will soon revolt at being deprived of almost all the rights of citizens.

The Newcomers

The proposition that "all men are created equal" was not only withdrawn from blacks and Indians. Social custom and economic practice also limited its application to immigrants. Employers and developers, like the railroads, welcomed the flood of population from Europe: there was a continent to populate, a wilderness to be tamed, and new industries rising. But working people feared the competition of the newcomers. From 1820, when statistics were first kept, until 1898, about 17 million immigrants came to the United States. Mostly they came from Western Europe—the British Isles, Germany, and Scandinavia.

A wave of immigration began in the 1840s, stimulated by the Potato Famine in Ireland. The Irish seemed a threat: they were hard workers, and other workingmen feared that, accustomed to a lower standard of living, they would accept lower wages. Furthermore, they professed the Catholic faith. The Irish and the German Catholics did not share Protestant scruples against beer and whiskey. They were pictured in cartoons as habitual drunkards. The immigrant Catholics were systematically denied the freedom to pursue happiness in their own way. They were excluded from all but menial jobs and denied entrance into established society.

In the 1840s, a group of nativist societies joined together as the Supreme Order of the Star Spangled Banner, demanding that twenty-one years' residence be required before an immigrant would be eligible for citizenship. Because of a passion for secrecy, they were called the Know-Nothing party. Although electing six governors in the mid-1850s, the party was destroyed by the issue of the expansion of slavery.

As the nineteenth century ended, improving conditions in Western Europe shifted the source of new Americans to Southern and Eastern Europe—Austria, Italy, and Poland. Each wave of newcomers was greeted with hostility by the earlier wave. The frontier was settled, and the newcomers went into the great cities, where they found solace from strangeness in the neighborhoods already settled by their fellow countrymen. A precinct captain from the local party organization soon called to introduce them to democracy.

Israel Zangwill wrote eloquently of America as a "melting pot," where all the oppressed peoples of the exhausted nations of Europe could gather, mingle, and create a new nation: all racial and cultural differences would be at least subdued, if not eliminated, to create a great people.

But what was the price? The price was conformity—in language, custom, dress, and attitude. The cost of breaking loose from the ties of the ethnic neighborhood was to become more American than the Americans, to compete furiously in the free-enterprise system, to abandon the comforts of one's former identity. The style of American life and society was set by the families who shared the racial characteristics and religious convictions of the original settlers: white, Anglo-Saxon, and Protestant.

This WASP domination was unquestioned throughout the nineteenth century. The Daughters of the American Revolution, an organization designating for purposes of society the "genuine" descendants of the colonial period, was not founded until 1890.

Civil War: To Achieve Equality, or to Preserve the Union?

The principle of the equality of all mankind, asserted in the Declaration of Independence, was denied in the Constitution. Could a nation founded on this contradiction survive? In a period of insignificant presidential leadership, the Union was held together by a series of political compromises worked out in Congress. But the question of what labor system should be extended into the new lands of the West could not be forever resolved by compromise.

There were a number of leaders in the Abolitionist movement who were convinced that any compromise was immoral. William Lloyd Garrison, the fiery Abolitionist leader, denounced the Constitution as "a covenant with death, and an agreement with Hell." He claimed that the Constitution should be immediately annulled. Garrison was condemned as an extremist by his colleagues. To their objections that his demands were impractical, he replied that politics could be the art of the possible, but his was the role of agitation, the art of the desirable. Garrison's moral crusade won new converts from the readers of Harriet Beecher Stowe's novel, Uncle Tom's Cabin.

The perception of chattel slavery as pure evil which should not be accommodated through compromise was particularly strong among women. The movement for women's equal political rights in America may be dated from a British antislavery conference in the 1830s. The American women in attendance were allowed seats on the balcony only after a curtain was installed to hide them from the males below. They realized that the practice of inequality had more than a racial dimension. The first woman's rights convention was held in Seneca Falls, New York, in 1848. The delegates, as part of a long list of grievances, complained that men had consigned them to a "dependent and abject life."

In 1849, the delegates to the California Constitutional Convention established a state government in which slavery was prohibited. This upset the delicate balance of the Missouri Compromise, which implicitly provided that each new free state should be admitted to the union in partnership with a new slave state. But the miners of '49 were not moral crusaders. Their intent was to prevent competition. Limitations on the rights of black men were included in the constitution, and the convention very nearly decided upon the exclusion of free black people from the state.

Californians were only following the lead of other "free" states. In 1813, Illinois ordered every free black to leave the territory under a penalty of thirty-nine lashes repeated every fifteen days. Ohio, Michigan, Iowa, and Wisconsin voted against Negro suffrage in the 1830s. In 1835, Tocqueville observed that

> the prejudice of race appears to be stronger in the states which have abolished slavery than in those where it still exists; and nowhere is it so important as in those states where servitude never has been known.

Kansas became a battleground for proslavery and antislavery forces; and the antislavery forces voted to exclude free blacks from the territory. In 1857, Oregon was admitted to the Union with a constitution that excluded free blacks from residence and from citizenship. An editorial proclaimed that "Oregon is a land for the white man."

The moral outrage of Garrison, even supported by the sentimentality of Mrs. Stowe, was not enough to lead a nation on to war. The ascendancy of the slaveholders in both the Democratic and Whig parties, and thus in the national government, led to the founding of the Republican party and growing national division. The white settlers in the new western lands wanted opportunity for themselves; they were little interested in the welfare of other races.

Abraham Lincoln was aware of this dominant public opinion. He treated the question of slavery with great caution. In responding to the southern challenge at Fort Sumter, Lincoln declared only that it was the duty of the North to preserve the Union.

Nevertheless, a large minority shared the Abolitionist perception of slavery as pure evil. Many had labored to subvert the slave system by operating an "underground railroad" that helped slaves to freedom. Abolitionist pressures to include freeing the slaves as an aim of the war were redoubled. When the northern armies met a series of defeats, the rate of volunteering in the Union Army declined. Abolitionists demanded that slaves be freed and black men used as troops. Fearing that some northern governors might withdraw their states' troops unless emancipation were made an aim of the war, Lincoln on September 22, 1862, announced that his intention, on January 1, 1863, was to declare free all slaves held in parts of the United States *not* in control of Union armies. The one-hundred day delay was an invitation to the Confederate states. By rejoining the Union, they could keep their slaves for a time, yielding to gradual and compensated emancipation. But the South was not interested in gradualism.

Northerners were alarmed at the prospect of a migration into their midst of newly freed blacks. This alarm, coupled with reverses suffered by the Union armies, was blamed for the widespread defeat of Republican congressional candidates in the November 1862 elections. The

Republican party declared its policy to be that the newly freed blacks would be deported to Africa, rather than encouraged to migrate northward. The details of this mass transportation were not worked out.

On January 1, 1863, Lincoln did issue the formal Emancipation Proclamation. It declared all slaves then within the Confederate lines to be free and invited them to join the Union Army. It served to win the support of England and other European nations for the North's blockade of southern ports, which denied cotton to the English textile industry. Northern reverses continued, and, for the troops, war goals made little difference. The need of survival was paramount—kill or be killed. Civil liberties have little place in warfare.

Lee surrendered to Grant at Appomattox, April 9, 1865.

In 1867, the white voters of Kansas, Ohio, and Minnesota rejected, in referendum votes, the proposition that black people be permitted to vote. In 1868, the voters of Michigan did the same.

But a bloody war had been fought. Six hundred thousand Americans were dead. The resources of a modern industrial state had been used for the first time to pit whole populations against each other. Weapons and tactics that would characterize twentieth-century warfare were developed—aerial observation from balloons, iron-clad battleships, trench warfare, the long-range bombardment of cities, destruction of transportation and manufacturing systems, the final triumph of numbers, technology, and industrial might over brilliant military leadership.

How could the bloodbath be justified?

As preserving the Union? Why was the Union worth preserving, unless the national government was better able to secure freedom and equality than the governments of the individual states? At Gettysburg, Abraham Lincoln made exactly this claim in justifying the sacrifices of the dead. But Lincoln was killed before he could lead a reunited America, and it is not certain that even Lincoln's political skills could have persuaded the South to join as partners in "a new birth of freedom."

Because it freed the slaves? The Republican party expected black peoples' votes forever after as a debt of gratitude. But the spirit of Abolitionist reform collapsed, and the promise of equality implicit in freeing the slaves was largely forgotten. Slavery had been regarded as a moral problem for the slave-owner, rather than a social problem for the slave. The freedman was abandoned as a matter of concern by the national government after 1877.

And why did the South fight on, stubbornly, until overwhelmed? To defend southern plantation culture and its finest flower, the southern woman, against a brutal northern assault? This myth was quickly manufactured, bathed in essence of magnolia, and exported to the North. To seem plausible, the myth had to include the idea that the lot of the black man sold into slavery had been rather comfortable—free from responsibilities, he spent his days in rhythmic labor, singing contentment for his status and praises for his master. This nonsense was very near the standard picture of the Old South published in northern periodicals by the end of the century. Southern writers felt compelled to establish a justification for the devastation of their region—and mythology served the purpose better than history.

The South was able to make up its losses in another way. Originally, the Constitution provided that a slave would count as three-fifths of a free citizen in reckoning the number of men to be sent to the House of Representatives. But only the white masters could vote. At the end of Reconstruction, when political rights were again taken away from the black man, the full population of the southern states counted toward representation in Congress, so the proportion of southern representatives increased. But only the white masters voted.[5]

Wounded Knee

Following the Confederate surrender, the United States Army turned its attention to the pacification, as it would now be called, of the native Americans — those same dark-skinned people who had greeted the first settlers, helped them survive the first winters, and were later betrayed. Most Puritans could not imagine members of another race being candidates for salvation. The Indians were pushed ever westward. With California booming, a transcontinental railroad built, and the prairie being broken up for homesteads, it was time to mop up the last resistance of those whose lands were being expropriated. In December 1890, the U.S. Cavalry fought the Sioux for the last time, at Wounded Knee, South Dakota. But that was hardly a battle; it was more nearly a slaughter; rampaging troops killed 153 old men, women, and children.

Unlike the freed black slave, the Indian was not deemed capable of taking a place in the larger society. If the black could achieve only second-class citizenship, the Indian could achieve none at all. He was told: Abandon your ways, and become like the white man, or be isolated. The survivors of the broken treaties, the betrayals, and the ambushes, were herded to reservations usually established upon the most rocky and inhospitable land. (When oil was later discovered on that barren land, the claim of the Indian upon it presented a minor embarrassment.)

For seventy days in 1973, the hamlet of Wounded Knee was occupied by militant Indians hoping to attract sympathy for their cause and protest the practices of the Bureau of Indian Affairs. They charged that the bureau administers Indian grazing lands to benefit white ranchers. The bureau often consults the tribal leaders, but the young militants charged that the elected leaders are Establishment-oriented "Uncle Tomahawks."

> In his 1973 State of the Union message, President Nixon had proposed that more of the authority of the Bureau of Indian Affairs be delegated to the councils of tribal elders. This was his equivalent, for Indians, of his plan to provide new power for "grassroots governments."

Defining the Rights of Citizens

No war is possible without suffering, and no victory is clearcut. If the Civil War was fought to perfect and implement the American ideal of equality, it must be reckoned a failure. Just as Jefferson realized that the assertions of the Declaration of Independence began, rather than ended, the political battle, we now know that equality must be achieved politically, and its meaning must be defined anew in each historical era. The Civil War changed American institutions enough to make the dream of equality still possible.

---

5. Section Two of the Fourteenth Amendment to the Constitution provided that a state's congressional delegation would be reduced in proportion to its denial to "male inhabitants . . . twenty-one years of age" of the right to vote. But the section was never enforced, nor was the Fifteenth Amendment's guarantee of the right to vote regardless of "race, color, or previous condition of servitude" between Reconstruction and the 1950s.

Some questions were settled for all time:

Chattel slavery was abolished. The Thirteenth Amendment of the Constitution achieved this in 1865: "Neither slavery nor involuntary servitude . . . shall exist within the United States. . . ."

The nature of the Union was established. Hereafter, it would be considered an "indestructible Union, composed of indestructible States" formed by the people themselves. Thus wrote the Supreme Court in 1869.[6] The contrary view, that the Union was but a league of states from which the members were free to withdraw, had once been expressed by New Englanders when they disagreed with policies of the national government. The idea was made into a theory by John C. Calhoun. It was acted upon by the southern states. And made into folly by the force of arms.

The rights of citizens would be decided by the national government; individuals could appeal to the national government to protect themselves against the power of local governments; minorities could seek protection against the outrages of the majority. This quickly came to mean that an appeal could be made to the judicial branch; the elected branches felt constrained by their conception of majority opinion.

From the beginning, it was implicit in the Constitution that Americans were citizens both of the United States and of the state in which they lived. But the Bill of Rights limited only the actions of the *national* government. In 1868, the Fourteenth Amendment to the Constitution recognized this dual citizenship. But it provided that:

> No State shall make or enforce any law which shall abridge the privileges or immunities of citizens of the United States; nor shall any State deprive any person of life, liberty, or property, without due process of law; nor deny to any persons within its jurisdiction the equal protection of the laws.

The Civil War established the principle of equality in the Constitution, realizing, in part, the promise of the Declaration of Independence. The point of both documents became that there are certain rights so important, so basic to a democratic society, that they cannot be modified by a democratic decision. It is not for the majority of the moment to define the rights of citizenship; that definition is embodied in the basic law of the land. It is as much the duty of the national government to protect the rights of a minority as it is to formulate policies in accord with the will of the majority.

But will the majority accept this limitation upon its authority? Who will restrain the majority?

What happens when the majority in a given jurisdiction—a county in Mississippi or a particular school district or the entire United States —joins in denying constitutional rights to a minority?

Consider the phenomenon of lynchings. Lynchings happen when a mob takes a person accused of real or imagined crimes away from the legal authorities for punishment without trial. The form taken by lynch murders has included mutilation, hanging, and burning alive. For three decades in the twentieth century, the number of lynchings in the Deep South varied annually with the price of raw cotton. As

6. *Texas* v. *White*, 7 Wallace 700 (1869).

the price sank lower, lynchings increased. This chilling statistic suggests that economic frustration was easily sublimated in racial violence. The Bill of Rights became irrelevant, for the locally elected law enforcement officials did nothing to protect the victim.

Shall we take comfort from the fact that lynchings in the classic mode are dying out? As of the present writing, the lynching of Charles Mack Parker at Poplarville, Mississippi, on April 26, 1959, is the last lynching in that classic pattern. The murderers of Parker have never been convicted.

Or consider whether the majority (and its designated officials) may require a minority to pay public homage to national symbols, even when their religious convictions prohibit acknowledging the authority asserted by human institutions. Can the officials of a public school district compel their students to pledge allegiance to the American flag, although such a pledge is contrary to the religious convictions of the child's parents?

The United States Supreme Court answered this question with a resounding negative in 1943, when it found unconstitutional a West Virginia requirement calling for a salute of the flag and pledge of allegiance, with a penalty of student expulsion and parental fine. The case involved the child of members of Jehovah's Witnesses. Said the Court:

> If there is any fixed star in our constitutional constellation, it is that no official, high or petty, can prescribe what shall be orthodox in politics, nationalism, religion, or other matters of opinion or force citizens to confess by word or act their faith therein.[7]

Has this "fixed star" been widely accepted by the public, or by the officials who manage the public schools? In 1969, in a midwestern town, a school principal reported that he had been approached by a Jehovah's Witness parent who insisted that her child not be forced to salute the flag. He claimed that he resolved the matter "brilliantly" by requiring the child to *hold* the flag while his classmates saluted it!

Freedom in an Industrial Society

By the last third of the nineteenth century, American society had been almost completely transformed. Population had settled on the expanse of the continent, occupying the West Coast and most of the interior. The number of persons needed to provide food for the nation was declining. Railroads spanned the continent. America had become a leading industrial nation.

Was the American ideal of equality relevant in a society so different from that known to Jefferson? The condition of the people was becoming *less* equal as entrepreneurs and financiers amassed profits that were neither taxed by government nor shared by workers. Cities were becoming the centers of culture for the few and degradation for the many. The "yeoman farmer" of Jefferson's day was vanishing, for farmers produced a single cash crop, rather than supplying most of their families needs. Men, women, and even children worked for as long as twelve hours per day in the factories.

The argument against government regulation of business was that such regulation would threaten that equality of opportunity valued so highly by Jefferson and Jackson. Support for this claim came from

---

7. *West Virginia State Board of Education v. Barnette*, 319 U.S. 624 (1943).

the most respected minds of the era. A group of social theorists, adopting the findings of Charles Darwin concerning the evolution of biological species, compared the world of private enterprise to a jungle. Unrestrained competition was necessary, they argued, so that the process of natural selection would weed out the inefficient, permitting the strong competitors to bring benefits to all. That the competitors who were weeded out suffered great hardship, or even death, was regrettable, but there was no way to repeal a law of nature.

Neither of these arguments impressed the farmer, who saw his profits skimmed away by manipulated railroad rates, the prices of his products determined by speculators, and interest rates on his borrowed capital set by distant forces and men he could not identify. Workers in the cities were just as aware of injustice, but they lacked the numbers of the farmers. The tentative efforts of labor to organize were crushed, as when Democratic President Grover Cleveland sent federal troops to end the bloody Pullman Strike in 1894. Conceptions of equality had not yet been adapted to the reality of industrial society.

The farmers turned to political action. Some of their demands seem mildly radical, even today, such as the call for the national government to purchase and operate the railroads. Others seem but a misguided interpretation of economic forces, such as the insistence of the People's (Populist) party upon the free coinage of silver as a means of increasing the supply of money. The reforms that appear uncontroversial today—following their eventual adoption—were aimed at providing more equal opportunity in the economic system by assuring a greater political voice for the people.

The direct election of senators was achieved with the adoption of the Seventeenth Amendment in 1913. But this was not as a result of Populist agitation. By then, the Progressive movement had enlisted many members of the Democratic and Republican parties. The Progressives were led by small-town lawyers, small businessmen, and other members of the white middle class. They, like the farmers, had seen the necessity for political action against the power of corporations, wealth, and "the interests." Also, like the farmers, they did not see government as a potential positive force in protecting economic equality, although European nations were beginning to use the authority of government to protect individual citizens against the uncertainties of industrial society. (Otto von Bismarck, the premier of Prussia, adopted a social security plan and national health insurance in 1883; England adopted important welfare measures in 1911.)

In America, direct benefits from government were scarcely considered. Government was still viewed as the potential enemy. The focus of reform was upon ending special privileges enjoyed by the wealthy; and Progressive reform came upon the demand of a politically organized majority.

The movement for women's rights, begun before the Civil War, made little progress after it. Some members of the middle class, like Elizabeth Blackwell, the first woman doctor, demonstrated the fallacy of male prejudices. But lower-class women were grist for the industrial mill. They worked twelve or fourteen hours a day in the sweatshops, earning six dollars a week, and then came home to domestic responsibilities. Political organization lay in the future.

Why did the Populist movement fail, and the Progressive movement succeed? Did the effort of the Populists to form a new and powerful political force vanish without a trace? Populism attempted to form a coalition between farmer and workers, but Americans had not formed a politically self-conscious working class. Progressivism was formed as a reaction to Populism when middle-class businessmen felt they were threatened by greedy corporations above and demanding workers below. The Progressives then achieved the adoption of many reforms urged by the Populists.

The Southern Reaction to Populism

The indelible mark left by Populism was in the South. The outcome in that region was the exact opposite of what the Populist leaders intended. The vision of the Populists was to join together citizens on the lowest rungs of the economic ladder, *regardless of race.*

For a decade following Reconstruction, relations between the races in the South were outwardly—and in daylight—less strained than in the North. (The Ku Klux Klan rode at night.) Blacks were served in the same room as whites in restaurants, saloons, and ice-cream parlors. A black man who could purchase a first-class railway ticket was permitted to ride in the first-class car. Nor was there a massive movement to deny the freedman his vote, although the honesty of vote-counting was frequently questioned.

The political pattern of those years was for the black man to support the more conservative elements of southern politics—in essence, the former slavemasters. The deepest resentment against blacks was held by the poor whites who feared them as economic competitors. A wave of lynchings that accompanied economic depression in the 1870s was led by lower-class whites, and other blatant expressions of racism came from the poorer and less well educated. The poor white was an unlikely political friend of the black. The former slave-owning class, in general, treated the freedman as an aristocrat would treat a social inferior—with consideration, with dignity, even with sympathy; but without forgetting the difference in station. Careful use of political patronage by appointing black leaders to secondary positions cemented this alliance.

Danny Lyon

The Populists threatened to destroy the arrangement. They preached that the common self-interest of white and black share-croppers should lead them to combine forces against the political interests of the landowners. Racial differences, they argued, should not blind men to economic realities; the wealthy were oppressing black and white alike. The Populists adopted a program calling for genuine political equality for the freedman, regulation of corporations and measures of economic equality.

The reaction of southern political leaders was to call forth all the latent power of racism. Systematic methods (literacy tests, or "grand-father clauses," which waive literacy tests for those whose ancestors voted) were devised to disenfranchise the black man without directly violating the Fifteenth Amendment. During the 1890s, southern states enacted legislation requiring segregation of the races in public places and in transportation facilities. Enforcement of the new order was undertaken by the white majority; during periods of the decade, the lynching of a black person was reported every two days. The Demo-cratic party of the South was conceived as the protector of white supremacy: the ruling classes substituted the politics of race for the politics of economic interest.

When Progressivism came to the South, it brought a wave of re-form measures, including primary elections to provide choice within the one-party system. But blacks were excluded from their benefits.

Up from Slavery

Booker T. Washington was, as the twentieth century dawned, the best known black American. As the principal of Tuskeegee Institute in Alabama, this son of slaves preached a gospel of hard work, rectitude, and honor. His biography, *Up from Slavery*, published in 1901, was cherished in hundreds of black people's homes. It was proof of what a single man, regardless of race, could achieve with his own hands and pure heart. He felt that the black man, through education, could earn the fruits of freedom implicit in emancipation.

In 1895, Booker T. Washington delivered a famous speech at the Cotton States Exhibition. As the Jim Crow laws requiring racial segre-gation spread across the South, blacks foresaw and protested the death of the promise inherent in emancipation. Washington coun-seled them to be patient, to educate themselves, to win the respect of the nation. Rather than seeking political or social equality, they should be content to live and work and learn separately, until they should be prepared for the responsibilities of freedom. Thrusting his hand in the air, with the fingers extended, Washington declared that, in economic development, the two races in the South could work

together as a single hand. But, in social matters, they could remain
as separate as the fingers.

White listeners in the audience stood on their chairs and cheered.
Washington's capitulation seemed to herald a new era of racial peace.

A few months later, the United States Supreme Court ruled in the
case of Homer Plessy, one-eighth Negro, who was ordered to sit in the
"colored" section of a railway coach, in accord with a law of Louisiana. Plessy argued that the Louisiana law was contrary to the
Thirteenth and Fourteenth Amendments to the United States Constitution.

The Court disagreed. While the Court majority admitted that the
intention of the two amendments was to "enforce the absolute equality of the two races before the law," they argued that racial segregation
certainly did not imply the superiority of one race over the other. To
reach this conclusion, the Court majority was forced to make an
excursion into the realm of psychology.

> We consider the underlying fallacy of the plaintiff's argument
> to consist in the assumption that the enforced separation of the
> two races stamps the colored race with a badge of inferiority. If
> this be so, it is not by reason of anything found in the act, but
> solely because the colored race chooses to put that construction
> upon it.[8]

As long as they were "equal," separate accommodations were constitutional. Justice John Marshall Harlan wrote a thundering dissent that still echoes in the dusty pages of the lawbooks and was
adopted by a unanimous Supreme Court in 1954.

> There is no caste here. Our Constitution is color-blind, and
> neither knows nor tolerates classes among citizens. In respect of
> civil rights, all citizens are equal before the law. The humblest
> is the peer of the most powerful. The law regards man as man,
> and takes no account of his surroundings or of his color when
> his civil rights as guaranteed by the supreme law of the land are
> involved. . . .
>   . . . What can more certainly arouse race hate, what more
> certainly create and perpetuate a feeling of distrust between
> these races, than State enactments which in fact proceed on the
> ground that colored citizens are so inferior and degraded that
> they cannot be allowed to sit in public coaches occupied by
> white citizens?[9]

Just as Justice Harlan perceived the evil effects of discrimination
sanctioned by law, the easy assumption of Booker T. Washington that
black Americans could somehow earn equality in the eyes of whites
was challenged within the black community. Dr. W. E. B. Du Bois, the
noted black historian, who supported Booker T. Washington's stand
in 1895, soon realized that the bondage of social custom would not be
so easily severed. His book, *The Souls of Black Folk*, published in 1903,
examined the "double consciousness" of black Americans, who were
technically and legally free but were surrounded by restraints upon
their very humanity and were forced to measure their own worth by
the standard of "amused contempt" provided by the white world.

Du Bois's book was credited with freeing the artistic expression of
black Americans from its dependence upon the slave experience. But
Du Bois also realized the need for concrete political action. In 1905, he

8. *Plessy* v. *Ferguson,* 163 U.S. 537 (1896).
9. Ibid.

met with a group of thirty prominent black people to found the "Niagara Movement," which, four years later, merged into the National Association for the Advancement of Colored People, dedicated to "aggressive action on the part of men who believe in Negro freedom and growth."[10] Du Bois left his faculty position at Atlanta University to become director of publicity and research for the NAACP.

Du Bois was convinced that the black man would win equality only through his own actions, not as a reward from the dominant forces in society. He wrote prophetically in 1903 that "The Problem of the twentieth century is the problem of the color line." Du Bois was referring not only to the United States, but also to the colonies of Africa then managed by white men, where the thrust for independence was yet to begin. After many years of battling for the rights of black men, Dr. Du Bois, despondent at the lack of real black progress, left the United States. He died in Ghana, honored as a prophet—but not in his own country.

The prophecy of Du Bois received little attention from American political leaders in 1903 or thereafter. Instead, the white establishment lavished its attention upon Booker T. Washington. He was invited to the White House by President Theodore Roosevelt (who wanted the United States to become a colonial power).

In the South, "separate but equal" was taken as a mandate for racial segregation in facilities ranging from public schools to drinking fountains. But the region was impoverished, and white officials elected by white voters made budget decisions. The separate black institutions never received enough money to be made "equal."

By the time of Woodrow Wilson's inauguration, Washington, D.C. was a Jim Crow town.

The Pinnacle of Progressive Reform

Although they led separate political parties, both Theodore Roosevelt and Woodrow Wilson must be counted as leaders of the Progressive reform movement. Each in his different way exerted remarkable democratic leadership. Roosevelt, the hearty outdoorsman, called for a "square deal"; Wilson, the austere idealist, sought to achieve a "new freedom." Roosevelt popularized conservation; Wilson formed the Federal Reserve Bank to stabilize the monetary system. Both men demonstrated again that the majority would respond to effective leadership, that the voters could understand and support changing concepts of equality.

In the economic sphere, both Wilson and Roosevelt achieved some success in breaking up monopolies. The Sherman Anti-Trust Act had been passed as early as 1890 but had been ineffective until used vigorously by Roosevelt and his successor, William Howard Taft. Wilson extended the attack on monopolies through the Clayton Act, passed in 1914. The basis of the policies of all three presidents was an effort to restore competition to private enterprise: equality of opportunity in the economy.

When the storm clouds gathered in Europe, and Wilson's last efforts to prevent America's involvement in the conflict failed, he turned the power of his moral leadership to unifying the nation. He called for a war to make the world safe for democracy. Other nations should participate in the dream of human equality. America entered the war as the culminating act of a long era of cautious domestic political reform supported by the rhetoric of freedom and equality.

10. Quoted in C. Eric Lincoln, *The Negro Pilgrimage in America* (rev. ed., New York: Bantam Books, 1969), p. 83.

Woodrow Wilson was careful to identify the enemy as the German leadership, rather than the German people. But Americans had read the atrocity stories of crimes committed in Belgium by the German soldiers; British and then American posters pictured "the Hun" as a menacing figure leaping out of the dim pages of history. Anti-German feeling engulfed the nation. The teaching of German as a foreign language was abandoned in most schools. American citizens of German origin were subjected to abuse; their homes were stoned, their businesses were boycotted, their forms of speech were ridiculed. Sauerkraut was renamed "liberty cabbage." The maximum effort needed to produce the equipment and ammunition to win the war required the enthusiasm of a united people. But that enthusiasm worked to destroy the very principle—liberty—that justified fighting the war.

The end of the war did not turn American minds to the need for achieving equality. Woodrow Wilson journeyed to Europe and found many of his ideals betrayed by the practical needs of achieving a peace settlement. He returned to America and failed to convince Congress and the American people of the need to participate in his greatest dream of all, the League of Nations. The battle destroyed his health. Then, as the sick and broken Wilson lay in the White House, Attorney General A. Mitchell Palmer launched an ardent persecution of persons suspected of disloyalty to the United States. With the success of the Bolshevik Revolution in Russia, a "red scare" of major proportions swept the nation. Radical spokesmen of every kind—particularly labor union leaders—were subjected to official abuse. Freedom of speech and freedom of the press were denied them, with little justification other than suspicion. And public opinion approved.

The Progressive era left a legacy in the U.S. Constitution. The Prohibition (Eighteenth) Amendment of 1919 symbolized the naive optimism of the reformers, only to be repealed in 1933. The Nineteenth Amendment, providing equality of voting rights, marked the end of a beginning.

The Progressive impulse included a concern for the state of working-class women and children by elements of the middle and upper-middle classes. Jane Addams, working in Chicago's Hull House, and young Eleanor Roosevelt, expanding her consciousness through social work in New York, were part of a new awareness. Education became available to women; they awakened to their own status, and they saw that legal discrimination was based as much upon sex as upon economics. Women were not allowed to own property, nor to raise their children after a divorce, and they were everywhere required to work for lower wages than men for comparable employment. The only way to win equal treatment was by winning the vote: the power of the vote could mean the ability to sway legislatures.

The Nineteenth Amendment was ratified in 1920, as a last gasp of the Progressive movement, a final achievement of the moral fervor that passed an Anti-Trust Act and led the nation into a world war. It was the men who yielded, a tribute to the vigor (and frequent good humor) of the Suffragist campaign. Some supported votes for women because they foresaw the defeat of the urban machines: the good judgment of their own wives would counterbalance the "controlled" vote of the immigrant masses.

Return to Normalcy

The sense of high moral purpose could not be sustained. It had been submerged by Palmer's raids upon civil liberties even before the Nineteenth Amendment was inscribed upon the books. Then came the election of Warren Harding, the rush back to "normalcy," widespread public participation in the stock market, and the speakeasy. The Ku Klux Klan was reborn, added anti-Semitism and anti-Catholicism to its banners, and wielded great political power in southern and western states. Another great change came in the American economy. Its focus shifted from production (railroads, bridges, heavy equipment, farm machinery) to consumption (automobiles, radios, refrigerators, toothpaste). In the scramble to participate in the joys of consumption, questions of freedom and equality were laid aside.

Black soldiers returning to southern towns following World War I, after they had seen Paris and learned that the whole world is not operated in the manner of Alabama and Mississippi, did not seem respectful enough to the whites who had never left those towns. It was as if they expected some credit, or even some improved status, for helping make the world safe for democracy. Many were lynched while still wearing their uniforms.

Government as Protector of Freedom

The stock market collapse of 1929 signaled a general collapse of the American — indeed, the world — economy. The collapse was as mystifying as it was total. Conventional economic theory held that wage rates were set by supply and demand. Workers were unemployed only when they refused to accept wages that would permit employers to make a reasonable profit. As the Depression deepened, however, millions could not find employment *at any wage at all.*

The confusion of economists was matched by the confusion of politicians. President Herbert Hoover, the great humanitarian who had fed the Belgian refugees, was a champion of "rugged individualism." In this view, the government dared not intervene in the functioning of the economic system, for free competition assured the benefit of all. He shared the belief of Jefferson and Jackson that government power was the greatest potential danger to freedom and that the Constitution existed to limit that power. He felt he could take no action that was not specifically provided for in the Constitution.

Meanwhile, in the Detroit of 1930, W. D. Fard founded the Nation of Islam, a religious organization based on the conviction that the white man is the devil and can only contaminate black men. The movement would grow slowly for a quarter of a century, until a man called Malcolm X, able to speak the language and comprehend the frustrations of the northern ghetto, would bring its message into the world like a bombshell.

Franklin D. Roosevelt was elected in 1932. An intellectual heir of Jefferson and Wilson, he did not accept the paralyzing theories of Herbert Hoover regarding presidential power. FDR tended to view the Constitution as an instrument available to the majority to work its will. He further stated that the emergency of economic collapse equaled any emergency caused by a war, and he claimed the emergency powers exercised by presidents in wartime.

At first, Congress agreed with President Roosevelt and largely supported him, but the Supreme Court did not accept his view of the Constitution. After a battle against the Court, which cost him the cooperation of Congress, Mr. Roosevelt won the agreement of the Court.

Then came World War II.

By then, the long parade of alphabetical laws and agencies was a fixture of the government landscape: NRA, SEC, WPA, PWA, CCC,

TNEC, AAA. What they added up to was an acceptance of the belief that the national government should become a *positive* force, able to intervene in society and the economy to protect the liberty of the individual and the welfare of groups.

Liberty itself took on a new dimension. The Depression had made clear that a modern industrial economy is ruled by vast and impersonal forces that the individual citizens and even large corporations are powerless to affect. Equality of opportunity had meant that no restraints would be imposed by government. Now it meant that government must take positive actions. The children of unemployed parents, denied food and thus life, would not have even an equality of opportunity, much less the freedoms guaranteed by the Bill of Rights.

The people responded to Roosevelt's leadership. They accepted the new dimension of liberty. When FDR met with Prime Minister Winston Churchill to formulate peace aims (the Atlantic Charter), he included "Freedom from Want" and "Freedom from Fear."

This began to give new meaning to the rights of "life, liberty, and the pursuit of happiness." It added a material dimension. It suggested that the role of government might be to establish a minimum level of food, clothing, and housing for every citizen, including those cast aside by the selective process of competitive enterprise, those retired in old age, and the children born to impoverished parents.

> President Roosevelt's humane instincts were warm and great. They could embrace all of mankind. But they did not lead him to sponsor legislation aimed at ensuring the equal rights of black Americans, who had been largely abandoned by the national government since the administration of Rutherford B. Hayes.
>
> Because of the dependable functioning of the seniority system, the congressional leaders Roosevelt had to work with were southern Democrats. This may be the reason why he did not risk civil rights legislation. He needed the support of the southerners for other programs, including his foreign policy. But the president was under no pressure from northern members of Congress. They regarded the "Negro problem" as a matter for the South. They saw it as a regional, not a national, dilemma.
>
> The needs of the war factories in the cities of the "Arsenal of Democracy"—Detroit, Chicago, Los Angeles, San Francisco-Oakland, Wichita—brought black families pouring out of the South. When A. Phillip Randolph of the Brotherhood of Sleeping Car Porters threatened to lead 50,000 marchers down Pennsylvania Avenue, President Roosevelt established the Fair Employment Practices Committee charged with preventing racial discrimination by firms holding government contracts.
>
> Black soldiers were segregated from whites in the armed forces. Japanese-American families were segregated within the United States in "relocation" camps.

As soon as the war ended, and the nation disarmed, the Cold War began. Communism was identified as the enemy; Senator Joseph McCarthy "exposed" the domestic influence of that enemy, providing new reasons for suspicion and division among the people. Those who had, a generation before, called for an expanded governmental concern for the welfare of individuals—the same sort of social justice characterized in the Atlantic Charter as "Freedom from Want" and "Freedom from Fear"—were now tarred with a label reading "Socialist" or "Communist."

One great scar upon the American memory was healed, however. In 1960, John Fitzgerald Kennedy was elected president. There was an underground campaign, never blessed by the Republicans, to awaken the same kind of ignorant hatred that had helped defeat Democrat (and Catholic) Al Smith in 1928. It failed. The impulse of Americans to divide and fight against each other on the basis of religion was diminishing.

No longer could you imagine a sign tacked to the White House fence reading "No Irish Need Apply." More than a century was needed for the Irish to win this symbolic acceptance.

How Long Can a Dream Prevail?

While American society was caught up in the feverish speculation of the 1920s, and Calvin Coolidge in the White House made a virtue of inactivity, black Americans were seeking some method to breach the wall of racial hatred. The first national campaign of the NAACP was directed at the United States Congress and sought federal legislation against lynchings. The measure was killed by southern filibusters, but the effort focused the glare of national publicity upon the South, and eventually the barbaric practice faded. (Brutality—sometimes murder "to prevent the prisoner's escape"—committed upon blacks by southern lawmen, the surrogates for southern society, became the substitute.)

The NAACP turned next to the courts. Painfully, on a city-by-city basis, court suits were used to force school officials to adhere to the "separate but equal" doctrine by equalizing the expenditure of public funds for the education of white and black students. When this effort began in 1933, the average expenditure per black child in the South was $12 per year, while the annual expenditure per white child was $45. The battle was waged in one school district at a time. Southern officials began voluntarily to equalize support for the black schools only when the doctrine of segregation itself was threatened with extinction.

In the 1930s, lawyers for the NAACP planned a cautious, gradual assault upon the precedent of *Plessy* v. *Ferguson*. Aware that all judges are familiar with legal education, they brought to the Court a series of cases concerning admission to state law schools. In 1938, the Court ruled that a state may not exclude blacks from its law school by paying their tuition in neighboring states.[11] To do so would deprive citizens of the equal protection of the laws, for a student should have the privilege of attending a law school in the state where he intends to practice.

11. *Missouri ex. rel. Gaines* v. *Canada,* 305 U.S. 337 (1938).

Several southern states hastily established separate law schools for blacks; but they were inferior in many ways. In 1950, the Court ruled unanimously that the new Texas law school for blacks was far inferior to the University of Texas Law School, which had far greater prestige, an alumni organization, and an excellent library, among other features.[12] The Court stopped short of ruling that *any* law school for blacks would be unequal to the established white school.

In 1954, the attention of the Court was turned to primary and secondary schools in districts that were becoming "equal" in terms of buildings, curricula, and the qualifications and salaries of teachers. Citing contemporary studies in psychology, the Court found that segregation denotes black inferiority and that "a sense of inferiority affects the motivation of a child to learn."

> We conclude that in the field of public education the doctrine of "separate but equal" has no place. Separate educational facilities are inherently unequal.[13]

The following year, the Court held another hearing to decide what relief should be granted. It ordered that the desegregation of the schools—the abolition of dual black and white school systems—should proceed "at all deliberate speed."[14] Lower federal courts would oversee the process.

Rebuffed in the U.S. Congress, knowing that no sympathy would be found in southern legislatures, and having won most of the presidential support that was possible without approval by Congress, the hopes of the NAACP were pinned upon the judicial process. The *Brown* decision of 1954 seemed a vindication of those hopes. But the voice of the Supreme Court did not thunder in the land. By 1963, only 0.8 percent of southern black children were attending integrated schools.

Meanwhile, a new generation of black Americans had known more education than their parents, and many had escaped the closed societies of small southern towns to learn the lonesome horror of big city slums. The separate education Booker T. Washington prescribed had been largely acquired, but it did not open up places in American society. The time came to heed the advice of Du Bois, who felt that blacks would have to win equality for themselves.

In December of 1955, Mrs. Rosa Parks was arrested in Birmingham, Alabama, for refusing to move to the back of the bus. Spontaneously, the blacks of Birmingham began a boycott of the segregated buses so complete and effective that the company sought a settlement. In the midst of bargaining, a federal court order affirmed that segregation in local transportation systems is unconstitutional.

From the Birmingham boycott emerged a new leader, Martin Luther King, Jr., who would give voice to black aspirations and become the champion of a tactic alien to the American experience: nonviolent direct action.

> Gandhi preached nonviolence as part of a deep religious faith and used it to win political victories over the British colonial administrators. He succeeded because, as George Orwell pointed out, the British had been taught to respect human life—a respect eliminated in peoples dominated by Hitlers and Stalins. The playing fields of Eton imbued a sense of decency, even if it was stuffy and inarticulate.

12. *Sweatt v. Painter*, 339 U.S. 629 (1950).
13. *Brown v. Board of Education of Topeka, Kansas*, 347 U.S. 483 (1954).
14. *Brown v. Board of Education*, 349 U.S. 294 (1955).

The nonviolence for which Martin Luther King was the spokesman did not operate upon the direct oppressor in the same way as Gandhi's. Sheriff "Bull" Connor's deputies and the hooded members of the Ku Klux Klan have not experienced the playing fields of Eton. But acts of nonviolent confrontation in the full glare of publicity could by-pass the immediate oppressor to engage the conscience of the un-committed, forcing them to decide which aspect of the American character should triumph. King wrote,

> Ever since the signing of the Declaration of Independence, America has manifested a schizophrenic personality on the question of race. She has been torn between two selves — a self in which she has proudly professed democracy and a self in which she has sadly practiced the antithesis of democracy.[15]

The American people had not lost their capacity for involvement. The pictures of fire hoses and vicious dogs turned against blacks who did nothing to defend themselves had an impact. The old sense of outrage that had fired the Abolitionists was reborn.

Some called it the second American revolution. The Montgomery bus boycott was followed by lunch-counter sit-ins, then the picketing of chain stores. Southern black students were joined by northern whites — as many as 70,000 demonstrators took part in 800 sit-ins in 1961. Freedom riders tested the enforcement of Supreme Court prohibitions against segregated transportation, and a Greyhound bus was set fire by whites outside Anniston, Alabama. Voter registration drives began in 1963, and the Mississippi Freedom Democratic party was founded.

Nonviolent direct action in the name of the American creed — Constitution, Declaration of Independence, and rulings of the Supreme Court — confronted southern laws and customs, and slowly they began to yield. The moral superiority of the nonviolent demonstrators was obvious to the world; and the North could still tell itself that this was a southern problem.

Burt Glinn

15. Lotte Hoskins, ed., "I Have a Dream": The Quotations of Martin Luther King, Jr. (New York: Grosset and Dunlap, 1968), p. 5.

In August, 1963, came a March on Washington and a meeting surrounding the Lincoln Memorial. Martin Luther King, the apostle of nonviolence, restated the American dream.

> I have a dream that one day on the red hills of Georgia the sons of former slaves and the sons of former slaveowners will be able to sit down together at the table of brotherhood.
>
> I have a dream that one day even the State of Mississippi, a state sweltering with the heat of injustice, sweltering with the heat of oppression, will be transformed into an oasis of freedom and justice. I have a dream that my four little children will one day live in a nation where they will not be judged by the color of their skin but by the content of their character. . . .[16]

President Kennedy issued a statement praising the peaceful demonstration, and congressmen displayed some interest. President Kennedy had shown, in a television speech in the spring of 1963, that he finally understood the urgency of the civil rights cause and would support it. But he was assassinated in November.

> In the northern ghettoes, where racism was not written into law but was practiced—sometimes absent-mindedly—by bureaucrats and private citizens, nonviolence held fewer promises. Segregation had meant not dual school systems, restaurants, and drinking fountains, but segregated inadequate housing and building trades unions closed to blacks. Integration had meant selected blacks escaping from the ghettoes to join white middle-class neighborhoods. Civil rights legislation didn't change things in the North, and frustrations mounted. Stokely Carmichael pointed out in 1966 that, because of the implicit assumption that decent housing and a decent way of life were available *only* in white neighborhoods, integration was but a psychological tool of white supremacy. The ghettoes needed organization, a sense of community, the creation of political and economic influence. Black Power.

John F. Kennedy was killed in Dallas.

A Civil Rights Act was passed in 1964.

Lyndon Johnson declared war on poverty, announced his determination to save the cities from decay, and won his reelection.

But all good purposes could not be achieved simultaneously. Increasingly, the war in Vietnam was more important than the War on Poverty or the battle against injustice.

Each summer became a "long, hot summer."

Langston Hughes had asked the question years before:

What happens to a dream deferred?

Does it dry up
like a raisin in the sun?
Or fester like a sore—
And then run?
Does it stink like rotten meat?
Or crust and sugar over—
like a syrupy sweet?
Maybe it just sags
like a heavy load.

Or does it explode?[17]

16. "I Have a Dream," reprinted in John Hope Franklin and Isidore Starr, eds., *The Negro in Twentieth Century America* (New York: Vintage, 1967), p. 146.
17. Copyright 1951 by Langston Hughes. Reprinted from *The Panther and the Lash*, by Langston Hughes, by permission of Alfred A. Knopf, Inc., and Harold Ober Associates, Inc.

Malcolm X, having outgrown the narrow philosophy of the Nation of Islam, still recognized as spokesman for the truth of the black experience, was struggling to establish a new organization that would acknowledge the possibility for justice in all races; he was killed by gunfire in 1965.

In 1968, Martin Luther King was killed by a lone sniper.

The explosion came.

After the riots and the demonstrations, the self-destruction of black ghettoes, the rise of George Wallace, all the civil rights acts, and the reports of commissions on violence, what had changed? Had the people accepted new meanings for equality? Was there a growing sense of national dedication to the principles of the Declaration of Independence?

Some of the barriers against equality were lowered. Television commercials were integrated, and then some of the programs. Large corporations hurried to display at least one black person in their front offices, and colleges agreed to offer programs of black studies. Public facilities in southern cities—but not in the towns—were integrated. Resistance stiffened in the North against integration in the schools and the building trades unions.

Vietnam was the first completely integrated war fought by the United States. Blacks and whites fought in the same units and shared the same facilities. Because white college students got deferments, more blacks were drafted. Black soldiers volunteered for the extra-pay crack combat units. For both these reasons, blacks did more than their share of the dying. At home, the income level of black Americans improved. But the income of white families grew by a greater proportion.

In California, Texas, Colorado, and Michigan, America's second largest minority, the Mexican-Americans, stirred into political consciousness. They began to glory in the name *Chicano*. Cesar Chavez succeeded, for the first time ever, in winning recognition for a union of migratory farm workers. In Denver, "Corky" Gonzales revealed that the entire American Southwest is the mystical region of Aztlán, historic home of the Chicano people. All others are interlopers.

After the atomic bomb brought Japan's surrender, the girls rushed to greet their men. Husbands plunged into the intrigues of their corporate organizations, and the wives settled into suburbia to raise kids.

But a reborn concern for the rights of minorities again caused women to think of themselves. Betty Friedan established that the highest calling of feminine consciousness is not necessarily realized through housework.[18] A new, diverse, and fascinating feminist move-

18. Betty Friedan, *The Feminine Mystique* (New York: Nortin, 1963).

ment was launched, as women attempted to free themselves, and men as well, from sex-bound stereotypes. Like other movements of the 1960s, its announced goal was not only equality, it was liberation.

The All-American Boy

How should the American people react to the Russian feat of a manned earth-orbiting vehicle? This is how it looked to the man who had to decide:

> Many of [President John F. Kennedy's] advisers told him that money spent on a large manned space flight program would not produce benefits for the United States as great as other possible uses of the same resources. Kennedy considered this advice, but ultimately decided that the power and pride of the American nation . . . required a program to establish the United States as the leading spacefaring country. He committed himself to that objective and came to view it as representative of some of the most basic motivations and aspirations of the people who had chosen him as their leader.[19]

A man on the moon (and safely returned) within the decade. That was the goal President Kennedy adopted and the commitment he made. It was a crystal clear ranking of priorities. And it was a possible goal: it called for the mastery of things, not of men. Once promised, and enough resources supplied, it could be achieved.

It was achieved on July 20, 1969, when Neil Armstrong radioed, "Tranquillity Base here. The Eagle has landed." Then, six and a half hours later, "That's one small step for a man, one giant leap for mankind."

Neil Armstrong! To an older generation that name stirred memories of a hundred afternoons, coming home from school and flopping in a living room chair, when the booming voice sang out of the radio to announce the continuing saga of "Jack Armstrong! Jack Armstrong! The All-American Boy!" Hero of his high school, the consummate athlete, filled with strength and purity and joy, Jack Armstrong represented a simpler, but now lost, American time, when Americans seemed to rise above any division caused by race or class or sex — or were blissfully ignorant of them.

19. John M. Logsdon, *The Decision to Go to the Moon: Project Apollo and the National Interest* (Cambridge, Mass.: MIT Press, 1970), pp. 180-181.

So Neil Armstrong was the first to land on the moon. The triumph of the American technological ego. ("Our purpose," the astronauts said, "is to interface with the machinery.") The astronauts personified the American, male, white, Anglo-Saxon, Protestant, practical mechanical mind that mastered mathematics and other arcane sciences in the full confidence of the inevitable triumph of Progress.

Thus man escaped the age-old bond of gravity, initiating a brave new era in space. It may have been a hollow victory. Does the only authentic American genius reside in the manipulation of things through technology, while our great political ideals, which claim a unique vision of the relationships between men, have failed to achieve their promise?

The Second Inaugural

When he stood on the steps of the Capitol to praise the coming of peace and describe the domestic achievements planned for his second administration, Richard Nixon appeared obsessed with the year in which that administration would end: 1976, the two-hundredth anniversary of the national foundation. Three times he mentioned the forthcoming anniversary, as if compelled to show that those who guide the national destiny today are worthy of their predecessors.

President Nixon made a passing reference to the need for tolerance among the people. "Let each of us," he said, "reach out for that one precious quality government cannot provide—a new level of respect for the rights and feelings of one another and for the individual human dignity which is the cherished birthright of every American."

The main theme of his speech was that the federal government must move away from a direct concern for the legal and material foundation of that sense of individual dignity. If the two great, and often conflicting, values that have dominated American history have been equality and achievement, the president seemed interested only in achievement—the kind of individual striving which, set in the proper organizational framework, can land an All-American Boy among the craters of the moon, and ignore children starving in Mississippi. Said President Nixon,

> Let us encourage individuals at home and nations abroad to do more for themselves and decide more for themselves. Let us locate more responsibility in more places. Let us measure what we will do for others by what they will do for themselves. . . .
>
> Let each of us remember that America was built not by government, but by people, not by welfare, but by work—not by shirking responsibility, but by seeking responsibility.
>
> In our own lives, let each of us ask—not just what will government do for me, but what can I do for myself?

The president called for a renewed pride in America's accomplishments. "Our children have been taught to be ashamed of their country," he said, "ashamed of their parents, ashamed of America's record at home and of its role in the world." But, in fact, the American system has provided "more freedom and more abundance" than any other in history.

The president concluded by asking for the blessing of God upon the national purpose and his own decision-making.

If the words of the inaugural address left any question, President Nixon submitted a budget to Congress that revealed his intention very clearly. His intention was to rebuild the structure of the executive branch by eliminating many agencies established to deal with human needs. Leading the list of abolished bureaus was the Office of Economic Opportunity, the flagship of Lyndon Johnson's federal fleet designed to battle poverty. President Nixon reported that most of the functions of the disestablished agencies would be assigned to the old-line departments. One program that had no immediate home was the one which provided federal assistance to lawyers who represent the poor in their contests with local power structures, thus making a giant leap toward realizing the ideal of equality before the law— which, in modern times, has to mean the equal right to the help of a lawyer.

President Nixon left the impression that his administration would no longer be concerned with the struggle to redefine and fill the promises of the Declaration of Independence with meanings appropriate to the post-industrial era.

Some of Lyndon Johnson's antipoverty agencies had indeed been hastily planned and fell far short of achieving their goals. But President Nixon left the impression that his second administration would offer nothing more than "benign neglect" to those groups still seeking to realize the promise of America. It looked as if government would be conducted for those who feel (with the encouragement of their favorite tax loopholes) that the promises of the Declaration of Independence have been achieved.

Perhaps the time had come to reverse a trend. Perhaps the continued concern of Washington for the welfare and comfort of individual citizens caused only bureaucratic confusion and a waste of taxes. Perhaps citizens should seek the fulfillment of the promises inherent in citizenship only through living and working in their local communities.

What could be more true to the spirit in which Jefferson wrote than to remind individuals that they are responsible for their own "life, liberty, and the pursuit of happiness"?

The suspicion remained that an eighteenth-century definition of those words does not fit the reality of the 1970s.

Some Lessons of Vietnam

Early in 1973, the promise of "peace at hand" made on election eve of 1972 was more or less realized. A cease-fire agreement, signed in Paris, provided for the withdrawal of American forces from Vietnam and the return of American prisoners of war.

Since nobody had surrendered and neither side could impose peace terms, the issues that had caused thirty years of armed conflict in Indochina remained unresolved. The agreement was ambiguous about the future, and the contracting parties were free to claim that their goals had been won. President Nixon said that it constituted "peace with honor."

Fighting of some kind was likely to go on, but at least the moral and physical agony and the economic drain of American involvement was coming to a temporary end. Where could one begin, in counting the cost of America's retrieval of "honor"? Sifting through all the photographs and memories and casualty lists and names of places and people: Presidents Eisenhower, Diem, Kennedy, Johnson, Thieu, Nixon; the Emperor Bao Dai, Madame Nhu; Ho Chi Minh; Generals Westmoreland and Lavelle, Captain Medina and Lieutenant Calley; the National Liberation Front, the Green Berets; Dien Bien Phu, Gulf of Tonkin, Hamburger Hill, Hue, My Lai, Haiphong; revelations of deliberate lying in high places, and careful self-deceptions in the Pentagon; where in all this were the lessons to be learned? Something had gone awfully wrong; but what? And why? And must it happen again?

A Question of Morality

Americans believe themselves to be a moral people. Our history is spangled with the stories of conflicts entered — and won — not in pursuit of mere wealth or power, but to serve a just cause. However, we have seldom been able totally to agree about what, in international relations, is right, and what is wrong. There have been some who claim that war is wrong, no matter what the cause; there have been great numbers who claimed the only sane course was to avoid engagement of any kind with the affairs of other nations. George Washington first recommended this policy.

One need not share either of these convictions to perceive the Vietnam War as immoral. A leading industrial nation was fighting against a far-away, and relatively tiny, nation mainly of peasants, whose existence had been largely unknown and which could hardly

constitute a direct threat to American security. At one time the justification for our actions in Vietnam was said to be our moral duty to
prevent the spread of communism into all of Southeast Asia. We
could count a large number of atrocities inflicted upon the resident
population by the National Liberation Front (NLF) guerrillas; even
the American embassy in Saigon was bombed. Our motives for intervening in Vietnam seemed no less noble than the reasons we fought
to halt the advance of communism in Korea.

Any search for the lessons of Vietnam comes up against the realization that quick moral judgments will not suffice. Indeed, a moral
groundwork for the investigation should be established at the outset:
*neither side can claim a monopoly upon physical agony or moral
insight.*

As a Moth to the Candle

Indochina became a French colony in the nineteenth century. During
World War II, it was occupied by Japanese forces, and the French
retreated. When the Japanese were defeated, the Vietnamese did not
desire the return of French colonial officials. Ho Chi Minh announced
the formation of the People's Republic of Vietnam in 1945. The
French attacked him in 1946. American policy at the time was turned
toward Europe, where the ravages of the war were being repaired. The
explosion of an atom bomb by Russia in 1949 convinced American
leaders that much greater military power had to be developed in
Europe to contain the expanding ambitions of Stalinist Russia. This
would require permitting West Germany to resume heavy industrial
production, as a preparation for German rearmament. And the forces
of NATO (North Atlantic Treaty Organization) needed strengthening.

With so many resources committed to Indochina, France felt unable to increase its contribution to NATO. Furthermore, because of
long-standing hatred for neighboring Germany, the French people
were not enthusiastic about the reestablishment of German industrial
capacity. However, French officials were so eager for aid in Indochina
that they were willing to revise their attitudes toward policy in Europe
in return. On December 23, 1950, the United States agreed to supply
"indirect" military aid to Vietnam, Cambodia, and Laos. The United
States took over the logistical support of the French forces in Indochina, without using American troops. The French soon afterward
announced plans for a European Economic Community, with West
Germany as a full partner. By October 1952, 200 shiploads of American military supplies had arrived in Saigon.

> The first American commitment in Indochina, therefore, was made
> during the early stage of the Cold War in large part to further our
> strategic purposes in Europe. Secondarily, it was a reaction to the
> Communist success in China. It had little to do with an analysis of
> the situation in Vietnam or even any knowledge of it. Not a half
> dozen Americans could speak Vietnamese.

The French Army lost ground steadily against the forces of Ho Chi
Minh. Proposals were made to send American troops to join this
ground war on the Asian land mass. In early 1954, Senator Edwin C.
("Big Ed") Johnson, a conservative Democrat from Colorado, denounced such proposals:

> The present crusade to send troops to Indochina, with its un-
> calculated cost and uncalculated result, is the most foolhardy
> adventure in all American history . . . to drift, drift, drift, closer
> and ever closer to the flaming candle, like some silly enchanted
> moth, is almost too fantastic for human minds to contemplate.[1]

When French troops were encircled at Dien Bien Phu, President Eisenhower overrode the advice of the National Security Council and
refused to send American planes and troops on a rescue mission.
Great Britain vigorously opposed American intervention (in contrast
to Korea), and President Eisenhower, after consulting congressional
leaders, decided not to employ the direct force of the United States in
support of the French colonial power. Critics of the Vietnam involvement have called this the last decent and wise decision made in
Washington concerning Vietnam.

Following the French surrender, the future of Vietnam was presumably settled by the Geneva Accords of 1954, which were signed
by Great Britain, Russia, France, the People's Republic of China,
Cambodia, and Laos. The United States attended the Geneva conference as an observer but did not sign the agreement. The Eisenhower
administration did not wish to be involved in "approving" a "surrender to Communism."[2] The United States promised not to violate
the agreement, which partitioned Vietnam at the seventeenth parallel.
The United States immediately did violate the Geneva agreement by
sending active military forces commanded by the legendary "ugly
American," Colonel Edward Lansdale. Soon after, Americans took
over the task of training the military forces of South Vietnam. Convinced that Ho Chi Minh would win, United States officials supported Ngo Dinh Diem in his decision to cancel the 1956 elections
promised by the Geneva agreement. American planners were convinced that, if Vietnam were controlled by Communists, the other
nations of Southeast Asia would fall to communism like a row of
dominoes.

To the extent that American activities were publicly discussed,
they were explained as steps taken to "resist Communist aggression."
In this view, the NLF guerrillas who controlled rural South Vietnam,
particularly at night, were invaders supplied by Ho Chi Minh in the
North. However, an anonymous Department of Defense research
worker concluded in the Pentagon Papers that the guerrilla activity
began spontaneously as pockets of local, rural resistance to the oppression and corruption of the Diem regime, and support came from
the North only upon request, and much later. Diem reversed previous
land reforms, returning land to former landlords; he had abolished
elected village councils; and he insisted on attempting to govern with
"outsiders"—persons who came from the cities, shared Diem's Catholic faith, and were eager to suppress Buddhism.

The number of American "advisers" in Vietnam grew from 900
during the Eisenhower administration to 17,000 during the Kennedy
administration. A tour of duty in Vietnam became a career expectation for Army officers. The effort in Vietnam was a permanent preoccupation of American military and foreign policy-makers; but they
never explained the depth of commitment, nor submitted its purposes
for reexamination. The bureaucratic mind regarded public opinion
as an object to be manipulated, not a voice to heed. The scope of the

1. Quoted by Leslie H. Gelb and Anthony Lake, "Role of the Congress," *New Republic*,
   February 10, 1973, p. 27.
2. Bernard B. Fall, "How the French Got Out of Viet-Nam," reprinted in M. G. Raskin
   and B. B. Fall, eds., *The Viet-Nam Reader* (New York: Random House, 1965), p. 84.

American effort was steadily expanded, although American intelligence reports suggested that such expansions would be futile.

The Pentagon researcher concluded that, as a nation, South Vietnam was largely the creation of, and existed because of, continuing support by the United States.

The firmness of the American commitment was redoubled in 1963 when the United States supported the coup prepared by leading generals to overthrow Diem. Although Lyndon Johnson hailed Diem as "the Winston Churchill of Asia" in 1961, within two years Diem's promotion of religious conflicts, and his unconcern for democratic procedures and reform, suggested that he was not the best champion of the anti-Communist cause. Rather than uniting his people against communism, Diem only reinforced the old divisions between country and city, rich and poor. American officials did not prevent the assassination of Ngo Dinh Diem.

When power struggles broke out between the Vietnamese generals to determine the permanent successor to Diem, American forces were drawn deeper into the war, as the United States propped up one shaky regime after another. Then, on November 22, 1963, President John F. Kennedy was himself assassinated in Dallas. Two days after taking office, President Lyndon Johnson proclaimed a continuation of the Kennedy policies in Vietnam. Secretary of Defense Robert McNamara and military officials made periodic inspection tours of Vietnam to return with reports of progress. There were, by March 1964, 25,000 U.S. "advisers" in Vietnam.

In early August 1964, with Barry Goldwater nominated by the Republicans and a presidential campaign in the offing, two U.S. destroyers suffered an "unprovoked" attack by North Vietnamese patrol boats in the Gulf of Tonkin. Within twelve hours, reprisal raids were mounted against North Vietnamese targets that, in fact, had been selected long before. The Johnson administration introduced a resolution that declared the support of the Congress for the determination of the president "to take all necessary measures to repel any armed attack against the forces of the United States and to prevent further aggression." The resolution passed easily, with only two senators voting against it (Morse of Oregon and Gruening of Alaska). The Tonkin Gulf Resolution entered American history.

The *Pentagon Papers* reveal that American planners felt the need of some sign of congressional approval for expanding the war. American forces had been supporting clandestine attacks upon North Vietnamese coastal positions for several months and attacked North Vietnamese islands in an amphibious operation on July 30. A North Vietnamese attack upon the American destroyers was not all that "unprovoked." But Congress passed the resolution on the basis of incomplete and misleading information supplied by the executive branch.

When leading congressmen became upset with the Johnson administration's interpretation of the Tonkin Gulf Resolution as supplying a blank check for whatever measures it deemed necessary in Vietnam, they were told by Undersecretary of State Nicholas Katzenbach that the resolution was the "functional equivalent of a declaration of war."

On June 24, 1970, the Senate voted 81-10 to repeal the resolution. President Nixon explained that the Tonkin Gulf Resolution was not particularly relevant; his constitutional authority as commander-in-chief empowered him to direct military operations in Vietnam in any case.

When President Johnson announced the attacks upon the destroyers in a television address, he also announced the reprisal air raids upon the North as a "limited and fitting" response. He said, "we seek no wider war."

As the presidential campaign was launched, Republican candidate Goldwater called upon the nation to acknowledge the existence of war in Vietnam. He recommended bombing North Vietnam to interdict logistical support for the Viet Cong and chemical defoliation of the jungle to destroy their hiding places. Supporters of President Johnson depicted Senator Goldwater as a "trigger-happy" warmonger, a dangerous man to have in control of the nuclear forces of the United States. President Johnson was reelected in a historic landslide. If he was not the "peace candidate," he certainly encouraged his own presentation as the most peaceable candidate.

The *Pentagon Papers* reveal that a White House strategy conference held on September 7, 1964—two months before the election—reached a consensus that intense bombing of the North would be essential to the military effort.

In August 1964, planning began for the intensive bombing of North Vietnam, with the code name Operation Rolling Thunder. The CIA and other intelligence agencies expressed doubt that any amount of bombing would break Hanoi's will. Nonetheless, the operation was launched as soon as the domestic political climate seemed favorable, in February of 1965. The operation was hardly launched before its usefulness was called into question. In April 1965, President Johnson made a secret decision that American ground forces would take the major responsibility for military operations. No reassessment of the goals of the American presence in Vietnam was made by the administration or offered to the public. On July 1, 1965, Undersecretary of State George Ball recommended deescalation as a prelude to withdrawal, but his memorandum was ignored by President Johnson.

American advisers, no matter how numerous, could not prevent the collapse and defeat of the Vietnamese Army. Only the American Army (and Navy and Marine Corps and Air Force) could hold back the advance of communism. On November 5, 1964, Assistant Secretary of State William Bundy had written a paper on the "problems of handling world and public opinion" which included the sentence, "We all feel the problem of proving North Vietnamese participation is less than in the past. . . ."[3]

In April 1965, the president was asked to place 82,000 troops in Vietnam; by July, he had authorized 193,000. The United States was committed to a ground war on the Asian land mass, which all military leaders since General Douglas MacArthur had counseled against.

The moth went to the candle.

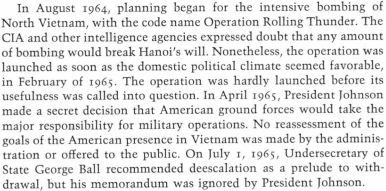

In 1940, when the Battle of Britain raged, the American people thrilled to the accounts of English bravery. The heroic efforts to preserve St. Paul's Cathedral against fire-bombing were told again and again. Winston Churchill's biting words were quoted. The more intensive the bombing, the more determined was the British will to resist; one could only admire this courageous people, the heirs of Shakespearean splendor.

Less noticed by the public were the conclusions of post-war American research teams, which held that the bombing of Germany by the Allies only stiffened the German will to resist.

3. From document number 84, New York Times Co. edition of *The Pentagon Papers* (New York: Bantam, 1971), p. 364.

When Operation Rolling Thunder, and its many successors, failed to bring North Vietnam to its knees, the American policy-makers were perplexed. How could a small, backward nation be so irrational?

The Long, Sad Story

The story of the United States effort in Vietnam from the first large-scale use of ground forces in 1965 until the signing of a cease-fire agreement in 1973 is long and dreary. The conflict settled into a war of attrition. Unlike World War I, it was not a static grinding of entrenched armies against each other. It was a war of movement, of ambush, of following trails through the jungle. The identity of the enemy was uncertain; friends of the daytime became enemies at night. It was warfare marked by few certain victories; a hamlet destroyed in one area did not prevent another from harboring the NLF. Bloody battles were fought for hills and villages that were never occupied.

The currency of battle became the body count. The computers were able to prove that victory was possible, because the armed forces of the enemy would eventually be destroyed, and there would be no enemy left. The computer could not distinguish between soldier and civilian dead, nor could it judge the honesty of the figures fed into it. It dealt only in numbers, not the human beings they represented. In Washington, doubts began to surface. Even Defense Secretary Robert McNamara eventually recommended an end to the bombing. He wrote to President Johnson on May 19, 1967,

> The picture of the world's greatest super-power killing or seriously injuring 1,000 non-combatants a week, while trying to pound a tiny backward nation into submission on an issue whose merits are hotly disputed, is not a pretty one. It could conceivably produce a costly distortion in the American national consciousness and in the world image of the United States —especially if the damage to North Vietnam is complete enough to be "successful."[4]

By the end of the year, Secretary McNamara was removed from his job, named by Lyndon Johnson to be president of the World Bank. McNamara had been an appointee of John Kennedy; President Johnson named Clark Clifford, an old friend (and "hawk") with whom he could be more comfortable, to be secretary of defense.

Then came the Tet offensive of early 1968, a major onslaught that took the Pentagon (and its computers) by surprise. The attack was

4. Document number 129, ibid., p. 580.

turned back, with heavy losses for the Communist forces, and President Johnson announced a victory. But the magnitude of the enemy effort demonstrated that their will to resist had hardly been dented, and they remained able to call upon plentiful reserves of men and weapons. Many of their weapons, made in the United States, were captured in battle. Others were manufactured in China and Russia, beyond the reach of the bombings.

Secretary-designate Clark Clifford began to doubt the wisdom of further escalation. General William Westmoreland, then the commander of American forces in Southeast Asia, requested an additional 206,000 troops, which he felt sure would bring "victory." To supply them would require mobilizing the reserve forces, tearing *voters* away from their jobs and families, when home opinion was unsettled and demonstrations against the war were at their peak. Clifford and his advisers reached the conclusion that not even 206,000 more troops — or any other conceivable number — could finally establish the authority of the Saigon government.

Finally, on March 31 (after Senator Eugene McCarthy's impressive show of strength in the New Hampshire primary election), Lyndon Johnson announced a bombing halt and, in an effort to unify the nation, withdrew from the election campaign, saying "I do not seek, and I will not accept, the nomination of my party."

Thus, at long last, the march of American forces, ever deeper into the quagmire of Vietnam, was halted. President Johnson refused to escalate further, and peace negotiations began in Paris. They would continue for more than four years. But Lyndon Johnson did not begin a withdrawal; he could only bequeath a stalemate to his successor.

His successor turned out to be Richard Nixon. Burdened by his association with LBJ, Hubert Humphrey for a time looked as if he would finish third, behind Nixon and George Wallace. In the end, his vote was only a hair less than Nixon's. Richard Nixon had a "secret plan" for bringing peace to Vietnam.

It turned out to be not all that peaceful. It was called "Vietnamization." It consisted of propping up the Saigon regime yet again, further training and equipping the Vietnamese army, supplying that small nation with one of the world's major air forces, and gradually winding down the commitment of American ground troops.

The Nixon policy did not abandon bombing. All useful military targets (except the North Vietnamese ports) had long since been destroyed; and the mining of Haiphong harbor eventually took place. A rain of bombs coming down through the overcast destroyed villages in a more impersonal way than the attacks like that of Lieutenant Calley's infantry platoon upon the hamlet of My Lai. The outcome was the forced urbanization of South Vietnam. The NLF had always been a rural force; driven to the cities as refugees, Vietnamese were available as unskilled laborers, as servants and bar girls for the Americans, and as political supporters for the Saigon regime. Thus was an agrarian village culture that had endured for two thousand years forced towards modernization. But the villagers were ill-equipped for urban life. Removal of American troops would remove their source of livelihood, for they lived off the needs and vices of the Americans.

Nixon's first term expired without peace. He made his historic visits to China and Russia to signal the determination of the United States to exist in the same world with Communist powers and offer them some kind of relationship other than blind hostility.

If Richard Nixon could exchange diplomatic smiles with the rulers of Russia and China, why were we fighting on in Vietnam? To "honor our commitments."

Finally, after an overly optimistic promise of peace offered by Henry Kissinger on the eve of the 1972 election, and heavy bombing during the Christmas recess of Congress, the cease-fire agreement came in 1973. It read very much like the provisions of the Geneva Accords of 1954.

What good had come out of the intervening nineteen years of conflict?

The United States promised foreign aid to both Vietnams, in order to repair the devastation of the land. How much more simple it would have been if the military might of the United States—those tons of bombs, those gallons of defoliants, those thousands of American young men zipped into bags and airlifted back home for burial—had never been employed to devastate the land.

Some Costs that Can Be Counted

Start with dollars. Even though shaky in international trading, the dollar is an entity we can all understand. Since large-scale American efforts began in Vietnam in 1965, the budgeted costs of the war have come to $137 billion. (Anyone can understand a dollar, but who can really comprehend a billion dollars?)

Bombs, then. The United States dropped approximately 7.1 *million tons* of bombs on North and South Vietnam. This is three times the tonnage of explosives dropped in World War II and Korea, combined. It means about 284 pounds of explosives for every person in the area know as Indochina. A number of unexploded weapons remain behind, making agriculture hazardous. The hooves of cattle are cut by metal fragments. Trees are full of shrapnel. In North Vietnam, American bombing destroyed nearly every bridge, miles of railroad track, and cut up most of the roads. Schools and hospitals, although not official targets, did not escape. There are millions of bomb craters that will be barren for at least a decade.

Defoliation? About six million acres of forest were sprayed. Some were completely and permanently destroyed. Twenty percent of the forest land of South Vietnam (our ally) was sprayed.

Or should the cost be reckoned in human lives? More than 773,000 "Communist" soldiers have been reported as killed; 124,000 South Vietnamese troops were killed from 1965 through 1973. The civilian dead are harder to estimate; one suggested figure is 400,000—the equivalent of the populations of Boston, Washington, and New Orleans. The wounded of both sides, military and civilian, total some 2.4 million. Many of them were permanently crippled.

The cost, in human lives, can be reckoned accurately for the United States. Not counting those missing in action, the Department of Defense reported that 45,928 American lives were lost. Three hundred thousand were wounded, half of them seriously enough to be hospitalized.

Back to dollars. Over the next half century, the U.S. government will pay at least $50 billion in benefits to the veterans of the war in Vietnam.[5]

But how do you make statistics real? Who are the human beings hidden in them? Consider Charley Stockbauer, posthumous winner of the Bronze Star, shipped home for burial in Mount Olivet Cemetery, St. Joseph, Missouri.

Charles T. Stockbauer received his notice to report for induction in 1969. He thought a lot, and he wrote an eighteen-page letter outlining his ideas about war and patriotism.

---

5. Statistics in this section are from Eliot Marshall and Tom Geoghegan, "Calculating the Costs," *New Republic*, February 10, 1973, pp. 21-22.

Philip Jones Griffiths

> War is only a word to soothe our conscience. But it doesn't work. War is still nothing more than murder. And murder is wrong no matter who says it can be justified.
>
> I realize that war will possibly never cease as long as we live in this world, as long as there are flags, there will be war. . . . The trouble in America is that because freedom is written down we think we have it.

Charley Stockbauer left the letter for his mother on the kitchen table, and then he left—for Canada. But Charley couldn't hack it. He worried about his young sisters, and what the neighbors might think, and he felt that he should not cause grief and shame for his family. Five days later, he came back, and he entered the Army. Within a year, Specialist 4 Stockbauer was dead, killed in action at age twenty-three. He died a hero. This fact was certified to his family by letters from the secretary of the Army, the chief of staff, half a dozen other generals, and President Richard M. Nixon.

His mother and sisters joined the Fellowship of Reconciliation. Every Wednesday afternoon, they marched against the war on the steps of the St. Joseph Post Office. It was the least they could do, to give some meaning to Charley's life—and death. After three years, Charley's mother only cried when some politician or general demanded victory in Vietnam so that the sacrifices of dead Americans would not be in vain.[6]

And what of the other side? Did not members of the NLF think at times upon war, death, and sadness? Here is one paragraph from the diary of an NLF medical officer named Mai Xuan Phong:

> The most precious thing for a man is his life, because one has only one life. One must, then, live in such a way that one does not have to regret the wasted years and months, that one does not have to be ashamed of a pitiful past, that one is able to say before passing away: my whole life, my whole strength have been devoted to the most elevated and the most beautiful cause —the struggle for the liberation of mankind. . . .[7]

6. From a dispatch of the New York Times Service published in the *San Francisco Chronicle*, February 5, 1973.
7. Raskin and Fall, *Viet-Nam Reader*, p. 229.

On other pages of the diary, Mai Xuan Phong recorded his joy at returning to the South for the purpose of freeing its people from the oppression of Ngo Dinh Diem and the United States of America. His diary was captured when the NLF camp in which Mai Xuan Phong served as medical officer was overrun by a unit of the Army of the Republic of Vietnam.

Some Costs that Are Not in Numbers

Of what value is the allegiance of the mother and sisters of Charles Stockbauer? They have not renounced America, but they will never again trust the national leadership. They can no longer view unquestioning patriotism as a virtue. What of the thousands who, unlike Charles Stockbauer, chose expatriation rather than induction but did not feel compelled by duty to return to family and country? The president of the United States has so far (August 1973) taken the position that amnesty is out of the question; any person avoiding his duty must pay a price, if he is to be readmitted to the privileges of citizenship. That price, suggests the president, is a prison term.

No amnesty for draft evaders, no amnesty for deserters, no admission that the policy-makers of the United States might have made a mistake. Yet the American people preferred to forget the war, and the combat veteran found no welcoming parades in his hometown when his tour of duty was complete.

The first real welcome was extended to the returning prisoners of war. Bands played, the red carpet was rolled out, and newspapermen got no interviews. The war had at last produced some heroes, and their status would not be jeopardized. Mostly, they were the pilots. Before capture, their war had been impersonal: they never saw individual human beings in the target areas, they never had to worry about how many of the dead were women, children, or civilians. A jet aircraft hurtling through the sky to launch explosives at a set of map coordinates is a study in technological competence. Caught up in the joy of technical performance for its own sake, the pilot needs little justification for his task. Some abstraction like "stopping communism" is perfectly adequate.

It was the ground troops, the grunts, who sometimes could not escape the moral implications of their acts. They had to deal with the people. One way out was the alternative of racism: all Vietnamese were "gooks," regardless of political affiliation; the Viet Cong and the Army of the Republic of Vietnam and the peasant woman tending a water buffalo in a field were all treated as members of a sub-human species. But this easy release could not always hide the perception of absurdity.

> The central fact of the Vietnam War is that no one really believes in it. The "larger purposes" put forth to explain the American presence—repelling an "outside invader," or giving the people of the South an opportunity "to choose their own form of government"—are directly contradicted by the overwhelming evidence a GI encounters that *he* is the outside invader, that the government he has come to defend is justly hated by the people he has come to "help," and that he, the American "helper" is hated by them most of all.[8]

Thus writes a psychiatrist who interviewed many Vietnam veterans. He describes their problems of adjustment, upon returning home

8. Robert Jay Lifton, "Home from the War: The Psychology of Survival," *Atlantic*, November 1972, p. 58.

after the experience of violent war. Universally, doubts arise in the minds of the men as to the purpose of American involvement in the conflict. They are caught up in a "survivor psychology." Knowing violence and corruption, they have seen the depths of degradation into which their own bodies and psyches can plunge. Yet they survived, when many others, both friend and foe, did not. There is no explanation for that survival, other than random chance. So the sense of guilt: why should I be spared? And the sense of identification with Lieutenant Calley of the My Lai Massacre—we were all doing those things, we're all guilty! The Vietnam Veterans United Against the War became an organization for the veterans to tell the truth of their experience, to lessen the feelings of guilt by confessing it, and to explain the folly of American policy.

How many young American men must build their future lives upon some recognition of, and adaptation to, the knowledge of having participated in a war of questionable purpose that was generally not supported by their own generation at home? Not counting those who served in neighboring areas like Cambodia, about *three million*.

One result of the loss of public support for the war was that employers did not go out of their way to hire Vietnam veterans. In a sluggish economy, this meant that many of the survivors of Vietnam did not find places in the economy when they returned. Why was the economy sluggish? Because political leaders beginning with Lyndon Johnson dared not ask for higher taxes to pay for the war, thus inviting inflation and recession.

And there was the question of drug addiction. Drugs were plentiful and cheap in Nam. They provided an escape from the guilt and confusion. According to the Senate subcommittee on veterans affairs, the American presence in Vietnam produced at least 100,000 heroin addicts. Instead of treating these men, the Army's policy was to identify them and discharge them from the ranks. Sent home, they faced an entirely different drug market. For many, crime was the only possible method of maintaining a habit.

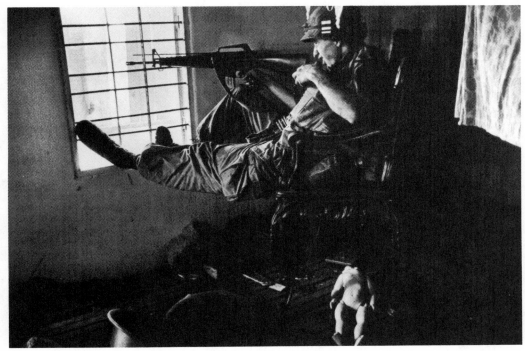

Philip Jones Griffiths

The devastation of the land and people of Vietnam was terrifying to contemplate. But the legacy of Vietnam in the United States was a long list of divisions among Americans made more serious by the drain of the war, of problems deferred, of resources squandered.

There was the division between generations:

Hey, hey, LBJ,
How many kids did you kill today?

or

Hell, No, We Won't Go!
Because the old men in Washington,
caught in an intellectual trap of their own making,
carving up the world into spheres dominated by good (us) or
    evil (them),
ordered the young to do the fighting.

There was the division between races,
which began long before the war and will continue long after,
but which the war dramatized,
because it was the blacks and Chicanos,
and other young men with little income,
who in the beginning accepted the will of their draft boards,
because they did not have the money or maybe the ambition to
    go to college.
The well-off sons of the middle and professional classes
    went to college and got a student deferment.

> Think how much the draft lottery quieted down the campuses. It ended uncertainty. Students knew their luck in advance. Once safe, they remained safe. No longer was there a personal reason to fight to end the war and the draft.

There was another war, the War on Poverty, declared by
Lyndon B. Johnson in the full glare of the presidential spotlight.
But its programs were hastily conceived and under-funded. The
energy and attention of the administration was increasingly
absorbed by Vietnam. Defeat in the War on Poverty was so obvious
as to require no announcement.

There was the division between those who continued to respect
and even revere the American flag, and those who used it as a
handkerchief. Many Americans were opposed to the war but
disgusted by the antiwar movement.

Some Truths about the Constitution

The Vietnam War did illuminate the present functioning of the Constitution.

The president has the power of initiative in foreign affairs. He is the commander-in-chief, and he can dispose the armed forces of the United States around the world according to his interpretation of American treaty obligations and executive agreements (which do not require the approval of Congress). He also has an informational network that he can use to his advantage, but which can make ghastly mistakes. (Remember the Bay of Pigs?)

The president is the chief diplomat. He controls official relationships between Washington and foreign governments; the ambassadors to foreign nations are his personal representatives, but he is free to bypass them, sending emissaries of the Kissinger type, or allowing agencies like the CIA to operate independently of the ambassador in a foreign nation.

But there is a paradox here. The American nation may attempt to dominate the actions and attitudes of other nations. But, regardless of our wealth and power, we cannot issue commands that ensure the cooperation of other peoples, much less their respect. For other nations are sovereign, and they need not bend to our will. Opponents to our involvement in Vietnam charged that both President Diem and President Thieu have been puppets of the American government. This was true in the sense that only American support maintained them in office. But they were puppets who danced on very frayed strings, as Thieu demonstrated by delaying conclusion of the cease-fire agreement.

As for Congress, it retained throughout the Vietnam conflict the power to halt it, by refusing the funds to pay for military operations. But Congress never exercised that power. Presidents Kennedy, Johnson, and Nixon were eager to accept the political responsibility—the accountability to the electorate—for the conduct of the war. Congress, as a collective body, was never willing to accept responsibility for inhibiting presidential action, in spite of the expressed convictions of Senators such as Ernest Gruening, Wayne Morse, George McGovern, Mike Gravel, Eugene McCarthy and William Fulbright that a tragic mistake was being made.

So presidents were not usurping powers assigned to Congress by the Constitution, except for the undeniable fact of waging a war that was never declared. But this was no new phenomenon. According to which engagements qualify for counting, at least 151 military conflicts have occurred that were never approved by Congress, since the Constitution was ratified. They range from the sea war with France (1798-1800) and the wars with the Barbary pirates of 1801-1805 through the Philippine rebellion of 1899-1901 and the Korean war to the Cambodian invasion of 1970.[9] According to research sponsored by Barry Goldwater, 96 of these conflicts involved fighting that lasted for more than thirty days.[10]

And what of the people? A president's power is normally based upon the support of public opinion, for the Constitution separates powers in a manner that will frustrate his will, unless other elements of government are sure the people support the president. Lyndon Johnson and his advisers felt that the responsibility should be shared by Congress; to insure the support of public opinion, they engineered the Tonkin Gulf Resolution, shortly before sending "dangerous" Barry Goldwater down to resounding defeat. But bombing of the North and escalation of the ground warfare began in 1965. It stimulated a movement of outraged protest.

Public support for the war effort in Vietnam was curiously like that for the war in Korea fifteen years earlier. The initial stages of the ground war—when the boys would be home by Christmas (of 1965!)—generated some enthusiasm, as citizens felt a certain glow of pride in their nation's show of power. But, as the months turned into years, and the costs in lives and dollars mounted, and no particular goal was achieved, public support drained away. The difference be-

9. These conflicts are listed in American Enterprise Institute, *The War Powers Bill* (Washington, D.C., April 17, 1972), pp. 47-55.
10. See J. F. Bibby and R. J. Huckshorn, eds., *Current Politics* (Minneapolis: Winston, 1973), p. 297.

tween the two cases was the public protest movement in the 1970s, which had not existed in the 1950s. Apparently it had very little effect on the degree of public support for the war.[11] In 1972, President Nixon neutralized the war as an issue by the withdrawal of ground troops.

When Is Tragedy Only a Mistake?

On March 15, 1973, with a mere three hundred officers in attendance at the ceremony in a Saigon theater, the United States Army in Vietnam furled its combat flag. A few bars of appropriately Oriental music were played by a brass band borrowed for the occasion from the Army of the Republic of Vietnam. At that point, some 5,500 American military men remained in Vietnam, compared to 500,000 in early 1968.

The war (or, more accurately, American participation in the ground war) ended with little ceremony. The entire conflict had been one which the United States attempted to wage without really admitting that it was happening. Perhaps the slight public notice of its ending was part of that same pattern. Once the prisoners of war were safely home, and the maimed veterans tucked away in hospitals to practice with their artificial limbs, the process of forgetting could begin. The nation could shake off the memory of Vietnam as if it had only been a bad dream—forgotten in daylight, it only caused a few screams at night.

But many wanted to remember. For the central mystery remained. How did it all happen? The war in Vietnam was not conceived by some mad Dr. Strangelove enamored of military weaponry; it was not conceived in secret in the dim recesses of the Pentagon. The commitment was begun in the Truman era and continued by succeeding presidents of the United States. Their advisers were not sinister Rasputins, or even Machiavellis. They were liberal professors, businessmen, and diplomats. The escalation of the war was indeed carried out by "the best and the brightest" minds thrust forward by the American political system.[12]

To understand what happened requires concepts of force and magnitude. The concept of tragedy, developed by the Greeks but applied to the American nation instead of to an individual leader, was readily available. In this view, America began with good intentions, with the best interests (as we understood them) of the Vietnamese as our goal. But our pride in power blinded us to the true nature of the conflict until our resources became overextended, and we were forced to withdraw with our goals unrealized. The fall of the hero is a fall into misfortune. Perhaps the American nation has not fallen into total misfortune, but 46,000 Americans and hundreds of thousands of Indochinese have paid with their lives. In the Greek view, the fall of the tragic hero results in his gaining new insight into his own nature and the nature of the world, so that he may receive honor as a prophet that he never commanded as a leader.

But it doesn't fit. It is hard to prove that American decision-makers even had admirable motives. The original commitment to an American presence in Vietnam was made to serve American interests in Western Europe. When the French were driven out of the country, America took over what had been the French role, eager to hold up the banner of the "free world."

11. See John E. Mueller, *War, Presidents, and Public Opinion* (New York: Wiley, 1973).
12. See David Halberstam, *The Best and the Brightest* (New York: Random House, 1972).

Philip Jones Griffiths

Americans came to Vietnam as the representatives of a different—and, in their own eyes, superior—culture and technology. It was at heart a colonial impulse. American leaders justified their actions as necessary to contain communism and quickly came to believe it. The best and the brightest became the victims of their own propaganda.

These politicians and advisers liked to think of themselves as realists, as men of action, as tough guys able to recognize the Communist menace and take action to thwart it. They were problem-solvers. They also regarded themselves as honorable men, and their attitudes reinforced each other: no individual could conceive of a group of honorable men participating in decisions that led to moral outrages. They soon invented an Orwellian language that hid from themselves the moral horrors of what they did.

The destruction of rural hamlets was known as "pacification." The first intensive bombing program was known as "Operation Rolling Thunder," as if the storm of explosives could not really maim and kill. Bombing raids during the bombing pause were called "protective reaction." The measure of the success of military expeditions and commanders, the proof of progress, the ray of light shining down the tunnel, was the body count or "kill ratio."

The ethically sensitive historians of the future will select the phenomenon of the body count as the perfect symbol of America's descent into evil. The body count manages to distill the essence of the American numbing, brutalization, and illusion into a grotesque technicalization: there is something to count, a statistic for accomplishment. I know of no greater corruption than this phenomenon: the amount of killing—any killing—becomes the total measure of achievement. And concerning that measure, one lies, to others as well as to oneself, about why, who, what, and how many one kills.[13]

13. Lifton, "Home from the War," p. 60.

Was there new wisdom that came to the American people—some new reluctance to impose a pattern of living upon other cultures, or some new humility about the value of mass production and the two-party system? American public opinion would not tolerate 25,000 ground troops in Vietnam, but it acquiesced in the presence of 100,000 men in the neighboring areas and in the Seventh Fleet.

The United States remained the dominant power in Southeast Asia. When American power would again be committed to war would be more nearly determined by leaders like Nguyen Van Thieu than by the Congress of the United States.

America will be paying the economic costs of Vietnam for years, if not generations. The price was in veterans' benefits, in economic instability, in the escalating domestic tensions made worse by the war, just as the war drained away the resources that could have been applied to ending them. This does not count the moral cost, the guilt, the screaming horror of thousands killed and maimed, or the loss of worldwide respect for, and domestic trust in, American leadership.

The greatest danger was that the Vietnam War would be forgotten, treated as a grotesque accident that cannot happen again. For it revealed some truths about the dark side of the American national character, and some realities about the operations of American political institutions, which must not be forgotten.

It may be too soon in the span of history to define with final certainty the lessons of Vietnam. But every American must seek the meaning of those lessons.

Power, Pride, and the People: Can Democracy Live by the Sword?

The uneasy cease-fire in Vietnam did not end the American presence in Southeast Asia. President Nixon's travels to Communist capitals seemed to promise a new and more fruitful relationship with the traditional enemy, but the military establishment prepared for World War III. The president's budget proposals indicated that he saw America's mission in the world as more important than seeking federal solutions to pressing domestic problems.

Questions about American military power and the meaning of patriotism were no longer so much a question of disagreement between fathers and sons. Instead, they were questions of the national destiny, and whether the people could influence it.

How had America come to appoint herself the guardian of the world's freedom? If the people found that mission futile, could they change it? Or did forces beyond the control of the people direct the national destiny?

The Duty of the State

Thomas Hobbes pictured men as yearning for the creation of order from the chaos of nature. This yearning led them mutually to abandon certain freedoms to form the compact bringing the state into existence. A primary duty of the state was to guard the safety of its inhabitants against outside enemies. Provision for "the common defense" was a purpose stated in the Preamble to the United States Constitution.

This promise of guardianship against external foes was a basic justification for the existence of the state. In return for the promise of security, men gave their allegiance to the state; love of country became a noble emotion, an offer of thanksgiving for safety achieved. To insure this security for their families and friends, young men gave up their lives in battle.

Nay, nay sweet England, do not grieve!
Not one of these poor men who died
But did within his soul believe
That death for thee was glorified.[1]

Hiroshima changed all that.

The Bomb brought to man the capacity to destroy his own planet. The offensive technology kept well ahead of the defensive capability.

---

1. From "How Sleep the Brave," by Walter de la Mare. Reprinted by permission of the Literary Trustees of Walter de la Mare and the Society of Authors as their representatives.

The United States government could no longer promise that its citizens could survive a determined, massive nuclear attack, for such an attack could not be stopped before it had done immeasurable damage, killing many millions and possibly rendering the continent uninhabitable. So the billions of dollars expended in the 1960s on nuclear hardware promised not safety, but revenge. The antagonist could be sure that a devastating attack would be answered by equal devastation.

The ultimate question concerning the survival of the human race was answered by Senator Richard Russell. "If we have to start over again with another Adam and Eve," he said, "I want them to be Americans and not Russians." This was at least an argument for training both male and female astronauts to pilot orbiting space satellites.

The Opinions of Mankind

The birth of the American nation, advertised in the Declaration of Independence, was attended by a concern for its proper place in the family of nations. Thomas Jefferson wrote that "a decent regard for the opinions of mankind" required that the reasons for the separation from England be set forth. The signers of the Declaration were well aware that the principles stated in it were capable of universal application, and that the world would be watching the American experiment. From the beginning, however, there was disagreement concerning the appropriate American role as the champion of those principles. Should America concentrate on achieving a successful democratic example, which other nations would be led to imitate, or should America provide actual leadership for the forces of democracy in all nations?

From the beginning, there was strong sentiment holding that America did have a mission to perform in the world; assertions of the sacred nature of that mission overlooked the weakness of the new nation and the pretentiousness of any claim to status as a world power.

In 1793, John Adams wrote a despairing note to his son:

> The Anti-Federal party, by their ox feasts and their civic feasts, their King-killing toasts, their perpetual insolence and billingsgate against all the nations and governments of Europe, their everlasting brutal cry of tryanny, despots, and combinations against liberty, etc., etc., etc., have probably irritated, offended, and provoked all the crowned heads of Europe at last; and a little more of this indelicacy and indecency may involve us in a war with all the world.[2]

Jefferson's growing party tended to assert that conflicts between nations are caused by the jealousies and ambitions of kings; a government responsible to the people would be devoted to peace, unless provoked by the surrounding monarchies. Adams disagreed. Pointing to the example of ancient Athens, he noted that democratic governments are more bloodthirsty than despotic ones, never resting content with mere protection, but seeking to expand their influence. While the despot is guided by cunning calculations of personal advantage (in which caution looms large), democracies are guided by the fluctuating passions of the majority. And the emotions of the majority are developed on the basis of less accurate information than the calcu-

2. John Adams to John Quincy Adams, December 22, 1793. Quoted in Page Smith, *John Adams* (Garden City, N.Y.: Doubleday, 1962), p. 845.

lations of the despot, for the attention of the democratic electorate is normally engaged by domestic matters. Only when international affairs are thrust upon their attention do the people assert their authority.

In the formation of America's first political parties, the influence of foreign relations was clear. Jefferson's Republicans were friendly toward the goals and ideals of the French Revolution. The Federalists of Washington and Adams were so appalled at the tactics of the revolutionaries that they soon became suspicious even of their goals.

Two related facts about the making of American foreign policy were clear at the time of George Washington's presidency. They have remained valid since, in spite of periods of national unity and national division, of decades of isolationism interspersed with times of intervention:

> Foreign policy has normally supplied issues, of greater or lesser importance, for the contests between American political parties.

> Politics has never stopped "at the water's edge."

Assure the Survival...of Liberty

The certainty that America should fulfill a special mission in the world, plus a certain oratorical eagerness for military conflict, suppressed with care by President John Adams, flowered into conflict with Great Britain when James Madison was president. The War of 1812 was at best a stalemate; it would have been a disaster, if the bulk of England's forces had not been engaged in fighting Napoleon. The war produced one victory—the Battle of New Orleans—after the treaty of peace had been signed. Because news of the treaty was received after news of the defense of New Orleans, it was easy to assume that Andrew Jackson's victory produced the treaty. For quite invalid reasons, the American nation experienced a new feeling of unity, a new assurance that it had a destiny to fulfill in the world.

That destiny was defined eloquently in 1960:

> Let the word go forth from this time and place, to friend and foe alike, that the torch has been passed to a new generation of Americans.
>
> Let every nation know, whether it wishes us well or ill, that we shall pay any price, bear any burden, meet any hardship, support any friend, oppose any foe to assure the survival and the success of liberty.

These words are from the Inaugural Address of President John F. Kennedy. Their resonant cadence almost hides a belligerent, even arrogant, tone. That tone was widely approved at the time. Reading them now, after an expensive stalemate and an uneasy cease-fire in Vietnam, they seem absurd. Is it really so easy to divide the world into "friends" and "foes"? Can we be so sure of universal acceptance of our definition of "liberty"? Can a desire to provide liberty for a foreign people justify the devastation of their land, the corruption of their culture, and the deaths of countless men, women, and children? Were the young men of the United States rightly asked to "pay any price"—including life itself—to assure to the people of a tiny, agrarian nation in Asia that they would enjoy the blessings of liberty, as defined by the United States, rather than such blessings as defined by themselves?

Such questions were not even asked in 1960. But the assumptions at the base of American policy led us into Vietnam and continued that fruitless conflict for thirteen more years.

There have been many diagnoses of an affliction from which America presumably suffers. One of the most persuasive analyses has been made by Senator J. William Fulbright:

> Power tends to confuse itself with virtue and a great nation is peculiarly susceptible to the idea that its power is a sign of God's favor, conferring upon it a special responsibility for other nations—to make them richer and happier and wiser, to re-make them, that is, in its own shining image. Power confuses itself with virtue and tends also to take itself for omnipotence. Once imbued with the idea of a mission, a great nation easily assumes that it has the means as well as the duty to do God's work.[3]

If the diagnosis rings true, the next step is to find a remedy. That will depend upon identifying the agent responsible for the malady. If America's "arrogance of power" has roots in our national history and is but the modern expression of attitudes formed before that power was developed, is there any way to isolate and treat the infection?

Americans have long offered simple explanations for the cause of war. When the nation was born, and during most of the nineteenth century, wars were regarded as but another sign of the decadence of European civilization—one of the evils the New World was destined to escape. When America nevertheless became embroiled in war, explanations were sought closer to home. In the 1930s, U.S. senators claimed that profit-hungry munitions makers were responsible for war. The modern version of that argument is more sophisticated. Modern militants, several responsible scholars, and at least one general, with a ritualistic citation of President Eisenhower's Farewell Address, identify the "military-industrial complex" as the baneful influence that squanders scarce resources on building ever more powerful weapons we dare not use.

And what of the people?

America Enters the World

After the illusory victory at New Orleans and the end of the War of 1812, American attention turned inward, to conquering the wilderness and exploiting its resources. The fact that this was made possible by the isolation of the North American continent between two massive oceans and the enforcement by the British Navy of world peace were conveniently forgotten. The separation of the United States from the nations of Europe and their continuing political conflicts nourished the conviction that, as a nation, the United States was morally superior. The Monroe Doctrine declared our interest in limiting European influence in the South American hemisphere. The wisdom of George Washington's warning against foreign alliances seemed to be proved in practice.

The question of whether America should simply provide an example for the world, or should lead actively in its affairs, was largely resolved in favor of isolationism.

Apparent emergence from this isolationist spirit only confirmed it. President William McKinley reluctantly agreed to war with Spain,

3. J. William Fulbright, *The Arrogance of Power* (New York: Vintage, 1967), pp. 3-4.

but only to free the Cubans from the oppression of their Spanish masters; it was strictly a humanitarian mission. Admiral Dewey's victory over the Spanish fleet in Manila Bay led to the occupation of the Philippines, and their annexation, almost by accident. But political leaders and the Protestant clergy discovered the hand of God at work; in their view, Manifest Destiny, not crass commercial motives, made the United States a colonial power.

The conviction grew that America's involvements with the rest of the world were singularly noble and disinterested. Unlike other nations, America only intervened to serve the interests of other peoples. President Woodrow Wilson sent two major expeditions into Mexico in an effort to install democratic practices in that country. An election had been held, but its outcome had favored General Huerta, and Wilson decided that it did not represent the true will of the Mexican people.

In 1955, the United States encouraged Ngo Dinh Diem in preventing elections, provided in the Geneva Accords, which would have allowed the people of both North and South Vietnam to choose their government. Ho Chi Minh probably would have won. Washington officials somehow knew that the selection of a Communist would not represent the true will of the Vietnamese people.

Woodrow Wilson invaded Mexico, and American presidents sent military forces to Vietnam, convinced of their own philanthropic motives.

Comments Garry Wills, "It is when America is in her most altruistic mood that other nations better get behind their bunkers."[4]

When the European balance of power collapsed in 1914, America first remained uninvolved, and Woodrow Wilson was reelected in 1916 on the slogan, "He kept us out of war." But the adherence of Wilson to an obsolete concept of the freedom of the seas, dramatic reports of German atrocities committed in Belgium, German submarine activity directed against American vessels, and the desperate needs of blockaded England combined with a moralistic sense of mission to bring the United States into the war on the side of the Allies.

The war consumed the full energies of modern industrial nations. For the American involvement to be effective, dedication of the American people to the struggle was required. Farmers in the wheat field and workers in the factory were even more important than the relatively small expeditionary force fielded by the United States. Woodrow Wilson provided the necessary motivation, well within the traditional American assumption of moral superiority. He announced that America sought no national advantages from the war. Her purpose would be to "make the world safe for democracy" and to assure establishment of the principle of "national self-determination."

America left her ocean-guarded stronghold to set right the affairs of the world. Wilson envisaged an international organization led by Americans entrusted with keeping world peace. But the Treaty of Versailles was riddled with compromise between the European victors over the spoils of victory. Wilson's noble purposes seemed betrayed. The same persons who supported participation in the war on idealistic grounds were led to reject the treaty and the League of Nations, because they were tainted by the political maneuvering of the European powers.

Nearly two decades ago, Louis Hartz summarized the essential ambivalence produced by America's confrontation with the world:

4 Garry Wills, *Nixon Agonistes* (New York: New American Library, 1971), p. 397.

We have been able to dream of ourselves as emancipators of
the world at the very moment that we have withdrawn from it.
We have been able to see ourselves as saviors at the very moment that we have been isolationists. Here, surely, is one of the
great American luxuries that the twentieth century has destroyed.[5]

If that mental luxury were destroyed, neither the people nor their
leaders were quick to recognize the fact. In 1919, America retreated
behind her oceans, disbanded her armies, and burned her surplus
military aircraft. The Army was reduced to a tiny cadre of professionals. When the Depression came, defense spending was attacked
as a waste of national resources, in spite of the well-reported emergence of Hitler's power. When Europe was again engulfed by war,
President Roosevelt moved toward involvement with great caution,
aware of the organized sentiment for maintaining an isolated position. Public opinion was divided. Only the Japanese attack on Pearl
Harbor ended that division; the nature of that attack stimulated support for a total effort by the people and suggested the policy of unconditional surrender.

Development of the atomic bomb was undertaken in a defensive
mood, for the principles were known to German scientists, and it
seemed probable that Germany would develop the weapon. The doctrine of unconditional surrender made the decision to use the weapon
against Japan almost inevitable.

With victory, the pressures to return to a peacetime basis were
intense. American political and military commanders felt compelled
to yield to demands of public opinion to "bring the boys home." Support for the United Nations was nearly unanimous among American
political leaders, who were determined to avoid a repetition of the
League of Nations fiasco. But the usefulness of the UN as a guarantor
of world peace was oversold to the American people, just as faith in
the friendliness of the Russian nation had been officially proclaimed
during the war, so that aid to the Communist ally would be supported.
The stage was set for further public disillusionment.

Within five years, America was at war in Korea.

American industrial might could defeat the Axis powers, but her
political influence could not maintain peace. And American public
opinion seemed a major obstacle. It was characterized by alternations
between isolationism and aggressive belligerence; a propensity for
viewing world affairs in simple moralistic terms, ignoring political
realities; refusing to enter upon inevitable conflict when its scope
could be contained, yet rejecting any goal short of total victory once
the conflict began. Most important, the American record in the fifty
years following the war with Spain revealed an attitude that rejected
sustained involvement and leadership in world affairs, yet supported
military adventures in the belief that a single application of American
power could set a delinquent world to rights and permit America to
again withdraw to its internal concerns.

Walter Lippmann claimed that the blame for such errors rested
upon the malign influence of public opinion upon the foreign-policy
decisions of elected officials.

The unhappy truth is that the prevailing public opinion has
been destructively wrong at the critical junctures. The people
have imposed a veto upon the judgments of informed and responsible officials. They have compelled the governments, which

5. Louis Hartz, *The Liberal Tradition in America* (New York: Harcourt, Brace, 1955), p. 38.

> usually knew what would have been wiser, or was necessary, or was more expedient, to be too late with too little, or too long with too much, too pacifist in peace and too bellicose in war, too neutralist or appeasing in negotiation or too intransigent. Mass opinion has acquired mounting power in this country. It has shown itself to be a dangerous master of decisions when the stakes are life and death.[6]

In this interpretation, the people control national policy, yet their power brings disaster. The lesson of Vietnam is that public opinion can exert a veto power — Lyndon Johnson renounced reelection — but opinion can be influenced mightily, and, when the authorities base policy on ignorance or delusion, the public is not likely to be better educated than its leaders.

"Provide for the Common Defense"

Discussion of the provisions for military defense and the conduct of foreign relations by the United States government begins properly with the Constitution. As with any return to the Constitution, suspense comes from wondering if modern institutions can be recognized in its eighteenth-century language. In this case, as in others, some imagination is required to see the seeds of vast modern bureaucracies within the basic document.

The conduct of foreign relations is lodged with the executive. The founders realized that a nation must speak with but a single, authoritative voice in its dealings with other powers. The president, therefore, is designated as the person who shall "receive Ambassadors and other public Ministers" (Article II, Section 3), and the president is empowered to "make treaties." But treaties must be ratified by the senior branch of the national legislature; the president shall make treaties "by and with the Advice and Consent of the Senate,... provided two-thirds of the Senators present concur." Similarly, the president appoints ambassadors and other diplomats "with the Advice and Consent of the Senate" (Article II, Section 2). Thus the power of the president to speak with a single voice in foreign affairs was tempered by the knowledge that, at crucial points, he must persuade the Senate of the rightness of his policies. Furthermore, when dealings with foreign nations should fail, and war become the substitute for peaceful relationships, only Congress could declare it (Article I, Section 8, Paragraph 11).

To prevent the armed forces from becoming an independent power in the new nation, the president was made their commander-in-chief (Article II, Section 2). But the very existence of the armed forces rested with Congress, and, in fact, Congress was not permitted to appropriate funds for the support of an army for longer than two years at a time. The founders felt that a large standing army posed a threat to democratic institutions, for professional military leaders were unlikely to be patient with the delays of the democratic process.

6. Walter Lippmann, *The Public Philosophy* (Boston: Little, Brown, 1955), p. 20.

Rather, it was felt that reliance should be placed on the citizen-soldiers of the militia, which would be formed in each state and could be called up in time of need. The Minutemen of the Revolutionary War suggested the pattern.

The pattern prevailed for the first century and a half of America's existence. It has changed permanently only since World War II. The reasons for that change are many: technological advance, ideological conflict, and fear—possibly a seldom-expressed fear that the material luxury of America would make it a military target of the have-not nations; certainly a fear that America's system and all its riches might be overrun and conquered by a force labeled "International Communism."

Ironically, the United States developed a permanent and influential military establishment only when the development of nuclear weapons by our potential adversaries made it impossible to realistically guarantee "the common defense."

What Are Missiles For?

In midwestern wheat fields, in a circle of some seventy-five miles' radius, centered in Grand Forks, North Dakota, 150 Minuteman II missiles are buried in reinforced concrete silos. Each carries in its nose one or more nuclear warheads.

Remember the Minutemen? The citizen soldiers of the Revolutionary War who were prepared to kiss their wives and children goodbye and on a moment's notice grab the musket and join their friends to protect homes and families from the ravages of the redcoats? There is a famous statue of a Minuteman, standing, rifle in hand, peering out at danger. It was adopted by an insurance company as its symbol. Now the outline of this figure is imprinted upon the punched card which, when read by the computer in the launch-control capsule, programs the directional guidance systems of ten missiles with directions to take them to targets in China or Russia.

The 150 Minutemen around Grand Forks are the principal asset of the 321st Strategic Missile Wing. There are five similar wings deployed through the plains of North Dakota, South Dakota, Missouri, Montana, and Wyoming. If no preemptive enemy strike comes in, if all the electronic circuits work as designed, and if the natural deterioration brought to machinery by age has had no important effect, these six missile wings can hurl 1,000 Minutemen into the sky.

Each flight of ten missiles is tended by a crew of two officers who sit forty-six feet below the ground in a concrete and steel hardened room, waiting for World War III. Both must turn keys in the control console simultaneously to place their monstrous charges on the status of strategic alert. ("Monstrous" because each missile weighs 70,000 pounds, stands 59 feet high and, if launched, reaches a velocity of 15,000 miles per hour in three minutes.) To actually fire a squadron of fifty missiles requires the positive "vote" of two of its five two-man crews, who must decide if the war message coming into their command center, presumably triggered by the president of the United States, is in fact genuine.

One of the control officers stationed at Grand Forks was Major Danny Kinker, sixteen-year veteran of the United States Air Force, father of three teen-age children. Said Major Kinker of his job:

> Being a missileman is my profession. It's more than a job, really;
> it's a matter of dedication. I take tremendous pride in my work.
> I feel that every day I have done something worthwhile. I think

> that what we crew members think about most is this: that if we maintain a high level of readiness and a high level of proficiency—and the enemy knows it—then chances are we'll never have to play the real game.[7]

The thousand Minuteman missiles wait in their hardened silos, able to wage a war in which millions die but soldiers do not fight. Other missiles stand in Russia, aimed at the United States. The reason for missiles is to ensure that such a war will never be fought. It is called the Balance of Terror.

Relaxing Tensions

The leaders of nations, regardless of their political ideologies, do not relish the prospect of blowing up the world. They would rather be remembered for achieving benefits for their peoples; with the world gone, there would be nobody to remember.

Periodically, the nuclear superpowers have come together in recognition of the dangers of destructive war and have mutually agreed to limit certain activities. In 1963, a nuclear test-ban treaty was negotiated with Russia which prohibited testing nuclear weapons in the atmosphere; scientists had recognized radiation pollution as increasing to dangerous levels. No sooner was it announced than the Kennedy administration began an expanded program of underground testing.

After years of negotiations known as the Strategic Arms Limitation Talks (SALT), the United States and Russia signed a treaty limiting the further deployment of the anti-ballistic missile (ABM).

The Defense Department, preparing for the 1973 budget battle, asked for a number of new weapons systems, including the Trident missile-launching submarine (in case Russia should develop a defense against the current Polaris missile-launching submarine) and the B-1 bomber (which would be a manned backup to rely on in the unlikely event that hundreds of submarine- and land-based intercontinental ballistic missiles should fail to function).

With the Vietnam War ended, the Pentagon requested an *increase* in its annual budget, from $76 to $80 billion. We have to be superior to Russia in every kind of weapon, before agreeing to limit the production of any kind.

Fifteen percent of the American labor force works on defense contracts, with plants in nearly every congressional district.

President Nixon has said that economy in the federal budget should be achieved by cutting education and welfare programs, and he impounded funds already appropriated by Congress for these programs.

Portrait of American Militarism

General David M. Shoup, former commandant of the U.S. Marine Corps, once contrasted the scope of American military power with previous American practices. He noted that, before World War II, there were only a few thousand professional military men. Any use of the Army overseas was impossible without mobilization, and mobilization required a declaration of war or at least of emergency. Any unexpected need for a show of force in international relations was handled by the U.S. Navy and its Marine landing forces, used

7. Richard Pollak, "Missileland" *Harper's*, October 1969, p. 86.

Roger Malloch

to protect American lives and property from the perils of native
bandits and revolutionaries.

Now, however, we have numerous contingency plans involving large joint Air Force-Army-Navy-Marine task forces to defend U.S. interests and to safeguard our allies wherever and
whenever we suspect Communist aggression. We maintain
more than 1,517,000 Americans in uniform overseas in 119
countries. We have 8 treaties to help defend 48 nations if they
ask us to—or if we choose to intervene in their affairs. We have
an immense and expensive military establishment, fueled by a
gigantic defense industry, and millions of proud, patriotic, and
frequently bellicose and militaristic citizens.[8]

According to General Shoup, American militarism was developed
from, and is sustained by, four important influences: the large proportion of the public who are veterans of military service and regard
the use of military force in international relations as natural and
proper; the competence and prestige (at least until recently) of top
military leaders; the vast defense industry and its political influence;
and a sustaining mystique of militant patriotism and anticommunism.

The base of military experience in the population was established
by the length and needs of World War II (14.9 million veterans) and
the Korean War (5.7 million). Additional millions were trained in the
armed forces during peacetime. The total of 23 million military veterans constitutes 20 percent of the American adult population. For
many, military experience was the strongest influence shaping their
lives and attitudes. Memories of the inevitable physical hardships and
mental brutalization of military training and combat fade away, leaving nostalgia for the comradeship and a glow of pride in having defended one's country—even if only as a company clerk at Fort Ord,

8. "The New American Militarism," *Atlantic*, April 1969, p. 51.

California. Veterans of the military experience are likely to prescribe it for all young men; and the veterans' organizations, with 4 million members, have traditionally urged aggressive policies in international relations.

During and after World War II, military commanders elevated to the status of heroes held top governmental positions—Marshall, Eisenhower, and Ridgeway are a few. Military leaders are trained "to command large organizations and to plan big operations. They learn the techniques of influencing others. Their education is not, however, liberal or cultural," according to General Shoup.[9] The services are rigidly selective in promoting men into the top ranks. To reach them, it is helpful to establish a good combat record. It is even more important to establish one's single-minded devotion to the branch of the service and to its doctrines—doctrines which support claims to the superiority of that branch's particular mission and therefore its claims upon budgetary support.

The military leaders do not necessarily possess an ideologue's determination to oppose communism. They are merely men who justify their life and work by finding and engaging an enemy. Such men build an organization dedicated to the same purposes, and the organization soon develops a vitality and momentum that is separate from the guiding intelligence of any individual or group. Like any large bureaucracy, a military organization readily develops "information pathologies": subsidiary agencies responsible for supplying the facts which can form the basis of decisions are themselves limited by the outlook of the organization. Information that calls into question the central assumptions of the organization is not processed.

Observers on the ground in Vietnam knew that American goals there could probably never be achieved, that the body counts sent to the Pentagon computers were often fabricated, and that the Diem regime received no respect, much less affection, from the people. But such knowledge was seldom forwarded up the chain of command; for those who tried had been judged incompetent and lost their jobs. The higher the official, the less he was told that might question established policy; until the man kept in the most perfect ignorance by his elaborate system for information gathering was the commander-in-chief, Lyndon B. Johnson. Men who expressed doubts about Vietnam soon left his service.

It is not only military organizations that suffer from information pathologies. It is a weakness of human organizations.

Information pathologies make historical footnotes: the continuation of U-2 flights over Russia on the eve of Eisenhower's carefully planned and breathlessly awaited summit meeting with Khrushchev; the belief of the CIA that, because Fidel Castro is a Communist, the people of Cuba would be eager to rise up against him with the launching of a "friendly" invasion by expatriated Cubans; assurances given or perceived by Robert McNamara that each new escalation in Vietnam would be the last.

The accumulation of enough such historical footnotes, even when viewed as exceptions to the general rule of competence, led to a growing suspicion of the fallibility of the organizational mind. But a mere suspicion does not begin to dismantle a structure of interlocking military, industrial, and political enterprises, particularly when the mutual concern of the members of that structure is powered by the relentless drive of technological advance.

9. Ibid., p. 53.

The Spiral of Technology

The momentum of technological change in weaponry springs from a simple and quite human assumption: whatever destructive weapons can be conceived of should be built, for they can also be conceived and built by the opponent; the only way to deter their *use* is through the threat of retaliation. Thus is built the stockpile of increasingly sophisticated delivery systems for nuclear weapons. The American stockpile of atomic weapons provides the explosive equivalent of six tons of dynamite for each person on earth.

Those who have questioned the wisdom of the technological struggle have not fared well. The comfortable victory of the United States in the race with Germany to develop the atomic bomb was largely due to the scientific and organizational genius of J. Robert Oppenheimer. After the war, Oppenheimer became concerned with the possibility of survival in the atomic age, and he was not convinced that an attempt to construct the hydrogen bomb (twenty times as destructive as atomic bombs) should be made. At the height of the Cold War, when Senator Joseph McCarthy's charges of Communist influence in high government places were making daily headlines, the Atomic Energy Commission held a month-long security hearing and finally concluded by removing Oppenheimer from his position as chairman of the General Advisory Council of AEC. Because, in his youth, Oppenheimer had associated with members (including two relatives) of left-wing organizations (including the Communist party), he was branded as "a security risk."

Oppenheimer's past associations had been known when he was originally approved for leading the development of the atomic bomb. His doubts about the wisdom of the hydrogen bomb were the only new factor in the situation.

During the Eisenhower administration, nuclear weapons were praised as supplying "more bang for a buck." (It was surmised that some nuclear enthusiast in the Kremlin would be talking about "more rubble for a ruble.") This logic—natural to a modern industrial nation that would want to use resources to ensure production, rather than assigning workers to unproductive stand-by military duty—further supported the assumption that whatever could be conceived must be built.

By the 1960s, the realization grew that offensive nuclear weaponry was likely to be forever in advance of defensive hardware; and even the use of "tactical" nuclear weapons on a battlefield would call forth an intolerable retaliation. With the launching of long-range missiles assigned to the Air Force, the Army cast about for a new mission. It began to develop concepts variously called "counter-insurgency," "civic action," and "counter-guerrilla warfare." Highly placed officials of the Kennedy administration encouraged the development of these doctrines, and John F. Kennedy himself became the patron of the Green Berets.

At first, the needs of Vietnam seemed exactly appropriate for counter-insurgency techniques. It was a nation struggling to emerge into the modern world; the incumbent regime needed to demonstrate its concern for the needs of the peasantry. There were schools and hospitals to be built, wells to be dug, and hamlets whose loyalty might be won away from the NLF. There appeared to be an important constructive role for the military parallel to the mission of the Peace Corps in nations less torn by internal strife.

This kind of American activity went on for a long time, without making much difference; next, the American military took up the task of training and equipping the Army of the Republic of Vietnam. But the factions of South Vietnam could never abandon their intrigues long enough to unite in the great cause of defeating communism, so the U.S. armed forces took over the actual fighting.

Congress and the Defense Contractors

The Constitution establishes the responsibility of the executive branch for the day-to-day conduct of foreign affairs, as well as the management of the military forces. It assigns to Congress the role of consultation in the formulation of foreign policy. All this is summarized in the phrase "advise and consent."

Many critics, including several members of Congress, call upon Congress to reassert its right to be consulted and its duty to consult. Implicit in this call is the assumption that such consultation will prevent drastic mistakes on the part of the executive branch: no more Vietnams. In this view, Congress is closely in touch with the people, responding to their wishes and needs, while decisions and consultation within the executive branch are likely to be dominated by the special interests and pleading of the State Department and the Defense Department, specialized bureaucracies that are susceptible to information pathologies.

Walter Lippmann claimed that the people were at fault, and legislative bodies, responding to mistaken public opinion, usurped the appropriate role of the executive. Senator Jacob Javits represents the opposite persuasion: given the facts, he writes, the people and their legislators in Congress will counter-balance any arrogant tendencies of the executive. He calls for Congress to establish its own information-gathering organization so that it will no longer be dependent (as it was in the Tonkin Gulf incident) upon the information that the executive branch chooses to reveal.[10]

But Congress does not speak with a single voice. If more attention should be paid to Congress, should it be paid to the Senate Foreign Relations Committee of J. William Fulbright, or should it be paid to the House Armed Services Committee? Is there justification for the charge of General Shoup that the political influence of the defense industry is a source of American militarism?

Because of the pressure and complexity of modern legislative business, congressmen specialize: both House and Senate respect the expertise developed by their committees. A congressman who wins a seat on a powerful committee seldom abandons it for another assignment. With the working of time, granted the cooperation of the elec-

10. Jacob K. Javits, "The Congressional Presence in Foreign Relations," *Foreign Affairs* 48 (January 1970): 223.

torate in his district, he will probably enjoy the powers and privileges of the chairmanship. And, if he is assigned to the right committee, the congressman may come to enjoy the admiration of a special interest group that extends far beyond the borders of his own district.

The Immortality of Mendel Rivers

Lucius Mendel Rivers was born in Berkeley County, South Carolina, in 1905, where he was educated in the public schools, the College of Charleston, and the University of South Carolina. Admitted to the bar in 1932, he served in the state legislature from 1933 to 1936 and as a special attorney for the U.S. Department of Justice from 1936 until 1940. He was first elected to Congress in 1940 (when Franklin D. Roosevelt was winning his third term as president) from the First District of South Carolina, which is made up of nine counties surrounding the city of Charleston.

In 1969, there were seventeen Army, Navy, Marine, and Air Force installations in the district, which were said to account for 55 percent of Charleston's economy. Congressman Rivers did not claim credit for all the economic benefits bestowed on the area by the military, but his constituents returned him to every session of Congress as regularly as if he were the inventor of economic prosperity. Route 52 through Charleston is called Rivers Avenue, and, on Charleston's naval base, a housing project is named Menriv Park.

When the Johnson Administration first proposed a "heavy" ABM system, with a total price tag of $50 million, Sprint ABM sites were planned for forty-nine major population centers—and for Charleston, South Carolina, 228th largest city in the United States.

It was not only his own district that benefited from Mendel Rivers' meticulous attention to the needs of the Pentagon. Others were grateful for his annual attention to the bill authorizing military spending. The official biography of Congressman Rivers in the *Congressional Directory* recorded that, in 1965, he received the "Minute Man" Award of the Reserve Officers Association. In the same year, he received the Citation of Honor of the Air Force Association. He was an honorary member of the Fleet Reserve Association, the National Guard Association, and the Air Force Sergeants Association.

Mendel Rivers died in late 1970. He was succeeded by his own godson, thirty-year-old Mendel Davis. Davis argued that, because of his youth, he would be able to build up great seniority and be in a position to renew the flow of federal funds to the district. The next chairman of the Armed Services Committee was F. Edward Hébert of New Orleans, Louisiana, a recognized friend of the military. Hébert's district received at least $118 million in Department of Defense funds even in 1970.[11]

There is no guarantee that 100 senators and 435 congressmen will together be wise in discerning the national interest. Each is responsible to the electorate of his district, and to his own conscience. One time-honored way of showing one's concern for the home folks is to list the dollar value of all federal projects—from channel dredging to missile contracts—brought into the district during the legislator's tenure in Washington.

The term "logrolling" has been coined to apply to the practice of congressmen who vote for the projects in their colleagues' districts in return for votes favoring projects in their own. Traditionally, considering rivers and harbors legislation was the signal for an orgy of logrolling. But the term can be applied to any legislation that may

11. See M. Barone, G. Ujifusa, and D. Matthews, *The Almanac of American Politics* (Boston: Gambit, 1972), p. 301.

benefit individual districts. If nobody questions the wisdom of devoting national resources to a particular usage, the congressman is likely to perceive his first duty as winning as large a slice of the pie as possible for his own district.

For many years, military spending was treated in just this manner. Senator Gaylord Nelson complained in 1964:

> An established tradition . . . holds that a bill to spend billions of dollars for the machinery of war must be rushed through the House and the Senate in a matter of hours, while a treaty to advance the cause of peace, or a program to help the underdeveloped nations . . . guarantee the rights of all our citizens, or . . . to advance the interests of the poor must be scrutinized and debated and thrashed over for weeks and perhaps months.[12]

Robert McNamara had come to the Pentagon by 1964, along with a team of management experts from the Ford Motor Company, and there was much talk of the restoration of civilian control over the sprawling and complex military organization. What McNamara brought were improved techniques of management, including the cost-benefit technique of budgetary analysis. He did not bring questions about the propriety of military expenditures in general. During his seven years at the Pentagon, the level of defense spending increased by $20 billion.

As for the military leaders, they were exponents of the bureaucratic truth. They rose to the top positions in part because of their ability to voice the doctrines that justified the existence and continued growth of their organizations, and the habit continued even after they had retired from these positions. In 1968, General Curtis E. LeMay, former head of the Air Force, wrote:

> It is necessary to understand that Vietnam is part of a much larger and much longer war—a war between Communism and the Free World. . . . Although the war has many facets, it has but one objective: Communist control of the entire world.
> . . . I sincerely believe any arms race with the Soviet Union would act to our benefit. I believe that we can out-invent, out-research, out-develop, out-engineer, and out-produce the USSR in any area from sling shots to space weapons, and in so doing become more and more prosperous while the Soviets become progressively poorer. This is the faith I have in the free enterprise economy.[13]

In Search of a Conspiracy

General LeMay's faith in free enterprise was no more surprising than his disdain for communism. But his knowledge of economics was incomplete, if he felt that free enterprise guaranteed superior weaponry for the United States.

The benefits of free enterprise are, in one way or another, related to competition. The customer benefits when several firms compete against each other for his business. The firms are compelled to develop efficiencies of management and production that result in the price being lowered. If he can inspect for quality, the customer can accept the lowest bid and relax in the confidence that the managers of the enterprise are responsible for setting a price that will assure a

12. Quoted in John Kenneth Galbraith, "How to Control the Military," *Harper's*, June 1969, p. 38.
13. From Curtis E. LeMay, *America Is in Danger,* quoted in ibid., p. 37.

reasonable return to the stockholders, yet be below that offered by competing firms.

This situation—when several firms are equally capable of producing the desired commodity, and the prices offered by each are common knowledge—holds true in the case of what the economists call "perfect competition." It has not been the situation in the defense industry for many years. Before World War II, the Army Air Force announced a competition for the design of a long-range bomber, listing the minimum characteristics desired, in range, speed, altitude, and payload. Several firms entered the competition, and Boeing produced the first version of the aircraft that would win fame as the B-17, or Flying Fortress. (Because of an accident during the tests, it did not win the competition.) In the 1970s, with the pace of technological development accelerating, this leisurely process is no longer possible. Weapons systems are so complicated, and the requirements they must meet so changing, that the conception of designs normally takes place through interaction between military and industrial representatives at the engineering level. When the time comes to award a contract, there are only one or two companies capable of producing the design. Rather than the separateness between customer and firm from which the benefits of free competition flow, there is the phenomenon of interacting bureaucracies—huge industrial firms in contact at many levels with military men who represent the only possible purchaser of their wares. The situation is probably little different in the Soviet Union, where not-quite-separate bureaucracies interact with each other in the same manner. That the industrial firm is owned by the state probably makes little difference.

Now, it would seem, we are on the trail of the infamous military-industrial complex. Retired military men are employed by defense contractors to handle "customer relations"—the only customers being their friends and former colleagues in the Navy or Air Force.

This fact adds fuel to the old American contention that wars and preparation for wars result from the desire of individuals for private profit: industrialists conspiring with military leaders to feather each other's nests, supported by key congressmen.

"The reality," writes John Kenneth Galbraith, "is far less dramatic."

> The reality is a complex of organizations pursuing their sometimes diverse but generally common goals. The participants in these organizations are mostly honest men whose public and private behavior would withstand public scrutiny as well as most. They live on their military pay or their salaries as engineers . . . and would not dream of offering or accepting a bribe. . . .
>
> The men who comprise these organizations call each other on the phone, meet at committee hearings, serve together on teams or task forces, work in neighboring offices in Washington or San Diego. They naturally make their decisions in accordance with their view of the world—the view of the bureaucracy of which they are a part. The problem is not conspiracy or corruption but unchecked rule. And being unchecked, this rule reflects not what is best for the United States but what the Air Force, Army, Navy, General Dynamics, North American Rockwell, Grumman Aircraft, State Department representatives, intelligence officers, and Mendel Rivers and Richard Russell believe to be best.[14]

14. Ibid., pp. 34, 35. Since Galbraith wrote, Rivers and Russell have died, replaced by Congressman Hébert and Senator John Stennis of Mississippi. The situation is unchanged.

An awareness that competition was less than perfect in defense contracting led to the development of the "cost plus" contract during World War II. Congressional investigations in the 1930s of World War I profiteering so embarrassed industrialists that many supported the isolationist movement. When the war came, they welcomed the "cost plus" arrangement. It prevented defense contractors from making an exorbitant profit by assuring them a modest, fixed profit in excess of costs.

Studies of these contracts revealed, not surprisingly, that the guaranteed profit provided no incentive to hold down costs. Companies simply did not develop the economies and efficiency which would alone assure them of a profit under a normal contract. One of Robert McNamara's reforms was to change to contracts that provided a fixed fee. To earn a profit, the company had to hold its costs below that fee, and contracts were awarded to the lowest bidder. Companies soon discovered that they could submit an unprofitable low bid to win the contract, then swing into the profit column through contract renegotiations as development of the system brought requests for changes and new capabilities from the armed services who would use the system. This process created the cost overruns in the F-111 and C5A aircraft, among others. Once the design was completed, however, the fee could not be raised, even if the volume of orders was suddenly increased, straining productive capacity, or the general economy became inflated, with the wages of skilled labor rising dramatically.

The Vietnam War was nearly an economic disaster for the firms that were the top five defense contractors in 1965, when the Vietnam buildup began. One—Douglas Aircraft—was forced into a merger, and the other four saw their earnings per share fall dramatically in the following four years. For one example, in 1968, General Dynamics ranked as the leading defense contractor. On the basis of total revenue for the year, it ranked thirty-fourth among U.S. corporations. But its rank based on total profit was two hundred twentieth.[15]

Most defense contractors would find peace more profitable than war; it would be easier to pass the costs of inflation along to the civilian consumer. As for military contracts, the profit comes from developing prototype weapon systems (with cost overruns), which are forever being refined to keep pace with technological advance, rather than in mass producing a given design. It seemed at least arguable that involvement in, and the duration of, the Vietnam War could not be blamed on the munitions makers, provided they were rational men.

And what of the people?

15. George E. Berkeley, "The Myth of War Profiteering," *New Republic*, December 20-27, 1969, p. 16.

The Politics of Foreign Policy

The people do not speak with a single voice. Various spokesmen compete for their attention and support, and they respond to those who
best articulate their convictions, their passions, and their fears. When
such a spokesman also leads a political organization, change becomes
possible.

As with domestic issues, questions of the direction of foreign affairs
have been part of the contest between the political parties. For it is
only through an election that the people may exercise their ultimate
control over the government.

The most striking fact about the use of foreign-policy issues in
American elections is that this has been a politics of revenge — rather
than debating alternative courses or new approaches, the party in
power has been punished for the results of its foreign policies, whether
those results could have been avoided or not. Parties must seek a
renewal of their mandate on the basis of past performance in domestic
affairs, also. But the orientation to the past is striking in foreign affairs:

> The most vociferous isolationist politicians in the 1930s were
> Republicans, largely from the Midwest, many of whom, like the
> La Follettes of Wisconsin, were quite progressive in their attitudes
> toward domestic issues. In the atmosphere created by Senate
> investigations of the profits of World War I munitions makers,
> Congress passed the Neutrality Act of 1935, which banned the
> shipment of war materials to belligerents. In essence, it was a
> declaration by Congress that vindicated the judgment of those
> few congressmen who voted against entry into the war in 1917.

> As World War II neared its conclusion, Democrats cited the
> Republican record in scuttling the League of Nations and in
> embracing isolationism; they hinted that Republicans could not
> be trusted to secure the peace.

> As respected a figure as Senator Robert A. Taft joined the
> Republican chorus of claims that China had somehow been
> betrayed into the hands of Mao's Communists by the Democratic
> foreign policy. The charge that the Democrats "lost China"
> included the arrogant assumption that China was somehow ours
> to lose.

> As the Korean War was prolonged, partly because early success
> led to an expansion of its objectives, it grew increasingly
> unpopular. "Communism, Corruption, and Korea" was the slogan
> on which the Republicans rode to victory with Dwight Eisenhower
> in 1952.

> When Russian armies invaded Hungary, snuffing out a flicker of
> freedom, and the United States did not intervene, Democrats
> shamed the Republicans for promising to "roll back" communism
> in their 1952 platform. (The Democratic platform made the same
> promise, but less stridently.) A Democratic administration later
> watched silently while Russian tanks rolled into Prague.

> Richard Nixon rode into office in 1968 on the crest of public dis-
> satisfaction with the human costs of the Vietnam War. He did not
> initiate public discussion of alternative ways of extricating
> American forces; he was able to gather support from both "hawks"
> and "doves."

When President Nixon later journeyed to Russia and China as the signal for a thaw in the Cold War, commentators suggested that only Richard Nixon, with his long record of anticommunism, could have won public support for a relationship with the leading Communist powers. A Democratic administration, they suggested, would have been too burdened by charges of past "softness" on communism to accomplish the new accommodation with the traditional "enemy."

In this catalog of partisanship, there is one period that seems, on the surface, to be an exception. It is the period of 1947 and 1948, when the Truman Doctrine, the Marshall Plan, the North Atlantic Treaty Organization (NATO), and the general structure of postwar foreign policy was constructed. It was a policy aimed at restoring war-ravaged Europe to economic and political health, while containing the expansion of Stalin's communism. It has been called the most creative period of American foreign-policy-making in the twentieth century.

These policies were formulated through a cooperation more deep than the normal definition of "advice and consent" between the Truman administration and a Republican-controlled Congress. Congress was largely represented by Senator Arthur H. Vandenberg of Michigan, then chairman of the Senate Foreign Relations Committee. In effect, Dean Acheson at the State Department yielded to Vandenberg nearly a veto power over a certain range of decisions. Because the Senate had a voice in making the decisions, senators were able to support and justify the policies before the nation.

At this time, there was much talk of a "bi-partisan foreign policy" and much use of the slogan, "politics stops at the water's edge." In fact, there were compelling reasons for the two parties to cooperate in the field of foreign policy, while battling over domestic issues. President Truman was perceived as being in serious political trouble. He wanted at least to achieve acceptance of his foreign-policy recommendations. The Republicans expected to win the presidency in 1948, probably with Senator Robert A. Taft as their candidate. They were eager to bury the isolationist image by demonstrating their responsibility in the management of foreign policy. So the bi-partisan foreign policy of the time did not result from a renunciation of partisanship, but it did result from the functioning of government institutions in a manner close to that suggested in the Constitution—foreign policy being made by the executive, aided by constant consultation with the legislature. And the main effect of bi-partisanship was to limit public attacks on an international involvement unprecedented for peacetime.

The program of aid to Western Europe achieved its major goals, but the Cold War mentality it fostered led to difficulties. The simplistic perception of the world as being divided into two hostile camps —"Communist" and "free"—failed to account for other powerful forces in the affairs of nations, particularly the drive of regions of Africa and Asia for independence from their former colonial masters, and the striving of peoples in the southern part of the globe to achieve the benefits of industrial society displayed in the northern hemisphere. The United States found itself supporting existing regimes with uncertain popular support, as long as they had declared their opposition to communism, in efforts to defeat the forces of social change.

One of America's dubious friends was the dictator of Cuba, Fulgencio Batista. When Fidel Castro's revolution succeeded, he came to power as an enemy of the United States. Yet that need not have been; the Bay of Pigs need not have been; the Cuban Missile Crisis need not have been.

Another was Generalissimo Franco, dictator of Spain. There was no doubt of his anticommunism, but he could hardly be called a friend of the Bill of Rights.

Another was President Diem of Vietnam . . .

Making Democracy Safe for the World[16]

The people do not speak with a single voice. Instead, there are spokesmen for various factions, interests, and convictions. When this state of affairs prevails in the formation of foreign policy, the process is quite like that through which domestic policy is made. But there is an important difference. The motives of the groups concerned with domestic policy are more clear, and their ability to understand both the limits of the situation and their own best interests are more certain.

For example:

A congressman who urges that a particular weapons system be awarded to the Navy may want the plant in his district to build it.

The officer of a veterans' organization who urges a belligerent course in international relations may speak out because of over-compensation for the fact that he himself never served in real combat, rather than because of special knowledge of the situation.

The German-Americans who most opposed intervention in World War II remembered the hysteria directed against German-Americans during World War I, and became isolationists.

Americans have yet to outgrow the sense of superiority nourished by centuries of isolation and technological leadership; it is that sense which permitted the labeling of all Asians as "gooks" and many Americans to remain undisturbed by what the massacre at My Lai revealed about the senseless savagery of the Vietnam conflict.

That same sense of superiority is easily turned against other Americans, particularly those charged with official responsibilities; opponents of the involvement in Vietnam sought polarization of attitudes on the most rigid moral grounds, which could conclude logically only by making every policy unacceptable.

The result of such influences is that the long-range development of American foreign policy, taking place in the arena of public discussion, has proven unsatisfactory.

When there is time for planning, there is time for disagreement. Since there is nothing in American culture to limit the course of disagreement, disagreement spreads. It spreads among all individuals who have the interest and the resources. It ultimately becomes public and involves all of the engines and motives of public politics, as well as all the unpredictability of publicly made decisions.[17]

16. For this inversion of Woodrow Wilson's famous phrase, I am indebted to Theodore J. Lowi, as I am for much of what follows. See his *The End of Liberalism* (New York: Norton, 1969), Chapter 6.
17. Ibid., p. 161.

Philip Jones Griffiths

Public officials have had to manipulate public opinion in order to achieve the degree of support from all interested parties necessary to launch new action. This has required exaggerating the importance of some dangerous element in the international situation, as well as exaggerating the usefulness of policies designed to meet that danger.

Since World War II, key phrases have been developed to over-dramatize dangers: "Cold War," "iron curtain,"[18] "brink of war," "massive retaliation," "bamboo curtain," "world Communist conspiracy," and "Godless Communism." President Kennedy's inaugural address can be read as a more skilled and subtle effort to achieve a national consensus in favor of devoting new attention and resources to foreign affairs.

Overselling the usefulness of a particular remedy has been common in the same period. Each new signing of a treaty, creation of an international organization, or development of a foreign-aid program has been advertised as crucially important. Official enthusiasm was generated for the United Nations; when it could not protect Europe, new enthusiasm was generated for NATO. The Alliance for Progress was announced as if it could be counted upon to lift Latin America into the industrial age, guaranteeing free elections in the process.

When the United States chose to intervene in behalf of the narrowly based regime of President Diem, the intervention was justified on the basis of the Domino Theory: if this corner of Asia should go Communist, the rest would soon follow. Each increase in the military commitment required a darker projection of the disasters that would come with military defeat. Finally, however, the request of General Westmoreland for 206,000 more troops was denied. An overheated economy and a people increasingly certain that no national benefits resulted from the sacrifices being made in Vietnam would no longer

18. The phrases "Cold War" and "iron curtain" were coined by Winston Churchill, the former British prime minister. But the British never took them as seriously as did the Americans.

tolerate sending its young men to die. Later, President Nixon acted successfully upon the presumption that the people would tolerate continued bombing, as long as only a few planes were shot down.

> One hundred and seventy-five years before, based on his reading of Thucydides' account of the fall of Athens, John Adams questioned the propensity of democracies to live in peace.

Yet, in times of crisis, when the stakes were high and time was short, American policy-makers tended to function surprisingly well. Since World War II, sound decisions were made in response to the blockade of Berlin, the invasion of Korea, the French request for help at Dienbienphu, and the threat posed by Soviet missiles stationed in Cuba, to name leading examples. President Nixon's decision to invade Cambodia (made without congressional consultation) should be excluded from the list of sound responses. Even if history judges the Cambodian operation a military success, its cost in domestic turmoil was enormous and perhaps permanent. For Lyndon Johnson in 1964 and Richard Nixon in 1968 were elected as peace candidates—yet both expanded the war. The effectiveness of the presidential office depends upon public trust.

These sound decisions were made by an elite. But it was not the familiar military-industrial complex which acted. The elite has been composed of the president, his chief advisers, heads of executive departments, and congressmen called in for consultation. *They have been the officials designated by the Constitution.* Far from being the representatives of private industrial power, they have been the men who must submit their record for public judgment at the next election. In times of crisis, the machinery for the development of foreign policy has functioned very much in the manner envisaged by the founding fathers. The Vietnam War grew out of a commitment first made in 1950. Policy-makers never reexamined the assumptions upon which it was made. Vietnam was not recognized as a crisis, until too late.

This success of crisis decisions and failure of decisions reached gradually suggests tentative conclusions:

> The constitutional machinery for foreign-policy-making can work well, if the circumstances are appropriate.

> The check provided by the electoral process upon public officials can lead them to disregard the special pleadings of both industrial and governmental bureaucracies. On the other hand, electoral considerations may inspire officials to systematically misinform both the public and Congress. Public officials may be enslaved by myths.

> Public leaders articulate these myths when they struggle to achieve a consensus by overdramatizing both dangers and remedies; and they must be held responsible for the dead hand of mythology upon foreign-policy formation, particularly when they come to believe their own propaganda, as in Vietnam.

Studies of public opinion show that support for the president rises in times of international crisis. They show further that the people accept innovations in foreign policy with good grace. The people have accepted a degree of involvement with the external world as inevitable. Therefore, the problem of foreign policy seems to be more a question of leadership than of inadequate institutions.

Call for a Reassessment

Republican Senator Charles Mathias of Maryland called for the repeal of congressional actions arising from the Cold War—the State of Emergency proclaimed in 1950, when the Korean War began, and never repealed; the Quemoy-Matsu-Formosa resolution of 1955; the Cuban resolution of 1962; and the 1964 Gulf of Tonkin Resolution. Mathias declared that it was time to "start clearing away the debris of Cold War dogmas and resolutions that encumber and stultify our policies today."

The containment of communism had been the well-spring of American foreign policy for more than twenty years. "As we enter the seventies," Mathias said, "we should reappraise the domestic requirements of our inevitable embroilments in world tensions and difficulties."[19]

Meanwhile, Republican Senator Jacob Javits pointed out that some "5,000 international agreements reached by the Executive since 1946 have done much to shape the nature of America's position in the world."[20] And he again endorsed the National Commitments Resolution, passed by a vote of 70-16 in the Senate on June 25, 1969. Defining a national commitment as the use of, or promise to use, American armed forces or financial aid on foreign soil, the Senate declared its sense that

> a national commitment by the United States results only from affirmative action by the Executive and Legislative branches of the United States Government by means of a treaty, statute, or concurrent resolution of both Houses of Congress specifically providing for such commitment.

Perhaps the Senate could not guarantee that there would be no more Vietnams. But it could and did declare its intention of never approving another Gulf of Tonkin Resolution. The senators hoped they would no longer be asked to approve wars only after they began. It was not clear whether this new insistence upon the constitutional authority of Congress in the making of foreign policy meant that the president would deal with foreign relations hereafter on the basis of new wisdom. The decision to invade Cambodia, the bombing of North Vietnam at Christmastime, 1972, and the bombing of Cambodia until a cut-off date of August 15 was agreed upon with Congress, suggest that the authority of the commander-in-chief has few limits, at least in the short run.

19. *New York Times*, December 9, 1969.
20. Javits, "The Congressional Presence in Foreign Relations," p. 233.

The Pride of Self

With nuclear destruction the instant price of miscalculation, did it
really matter whether foreign policy was being conducted in accord
with the Constitution? Was the discussion of interrelationships between military men, Congress, and the defense industry perhaps, in
a deeper sense, irrelevant?

Reinhold Niebuhr, the theologian, offered one answer:

> After the successful moon shot, the triumphant President Nixon,
> speaking at a White House reception for foreign exchange
> students, exulted: "Any culture which can put a man on the
> moon is capable of gathering all the nations of the earth in
> peace, justice, and concord." He was so persuaded by this con-
> clusion, weighted with error, that he repeated this hope and
> promise in all the capitals of Asia.
>
> The error of the President has persisted in Western culture
> since the eighteenth century. Quite simply, it is the error of
> identifying the self with the mind. When the mind considers,
> studies and conquers nature, then it is pure mind. The self with
> its pride, passion, and interests does not enter when man frees
> himself from the limitations of nature. But when there is the
> problem of relating man to man and nation to nation, then the
> mind becomes the servant of the self's hopes, ambitions, pride
> and fears. Reason cannot simply annul or reduce the self's
> ideologies. An ideology is, in fact, a corruption of the reasoning
> process in the interest of self, individual or collective.
>
> . . . No doubt there were as many skeptics in the capitals of
> Asia as among the foreign students at the reception.[21]

*Because it is bound up in feelings of national pride and personal
patriotism, foreign policy is likely to be surrounded by limited views
of the world that pervert decisions. These attitudes become more influential and dangerous when the process used to reach decisions
becomes more public.*

Three types of attitude are particularly dangerous:

*Assumptions that justify the existence of bureaucracies,
particularly military bureaucracies, and dominate their
information-gathering subsystems.*

*Convictions of the moral superiority of the American political
or economic systems — but convictions of the immorality of those
systems can be just as damaging, if they prevent an examination
of the real situation.*

*Conceptions used to overdramatize both international dangers
and their proposed remedies, which may become accepted by the
very officials who mouth them as guidelines for policy.*

*The first step in avoiding the dangers which adhere to such attitudes
is to recognize that, regardless of the role of truth in stimulating their
original development, they have acquired the emotional impact of
myths. When accepted uncritically, they destroy any ability to know
the full truth of the world.*

*If the leaders of a democracy cannot recognize this fact, there is
little hope that the people will do so.*

21. "The President's Error," *Christianity and Crisis*, September 15, 1969, pp. 227-228.

Philip Jones Griffiths

The Places We Live

Acting out our sense of mission in the world and even the universe, America sent manned spacecraft to the moon and spent billions in an unsuccessful effort to subdue a peasant people in Asia. With the attention of national leaders focused outward, disorder grew at home. In the 1960s, the explosions came—in the cities, on the campuses, and in the consciousness of urban groups.

A determination to improve the quality of American city life could not be so easily implemented as a decision to go to the moon. Community life—the safety of the streets, the quality of education and recreation—depends on the performance of state and local governments, operating in the tangled web of relationships that is the American federal system. President Nixon proposed a major revision of federal relationships. This was small comfort to cities facing the threat of a strike by teachers or firemen.

What does federalism have to do with the places Americans live?

Politics, Planning, and the Urban Poor

On a Block in the Bronx

There was a time when dense urban neighborhoods—call them slums—served as processing centers. Immigrants came from Europe, or in from the countryside, and they stayed in the low-rent districts while they learned the ropes of urban living and found jobs. There were sweatshops in the neighborhood, so those willing to work could find employment. Eventually they or their children would find a better job and move on to a better neighborhood, and cast off the language and habits of the ethnic neighborhood. It is a story as old as, and related to, the American Dream of Success.

Success is seldom possible any more. The new arrivals in the cities—blacks up from the South, whites from Appalachia, Puerto Ricans, the second generation of families unable to escape those same neighborhoods—are trapped as much by economics as by race. The horrors of the sweatshops are gone now, and there is nothing to take their place. People move into decaying neighborhoods, expecting to reside there only temporarily, never investing the place with care or pride; then, when they are unable to leave, they are trapped in a cycle of despair.

Herb Goro has published a documentary photographic essay about the residents of a single block in the Bronx. His pictures, which capture the mood of their subjects and the poverty of the place, are accompanied by transcribed tape recordings of interviews with the residents.

He begins with the block worker, employed by a neighborhood community organization. Says the block worker,

> In this community as such, there is no community . . . it's just a place where they stop over and find a place to live—for a temporary type of period. The people come here from the Deep South, and from other places—Puerto Rico—and they stop here and they accept these fantastically high rents to landlords. They accept bad living standards. They accept health problems and things like this . . .; the reason for this is that they have no choice.
>
> . . . I think the housing problem is like where the kid grows up with rats jumping all over his bed, waking up in the middle of the night and something's crawling on his foot; lifts the covers up, man, and there it is—a ten- or twelve-inch rat, and don't tell me it doesn't happen. I know people that become so accustomed to things of this nature that you ask them, "Do you have rats or mice in your house?" and they answer "Yeah. Only one comes in my bedroom at night." Like nothing's happening. Only one. So like, you know, for yourself, for one rat to come in my house would be for me to pack my things and leave. But for these people, they become so exposed and so, like I say, people on the whole adapt.
>
> The Sanitation Department is sort of like an organization that is not particularly interested in what the ghetto looks like. These men feel that they do their job. . . . They just don't feel that these garbage-filled lots are their problem. . . . We've requested more pickups per day, but they claim to be short-handed on men and equipment. . . . The garbage in the lot breeds health problems. . . . It's sort of like the decaying stink of garbage that lies decaying in this lot. And these fumes constantly seep in through your window, you know, in the summertime in 90-degree weather. It's just constantly decaying, night and day. You're going to get sick.

The mothers of the block also spoke of its problems—the crime, the violence, and the vacant lot filled with garbage—

> The kids play in that lot . . . and somebody throws garbage from the windows down to the lot where the kids are playing. . . . One day the Sanitation men came and all they did was push the garbage back, and a week later it was the same. Every night there is a fire in the lot. Last night, three times. And the kids set

> fires to the buildings next door, the ones that were abandoned. This happens every night. So I can't sleep. I'm afraid that the building will burn down while I'm sleeping.

Another mother adds,

> We have like junkies. Dope addicts. We have winos laying in the streets. There are fights and killings all up and down the street. Right out here on Third Avenue. On this block. In the past year there have been three or four killings on this block. This summer there was a man shot right here on the corner by the subway. . . .
>
> When the Negroes say prejudice nobody pays much attention. But you would be surprised at how much prejudice the Spanish people have against the Negroes. And those are the two races that should be the closest together because we really are the underdog.

And always there are the rats.

> Listen, I've had rats falling in my bathtub. I had to go and buy four big rattraps and I've caught as high as nine big rats. Not mice, rats. Rats that cats would be afraid to tackle. We had to nail down the traps so the rats won't take them away. And they were pulling and pulling, and I found them when they strangled themselves to death. I saved some to show the landlord when he came in. I had the exterminator, but he didn't do nothing. He'd come in and put a little mice feed and spray a little bit and leave.

And every night you hear the rats fighting.[1]

Was there no way to clean up the vacant lot, to drive out the rats, to cure the health problems? The sanitation worker explained that they did not have the time both to sweep up trash and load it onto the truck. The landlord explained that the vacant lot did not belong to him, it belonged to the city, and the city should be responsible. The block worker explained that, when some of the people arrived in the neighborhood from a rural area, they would not understand that trash should not be thrown out of a window. When the mothers learned it, they had trouble teaching the children. Children would be sent to take trash to the bin; they would throw it out of the hallway window, then sit on the windowsill for ten or fifteen minutes before returning to their mothers. The block worker explained that the children had seen winos throwing trash from the windows of their own building; when everyone did it, why bother to be different?

On a freezing January night, a fire caused by an electric heater completely destroyed one of the two ancient brick and frame buildings on that block in the Bronx. The tenants were housed in a hotel until they could be placed by the New York City Department of Relocation.

The Story of Pruitt-Igoe

The buildings on that block in the Bronx were antiquated tenements. There can be little anguish over their demise. In New York and other cities, housing has been provided specifically for the poor, with the help of federal funds.

---

1. Quotations are from Herb Goro, *The Block* (New York: Random House, 1970), pp. xii-xiv, 42, 44.

One way to provide housing for the poor—recognizing that, in most cases, the poor are not to blame for their own poverty—would be for the government to pay part or all of their rent for facilities available to anyone. This method is widely used in Europe, but it has barely been tried, and that only quite recently, in the United States. The American insistence upon self-reliance (the value of achievement) prevents citizens, public officials, and even architects from admitting that the poor may not be to blame for their poverty. Their instinct has been to separate the poor from the rest of society. The construction of public housing has been tied to the clearance of slums. Tear down the rotting old buildings; a few years later, new buildings will rise in their place.

> Those rotten old buildings were the only home their tenants had. Never mind; the tenants will be relocated to further overcrowd some other slum while the bulldozers and architects and construction workers do their jobs.

The urban renewal program gave to city government the power to take private slum property, destroy the buildings, and then sell the property, or lease it, to private developers. So the new buildings seldom provided housing for the same class of people the bulldozer had displaced. More frequently, expensive middle-class apartments were built, or even office buildings and shopping centers. American core cities were rebuilt, their former residents shoved off to other slums and forgotten. Most of these former residents were members of racial minorities, and they referred to urban renewal as "nigger removal." But the phrase "institutionalized racism" did not find its way into the textbooks for a long time.

One of the cities that took seriously its responsibility for housing the poor was St. Louis, Missouri. The design of its Pruitt-Igoe project was considered a model solution to the problem, and it won a 1958 award for excellent architectural design. Dwight Eisenhower was president then, public affairs were calm after a period of turbulence, and no destructive domestic issues were on the political agenda. Pruitt-Igoe was first intended as a segregated project: Pruitt for blacks, and Igoe, across the street, for whites. But a court decision prevented that. First occupied in 1954, it was integrated for a while but quickly came to be occupied exclusively by blacks. Soon after 1958, Pruitt-Igoe developed the highest vacancy rate of any public housing project in the nation. Tenants regarded it as a last resort in the search for a place to live.

Pruitt-Igoe consisted of thirty-three eleven-story slab-shaped brick apartment buildings, providing space for some 10,000 people. The buildings were dispersed over their crowded grounds, for the architects were enthralled by the vision of towers rising up out of open space, equating open space with clear air and other rural virtues. The design gave no suggestion that any part of the open space was assigned to any particular building or group of tenants. There was no suggestion of either ownership or responsibility, and the space was as accessible to the surrounding area as to the tenants themselves. It soon became littered with broken glass and an area to be avoided at night.

The apartments themselves were designed as monuments to insensitivity—as if the architects were determined to show their tenants as a special species, undeserving of normal human dignity. The elevators stopped only on the fourth, seventh, and tenth floors. The elevators themselves opened directly onto breezeways at the street level, so that no tenant was able to monitor the passage of strangers into or out of his building. Access routes into the buildings provided for the tenants no sense of possession or responsibility. The stark buildings were institutions, stating by their design that the poor should be put in their place. The design also made the tenants vulnerable to prowlers from outside. The hallways, stairwells, and elevators of Pruitt-Igoe, unsupervised and untended, became stained by human urine and the location for frequent rapes and muggings.

The Pruitt-Igoe experience was typical of high-rise public housing projects. Statistical studies show that the incidence of serious crime — the number of murders, rapes, and muggings per thousand population — increases with the number of floors in the building. The most terrifying crimes are committed in the unsupervised public spaces of the buildings — elevators, halls, lobbies, and stairs.[2]

There are, of course, very successful high-rise apartment buildings housing middle- and upper-class tenants. What assures their success is the uniformed doorman who guards all points of entry with closed-circuit television, summons taxicabs, and helps tenants in with their packages.

Publicly subsidized housing cannot afford a uniformed staff; taxpayers, who largely cannot afford them for themselves, would be the first to complain. Knowing that maintenance funds would be scanty, the designers of public housing in the 1950s added certain features that raised the cost of original construction. Considerable attention was given to making the Pruitt-Igoe project as indestructible as possible. Glazed tiles were used in the hallways — the same tiles that are used in mental hospitals and prisons — for their easy washability. "Indestructible" plastic shields were installed over the outdoor and hallway light fixtures.

Prisoners do not react favorably to their prisons. The glazed tile and the light shields came to be seen as challenges. Eventually, the tiles were ripped out of the walls, and the lightbulbs were broken. Mailbox doors were ripped off, and every other kind of vandalism was perpetrated upon the offensive structures.

By 1972, only 713 of the originally constructed 2,190 units at Pruitt-Igoe remained occupied. The St. Louis Housing Authority Board of Commissioners, faced with rising costs, falling income, and an inadequate federal subsidy, first determined to close down all nine of the city's conventional public housing projects. Then they unsuccessfully petitioned the federal Department of Housing and Urban Development (HUD) to take over ownership of the projects.[3]

A study based on extensive interviews with some residents of the Pruitt-Igoe project has been published. It displays the separate culture of poverty developed there and the means adopted by families, and particularly children, to survive. It is called *Behind Ghetto Walls.*[4]

Lives are shaped by their environment; and the beginning of freedom is to be able to choose one's environment. As one student of public housing has written,

> Living units are assessed by tenants not only on the basis of size and available amenities but on the basis of the life styles they symbolize and purport to offer. . . . As with most of American society, low-income groups aspire to the life style symbolized by [the two-story row house] and by the suburban bungalow. They view the row house as more closely resembling the individual

2. Oscar Newman, *Defensible Space: Crime Prevention through Urban Design* (New York: Macmillan, 1972), pp. 22-50.
3. Sally Thran, "No Room for the Poor," *Commonweal*, January 25, 1973, p. 292.
4. Lee Rainwater, *Behind Ghetto Walls: Black Families in a Federal Slum* (Chicago: Aldine, 1970).

family house than the apartment within a communal building. A piece of ground adjacent to a unit, provided for the exclusive use of the family, is cherished and defended, regardless of how small.[5]

Housing projects like Pruitt-Igoe aren't being planned any more. By 1972, the slogan and policy of public housing authorities—including HUD—was the "economic mix." Rather than stigmatize the poor by segregating them, the hope is to meld poor people with working-class and lower-middle-class families, who will set an example of pride in their homes and respect for property.

In St. Louis, the managers of projects that practice the new policy will admit up to 10 percent of their tenants from the welfare rolls. The result is that many poor people must go without decent housing, crowding in with relatives instead. New housing is not being constructed fast enough to house the poor people who need it.

The "economic mix" policy was developed by former HUD Secretary George Romney for the suburbs; the cities will soon contain an insufficient number of financially independent families for the poor to be mixed with. But the suburbs aren't very interested, and President Nixon declared in June 1972 that "forced integration of the suburbs is not in the public interest."[6]

> In April 1972, building C–15 at Pruitt-Igoe was destroyed in ten seconds—at a cost of $67,000—by carefully placed charges of dynamite. The ultimate act of vandalism was thus performed by the housing authority that owned the building. Destruction of the building would make room for a park and playground. The authority planned to destroy several other buildings, as well, to reduce the density (families per acre) of the project. Critics of high-rise public housing suggest that all thirty-three buildings be leveled.

Farewell to Mayor Lindsay

> *From the* New York Times, *March 11, 1973:* Seven years ago he triumphantly entered City Hall as a fresh new face, a hot political property, the man on the white horse who would smite the municipal dragons plaguing New York and its sister cities around the nation—crime, corruption, middle-class migration, mismanagement and bloated budgets. Last week, John Lindsay bowed to the torments of America's second toughest job and announced that he would not seek a third term.
>
> "This decision is based on personal considerations and is final," he said without a trace of bitterness or any emotion other than relief. "Eight years is too short a time" for the work that still has to be done, "but it is long enough for one man."

What happened in seven years to destroy the high hopes with which John V. Lindsay began? Before answering that question, it is essential to point out his great accomplishment: during those seven years, New York did not burn down. In a period when city after city erupted in riot and looting, Lindsay somehow kept the lid on in New York. Partly by his famous walking tours in the ghettos, partly because of

5. Oscar Newman, *Defensible Space*, p. 106.
6. For a discussion of the crisis in urban housing stimulated by the destruction of the building at Pruitt-Igoe, see Alex Poinsett, "Countdown in Housing," *Ebony*, September 1972, pp. 60–68. President Nixon's statement is quoted here, among other sources.

his use of federally supported programs to alleviate suffering in the decaying neighborhoods, partly by showing that he cared, John Lindsay kept the lid on.

Somebody asked Dean Rusk his greatest accomplishment as secretary of state. He replied that, for all those long years, the nuclear beast was kept in its cage. The ability to destroy the world was possessed by at least two nations, but it was not used.

Only Vietnam was laid waste.

John Lindsay was plagued by troubles. One of his troubles was that the civic employees of New York—from trash collectors to school-teachers—are civil servants, their jobs secure from direct influence by Mayor Lindsay. And they are organized, ready to use collective bargaining to protect their wages and conditions of employment. As businesses and middle-class residents fled to the suburbs, Lindsay faced a series of strikes by municipal workers—policemen, teachers, garbage collectors (many of whom live in the suburbs)—eager to protect their earning capacity in the face of national inflation. Settling those strikes was particularly costly for the city in a time of declining revenues.

Lindsay, then a Republican, was first elected on a "fusion" ticket. He was nominated by both his own party and the Liberal party, an organization that has existed for four decades in New York, its mainstay the garment workers and their union leaders, to support liberal causes but avoid contamination by association with the leadership of the regular Democratic organization (remember Tammany Hall?). It was the same coalition that nominated and elected the legendary Fiorello La Guardia, the half-Italian "Little Flower" who learned to speak Yiddish from his mother. In fact, the Liberal party, which was in danger of becoming an adjunct to the Democratic party, which it had supported since La Guardia, preserved itself a while longer as an independent and viable political force by supporting Lindsay in 1966.

Mayor Lindsay moved to consolidate his support among the city's liberal constituency—the blacks and Puerto Ricans of the slums, the fashionable "limousine liberals" of Park Avenue, and Jewish union members. He soon became embroiled in conflict with Republican Governor Nelson Rockefeller; any mayor of New York must do battle in Albany to win state support for the city. In 1970, when the time came for election to his second term, Lindsay was defeated in his own Republican party primary. Many New Yorkers felt that his administration had devoted its major energies to mollifying the ghettos, rather than protecting middle-class comforts and safety. Both the Republican and Democratic primary elections produced candidates of a conservative, "law 'n order" approach to the city's problems. Mayor Lindsay did not attempt to win on municipal issues alone. Recognizing the growing opposition of New Yorkers to the Vietnam War, he campaigned against the Republican administration's foreign policy. This injection of questions that no city administration can solve apparently won back some of New York's traditional liberals, who were reluctantly preparing to vote for one or the other of the conservative candidates. Lindsay won the three-way contest with a scant 42 percent of the vote.

Feeling isolated from his former party, John Lindsay in 1972 declared himself a Democrat and launched a campaign for promotion from the nation's "second toughest job" to its toughest. His quest came to an end with the Florida Democratic presidential primary election.

Ironically, Governor Rockefeller promoted for a time in 1973 the candidacy of former Mayor Robert Wagner as the prospective nominee of both the Republican and Liberal parties and thus Lindsay's successor. Wagner—a Democrat—had been the very mayor replaced in 1966 by Lindsay, who argued that the city required new, youthful, and vigorous leadership. Only Robert Wagner's firm refusal to participate prevented the arrangement of a new fusion ticket with Wagner at its head.

The Accomplishments of Mayor Daley

The story of frustration and failure that characterizes the administration of America's large cities was not universal. One great city had a veteran mayor supported by the major newspapers of his city, the downtown businessmen, the taxpayers, and organized labor. He was periodically reelected with a substantial vote from the ghettos, and—because of his friendliness with labor—was able to provide such civic services as refuse collection, street repair, and public work at a lesser cost than in many other cities. His name was Richard J. Daley. The city was Chicago.

Mayor Daley is not normally considered a hero by the academic community. His national reputation stems from the Democratic National Convention of 1968, when Daley was a substantial influence in the convention, and his policemen confronted the young people and others who sought to turn the Democratic party around and onto the path of peace. The history of Mayor Daley, and the record of his accomplishments, is much more extensive than the vivid images of stones and tear gas and police clubs outside the Hilton Hotel. Some of those who accepted Mayor Daley as a figure of hate in 1968 have taken a second look at Chicago. They find that it works in a way that other cities do not.

Nurtured throughout his adult life by the Chicago Democratic organization, which he in turn served faithfully, Richard Daley became chairman of the Cook County Democratic party in 1953. In 1955, he was first elected as mayor. His power comes from the combination of the two positions. The Democratic organization in Cook County consists of some 35,000 persons who make their living from politics—some, but not all, as employees of the city of Chicago. This is old-style political patronage, and Mayor Daley is a past master of its manipulation. Loyalty to the party comes first, the welfare of the city second. That may be a better arrangement than in other cities, where separate groups of civic employees have pursued their own welfare, with little thought for the city's good.

Mayor Daley launched a program of public works aimed at revitalizing the downtown business area, thus winning endorsement (and campaign contributions) from contractors and businessmen. Supporting the police force materially and with law-and-order rhetoric, Daley has kept the support of the working-class "white ethnics." Peace in the ghettos has been purchased by infiltrating the neighborhood gangs with informers and providing jobs for blacks at the lowest rung of the city ladder.

Living a modest personal life, Mayor Daley has operated to maximize his political power, rather than his personal wealth. That power has grown as he has arranged further rewards for the already powerful elements of the Chicago business and economic structure. He has not used his power to redistribute wealth or political power; on the contrary, he has tended to solidify the existing structure of influence.

His gift to the poor has been an orderly society, not a free or open or equalitarian one.

Could Mayor Daley have used his power to become a political prophet, leading the disadvantaged faithful out of the urban wilderness? Or did his power come to him only because he did *not* confront the basic human problems of the core city—racism, segregation, dilapidated housing, miserable health services, expensive public transportation, and a collapsing public educational system?

The easiest answer is the cynical one. Mayor Daley's accomplishment may be viewed as keeping the poor under control while assuring that the system will arrange modest, but increasing, payoffs for those who already benefit from the city's operations. In his failure to confront the social problems of his city, Mayor Daley's organization operates to reward those interests that profit from the further decay of the city. It does not stimulate forces that could profit from rebuilding the city into a real community.

Mike Royko, Mayor Daley's very unofficial biographer, has suggested that the Daley system could be exported. He proposes to

franchise Mayor Daley. Just as Colonel Saunders sells fried chickens everywhere, our City Hall can sell Machine Government everywhere. For a percentage of a city's taxes—10 percent would be fair—Chicago's Machine would teach the floundering administrations in other cities our efficient ways, setting up model governments much like ours. . . . And atop every City Hall in the country, there would be a big sign proclaiming: "Chicago-Style Government—The Pickins are Good."[7]

That was no prescription for a place like Newark, New Jersey, with perhaps the highest tax rate in the nation, from which nearly all visible resources have already departed.

Moving the States to Action

These pictures of urban despair leave out a crucial governmental element. Ours is, after all, a federal system; the nation is made up of fifty states. Surely, state governments are concerned with the health of the cities within them; surely the national government can persuade the states to launch programs, with federal support, aimed at rescuing the cities.

It is true that, for the last three decades, urban problems have concerned politicians and bureaucrats throughout the nation: in the national government, in state governments, and in the cities themselves. When the elected representatives agree on a program, the bureaucrats at various levels cooperate in administering it, as local governments administer the welfare program, which draws financial support from Washington. Whether the various levels of bureaucracy interpret the legislation in the same way is another question.

But how responsive are the states to federal programs designed to meet specific needs, as defined by the federal government? Michael D. Reagan cites the example of the highway beautification program. Desecration of both urban and rural landscapes by the erection of advertising signs along federally financed roads had become a national scandal. Washington attempted to do something about it, but the lobbyists for the billboard industry were more powerful in state capitals than in Washington.

7. Mike Royko, "Selling Daley to the Nation," *Chicago Daily News*, April 9, 1971, quoted in *City* (May-June 1971), p. 61.

Sometimes the carrot needs to be supplemented by the stick: the highway beautification program provides an example. A 1958 statute offered to the states a 1 percent bonus on Interstate System highway grants if they controlled outdoor advertisements along the Interstate roads in accord with agreements filed with the Federal Highway Administration. By 1965, only twenty states had entered into bonus agreements and President Johnson changed the system by submitting legislation (quickly enacted) that imposed a 10 percent penalty on states that did not elect to control outdoor advertising and junkyards in accord with federal standards. As of September 1971 forty-seven states had enacted advertising laws. . . . It takes a lot to get the states to act![8]

The Appetite of the Automobile

Henry Ford had a dream. He dreamt of making an automobile — relatively cheap, dependable, and easy to maintain — that the common man could buy. Henry Ford had a technique — mass production — that made his dream come true. The Model T brought mobility to a nation, except when the rains came and turned the roads into impassable mud. State legislatures reacted to public pressures and developed paved highways. Congress soon hurried to help.

Burk Uzzle

8. Michael D. Reagan, *The New Federalism* (New York: Oxford University Press, 1972), pp. 117-118.

During the Eisenhower administration, highway planning reached its zenith. The national government committed itself to providing states with 90 percent of the cost of constructing 42,500 miles of super-highways—mostly four or more lane freeways—to link all parts of the nation, the program to be completed in 1974. During that same period, urban mass-transportation systems and railway passenger service continued their decline towards bankruptcy with little attention from Washington.

States built those sections of the Interstate system which would link suburbs conveniently with downtown business districts, incidentally making public transit less attractive to commuters. These urban super-highways plunged over and through the run-down housing of the central cities, destroying neighborhoods and consuming land. Only in 1968 did the national government add provisions which require persons displaced by highway construction to be given real help in finding a new place to live.

In city after city, the air grew foul with the burden of materials discharged by industry and by automobile exhausts. Henry Ford's dream of an inexpensive car for every man had by then been modified by the appeal to basic instincts (express your masculinity, buy a Thunderbird), annual model changes, the appeal of the four-wheeled status symbol, and rapid depreciation. Anyone could have a large and complicated automobile, if it were a few years old. Only European,

Charles Harbutt

and then Japanese, competition forced Detroit to offer smaller models.

Henry Ford's dream produced a nightmare for American cities: air pollution; destruction of the city's heart by concrete ribbons and ramps and interchanges; and the abandonment of the urban transit systems, as streetcar tracks were ripped up to make smooth streets, while passenger ferries were replaced by bridges and tunnels. Cars made living in the suburbs easier, and trucks made regional shopping centers and the decentralization of industry possible.

In 1973, America faced an energy crisis. There was talk of rationing gasoline in specific areas. The Environmental Protection Agency proposed listing the gas mileage (such as eight or nine miles per gallon for autos weighing 5,000 pounds) on the price stickers of new cars.

> In his later years, Henry Ford devoted much attention to the creation of Greenfield Village, near Dearborn. It is a monument to the lifestyle of nineteenth-century small-town America, destroyed by the automobile.

The Attractions of Suburban Life

Ramona Heights (not its real name) is a neighborhood, or tract, in Orange County, California. Its homes are valued at $45,000 to $65,000; schools, churches, and a shopping center are close by. The husbands work at the cluster of aerospace firms at the Orange County airport, or at businesses in the northern part of Orange County. A few drive 90 miles each day, commuting to Los Angeles.

Ramona Heights occupies a bluff half a mile inland from the Pacific ocean. The prevailing breeze from the sea keeps polluted air away from the neighborhood. The residents like it; except for the 1970-71 depression in the aerospace industry, the neighborhood is stable, with a slow turnover in home ownership. The residents have personalized their tract homes by individual landscaping and painting.

Maureen Barbera, mother of three, a former model married to a computer engineer, explains why she likes to live there.

MAUREEN: *I think it's a very easy life. The concerns are few. I'm always comparing myself back with what I think I would be feeling in Pasadena if we were there. Such as I can go to sleep happily at night without thinking that there was someone who was going to be coming in the door. And I don't have to worry about the schools. . . . I think the people here are quite congenial. It's healthy, it's happy; so far we have money to afford it.*

Maureen realizes that big cities have problems. She is grateful that, living in Ramona Heights, she doesn't have to think about them very much. When asked if she would approve of publicly subsidized housing being constructed in her neighborhood, she replied that she would not oppose it in principle, but she would try to sell her house and move to a neighborhood where there was none.

Other residents of Ramona Heights take a more active interest in urban problems. One of them is Martha Weeks, born in the Depression on a midwestern farm, who is now married to an aeronautical designer. When asked about President Nixon's 1969 proposal for reforming the welfare system, she answered,

MARTHA: *I'm not sure I have the knowledge to say. Because I took our daughter when she was six years old into Santa Ana to show her poverty, and she said, "Well, why don't"* — children her age were play-

ing in the dirt—"we take them home! We've got grass and parks and everything."

She couldn't understand it, and I found myself not being able to explain it to her. . . . That's why I'm one of the people that voted President Nixon into office. I thought he would have the knowledge to make these decisions for me, because I'm not capable of making them along that scope, although I've seen enough poverty in the Midwest as I was growing up.

The parents of Ramona Heights cultivate their gardens and take their families to the beach, plagued only a little by the suspicion that their children are not becoming acquainted with the full reality of the world. Down the street from the Weeks live Arthur and Tina Roybal. Tina is a teacher in the local city schools, and Arthur is an administrator in the county office of education.

TINA ROYBAL: I would like to live in a more ethnically represented community. If I had had this choice, say five years ago, and knew what I know now, I don't think I would have selected this area.

ARTHUR ROYBAL: We both feel that this is a very sterile community. I think our kids are losing one heck of a lot, by the protective environment we have. All life is not a Disneyland. And I think in Ramona Heights all life is a Disneyland.

TINA: It's not giving them a wide view of things as they really are, really. It's our little white tower. Yet, what do you do? Take them down to Main Street?

ARTHUR: That wouldn't solve it, no.

What does the future hold for relations between the cities and their suburbs?

"If you're not part of the solution, you're part of the problem."

Farewell to Mayor Stokes

Carl B. Stokes was elected mayor of Cleveland, Ohio, by a narrow margin in 1967. He was the first black mayor of a major American city, and his election seemed to promise great changes in an era of urban tension. The population of Cleveland was about 43 percent black, but the voting population was between 35 and 40 percent black. His election was made possible by support within the white business community. No miracles occurred in Stokes' first term, but he was able to win reelection in 1969 by an equally narrow margin.

Miracles may be necessary to save Cleveland. In 1960, it was America's eighth largest city, with a population of 876,000. In the following decade, it lost more than 100,000 people who fled to the suburbs, and lost more than 10 percent of its industrial tax base, as the jobs followed white workers into suburbia.

Cleveland's municipal workers, like those of New York, decided to protect their interests while the city still had resources to spend. In 1970, garbage collectors and bus drivers went on strike, and the city settled the disputes by increasing city employees' salaries at the cost of a $15 million annual budget increase. Policemen and firemen initiated an amendment to the city charter, approved by the voters, which guaranteed them a pay scale 3 percent higher than that paid by any other city in Ohio.

Mayor Stokes received federal grants for specific projects from Washington with little difficulty. In his first administration, he built 5,200 units of public housing, more than Cleveland had provided in the preceding thirty years. He instituted job-training programs, passed a tough air-pollution code, and increased expenditures for health facilities and law enforcement. To revitalize the city, he launched a program aimed at raising $12 million in private contributions. About half that sum was raised, but then the effort collapsed.

Mayor Stokes' troubles were mounting. Policemen were still bitter because, in 1968, he had called white policemen out of black neighborhoods after a riot in which ten persons were killed, including three policemen. He was committed to establishing public housing on a firm basis through the policy of "economic mix," by constructing public housing units in stable neighborhoods. White residents of the west side opposed his plans (for an economic mix would mean a racial mix as well), and so did middle-class blacks when low-cost housing was proposed for their neighborhood. The Cleveland City Council is elected by districts; Stokes charged that they tend to represent local interests, rather than concentrating on citywide policies. White city councilmen counter-charged that Stokes represented the city blacks and ignored the white population.

In order to meet the increased costs of city government, including the higher municipal salaries, Stokes proposed increasing the city income tax (levied on all who are paid in the city, regardless of where they live) from 1 percent to 1.8 percent and to retain all the proceeds in the city, rather than sharing them with the suburbs. Voters defeated the proposal in November 1970, with black neighborhoods supporting Stokes and white neighborhoods opposing him. In 1971, 1,700 city employees had to be laid off, curtailing garbage collections and eliminating street sweepers entirely. The police academy was closed; no new trainees would replace men retiring from the force.

The white business leaders withdrew their support of Carl Stokes. But it had never been very strong. Dr. Kenneth W. Clement, Stokes' one-time campaign manager, charged that "business supported Stokes because they wanted to keep the plantation quiet more than they wanted progress."[9]

In April 1971, Mayor Stokes announced that he would not be a candidate for reelection.

President Nixon Declares a Victory

As one of a series of radio addresses making up his public report on the State of the Union, President Nixon declared on March 4, 1973, that America's urban crisis is over. In spite of talk that urban life is on the brink of collapse, he said, "today, America is no longer coming apart."

9. Quoted in "The Troubles That Face Carl Stokes," *Business Week*, December 19, 1970, p. 46.

Bob Adelman

A principal reason for this new optimism was a recent set of crime statistics. It showed that the rate of reported major crimes had declined in more than half of the nation's largest cities. (He did not mention that the population of many of those cities is declining, and that the crime rate in most of their suburbs is increasing.) The president also mentioned increasing cleanliness (or lessened pollution) of the urban air, a decline in the number of persons living in substandard housing, and the fact that "once again the business world is investing in our downtown areas." And the number of urban riots has declined.

> What does all this mean for community life in America? Simply this: The hour of crisis has passed. The ship of state is back on an even keel, and we can put behind us the fear of capsizing.[10]

The most hopeful news President Nixon had to offer the cities was his plan to change the nature of federal help to the cities. He claimed that federal urban programs, planned and administered in Washington, had proven costly but produced few results. His plans for sharing federal revenues would reverse that pattern and return the power of planning and decision-making to "grassroots government." "The time has come," he said, "to reject the patronizing notion that Federal planners, peering over their pencils in Washington, can guide your lives better than you can."

In other speeches, and in his budget message to Congress, President Nixon made it clear that he intended nothing less than a restructuring of American federalism. For the cities, this would mean a withdrawal of direct national involvement in their problems. Instead, by sharing federal revenues — particularly from the income tax — Washington would help finance the solutions planned locally on the basis of local needs.

10. Quotations from President Nixon's speech are as reported in the *New York Times*, March 4, 1973.

As American involvement in Vietnam deepened, several war critics resolved the problem of protecting American prestige, while withdrawing from stalemate. They suggested that we simply declare victory and then bring home the troops.

Some would say that President Nixon adopted this scenario for Vietnam, but only after long delays and needless violence.

Did he also adopt it for America's cities?

The City as Reservation

Knowingly or not, President Nixon may have been assigning a new role to the cities. Norton Long has described it.

> The city is not a ship that will finally sink and have it over with. . . . The older city will inevitably remain, and it will have to find new specialties to justify its continued existence (such as it may be). It is now finding such specialties, and perhaps the most noteworthy of these is as an Indian reservation for the poor, the deviant, the unwanted, and for those who make a business or career of managing them for the rest of society. . . .
>
> The magic remedy for those who knowingly or unknowingly accept the city's future as an Indian reservation is federal or other revenue sharing. The term "sharing" disguises the fact that this is a transfer payment from the outside society. Insofar as it is not an act of pure charity, it is for services rendered, because no export of goods is involved. . . . Part of this payment—as with the Bureau of Indian Affairs—goes for the subsistence and needs of the natives, another part to the keepers, and still another to those who can somehow make a profit in this business. . . . Business and the productively employed, seeking escape from tax burdens, poor services, and crime, migrate or suburbanize. Even the keepers suburbanize. Black teachers and policemen follow whites to the suburbs.[11]

America in the 1970s contained a remarkable variety of places to live. They ranged from country estates and Texas ranches with oil pumping out of the ground to rat-infested tenements in the core cities. But most Americans chose to live in the suburbs, in single-family houses, with lawns and nearby parks. They preferred not to think too much about the problems of the cities they drove through or over to get to work.

Surrounded by filth and decay, the residents of the inner cities had the miracle of television to remind them that there is in America a rich variety of affluent life styles from which well-off families may select. But the dwellers in the core cities cannot choose. They have no alternatives.

When will the next wave of riots come?

11. Norton E. Long, "The City as Reservation," *The Public Interest* 25 (Fall, 1971): 32–33.

REFLECTIONS 10

Politics in Cities, Suburbs, and States

Two events in March 1973 highlighted the problems of America's cities. In Washington, President Nixon announced that "the hour of crisis has passed" in American community life. Financial support will come in the form of federal revenue sharing. Cities need no longer suffer from "extravagant, hastily passed measures" administered from Washington but "producing few results" on the local level.

In New York, Mayor John V. Lindsay announced that he would not seek reelection. Lindsay was described as "one of the last of the glamor politicians of the 1960s." He had spent seven years dealing with the problems of America's largest city: crime, drug addiction, race relations, rising welfare rolls, unemployment, the declining tax base, and the flight of middle-class residents to the suburbs. Those problems remained, and they were measurably worse, in 1973.

New York's problems were statistically more severe than those of cities with smaller populations, but typical of the troubles of America's cities. Crime was not the only problem to invade the surrounding suburbs—think of air and water pollution, the loss of open space, and recurring financial troubles in the public school system. Could these issues be handled by the many units of local government in the metropolitan areas, or would the suburbs shirk involvement in the cities' problems until new explosions came?

President Nixon assured us that revenue sharing would return the problem-solving function to "grassroots government." He presumably referred to the governments of America's towns, cities, counties, and states.

How healthy were the grassroots?

What Is a City?

Cities are synonymous with civilization.

Western civilization was born and knew its first flowering in the cities of ancient Greece.

Cities were associated with the development of tolerance and self-governing institutions. The farmer linked to the soil, imprisoned by the cycle of the seasons, responsible for servicing the daily needs of his animals, had no leisure time for cultivating the arts, or learning compassion for his fellow men.

Cities began as the marketplace for agricultural commerce and became the marketplace of artifacts and ideas.

Cities provided the optimum environment for stimulating the co-operative endeavors of men through loyalty to a community purpose. (The nation-state, vast in extent and terrible in its ambitions, is a more recent invention in the history of man.) The very word politics derives from πολις (polis), the word for the Greek city. In the Greek sense, politics refers to the relationships between men which enable them to pursue the good life together.

Cities are the home of liveliness and diversity. They house people of every age, occupation, and economic status.

Cities are where performers seek their audiences. They can be a home of laughter, where each new day brings the possibility of joy.

Cities provide a home for the most respected minds of the age as well as a refuge for the dissenters who are creating the next age.

Cities have been all these things. They have also been the hiding place of pestilence, the breeding ground of violence, the home of poverty, and vast garbage heaps.

What Are American Cities?

In the 1970s, American cities are The Problem.

One style of racial discrimination, in southern towns, was legal and public. Changing the laws was relatively easy — it only took sixty years. In the cities of the North, discrimination is more subtle, and it is private. Because it is not explicitly supported by the law, people in the North like to tell themselves that it doesn't exist.

When renewal of the central cities is attempted, the best efforts of the architects and planners frequently yield only a cold sterility that defeats the joyousness inherent in cities.

Cities are bankrupt, defeated by the political power of their suburban neighbors.

Cities are losing population. Developers can no longer earn a profit by building housing. Only office buildings are profitable in the core cities. They bring office workers in from the suburbs who strain the city's transportation facilities and add to the burden of its waste-disposal systems and increase air and noise pollution. The increasing cost of those systems is usually paid for by the declining city population.

The problems created by cities and their surrounding satellites were not anticipated by the men who established our federal structure. Urban problems have changed the nature of federalism in directions they could not have anticipated. Population growth and developments in the economic system have created sprawling urban areas that the traditional boundaries of the states cannot contain. The 1970 census revealed that the fifty most populous urbanized areas provided living space for 87,209,600 people. Fourteen of them, housing some 38,037,000 persons, included areas in two or more states.

The Changing Nature of the Federal System

Except for providing that states could cede ten square miles of territory for the establishment of the seat of the federal government[1] (which resulted in the District of Columbia), cities are not mentioned in the Constitution. The federalism established by the Constitution was an association between the states and the national government, and the first thirteen states existed before the national government was formed. In ratifying the Constitution, they retained their status as sovereign states, for the Constitution assigns ("delegates") the authority to make decisions in certain matters to the national govern-

1. Article I, Section 8, Paragraph 17.

ment, and all others are reserved for the states. In order to clarify this relationship, the Tenth Amendment was added as part of the Bill of Rights in 1791, to assure the people of the ratifying states that their rights would not be infringed by the newly created central government. However, Article VI, Section 2, of the Constitution provided that the laws of the United States "shall be the supreme Law of the Land," and the theory which held that states could implement their sovereign status by withdrawing from the Union was settled through force of arms by the Civil War.

State governments are unitary; they are not federal associations of cities, towns, and counties. Cities, and other units of local government, created for administrative convenience by the state legislatures, are not sovereign. For they can also be disbanded by state legislatures. In fact, this power of the states has been much diluted by the tradition of home rule. States establish procedures for the approval of city charters to set up governmental machinery which thereafter becomes practically independent of the state. Nevertheless, the states are the basic components of the federal system. For the national government to deal directly with cities (as in grants for urban renewal) or with counties (as in supporting sewage-treatment plants) would have been unthinkable to the authors of the Constitution. But such programs have been in operation for many years.

The Tenth Amendment states a "literary theory" of federalism, which some readers of the Constitution admire, but it has been destroyed by the march of events. Although states remain responsible—through their agents, the local governments—for the regulation of human relationships (marriage, inheritance, education, the selling of property, the licensing of businesses, protection from fire, and the apprehension of criminals), nearly all these functions of government are affected by actions of the U.S. Congress, the federal bureaucracy, or decisions of the Supreme Court. The federal government, for example, has ruled that states cannot prohibit interracial marriages; it collects a tax on inheritances; it finances eductional programs; it regulates the trade in stocks of corporations and investigates the safety of products; and it subsidizes the purchase of equipment by local police departments.

The financing of state and local governments through federal grants-in-aid has created a financial tangle that belies the literary theory of federalism. In the famous metaphor of Morton Grodzins, American federalism is no longer like a layer cake, with each level of government making its own decisions (and each capable of culinary integrity).[2] Rather, it is like a marble cake, with the tendrils of federal influence reaching throughout the batter, distinct but essential. That is, decisions concerning a particular purpose or function of government are made at all levels of government, and the various levels typically cooperate in implementing public policies.

As for the Tenth Amendment, the Supreme Court has held that it is little more than a truism, meaning "that all is retained which has not yet been surrendered."[3] But that was in 1941. President Nixon has new ideas about federalism.

The authority to interpret the constitutional meaning of federalism resides with the Supreme Court in Washington, to which the states may appeal. For the states, this is like playing a World Series game with the other team's captain and manager serving as umpires.

2. Morton Grodzins, "The Federal System," in President's Commission on National Goals, Goals for Americans (Englewood Cliffs, N.J.: Prentice-Hall, 1960).
3. U.S. v. Darby, 312 U.S. 100 (1941).

State Government: Assets and Liabilities

When President Franklin D. Roosevelt's programs brought hope for relief from economic misery, as well as expanding the scope of the federal government by assuming responsibilities the states were incapable of meeting, state governments were widely regarded as beyond reform. Hopes for governmental achievement were pinned to the New Deal, in the belief that more and more functions would be assumed by Washington and that the states would fade and die, as anachronistic appendages on the body politic.

American state governments were beset by problems then, and they still are. Most states function under constitutions written in the nineteenth century under the spell of Populist and Progressive distrust of the political process. State legislators tend to be poorly paid, to lack professional clerical or research assistance, and to operate in an atmosphere of public apathy (for public attention is captured by local, national, and international affairs). Several state legislatures are limited by their constitutions to infrequent meetings, in the apparent conviction that the longer legislators are kept out of the capital, the less damage they can do.

Just as the legislative branch of state government tends to be part-time, amateur, and restricted in authority, the influence of the executive is often hopelessly fragmented. States tend to elect several administrative officials—governor, lieutenant governor, treasurer, secretary of state, controller, attorney general—independently of each other. The result is that the executive branch is unlikely to speak with a single voice or to pursue a unified policy. Because state governments have a relatively low level of public visibility, their decisions are more likely to be dictated by the lobbyists for special interest groups than are the policies formulated by Congress.

In spite of these shortcomings, state governments have, almost unnoticed, developed bureaucratic competence unknown to them thirty or forty years ago, for the pattern of the New Deal and its successors was to finance specific programs which were administered by state and local governments. That competence is a national resource which must be developed.

The state governments, far from fading, provide an important ingredient in the "marble cake" of federalism. They raise money from taxes they do not spend, allocating it to local units. They spend money they do not raise, receiving it from Washington. They build highways and try to control air pollution, staff penitentiaries and try to rehabilitate criminals, administer colleges and adopt textbooks for local school boards. The states are permanent fixtures of the governmental landscape.

Furthermore, there have been signs of new vitality in state government. Several state constitutions have been revised in recent years, prodded by such organizations as the National Municipal League, with considerable positive effect. The Supreme Court's decisions establishing "one-man, one-vote" as the rule for legislative apportionment have meant that the boundaries of legislative districts must be changed after every federal census.[4] Even if this principle has not proven to be the salvation of the cities, as some of its proponents once claimed, it assures that the faces of the state legislators are more likely to change, and they are likely to be more in touch with their constituents. And legislatures have been voting themselves decent salaries, as well as clerical and research staffs that are independent of the executive branch. At least in the larger states, voters have accustomed themselves to professional, full-time legislatures, rather than

4. See above, Chap. 5, pp. 202-207.

the amateur, part-time concept of the legislator's role developed in the nineteenth century. However, with national television networks providing news for most of the population, state legislatures receive comparatively little public attention. Special-interest lobbyists operate more blatantly in state capitals than they can in Washington.

Can state governments really be called grassroots governments? The bureaucracy in Sacramento or Albany or Lansing can seem as remote and unresponsive to the citizens of California or New York or Michigan as federal employees in Washington, D.C.

American Cities in Political Thought and Action

In the 1970s, the compelling drama, the challenge to American ideals, and the testing ground of a post-industrial democracy are in the cities. Intertwined in relationships with other governmental elements—federal, state, and the municipalities encircling them in a suburban ring —the cities are the place of action, where the future of America, if there is to be one, is taking shape. The urban crisis, which seems permanent and insoluble, is uniquely a product of the twentieth century.

To understand the cities' present, and to get a view of their alternative possible futures, a look at their past is necessary.

The Agrarian Tradition
The authors of the Constitution were men of substance and civility. They were, in the best sense, *urbane*. This did not mean, however, that they greatly admired cities, or that they felt that America should develop urban centers to rival London and Paris. Considerable sentiment held that the citizenry of independent judgment necessary to the proper functioning of democracy could only be achieved in a nation in which landed property was widely distributed—a nation of small farmers. The most vigorous statement of this view was made by the man conspicuously absent from the Constitutional Convention, Thomas Jefferson.

> While we have land to labour then, let us never wish to see our citizens occupied at a workbench . . . let our workshops remain in Europe. It is better to carry provisions and materials to workmen there, than to bring them to the provisions and materials, and with them, their manners and principles. The loss by transportation of commodities across the Atlantic will be made up in the happiness and permanence of government. The mobs of great cities add just so much to the support of pure government, as sores do to the strength of the human body.[5]

This passage is from Jefferson's *Notes on Virginia*, written in 1781 in response to a Frenchman's questions about his native land. Long before Jefferson became president, he acquiesced in the development of American manufacturing on grounds of national security. The hostility of England to the new American nation, and the general dangers of international affairs, indicated that the United States should become self-sufficient in all realms of endeavor. But cities were only to be permitted as necessary, not welcomed as desirable.

The first census, in 1790, revealed that just 10 percent of Americans lived in cities; by 1860, the percentage had grown only to 25 percent. For the first century of American democratic institutions, their development was in the hands of a rural majority. Jefferson's dislike of cities became a recurrent theme in American political and social thought. The agrarian ideology of the independent man unfettered by government intervention became an element in the philosophy of laissez-faire capitalism. It served well those captains of industry whose operations created urban America.

The strength of the agrarian ideology did not wane, even when city dwellers became a majority. In the nineteenth and early twentieth centuries, political movements gained much of their strength from identifying the city as the home of the enemy:

> Defenders of slavery argued that the slave in the field was more healthy in body and soul than the wage earner in the city. Jefferson's dislike of cities was used to contradict his proposition that all men are created equal.

> Populism under the leadership of William Jennings Bryan was essentially an agrarian revolt against the presumed moral degeneracy of the cities.

> The Progressive movement was strongest in rural areas and small towns; it contained more than a hint of disdain for the cities' immigrant laborers.

> The Anti-Saloon League was strongest in country churches; the city, after all, was the home of the saloon.

> When the Ku Klux Klan was reborn in the 1920s, its emphasis on native Americanism expressed fear and hatred of the cities.

> The presidential campaigns of Al Smith, the Catholic Tammany Hall Democrat who opposed Prohibition, in 1924 and 1928, were in part a contest between urban America on one side and rural and small-town America, on the other. The cities lost. Calvin Coolidge, the 1924 winner, had an annual picture taken on a farm to renew symbolic ties with the soil. Herbert Hoover, the 1928 winner, was born in West Branch, Iowa, and became the spokesman of rugged individualism.

5. Quoted in Max Beloff, *Thomas Jefferson and American Democracy* (New York: Collier Books, 1962), p. 82.

Who Understands the Cities?

The historic strain of anti-urban sentiment, and its political success, provided all the justification needed by state legislatures when they ignored city growth in the apportionment of state legislative seats and congressional districts. The practice grew increasingly scandalous for half a century before the Supreme Court intervened.

Not all attitudes toward cities were simple negativism. Yet, even when reformers regarded the cities with sympathy and hope, they failed to understand them. The Progressives were appalled by the corruption of urban party organizations. Seeing only the corruption, they failed to understand that essential social services were performed by the city machines which the public ideology did not permit government itself to attempt. City machines served as employment agencies, as the managers of charitable enterprises, as social organizations, and as the partner of the public schools in the political socialization process of immigrant families. The machines were usually both human and humane.

The Progressives saw parties, and party politics, as evil. They wanted to replace politics with administration, and overrule corruption (and humanity) with efficiency. The Progressive movement had the establishment of nonpartisan local elections as a principal rallying cry. The movement was partially successful in the Midwest (Chicago excepted) and nearly totally successful in the West. But the partisan habits of New York and Philadelphia prevailed.

If city politics were not understood, it should be no surprise that other attributes of the city were unappreciated. Reformers who visited crowded urban neighborhoods did not recognize the important functions of preserving vitality, excitement, and public order performed by mixed land use and the variety of enterprises and peoples. They saw only the crowding.

As one result, the infant profession of city planning was staffed by people who did not understand cities and were, in many cases, hostile to their very nature. This outcome was not unique to the United States. Ebenezer Howard, pioneer English planner of the turn of the century, hoped to convert cities into a working-class version of the country squire's home, and the cult of "greenbelts" was founded. France's Le Corbusier adapted that notion to the motor age, designing towers in a park served by great arching freeways; his vision influenced the architects of the Pruitt-Igoe project in St. Louis. Daniel Burnham of Chicago inspired the construction of a hundred civic centers that isolate government from the other activities of the city and are quickly surrounded by slums.

In the hands of the planners, "unstudied, unrespected, cities have served as sacrificial victims."[6]

Local Government: Administration, Not Politics

Possibly because the Constitution did not mention city government, while that document was regarded as settling most questions of political structure, big city government in the United States developed haphazardly. By 1900 it was dominated by party machines which made corrupt alliances with big business in such matters as street railway franchises and lighting contracts. (Methods for regulating business were not specified in the Constitution, either.)

Progressives saw the urban political machine as the essence of civic degeneracy. They sought—by political means—to replace city politics

6. Jane Jacobs, *The Death and Life of Great American Cities* (New York: Random House, 1961), p. 25. Mrs. Jacobs's persuasive analysis should be read by everyone interested in how cities work.

with professional administration. The two most persuasive devices they proposed were nonpartisan local elections and the city manager form of government. The manager replaces the mayor, traditionally a political animal, with the skills of professional public administration. The manager serves at the pleasure of the city council, which makes decisions of broad policy. The council is made up of leading citizens so well established that they need no salaries and are not tempted by graft. The entire system is insulated—at least in theory—from the effect of political developments outside its boundaries when the councilmen are elected without party labels. Nonpartisan elections need not be joined with the council-manager form of government. But the combination tends to make a city government that resists not only petty graft but also several normal functions of the democratic process.

By 1960, the manager form had been adopted by a majority of the medium-sized cities in the United States, while the traditional form of mayor and council was retained by a majority of the very large cities and the very small cities. Apparently, the largest cities required an adept politician at their head who could resolve conflicts between a variety of groups and demands; the middle-sized cities were homogeneous enough to sustain the myth that professional techniques can substitute for political bargaining in all but the most crucial decisions; in the smallest municipalities, the local power structure was so well established, and the local folkways so eccentric, that a trained professional making decisions by the book would only get himself into trouble.[7]

The conviction of the Progressive reformers that politics should be replaced by administration had not done irrevocable damage. Cities gravitated toward the governmental form that was appropriate for their size and political circumstances. This did not mean that cities were uniformly well governed, for the quality of city government depended on the competence of its leadership, the interest and good sense of the people, and the adaptability of local institutions and traditions to the problems of change.

In metropolitan areas, political institutions, and thus the influence of the democratic process, were hopelessly fragmented. Not only were the central cities strangled by a ring of suburbs; special needs of metropolitan areas were served by commissions and authorities (ranging from the Port Authority of New York to California's mosquito abatement districts) which overlapped political boundaries. In a typical metropolitan county, police protection and administrative services might be provided by a municipality; fire protection by a volunteer district with quite separate boundaries; water by yet a different district (and the water board might not agree with the fire commissioners as to the location and need for hydrants); roads would be maintained by the county; garbage be collected by a private business; and a separate sanitation district be struggling, with the urging of the state department of health, to construct adequate sewers for the area.

Thus the housekeeping tasks of civilization are divided among different agencies holding jurisdiction over separate but overlapping areas. Each of the boards or commissions is formally responsible to the people, either through election, or through appointment by elected officials, such as city councils or county boards of supervisors. Each is empowered to tax the people to finance the services provided. These agencies may be staffed by competent professionals trained to discharge well their narrow responsibilities. But there is no device for

7. See John H. Kessel, "Government Structure and Political Environment: A Statistical Note about American Cities," *American Political Science Review* 56 (September 1962): 615–620.

coordinating the response of the various agencies to the needs of the people, and no way for the people to determine the development of fragmented governmental services.

The growth of population and the increasing complexity of governmental tasks has placed intolerable strains upon America's local governments. City government was swept by a wave of reform in the early twentieth century. The single major city which retains a nineteenth-century machine—Chicago—seems better equipped for survival than does New York. But this is a financial judgment. It does not mean that the citizens of Chicago know more joy or culture.

In general,

> The nation's courthouses and city halls have often seemed to lack the vision and dedication—as well as the financial resources—to diagnose conditions, devise solutions, and make vigorous responses. New functions needed to meet new situations are neglected by most local units, and old functions are conducted without benefit of new techniques. By default, initiatives have commonly been left to more resourceful federal forces. Cast in an archaic mold, unable to cope with new issues, many—if not most—local governments are centers of strenuous resistance to change of any kind.[8]

Three cheers for grassroots government!

The City Was Always a Boiling Pot

Much of the anti-urban feeling expressed in American politics after the turn of the century represented a rear-guard reaction to the fact of urbanization. It was a nostalgia for the simpler life of the past. The mechanization of agriculture turned rural attention to the opportunities of the city: industry, commerce, education, and culture. The surplus children of the one-family farms headed toward the cities, and the small towns that had a vital role as railway junctions emptied and died with the coming of cars and trucks. Although they gave their political allegiance to Coolidge and Hoover, Americans were also voting with their feet. They were voting for a taste of city life. Then a move to the suburbs.

The cities were in ferment.

8. Committee for Economic Development, *Modernizing Local Government: To Secure a Balanced Federalism.* (New York: Committee for Economic Development, 1966), p. 9.

Bruce Davidson

> The city was never a melting pot. It was always a boiling pot.
> ... Many problems were indeed settled peacefully. For many
> others violence was required; it was an integral part of urban
> life from the start. Still more often problems were solved neither
> by peaceful adjustment nor by confrontation. The pot simply,
> and quite literally, boiled over. For many escapees there was the
> West, but for most there was escape to the suburbs. In no sense
> is this a new pattern.
>
> ... The reasons for growth through escape to the periphery
> were also the same, even before the Automobile Age. The rea-
> sons were hate and fear, an age-old treadmill. Yankees hated
> Germans and Irish, and Yankees escaped to whatever was a
> suburb at the time of the escape. Germans and Irish hated and
> feared Jews, Italians, Bohemians, Poles and Greeks—and they
> escaped. All of them hated and feared the varieties of poor white
> trash, who inherited the third and fourth generations of central
> ruins in the wake of their escaping predecessors. Common fear
> and hatred of the Negro is one more turn in the cycle. . . .[9]

The internal combustion engine made Detroit the center of a
technology that conquered the developed world. In the very process
of creation, however, it destroyed Detroit as a city. Before a diversity
of peoples could form at the center and through their very abrasive-
ness create the tolerance that is essential to urban vitality, the urge
to decentralize took command, and automobiles supplied the means.
Detroit, with a center that hardly attracts a public after seven o'clock
at night, became an ever-growing circle of failing suburbs ("slurbs")
that provide low-density housing—the absurd realization of Jefferson's society of small landholders; each dilapidated house on 5,000
square feet of land—but hardly any of the stimulation of the spirit or
celebration of the arts that make a city worthy of the name.

9. Theodore J. Lowi, *The End of Liberalism* (New York: Norton, 1969), p. 194.

Like the towns spreading outward from Detroit, other suburbs adopted population density as the single important determinant of the quality of life. Across America, thousands of municipalities adopted zoning codes that began, in typical fashion, "'AAA—single-family dwellings each contained on a minimum of 15,000 square feet. . . .'" Thus was the Jeffersonian mystique reincarnated. The amount of land was identified with the achievement of the good life, even when the land was not used to achieve economic independence through agriculture.

But it was not so simple. Population densities are less in Bedford-Stuyvesant than in Harlem; both are scenes of poverty and squalor; but Harlem has a developed culture which holds it together as a community, while Bedford-Stuyvesant does not. The myth of low population density as the route to happiness was destroyed by the Watts riots. Watts is a Los Angeles neighborhood of one- and two-story houses, a third of them owned by their occupants, each standing on its separate lot. In 1964, Los Angeles was labeled the best city in the country for black housing—according to traditional statistical measures—by the Urban League. Yet the six days of rioting in Watts in the summer of 1965 took 34 lives, injured 1,032 people, and destroyed $40 million of property. Low population density does not prevent the growth of frustration and despair, accented by racism; separation from one's neighbors may reinforce that despair.

Some cities are revising their zoning codes to permit the construction of planned developments that are more than detached houses gathered in the dull blocks defined by parallel concrete streets. Living units may share walls, yet be designed to assure privacy. This yields land for pedestrian paths, trees, and readily accessible playgrounds (or mini-parks). Some of these codes permit the variety of living accommodations needed for the population diversity that assures liveliness and interest.

But such developments remain expensive. Developed for profit, they serve only upper-middle-class suburbanites. True diversity of population will come only with massive rent subsidies supported by public policy—and the suburbanites usually oppose such policies.

The Suburban Myth

The 1970 census revealed what had long been predicted: the flight from the cities was unabated, and the plurality of the American population now lives in the suburbs.

The shift in the balance of population suggested a shift in the political balance of power. Commentators hastened to explain the "suburban vote." Many of them had recourse to a convenient image of suburbia, which had been formulated in the 1950s by journalists and popular social critics and had been so well implanted in the minds of intellectuals that the careful work of many sociologists in the 1960s could not dislodge it.

The myth of suburbia was formulated in the years following World War II, when housing tracts marched across the suburban landscape. The houses, built hastily from similar plans, looked quite alike; it seemed logical to assume that their occupants thought and acted alike. Analyses of the Eisenhower election of 1952 suggested that suburbanites vote Republican, concluding that a move to suburbia and a mortgaged home tends to convert Democrats into Republicans. Overlooked in the analysis was the fact that the cities also voted heavily for the Republican ticket in 1952; almost everybody liked Ike.

Studies of individual suburbs were subsequently published. They focused on middle- and upper-middle-class areas, which were populated by "organization men"[10] scrambling up the corporate ladder. Indeed, these men were found to exhibit personality characteristics that were new in America. Rather than acquiring tastes and planning careers that were based on an inner sense of rightness and self-respect, they absorbed opinions and values from those around them. They were "other-directed."[11] They lived in houses with picture windows; but the window had no view except for identical houses across the street. The picture windows functioned only to display the house-holder's possessions to passers-by and prove his ability to acquire the currently stylish possessions.

The suburban myth ignored the fact that all suburbs are not alike. In fact, variety is as great among suburbs as it is among cities. There are working-class suburbs, as well as middle-class suburbs; there are relatively poor, as well as rich, ones; not all of them are the home of young families, for entire towns have been developed to which only the retired are admitted. There are industrial suburbs, containing the businesses that have followed their executives, and brought their white workers, to suburbia. The attitudes (political and otherwise) found in suburbia tend to vary greatly according to the social and economic characteristics of the particular suburb. A remarkable variety of political viewpoints can be found within a few blocks of each other in a single suburban tract.[12] On national and state issues, the suburban vote is far from monolithic.

> The crucial question is: must the suburbs remain sworn enemies of the central cities that nurture them? Or can entire metropolitan areas somehow work together, before it is too late?

Charles Harbutt

10. William H. Whyte, Jr., *The Organization Man* (New York: Simon and Schuster, 1956).
11. David Riesman et al., *The Lonely Crowd* (New Haven: Yale University Press, 1950).
12. For a demonstration of this diversity in a tract in Orange County, California—considered the heartland of ultraconservatism — see Karl A. Lamb, *As Orange Goes: Twelve California Families and the Future of American Politics* (New York: Norton, forthcoming).

The Strangulation of the Cities

Was the race outwards from the city center propelled exclusively by hate and fear? In many cases, there was a conscious choice of positive values. Young parents adopt a suburban life-style because it seems designed to fulfill a family-centered ethic. How many dreary subdivisions have been defended by their residents in all sincerity as "a great place to bring up children!" And, as soon as the new residents move in their furniture, they develop a list of babysitters, so they can escape the children for an evening and return to the big-city scene.

The suburb, like the entire metropolitan area of which it is a part, achieves meaning from its relation to the central city, which supplies the cultural and commercial resources that the suburbanite draws upon in his daily job and his weekend entertainment. The metropolitan area remains a single area economically and culturally, leap-frogging the boundaries of states, counties, and municipalities, with the internal combustion engine making possible that unity by facilitating the participation of all in the attractions of civilzation.

But politics is concerned with paying the costs of civilization: providing transportation and waste removal, supervising the construction of housing. Because his town is separately incorporated, the suburbanite escapes paying many of those costs. The central cities are strangled by the ring of independent municipalities surrounding them.

The great cities of America have lost population in the last decade because of the flight to the suburbs and the conversion of former dwelling space to commercial uses. The consolidation of the five boroughs of Manhattan to form greater New York City took place in 1898; no further territory has been annexed since then. Similar accounts could be given of Chicago, Philadelphia, Baltimore, Pittsburgh, San Francisco, and Cincinnati. Los Angeles is an exception, but it is a city whose outlines were not firm before the advent of the automobile, and many charge that it remains a city in name only—"twenty-seven suburbs in search of a city."

The fact that suburbs incorporate as independent municipalities has other important political and social consequences:

The attention of the suburbanite is distracted from metropolitan problems to focus narrowly upon those institutions that attracted him to suburbia.

Political energies are drawn into contests over the administration and curriculum of the public schools, for they are a key factor in making the town a good place to bring up children.

The racial makeup of the suburb can be controlled implicitly through zoning regulations which require a large and expensive amount of land for each house and thus eliminate all but the most wealthy from residence.

A concern for the quality of the schools is bound up in the concern for maintaining property values; if the school is integrated, many parents may decide that the town is no longer so good a place for the children.

The intense localization of political concerns, coupled with the barrage of information about national political issues from the mass media, may make the suburbanite insensitive to political developments on the state level. Yet he owes the allegiance of citizenship to the state, not to the suburb. Governors and state legislators become known for their attitudes on issues—school curricula, safety in the streets—which are really local issues, while the bureaucracies of the state continue unabated the building of highways and shortsighted management of public resources, safe from public attention.

Theodore Lowi has proposed that the boundaries of school districts in the Chicago area be redrawn so that each district originates in the black ghetto and extends like a wheel spoke reaching out to a rim in the heart of suburbia. Districts would reach as far north as Glencoe, as far west as Glen Ellyn and as far south as Flossmoor. With busing, every school in every district would be assigned a black population of 15 percent.[6] This would assure black children of a chance to break out of the cycle of cultural deprivation and white children a chance to break out of the cycle of fear and guilt fostered by racial separatism. With the issue of school integration settled, guaranteed that no school would be flooded by a black majority, suburbanites would take a more relaxed attitude toward the gradual integration of housing; and property values—so dependent on perceived advantages for the children—would be preserved.

The proposal pursues the logic of a single fact: the residents of a metropolitan area that is a single economic and cultural unit should not escape responsibility for the political problems of that area by retreating behind artificial suburban boundaries.

But a single metropolitan area contains hundreds of independent and semi-autonomous "grassroots governments," each serving a limited vision of local needs and showing no concern for the welfare of the entire region.

The New York metropolitan area is served by 1,400 units of government.

Some enthusiastic supporters saw great promise for the cities in the Supreme Court's "one man, one vote" reapportionment decisions. They argued that cities were denied appropriate political power in state legislatures that overrepresented rural areas. But in many states, reapportionment according to population meant new political power for the burgeoning suburbs. And the suburban representatives could be even less sympathetic to city needs than the farmers, who at least regarded the cities as their markets. The suburbanites went to the suburbs to escape the city's problems and were not interested in sharing the costs of their solution.

It is now clear that the apportionment of legislative bodies into districts of equal population is not, by itself, the keystone of strong or effective state and local government.

Help from Washington

The economic collapse triggered by the stock market crash of 1929 brought the major institutions of American society to the edge of destruction: the banking system, state and local governments, and the rudimentary arrangements for private and public charity that provided such assistance as was available for the elderly, the disabled, and the unemployed. Dedicated to limiting governmental authority, the American Constitution did not provide machinery for responding

13. Lowi, *The End of Liberalism,* pp. 275-280.

to nationwide economic disaster. Or so the Supreme Court later claimed.[14]

Within a few days of his inauguration, FDR proposed legislation to restore the banking system. Next came programs to provide employment through public works projects, to support sagging agriculture, to develop the Tennessee Valley, to regulate the stock market, to refinance home mortgages, and to restore "free competition" to the economy under the banner of the National Recovery Administration. Only in 1935 did the Social Security Act provide the first federal support to the blind, the disabled, and fatherless families with dependent children.

None of these programs was designed to aid cities *as cities;* rather, they were aimed at specific problems which plagued the cities and the countryside alike. And, while opponents of the federal programs cried that they were destroying the federal system by centralizing authority in Washington, many federal programs provided grants-in-aid to the states, in place of dealing directly with the recipients of aid, and, in other cases, programs were administered by existing state authorities. Thus, while a generation was told that state governments were a vanishing anachronism, state governments were developing professional bureaucracies and administrative competence unknown before the New Deal.

This development of new competence was largely overlooked by the spokesmen of interest-group liberalism, oriented towards federal solutions, who could see only the shortcomings of the states. Indeed, federal grants frequently served purposes for which they were not intended, either because of inadequate conception in Washington, or deliberate policy choices made by their recipients.

More recently, in both North and South, local authorities involved in the programs of slum clearance and urban renewal used them to concentrate minority populations in the ghettos. The impact of federally guaranteed mortgage insurance was to subsidize the growth of the white suburbs. Congress had not prohibited such use of the programs, and the separate agencies administering various special programs were ill-equipped to discover a single national purpose when Congress could not find one.

Furthermore, as the suburbs grew in wealth and power, there was a renewal of conflict between the cities and the state legislatures. Often this conflict was reinforced by political confrontations, as Republican governors of Illinois confronted the Democratic machine of Chicago, or the politicians of upstate New York out-maneuvered the administration of New York City.

In the face of such political realities, the cities approached Washington directly, by-passing the state capitals. Since the time of Franklin D. Roosevelt, the necessity of forging a winning coalition in the Electoral College has made presidential candidates particularly sensitive to the needs of cities, for the vote of minorities—both racial and religious—living in the big cities held the political balance of power in several large states.[15]

The Democratic presidents who followed Franklin D. Roosevelt attempted to make a meaningful response to the needs of their urban constituents, and Republican Dwight Eisenhower made no effort to dismantle the programs begun by his predecessors. But each new national administration merely added to existing programs. There was no effort to consider the problems of the cities anew, no suggestion that the premises underlying federal urban programs should be re-

14. See above, pp. 197–199, for an account of the contest between the New Deal and the Supreme Court.
15. This poses a strong argument against the direct election of the president.

examined. The programs, and the Washington offices that administered them, grew. They grew in number, in budget, in personnel, and
in bureaucratic complexity. A new cabinet-level agency, the Department of Housing and Urban Development, was created. But just as
many urban programs were managed by the Department of Health,
Education, and Welfare, while the food stamp program (intended to
prevent starvation) was assigned to the Department of Agriculture,
which tends to be most sympathetic to the concerns of corporate
farmers. City governments maintained full-time offices to keep track
of available federal programs and procedures for applying for them.
A few mayors based their reputations for effectiveness upon the ability to find money in Washington, but many found the applications,
and the federal rules governing the administration of grants-in-aid,
too complicated to bother with. There were 530 different grant programs in 1970.

Poverty and the Cities
One of the programs that President Nixon would later see as mistaken
was the Community Action Program (CAP) of the Office of Economic
Opportunity. The legislation included the statement that grants made
by the program would require the "maximum feasible participation"
of local residents. The phrase received little notice during congressional debate. The drafters (members of the Johnson Administration)
said that its purpose was to ensure that southern blacks would not be
excluded from the benefits. In fact, they had accepted an academic
theory which holds that participation is essential to social change.

CAP established advisory groups on a neighborhood basis in direct
contact with the Washington-based administrators, by-passing the
city governments. Mayors reacted with hostility and suspicion. By
concentrating on tiny areas, action proposals were focused on narrow
and particular demands, rather than significant reforms. The advisory
groups were established with great public fanfare. When the money
came, it was never enough, and its impact upon poverty remained
negligible. CAP yielded the highest possible expectations and the
greatest possible disappointments: the "maximum feasible
misunderstanding."[16]

The shattering discovery of the Depression was that the economy
does not guarantee employment to all men able and willing to work.
Unemployment, and resulting poverty, struck at random in the 1930s,
as the result of local conditions and the misfortunes of private enterprises. Unemployment compensation and other welfare measures
were developed to protect individuals against the random accidents
of the economic system.

In present-day America, poverty does not strike at random. It results from the impact upon individuals of a series of experiences:
welfare-dependent families; inadequate ghetto schools; racial barriers
in employment and housing; the flight to the suburbs of energetic
young families, followed by businesses; the elimination of unskilled
jobs by advancing automation; and the exhaustion of natural resources such as the veins of coal in Appalachia.

These are the causes of poverty. To eliminate them involves nothing less than changing the system that chains some Americans to the
culture of poverty because of their race, their lack of education, and
their place of residence.

16. Daniel P. Moynihan has told the story of CAP in *Maximum Feasible Misunderstanding*
(New York: Free Press, 1969). The analysis here also depends on Lowi, *The End of Liberalism*, pp. 226–249.

Of Government and Taxes

The performance of the component governments within the federal system is related to the separate systems of taxation that each developed in response to historical forces. Some taxes appear more fair than others, depending on one's standard of fairness. Should the burden of financing government fall heaviest on those most able to pay, or should it fall more heavily upon those who benefit from its services? Such questions are of interest to philosophers and economists, but they seem academic to the mayors of large American cities. The mayors will take money wherever they can find it.

The Income Tax: A Federal Monopoly
The federal tax system as it now exists is a fairly recent development. For America's first 120 years, the national government relied almost exclusively on excise taxes, levied on the sale of particular commodities, such as whiskey, tobacco, or gasoline. This revenue was supplemented by the income from customs duties (or tariffs) imposed upon goods imported from foreign nations. From the beginning, excise taxes were recognized as placing an unfair burden on the poor; the Whiskey Rebellion of 1794 was a revolt by farmers against just such a tax. An income tax was used to meet the emergency of Civil War, but it lapsed in 1872. Within two decades, the public recognized the extremes of wealth and poverty created by that era and demanded that the wealthy pay a greater share of governmental costs. The income tax was reinstated in 1894, only to be declared unconstitutional in 1895.[17] The Supreme Court decision was nullified by adoption of the Sixteenth Amendment in 1913, and a personal income tax was enacted that same year. Together with the corporate income tax, enacted in 1909, it forms the backbone of the federal revenue system.

The income tax rate established in 1913 was 1 percent, with a surtax of up to 6 percent, after figuring exemptions. The theoretical maximum rate rose to 94 percent during World War II; it is now 70 percent.

But the tangle of exemptions, special privileges, tax concessions for particular enterprises, and special methods of figuring income have grown since 1913 and created two new professions: the tax accountant, and the tax lawyer.

In the economist's language, the federal income tax is *elastic*. Its yield varies with prosperity. When the national product increases, reflected by personal and corporate income, so does federal revenue. At present, revenue from the income tax increases at least $7 billion a year, with no increase in the rates.[18] Because federal financing is more dependable, state and local governments have long sought help from Washington.

By 1971, thirty-nine states had also enacted income taxes. The rates, however, were kept low or moderate. States compete against each other, fearing high tax rates will drive productive businesses or individuals to locate elsewhere. If their investment in that particular state is too profound to be easily uprooted, such enterprises will try to send more congenial representatives to the state capital.

17. See above, p. 194, for an account of *Pollock* v. *Farmer's Loan and Trust Company*.
18. Michael D. Reagan, *The New Federalism* (New York: Oxford University Press, 1972), p. 105.

The federal government enjoys a virtual monopoly of the income tax, or at least monopolizes its two advantages of being graduated (taxing heaviest those who can afford to pay) and elastic. State income taxes are very pale imitations.

Financing State Governments

From colonial times until the Depression of the 1930s, the main source of both state and local taxation was the general property tax —a tax upon land and the improvements constructed on it. During the Depression, there were many tax delinquencies, for owners had no cash to pay taxes. The states turned to other, more dependable sources of revenue. Local governments—cities, counties, and townships—claimed the property tax for their own.

States turned to excise taxes, which were often approved by the voters when their proceeds were reserved for a specific purpose, such as the dedication of gasoline tax revenues for road-building, or the provision of cigarette taxes for education. But such taxes had limits, and many states had recourse to general sales taxes, which added a tax to whatever items were purchased in a retail store.

The principal objection to such taxes is that they are regressive. Their burden falls most heavily on those least able to pay. Poor people must spend their entire income to acquire the amenities of life, while the rich invest a portion of their income, or save it. If all purchases are taxed at a uniform rate, the poor family will pay a much larger proportion of its income in sales taxes than will a wealthy family. In some states, this bitter result of the sales tax is eased by exempting "essential" products (such as food, milk, clothing, and prescription drugs—but never beer or cosmetics) from the sales tax.

As noted above, thirty-nine states have seen fit to add modest income taxes to their repertoire of revenue-gathering.

Problems of the Property Tax

When a tax was first levied upon land in colonial America, it was an equitable tax. In an economy of farmers and small merchants, the ownership of land and its improvements (real estate) was a measure of a family's productivity, and thus of its ability to pay. This is no longer true. Think of the retired couple, living on a fixed income, who buy a cottage in a quiet suburban hamlet. The developers come, young families move in, and the school tax rate climbs steadily. Or consider a divorced wife with small children who receives nothing but the mortgaged house in the settlement. The busiest tax assessor imaginable cannot keep up with changing values, and property owners resent the resulting inequities.

National and state legislators respond to the intense and well-organized pressures of groups demanding costly services, despite the more diffuse grumbling of taxpayers. The property tax rate is usually voted on directly, in such cases as approving bond issues for the construction of new school buildings. The citizen is then able to vote directly against new taxation. School districts are the most frequent victims of general taxpayer discontent.

Large cities have been forced to seek other revenue sources. Some have imposed sales taxes in addition to the sales taxes imposed by their states. Some have added small taxes upon income. A few have attempted to impose "commuter taxes," collected from the paychecks of persons who work in the city (and thus burden its facilities during the daytime) but who live elsewhere, with the reasonable claim that persons who earn their livelihood in the city should help sustain it.

This sets the suburbs to screaming.

The fiscal reality of federalism is that the national government has the most efficient system of gathering revenue. (Whether the federal tax burden is equitably shared is another question.) But the maintenance of an environment that will support civilization is the responsibility of local governments.

The large cities, one by one, are going bankrupt.

Toward a "New Federalism"

When Richard Nixon was first elected president in 1968, he had not offered a package of new programs for the salvation of the cities. He did not owe his election to urban minorities; he did not need to make a symbolic show of attacking their problems. On the advice of his then chief domestic adviser, Daniel P. Moynihan, he determined to make no immediate sharp breaks with the previous administration. Since he had been elected by only a plurality in a three-way contest, an emphasis on governmental continuity looked best. Domestic considerations were soon overshadowed by the problems of achieving "peace with honor" in Vietnam. Some notable domestic proposals—including revenue sharing—were made in 1969, but they were not pursued vigorously in Congress.[19]

President Nixon's first term was nearly completed before he could claim congressional approval of a major new domestic policy. Congress passed a version of his proposal for general revenue sharing in late 1972. The idea of general revenue sharing was to provide funds raised through the federal income tax to state and local governments for which they need not apply, to be spent without restrictions from Washington. Made retroactive to January 1, 1972, this legislation provided $5.3 billion dollars for state and local units of government in 1972, with similar amounts authorized through 1976. It was a bonanza for some small cities, counties, and townships. But the big-city mayors complained that President Nixon's concurrent withdrawal of the categorical grant programs would place increased burdens upon local taxpayers and drive large cities to collapse.

Such criticism—which could not be accepted completely until the President's proposals for "special revenue sharing" should be revised and passed by Congress—were very far from the enthusiasm that the concept of revenue sharing originally generated. Conservatives favored the concept because it promised to reduce total government spending and ease the political problems of local governments by lowering the hated property tax. They assumed that federal monies previously sent to the cities for specific programs in accord with federal guidelines (the "categorical grants") would be diverted to the revenue sharing program. Liberals, on the other hand, presumed that shared revenues would be added to whatever funds the federal government was already providing. The ordinary and unglamorous functions of local government, such as garbage collecting, could be supported with federal money, and the cities could then expand the programs first

19. President Nixon's Family Assistance Plan is described extensively below, pp. 437–450.

established because of the stimulus of federal grants, such as urban renewal, training the chronic unemployed for municipal jobs, and providing preschool ("Head Start") education for ghetto children.

Perhaps mindful of these diverse assumptions, President Nixon advertised revenue sharing as something of a panacea. In his State of the Union message for 1971, he proposed a "New American Revolution" that would provide a New Federalism through the medium of revenue sharing. Recognizing the superior tax-gathering abilities of the federal government, he said, "Let us put the money where the needs are. And let us put the power to spend it where the people are." This was followed by a February 4, 1971 message to Congress on revenue sharing, proclaiming it "a program under which we can enjoy the best of both worlds." It would, he said, "combine the efficiencies of a centralized tax system with the efficiencies of decentralized expenditure." He elaborated,

> Giving states and localities the power to spend certain federal tax monies will increase the influence of each citizen on how those monies are used. It will make government more responsive to taxpayer pressures. It will enhance accountability.

The president stated that local governments have been forced to do those things that Washington felt were necessary, rather than meeting needs as defined by the local political process. Revenue sharing would decrease the scope and authority of the Washington bureaucracy and "reverse the flow of power," returning it closer to the people.

If the president were to pursue ruthlessly the logic of this rhetoric, it would substantially modify the Grodzins model of marble-cake federalism. As the national government retreated from the supervision of the local governmental programs, the federal system would again become something like a layer cake. The policy area of each layer of government would be more carefully and exclusively defined. The national government would supply only baking powder—money—for the entire cake.

Marble-cake federalism originally developed because state and local governments were unable to meet the demands placed on them by economic depression. It was continued because of a conviction that problems which have a local impact—unemployment, inadequate education, racism, or pollution—are national in scope and will eventually yield only to national solutions. A citizen of California or Ohio, for example, has an interest in the quality of the public schools in Alabama. Migration between the states is unrestricted. When the sharecropper's child from Alabama seeks his fortune in the North or West, but is functionally illiterate, he will be unprepared for employment and can only seek admission to the welfare rolls.

If President Nixon's shared revenues would replace categorical grants for community services, the mayors of large cities would oppose the program. They were using federal funds to keep the lid on in the ghettos through programs which the wealthier voters in their cities would not support through increased taxes. As the drive for congressional passage of general revenue sharing was organized in 1969, the mayors were given assurances that categorical grant programs would be retained. They lobbied vigorously for two years in behalf of revenue sharing. The bill was passed by the Senate (which has two representatives per state, regardless of population or degree of urbanization) with a formula favoring the less-populated states in the allocation of funds. The House of Representatives adopted a formula providing much greater support for the urban states. Charged with reconciling the two versions, the conference committee proposed that states utilize whichever formula would bring the most money. The bill provided that two-thirds of each state's share would "pass through" the state capital and be allocated directly to units of local government. The bill provided for the sharing of $30 billion over a five-year period, thus freeing local governments from planning problems that result from the uncertainty of annual congressional appropriations. Final action on the bill was completed on October 13, 1972.

In January 1973, President Nixon sent his message to Congress concerning the 1974 budget. It provided for substantial reorganization of the executive branch, including the abolition of the Office of Economic Opportunity (OEO), which administered many grant programs dealing with poverty and other big city problems. Some of OEO's functions would be assigned to established cabinet departments. On February 4, the United States Conference of Mayors and the National League of Cities issued an analysis of the budget, which stated that "the President's promise has been breached." Specifically, the report charged, cutbacks in urban renewal, Model Cities, and public employment programs would withdraw $2.5 billion in anticipated revenues from the cities. They said that the president's plan to "slow inflation, avoid tax increases, and revamp the federal grant system . . . places a disproportionate share of the economic burden on cities and local taxes."[20]

President Nixon could not implement his New Federalism without a fight.

Skirmishes

A federal judge ruled that the Office of Economic Opportunity could not be closed on the basis of an executive order, for it was established by Congress. The administration decided not to appeal the decision, since the case could raise issues about the impoundment of funds in a manner unfavorable to the administration. Furthermore, if Congress appropriated no funds for 1974 OEO operations, the agency's continued "existence" would be only symbolic.

Kenneth R. Cole, Jr., executive director of the President's Domestic Council, stated that the administration had no intention of making the cities substitute general-revenue-sharing funds for the monies formerly received through categorical grant programs. Such support would come from special revenue sharing yet to be enacted by Congress. This would provide funds to local governments for specific — but broadly defined — purposes: education, law enforce-

20. Quoted in *Congressional Quarterly*, Feb. 10, 1973, p. 267.

ment and criminal justice, manpower training, and urban community development. They would replace some seventy categorical grant programs.

The U.S. Conference of Mayors charged that, even if special revenue sharing were enacted, the funds budgeted would be so much less than the programs being replaced that local governments would receive far less help from Washington than they had gotten in 1971.

The first special revenue-sharing proposal submitted by the administration included a formula for the allocation of funds, which the Washington lobbyist for the San Francisco city government said would be a bonanza for the Bay Area suburbs but a disaster for San Francisco.

Robert C. Wood, President of the University of Massachusetts, but formerly Lyndon Johnson's secretary of Housing and Urban Development, described the New Federalism as "a new version of the old shell-game — whichever shell you look under, the federal funds you thought were there have vanished."

A number of states, including California and New York, discovered during 1973 that they would have budgetary surpluses, although the states had joined the cities in demanding revenue sharing. The surpluses resulted from revenue sharing, from overestimating the impact of inflation upon costs, and from other causes. Some states considered reducing taxes. None proposed giving the surplus to their cities.

Lament for a Dying Program

Dudley Post, an employee of Boston's Model Cities agency, wrote in sorrow and anger of the Nixon administration's phasing out of the program.

> "We have run out of patience with Model Cities," presidential aide John Ehrlichman has said. And yet, ironically, this very program was one of the first examples of the comprehensive local planning that is needed if the administration's revenue sharing ideas are to work; it tested and demonstrated the concept of decentralized power which the President favors.[21]

The Model Cities program was launched with passage of the Demonstration Cities and Metropolitan Development Act in 1966. Its purpose was to get federal money into urban neighborhoods, launch programs based on local planning for local needs, and make a measurable impact on the quality of its residents' lives. Cities were given one year to prepare plans and applications, with the anticipation of a five-year period of operation. Original planners wanted to limit the program to just eight cities, but no congressman cares to admit that some other district has a city more deserving than his own. The program was provided for 75 cities in its first year and expanded in its second to 147. In every city, program responsibilities were divided between the professional bureaucrats of the city administration and an elected citizen's committee. The Model Cities grant was viewed as seed money. Further grants were to be attracted from the regular cabinet departments of Health, Education, and Welfare, or Housing and Urban Development.

21. Dudley Post, "Requiem for Model Cities," *New Republic*, April 14, 1973, p. 13.

Mr. Post complained that this supplemental support was always meager, for the established bureaucracies look upon Model Cities as an upstart. (How will the component parts of OEO fare, when farmed out to traditional departments?) And Model Cities' own bureaucracy treated the program too much like a categorical grant, with lengthy guidelines and review processes; Chicago's application was 2,500 pages long. Nevertheless, the program did have an impact upon the model neighborhoods. Activities in Boston included preparing adults to enter college; drug education; rehabilitation ("home improvement") loans to homeowners; code enforcement against landlords; and financing for black business. The agency's proudest accomplishment was a chain of neighborhood family health centers.

No lasting monuments were erected. Instead of new construction, the Model Cities program has improved the quality of people's lives and given new vitality to neighborhoods. Perhaps because of the lack of dramatic new construction, Mr. Ehrlichman's impatience is understandable; but it was formed too hastily, and the program's concept should have a new chance to prove itself.

Mr. Post concludes,

> Explanations for urban ills depend more on the observer's profession than on any body of objective fact. Planners bemoan the sprawl and waste of uncontrolled development, journalists blame corruption and inefficiency of city government, sociologists point to alienation and rootless mobility, architects see the ugliness of buildings and obsolete street plans, political scientists see the fragmentation of power in the metropolitan region. The point is we don't know what works. And we won't know unless we give such experiments as Model Cities time and money to prove themselves.[22]

Some Signs of Hope

Largely unnoticed by the nation at large, essentially unreported by the news media in the midst of daily crises, there are examples demonstrating that public apathy can be overcome and that governmental institutions need not remain frozen in archaic patterns.

There are metropolitan-area governments with varying degrees of authority. The government of Dade County, Florida, does not provide a utopian local government, but it is an important example of the possibility of regional government free from the fragmenting effects of municipal domination. In Minnesota, the "Twin Cities" of Minneapolis and St. Paul began modestly by sharing their planning for sewage disposal and started to build further areas of cooperation.

22. Ibid., p. 15.

There are multistate arrangements. In the East, the Appalachian Regional Council was formed to help an entire region break out of economic stagnation, overcoming the limitations of separate sovereign boundaries. Impatient for more dramatic results, the Nixon administration cut its funding support from the 1974 budget. In the West, California and Nevada managed to form the Tahoe Regional Planning Compact, establishing a commission to adopt plans for the conservation of the environment of the Tahoe Basin on the boundary of the two states. If action were quick, and the right decisions were made, it might still be possible to save Lake Tahoe from being killed ecologically by the pollution of human wastes.

Important new approaches were launched within the states. New York State established an Urban Development Corporation with broad powers—including the ability to override local building codes—which had the potential ability to create entire new cities, marrying public authority with private finance. In California, San Francisco and its surrounding suburbs formed the Bay Area Rapid Transit District to construct the first new subway system to be built in America in half a century. There was still a chance that San Francisco could avoid the fate of Los Angeles—obliteration of the land by the concrete and steel expanse of freeway interchanges and destruction of the air by automobile engine emissions. But the provision of rapid transit would accelerate the building of the office buildings that were filling up the skyline and usurping the view from San Francisco's hills.

During the sixties, a new breed of big-city mayors came on the scene, tough-minded and responsive to public opinion. Cavanaugh of Detroit, Stokes of Cleveland, Lindsay of New York, and Alioto of San Francisco were among their numbers. But their best efforts did not foresee or prevent the ghetto riots, and by the end of the decade, several (including Cavanaugh, Lindsay, Stokes and New Haven's Richard Lee) were retiring. But the ghetto riots at least made important segments of the public aware of racial discrimination and poverty, even if no quick solutions were forthcoming. In Detroit, leading industrialists tackled the problem of city rebuilding and attempted to supply jobs to the chronically unemployed. Black mayors were elected in Cleveland and in Gary, Indiana. They could not work miracles, for the urban financial crisis remained. But their election at least gave the ghettos an alternative to despair. In Oakland, the Black Panther party entered electoral politics and placed Bobby Seale in the run-off against incumbent Mayor Reading. Seale lost, but the party was established as an important—and respectable—force in local affairs.

The new awareness of ecological issues made citizens look around them at the decay of their communal life. In California, an initiative measure was passed intended to preserve the remaining coastline against the horrors of hasty development. Further growth was resisted by Ft. Lauderdale, Florida. In Washington, Congress narrowly defeated a proposal to permit the use of the federal gasoline tax to finance urban transit systems: next time around, the power of the highway lobby might be broken.

The flight to the suburbs continued.

As American ground forces withdrew from Asia and trade agreements were negotiated with Russia, national attention turned inward. Issues discussed in dusty political science texts became matters of public controversy. They were questions as old as Aristotle yet as fundamental now as then:

What is the optimum number of citizens who can share the living space of a city, providing diversity and a rich cultural life, yet retaining a sense of community?

How may the good order of the city's life and the safety of its streets be preserved without limiting the liberty of its citizens?

How may the influence of established local power centers be challenged without rending the fabric of society?

How can city planning be conducted in a manner that places human values first?

What new governmental forms can win public support as they lead all the citizens of a metropolitan area to share responsibility for its problems?

What is the proper balance between local planning and national administration — in short, what should be the nature of federalism?

The rhetoric of President Nixon's New Federalism did not offer serious answers to these questions. Returning power to grassroots governments would be futile, if the roots were shriveled and dead. Early reactions to general revenue sharing suggested that the big cities were invited to share the rhetoric but that the funds would be inadequate.

Some corrective to the bland assumptions of federal omnipotence made by previous administrations was necessary. Perhaps the sub-urban plurality (which some said was the cornerstone of the Nixon majority) indeed wished a retrenchment of the federal investment in urban survival, forgetting that only their core cities give meaning to the suburbs.

Simply to declare the end of the urban crisis solved no problems at all.

CHAPTER 11

The People, Maybe

IMAGES 11

Epitaph for
Two Revolutions

REFLECTIONS 11

Politics and Change:
What Is the Power
of the People?

Epitaph for
Two Revolutions

*Abraham Lincoln defined it: government of the people, by the people,
and for the people. Yet where, among all the bureaus and agencies
and city halls and polling booths and welfare offices and television
news commentaries and presidential addresses on the state of the
Union — where in the orders issued to pilots going off to bomb Cambodia — where in the statistics on unemployment — where in all the
vast and complicated federal, state, and local governments in the
United States of America — is the place where the needs and desires of
the people really make a difference?*

*Does government develop a course and an inertia of its own,
which, once established, can hardly be deflected? Or can the people
really control that direction?*

The Death of a Guaranteed Income

On February 24, 1973, President Richard M. Nixon delivered a radio
address. He began with these words:

> Good afternoon.
>
> At the beginning of each new year, as we reflect on the state
> of our American Union, we seek again a definition of what
> America means. Carl Sandburg came close to capturing its real
> meaning in three simple words that became the title for one of
> his greatest poems: "The People, Yes."
>
> America has risen to greatness because again and again when
> the chips were down, the American people have said yes — yes to
> the challenge of freedom, yes to the dare of progress, and yes to
> the hope of peace — even when defending the peace has meant
> paying the price of war.
>
> America's greatness will endure in the future only if our
> institutions continually rededicate themselves to saying yes to
> the people — yes to human needs and aspirations, yes to democ-
> racy and the consent of the governed, yes to equal opportunity
> and unlimited horizons of achievement for every American.
>
> It is in this spirit of rededication that I will send to the Con-
> gress in the next few days the fourth section of my 1973 State of
> the Union report — a message on the progress we have made, the
> steps we now must take, in helping people to help themselves
> through our federal program for human resources.

After outlining the achievements of his own administration in the field of human resources—social security benefits paid, newly integrated school districts, veterans' benefits, health care for the elderly, and money spent on civil rights activities—President Nixon criticized the "utopian" efforts of federal programs during the 1960s. Those programs, he said, ignored local governments, paid lavish wages to persons, like social workers, "who make a profession out of poverty," but accomplished little improvement in the status of the poor. Said the president,

> We must do better than this. The American people deserve compassion that works—not simply compassion that means well. They deserve programs that say yes to human needs by saying no to paternalism, social exploitation, and waste.[1]

President Nixon was so pleased with Sandburg's title and his own interpretation of its meaning that he repeated the same words in his March 1 message to Congress.

Carl Sandburg's book-length poem offers a panoramic view of the American people, celebrating their vitality and diversity. *The People, Yes* contains a vast range of images and ideas. Its central theme, however, is that the American people are stronger than their institutions. They will survive the injustices of the economic system and the machinations of the politicians and will see through shoddy appeals to the flag. The idea of war being the price of peace was foreign to the 1930s pacifist spirit of Sandburg's poem. At one point, he wrote,

> The little girl saw her first troop parade and asked,
>   "What are those?"
>   "Soldiers."
>   "What are soldiers?"
>   "They are for war. They fight and each side tries to kill as many
>   of the other side as he can."
> The girl held still and studied.
>   "Do you know . . . I know something?"
>   "Yes, what is it you know?"
>   "Someday they'll give a war and nobody will come."[2]

What the President Didn't Mention

The headlines made by the president's speech were based on what he left out, not what he included. He made no mention of the Family Assistance Plan (FAP), the major proposal of his first administration for reforming the welfare system. President Nixon had announced FAP—on national television—in 1969. He said it would break into the cycle of poverty and release families from dependence upon public assistance. After an initially greater federal outlay of funds, it would bring the burgeoning cost of welfare under control, by restoring initiative and a sense of self-worth—and a minimum income—to poor families.

Congress did not immediately enact the program.

In 1970, President Nixon's campaign to increase the number of Republicans in Congress failed completely. His tactics were based on stimulating negative responses to the cultural alternatives personified by the antiwar movement. President Nixon prepared a new

1. White House text of the president's speech, as reprinted in *Congressional Quarterly*, March 3, 1973, p. 441.
2. Carl Sandburg, *The People, Yes* (New York: Harcourt Brace Jovanovich, 1939), p. 43.

approach to Congress for his 1971 State of the Union message—which he delivered in person. He challenged Congress to work with him in achieving "six great goals." Together, he said, they could achieve a "New American Revolution." A mainstay of the revolution was the 1969 proposal for welfare reform.

A version of FAP was passed by the House of Representatives. The bill died in the Senate Finance Committee.

In the 1972 presidential campaign, George McGovern proposed the redistribution of the national income in the form of a liberal guaranteed annual income. FAP was also a guaranteed annual income, with added work incentives. Candidate McGovern's proposal drew much public criticism; he was soundly defeated in November.

In 1973, President Nixon withdrew the FAP proposal by not even mentioning it to Congress.

Thus ended the most radical component of the "New American Revolution" advertised in 1971.

What was it all about?

Defeat in the War on Poverty

The American Dream—Horatio Alger's heroes rising from the gutters to the brokerage houses or, alternatively, a sober and responsible citizen earning his wages, paying his taxes, and settling into the comfortable life of the consumer—what happens when the dream does not come true? How does the Land of Plenty react to the reality of poverty in its midst?

It does not question the justice of measuring every man's worth by the value of his labor in an economy devoted to the relentless pursuit of private profit. Just as the reforms of the New Deal did not question the basic premises of the system, the growing welfare bureaucracy does not question the system of which it is a part. The concern of the social worker is for the individual—to counsel him, to analyze him, to prepare him for labor. The basic assumption has been that one who is unable to live by the American Dream is sick—he needs treatment. Rather than attack the combined cause and symptom of poverty—low income—professional welfare service as it has developed in the United States is a matter of extending social services to poor individuals who are identified and pass the tests of qualification. This is the "services strategy" for dealing with poverty. Government provides services to the poor, which may alleviate their present suffering and prepare them—or their children—for future employment.

The various programs of President Johnson's War on Poverty—from Head Start to Work Study—were of this kind. They were expensive programs, and they scored many human successes, but the money mostly went to middle-class teachers and administrators.

> This is a "war" *on poverty*—the very nature of such a proposal requires an exposure of "the enemy" in its human form. In addition, separation of the poor creates a donor-donee relationship whether it exists between the income-tax-paying middle and upper classes and the low income earners, or the social worker and his client. In the context of American social philosophy, such a situation enhances the self-image of the well-to-do and places a stigma of failure and dependency upon aid recipients. Above all, it is "the American way" to approach social welfare issues, for it places the burden of responsibility upon the individual and not upon the socio-economic system.[3]

3. Elinor Graham, "The Politics of Poverty," reprinted in M. Gettleman and D. Mermelstein, eds., *The Great Society Reader* (New York: Random House, 1967), p. 216.

When the welfare system was given national direction and support for the first time by the New Deal's Social Security Act, programs were established to serve individuals who suffered hardships as a result of the random accidents that occur within a modern society and render individuals unable to contribute to or compete within it. Federal grants helped the states provide for the disabled, the blind, and the children of widows. Aimed at keeping families together, the Aid to Dependent Children program provided allowances for families with no male breadwinner. It allowed widows and the wives of the unemployed or disabled to care for their own small children, instead of sending them to orphanages. In 1950, aid was also extended to the mothers, and the program was renamed Aid to Families with Dependent Children (AFDC). It became the main federal program in support of the American family, and the policies established in the states by its administrators were the only "national" policy concerning families. But those policies were uneven. In Mississippi, AFDC payments were $8.50 a month per child. As the poor, driven from the land their fathers had worked by the mechanization of agriculture, flocked to (mostly) northern cities, fathers found that they could not find employment adequate to support their children. For the wives to receive AFDC support, the fathers had to leave their families. In 1940, 30 percent of welfare families had an absent father; by 1969, the figure was 70 percent. In twenty-six states, mothers were denied AFDC payments when an adult male was present in the household, regardless of whether he was able to find employment. If the head of the household (mother or father) found work, welfare payments were cut by an amount equivalent to the salary received. The result of the national policy on families was to destroy families.

Welfare was not the only dilemma of the cities. Beginning with the Watts riot of 1965, flames, destruction, looting, and death swept the major cities of America, as the anger of impoverished blacks exploded. The fear that American society was coming apart at the seams was the emotional backdrop of the 1968 election.

Richard Nixon had offered few specific alternatives to Democratic antipoverty programs during the 1968 campaign. Now he needed a plan that would demonstrate the ability of the new administration to solve human problems.

A Sound Idea

John Maynard Keynes once remarked upon the propensity of those who are hostile to social science to think within the framework established by all-but-forgotten social scientists. Indeed, he wrote, ranting demagogues who imagine they hear the voice of God frequently hear only the echoing words of a long-buried economist. Adam Smith published *The Wealth of Nations* in 1776, the year of the Declaration of Independence; intellectual historians would find it difficult to prove which event had the more profound influence on human thought.

Therefore, when economists reach something like agreement on a new idea, it is time to take that idea seriously. In the late 1960s, economists did reach something like agreement on the value of the guaranteed annual income concept. Welfare economists of the Left supported the idea; and Milton Friedman of the Right supported it too, provided it could be used to replace existing arrangements for the payment of welfare.

Friedman's version of the idea was called "the negative income tax": until an individual or family reached a certain income level, it would file its tax return and receive a payment from the government, rather than being asked to pay. Each family would be guaranteed a basic floor of support, even if its members were unable to find work. When they were employed, some of the earnings above that level would be retained, thus insuring a reward for initiative. Gradually, as earnings increased, government support would be reduced, until finally the near edge of comfort would be reached, the positive income tax would reassert itself, and the worker would be required to begin contributing to the support of the government.

The scheme had several attractions:

Simplicity of administration, doing away with the complex regulations concerning eligibility for welfare, and much of the bureaucracy needed to apply them.

Increased freedom of choice for the poor person. Rather than special programs supplying such items as surplus foods, there would be money.

Protection of initiative. No longer would a wage-earner on welfare face the possibility of a 100 percent tax upon his salary.

Protection of the family. Fathers would no longer be required to abandon their families so that their children could receive AFDC payments.

During 1968, the concept of the guaranteed annual income was widely discussed. It found its way into the columns of *Time, Newsweek,* and *Look.* (It was possible for an idea to be so "hot" that it was discussed by all three, without a conspiracy among the editors.)

On several occasions, members of the Johnson administration proposed a guaranteed annual income. It was always rejected, either by bureaucratic superiors, or by the White House itself. During the 1968 presidential election campaign, Richard Nixon said he was against it.

Tory Men With Liberal Principles

For the first six months, domestic policies received little public discussion by the Nixon administration. The silence concealed a ferment of debate. At the Department of Health, Education, and Welfare, civil servants again put forward proposals—as they had to President Johnson—for a guaranteed annual income. Robert Finch, then the secretary of HEW, received them with enthusiasm. At the White House, they found a champion in Daniel P. Moynihan, who had been a sub-cabinet official in the Kennedy and Johnson administrations and served President Nixon as adviser on urban affairs.[4] The president was prepared to abandon the "services strategy" in favor of an "income strategy." That meant striking at the root of poverty, not its secondary symptoms. It meant redistributing the national income. This was not an idea calculated to warm the cockles of conservative Republican hearts. (The Democrats had the chance, but never proposed it. Too radical.)

Most members of the president's new cabinet opposed the concept. So did the "political cadres," the men who organized and orchestrated the 1968 campaign and were now worrying, in the White House, about how to construct a "new conservative majority." Final consideration came at a meeting at Camp David, when Richard Nixon declared, "the present welfare system is a disaster, and I'm not going down that road another step."

The complex legislative proposal was hammered out by the bureaucracy. It was presented publicly by President Nixon in a 35-minute television speech on August 8, 1969.

The president began by underscoring the disasters of the current welfare system:

> During last year's election campaign, I often made a point that touched a responsive chord wherever I traveled.
>
> I said that this nation became great not because of what government did for people, but because of what people did for themselves. . . .
>
> Whether measured by the anguish of the poor themselves, or by the drastically mounting burden on the taxpayer, the present welfare system has to be judged a colossal failure.
>
> Our states and cities find themselves sinking in a welfare quagmire, as caseloads increase, as costs escalate, and as the welfare system stagnates enterprise and perpetuates dependency. What began on a small scale in the depression thirties has become a monster in the prosperous sixties. The tragedy is not only that it is bringing states and cities to the brink of financial disaster, but also that it is failing to meet elementary human, social, and financial needs of the poor.
>
> It breaks up homes. It often penalizes work. It robs recipients of dignity. And it grows.[5]

The growth was dramatic—three million persons added to the welfare (AFDC) rolls in the preceding eight years, another four million to be added by 1975. "The financial cost will be crushing," he said, "and the human cost will be suffocating."

President Nixon proposed abolishing AFDC and replacing it with the family assistance system—"a foundation under the income of every American family with dependent children that cannot care for itself—wherever in America that family may live." The level of support for welfare families would be increased in twenty (mostly southern) of the fifty states, but in no state would it be reduced. The support would be combined with incentives to work. "What America needs now is not more welfare, but more 'workfare.' "

4. The origins of the Family Assistance Plan, and its disposal in the 91st Congress, have been recounted by Moynihan in *The Politics of a Guaranteed Annual Income* (New York: Random House, 1973).

5. The text of the speech was published in the *New York Times*, August 9, 1969, p. 10. The section dealing with FAP is reprinted in Moynihan, *The Politics of a Guaranteed Annual Income*, pp. 220-226.

The president next reminded his listeners that he had opposed the concept of "guaranteed income" during the presidential campaign. He added:

> I oppose it now and will continue to oppose it. A guaranteed income would undermine the incentive to work; the family assistance plan increases the incentive to work. A guaranteed income establishes a right without responsibilities; family assistance recognizes a need and establishes a responsibility. It provides help to those in need, and in turn requires that those who receive help work to the extent of their capabilities. There is no reason why one person should be taxed so that another can choose to live idly.

In fact, the president was proposing exactly that—a guaranteed income for families with children. Daniel Moynihan explained later that President Nixon knew very well what he was proposing—but he was proposing it to Middle America, not to welfare families. Therefore, he avoided the poisonous label by denying its applicability. Moynihan writes that the president's words were justified, for his proposal was not a guaranteed income in the meaning the public had come to attach to that term.[6] Its basic purpose was to supplement the income of the working poor, and thus abolish poverty, according to the federal definition of poverty. Establishing a basic floor under family income, it would continue to supplement earned income, until wages had risen high enough to bring the family above the "poverty line." The sliding scale thus established would look like this for a family of four:

Earned Income	Benefit	Total Income
$ 0	$1,600	$1,600
720	1,600	2,320
1,000	1,460	2,460
1,500	1,210	2,710
2,000	960	2,960
2,500	710	3,210
3,000	460	3,460
3,500	210	3,710
3,920	—	3,920

There was, however, a condition. Both men and women applicants (except the mothers of pre-school children) would be required to register for work training or for employment. If they refused the offer of a job through the agency, their *individual* share of the family assistance benefit would be cut off; the children would receive support in any case. There would be an expansion of job training centers, with a $30 per month incentive for the head of the family to take job training. And the federal government would provide 90 percent of the funding for an expanded system of child-care centers, so that even mothers of pre-school children would be able to work. Said the president, "with such incentives, most of the recipients who can work will want to work. This is part of the American character."

As if this would still be too substantial a pill for his constituents to swallow, the president provided some sugar coating in the form of the three additional programs which completed what he called his welfare "package."

6. Moynihan, *The Politics of a Guaranteed Annual Income*, p. 11.

A "careful, phased transfer" of the responsibility for providing and managing job training centers away from Washington and into the hands of state and local governments, together with an expansion of training centers to provide for an additional 150,000 trainees. "For the first time . . . administration of a major established federal program would be turned over to the states and local government, recognizing that they are in a position to do the job better."

A reorganization of the Office of Economic Opportunity, most criticized agency in Lyndon Johnson's War on Poverty, to center its attentions upon research, rather than operation.

A proposal that, beginning in 1972, the federal government begin to provide funds for state and local governments. Such schemes of "revenue sharing" had long been called for, because of the superior ability of the national government to raise taxes, but President Nixon was the first to propose it. He recommended a "pass through" so that an appropriate share of funds would go directly to local governments without skimming by state legislatures. Only $1 billion would be so distributed in 1972, but the total would grow quickly after that.

The president's speech was a mixture of substance and symbolism, of appeals to rugged individualism and nods toward humanitarian instincts. On balance, the substance was nearly revolutionary in the changes it would bring to the welfare system; the tone was more appropriate to an audience of accountants than to one of benefactors.

Pleased with favorable initial reactions, President Nixon was reported as telling a friend, "Tory men with liberal principles are what has enlarged democracy in this world."[7]

> Tory men with liberal principles! The prototype was Benjamin Disraeli, novelist and dandy, author of the Reform Act of 1867 (which gave the vote to the working man), original swinger of the Victorian Era, and favorite minister of the Queen. Disraeli perceived that the Conservative party could at the same time reassure men of wealth because of the upper-class origins of its leaders and win the support of the working class by passing needed reforms before the Liberal party could propose them. Both his novels and his political activities revealed a deep sympathy for the suffering of factory workers. He labored to preserve capitalism by reforming it.
>
> He also secured British interests in the Suez Canal, made his Victoria Empress of India, and originated the phrase, "peace with honour."

Reactions: The Public

The Family Assistance Plan was greeted with immediate enthusiasm by the press. Editorials praising it appeared in national journals and local newspapers. The chance of doing something—anything—about the "welfare mess" appealed to some editors; others were turned on by the possible restoration of the work ethic; a few praised the goal of achieving a more equitable distribution of the national income.

Recognizing the innovative nature of the proposal, public opinion analysts were soon in the field. Gallup was asking questions within a week, and Lou Harris reported first results within a month. A remark-

7. "Nixon's New Deal," *Newsweek*, August 18, 1969, p. 17.

Bruce Davidson

ably large number of people had heard of the proposals — from two-thirds to three-fourths. Gallup found that 65 percent of those who had heard of the proposal favored it, with 20 percent opposed and only 15 percent holding no opinion.[8] In late 1969, Harris asked an unusually large sample their opinion of "the Nixon welfare plan — which would give every family on welfare $1,600 a year with a provision that anyone able to work either enter a job training program or get a job." This was an exaggeration of the bill's work provision, which may have influenced the respondents. Seventy-nine percent favored the plan, 13 percent opposed it, and only 8 percent were uncertain or had no opinion.[9]

The favor with which the plan was received did not vary dramatically with age, region, income level, or party affiliation. The American people, as a people, reacted favorably to the plan — at least as they understood it.

Supporting FAP was not an active matter. No suburban housewives marched to demand its enactment; businessmen did not pound legislative desks in its behalf; rural congressmen did not fear defeat if they opposed it. In gaining passive public acceptance, the president had only begun.

Reactions: The Groups
Public acceptance of the plan, as measured by the pollsters, would not determine the outcome. Only when proposed legislation generates such enthusiasm (or outrage) that hundreds of thousands of citizens write spontaneously to their congressmen does the public directly influence the outcome of legislation — and even that influence may be fleeting and soon forgotten, as the history of gun-control legislation shows.[10]

8. Moynihan, *The Politics of a Guaranteed Annual Income*, p. 268.
9. Bayard Hooper, "The Real Change Has Just Begun," report of a Lou Harris-Life poll, *Life*, January 9, 1970, p. 106.
10. See above, pp. 255–269.

The normal sources of outside influence upon the decisions of Congress are the organized groups that speak, or claim to speak, for particular interests within the population. The lineup of those groups on FAP held some surprises.

Labor organizations were not enthusiastic. Their preferred solution to poverty was to raise the minimum wage, and, at the time, they favored a minimum of $2 per hour. If this should drive certain employers out of business, and reduce the number of available jobs—well, marginal employers in a competitive system do not deserve to survive. But labor leaders were aware of the crisis in the welfare program, and they did not generally oppose the plan. Their acceptance was passive, like that of the general public.

Business was divided. The National Association of Manufacturers supported the plan vigorously, praising its potential for restoring the work ethic. The United States Chamber of Commerce, on the other hand, claimed that the work incentive features of the plan could not be properly administered and would never achieve their goal.

The national leadership of religious organizations responded warmly to the proposal. The National Council of Churches quickly endorsed it, and the National Conference of Catholic Charities called upon the faithful to work for its passage. Jewish leaders welcomed the plan and advised the administration leaders on tactics to win support for it in Congress. However, the endorsement of religious lobbyists in Washington did not light a fire of fervor among the parishioners of those denominations in the provinces. Middle-class churchgoers were capable of understanding the dilemma of welfare families on an intellectual level, but their own emotions and comfort were not engaged by the issue. Such an engagement is necessary before citizens *demand* a government program. Black organizations began to oppose FAP, and the Protestant organizations wavered in their support. Race was the compelling issue of the time, and white Protestant lobbyists had no intention of offending black Protestants.

Burk Uzzle

Who was directly involved with the plight of welfare families? The families themselves, and their social workers. As for the welfare workers, they were middle-class professionals accustomed to seeking in the Democratic party an increased governmental commitment to the amelioration of poverty. Many favored the concept of a guaranteed annual income, but they were suspicious of FAP's work provisions, and they were not inclined to place much trust in President Nixon or his party. The national leaders of their professional association denounced the plan. The denunciation gained increasing vigor as their black clients attacked the plan.

The organization that proclaimed itself the spokesman for welfare families was the National Welfare Rights Organization (NWRO). It had been formed in 1967 to articulate the concerns of welfare recipients—recipients of AFDC, not the guaranteed income of FAP. The membership was centered in New York and was overwhelmingly made up of black welfare mothers. Led by a brilliant and energetic black man, George A. Wiley, the organization proceeded on the assumption that the best way to overcome the stigmatization of dependency status was to proclaim dependency and capitalize upon it. Local chapters of NWRO organized to qualify more relief recipients for the welfare rolls and to improve the treatment received from welfare offices. Many local chapters were initiated and supported by the legal aid services of federal antipoverty agencies.

Following news reports intensively, NWRO was aware of the general provisions of FAP even before it was proposed by the president. FAP provided the bulk of its benefits for poorer states, particularly in the South; the best New York could hope for was to receive as much —but no more—federal assistance through FAP as it had through AFDC. Furthermore, the chief beneficiaries of FAP were the working poor. The working poor were not enrolled in NWRO. The most important aspect of FAP, in the eyes of many of its supporters, was the sliding scale of benefits, which permitted half of every dollar earned above the subsistence level to be retained by the earner; it saw most families as receiving income both from FAP and from work.

But NWRO concentrated on the benefits provided to a family in which there was no worker. They argued with justice that $1,600 a year was not enough to sustain a family of four; this was far below New York's minimum level of support. (However, support levels would not be reduced in any state; the difference between $1,600 and the established state minimum would be paid by the state, with federal help.)

The day *before* President Nixon made his televised proposal of FAP, the White House received a letter signed by the leaders of NWRO which declared:

> This plan is anti-poor and anti-black. It is a flagrant example of institutionalized racism.[11]

NWRO quickly developed a position. The organization was not opposed in principle to a guaranteed annual income. But the $1,600 of the Nixon proposal was inadequate. NWRO first suggested that the minimum support level should be raised to $5,500 for a family of four. But the cost of living increased, and $6,500 was defined as the amount a four-person family should receive as a matter of right when it was unable to develop assets of its own; "$6,500 Or Fight" became the rallying cry. NWRO never mentioned that this support level would require $71 billion and a surtax on incomes of 78 percent.

11. Moynihan, *The Politics of a Guaranteed Annual Income*, p. 226.

The natural constituency for the FAP proposal was the working poor. More than half were white, and more than half lived in the South. But they had no organization. They were proud people suspicious of "charity." And they were widely scattered throughout the United States.

The NWRO soon claimed to speak not only for the AFDC recipients but also for the *potential* recipients of FAP benefits. Black welfare mothers did march in demonstrations against the FAP proposal.

> FAP could not be adopted without an organized constituency to demand it. But FAP had to be adopted before the working poor would recognize their common interest and organize to protect it.
> The chicken, or the egg?

FAP in Congress

That FAP could survive the legislative process—committee deliberations, recommendations, floor debate, and final passage in both houses—seemed a long shot, but not an impossibility. No small source of trouble was uncertainty as to whether congressmen and the public completely understood the bill. It was not only a welfare reform bill; it provided a substantial redistribution of the national income. It dealt with the fundamental issues of politics as practiced in America: who gets what, when, where, and why; and how do they vote as a result?

President Nixon was convinced that the only way to bring the South into the mainstream of American life was to attack its poverty. One-third of the citizens of Mississippi would have been eligible for FAP benefits. But how would the established ruling elites of southern states maintain their domination, if southern poverty were frontally attacked? Governor Lester G. Maddox of Georgia summarized one reaction very neatly:

> You're not going to be able to find anyone willing to work as maids or janitors or housekeepers if this bill gets through, that I promise you.[12]

No explicit mention of race, but the hint is there: if FAP were approved, it would be hard to keep the blacks in their place. Southern congressmen did not greet the proposal with enthusiasm.

Meanwhile, northern liberal Democrats complained that the bill largely benefited the South and would do little for their own states. To support the proposal was to risk condemnation by NWRO, which could permanently tarnish a liberal image. At the other extreme of the congressional spectrum, conservative Republicans were upset, claiming that resentment against welfare spending had a major role in electing President Nixon. How could he propose adding 13 million more people to the welfare rolls, when the working poor hadn't voted for him in the first place? FAP was under fire from both the right and the left. Its chances rested with the moderate middle.

The moderate middle prevailed in the House of Representatives, more or less in spite of itself. By definition, "moderates" have neither ideological fervor nor organizational cohesiveness. The bill passed in the House because of Wilbur Mills. As a revenue bill, FAP was considered by the Ways and Means Committee. Chairman Mills approached the bill with an open mind, and, during hearings with the administration proponents of the bill, mastered its details. He decided

12. Quoted in ibid., pp. 378–379.

to support the bill, and the committee members persuaded themselves to join him. The committee changed some details but did not modify the basic thrust of the proposal. Mills persuaded the House leadership to endorse a closed rule, granted by the Rules Committee, which denied opponents the chance of offering crippling amendments on the floor.

Support for the bill came from diverse, and contrasting, motives. Northern liberal Democrats complained that $1,600 was inadequate, but recognized that some start must be made toward replacing AFDC. Congressman John W. Byrnes of Wisconsin, ranking Republican member of the Ways and Means Committee, quietly rounded up partisan—but reluctant—support from conservative Republicans for the Republican president's proposal. Southern conservative Democrats complained that the work incentives of the bill would be inadequate, so the leadership accepted an amendment symbolically strengthening the bill's language on work. In spite of their various misgivings, the consensus of the members of the House was to give FAP a chance to prove itself. On April 16, 1970, the bill was passed by the House of Representatives by a vote of 243 to 155.

Administration sponsors of the bill were euphoric. They knew the Senate was a more liberal body than the House; if the House passed the measure, the Senate was sure to follow. But did the normal division of attitudes and measures into "liberal" and "conservative" apply to FAP? Conservatively oriented publications thought so; the barrage of criticism aimed at the "radical" purposes of the bill was redoubled. At the same time, Senate liberals heeded the claims of NWRO and others that the bill was inadequate.

The Senate Finance Committee opened hearings almost immediately. The House Ways and Means Committee (which has the constitutional responsibility for "originating" money bills) has a membership representing nearly every section of the nation, with a permanent staff and a highly respected career chairman in Wilbur Mills. By contrast, the Senate Finance Committee had recently acquired a new chairman in the person of Russell Long of Louisiana. Its staff was relatively new and had no experience at all in welfare matters or questions of income distribution. Furthermore, the attitude of the Finance Committee was largely determined by southern senators, whose region faced the greatest social change from FAP's income redistribution features, and senators from sparsely populated western states, which had little direct contact with welfare problems.

Chairman Long chose to treat FAP as essentially a welfare reform measure. To the administration, "reform" meant breaking into the cycle of dependency. To Senators Long and John J. Williams of Delaware, "reform" meant cleaning up welfare abuses—making it harder for recipients, through fraud, to gain a combination of benefits which the legislation never intended. Long's investigation unearthed the most horrifying examples of the abuse of AFDC by a few of its recipients. Administration spokesmen had to admit that FAP was not aimed directly at eliminating those possibilities for abuse. Far from welcoming FAP, the Finance Committee was essentially hostile to *any* scheme of welfare.

But the Senate does not depend on its committees for final decisions to the extent that the House does, so the administration hoped for a vote by the full Senate. With the plan under attack from both the left and the right, the moderate Senate center did not prevail. As was the case with general public opinion, their support for FAP was passive, not active; measures which might have forced the bill from the committee to the Senate floor for a decision were not taken.

Then, in June, President Nixon invaded Cambodia, and the attention of the administration and the nation swung away from FAP.

In the 92nd Congress, a modified version of FAP was again passed by the House, and it was given a sense of high priority by assigning it the number "HR 1." But the bill died again in the Senate Finance Committee.

Daniel P. Moynihan wrote, with something like a cry of discovery, that the executive branch is more or less organized to gather the information that makes decisions possible. But Congress, at the core of its being, is concerned with *representation*: as long as the individual legislator feels he has demonstrated his responsiveness to the dominant groups in his district, he is happy to avoid making decisions. Decisions make political enemies.

> The Family Assistance Plan died. President Nixon buried it, while quoting Carl Sandburg, early in 1973. Who was to blame? It was perhaps overstating the case to describe the proposal as "revolutionary"; but it was potentially the most significant social welfare legislation in forty years, presented in complicated language and surrounded by the evocation of conflicting symbols. Manipulation of those symbols won public acquiescence but did not create a constituency that would demand its passage and overcome Senate resistance. Was this failure the fault of the people? Or was it the fault of their leaders?

Decade of Defiance: The Death of SDS

The rise and fall of the Family Assistance Plan was related to other events. President Nixon's renewed insistence that the plan be passed in 1971 came after a resurgence of liberal sentiment among those who bothered to vote in the 1970 congressional elections. His abandonment of the plan in early 1973 was a celebration of his 1972 landslide reelection by a coalition that was united at least in its opposition to the pace of social change and its revulsion against the challenge to traditional American values posed by blacks, women, and radical students.

By then, the defiance of radical students was mostly over. It had lasted for ten years. The tone of radical activity for that decade was set by the Students for a Democratic Society (SDS),[13] an organization of college students "on the left," concerned for the future of their country, diagnosing its ills, and making progressively more violent attempts to achieve remedies.

The symbolic end of SDS came on March 6, 1970, in an elegant townhouse at 18 West Eleventh Street in Greenwich Village. It was occupied by eight members of the Weatherman faction of the already disintegrated SDS. All were middle- and upper-class young people, the alumni of, or drop-outs from, expensive colleges. All were convinced that the American system's hopeless corruption could be challenged only by the violent acts of underground revolutionary cells striking out without warning. That morning, two of them were making crude bombs in the cellar. Wires were crossed; 100 sticks of dynamite exploded; the house collapsed and burned; three young revolutionaries were buried in the rubble.

13. Kirkpatrick Sale has written a definitive history of the Students for a Democratic Society in his *SDS* (New York: Random House, 1973). This truncated account of the organization depends on his book; "Decade of Defiance" is the title of Sale's introduction.

I: Origins, and a Statement

Ten years earlier, in the spring of 1960, Students for a Democratic Society was born by applying a new name to the tattered remnants of an earlier campus organization, which had been founded in 1905 as the Intercollegiate Socialist Society, and had attracted persons like Norman Thomas, Walter Lippmann, and Edna St. Vincent Millay to undergraduate membership, awakening middle-class youth to social responsibility. In 1921, when the success of Lenin made "socialism" a term of evil to Middle Americans, the name was changed to the Student League for Industrial Democracy. The League became an important campus presence during the 1930s and was supported by organized labor. After World War II and the retreat from political action associated with the era of Senator Joseph McCarthy, the League was moribund. But the change of name brought new vigor. SDS was ready to build a new organization out of the quickening campus mood of the 1960s.

The major organizational meeting of SDS took place at Port Huron, Michigan, in the spring of 1962. Its main accomplishment was the drafting of the *Port Huron Statement,* the SDS manifesto which became the rallying cry of the student left. It provided both a diagnosis of the ills of American society, and prescription for the remedy of "participatory democracy." It identified its authors as children of affluence who found America's true ideals betrayed. It was a statement of singular strength and beauty, based on a conception of the relationship between the people and their institutions that was rather different from the definition offered by President Nixon in 1973 as an interpretation of Sandburg's *The People, Yes:*

> We regard *men* as infinitely precious and possessed of unfulfilled capacities for reason, freedom, and love. In affirming these principles we are aware of countering perhaps the dominant conceptions of man in the twentieth century: that he is a thing to be manipulated, and that he is inherently incapable of directing his own affairs. We oppose the depersonalization that reduces human beings to the status of things. . . .
>
> We would replace power rooted in possession, privilege, or circumstance by power and uniqueness rooted in love, reflectiveness, reason, and creativity. As a *social system* we seek the establishment of a democracy of individual participation, governed by two central aims: that the individual share in those social decisions determining the quality and direction of his life; that society be organized to encourage independence in men and provide the media for their common participation. . . .
>
> In social change or interchange, we find violence to be abhorrent because it requires generally the transformation of the target, be it a human being or a community of people, into a depersonalized object of hate. It is imperative that the means of violence be abolished and the institutions—local, national, and international—that encourage nonviolence as a condition of conflict be developed.[14]

II: Organizing, a False Start, and a March

The statement was circulated in mimeographed form, 66 pages long. The tiny national office in New York could not keep up with the demand for copies. SDS was opposed to centralization and bureaucracy,

14. From an excerpt of the Port Huron Statement reprinted in Michael Leiserson, *The End of Politics in America* (Boston: Little, Brown, 1972), pp. 233-234.

and the concept of a national office was a contradiction. But SDS could not, at that point, imagine an organization without a headquarters.

The *Port Huron Statement* attracted some new members, but events attracted more. The Cuban missile crisis proved that the United States government could indeed contemplate the nuclear destruction of the world. SDS claimed that the ruthlessness of American imperialism was duplicated in the treatment accorded blacks and the poor at home. The civil rights movement was entering its initial militant stage, with sit-ins on buses and at lunch counters, and the Student Nonviolent Coordinating Committee emerged as the organizational leader. SDS considered sending its forces (white, northern, middle-class students) into the South, but young Stokeley Carmichael advised them that black students should be left free to work it out on their own. SDS offered an alternative mode of involvement.

The main activity for the summer of 1963 was an attempt to organize poor people, both black and white, in northern cities. It was called the Economic Research and Action Project. Its purpose was to enable the urban poor to present a united front when making demands upon the established power structure. The plan achieved some success in Chester, Pennsylvania (near Swarthmore College), and was soon expanded into ten cities.

The Action Project brought college youth into the slum to share its life. They made a commitment, not just a visit. The project was a failure, in terms of its own goals, for the poor showed no particular haste to accept the leadership and advice of these affluent students. Even when they did, city administrations proved intractable and the press hostile. By 1965, the project was over. Its main accomplishment was to radicalize those who took part in it. Members of SDS became increasingly convinced that the system would not yield to ordinary pressures for reform.

The 1964 SDS national convention was divided into three factions:

Those who felt SDS should concentrate on developing the
political consciousness of students on their own campuses,

Those who felt SDS should continue organizing work among
the poor, and

Those who hoped to make an impact through the electoral
process.

The last group was the smallest and was regarded as the right-wing faction. Appalled at the candidacy of Barry Goldwater, they invented the slogan "Part of the Way with LBJ" and supported Lyndon Johnson's reelection with stated reservations. But most SDSers attending the convention were already convinced of the irrelevance of electoral politics.

Events again took over. In September of 1964, students at the University of California in Berkeley, calling themselves the Free Speech Movement, began action that after three months of turmoil forced the administration to reopen an area of the campus for organizations to conduct political recruitment, after a futile attempt to ban them. That was the official issue. The larger issues were the powerlessness of undergraduates to make decisions affecting their lives and the perceived sell-out of universities to the dominant interests in society, particularly the "military-industrial complex." SDS was the only national organization to recognize the potential meaning of the Berkeley events. SDS offered to students on other campuses an explanation

Charles Harbutt

of the universities' failure and a promise of action. Action was better than debate.

Then, in the spring of 1965, dramatic escalation began in Vietnam. SDS was the main sponsor of an antiwar march which brought more participants than ever before to a Washington demonstration. But it remained orderly; the time for violence was not yet.

Lyndon Johnson stayed home on his ranch in Texas.

It is hard to recall that dim past of April 1965, when 15,000 marched. Hard to recall, because so many other marches and confrontations were to follow, and individual events grow blurred in memory. But it is easy to remember that a cease-fire was not accomplished in Vietnam until 1973.

III: Leading the Resistance

The SDS summer convention of 1965 was larger than ever, and the delegates were of a new kind. Those who remembered the warm glow of idealism that surrounded the *Port Huron Statement* were no longer in control. Celebrants of the counter-culture were there in force; marijuana and drugs were prevalent for the first time. Many of the delegates only knew SDS as the sponsor of the protest march in Washington, but they knew the situation on their own campuses. They wanted action.

Action they got. SDS organized simultaneous antiwar marches in ninety cities on October 15 and 16, in which some 100,000 persons participated. SDS was now identified by Lyndon Johnson's attorney general and by hawkish senators as the master organization attempting to foment campus revolt and undermine the draft. By December, SDS had nearly 5,000 members, but the national headquarters was perplexed; the "master plan" attributed to SDS by the press did not exist.

The campus revolt was fomented by the government. In the spring
of 1966, the Johnson administration decided to draft college students
—those with the poorest grades—for service in Vietnam. The student
deferment was no longer a hiding place. Local SDS chapters, without
guidance from national headquarters, began demonstrating against
college administrations to prevent them from sending class rankings
to the Selective Service System. What could be greater proof of the
universities' complicity with the war machine than that they would
help designate which of their own students should be drafted? A five-
day sit-in at the University of Chicago did not accomplish its immediate objectives, but it established the pattern. Universities were
seen, not as beneficent, liberal institutions, but as cogs in a destructive
machine. The appropriate response was to resist, and the experience
of the civil rights movement supplied a tactic: the sit-in. Government
agencies began the search for alternatives which would eventually
yield an all-volunteer army.

The 1966 SDS convention evolved the concept of student power.
It marked the return of the organization from reform and confrontation efforts in the world outside the campus to concentrate upon the
radicalization of students. SDS wanted to build a generation committed to radical social change; its leading program was called the
Radical Education Project. The universities responded with offers of
educational reform, student representation on key committees, and
similar changes. Some universities eliminated South African and defense firms from their investment portfolios. But the charge of complicity on the part of universities was basically a point about the larger
society. Students acted out their concerns in whatever manner presented itself: sit-ins, or picketing a Marine recruiter, or boycotting
campus elections. One of the more widely publicized events was the
trapping of Defense Secretary Robert McNamara in his car at Harvard.
By then, SDS had 30,000 members in 265 local chapters.

Massive demonstrations at the University of Wisconsin to block
the access of recruiters from the Dow Chemical Company took place

Leonard Freed

in 1967. It was one of the pattern-setting campus actions; tear gas was used for the first time on a college campus. SDS remained the national, political organization of campus youth; but college students, the counter-culture, hippies, and even long hair were national news. *Time* named college youth "Man of the Year" in its annual cover story. Two precedent-setting resolutions were passed at the 1967 SDS convention: one recognized male chauvinism and the legitimate claim of women's liberation; the second demanded immediate withdrawal from Vietnam, not mere negotiation. "Man of the Year" strikes back!

The resistance grew. The action was in the streets, on the campus, and in Washington. Nineteen sixty-seven was the year of the March on the Pentagon. Draft cards were burned. Young men chose jail or expatriation as alternatives to military service.

1968 was the year of violence, the turning away from American to foreign models. The year began with some members of SDS visiting Cuba. Posters of Che Guevara, Mao Tse-Tung, and Fidel Castro decorated SDS meetings. After Eugene McCarthy's good showing in the New Hampshire primary, and the entry of Robert Kennedy into the race for the nomination, there was campus talk of "giving the system one last chance." But the SDS leadership was committed to the belief that mere liberal reform (which Kennedy promised) would be ineffectual except as a tactic to delay the final revolution. On April 4, Martin Luther King was shot in Memphis. The ghettos exploded; SDS spokesmen argued that the system did not deserve another chance. In the first six months of the year, there were 221 major demonstrations at 110 colleges and universities. One of the longest and most publicized was at Columbia University in New York. Lyndon Johnson and the House Committee on Un-American Activities attacked SDS. FBI Director J. Edgar Hoover said that Communists were active in its leadership. Several FBI agents had already infiltrated SDS; a few organized new campus chapters.

The demonstrations at the Democratic National Convention in Chicago were not planned by SDS, although SDS "alumni," including co-founder Tom Hayden, were involved. SDS sent in organizers to recruit young McCarthy supporters away from electoral politics and into the revolution. The police riots radicalized students much more effectively than SDS rhetoric. A conviction grew that "black power" and "youth power," joining in the streets, could be the vehicle of revolt.

While the nation was caught up in the three-way contest between Humphrey, Nixon, and George Wallace, the SDS national convention took place in a different world. A seminar on sabotage and explosives drew the policemen, FBI agents, and other infiltrators away from the serious business of the convention. That business was never really concluded because of a frontal assault upon the machinery of SDS by the Progressive Labor party (PL), a group then centered largely in New York, which used Old Left analyses and sought an alliance between students and workers as the vehicle for social change. PL did not wish to combat the Vietnam War with such vigor as to offend the hardhats. The national headquarters group attempted to expel PL from the convention. The resolution was defeated, and PL stayed on, attempting to impose its politics on SDS. PL needed student members, for it was failing to attract industrial workers. When this contest moved into the local chapters, some members simply dropped out of SDS, rather than face the contest: the New Left was supposed to mean harmony, yet they were being asked to choose between contesting ideologies.

The fall of 1968 was a time of violence on campus, and a time of expansion in SDS membership. Membership reached a peak of between 80,000 and 100,000 in more than 350 local chapters. At national headquarters, the staff was busy handling inquiries from the media, fending off the efforts of the PL group, and trying to become a revolutionary force. The action was in the local chapters; the national bureaucracy could not determine what would be done in the name of SDS. Not realizing that the force of campus violence was temporarily spent, SDS leaders called for a student strike on election day. The posters read:

> THE ELECTIONS
> DON'T MEAN SHIT.
> VOTE WHERE THE POWER IS.
> OUR POWER
> IS IN THE STREET.

Not a single high school or college was successfully closed down.

At the 1968 SDS convention, the increasing influence of PL was countered by agreeing that SDS would no longer attempt to define anew the nature and meaning of white, middle-class, "post-scarcity" American college students. Rather than attempting to seek the relevance for the 1970s of the insights written in the *Port Huron Statement*, SDS voted to accept as its guiding ideology a version of traditional Marxism.

It was the beginning of the end.

IV: Underground in Amerika

The final struggle for the tattered soul of SDS came at the national convention of 1969. Progressive Labor forces numbered perhaps a third of the delegates. PL was strictly Old Left; it disdained the Black Panthers' breakfast program for schoolchildren and campus efforts to make ROTC voluntary or create co-ed dormitories as ameliorative efforts that could only inhibit the development of political consciousness and postpone the inevitable revolt of the working class. PL was committed to forging an alliance between students and workers, ignoring a major lesson of the 1968 election. Non-student voters of college age—who went to the factory, not to college—gave George Wallace his greatest support outside the South. The SDS constituency was smaller than it seemed.

The national leaders distributed a statement exposing the errors of the PL faction. It began with a phrase from Bob Dylan, "You don't need a weatherman to know which way the wind blows." The point was that the young did not need the rigid discipline and direction of the PL hierarchy to know what the making of a revolution would require. After a tense and noisy meeting in the Chicago Coliseum, Bernadine Dohrn led a walkout of the anti-PL forces which caucused in an adjoining room, announced that they represented the true SDS, and expelled the adherents of the Progressive Labor party, who of course did not accept expulsion. Weatherman was born.

That summer, Weatherman cells established communes based on abolishing middle-class practices such as monogamy, privacy, and property in order to concentrate on developing revolutionary consciousness. They also attempted to recruit ghetto teen-agers into the revolution by convincing them that American materialism can lead only to corruption and that individuals should be prepared to give up their lives to build the revolutionary force. The teenagers decided the college students were crazy.

In October 1969 came the "Days of Rage," planned as an uprising of a people's army against "the pig power structure." Only 300 people came to the revolution. They broke a lot of windows with chains and clubs before they were thoroughly subdued by the Chicago police. The *Port Huron Statement* had deplored violence because it requires "the transformation of the target, be it a human being or a community of people, into a depersonalized object of hate." The Weathermen felt that their best efforts to change the system had been rebuffed; that they had no role, as whites, to play in the black revolution; and that the working class was hopelessly corrupted. The only answer was to go underground, then to strike out unexpectedly. Their rhetoric became a symphony of hate: "pig Amerika" was the target.

During the 1969–1970 school year, major bombings related to "campus disturbances" occurred at the rate of at least one a day throughout the nation. When Weathermen were involved, they delivered messages explaining the symbolic reason for this particular target. These explanations were largely ignored. The press covered the destruction of property and the threat to life. The notion that the destruction of innocent peasants by napalm could somehow be avenged by planting a bomb in a bank never won wide public understanding, much less sympathy.

V: The Aftermath

Student activism in the 1960s could claim major achievements: students were able to live more free and open lives within their universities, and the faculties engaged in less military research; Lyndon Johnson was forced to withdraw from the 1968 electoral contest; the draft was finally abolished; and eighteen-year-olds won the right to vote. Thousands of students questioned the creed of individual achievement and ruthless economic competition that their parents and even their older brothers and sisters had lived by.

The Nixon administration was not able to handle that challenge on an intellectual level; instead of beginning a dialogue with youth, the president demanded evidence of foreign influence upon the student movement. After lengthy investigation, the CIA reported there was no significant contact between foreign governments and domestic radicals. The president asked the FBI to set up offices in foreign countries and conduct the investigation all over again.

In reaction to the terrorism of 1968 to 1970, a belief grew within the White House staff that the violent rejection of national policies could only be countered by the kind of tactics normally used to frustrate the secret operations of some foreign government. This grew into a distrust of political opposition and, by inference, of the people themselves. In 1972, a campaign group lodged in the White House itself, originally established to protect national security, launched illegal operations aimed at the opposition party. The scope of those operations were only revealed by the Watergate investigations of 1973.

Thus, while the SDS never succeeded in establishing a "democracy of individual participation," the essentially self-destructive acts of the Weathermen helped initiate a chain of events with profound implications for American politics.

For a time, SDS symbolized the frustrations of a generation and its judgment upon the structure of power. To change that structure, it was necessary to enlist the aid of the people. That required approaching the people as Americans—with a certain pride in citizenship, a certain fondness for their region, and a deep attachment to such symbols as the flag and the Declaration of Independence. The people could not understand a group that proclaimed as heroes such then declared enemies as Mao, or adopted tired Marxist theories to justify their tactics. The bombing of public buildings not only offended a bourgeois fondness for property; it outraged a simple sense of decency.

When former Vice President Agnew described the student activists as "elitist," he meant that they had grown out of touch with the people.

The people retained a sense of decency. When indicted for income tax evasion—the failure to report income from tainted gifts he received—Agnew resigned, rather than face the full agony of public disgrace himself, or further tarnish the troubled Nixon administration.

He also wanted to stay out of jail.

Two failed revolutions, then. Richard Nixon's effort to attack poverty by achieving a modest redistribution of the national income; the efforts of SDS to remake democratic institutions. Both calling upon the people for support, both failing to generate the public enthusiasm essential to success.

What does it take, in America, to achieve social and political change?

Politics and Change:
What Is the Power
of the People?

As its two-hundredth anniversary drew near, the United States did not reexamine its principles or modernize its values to make them appropriate guides for the future. The opening years of the 1970s were, instead, spent in recovering from the previous decade's turmoil.

In the 1960s, group after group called stridently for revolutionary change. Society was in ferment, but the political system did not adapt to social change. In 1972, President Nixon claimed that the electoral majority demanded diminished federal support for social change, such as racial integration. His "new federalism" offered federal financial support for solutions planned by "grassroots governments" in place of national action to resolve national problems.

By returning to a conception of federalism closer to that of the founding fathers, was President Nixon abandoning a national quest based on the noble principles of the Declaration of Independence? The student movement of the 1960s, inspired and guided by the SDS, was only a memory. The most appealing part of Mr. Nixon's abortive 1971 "New Revolution"—The Family Assistance Plan—was dead. The voters approved the demise of both.

Americans are not equipped by experience to understand revolutions, and they have seldom proved hospitable to revolutionaries. When that fact is understood, the power of the people to achieve political change comes into clearer focus.

Echoes of a Revolution that Never Was

If a revolution is defined as the complete overthrow of an existing political system, then the American Revolution wasn't one. It was more closely akin to a *reinstatement*. The conflict with England which preceded the Declaration of Independence revolved around the demand that Americans be permitted to enjoy the rights of Englishmen, which they had done for more than a century and a half, until those rights were abrogated by George III. They complained of the usurpation of powers, long exercised by the colonial legislatures, by the Royal Governors. For tactical reasons, the rights asserted in the Declaration were stated in universal terms. There was no intention of overthrowing the political system or social structure existing in the colonies. Only the ties with the mother country were to be cast off. Those ties had grown very loose over the years, and the colonists found the tightening of them by the British monarch intolerable.

When the rebellion against England succeeded, the United States
was left with a statement of universal rights in the Declaration of
Independence, without the necessity of destroying dominant social
classes to establish the validity of those rights. (Those choosing loyalty to the British monarch emigrated, largely to Canada.) Therefore,
America was not burdened by the traditions and institutions of feudalism, which were replaced in Europe only through violence. Alexis
de Tocqueville perceived this central truth of the American experience. Americans, he wrote, were "born equal." Their equality was
achieved at the same time as their national consciousness. There was
no sense of conflict between recognized social classes, no sense of a
unity of a lower class brought about by the oppression of their masters. In the time of Andrew Jackson, when Tocqueville wrote, there
were clear economic inequalities among Americans, but these were
little reflected in American social and psychological attitudes. Years
before, Governor Hutchinson of Massachusetts complained that a
"gentleman" did not meet even "common civility" from his in-
feriors.[1] Before and after the revolt against England, America was a
thoroughly bourgeois society; even the aristocrats of Virginia and
along the Hudson River had to compete furiously in the capitalistic
marketplace to retain their positions.

Thus America lacked the tension between the old order and the
new, the conflict between the social classes, which in Europe stimulated violence and the justification of violence. For practical purposes,
the questions which political philosophy confronted in Europe were
already settled in the United States. They were settled by the Declaration of Independence; and their implications for the structure of government were realized a few years later in the Constitution. All
questions of morality implicit in the enterprise of governing seemed
to be answered; it only remained to work out the details. It was no
accident that a "cult of the Constitution" quickly developed, and the
Supreme Court met with little resistance when it took unto itself the
authority of ultimate interpretation. The parallel with religious history is clear. The founding fathers were the law givers; the nine justices were the high priests who applied the law to daily circumstances.
A structure of legalism was erected upon the corpse of philosophy.

Thus the Constitution became the source of legitimacy of
American government. For many, it was a mystical symbol that
needed no explanation. If an explanation were required, it was this:
the eternal truths of human society stated in the Declaration of
Independence were realized in the Constitution, which was a social
contract formulated by the American people as a people, as well as
by the states as states. Decisions issuing from this government were
right, just, and should be obeyed, for they were formulated through a
democratic process in which equal citizens were free to participate.

Being "born equal," without explicit recognition of the reality of
social classes, handicapped the Americans when they encountered
European philosophies based on that recognition. Socialism, and later
communism, were initially condemned not so much for being *evil* as
for being *incomprehensible*. Since America achieved official freedom
and equality without the necessity of a true revolution, the American
mind had difficulty understanding those who called for revolution.
(The First Amendment protected their call, as long as it remained an
abstract doctrine.)[2]

---

1. Quoted in Louis Hartz, *The Liberal Tradition in America* (New York: Harcourt, Brace,
1955), p. 55. My debt to Hartz in this analysis will be obvious to his readers.
2. See above, pp. 180–184, 195–200, and 204, for a discussion of freedom of speech.

The First Great American Ideology

Americans were "born equal," assured of equality and able to entertain unlimited ambitions, even if economic conditions threatened to make those ambitions unreal. (The slave didn't count. Neither did the Indian.) Contrasting themselves to French society, with its four recognized classes or "estates," the Americans declared, "we are all of the same estate." The farmer on the frontier, the shopkeeper in the city, the craftsman in his workshop, and even (with some reservations) the planter on his plantation could all join in this declaration as the nineteenth century dawned. The New World had produced a New Man.

The Marxist critic may attempt to dismiss this historical moment by applying the Marxist epithet, "false consciousness." In the Marxist analysis, no reality is greater than the reality of social class. In America, the subjective feeling was much more powerful. Denying that social origins or social status could limit his individual achievement, the American at that historical moment effectively suspended the impact of such limitations, and the reality which Horatio Alger would elevate into myth was born.

The single most important influence upon the thought of the nation's founders was probably the philosophy of John Locke. Locke's liberalism focused its attention upon the relationship between the individual and the state. The state existed to preserve the life, liberty, and property of the individual, and the rights of the individual were defined as limitations upon the state. No account was given of other social realities. Locke did this because the feudal tradition had emphasized such realities—family, church, social status—to the near exclusion of the individual, and Locke was attempting to restore the individual to a place of importance. But Americans had not experienced feudal institutions. Adopting Locke as their patron, Americans built a government on the fallacious assumption that the whole of political and social reality is encompassed in the relationship between the individual and the state:

Any relationship between the individual and his church is rendered politically inconsequential by guaranteeing religious freedom.

The state is concerned with education, to make individuals capable of performing the duties of citizenship; educational institutions are not seen as an independent social force.

The role of the family is largely forgotten, for the state deals only with individuals.

And, with all ethical questions solved and their solutions emblazoned in the Declaration and the Constitution, the Americans turn their attention to questions of detail and technique, which do not depend upon a reexamination of the basic premises. This habit is called "pragmatism."

Capitalism and the Liberal State

Because Lockean liberalism was based upon suspicion of the power of the state, it was insensitive to the accumulation of power in private hands. Liberalism became the ideal handmaiden of industrial capitalism.

Although the Declaration of Independence had been couched in terms of political rights, the complaints of the colonists had been in large measure against economic control. The mercantilist policies of England controlled the trade of the colonies. Adam Smith's *Wealth of Nations*, published in 1776, called for free trade and decried any government interference in economic matters. It was perhaps more widely read in America than in England. It neatly matched the suspicion of governmental power derived from Locke, and it reinforced the passion for thrift and individual accomplishment that were part of the Protestant ethic. Smith claimed that, when many individual entrepreneurs seek to maximize their individual profit unrestrained by government, an "invisible hand" operates in the free economy to assure the greater good of all society. As it became the public ideology, Smith's doctrine was known as laissez faire capitalism. It was an ideology in Niebuhr's sense: a corruption of the reasoning process in the interest of self.[3] Further reinforced by notions of the morality of private property and the sanctity of contracts, laissez-faire swept all before it, including eminent social philosophers (the Social Darwinists) and the Supreme Court of the United States.

The spiral of technological advance, the abundance of raw materials as the nation expanded westward, and the concept of laissez faire combined to produce the industrial giant known as the United States of America. Although the face of society was transformed, and the contrast between rich and poor became more striking, the Constitution was regarded as the repository of all governmental wisdom. In the shadow of its presence, the corporation became the dominant force in the economy and the society, unfettered by public regulation. Corporate ownership was divided among the stockholders, but the corporation alone was responsible for debt or failure, and the greatest rewards went to the managers. When the corporation was defined as a person, it was found to enjoy the rights guaranteed by the Fourteenth Amendment!

> The corporate form developed as a result of its success in meeting the need for rapid industrial expansion, with its promise of plenty in an economy of scarcity. The invention of the limited liability joint stock company ensured that risk-taking was maximally rewarded and minimally penalized for failure. In the absence of broad gauge social planning to develop industry, a premium was placed on the entrepreneurial skills needed to set up factories; rather than hedge the freedom of the entrepreneur by forcing him to confront the problem of social planning and social purposes, either within his plant or in society, he was conveniently left to concern himself with profits. The social structure formed in an earlier age was capable of containing the chaotic effects of this for a while. Subsequent legislation limited the resulting grosser deprivations of the system, while allowing the subtler effects—alienation, regimentation, class division— to be perpetuated throughout society.[4]

Throughout most of the nineteenth century, during times of economic prosperity, hardly a voice was heard from the people to protest the human cost of developing industrialism. Laissez faire ruled because the lesser members of the system had little sense that their status could be permanent. The expanding frontier beckoned, with

3. The concept is introduced above, p. 388.
4. C. George Benello, "Participatory Democracy and the Dilemma of Change," in P. Long, ed., *The New Left: A Collection of Essays* (Boston: Porter Sargent, 1969), p. 411.

its promise of a new start. The dissatisfied employee was free to found his own enterprise. Workers did not think of themselves as working-men but as apprentice capitalists.

As transportation developed, farmers did not live in partnership with the land in the manner Jefferson envisaged. Increasingly, they drained its fertility and then moved on to new opportunities. With the emphasis on raising cash crops, they, too, were independent entre-preneurs.

The impact of the Civil War merely accelerated the growth of corporate power, and the zenith of laissez faire came in its aftermath.[5] When periodic economic recessions occurred, political discontent was voiced, and the corporations were its target. But the public and its leaders were enthralled by the laissez-faire ideology.

Discontent died as times improved, and Americans returned to the capitalistic scramble. Discontent that could survive an upswing in the trade cycle came only in the closing decade of the century, and William Jennings Bryan was its spokesman. The Democratic party adopted Bryan and his populist program. But Bryan's cure-all remedy, the free coinage of silver, did not attract the support of his potential constituency among the workingmen of the East.

Labor organization gained momentum around the turn of the cen-tury, and the long series of bloody battles began. The very name of the International Workers of the World (a pioneer union) suggested its alien inspiration. The immediate result was to stimulate the for-mulation of the Progressive movement, as members of the middle class feared that their share of the national bounty might be ground down by the organizing workers on one hand and the power of the corporations on the other.

Political Change through Critical Elections
Adjustments by the American political system to economic and social development have not been accomplished by revolutionary leaders demanding the overthrow of the system. Such movements have served to warn major party leaders of the need for change. When change comes, it is made in the name of furthering traditional values and preserving the Constitution, while satisfying the political de-mands of powerful, dissident groups. The vehicle for change has been the critical election.

Thomas Jefferson entered the presidency with the support of frontiersmen who resented the economic power of the merchants and financiers of the seacoast. He also expressed opposition against the Alien and Sedition Acts of John Adams's administra-tion, which seemed to negate the Bill of Rights. His dual cause: more equal economic opportunity and protecting the rights of the people.

Andrew Jackson voiced the complaints of farmers, frontiersmen, and workers against monopolized economic power in the form of the U.S. Bank. He also expressed the conviction that the common man is capable of managing his own affairs, rather than assigning leading roles in national government to the aristocracy (whether from Virginia or Massachusetts), which had previously claimed the White House. His causes: democratic equalitarianism and more equal economic opportunity.

5. This was the national economic impact of the Civil War. For a discussion of the signifi-cance of the war, see pp. 323–327, above.

Abraham Lincoln was elected by the new Republican party, a sectional alliance united by its opposition to the extension of slavery into the new territories; freedom, equality, economic opportunity, and the ascendancy of the small landowner against the slavocracy were the mixed motives of the coalition.

The election of William McKinley in 1896 ended the Populist insurgence of small farmers and workingmen, establishing the Republican party as the normal majority. But reformist sentiment quickly arose as a middle-class movement within the dominant party, directed at what Theodore Roosevelt called "the malefactors of great wealth." Its aim was to control economic monopolies in order to assure equality of opportunity, particularly for small businessmen. The Progressives moved toward the destruction of urban party organizations without appreciating the crucial services performed by party organizations for the urban, immigrant workingman.

Each of these critical elections, which adapted the political system to changing reality, occurred under two banners: furthering freedom and equal opportunity—the inalienable rights of the Declaration of Independence—and limiting the dominance of economic elites. Rather than using the power of government in a positive manner, responding directly to the needs of the people, their purpose was to limit the oppressive power of private institutions. Their goal was to make individuals better able to achieve economic success for themselves.

Each of these four critical elections featured a mixture of idealism and self-interest on the part of the voters. Each of the winning candidates—including McKinley, champion of the full dinner pail—articulated both the hopes and the fears of the people. Each of the four campaigns drew its intellectual justification from the first great American ideology, which held that the first duty of government was to preserve the freedom of the marketplace. The "invisible hand" of the marketplace would provide the greatest good for society.

The New Deal and a New Ideology

The invisible hand did not save the stock market from the reward of folly. Its collapse in 1929 triggered a profound dissolution of the entire economy. Still devoted to Lockean liberalism, Herbert Hoover—and the leading political and financial minds of the country—were helpless. For they saw the central intention of the Constitution as being to limit the scope, while prescribing the form, of government. Their sense of helplessness was felt by the people, but there was no widespread turning toward "alien" remedies like socialism.

Franklin D. Roosevelt did not bring to the White House any penchant for challenging basic premises. Public despair brought a call for the expansion of the scope of government, and the New Deal yielded to that call in a pragmatic manner. The first effort toward national action to bring prosperity was the National Industrial Recovery Act. Its theory was as much derived from Locke and Adam Smith as was Herbert Hoover's philosophy. It was based on the assumption that economic collapse resulted from unfair competitive practices indulged in by certain firms; it was necessary to restore the free market. Representatives of each industry were convened to agree on a code of fair competition which would govern that industry. The code was then added to the regulations of the National Recovery Administration, with the force of law. In effect, Congress *delegated* to the industry itself any authority it might have to regulate that industry.

Based on a diagnosis of economic ills that was erroneous, the NIRA, after an initial rally due to public enthusiasm, was revealed as totally ineffective. There was no great distress in the government when the Supreme Court found it to be unconstitutional.[6]

Invalidation of the NIRA meant that other remedies should be applied, but no new examination of basic premises was attempted. Organized labor had been awarded a "slice" of the National Industrial Recovery Act in its Section 7A; this was expanded and rewritten in the Wagner Act, which became known as the Magna Carta of American Labor. It guaranteed the right of unions to organize and to bargain collectively; government supervision of union elections was provided, and many anti-union practices of business were prohibited. Again, rather than public power being used to intervene in the operation of the economy, public authority was used to protect the ability of private organizations to bargain with each other in the marketplace.

This "solution" of the problems of labor was but an extension of the practices being developed for agriculture even before the New Deal.

> That agricultural affairs should be handled strictly within the agricultural community is a basic political principle established before the turn of the century and maintained since then without serious reexamination. As a result, agriculture has become neither public nor private enterprise. It is a system of self-government in which each leading farm interest controls a segment of agriculture through a delegation of national sovereignty. Agriculture has emerged as a largely self-governing federal estate within the Federal structure of the United States.[7]

The organization of agriculture has totally excluded the rural poor. When Roosevelt's New Deal attempted to help the rural poor, it was found that this purpose was so foreign to the Department of Agriculture that an entirely new agency, the Farm Security Administration, was required. Congress established the new agency but systematically starved it of appropriations; it expired quietly with the outbreak of World War II.

As with agriculture, so too with other special interests. Rather than a small number of agencies, responsible to the elected officials of government and hence ultimately to the people, the trend of government since the New Deal has been the creation of a large number of semi-autonomous, client-oriented, highly specialized agencies chartered originally by Congress and largely divorced from either congressional or administrative control.

The New Deal developed the concept of the positive state, and therefore an enormous expansion of the scope of government, in response to public recognition that no invisible hand operated to preserve society and the economy against disaster. The Lockean conviction that the single important relationship was between the individual and the state was clearly out of date in the complex organization of twentieth-century America, and a substitute conception quickly developed.

---

6. *Schecter Poultry Corp.* v. *United States*, 295 U.S. 495 (1935). See above, p. 198.
7. Theodore J. Lowi, *The End of Liberalism* (New York: Norton, 1969), p. 103. This provocative book should be read by every serious student of American politics.

An important insight of American political science held that men of like interests naturally combine into groups to further their political interests; it is possible to conceive of these groups as the only meaningful units of politics. Because they are many in number and diverse in outlook, they are said to bring the quality of "pluralism" to society.

What began as an *hypothesis* about the nature of American politics was soon accepted as a *description* of the political world, as the evidence of the ubiquitous operations of interest groups came flooding in. Political scientists discovered that their former concern for law and formal institutions had not explained the political process, and they seized upon the interest group as a concept with great explanatory power. Several political scientists began to justify the clash between interest groups as providing something akin to an invisible hand that maintained the equilibrium of the political system. Grant McConnell wrote of this development:

> This attribution of almost all virtue to the institutionalization of what another era might have seen as narrow selfishness is a remarkable phenomenon, particularly since it comes from some of the more generous minds of our time.[8]

Accepting the hypothesis of pluralism as the key to political reality brought into being a new public ideology. We may identify it as "interest-group liberalism."

Laissez faire had denied the authority of the people *as a people* to control their own destiny, claiming that such attempts would only disturb the natural regulatory mechanism of the marketplace. Interest-group liberalism also functioned to deny the authority of the people *as a people* to control their own destiny. It shared Locke's suspicion of governmental power. Seeing the relationship between government and the group as the single most important relationship, it increasingly cast government in the role of impartial referee, assigned the task of assuring that contending groups resolve their differences to their mutual satisfaction and with little obvious damage to the public interest. In fact, many groups came to exercise the authority of government within their limited spheres. The ideology of interest-group liberalism saw political parties not as vehicles for the forging and expression of the public will but rather as master groups that acted as brokers between special interests, charged with their "aggrandizement" into public policy.[9]

The outlook of interest-group liberalism was as limited in its own way as had been that of laissez faire. This fact was obscured for twenty years by a noisy controversy between the fading ideology and the emerging one.

Laissez faire, a product of nineteenth-century liberalism, was tagged "conservatism."

"Liberalism" was appropriated for its name by the new ideology, and identified with the values defined in the Declaration of Independence.

An Ever-Growing Pie
Developed in a time of economic distress, the new ideology of interest-group liberalism was as devoted to the exploitation of the en-

8. Grant McConnell, *Private Power and American Democracy* (New York: Knopf, 1967), p. 353.
9. The pluralist analysis has been challenged by the elitists. See Chapter 7, pp. 288-292.

vironment and the acquisition of material rewards as laissez-faire capitalism. Yet, because it was based on facilitating the pursuit of their special interests by specific groups, it shied away from the use of public authority (responsible to all the people) to determine that one interest was superior to another, that one claim was more deserving than another. This determination was made only through the clash of interests, and the group which could marshall the most impressive array of political influence at a given time would win that particular round of the continuing battle. The power of the strongest existing groups was reinforced.

Interest-group liberalism, therefore, is not capable of establishing a new pattern of sharing between the interests in society. It does not take the pie of national resources and reallocate them into different sized slices. It contains new political pressures by yielding to the demands of new organizations without reducing the status of existing organizations. Therefore, pluralism depends upon the expansion of the total national economy and productivity. It does not take from an established interest to supply an emerging one.

For example:

In spite of the official schedule of income tax rates, which is steeply graduated, there are so many provisions for special interests (depletion allowances, lower tax on capital gains, no tax on family foundations, etc.) that men of wealth have little trouble becoming wealthier. A public outcry resulted in the modification of these special benefits in 1969, but Congress recognized that they were built into the economy, and the reforms were timed to take effect gradually.

The Social Security system is rightly considered an important achievement of the New Deal. It is an insurance system in which both worker and employer pay premiums. No contribution by the rest of society through the government budget need be provided, and workers are only eligible for benefits after they have paid premiums for a period of years. It is not a scheme for the redistribution of wealth.

Semi-independent agencies (such as the Food and Drug Administration, the Federal Communications Commission, and the Federal Aviation Agency) established to regulate specific industries are constantly being exposed by journalists for being dominated by the attitudes and some of the personnel of the very industries they are assigned to guard. But the exposés seldom change anything.

Two glaring oversights in the ideology of interest-group liberalism blind it to important social realities and make it an inappropriate guide to the development of governmental organizations and policies in the 1970s:

Because it deals with organized interests, it is handicapped in dealing with the needs of inarticulate groups which do not present themselves according to the rules of pluralism, including consumers, the rural poor, migratory farm workers, and the urban poor. There was no organized group ready to demand enactment of President Nixon's Family Assistance Plan.

Since interest-group liberalism is concerned above all with the instincts of exploitation and acquisition, its premises exclude the fact that the supply of national resources is becoming exhausted, the environment is becoming polluted, and that, in the coming era, American government must labor to limit certain kinds of production, rather than increasing all kinds.

President Nixon and the American Dream

The two great ideologies of American life managed to entwine doctrines of political right with convictions about economic organization. First rampant capitalism and then interest-group liberalism produced an abundance unknown in the history of mankind. Both were philosophies of exploitation, assuming that endless natural resources awaited development by men for their own use and comfort. When the system exploited other men, reserving all the profits to a small group, political action painfully achieved adjustments which either distributed the system's rewards on a wider basis, or encouraged dissident groups to feel that their competitive chances had been restored.

The monument of the New Deal was the American labor movement, which, at the instant of achieving success, also acquired respectability, by abandoning European notions of the class struggle and settling down to carve out its own empires of exploitation. American society developed a class structure quite like that of other industrial nations:

> *The upper class*, of inherited wealth, owner of great enterprises, claiming influence in the seats of government, and possessing its own schools, churches, and charities;

> *The middle class*, made up of shopkeepers and professional men, the doctors and lawyers and bond salesmen and labor union officials, and the public school teachers who implanted the values of the middle class in their charges;

> *The working class*, with its simpler joys and lesser education, possessing skills which commanded increasing wages because of the ability to withhold them through a strike. After a generation, workers were receiving incomes as good or better than those of the middle class, and acquiring middle-class burdens: a suburban home, crabgrass, and an annual vacation.

Because the notion of permanent social classes was foreign, however, the workingman identified his own virtues with middle-class values, and a real aristocracy never developed. Whatever developed that was the equivalent of an aristocracy never publicly claimed superiority over less affluent, or less pedigreed, families. We were a thoroughly bourgeois nation.

But this structure left out the tenant farmers of the South and families living on eroded acres in Appalachia who could not organize to force greater rewards from the system. For the last four decades, they have been driven from their land to the slums of great cities. Nor did this structure allow for the technological change that was making the world of work more complicated, increasing the educational requirements for entry into most occupations, and automating industry to the point that fewer employees were needed to assure basic industrial productivity. There was a massive shift of workers from industry into the service fields, from dry cleaning to tree spraying. The economy changed from an emphasis on production to an emphasis on consumption. The entire system depended on the stimulation of consumer desires for the products of an ever-expanding technology.

The change began after World War I, was obscured by the suffering of the Depression, but was accomplished after World War II. America became a post-industrial society. Walter Dean Burnham has borrowed terminology from David Apter to explain that, in modern America, the structure of social classes has been substantially reorganized.[10] It now consists of:

The technologically competent, who manage large organizations, oversee the further developments of technology, plan advertising campaigns, conduct research, and either use computers themselves, or employ people who use computers, for functions ranging from simple bookkeeping to the design of guided missiles. Highly educated, this class includes much of, but is not limited to, the old upper class. One of the divisions within it is created by conflicting attitudes about the duty of this class to the other elements of society. Those who have newly arrived in these higher circles feel that every individual should be required to achieve wealth (or even subsistence) strictly on his own — emphasizing the value of achievement. Those who have lived with their wealth long enough to be comfortable with it support government programs aimed at improving the welfare of society's least fortunate members — emphasizing the value of equality.

The technologically obsolescent, those who have achieved comfort in the present system but are threatened by further technological change. They include assembly-line workers, bank clerks (and some bank presidents), salesmen, construction workers and other union members, small tradesmen threatened by national chain stores, and the elites of small towns and cities that are dying because of population movement into the sprawling metropolitan areas on the East and West coasts. They are engineers unable to keep up with developments in their own fields. They are the Middle Americans.

The technologically superfluous, those members of society who have no skills to offer, and no services to perform, for the system. They live on small, eroded farms, in the ghettos of large cities, and on Indian reservations. There are no secure roles for them in a technological society, for the kind of labor that requires pure strength has been taken over by machines. With no skills to sell, the members of this underclass receive no rewards from a free-enterprise economy. But their lack of saleable skills — reflecting a lack of education and training, or a lifetime in agricultural labor before they were uprooted from the soil — hardly results from the failure of personal ambition.

10. Walter Dean Burnham, *Critical Elections and the Mainsprings of American Politics* (New York: Norton, 1970), p. 138ff. Apter's work is his essay in *Ideology and Discontent* (Glencoe, Ill.: Free Press, 1964).

Politics Transformed

According to Burnham, the shape of American politics has been transformed by this change in the class structure. Clinging to attitudes formulated during the New Deal, a great many of the technologically competent have formed a political alliance with the technologically superfluous. Possibly from a sense of duty, but certainly from a sense of guilt, members of this uppermost social class have determined that persons on the lowest rung of society's ladder have no skills to contribute to the work of the technological system; nevertheless, as Americans and humans, they deserve a share of its output. The nature of this alliance was clearest in the 1972 Democratic Convention, but there are liberal Republicans, the current generation of the established families of wealth, who feel the same way. Recognizing the human injustices of the system, they are willing for certain members of society to receive *something for nothing*.

John Lindsay's reelection as Mayor of New York in 1970 was supported by this coalition of the upper and lower social strata. But he only won because the Middle American vote was split by two other candidates.

The children of wealthy families were long ago placed in private schools; their families need not suffer from the integration of the public schools. If the policy of "economic mix" places publicly subsidized housing in the suburbs, it will not disturb neighborhoods which house one family on each five acres of land. The poor people will be sprinkled among the dwellings of the technologically obsolesent. Racial integration comes painfully to white neighborhoods on the fringe of the black ghetto; it does not bother the country estate. Most importantly, the cost of increasing social services is paid by middle Americans through the income tax. The wealthy have loopholes and depletion allowances and capital gains privileges, so they need not pay a proportionate share of the cost of their own charitable impulses.

The Middle Americans adhere to the value of achievement, convinced that individuals must succeed on their own, with no help from society, beyond the public schools. Many of them are the children or grandchildren of immigrants who made their way to comfort through their own efforts. They see the rewards for those efforts being eaten away by rising taxes and inflation. They feel crowded in their positions, both at work and in their neighborhoods, by the upward thrust of blacks and other minorities who are attempting to achieve middle-class status. Above all, they resent the fact that certain groups in society — black unwed mothers, for example — apparently receive something for nothing.

Throughout the decade of the 1960s, public attention focused upon the social revolution of changing lifestyles, the demand for equality in civil rights, and the campus revolt. White Middle Americans who resented the unsettling of their neighborhoods by racial change, who deplored the destruction of property by campus demonstrators, and who could not comprehend the lifestyle of an unwed mother, were told that their resistance to change stemmed from racial bigotry, and that they were betraying the meaning of the Declaration of Independence. They knew that the cost of social change fell heavily upon themselves, and their resentment grew. It was expressed as a disdain for the recipients of welfare, hatred for hippies, and a turning away from political leaders who urged yet further accommodations to the needs of those who could contribute nothing to the work of the technological system.

Resentment can be a powerful political force. Particularly when, as in this case, those harboring the resentment are a numerical majority within a democratic electorate.

> In 1968, George Wallace articulated the resentment of the Middle Americans, with his attacks on social planners and the welfare system. Only a great effort by the leaders of organized labor prevented massive desertions to Wallace from the Democratic party.

> In 1972, George McGovern (who proposed an allowance of $1,000 a year for every person in the United States) was perceived as an agent of this alliance between the upper class and the lower class. The labor leadership was urged by AFL-CIO President George Meany to remain neutral, which many did, and workingmen deserted George McGovern in large numbers. Not all Nixon voters deserted the Democratic party, however, and an opposition Congress returned to share the power of government with a Republican president.

Professor Burnham sees the most likely prospect for the future of American politics to be a period of fascism. He predicts that the "urban populist" middle group, so responsive to the appeal of George Wallace, will insist upon turning back the march of minorities toward equality and demand the repression of cultural and political dissent. Still adherents of the American Dream, the technologically obsolescent hope that they themselves, or at least their children, will be able to ascend into the highest circles. Frustrations resulting from their present position are blamed upon the poor, who threaten from below. Identifying with the materialistic values of those above, they fail to perceive that the technologically competent should be paying a larger share of the costs of a changing society.

But was the national mood, as expressed in President Nixon's landslide, really a mood that demanded harsh repression that would fit Professor Burnham's prediction of fascism? According to Kevin Phillips, prophet of the Republican majority, that mood was largely negative:

> Thanks to the failures of the liberal establishment in the 1960s—in everything from busing, the welfare explosion, don't-blame-the-criminal sociology, and mockery of patriotism to flagrant cultural elitism—the bonds that unite the New Majority are largely negative: there are a lot of things that people *just don't want done any longer.*[11]

President Nixon's "new federalism," which withdraws national concern for urban problems but promises money to help local governments with them, and his dismantling of OEO and other agencies, can be seen as a response to this mood. It can hardly be labeled "fascism."

The Inevitability of Richard M. Nixon
Garry Wills has written a social and intellectual commentary on twentieth-century America centered upon the career of Richard Nixon.[12] What other writers have treated as mystery—how Richard

11. Kevin Phillips, "Conservative Chic," *Harper's*, June 1973, p. 70. Emphasis in the original.
12. Garry Wills, *Nixon Agonistes: The Crisis of the Self-Made Man* (New York: New American Library, 1971).

Nixon, narrowly losing the presidency in 1960, soundly beaten for
the governorship of California in 1962, rose from the ashes of bitter
defeat to be elected president—he treats as no mystery at all. The
election of Richard Nixon was inevitable. For Richard Nixon personifies the classic liberalism that was formulated by John Locke and
adopted by the founding fathers; the liberalism that was applied to
economics by Adam Smith, to morality by Ralph Waldo Emerson,
to the value of ideas by John Stuart Mill, to foreign policy by Woodrow Wilson, and to interest groups by the New Deal. Wills feels that
the reemphasis of this traditional American conviction was imper-
fectly articulated by the Eisenhower administration and was a hidden
influence behind the thought of the "tough-minded" academic advisers of John F. Kennedy, who advertised "the end of ideology" yet
led us ever deeper into the quagmire of Vietnam.

Liberalism insists that the highest duty of government is to assure that equality of opportunity exists for its citizens. Their free
competition against each other, and free competition between the
organizations they form, will assure the good of all. An invisible
hand produces the advancement of society out of the relentless
striving of its individual members.

Never mind that the mythical nature of the invisible hand was
demonstrated for all to see in 1929. Never mind that American society, and the surrounding world, have become a complex tangle of
interdependent nations, groups, corporations, cartels, universities,
and even tribes. An insistence upon the value of individual achievement cuts through all the complexities. It denies that the purpose of
democratic government is related to the implementation of the will
of the people, expressed somehow by an entire people. Returning to
the conviction of the Puritans that each man is responsible for his
own salvation, it denies the possibility of wise policies seeking salvation for society.

Richard Nixon was our inevitable president because he personifies
in his career the American Dream of self-reliance, of progress from
poverty to affluence. More than the Declaration of Independence and
the Bill of Rights, this vision of self-reliance has been the American
creed. And it is based on worn-out myths.

There are groups in America which insist upon abandoning those
myths. There are the ecologists, who know that an ethic of unlimited
exploitation must conclude by consuming all natural resources, with
the ultimate collapse of the planet. There are apostles of a new open-
ness in human relationships, who call for communication across the
barriers of status and would subvert traditional distinctions based on

the power to earn. There are the young people, secure in familial support, who disdain the competitive struggle of the marketplace, and even that between the sexes, to live in cooperative harmony with each other and with nature. It doesn't always work, but what outrages those Americans who have lived their lives by the old myths is that the young people get to try something different.

Richard Nixon spoke for those who would restore the old myths, pretending that they still provide guides to action in the real world. Garry Wills concludes with ironic optimism:

> Nixon, by embodying that creed, by trying to bring it back to life, has at last reduced it to absurdity.

The World of Watergate

The tone of an administration is partly established by the president's close associates. Ideological conviction as a driving force behind the New Deal was not supplied by Franklin D. Roosevelt, the happy pragmatist. It came from men like Harry Hopkins, Henry A. Wallace, and Thomas G. Corcoran.

It is instructive to examine the backgrounds and convictions of any group of presidential intimates, to see if they possess an orientation which defines and influences the president's attitudes. It is doubly instructive in the case of Richard Nixon, for some of his highest-ranking helpers were dismissed because of their implication in the Watergate scandals.

A remarkable number of the men brought into high government posts by President Nixon came from a particular area of the United States—the "southern rim," that area of recent economic boom stretching from Florida across Texas and Arizona to southern California. According to Kevin Phillips, half the White House staff once worked at Disneyland, the temple of technological image-production. They moved on to public relations firms, or large, technologically advanced industries that are heavily engaged in defense contracting. Most were trained as lawyers, which gave weight to their promises to restore "law and order."

These men were clearly members of the technologically competent class. Furthermore, they were members of its "newly arrived" division, who did not share with the established families a sense of social responsibility. The official concern for an energy crisis has been seen as an effort by businessmen from the southern rim and their friends in government to protect the high profits of the oil industry and extend the time limit for achievement of antipollution standards by the utilities. Although their own enterprises often depend on federal contracts and subsidies, they are conservative in outlook and oppose the payment of government subsidies to individuals who cannot succeed in the free competitive market. They tend to believe in a strong military posture (defense contracts!) coupled with a reduction in the scope and expense of domestic programs.

Even more than Richard Nixon, Lyndon Johnson represented this geographical region. Johnson brought some business leaders from the southern rim into government. But Richard Nixon shared more completely their view of the world, and their immigration into Washington increased apace with his inauguration. John Ehrlichman (California lawyer) and Robert Haldeman (Los Angeles public relations man) became his top White House assistants for domestic affairs, while Richard Kleindienst (Arizona lawyer) became Attorney Gen-

eral and George Bush (Texas oilman) became co-chairman of the
Republican National Committee. Press Secretary Ronald Ziegler was
a California public relations man. Some 50 other top officials from
the southern rim could be listed. When the Nixon staff was reorganized for the second term, that region was the dominant source of
personnel.[13]

If Richard Nixon was an inevitable president, elected as defender
of an obsolete American creed that millions still cling to, then his
"southern strategy" of winning the allegiance of powerful figures in
that region, where the creed remains most influential, was a foregone
conclusion.

> The southern rim is the last frontier for free-wheeling, exploita-
> tive capitalism. Wages are lower there, and organized labor less
> powerful. Contrasts between wealth and poverty are greater. If the
> people of the nation recognize such a pattern of enterprise as de-
> structive, they should have the power to limit its operations, rather
> than seeing its leaders installed in Washington's seats of power.

When the Watergate revelations reached so close to his own door
that earlier denials of White House involvement were rendered "inoperative," President Nixon announced the firing of White House
counsel John W. Dean III and the resignation of top assistants Haldeman and Ehrlichman. Attorney General Kleindienst resigned soon
afterwards.

Mr. Nixon named Elliot Richardson to replace Kleindienst. Richardson was put forward as the Republican party's single shining
example of incorruptible integrity. A former secretary of HEW, and

Mark Godfrey

13. See Kirkpatrick Sale, "The World Behind Watergate," *New York Review of Books*, May
3, 1973. Sale charges that a number of the Nixon officials — and his close personal friend,
"Bebe" Rebozo — have been involved in ethically questionable business dealings. Kevin
Phillips writes that "The Nixon Administration is closely allied with the burgeoning
affluence of California, the South, and the Southwest." Phillips, "Conservative Chic,"
p. 66.

briefly secretary of defense, he was named as attorney general and assigned full responsibility for investigating and prosecuting the Watergate scandals. Note the symbolism. Richardson is not from the southern rim; he is a Boston aristocrat, the politically active son of an old, established family. Richardson named Archibald Cox, a Boston Democrat and Harvard law professor, as the Watergate prosecutor.

This circumstance suggests one meaning of the Watergate scandals. The investigations implicated the leading southern rim operators in the White House, discrediting the ideology which guided their actions. Their pursuit of partisan advantage, overriding any concern for morality, legality, or common sense—for what was really worth overhearing at the Democratic National Committee?—revealed the moral bankruptcy of the American dedication to unregulated competition between individuals, corporations, and political organizations.

This may seem an overly philosophical interpretation of what can be more simply described as the Republican champions of law and order getting caught breaking the law. If the interpretation is accurate, however, and many Americans may be led by the Watergate revelations to recognize the absurdity of a post-industrial America clinging to the achievement value and its corollary, interest-group liberalism, important questions remain:

What can the people do to change the direction of their government and the ideology that motivates its decisions? What is the power of the people?

If the people can initiate such change, will they choose wise alternatives? What interests or emotions are most likely to persuade the majority?

The Power of the People

The obvious power of a democratic electorate is the ability to turn out of office an administration that displeases it. But this can be done only when the calendar decrees an election; there is no provision for a vote of "no confidence" by the people, or by Congress. Is this ability to pass periodic judgment upon the incumbent's record only negative? No—there are positive alternatives. When a relationship of trust is established between the people and an inspiring leader, change is possible. The factionalism of Congress and the ability of powerful groups to counterbalance each other's influence can be negated by presidential authority that is backed by nearly united public opinion.

The potential for stagnation implicit in the separation of powers usually predominates. The most likely outcome is the protection of the status quo; change will be gradual and incremental; the structure of power and wealth will be unaffected; and the dominant ideology will continue. American national government (after which the state governments are modeled) responds sluggishly to changing convictions on the part of the people. The founders wanted it this way.

The rigidities of the Constitution can be dissolved by the actions of a president who acts in accord with a national mood that Congress shares. This happened in the first hundred days of the New Deal, when Franklin D. Roosevelt transcended the limitations of laissez-faire and offered release from despair. It happened again in the early months of Lyndon Johnson's presidency, when the national feeling of guilt at the murder of John F. Kennedy was translated by Congress into a remarkable record of domestic legislation.

Charisma

What is the quality of inspirational political leadership that persuades men to abandon self-interest in the service of a higher cause? Social science has contributed an important concept to describe this phenomenon. It is the concept of *charisma*, as developed by sociologist Max Weber.[14]

Weber distinguishes three kinds of authority in human social relationships:

Traditional authority, such as that exercised by fathers in some families, or by tribal chieftains in primitive societies;

Bureaucratic authority, which provides administration according to established rules in a settled organization;

Charismatic leadership, based on the psychological relationship between leaders and followers, which can achieve social change.

Literally, charisma means "the gift of grace." The term comes from the study of innovations in the structure and practice of religions. It designates the leader—often self-appointed—who is perceived by his followers as the spokesman for forces and realities greater than himself. The charismatic leader:

Cuts through the humdrum routine of bureaucratic authority, promising freshness, vigor, and change;

Binds followers to him with an intense personal loyalty, often stimulating a passionate opposition;

Founds organizations which live on long after him, but sink into bureaucratic routine;

Is sustained by the psychic bond between himself and his followers;

Can be dedicated to evil causes, rather than good ones—think of Adolf Hitler.

The truly charismatic American presidents (Washington, Jefferson, Lincoln, Wilson, and the two Roosevelts) have been hailed by historians as the greatest occupants of the office. They were men of decent instincts, with varying talents for political deviousness. An American president cannot operate on charisma alone. He is the chief executive officer and must administer a far-flung bureaucracy. To change the habits of the bureaucrats, to give a new sense of purpose and direction to whole departments and agencies, the president must be accepted as charismatic leader by the bureaucrats, as well as the voters.

Franklin D. Roosevelt combined sure political instincts and remarkable charisma. Although he broke the then accepted rules of administration, he was an administrative genius.

14. H. H. Gerth and C. Wright Mills, tr. and ed., *From Max Weber* (New York: Oxford University Press, 1958), pp. 51-58, 246ff.

In a memorable television interview during his first term, Richard Nixon confessed that he does not possess those qualities described as charismatic. Rather than attempting to measure that mystical relationship, he suggested that critics should judge his administration by its performance.

The dilemma of political leadership which Mr. Nixon thus acknowledged was obscured during the 1972 campaign because so few voters perceived George McGovern as a plausible alternative.

Power, or Authority?

The source of any president's power is the Constitution of the United States. The people of the United States are the source of his authority. His victory in an election may demonstrate the strength of his relationship with the people at a particular time, but it must be a continuing relationship, touched by charisma, for power and authority to be blended.

> Power and authority should, of course, go hand-in-hand. Authority invests power with dignity and honor and even a kind of sacredness. Without that mantle of authority, kings become tyrants, and the strong become bullies. By the same token presidents become suspicious and insecure and everywhere see threats which must be met and turned aside by unscrupulous guile and cunning. . . . When one senses a loss of authority, the temptation to use raw power to repair it is perhaps as irresistible as, in the long run, it is futile.[15]

Richard Nixon came to office at a time when the authority of government and authority on every level of American society was held in question by large segments of the American people. He tended to approach the problems of political leadership as applications of power, rather than as exercises of authority. In his first term, his primary instrument of "leadership" in Congress was the veto power. In his second term, he asserted his power to impound funds appropriated by Congress with a vigor unused by previous presidents, and he asserted "executive privilege" to prevent his aides from testifying before congressional committees in a manner undreamt of by George Washington, who originated the practice. Although he approached the leaders of Russia and China on the basis of shared interests, President Nixon used raw power in Southeast Asia: he bombed Vietnam until a cease-fire was signed, and he bombed Cambodia until Congress twice voted to cut off funds to support it.

Investigations into the Watergate scandals suggested that this mood—the reliance upon power, not authority—pervaded the consciousness of the men who surrounded President Nixon. Perhaps they were the embattled defenders of an outmoded laissez-faire ideology. Perhaps they merely loved power. Clearly, they did not understand the source of democratic authority as a continuing two-way relationship with the people. With his apparent blessing, they shielded the president from contact with the press, congressmen, and the public. They treated his every public appearance as a problem in image-making, denying Mr. Nixon that direct contact with the people so essential to two-way communication. The staff spent some energy drawing up lists of "enemies" of the White House, who should be excluded from any contact with it; some wished to punish these enemies

15. Page Smith, " 'Cogito Ergo Sum' . . . and Then Came Watergate," *Los Angeles Times*, June 11, 1973, Part II, pp. 6-7.

through the power of government. Both individuals and groups were named. They were as diverse as athlete Joe Namath, Senator Edmund Muskie, the staff of *The Washington Post,* and the National Welfare Rights Organization.

The voice of the people is heard in an election; but what if the election is rigged? The most shocking Watergate revelations concerned the eagerness of some of Mr. Nixon's aides to subvert the electoral process. When it came to achieving the 1972 landslide, some of them regarded the restraints of the Constitution as mere inconveniences.

When White House functionaries attempted to employ government agencies (the CIA, the FBI, and the Internal Revenue Service) to harass the administration's enemies, the bureaucracies balked, as good bureaucracies should. Civil servants did not wish to imbue their work with a partisan bias. But a group directed from the White House burglarized the office of Daniel Ellsberg's psychiatrist. They were later arrested while attempting to install electronic surveillance equipment ("bugs") at the Democratic National Committee Headquarters in the Watergate apartments. Bribery was then undertaken to obstruct justice and hide the involvement of the White House in the incident. Other members of the White House staff used their influence in the councils of governments to benefit specific corporations or industries, often in return for campaign contributions.

So far were they from understanding the quality of persuasion that establishes the legitimacy of authority that the men closest to the president treated lesser members of the staff, congressmen of their own party, and the public at large, with casual arrogance. The attempts of the president's men to use the power of their offices in such a manner has been called a preview of dictatorial government. But a vital element was missing: the approval of the people. Power was not united with authority. The exposure of the Nixon aides by a free and aggressive press, together with their prosecution by the judicial, and their investigation by the legislative, branches of government, suggested a fundamental health in the system. The investigations of Watergate could be seen as a vindication of the judgment of those who wrote the Constitution and its First Amendment: the separation of powers, together with the freedoms of speech and of the press, can and do serve the people.

The Ultimate Sanction: Impeachment

In reelecting President Nixon by a landslide, the people did not grant him the authority of an unlimited mandate. This fact was underlined by the simultaneous election of a Democratic majority to Congress.

The Watergate hearings (controlled by that Democratic majority, who wisely encouraged the Republicans to do most of the talking) suggested that the secret conduct of President Nixon's aides, who had become the equivalent of eighteenth-century court favorites, when exposed to public view, deeply offended a sense of decency held by the people. Such a sense of decency can displace public cynicism about politicians. It is outraged at discovering a blatant attempt to manipulate the people's judgment. A sense of democratic decency insists on the right of the people, as a whole people, to control their own fate. It offers contempt to those who would treat the people with contempt. When Spiro T. Agnew resigned as Vice President, he said he wanted to save his family and the nation from the agony of a long trial. He did not care to experience the full force of public condemnation.

But a handful of resignations does not change the convictions or direction of an administration. The Constitution provides for the voice of the people to be heard through elections only at stated intervals. If high officials deeply offend the people, their representatives in Congress can apply the ultimate sanction: removal from office through impeachment. A majority of the House of Representatives can impeach a president, and two thirds of the Senate can convict him, with the Chief Justice of the United States presiding at the trial.

It is a drastic measure. Impeachment is not a weapon for the people to use against mere incompetence or arrogance. The Constitution provides that it shall be invoked against "Treason, Bribery, or other high Crimes and Misdemeanors." The founding fathers provided the people with an ultimate sanction against their elected officials, but they wished to avoid the abuses which the impeachment process had developed in eighteenth-century England. The only outcome of a conviction following impeachment can be removal from office. The person thus removed can then be indicted for committing actual crimes and tried in a court of law. Impeachment amputates the offending limb of government, rather than treating its infection.

The constitutional provisions suggest, but they do not state, that a president may be impeached for politically offensive actions which are not, in the strictest sense, illegal. Confusion over this point has given pause to those urging impeachment proceedings in the past and contributed to the acquittal of President Andrew Johnson. In the Watergate testimony, however, persons very close to the president were implicated in clearly illegal acts: wiretapping, bribery, burglary, and a conspiracy to obstruct justice, among others.

American political campaigns have never been rational debates conducted by gentlemanly rules. Casual spying in the camp of the opposition has been something of a tradition. Democrats have played "dirty tricks" upon Republicans, and vice versa; in 1964, Richard Tuck smuggled pretty models, who were pro-Johnson, onto the Goldwater campaign train and had them distribute phony releases to the press. Never had such a concerted attempt to subvert the operations of the opposition party been made as was undertaken by the Nixon campaigners in 1972. The irony, of course, was that it was all unnecessary: in retrospect, the landslide reelection of President Nixon seems inevitable. That the activities were felt to be necessary suggests a failure to trust the wisdom of the electorate, a fondness for manipulation, and a contempt for the people.

The Lessons of Watergate

It was revealed that Nixon's presidential conversations were routinely tape recorded, and the Senate committee demanded access to the crucial tapes. The president refused, asserting "executive privilege" based on the constitutional concept of the separation of powers. There was talk of a constitutional crisis. Rather than confront the executive directly, however, Congress referred the matter to the courts. The judicial branch was once again called upon to settle a conflict between the executive and the legislature. A presidential press secretary announced that the president would obey the law.

> The system remains one of separated powers. Although he is surrounded by courtiers, our elected monarch does not assert a royal prerogative to be above the law. To retain the authority that makes his constitutional powers meaningful, a president must keep the general support of the people. The people rejected "the divine right of kings" in 1776.

When the Senate committee recessed its investigation in the summer of 1973, the best prediction was that President Nixon would continue in office. His authority in domestic affairs would be gravely damaged. Persuading congressmen and bureaucrats to accept his vision of policy would be difficult, for they would see that he did not have the full trust of the people. His power to seize the initiative in foreign affairs would remain intact, but the scandals had eroded the prestige of the United States within the family of nations. Diplomatic victories would be hard to achieve, and Congress would be increasingly reluctant to fund military adventures.

The Watergate hearings provided a morality play for the American people, but did not point the way to basic institutional change. Congress would not gain awesome power in place of the executive branch. The American system depends upon a strong executive. The legislative branch, bent on representing diverse communities, cannot formulate a single will that has any hope of competing with the determination of the executive. Hopefully, stringent new laws would regulate campaign financing so severely that both parties could emerge from the cloud of suspicion that their policies are purchased by special interests. But the first new legislation passed by the Senate —nearly unanimously—was rather mild. Future presidents—and Richard Nixon himself—would be more poignantly aware of the danger of becoming isolated in the White House by the very staff organizations designed to gather information. Finally, a more tenderhearted concern for fair campaign practices could be stimulated, after discovering that the people's sense of democratic decency has yet to be anesthetized.

> The ultimate sanction of impeachment remains available; that fact itself may limit the assertions of power by public officials, in times like the present when the authority of government is uncertain. In the future, as in the past, the power of the people will normally be exercised through the electoral process. When power is joined with charismatic authority, change is possible.

Political Change and Middle America

If the ultimate power of the people to affect the direction of the nation is conceded, an important question remains: what causes and emotions will win their allegiance? Predictions for the future range

from repressive fascism to a cultural revolution in the name of freedom. The evidence is as contradictory as the predictions.

If asked to comment on Garry Wills's thesis that Richard Nixon
may demonstrate the absurdity of interest-group liberalism, Professor
Burnham might claim that Middle America, wedded to the economic
struggle, is incapable of recognizing the inappropriateness of the
competitive ethic. If that ethic should be temporarily eclipsed, they
would demand that it be re-imposed with the force of fascism. (A nice
contradiction: free enterprise imposed by force.)

Fascism has taken many forms. At a minimum, it suggests a society
in which the liberties of the people are restricted, dissent is suppressed, racial hatred is encouraged, and government operates in a
manner that further enriches its leading industrial managers. Fascist
governments are built upon popular movements. If they are not installed by a majority, they are supported by a substantial, and fanatic,
minority. A prediction of fascism for America must stand or fall on
the quality of the presumptions it makes about the political convictions and desires of the technologically obsolescent class—Middle
America, the current majority. Professor Burnham's implicit assumptions about the selfishness of the motives of this middle group are
not very flattering. He assumes that their resentment against the
"welfare chiselers" and their dismay at the economic achievements
of other minority-group citizens far outweigh their dedication to abstract principles such as freedom and equality. He views the suburbs
as tight little islands, shutting themselves off from any sympathy for
the needs of the cities or of the poor. He assumes that appeals to
racism and envy by political leaders cannot fail to strike a responsive
chord.

Every measure of public opinion indicated widespread, but passive, support for President Nixon's proposed Family Assistance Plan.
Even voters who knew they would have to pay its costs tended to
support it. Perhaps they thought it would substitute "workfare" for
welfare. But they were willing at least to tolerate a redistribution of
the national income to support poor families. This can hardly be
labeled an ungenerous impulse.

Professional students of public attitudes—who must treat complex
human beings as a system of punched holes on a computer card—indeed support the claim that Americans hold many convictions that,
if acted upon, would tend to negate the values of freedom and equality. Racial bigotry is demonstrably present among Americans, although it is neither so strong nor so widespread as it was even in
1964; and, since World War II, there has been a massive shift in white
attitudes toward accepting racial equality as a national goal.[16] How-

16. See Angus Campbell, *White Attitudes toward Black Americans* (Ann Arbor: Institute for
Social Research, University of Michigan, 1971), Chapters 7 and 8.

ever, the growing public cynicism toward government officials—"all politicians are crooks"—fosters a climate in which citizens are likely to feel that all others in the system are motivated by narrow, selfish interests. They will pay little attention to the invocation of abstract ideals, for the person mouthing them is bound to be insincere. As the Watergate disclosures increased in tempo, a Gallup poll revealed that 41 percent of the electorate believed President Nixon knew about the Watergate break-in before it happened. Yet, at that time, 53 percent of those interviewed felt that the incident was "just politics" of the kind engaged in by both parties.[17]

Experience in advertising agencies (think of H. R. Haldeman) need not provide an education in the nuances of politics. Ad men may assume that the role of political leadership is like that of Madison Avenue—to measure, and then manipulate, public opinion, rather than inspiring and formulating it. Their concepts of motivation may lead them to approach the public through their least admirable traits and desires. Public opinion is measured by asking questions of a representative sample. Survey researchers have a good record of finding in the public those attitudes they are looking for. But the half-hour survey interview gives little indication of the intensity with which opinions are held, no sure indication as to whether those opinions are likely to become the basis for action, and no clue at all about the contradictory opinions which the individual may simultaneously adhere to. In fact, the desire for consistency in our ideas is an academic hangup which bothers most people not at all.[18]

This suggests that a variety of emotions and motives are involved in politics. Immediate selfish interest may be displaced by a desire to serve one's country, one's fellow men, or "generations yet unborn." Hundreds of thousands of young men enlisted in the U.S. Army in response to Abraham Lincoln's appeal to preserve the Union; the Japanese attack upon Pearl Harbor had the same impact. Hatred and resentment can be powerful forces in politics; so can idealism or—excuse the word—patriotism.

Psychiatrist Robert Coles has conducted research among the families of factory workers for more than a decade, in both North and South, among both blacks and whites. He has interviewed families in great depth, getting to know them thoroughly, not attempting to describe their attitudes until he has been their friend for five years. Coles reports that there have indeed been times, during his interviews, when he has listened to his respondents and recognized their words as meriting the labels that social critics apply so casually to the electorate—such as "white racist," or "alienated." He has even listened to an "authoritarian personality." But the full fabric of individual lives is so complex, and so many strands of personal experience and psychological and economic pressures are woven into individual attitudes, that labels simply don't stick. The man who sounds like a white racist one day will be a rock-hard New Dealer the next.[19]

17. Gallup Poll, *The San Francisco Chronicle*, April 23, 1973. This survey was conducted before President Nixon's April 30th denial of involvement in Watergate. By June, only 43 percent viewed the incident as "just politics."
18. For a critique of cognitive consistency theories, see Daryl J. Bem, *Beliefs, Attitudes, and Public Affairs* (Belmont, California: Brooks/Cole, 1970), Chapter 4.
19. Robert Coles, "Understanding White Racists," *New York Review of Books*, December 30, 1971, pp. 12ff. Coles' experience was duplicated by the present author, when conducting depth interviews of affluent suburbanites.

Overriding all the cynicism directed toward politicians of the moment is a faith in American institutions, a simple sense of what constitutes decent behavior by public officials, and a desire for fairness in social relationships.

A Suggestion from France

Jean-Francois Revel specializes in holding up the accepted ideology to the light of reality and castigating the intellectuals who cling to outmoded ideas. He visited the United States in 1969 and 1970. He wrote a book attacking the negative image of America held by European intellectuals in general and their ideas about the process of social change in particular. He reported that a revolution (defined as a change in cultural and social reality leading to greater equality) has begun in the United States, and its outcome will determine the future of the world.

In Revel's view, the Marxists of the traditional Left do not understand modern social change. The Marxist vision of a workers' revolt continually recedes as a possibility. In the United States, he finds, cultural, social, and limited political change is going on. It is not happening according to the rules. It is not following a Marxist blueprint, and it is not fueled by religious fervor or sanction.[20]

It is helped by the media. American television, he reports, is more free and open and inclusive than anything imagined in France. Thus the report of a pocket of protest in Berkeley can inflame and inspire students in Dubuque. The same with new styles of dress and music and love; the same for new movements seeking to develop a black, or Chicano, or women's consciousness. American society exhibits a freedom and variety that astonishes Europeans.

The United States is in a ferment which is ultimately healthy and which is changing reality. The ferment is cultural; it challenges the ethic of exploitation. This cultural change is what rendered the American Dream as defined by Richard Nixon so obsolete.

It takes a Frenchman to call what has been happening in America a revolution. Americans are uncomfortable with revolutionaries. But cultural and social change seeking the great goal of equality promised by the Declaration of Independence—extended to include racial and sexual equality—is well within the mainstream of political change in America.

Americans live a revolution best when they fail to recognize it.

A Suggestion from the Record

Notable political leaders in American history—particularly those carried into office by the realignments identified as critical elections—have addressed the electorate in mixed accents. They have served the interests of groups which, left behind by the developments of the social and economic systems, have sought to regain a share of status, or at least renewed opportunity. At the same time, they have modernized the political system by redefining the eternal American political verities, stated in the Declaration of Independence. They have reached the electorate more often through noble motives than through base ones. Rather than pandering to public opinion, they have sought to inform and shape it to support policies designed to benefit the entire nation.

20. Jean-Francois Revel, *Without Marx or Jesus* (New York: Doubleday, 1971).

The American presidents who most blatantly invited special interests to sup at the White House table, and who permitted corruption to flourish in high places—Ulysses S. Grant and Warren G. Harding—have been treated harshly by history.

The People Will Live On

Presidents Grant and Harding each held office during a time of the ascendancy of the competitive ethic. The robber barons of the post-Civil War era were developing the style of life that would give its name to "The Gilded Age." Elected because of his stature as an heroic general, President Grant was politically inept. But he gloried in the company of, and favors extended by, the wealthy. President Harding was not only politically inept; he was not very bright. In each case, the praises of laissez-faire liberalism were sung in the White House, while individual entrepreneurs sought special advantages by corrupting lesser officials.

Neither Grant nor Harding demonstrated to the people the absurdity of the dominant ideology. Grant was followed by Rutherford B. Hayes, whose election was finalized only by the compromise of 1877. Hayes did not possess charismatic authority, and the presidency was eclipsed by Congress for the rest of the century. Harding was followed by "Silent Cal" Coolidge, whose dour New England visage supplied an aura of rectitude for an era of feverish economic speculation.

However, Garry Wills tells us that Richard Nixon may demonstrate the absurdity of the competitive ethic in the modern world. Perhaps the third time is the charm. Certainly there are signs that massive changes in American attitudes are taking place; Jean-Francois Revel cites the evidence. There is a growing awareness of the preciousness of our natural resources; the United States is launched upon a new and promising course in international relations, with the approval of the people; the unfinished process of making a nation from the diverse races and national backgrounds of the American people makes slow progress. This is accomplished by a growing tolerance of diverse life styles, rather than requiring the dull conformity once known as the "melting pot."

The people can grow in wisdom. They can be motivated by generous instincts, as well as by selfish ones. The search for the modern meaning of the promises of the Declaration of Independence can still go forward. The people remain stronger and even somehow wiser than the politicians of the moment.

The most important power of the people is this: they will endure.

The people will live on.
The learning and blundering people will live on.
They will be tricked and sold and again sold
And go back to the nourishing earth for rootholds,
The people so peculiar in renewal and comeback,
You can't laugh off their capacity to take it.[21]

21. Carl Sandburg, *The People, Yes*, p. 284.

APPENDIX

The Fundamental Charters

This book has been about the people, not the Declaration of Independence or the Constitution. But the destiny of the American people is bound up with the fate of these two documents.

They are reprinted here with notes indicating some of the pages in the text where the principles they enunciate are important to the narrative. Those points are numerous, for each age must define the promises of these documents anew and labor to achieve them.

Since this book was not written as a commentary upon the Declaration or the Constitution, many of their phrases play no part in it. (What is a Letter of Marque? What is Corruption of Blood?) Nevertheless, this appendix may demonstrate their importance to the people — in history, in the 1970s, and for "generations yet unborn."

The Declaration of Independence

In Congress, July 4, 1776. A Declaration by the Representatives of the United States of America, in General Congress assembled.

Thomas Jefferson, the author, was influenced by John Locke: 23, 103, 316–317, 461; contrast with Hobbes' pessimism: 23, 229–231, 317, 365; Jefferson as an agrarian: 413–414

Ambivalence of America toward her role in the world: 366–371

Equality
in the Declaration is statement of the American ideal: 23, 299, 317, 458–460, 464, 483
not extended to women: 307–309, 329, 334, 342; or to blacks: 24, 66, 317, 320, 325, 335, 339–342; or to Indians: 28, 317, 320, 326; or to immigrants: 322–323
denied by the Constitution when it condoned slavery: 24, 28, 317–319
contradicted by the value of achievement: 26–28, 31, 58, 396, 439, 444, 462, 469, 472; Jefferson anticipated an "aristocracy of merit": 24, 321
school desegregation is one means of realizing the ideal: 6, 113, 338, 422
"melting pot" idea of: 34, 323, 484
changing concepts of: 316–344

When in the Course of human Events, it becomes necessary for one People to dissolve the Political Bands which have connected them with another, and to assume among the Powers of the Earth, the separate and equal Station to which the Laws of Nature and of Nature's God entitle them, a decent Respect to the Opinions of Mankind requires that they should declare the causes which impel them to the Separation.

We hold these Truths to be self-evident, that all Men are created equal, that they are endowed by their Creator with certain unalienable Rights, that among these are Life, Liberty, and the Pursuit of Happiness — That to secure these Rights, Governments are instituted among Men, deriving their just Powers from the Consent of the Governed, that whenever any Form of Government becomes destructive of these Ends, it is the Right of the People to alter or to abolish it, and to institute new Government, laying its Foundation on such Principles, and organizing its Powers in such Form, as to them shall seem most likely to effect their Safety and Happiness. Prudence, indeed, will dictate that Governments long established should not be changed for light and transient Causes; and accordingly all Experience hath shewn, that Mankind are more disposed to suffer, while Evils are sufferable, than to right themselves by abolishing the Forms to which they are accustomed. But when a long Train of Abuses and Usurpations, pursuing invariably the same Object, evidences a Design to reduce them under absolute Despotism, it is their Right, it is their Duty, to throw off such Government, and to provide new Guards for their future Security.

Colonists distressed by arbitrary
executive power: 100

Such has been the patient Sufferance of these Colonies; and such is now the Necessity which constrains them to alter their former Systems of Government. The History of the present King of Great-Britain is a History of repeated Injuries and Usurpations, all having in direct Object the Establishment of an absolute Tyranny over these States. To prove this, let Facts be submitted to a candid World.

He has refused his Assent to Laws, the most wholesome and necessary for the public Good.

He has forbidden his Governors to pass Laws of immediate and pressing Importance, unless suspended in their Operation till his Assent should be obtained; and when so suspended, he has utterly neglected to attend to them.

He has refused to pass other Laws for the Accommodation of large Districts of People, unless those People would relinquish the Right of Representation in the Legislature, a Right inestimable to them, and formidable to Tyrants only.

He has called together Legislative Bodies at Places unusual, uncomfortable, and distant from the Depository of their public Records, for the sole Purpose of fatiguing them into Compliance with his Measures.

He has dissolved Representative Houses repeatedly, for opposing with manly Firmness his Invasions on the Rights of the People.

He has refused for a long Time, after such Dissolutions, to cause others to be elected; whereby the Legislative Powers, incapable of Annihilation, have returned to the People at large for their exercise; the State remaining in the mean time exposed to all the Dangers of Invasion from without, and Convulsions within.

He has endeavoured to prevent the Population of these States; for that Purpose obstructing the Laws for Naturalization of Foreigners; refusing to pass others to encourage their Migrations hither, and raising the Conditions of new Appropriations of Lands.

He has obstructed the Administration of Justice, by refusing his Assent to Laws for establishing Judiciary Powers.

Compare Article I, Section 6,
Article II, Section 5, and
Article III, Section 1, of the
Constitution.

He has made Judges dependent on his Will alone, for the Tenure of their Offices, and the Amount and Payment of their Salaries.

Following Locke, Americans
identify government as the chief
danger to liberty: 23, 317, 461, 464

He has erected a Multitude of new Offices, and sent hither Swarms of Officers to harrass our People, and eat out their Substance.

He has kept among us, in Times of Peace, Standing Armies, without the consent of our Legislatures.

Civilian control of the military:
94–95, 101

He has affected to render the Military independent of and superior to the Civil Power.

He has combined with others to subject us to a Jurisdiction foreign to our Constitution, and unacknowledged by our Laws; giving his Assent to their Acts of pretended Legislation:

For quartering large Bodies of Armed Troops among us:

Compare Amendment III of the
Constitution.

For protecting them, by a mock Trial, from Punishment for any Murders which they should commit on the Inhabitants of these States:

For cutting off our Trade with all Parts of the World:

"Taxation without
representation": 319

For imposing Taxes on us without our Consent:

Compare Article III, Sect. 2,
para. 3, and Amendment V of the
Constitution.

For depriving us, in many Cases, of the Benefits of Trial by Jury:

For transporting us beyond Seas to be tried for pretended Offences:

For abolishing the free System of English Laws in a neighbouring Province, establishing therein an arbitrary Government, and enlarging its Boundaries, so as to render it at once an Example and fit Instrument for introducing the same absolute Rule into these Colonies:

For taking away our Charters, abolishing our most valuable Laws, and altering fundamentally the Forms of our Governments:

For suspending our own Legislatures, and declaring themselves invested with Power to legislate for us in all Cases whatsoever.

He has abdicated Government here, by declaring us out of his Protection and waging War against us.

He has plundered our Seas, ravaged our Coasts, burnt our Towns, and destroyed the Lives of our People.

He is, at this Time, transporting large Armies of foreign Mercenaries to compleat the Works of Death, Desolation, and Tyranny, already begun with circumstances of Cruelty and Perfidy, scarcely paralleled in the most barbarous Ages, and totally unworthy the Head of a civilized Nation.

He has constrained our fellow Citizens taken Captive on the high Seas to bear Arms against their Country to become the Executioners of their Friends and Brethren, or to fall themselves by their Hands.

Puritan attitude toward the Indians: 28, 320

He has excited domestic Insurrections amongst us, and has endeavoured to bring on the Inhabitants of our Frontiers, the merciless Indian Savages, whose known Rule of Warfare, is an undistinguished Destruction, of all Ages, Sexes and Conditions.

Right of petition: 135–136, 279–280; compare Amendment I of the Constitution.

In every stage of these Oppressions we have Petitioned for Redress in the most humble Terms: Our repeated Petitions have been answered only by repeated Injury. A Prince, whose Character is thus marked by every act which may define a Tyrant, is unfit to be the Ruler of a free People.

Nor have we been wanting in Attentions to our British Brethren. We have warned them from Time to Time of Attempts by their Legislature to extend an unwarrantable Jurisdiction over us. We have reminded them of the Circumstances of our Emigration and Settlement here. We have appealed to their native Justice and Magnanimity, and we have conjured them by the Ties of our common Kindred to disavow these Usurpations, which, would inevitably interrupt our Connections and Correspondence. They too have been deaf to the Voice of Justice and of Consanguinity. We must, therefore, acquiesce in the Necessity, which denounces our Separation, and hold them, as we hold the rest of Mankind, Enemies in War, in Peace, Friends.

New national government not established: 318

Concept of a social contract: 188, 229–232, 460

We, therefore, the Representatives of the UNITED STATES OF AMERICA, in General Congress, Assembled, appealing to the Supreme Judge of the World for the Rectitude of our Intentions, do, in the Name, and by Authority of the good People of these Colonies, solemnly Publish and Declare, That these United Colonies are, and of Right ought to be, *Free and Independent States;* that they are absolved from all Allegiance to the British Crown, and that all political Connection between them and the State of Great-Britain, is and ought to be totally dissolved; and that as *Free and Independent States,* they have full Power to levy War, conclude Peace, contract Alliances, establish Commerce, and to do all other Acts and Things which *Independent States* may of right do. And for the support of this Declaration, with a firm Reliance on the Protection of divine Providence, we mutually pledge to each other our Lives, our Fortunes, and our sacred Honor.

The Constitution
of the United States of America

The separate paragraphs of each section are not numbered in the Constitution. Numbers are added here to facilitate discussion. For easier reading, the original capitalization has been modernized.

Constitution as a social contract: 188, 231–232, 460

Definition of "justice": 234

"Common defense" cannot be guaranteed in nuclear age: 365–366, 372

Many of these purposes are achieved by the states, if at all: 231, 393

Separation of powers
basic principle of Constitution, usually protects status quo: 24, 25, 63, 70, 85, 102, 105, 120–125, 147–148, 153–154, 271, 278, 282, 361, 475
concept was Montesquieu's: 99–100
expounded by Madison: 63
political parties overcome, to make Constitution workable: 51, 63, 70, 86, 102, 105, 463–466
some governments work well without: 21, 100, 148, 277

Roles envisaged by the founders for the House and the Senate have been reversed: 147–151, 153

Ownership of property not made a requirement for voting: 319

This provision was superseded by Amendment XIV, Section 2: 325–326

Condoning slavery in the Constitution denied the equality asserted in the Declaration: 24, 28, 317–319

Changing role of the Speaker: 155–156

Impeachment: see notes to Article I, Section 3, paragraph 7.

Direct election of Senators secured by Amendment XVII: 149, 151, 329

Senate represents states as states: 149, 151, 161, 318, 428

We, the People of the United States, in Order to form a more perfect Union, establish Justice, insure domestic Tranquility, provide for the common defense, promote the general Welfare, and secure the Blessings of Liberty to ourselves and our Posterity, do ordain and establish this Constitution for the United States of America.

Article I

Section 1. All legislative powers herein granted shall be vested in a Congress of the United States, which shall consist of a Senate and House of Representatives.

Section 2. 1. The House of Representatives shall be composed of members chosen every second year by the people of the several states, and the electors in each state shall have the qualifications requisite for electors of the most numerous branch of the state legislature.

2. No person shall be a representative who shall not have attained to the age of twenty-five years, and been seven years a citizen of the United States, and who shall not, when elected, be an inhabitant of that state in which he shall be chosen.

3. Representatives and direct taxes shall be apportioned among the several states which may be included within this Union, according to their respective numbers, which shall be determined by adding to the whole number of free persons, including those bound to service for a term of years, and excluding Indians not taxed, three-fifths of all other persons. The actual enumeration shall be made within three years after the first meeting of the Congress of the United States, and within every subsequent term of ten years, in such manner as they shall by law direct. The number of representatives shall not exceed one for every thirty thousand, but each state shall have at least one representative; and until such enumeration shall be made, the state of New-Hampshire shall be entitled to chuse three, Massachusetts eight, Rhode-Island and Providence Plantations one, Connecticut five, New-York six, New-Jersey four, Pennsylvania eight, Delaware one, Maryland six, Virginia ten, North-Carolina five, South-Carolina five, and Georgia three.

4. When vacancies happen in the representation from any state, the Executive authority thereof shall issue writs of election to fill such vacancies.

5. The House of Representatives shall chuse their Speaker and other officers; and shall have the sole power of impeachment.

Section 3. 1. The Senate of the United States shall be composed of two senators from each state, chosen by the legislature thereof for six years; and each senator shall have one vote.

2. Immediately after they shall be assembled in consequence of the first election, they shall be divided as equally as may be into three classes. The seats of the senators of the first class shall be vacated at the expiration of the second year, of the second class at the expiration of the fourth year, and of the third class at the expiration of the sixth year, so that one-third may be chosen every second year; and if vacancies happen by resignation, or otherwise, during the recess of the Legislature of any state, the Executive thereof may make temporary appointments until the next meeting of the Legislature, which shall then fill such vacancies.

3. No person shall be a senator who shall not have attained to the age of thirty years, and been nine years a citizen of the United States, and who shall not, when elected, be an inhabitant of that state for which he shall be chosen.

4. The Vice-President of the United States shall be President of the senate, but shall have no vote, unless they be equally divided.

5. The Senate shall chuse their other officers, and also a President pro tempore, in the absence of the Vice-President, or when he shall exercise the office of President of the United States.

6. The Senate shall have the sole power to try all impeachments. When sitting for that purpose, they shall be on oath or affirmation. When the President of the United States is tried, the Chief Justice shall preside: And no person shall be convicted without the concurrence of two-thirds of the members present.

7. Judgment in cases of impeachment shall not extend further than to removal from office, and disqualification to hold and enjoy any office of honor, trust or profit under the United States; but the party convicted shall nevertheless be liable and subject to indictment, trial, judgment and punishment, according to law.

Section 4. 1. The times, places and manner of holding elections for senators and representatives, shall be prescribed in each state by the legislature thereof; but the Congress may at any time by law make or alter such regulations, except as to the places of chusing Senators.

2. The Congress shall assemble at least once in every year, and such meeting shall be on the first Monday in December, unless they shall by law appoint a different day.

Section 5. 1. Each house shall be the judge of the elections, returns and qualifications of its own members, and a majority of each shall constitute a quorum to do business; but a smaller number may adjourn from day to day, and may be authorized to compel the attendance of absent members, in such manner, and under such penalties as each house may provide.

2. Each house may determine the rules of its proceedings, punish its members for disorderly behaviour, and, with the concurrence of two-thirds, expel a member.

3. Each house shall keep a journal of its proceedings, and from time to time publish the same, excepting such parts as may in their judgment require secrecy; and the yeas and nays of the members of either house on any question shall, at the desire of one-fifth of those present, be entered on the journal.

4. Neither house, during the session of Congress, shall, without the consent of the other, adjourn for more than three days, nor to any other place than that in which the two houses shall be sitting.

Section 6. 1. The senators and representatives shall receive a compensation for their services, to be ascertained by law, and paid out of the treasury of the United States. They shall in all cases, except treason, felony and breach of the peace, be privileged from arrest during their attendance at the session of their respective houses, and in going to and returning from the same; and for any speech or debate in either house, they shall not be questioned in any other place.

2. No senator or representative shall, during the time for which he was elected, be appointed to any civil office under the authority of the United States, which shall have been created, or the emoluments whereof shall have been encreased during such time; and no person holding any office under the United States, shall be a member of either house during his continuance in office.

Section 7. 1. All bills for raising revenue shall originate in the house of representatives; but the senate may propose or concur with amendments as on other bills.

2. Every bill which shall have passed the house of representatives and the senate, shall, before it become a law, be presented to the president of the United States; if he approve he shall sign it, but if not he shall return it, with his objections to that house in which it shall have originated, who shall enter the objections at large on their journal, and proceed to reconsider it. If after such reconsideration two-thirds of that house shall agree to pass the bill, it shall be sent, together with the objections, to the other house, by which it shall likewise be reconsidered, and if approved by two-thirds of that house, it shall become a law. But in all such cases the votes of both houses shall be determined by yeas and nays, and the names of the persons voting for and against the bill shall be entered on the journal of each house respectively. If any bill shall not be returned by the President within ten days (Sundays excepted) after it shall have been presented to him, the same shall be a law, in like manner as if he had signed it, unless the Congress by their adjournment prevent its return, in which case it shall not be a law.

3. Every order, resolution, or vote to which the concurrence of the Senate and House of Representatives may be necessary (except on a question of adjournment) shall be presented to the President of the United States; and before the same shall take effect, shall by approved by him, or, being disapproved by him, shall be repassed by two-thirds of the Senate and House of Representatives, according to the rules and limitations prescribed in the case of a bill.

Section 8. The Congress shall have power

1. To lay and collect taxes, duties, imposts and excises, to pay the debts and provide for the common defence and general welfare of the United States; but all duties, imposts and excises shall be uniform throughout the United States;

2. To borrow money on the credit of the United States;

3. To regulate commerce with foreign nations, and among the several states, and with the Indian tribes;

4. To establish an uniform rule of naturalization, and uniform laws on the subject of bankruptcies throughout the United States;

5. To coin money, regulate the value thereof, and of foreign coin, and fix the standard of weights and measures;

6. To provide for the punishment of counterfeiting the securities and current coin of the United States;

7. To establish post offices and post roads;

8. To promote the progress of science and useful arts, by securing for limited times to authors and inventors the exclusive right to their respective writings and discoveries;

9. To constitute tribunals inferior to the supreme court;

10. To define and punish piracies and felonies committed on the high seas, and offences against the law of nations;

11. To declare war, grant letters of marque and reprisal, and make rules concerning captures on land and water;

12. To raise and support armies, but no appropriation of money to that use shall be for a longer term than two years;

13. To provide and maintain a navy;

14. To make rules for the government and regulation of the land and naval forces;

15. To provide for calling forth the militia to execute the laws of the union, suppress insurrections and repel invasions;

16. To provide for organizing, arming, and disciplining, the militia, and for governing such part of them as may be employed in the service of the United States, reserving to the States respectively, the appointment of the officers, and the authority of training the militia according to the discipline prescribed by Congress;

17. To exercise exclusive legislation in all cases whatsoever, over such district (not exceeding ten miles square) as may, by cession of particular States, and the acceptance of Congress, become the seat of the government of the United States, and to exercise like authority over all places purchased by the consent of the legislature of the state in which the same shall be, for the erection of forts, magazines, arsenals, dock-yards, and other needful buildings;—And

18. To make all laws which shall be necessary and proper for carrying into execution the foregoing powers, and all other powers vested by this constitution in the government of the United States, or in any department or officer thereof.

Section 9. 1. The migration or importation of such persons as any of the states now existing shall think proper to admit, shall not be prohibited by the Congress prior to the year one thousand eight hundred and eight, but a tax or duty may be imposed on such importation, not exceeding ten dollars for each person.

2. The privilege of the writ of habeas corpus shall not be suspended, unless when in cases of rebellion or invasion the public safety may require it.

3. No bill of attainder or ex post facto law shall be passed.

4. No capitation, or other direct, tax shall be laid, unless in proportion to the census or enumeration herein before directed to be taken.

5. No tax or duty shall be laid on articles exported from any state. No preference shall be given by any regulation of commerce or revenue to the ports of one state over those of another: nor shall vessels bound to, or from, one state, be obliged to enter, clear, or pay duties in another.

6. No money shall be drawn from the treasury, but in consequence of appropriations made by law, and a regular statement and account of the receipts and expenditures of all public money shall be published from time to time.

7. No title of nobility shall be granted by the United States;—And no person holding any office of profit or trust under them, shall, without the consent of the Congress accept of any present, emolument, office, or title, of any kind whatever, from any king, prince, or foreign state.

Section 10. 1. No state shall enter into any treaty, alliance, or confederation; grant letters of marque and reprisal; coin money; emit bills of credit; make any thing but gold and silver coin a tender in payment of debts; pass any bill of attainder, ex post facto law, or law impairing the obligation of contracts, or grant any title of nobility.

2. No state shall, without the consent of the Congress, lay any imposts or duties on imports or exports, except what may be absolutely necessary for executing its inspection laws; and the net produce of all duties and imposts, laid by any state on imports or exports, shall be for the use of the Treasury of the United States; and all such laws shall be subject to the revision and controul of the Congress. No state shall, without the consent of Congress, lay any duty of tonnage, keep troops, or ships of war in time of peace, enter into any agreement or compact with another state, or with a foreign power, or engage in war, unless actually invaded, or in such imminent danger as will not admit of delay.

Article II

Section 1. 1. The executive power shall be· vested in a President of the United States of America. He shall hold his office during the term of four years, and, together with the vice-president, chosen for the same term, be elected as follows.

Each state shall appoint, in such manner as the legislature thereof may direct, a number of electors, equal to the whole number of senators and representatives to which the state may be entitled in the Congress: but no senator or representative, or person holding an office of trust or profit under the United States, shall be appointed an elector.

This paragraph has been superseded by Amendment XII.

The electors shall meet in their respective states, and vote by ballot for two persons, of whom one at least shall not be an inhabitant of the same state with themselves. And they shall make a list of all the persons voted for, and of the number of votes for each; which list they shall sign and certify, and transmit sealed to the seat of the government of the United States, directed to the president of the senate. The president of the senate shall, in the presence of the senate and house of representatives, open all the certificates, and the votes shall then be counted. The person having the greatest number of votes shall be the president, if such number be a majority of the whole number of electors appointed; and if there be more than one who have such majority, and have an equal number of votes, then the house of representatives shall immediately chuse by ballot one of them for president; and if no person have a majority, then from the five highest on the list the said house shall in like manner chuse the president. But in chusing the president, the votes shall be taken by states, the representation from each state having one vote; a quorum for this purpose shall consist of a member or members from two-thirds of the states, and a majority of all the states shall be necessary to a choice. In every case, after the choice of the president, the person having the greatest number of votes of the electors shall be the vice-president. But if there should remain two or more who have equal votes, the senate shall chuse from them by ballot the vice-president.

2. The Congress may determine the time of chusing the electors, and the day on which they shall give their votes; which day shall be the same throughout the United States.

3. No person except a natural born citizen, or a citizen of the United States, at the time of the adoption of this constitution, shall be eligible to the office of president; neither shall any person be eligible to that office who shall not have attained to the age of thirty-five years, and been fourteen years a resident within the United States.

This section has been modified by Amendment XXV

4. In case of the removal of the president from office, or of his death, resignation, or inability to discharge the powers and duties of the said office, the same shall devolve on the vice-president and the Congress may by law provide for the case of removal, death, resignation or inability, both of the president and vice-president, declaring what officers shall then act as president, and such officer shall act accordingly, until the disability be removed, or a president shall be elected.

5. The president shall, at stated times, receive for his services, a compensation, which shall neither be encreased nor diminished during the period for which he shall have been elected, and he shall not receive within that period any other emolument from the United States, or any of them.

6. Before he enter on the execution of his office, he shall take the following oath or affirmation:

"I do solemnly swear (or affirm) that I will faithfully execute the office of president of the United States, and will to the best of my ability, preserve, protect and defend the constitution of the United States."

Section 2. 1.The president shall be commander in chief of the army and navy of the United States, and of the militia of the several States, when called into the actual service of the United States; he may require the opinion, in writing, of the principal officer in each of the executive departments, upon any subject relating to the duties of their respective offices, and he shall have power to grant reprieves and pardons for offences against the United States, except in cases of impeachment.

2. He shall have power, by and with the advice and consent of the senate, to make treaties, provided two-thirds of the senators present concur; and he shall nominate, and by and with the advice and consent of the senate, shall appoint ambassadors, other public minister and consuls, judges of the supreme court, and all other officers of the United States, whose appointments are not herein otherwise provided for, and which shall be established by law. But the Congress may by law vest the appointment of such inferior officers, as they think proper, in the president alone, in the courts of law, or in the heads of departments.

3. The president shall have power to fill up all vacancies that may happen during the recess of the senate, by granting commissions which shall expire at the end of their next session.

Section 3. He shall from time to time give to the Congress information of the state of the union, and recommend to their consideration such measures as he shall judge necessary and expedient; he may, on extraordinary occasions, convene both houses, or either of them, and in case of disagreement between them, with respect to the time of adjournment, he may adjourn them to such time as he shall think proper; he shall receive ambassadors and other public ministers; he shall take care that the laws be faithfully executed, and shall commission all the officers of the United States.

Section 4. The president, vice-president and all civil officers of the United States, shall be removed from office on impeachment for, and conviction of, treason, bribery, or other high crimes and misdemeanors.

Article III

Section 1. The judicial power of the United States, shall be vested in one supreme court, and in such inferior courts as the Congress may from time to time ordain and establish. The judges, both of the supreme and inferior courts, shall hold their offices during good behaviour, and shall, at stated times, receive for their services, a compensation, which shall not be diminished during their continuance in office.

Section 2. 1. The judicial power shall extend to all cases, in law and equity, arising under this constitution, the laws of the United States, and treaties made, or which shall be made, under their authority; to all cases affecting ambassadors, other public ministers and consuls; to all cases of admiralty and maritime jurisdiction; to controversies to which the United States shall be a party; to controversies between two or more States, between a state and citizens of another state, between citizens of different States, between citizens of different States, between citizens of the same state claiming lands under grants of different States, and between a state, of the citizens thereof, and foreign States, citizens or subjects.

2. In all cases affecting ambassadors, other public ministers and consuls, and those in which a state shall be party, the supreme court shall have original jurisdiction. In all the other cases before mentioned, the supreme court shall have appellate jurisdiction, both as to law and fact, with such exceptions, and under such regulations as the Congress shall make.

3. The trial of all crimes, except in cases of impeachment, shall be by jury; and such trial shall be held in the state where the said crimes shall have been committed; but when not committed within any state, the trial shall be at such a place or places as the Congress may by law have directed.

Section 3. 1. Treason against the United States, shall consist only in levying war against them, or in adhering to their enemies, giving them aid and comfort. No person shall be convicted of treason unless on the testimony of two witnesses to the same overt act, or on confession in open court.

2. The Congress shall have power to declare the punishment of treason, but no attainder of treason shall work corruption of blood, or forfeiture except during the life of the person attainted.

Article IV

Section 1. Full faith and credit shall be given in each state to the public acts, records, and judicial proceedings of every other state. And the Congress may by general laws prescribe the manner in which such acts, records and proceedings shall be proved, and the effect thereof.

Section 2. 1. The citizens of each state shall be entitled to all privileges and immunities of citizens in the several states.

2. A person charged in any state with treason, felony, or other crime, who shall flee from justice and be found in another state, shall, on demand of the executive authority of the state from which he fled, be delivered up, to be removed to the state having jurisdiction of the crime.

3. No person held to service or labour in one state, under the laws thereof, escaping into another, shall, in consequence of any law or regulation therein, be discharged from such service or labour, but shall be delivered up on claim of the party to whom such service or labour may be due.

Section 3. 1. New states may be admitted by the Congress into this union; but no new state shall be formed or erected within the jurisdiction of any other state; nor any state be formed by the junction of two or more states, or parts of states, without the consent of the legislatures of the states concerned as well as of the Congress.

2. The Congress shall have power to dispose of and make all needful rules and regulations respecting the territory or other property belonging to the United States; and nothing in this Constitution shall be so construed as to prejudice any claims of the United States, or of any particular state.

Section 4. The United States shall guarantee to every state in this union a Republican form of government, and shall protect each of them against invasion; and on application of the legislature, or of the executive (when the legislature cannot be convened) against domestic violence.

Article V

The Congress, whenever two-thirds of both houses shall deem it necessary, shall propose amendments to this constitution, or, on the application of the legislatures of two-thirds of the several states, shall call a convention for proposing amendments, which, in either case, shall be valid to all intents and purposes, as part of this constitution, when ratified by the legislatures of three-fourths of the several states, or by conventions in three-fourths thereof, as the one or the other mode of ratification may be

proposed by the Congress; Provided, that no amendment which may be made prior to the year one thousand eight hundred and eight shall in any manner affect the first and fourth clauses in the ninth section of the first article; and that no state, without its consent, shall be deprived of its equal suffrage in the senate.

Article VI

1. All debts contracted and engagements entered into, before the adoption of this Constitution, shall be as valid against the United States under this Constitution, as under the confederation.

2. This constitution, and the laws of the United States which shall be made in pursuance thereof; and all treaties made, or which shall be made, under the authority of the United States, shall be the supreme law of the land; and the judges in every state shall be bound thereby, any thing in the constitution or laws of any state to the contrary notwithstanding.

3. The senators and representatives beforementioned, and the members of the several state legislatures, and all executive and judicial officers, both of the United States and of the several States, shall be bound by oath or affirmation, to support this constitution; but no religious test shall ever be required as a qualification to any office or public trust under the United States.

Article VII

The ratification of the convention of nine States, shall be sufficient for the establishment of this constitution between the States so ratifying the same.

Articles in addition to, and Amendment of the Constitution of the United States of America, proposed by Congress, and ratified by the Legislatures of the several States, pursuant to the fifth Article of the original Constitution.

(Dates of ratification are shown in parentheses.)

Article I (1791)

Congress shall make no law respecting an establishment of religion, or prohibiting the free exercise thereof; or abridging the freedom of speech, or of the press; or the right of the people peaceably to assemble, and to petition the Government for a redress of grievances.

Article II (1791)

A well regulated Militia, being necessary to the security of a free State, the right of the people to keep and bear Arms, shall not be infringed.

Article III (1791)

No Soldier shall, in time of peace be quartered in any house, without the consent of the Owner, nor in time of war, but in a manner to be prescribed by law.

Article IV (1791)

The right of the people to be secure in their persons, houses, papers, and effects, against unreasonable searches and seizures, shall not be violated, and no Warrants shall issue, but upon probable cause, supported by Oath or affirmation, and particularly describing the place to be searched, and the persons or things to be seized.

Article V (1791)

No person shall be held to answer for a capital, or otherwise infamous crime, unless on a presentment or indictment of a Grand Jury, except in cases arising in the land or naval forces, or in the Militia, when in actual service in time of War or public danger; nor shall any person be subject for the same offence to be twice put in jeopardy of life or limb; nor shall be compelled in any criminal case to be a witness against himself, nor be deprived of life, liberty, or property, without due process of law; nor shall private property be taken for public use, without just compensation.

Article VI (1791)

In all criminal prosecutions, the accused shall enjoy the right to a speedy and public trial, by an impartial jury of the State and district wherein the crime shall have been committed, which district shall have been previously ascertained by law, and to be informed of the nature and cause of the accusation; to be confronted with the witnesses against him; to have compulsory process for obtaining witnesses in his favor, and to have the Assistance of Counsel for his defence.

Article VII (1791)

In Suits at common law, where the value in controversy shall exceed twenty dollars, the right of trial by jury shall be preserved, and no fact tried by a jury, shall be otherwise re-examined in any Court of the United States, than according to the rules of the common law.

Article VIII (1791)

Excessive bail shall not be required, nor excessive fines imposed, nor cruel and unusual punishments inflicted.

Article IX (1791)

The enumeration in the Constitution, of certain rights, shall not be construed to deny or disparage others retained by the people.

Article X (1791)

The powers not delegated to the United States by the Constitution, nor prohibited by it to the States, are reserved to the States respectively, or to the people.

Article XI (1798)

The judicial power of the United States shall not be construed to extend to any suit in law or equity, commenced or prosecuted against one of the United States by Citizens of another State, or by Citizens or Subjects of any Foreign State.

Article XII (1804)

The Electors shall meet in their respective states, and vote by ballot for President and Vice-President, one of whom, at least, shall not be an inhabitant of the same state with themselves; they shall name in their ballots the person voted for as President, and in distinct ballots the person voted for as Vice-President, and they shall make distinct lists of all persons voted for as President, and of all persons voted for as Vice-President, and of the number of votes for each, which lists they shall sign and certify, and transmit sealed to the seat of the government of the United States, directed to the President of the Senate;—The President of the Senate shall, in the presence of the Senate and House of Representatives, open all the certificates and the votes shall then be counted;—The person having the greatest number of votes for President, shall be the President, if such number be a majority of the whole number of Electors appointed; and if no person have such majority, then from the persons having the highest numbers not exceeding three on the list of those voted for as President, the House of Representatives shall choose immediately, by ballot, the President. But in choosing the President, the votes shall be taken by states, the representation from each state having one vote; a quorum for this purpose shall consist of a member or members from two-thirds of the states, and a majority of all the states shall be necessary to a choice. And if the House of Representatives shall not choose a President whenever the right of choice shall devolve upon them, before the fourth day of March next following, then the Vice-President shall act as President, as in the case of the death or other constitutional disability of the President. The person having the greatest number of votes as Vice-President, shall be the Vice-President, if such number be a majority of the whole number of Electors appointed, and if no person have a majority, then from the two highest numbers on the list, the Senate shall choose the Vice-President; a quorum for the purpose shall consist of two-thirds of the whole number of Senators, and a majority of the whole number shall be necessary to a choice. But no person constitutionally ineligible to the office of President shall be eligible to that of Vice-President of the United States.

Article XIII (1865)

Section 1. Neither slavery nor involuntary servitude, except as a punishment for crime whereof the party shall have been duly convicted, shall exist within the United States, or any place subject to their jurisdiction.

Section 2. Congress shall have power to enforce this article by appropriate legislation.

Article XIV (1868)

Section 1. All persons born or naturalized in the United States, and subject to the jurisdiction thereof, are citizens of the United States and of the State wherein they reside. No State shall make or enforce any law which shall abridge the privileges or immunities of citizens of the United States; nor shall any State deprive any person of life, liberty, or property, without due process of law; nor deny to any person within its jurisdiction the equal protection of the laws.

Section 2. Representatives shall be apportioned among the several States according to their respective numbers, counting the whole number of persons in each State, excluding Indians not taxed. But when the right to vote at any election for the choice of electors for President and Vice President of the United States, Representatives in Congress, the Executive and Judicial officers of a State, or the members of the Legislature thereof, is denied to any of the male inhabitants of such State, being twenty-one years of age, and citizens of the United States, or in any way abridged, except for participation in rebellion, or other crime, the basis of representation therein shall be reduced in the proportion which the number of such male citizens shall bear to the whole number of male citizens twenty-one years of age in such State.

Section 3. No person shall be a Senator or Representative in Congress, or elector of President and Vice President, or hold any office, civil or military, under the United States, or under any State, who, having previously taken an oath, as a member of Congress, or as an officer of the United States, or as a member of any State legislature, or as an executive or judicial officer of any State, to support the Constitution of the United States, shall have engaged in insurrection or rebellion against the same, or given aid or comfort to the enemies thereof. But Congress may by a vote of two-thirds of each House, remove such disability.

Section 4. The validity of the public debt of the United States, authorized by law, including debts incurred for payment of pensions and bounties for services in Suppressing insurrection or rebellion, shall not be questioned. But neither the United States nor any State shall assume or pay any debt or obligation incurred in aid of insurrection or rebellion against the United States, or any claim for the loss or emancipation of any slave; but all such debts, obligations and claims shall be held illegal and void.

Section 5. The Congress shall have power to enforce, by appropriate legislation, the provisions of this article.

Article XV (1870)

Section 1. The right of citizens of the United States to vote shall not be denied or abridged by the United States or by any State on account of race, color, or previous condition of servitude.

Section 2. The Congress shall have power to enforce this article by appropriate legislation.

Article XVI (1913)

The Congress shall have power to lay and collect taxes on incomes, from whatever source derived, without apportionment among the several States, and without regard to any census or enumeration.

Article XVII (1913)

Section 1. The Senate of the United States shall be composed of two Senators from each State, elected by the people thereof, for six years; and each Senator shall have one vote. The electors in each State shall have the qualifications requisite for electors of the most numerous branch of the State legislatures.

Section 2. When vacancies happen in the representation of any State in the Senate, the executive authority of such State shall issue writs of election to fill such vacancies: Provided, That the legislature of any State may empower the executive thereof to make temporary appointments until the people fill the vacancies by election as the legislature may direct.

Section 3. This amendment shall not be so construed as to affect the election or term of any Senator chosen before it becomes valid as part of the Constitution.

Article XVIII (1919)

Section 1. After one year from the ratification of this article the manufacture, sale, or transportation of intoxicating liquors within, the importation thereof into, or the exportation thereof from the United States and all territory subject to the jurisdiction thereof for beverage purposes is hereby prohibited.

Section 2. The Congress and the several States shall have concurrent power to enforce this article by appropriate legislation.

Section 3. This article shall be inoperative unless it shall have been ratified as an amendment to the Constitution by the legislatures of the several States, as provided in the Constitution, within seven years from the date of the submission hereof to the States by the Congress.

Article XIX (1920)

The right of citizens of the United States to vote shall not be denied or abridged by the United States or by any State on account of sex.
Congress shall have power to enforce this article by appropriate legislation.

Article XX (1933)

Section 1. The terms of the President and Vice President shall end at noon on the 20th day of January, and the terms of Senators and Representatives at noon on the 3rd day of January, of the years in which such terms would have ended if this article had not been ratified; and the terms of their successors shall then begin.

Section 2. The Congress shall assemble at least once in every year, and such meeting shall begin at noon on the 3rd day of January, unless they shall by law appoint a different day.

Section 3. If, at the time fixed for the beginning of the term of the President, the President elect shall have died, the Vice President elect shall become President. If a President shall not have been chosen before the time fixed for the beginning of his term, or if the President elect shall have failed to qualify, then the Vice President elect shall act as President until a President shall have qualified; and the Congress may by law provide for the case wherein neither a President elect nor a Vice President elect shall have qualified, declaring who shall then act as President, or the manner in which one who is to act shall be selected, and such person shall act accordingly until a President or Vice President shall have qualified.

Section 4. The Congress may by law provide for the case of the death of any of the persons from whom the House of Representatives may choose a President whenever the right of choice shall have devolved upon them, and for the case of the death of any of the persons from whom the Senate may choose a Vice President whenever the right of choice shall have devolved upon them.

Section 5. Sections 1 and 2 shall take effect on the 15th day of October following the ratification of this article.

Section 6. This article shall be inoperative unless it shall have been ratified as an amendment to the Constitution by the legislatures of three-fourths of the several States within seven years from the date of its submission.

Article XXI (1933)

Section 1. The eighteenth article of amendment to the Constitution of the United States is hereby repealed.

Section 2. The transportation or importation into any State, Territory, or possession of the United States for delivery or use therein of intoxicating liquors, in violation of the laws thereof, is hereby prohibited.

Section 3. This article shall be inoperative unless it shall have been ratified as an amendment to the Constitution by conventions in the several States, as provided in the Constitution, within seven years from the date of the submission hereof to the States by the Congress.

Article XXII (1951)

Section 1. No person shall be elected to the office of the President more than twice, and no person who has held the office of President, or acted as President, for more than two years of a term to which some other person was elected President shall be elected to the office of the President more than once. But this Article shall not apply to any person holding the office of President when this Article was proposed by the Congress, and shall not prevent any person who may be holding the office of President, or acting as President, during the term within which this Article becomes operative from holding the office of President or acting as President during the remainder of such term.

Section 2. This article shall be inoperative unless it shall have been ratified as an amendment to the Constitution by the legislatures of three-fourths of the several States within seven years from the date of its submission to the States by the Congress.

Article XXIII (1961)

Section 1. The District constituting the seat of Government of the United States shall appoint in such manner as the Congress may direct:
   A number of electors of President and Vice President equal to the whole number of Senators and Representatives in Congress to which the District would be entitled if it were a State, but in no event more than the least populous State; they shall be in addition to those appointed by the States, but they shall be considered, for the purposes of the election of President and Vice President, to be electors appointed by a State; and they shall meet in the District and perform such duties as provided by the twelfth article of amendment.

Section 2. The Congress shall have power to enforce this article by appropriate legislation.

Article XXIV (1964)

Section 1. The right of citizens of the United States to vote in any primary or other election for President or Vice President, for electors for President or Vice President, or for Senator or Representative in Congress, shall not be denied or abridged by the United States or any State by reason of failure to pay any poll tax or other tax.

Section 2. The Congress shall have power to enforce this article by appropriate legislation.

Article XXV (1967)

Section 1. In case of the removal of the President from office or his death or resignation, the Vice President shall become President.

Section 2. Whenever there is a vacancy in the office of the Vice President, the President shall nominate a Vice President who shall take the office upon confirmation by a majority vote of both houses of Congress.

Section 3. Whenever the President transmits to the President pro tempore of the Senate and the Speaker of the House of Representatives his written declaration that he is unable to discharge the powers and duties of his office, and until he transmits to them a written declaration to the contrary, such powers and duties shall be discharged by the Vice President as Acting President.

Section 4. Whenever the Vice President and a majority of either the principal officers of the executive departments or of such other body as Congress may by law provide, transmit to the President pro tempore of the Senate and the Speaker of the House of Representatives their written declaration that the President is unable to discharge the powers and duties of his office, the Vice President shall immediately assume the powers and duties of the office as Acting President.

Thereafter, when the President transmits to the President pro tempore of the Senate and the Speaker of the House of Representatives his written declaration that no inability exists, he shall resume the powers and duties of his office unless the Vice President and a majority of either the principal officers of the executive department or of such other body as Congress may by law provide, transmit within four days to the President pro tempore of the Senate and the Speaker of the House of Representatives their written declaration that the President is unable to discharge the powers and duties of his office. Thereupon Congress shall decide the issue, assembling within 48 hours for that purpose if not in session. If the Congress, within 21 days after receipt of the latter written declaration, or, if Congress is not in session, within 21 days after Congress is required to assemble, determines by two-thirds vote of both houses that the President is unable to discharge the powers and duties of his office, the Vice President shall continue to discharge the same as Acting President; otherwise, the President shall resume the powers and duties of his office.

Article XXVI (1971)

Section 1. The right of citizens of the United States, who are 18 years of age or older, to vote shall not be denied or abridged by the United States or any state on account of age.

Section 2. The Congress shall have the power to enforce this article by appropriate legislation.

Article XXVII (Proposed by Congress Mar. 22, 1972; ratification by the states incomplete.)

Section 1. Equality of rights under the law shall not be denied or abridged by the United States or by any State on account of sex.

Section 2. The Congress shall have the power to enforce, by appropriate legislation, the provisions of this article.

Section 3. This amendment shall take effect two years after the date of ratification.

INDEX